Novels for Students

National Advisory Board

Novels *for Students*

Presenting Analysis, Context, and Criticism on Commonly Studied Novels

Volume 24

Ira Mark Milne
Project Editor

Foreword by Anne Devereaux Jordan

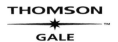

THOMSON
GALE

Detroit • New York • San Francisco • New Haven, Conn. • Waterville, Maine • London

THOMSON
GALE

Novels for Students, Volume 24

Project Editor
Ira Mark Milne

Editorial
Anne Marie Hacht, Sara Constantakis

Rights Acquisition and Management
Edna Hedblad, Lisa Kincade, Tracie Richardson, Kim Smilay

Manufacturing
Rita Wimberley

Imaging
Leitha Etheridge-Sims, Lezlie Light, Mike Logusz, Dan Newell

Product Design
Pamela A. E. Galbreath

Vendor Administration
Civie Green

Product Manager
Meggin Condino

For more information, contact
Thomson Gale
27500 Drake Rd.
Farmington Hills, MI 48331-3535
Or you can visit our Internet site at
http://www.gale.com

ISBN-13: 978-0-7876-6947-8
ISBN-10: 0-7876-6947-4
ISSN 1094-3552

Printed in the United States of America
10 9 8 7 6 5 4 3 2 1

Table of Contents

The Informed Dialogue: Interacting with Literature

When we pick up a book, we usually do so with the anticipation of pleasure. We hope that by entering the time and place of the novel and sharing the thoughts and actions of the characters, we will find enjoyment. Unfortunately, this is often not the case; we are disappointed. But we should ask, has the author failed us, or have we failed the author?

We establish a dialogue with the author, the book, and with ourselves when we read. Consciously and unconsciously, we ask questions: "Why did the author write this book?" "Why did the author choose that time, place, or character?" "How did the author achieve that effect?" "Why did the character act that way?" "Would I act in the same way?" The answers we receive depend upon how much information about literature in general and about that book specifically we ourselves bring to our reading.

Young children have limited life and literary experiences. Being young, children frequently do not know how to go about exploring a book, nor sometimes, even know the questions to ask of a book. The books they read help them answer questions, the author often coming right out and *telling* young readers the things they are learning or are expected to learn. The perennial classic, *The Little Engine That Could, tells* its readers that, among other things, it is good to help others and brings happiness:

> "Hurray, hurray," cried the funny little clown and all the dolls and toys. "The good little boys and girls in the city will be happy because you helped us, kind, Little Blue Engine."

In picture books, messages are often blatant and simple, the dialogue between the author and reader one-sided. Young children are concerned with the end result of a book—the enjoyment gained, the lesson learned—rather than with how that result was obtained. As we grow older and read further, however, we question more. We come to expect that the world within the book will closely mirror the concerns of our world, and that the author will *show* these through the events, descriptions, and conversations within the story, rather than *telling* of them. We are now expected to do the interpreting, carry on our share of the dialogue with the book and author, and glean not only the author's message, but comprehend how that message and the overall affect of the book were achieved. Sometimes, however, we need help to do these things. *Novels for Students* provides that help.

A novel is made up of many parts interacting to create a coherent whole. In reading a novel, the more obvious features can be easily spotted—theme, characters, plot—but we may overlook the more subtle elements that greatly influence how the novel is perceived by the reader: viewpoint, mood and tone, symbolism, or the use of humor. By focusing on both the obvious and more subtle literary elements within a novel, *Novels for Students* aids readers in both analyzing for message and in determining how and why that message is communicated. In the discussion on Harper Lee's *To*

Kill a Mockingbird (Vol. 2), for example, the mockingbird as a symbol of innocence is dealt with, among other things, as is the importance of Lee's use of humor which "enlivens a serious plot, adds depth to the characterization, and creates a sense of familiarity and universality." The reader comes to understand the internal elements of each novel discussed—as well as the external influences that help shape it.

"The desire to write greatly," Harold Bloom of Yale University says, "is the desire to be elsewhere, in a time and place of one's own, in an originality that must compound with inheritance, with an anxiety of influence." A writer seeks to create a unique world within a story, but although it is unique, it is not disconnected from our own world. It speaks to us *because* of what the writer brings to the writing from our world: how he or she was raised and educated; his or her likes and dislikes; the events occurring in the real world at the time of the writing, and while the author was growing up. When we know what an author has brought to his or her work, we gain a greater insight into both the "originality" (the world of the book), and the things that "compound" it. This insight enables us to question that created world and find answers more readily. By informing ourselves, we are able to establish a more effective dialogue with both book and author.

Novels for Students, in addition to providing a plot summary and descriptive list of characters—to remind readers of what they have read—also explores the external influences that shaped each book. Each entry includes a discussion of the author's background, and the historical context in which the novel was written. It is vital to know, for instance, that when Ray Bradbury was writing *Fahrenheit 451* (Vol. 1), the threat of Nazi domination had recently ended in Europe, and the McCarthy hearings were taking place in Washington, D.C. This information goes far in answering the question, "Why did he write a story of oppressive government control and book burning?" Similarly, it is important to know that Harper Lee, author of *To Kill a Mockingbird,* was born and raised in Monroeville, Alabama, and that her father was a lawyer. Readers can now see why she chose the south as a setting for her novel—it is the place with which she was most familiar—and start to comprehend her characters and their actions.

Novels for Students helps readers find the answers they seek when they establish a dialogue with a particular novel. It also aids in the posing of questions by providing the opinions and interpretations of various critics and reviewers, broadening that dialogue. Some reviewers of *To Kill A Mockingbird,* for example, "faulted the novel's climax as melodramatic." This statement leads readers to ask, "Is it, indeed, melodramatic?" "If not, why did some reviewers see it as such?" "If it is, why did Lee choose to make it melodramatic?" "Is melodrama ever justified?" By being spurred to ask these questions, readers not only learn more about the book and its writer, but about the nature of writing itself.

The literature included for discussion in *Novels for Students* has been chosen because it has something vital to say to us. *Of Mice and Men, Catch-22, The Joy Luck Club, My Antonia, A Separate Peace* and the other novels here speak of life and modern sensibility. In addition to their individual, specific messages of prejudice, power, love or hate, living and dying, however, they and all great literature also share a common intent. They force us to *think*—about life, literature, and about others, not just about ourselves. They pry us from the narrow confines of our minds and thrust us outward to confront the world of books and the larger, real world we all share. *Novels for Students* helps us in this confrontation by providing the means of enriching our conversation with literature and the world, by creating an *informed* dialogue, one that brings true pleasure to the personal act of reading.

Sources

Harold Bloom, *The Western Canon, The Books and School of the Ages,* Riverhead Books, 1994.

Watty Piper, *The Little Engine That Could,* Platt & Munk, 1930.

Anne Devereaux Jordan
Senior Editor, TALL
(Teaching and Learning Literature)

Introduction

Purpose of the Book

The purpose of *Novels for Students (NfS)* is to provide readers with a guide to understanding, enjoying, and studying novels by giving them easy access to information about the work. Part of Gale's "For Students" Literature line, *NfS* is specifically designed to meet the curricular needs of high school and undergraduate college students and their teachers, as well as the interests of general readers and researchers considering specific novels. While each volume contains entries on "classic" novels frequently studied in classrooms, there are also entries containing hard-to-find information on contemporary novels, including works by multicultural, international, and women novelists.

The information covered in each entry includes an introduction to the novel and the novel's author; a plot summary, to help readers unravel and understand the events in a novel; descriptions of important characters, including explanation of a given character's role in the novel as well as discussion about that character's relationship to other characters in the novel; analysis of important themes in the novel; and an explanation of important literary techniques and movements as they are demonstrated in the novel.

In addition to this material, which helps the readers analyze the novel itself, students are also provided with important information on the literary and historical background informing each work. This includes a historical context essay, a box comparing the time or place the novel was written to modern Western culture, a critical essay, and excerpts from critical essays on the novel. A unique feature of *NfS* is a specially commissioned critical essay on each novel, targeted toward the student reader.

To further aid the student in studying and enjoying each novel, information on media adaptations is provided, as well as reading suggestions for works of fiction and nonfiction on similar themes and topics. Classroom aids include ideas for research papers and lists of critical sources that provide additional material on the novel.

Selection Criteria

The titles for each volume of *NfS* were selected by surveying numerous sources on teaching literature and analyzing course curricula for various school districts. Some of the sources surveyed included: literature anthologies; *Reading Lists for College-Bound Students: The Books Most Recommended by America's Top Colleges;* textbooks on teaching the novel; a College Board survey of novels commonly studied in high schools; a National Council of Teachers of English (NCTE) survey of novels commonly studied in high schools; the NCTE's *Teaching Literature in High School: The Novel;* and the Young Adult Library Services Association (YALSA) list of best books for young adults of the past twenty-five years.

Input was also solicited from our advisory board, as well as from educators from various areas.

From these discussions, it was determined that each volume should have a mix of "classic" novels (those works commonly taught in literature classes) and contemporary novels for which information is often hard to find. Because of the interest in expanding the canon of literature, an emphasis was also placed on including works by international, multicultural, and women authors. Our advisory board members—educational professionals—helped pare down the list for each volume. If a work was not selected for the present volume, it was often noted as a possibility for a future volume. As always, the editor welcomes suggestions for titles to be included in future volumes.

How Each Entry Is Organized

Each entry, or chapter, in *NfS* focuses on one novel. Each entry heading lists the full name of the novel, the author's name, and the date of the novel's publication. The following elements are contained in each entry:

- **Introduction:** a brief overview of the novel which provides information about its first appearance, its literary standing, any controversies surrounding the work, and major conflicts or themes within the work.
- **Author Biography:** this section includes basic facts about the author's life, and focuses on events and times in the author's life that inspired the novel in question.
- **Plot Summary:** a factual description of the major events in the novel. Lengthy summaries are broken down with subheads.
- **Characters:** an alphabetical listing of major characters in the novel. Each character name is followed by a brief to an extensive description of the character's role in the novel, as well as discussion of the character's actions, relationships, and possible motivation.

  Characters are listed alphabetically by last name. If a character is unnamed—for instance, the narrator in *Invisible Man*—the character is listed as "The Narrator" and alphabetized as "Narrator." If a character's first name is the only one given, the name will appear alphabetically by that name.

  Variant names are also included for each character. Thus, the full name "Jean Louise Finch" would head the listing for the narrator of *To Kill a Mockingbird,* but listed in a separate cross-reference would be the nickname "Scout Finch."
- **Themes:** a thorough overview of how the major topics, themes, and issues are addressed within the novel. Each theme discussed appears in a separate subhead and is easily accessed through the boldface entries in the Subject/Theme Index.
- **Style:** this section addresses important style elements of the novel, such as setting, point of view, and narration; important literary devices used, such as imagery, foreshadowing, symbolism; and, if applicable, genres to which the work might have belonged, such as Gothicism or Romanticism. Literary terms are explained within the entry but can also be found in the Glossary.
- **Historical Context:** This section outlines the social, political, and cultural climate *in which the author lived and the novel was created.* This section may include descriptions of related historical events, pertinent aspects of daily life in the culture, and the artistic and literary sensibilities of the time in which the work was written. If the novel is a historical work, information regarding the time in which the novel is set is also included. Each section is broken down with helpful subheads.
- **Critical Overview:** this section provides background on the critical reputation of the novel, including bannings or any other public controversies surrounding the work. For older works, this section includes a history of how the novel was first received and how perceptions of it may have changed over the years; for more recent novels, direct quotes from early reviews may also be included.
- **Criticism:** an essay commissioned by *NfS* which specifically deals with the novel and is written specifically for the student audience, as well as excerpts from previously published criticism on the work (if available).
- **Sources:** an alphabetical list of critical material used in compiling the entry, with full bibliographical information.
- **Further Reading:** an alphabetical list of other critical sources which may prove useful for the student. It includes full bibliographical information and a brief annotation.

In addition, each entry contains the following highlighted sections, set apart from the main text as sidebars:

- **Media Adaptations:** a list of important film and television adaptations of the novel, including source information. The list also includes stage adaptations, audio recordings, musical adaptations, etc.

- **Topics for Further Study:** a list of potential study questions or research topics dealing with the novel. This section includes questions related to other disciplines the student may be studying, such as American history, world history, science, math, government, business, geography, economics, psychology, etc.
- **Compare and Contrast Box:** an "at-a-glance" comparison of the cultural and historical differences between the author's time and culture and late twentieth century/early twenty-first century Western culture. This box includes pertinent parallels between the major scientific, political, and cultural movements of the time or place the novel was written, the time or place the novel was set (if a historical work), and modern Western culture. Works written after 1990 may not have this box.
- **What Do I Read Next?:** a list of works that might complement the featured novel or serve as a contrast to it. This includes works by the same author and others, works of fiction and nonfiction, and works from various genres, cultures, and eras.

Other Features

NfS includes "The Informed Dialogue: Interacting with Literature," a foreword by Anne Devereaux Jordan, Senior Editor for *Teaching and Learning Literature* (*TALL*), and a founder of the Children's Literature Association. This essay provides an enlightening look at how readers interact with literature and how *Novels for Students* can help teachers show students how to enrich their own reading experiences.

A Cumulative Author/Title Index lists the authors and titles covered in each volume of the *NfS* series.

A Cumulative Nationality/Ethnicity Index breaks down the authors and titles covered in each volume of the *NfS* series by nationality and ethnicity.

A Subject/Theme Index, specific to each volume, provides easy reference for users who may be studying a particular subject or theme rather than a single work. Significant subjects from events to broad themes are included, and the entries pointing to the specific theme discussions in each entry are indicated in **boldface.**

Each entry may have several illustrations, including photos of the author, stills from film adaptations, maps, and/or photos of key historical events, if available.

Citing Novels for Students

When writing papers, students who quote directly from any volume of *Novels for Students* may use the following general forms. These examples are based on MLA style; teachers may request that students adhere to a different style, so the following examples may be adapted as needed.

When citing text from *NfS* that is not attributed to a particular author (i.e., the Themes, Style, Historical Context sections, etc.), the following format should be used in the bibliography section:

> "*Night.*" *Novels for Students.* Ed. Marie Rose Napierkowski. Vol. 4. Detroit: Gale, 1998. 234–35.

When quoting the specially commissioned essay from *NfS* (usually the first piece under the "Criticism" subhead), the following format should be used:

> Miller, Tyrus. Critical Essay on *Winesburg, Ohio. Novels for Students.* Ed. Marie Rose Napierkowski. Vol. 4. Detroit: Gale, 1998. 335–39.

When quoting a journal or newspaper essay that is reprinted in a volume of *NfS,* the following form may be used:

> Malak, Amin. "Margaret Atwood's *The Handmaid's Tale* and the Dystopian Tradition," *Canadian Literature* No. 112 (Spring, 1987), 9–16; excerpted and reprinted in *Novels for Students,* Vol. 4, ed. Marie Rose Napierkowski (Detroit: Gale, 1998), pp. 133–36.

When quoting material reprinted from a book that appears in a volume of *NfS,* the following form may be used:

> Adams, Timothy Dow. "Richard Wright: Wearing the Mask," in *Telling Lies in Modern American Autobiography* (University of North Carolina Press, 1990), 69–83; excerpted and reprinted in *Novels for Students,* Vol. 1, ed. Diane Telgen (Detroit: Gale, 1997), pp. 59–61.

We Welcome Your Suggestions

The editor of *Novels for Students* welcomes your comments and ideas. Readers who wish to suggest novels to appear in future volumes, or who have other suggestions, are cordially invited to contact the editor. You may contact the editor via e-mail at: **ForStudentsEditors@thomson.com.** Or write to the editor at:

Editor, *Novels for Students*
Thomson Gale
27500 Drake Road
Farmington Hills, MI 48331–3535

Literary Chronology

1877: Hermann Hesse is born on July 2 in the small town of Calw, in the German state of Württemberg.

1897: William Faulkner is born on September 25 in New Albany, Mississippi.

1897: Thornton Wilder is born on April 17 in Madison, Wisconsin.

1898: C. S. Lewis is born on November 29 in a suburb of Belfast, Ireland.

1926: Alison Lurie is born on September 3 in Chicago.

1927: Hermann Hesse's *Steppenwolf* is published.

1927: Thornton Wilder's *The Bridge of San Luis Rey* is published.

1928: Thornton Wilder is awarded the Pulitzer Prize for his novel *The Bridge of San Luis Rey.*

1932: William Faulkner's *Light in August* is published.

1932: John Updike is born on March 18 in Reading, Pennsylvania, located in what is known locally as Pennsylvania Dutch country.

1938: Judy Blume is born on February 12 in Elizabeth, New Jersey.

1938: Joyce Carol Oates is born on June 16 in Lockport, a small town in rural western New York State, similar to the setting of many of her works.

1944: Marilynne Robinson is born in Sandpoint, Idaho, probably in 1944 (though 1943 and 1947 are also reported).

1946: Hermann Hesse is awarded the Nobel Prize for Literature.

1947: Keri Hulme is born on March 9 in Christchurch, New Zealand.

1950: C. S. Lewis's *The Lion, the Witch and the Wardrobe* is published.

1955: Barbara Kingsolver is born on April 8 in Annapolis, Maryland.

1960: Jeffrey Eugenides is born on March 8 in the affluent Detroit suburb of Grosse Pointe, Michigan.

1962: William Faulkner dies of a heart attack on July 6 in Byhalia, Mississippi.

1962: Hermann Hesse dies from a cerebral hemorrhage on August 9 at the age of eighty-five in Montagnola.

1963: C. S. Lewis dies on November 22, one week short of his sixty-fifth birthday.

1975: Judy Blume's *Forever . . .* is published.

1975: Thornton Wilder dies of a heart attack in his sleep on December 7 in Hamden, Connecticut.

1984: Alison Lurie's *Foreign Affairs* is published.

1984: Keri Hulme's *The Bone People* is published.

1985: Alison Lurie is awarded the Pulitzer Prize in fiction for *Foreign Affairs.*

1996: Joyce Carol Oates's *We Were the Mulvaneys* is published.

1997: John Updike's *Toward the End of Time* is published.

1998: Barbara Kingsolver's *The Poisonwood Bible* is published.

2002: Jeffrey Eugenides's *Middlesex* is published.

2003: Jeffrey Eugenides is awarded the Pulitzer Prize in fiction for *Middlesex*.

2004: Marilynne Robinson's *Gilead* is published.

2005: Marilynne Robinson is awarded the Pulitzer Prize in fiction for *Gilead*.

Acknowledgments

The editors wish to thank the copyright holders of the excerpted criticism included in this volume and the permissions managers of many book and magazine publishing companies for assisting us in securing reproduction rights. We are also grateful to the staffs of the Detroit Public Library, the Library of Congress, the University of Detroit Mercy Library, Wayne State University Purdy/Kresge Library Complex, and the University of Michigan Libraries for making their resources available to us. Following is a list of the copyright holders who have granted us permission to reproduce material in this volume of *NFS*. Every effort has been made to trace copyright, but if omissions have been made, please let us know.

COPYRIGHTED EXCERPTS IN *NFS*, VOLUME 24, WERE REPRODUCED FROM THE FOLLOWING PERIODICALS:

The Christian Century, v. 114, November, 1997. Copyright © 1997 by the Christian Century Foundation. All rights reserved. Reproduced by permission.—***College Literature***, summer, 2003. Copyright © 2003 by West Chester University. Reproduced by permission.—***Critique***, v. 33, winter, 1992; v. 45, summer, 2004. Copyright © 1992 by Helen Dwight Reid Educational Foundation. Reproduced with permission of the Helen Dwight Reid Educational Foundation, published by Heldref Publications, 1319 18th Street, NW, Washington, DC 20036-1802.—***Europe Intelligence Wire***, June 8, 2005. Copyright Guardian Newspapers Limited 2005. Reproduced by permission of Guardian News Service, LTD.—***First Things: A Monthly Journal of Religion and Public Life***, March, 2005. Copyright 2005 Institute on Religion and Public Life. Reproduced by permission.—***Hecate***, v. 14, May 31, 1988. Copyright Hecate Press, English Department. Reproduced by permission.—***International Fiction Review***, January, 2002. Copyright © 2002 International Fiction Association. Reproduced by permission.—***Key West Review***, v. 1, spring, 1988 for "Alison Lurie: An Interview," by Liz Lear. Reproduced by permission of the author.—***Modern Fiction Studies***, v. 48, fall, 2002. Copyright © 2002 The Johns Hopkins University Press. Reproduced by permission.—***The Nation***, October, 1996. Copyright © 1996 by *The Nation* Magazine/The Nation Company, Inc. Reproduced by permission.—***The New Republic***, v. 191, October 8, 1984; v. 217, November 17, 1997; v. 227, October 7, 2002. Copyright © 1984, 1997, 2002 by The New Republic, Inc. All reproduced by permission of *The New Republic*.—***School Library Journal***, v. 42, June, 1996. Copyright © 1996. Reproduced from *School Library Journal*, a Cahners/R. R. Bowker Publication, by permission.

COPYRIGHTED EXCERPTS IN *NFS*, VOLUME 24, WERE REPRODUCED FROM THE FOLLOWING BOOKS:

Burbank, Rex. From ***Thornton Wilder***. Twayne Publishers, 1978. Copyright © 1961, by Twayne Publishers, Inc. Reproduced by permission of the author.—Creighton, Joanne V. From "The 'I,' Which Doesn't Exist, Is Everything," in ***Joyce Carol Oates***, Twayne's United States Authors on CD-ROM, G. K. Hall & Co., 1997, previously published in 1992. Copyright © 1992 Twayne. Reproduced by permission.—Goldstein, Malcolm. From ***The Art of Thornton Wilder***. University of Nebraska Press, 1965. Copyright © 1965 by the University of Nebraska Press. Copyright © renewed 1993 by the University of Nebraska Press. All rights reserved. Reproduced by permission of the University of Nebraska Press.—Konkle, Lincoln. From "Judgment Day in the Jazz Age …," in ***Thornton Wilder: New Essays***. Edited by Martin Blank, Dalma Hunyadi Brunauer, and David Garrett Izzo. Locust Hill Press, 1999. © 1999 Martin Blank, Dalma H. Brunauer, and David Garrett Izzo. All rights reserved. Reproduced by permission of the author.—Manlove, Colin. From ***"The Chronicles of Narnia": The Patterning of a Fantastic Word***. Twayne Publishers, 1993. Copyright © 1993 by Twayne Publishers. All rights reserved. Reproduced by permission of Thomson Learning.—Martindale, Wayne, with Kathryn Welch. From "Food for the Soul: Eating in Narnia," in ***Narnia Beckons***. Edited and translated by Ted Baehr and James Baehr. Broadman & Holman Publishers, 2005. Copyright © 2005 by Theodore Baehr. All rights reserved. Reproduced by permission.

COPYRIGHTED EXCERPTS IN *NFS*, VOLUME 24, WERE REPRODUCED FROM THE FOLLOWING WEBSITES OR OTHER SOURCES:

From ***Contemporary Authors Online***. "Joyce Carol Oates," www.gale.com, Thomson Gale, 2006. Reproduced by permission of Thomson Gale.

Contributors

Bryan Aubrey: Aubrey holds a Ph.D. in English and has published many articles on twentieth century literature. Entries on *Foreign Affairs* and *Steppenwolf.* Original essays on *Foreign Affairs* and *Steppenwolf.*

Timothy Dunham: Dunham has a master's degree in communication and a bachelor's degree in English literature. Entry on *The Lion, the Witch and the Wardrobe*. Original essay on *The Lion, the Witch and the Wardrobe.*

Joyce Hart: Hart is a published author and a former teacher. Entries on *The Bone People*, *Forever . . .* , and *Toward the End of Time*. Original essays on *The Bone People*, *Forever . . .* , and *Toward the End of Time*.

David Kelly: Kelly is an instructor of creative writing and literature. Entries on *The Bridge of San Luis Rey* and *We Were the Mulvaneys*. Original essays on *The Bridge of San Luis Rey* and *We Were the Mulvaneys*.

Melodie Monahan: Monahan has a Ph.D. in English and operates an editing service, The Inkwell Works. Entry on *Gilead*. Original essay on *Gilead*.

Wendy Perkins: Perkins is a professor of American and English literature and film. Entries on *Light in August*, *Middlesex*, and *The Poisonwood Bible*. Original essays on *Light in August*, *Middlesex*, and *The Poisonwood Bible*.

Laura Pryor: Pryor has a B.A. from the University of Michigan and twenty years experience in professional and creative writing with special interest in fiction. Original essay on *Forever . . . .*

The Bone People

Keri Hulme

1984

The Bone People, published in 1984, is an unusual story of love. It is unusual in the telling, the subject matter, and the form of love that the story depicts. This is in no way a romance; it is filled with violence, fear, and twisted emotions. At the story's core, however, are three people who struggle very hard to figure out what love is and how to find it.

Hulme won New Zealand's Pegasus Prize for Literature (1984) for *The Bone People*. Then the book went on to win the prestigious Booker Prize (1985), a coveted literary award. *The Bone People*, which began as a short story, took Hulme twelve years to write. As of 2006, it was the only novel that she has published.

The Bone People has been praised for its story and for the way it is written, which is said to reflect the intonation and style of the Maori language. The story is, in fact, filled with allusions to the Maori culture and many of the challenges that the Maori people face, those common struggles caused by the colonization of an indigenous people. At the same time, however, the problems that are presented in this story have universal relevance. The story attempts to answer questions about how one heals deep-seated, emotional pain, how one becomes true to oneself, and how one finds love.

Author Biography

Keri Hulme was born on March 9, 1947 in Christchurch, New Zealand, to a mother of mixed

Maori and Scots heritage and an English father. Her father died when Hulme was eleven. By that time, she had already demonstrated her potential as a writer, creating poems and short stories and rewriting published stories that she thought she could improve. To encourage her daughter (the eldest of six siblings), Hulme's mother converted a sun porch into a writing studio. When Hulme was eighteen, she had a dream about a mute, mysterious boy with long hair and green eyes. From this dream, she modeled the character of Simon in her first novel. Like her protagonist, Kerewin Holmes, Keri Hulme identifies most with her Maori heritage. Also like her protagonist, Hulme left home early and worked odd jobs, one in a tobacco field, another for the New Zealand post office system. She spent one year at the University of Canterbury.

In 1972, at the age of twenty-five, Hulme decided to write full time. She had several short stories and poems published. In 1975, she won the Katherine Mansfield Memorial Prize for her short story "Hooks and Feelers." A few years later, she accepted the position of resident writer at Otago University, and later she also worked at the University of Canterbury.

Silences Between, published in 1982, was Hulme's first collection of poetry. *The Bone People* appeared in 1984. This novel first began as a short story, but it kept growing. Hulme received many rejections from publishers before a small collective of women decided to publish the book. They ran four thousand copies on the first printing, and the books sold out quickly.

Hulme's other works include a collection of short stories, *The Windeater* (1982), *Homeplaces* (1989), a collection of essays and photographs retaining to New Zealand, and a second collection of poems called *Strand* (1992).

Plot Summary

Prologue
The End At The Beginning
I Season Of The Day Moon

Keri Hulme's *The Bone People* is written in a nontraditional style. It begins with a prologue, which includes a poem and three short sections that serve as oblique introductions to the three main characters, although readers will only recognize this fact after they have completed the novel and then look back at the prologue again.

1 Portrait Of A Sandal

Kerewin Holmes, the protagonist of this story, falls asleep outside. When she awakens, she notices a sandal that lies at her feet. She curses the intruder who must have left it, a small shoe with a hole through the heel. Kerewin suspects it belongs to a child who must have stepped on something sharp and, from the footprints she finds, must have then limped away.

Kerewin lives on an isolated parcel of land in a house she has built in the shape of a tower. She has never invited anyone to visit her home.

Kerewin enters her house and spots a young boy sitting high in the midst of some bookshelves. Kerewin yells at him and soon discovers that the child cannot talk. The young boy wears a pendant that bears his name, phone number, and address. His name is Simon P. Gillayley.

Kerewin notices the boy has a piece of sharp wood stuck in his foot. She pulls it out and bandages his foot then tells him to go home. The boy communicates through hand gestures and short notes he writes on a pad. Kerewin feels something for the boy and invites him to stay for lunch. Afterward, she calls the boy's telephone number. She uses a radiophone, which has to go through an operator who says he will call Kerewin back when he reaches someone at the other end. The operator calls back later and says that the father is working late and he has not been able to reach the Tainuis, a couple that sometimes takes care of Simon while his father is away.

Kerewin tells Simon that he can stay until someone comes to pick him up. No one shows up until the next morning. Piri Tainui, a cousin of the boy's father, finally comes. Piri says that Joe, Simon's father, is still sleeping. Piri takes Simon home.

2 Feelers

The next day, Joe comes by to thank Kerewin and brings the boy with him. He also brings back the black chess queen that Simon has stolen from Kerewin's house. Joe explains how Simon constantly gets into trouble and also has a hard time at school. Joe is impressed that Kerewin was so good with Simon and is surprised that Simon asked to see her again.

Joe then tells Kerewin the story of how he found Simon, the victim of a shipwreck. Joe is not certain of Simon's age. He has had Simon for three years. Simon is probably between seven and nine years of age. Kerewin invites Joe and Simon to stay for tea (dinner).

Simon falls asleep. Joe and Kerewin play chess. A few days later, Simon turns up at Kerewin's home. Simon has brought Kerewin a gift, a string of semi-precious stones, which she refuses because she recognizes that the stones are an heirloom, an old rosary, possibly. Simon insists that the stones are his to give; Kerewin accepts graciously but also reluctantly, feeling unworthy of them.

Kerewin is an artist. In the past few years, she has been unable to paint. She tries to work out an image, while Simon is still there. Then she thinks about him and realizes that Simon has touched her, both physically and emotionally, something that she is unused to. She recoils from his touch, but at the same time, she also starts opening up to him.

Joe shows up and invites Kerewin to join him and Simon for tea at his house. They go to Joe's house. In the midst of the meal, Joe gets angry at Simon for sneaking a glass of wine. He threatens to beat the boy. Kerewin senses the tension and breaks it by complimenting Joe for the meal.

When Simon is ready for bed, he kisses Kerewin. She says it has been a long time since she has been kissed. The last was from her brother before the big family break up. She does not explain what happened then.

After Simon goes to bed, Joe tells Kerewin how he found the boy three years earlier. There had been a storm. A boat had crashed against the rocks. Two bodies were found. Then Joe found Simon and performed artificial respiration. Several of Simon's bones were cracked, and the boy was in shock and also had pneumonia. Simon would not let go of Joe's hand all the while he was in the hospital. Joe and his wife, Hana, decided to keep Simon.

Police never determine who the other two people were. The necklace of semi-precious stones that Simon had given to Kerewin used to belong to one the people who died. The necklace was found around the woman's neck. Simon clung to the necklace, not allowing anyone to take it from him during his first year with Joe.

Later, Kerewin asks Joe if he has ever taken a vacation. Joe tells her how he has tried, but nothing seemed to work out right with Simon. Kerewin tells Joe about a little beach shack that her family owns and suggests they all go there sometime.

3 Leaps In The Dark

Kerewin writes in her journal. She refers to herself as a "neuter human." She tells the journal she cannot paint. She refers to Simon as "a very unlikely but strangely likable brat." She admits that she wants to uncover Simon's history. She has done some research. The string of semi-precious stones is a rosary, and she has traced it to an Irish earl. Kerewin tells her journal that she witnessed Joe beating Simon.

Kerewin receives a letter from the earl in Ireland. He recognizes the rosary. It once belonged to his grandson, who has since been disinherited. This grandson once lived in New Zealand, but the earl wants nothing to do with him and asks that Kerewin not write again.

Later, Kerewin watches Simon build small structures on the beach made of bits of driftwood, shells, and grass. When finished, Simon leans his ear down on them and listens. He tells Kerewin that he hears music. Simon tells Kerewin to do the same. Kerewin is fascinated and wonders how Simon came to know how to do this. When Joe sneaks out one night to listen, he hears music, too. But the music scares Joe. He steps on the structure and smashes it. Joe never tells anyone that he has heard the music.

Joe calls Kerewin from the bar one night. Joe is drunk. He tells Kerewin there has been an incident. Joe does not know where Simon is. Kerewin looks around the town but cannot find Simon. She then goes to the bar and for the first time does not feel comfortable around Joe. Kerewin feels that Joe is lying about something or hiding something from her.

Kerewin goes home and finds Simon there. He is shivering. Kerewin sees that his eyes are swollen, and his lip is split. When Kerewin calls Joe, he denies hitting Simon.

Joe is afraid to tell Kerewin about how he beats Simon. He is concerned that if he does, it will ruin everything between him and Kerewin. Joe hopes that maybe the three of them may become a family. Shortly afterward, Simon gets into trouble again, and Joe beats him severely.

A few days later, Simon goes to Kerewin's place, but she is not there. Simon starts drinking from different bottles in Kerewin's kitchen. Kerewin finds him later slumped on the floor, totally drunk. She places him under a cold shower. Simon is revived, but he is totally disoriented and starts screaming. Kerewin realizes that she might have triggered feelings he had when he was shipwrecked. She sees the terror on Simon's face. When she takes off Simon's wet clothes, she also sees that he has been repeatedly beaten with a belt. Kerewin does not know what to do. She had not realized that the beatings Joe was giving Simon were so harsh. She does not want the responsibility of knowing. So she decides to say nothing to Joe or to anyone else about it. She resolves to keep Simon out of harm's way as best she can.

II The Sea Round

4 A Place To Sleep By Day

Kerewin, Joe, and Simon go to the beach hut belonging to Kerewin's family. Simon feels the tension between Joe and Kerewin and tries to break it by annoying Joe. Joe becomes angry and lunges for the boy, but now Kerewin sees a chance to protect Simon and gives Joe a fight she believes he deserves. Kerewin, a master at Aikido, takes on Joe and beats him.

Immediately after the fight, though, Kerewin feels sick, a sudden pain in her stomach. She sleeps all day but wakes up at sundown feeling better. Kerewin thinks it might be an ulcer. Later, Kerewin and Joe talk about how Joe beats Simon. Kerewin admits that she already knew about it. Joe promises never to hit Simon again unless Kerewin agrees that Simon needs it.

5 Spring Tide, Neap Tide, Ebb Tide, Flood

The next day, Kerewin talks Joe and Simon into going fishing on an old family boat. As they are getting onboard, the adults realize that this might be a traumatic experience for Simon. Once they get out on the water, Simon looks terrified and eventually vomits. The adults want to turn back for his sake, but Simon says that he feels better and insists that they continue on. Simon catches a huge groper but in the process gets the large fishhook stuck deep in his thumb. Kerewin wants to take Simon to a doctor, but Simon refuses to go, so Joe takes the hook out.

The next day, Joe talks about his childhood. He was given to his grandmother when he was three. Joe's grandfather used to beat him. Joe suspects he was beaten because he was dark-skinned like his grandmother, whom his grandfather did not like for her Maori ways.

Simon finds a badly hurt bird on the beach. He digs a hole then puts it out of its misery by hitting it with a stone. Then Simon sings to the bird. Kerewin witnesses the scene from a distance. Simon freezes in terror when he realizes that Kerewin has heard him singing. Simon is also surprised by his ability. When Kerewin hugs him, he realizes it is all right to sing and continues doing so all through the day. He sings melodies with no words.

6 Ka Tata Te Po

Kerewin is upset by a surprise visit from her brother. It is brief, but it stirs memories. Joe decides they may all need a change of scenery, so they go to a local bar. Kerewin eventually becomes bored with the place and starts to leave. As they are leaving, a local man insults Kerewin, Joe, and Simon. Kerewin goes into a fighting position. The bartender steps between Kerewin and the man. Just then, a fly buzzes between them. Without moving, Kerewin catches the fly, smashes it, and flings the dead insect in the direction of the man. The people in the bar are amazed by her quick reflexes. A couple days later, the trio pack up and leave for home.

Part III The Lightning Struck Tower

7 Mirrortalk

Joe comes around to Kerewin's house after a brief separation. Joe is happy. The Tainuis have welcomed him home. Joe tells Kerewin that he and Simon hope Kerewin will join their family. Kerewin takes Joe to her studio and shows him some of her old paintings. This is all she wants, she tells him. No people. No family. She just wants to paint again. She gives one of the paintings to Joe and tells him to remain her friend but not to come any closer. There is nothing wrong with her, she tells Joe. She has never felt good in relationships since she was a child. Joe is undaunted. He believes he will eventually win her over.

One night when he is drunk, Joe asks Kerewin to come to the bar. Kerewin is depressed and gets drunk and sick. Joe and Kerewin do not get along well, and they leave in foul moods.

8 Nightfall

Simon goes to Binny Daniels to get money but finds the man dead. Joe had told Simon not to go to Kerewin's, but he goes there anyway. Simon has stolen a special knife from Kerewin. She knows he has it, but Simon continues to deny it. Simon, upset about seeing Binny, punches out toward Kerewin. She hits him back. Simon punches at her twice more but misses, then he sees her favorite guitar and kicks it, smashing it. Kerewin yells at Simon to get out, and he leaves.

Simon walks along the shops in the little town, smashing every window. A policeman brings Simon home to Joe. Joe calls Kerewin before he lays a hand on Simon. Kerewin is still angry and tells Joe and Simon how she feels. Joe hangs up and beats Simon. Joe tells Simon that he has ruined everything.

9 Candles In The Wind

Simon had taken a piece of glass from one of the broken windows and, when Joe was beating him, had stabbed Joe in the stomach. Kerewin is at Joe's house, cleaning up the blood, wishing she had not reacted the way she had. Maybe she could have prevented all the misery. Three weeks pass, and Kerewin is packing. She cannot erase the images in her head, seeing Simon, his jaw and nose broken, a hole in his crushed skull. Simon is in the hospital. Joe is about to be sent to jail. Joe sells his house, and Kerewin plans to burn hers down.

IV Feldapart Sinews, Breaken Bones

10 The Kaumatua and the Broken Man

Months have passed, and Joe is out of jail. He gets off a bus in the middle of nowhere. Joe camps out on some open land above a beach. The next day, Joe walks until he comes to the edge of cliff. He can go no further unless he jumps down. He finally decides that if he survives it will be a sign that he should go on. He survives the jump but breaks his arm. He is found by a man called Tiaki Mira, who calls himself The Keeper.

The old man helps Joe to heal. He tells Joe that he has been waiting for him. Tiaki Mira has been told a secret by his grandmother, who raised him in the old Maori way. Tiaki cannot die until he has passed this secret on to another person. Tiaki has been waiting a long time, but now he knows he is near death. He passes the secret to Joe and then dies. Before dying, Tiaki signs over all his property to Joe.

Joe must protect the secret, which is the existence of an old ship that the ancient ones used to come to New Zealand. It is hidden in a pool of water on Tiaki's land. One night, there is an awful noise, and the land shakes. When Joe makes it over to the pool, he sees huge boulders have filled in the hole. The ancient ship is buried. There is no more reason for Joe to stay on this piece of land. He packs his things and leaves.

11 The Boy By His Own

The scene changes to the hospital. Simon is recovering slowly. He has had amnesia, but his memory is slowly returning. His crushed skull has cost him his hearing. Simon wants to go home. He does not understand why Joe and Kerewin do not come to see him.

Doctors try to get Simon to communicate. He only asks when he is going home. Tainui comes to visit, but he feels he cannot help the boy, who still needs a lot of therapy and rehabilitation. Simon is sent to a special hospital. People there try to find him a home, but Simon escapes.

12 The Woman At The Wellspring Of Death

Kerewin is sick, and she fears she is dying. She has that same ache in her stomach that she had at the beach with Joe and Simon. It will not go away. She tries to get medication, but doctors will not give her anything unless she allows them to examine her, which she will not permit. She is determined to heal herself or die. She camps out at the beach and suffers through her illness until close to death; the illness subsides, and she begins to heal. Then, as she recuperates, she decides it is finally time to go home.

Epilogue
Moonwater Picking

The final scene of the novel depicts a family reunion, both Kerewin's and Joe's. Simon is in the midst. Nothing is really explained, and sentences are only barely connected. Bits of conversation, sometimes without indicating who is saying what, complete the passage. There are hints of happiness in some corners, suspicion and anger in others. All the reader knows for sure is that Kerewin has survived her ordeal, Joe is back in the fold, and Simon has somehow managed to escape the authorities. They are all celebrating some unnamed occasion in an unidentified location. It is not certain that Joe, Kerewin, and Simon will remain together, but they are together in the final scene.

Characters

Binny Daniels

Binny Daniels is a misfit who remains on the periphery of the action. He is an old man who lures young boys to his rundown shack and takes advantage of them sexually. Simon goes to Binny when he needs money. Simon swears that Binny does not do anything to him in exchange for the money, but there are hints that this may not be true. Simon is the one who finds Binny dead toward the end of the story. Seeing the dead body triggers

Simon, prompting Simon to break Kerewin's guitar and smash the shop windows.

Hana Gillayley

Hana, the deceased wife of Joe Gillayley, was a nurse and had mothered one child, who died from influenza. Hana was pregnant with a second child when she too contracted influenza and died. It was Hana who encouraged Joe to bring Simon into the family.

Joe Gillayley

Joe Gillayley takes the shipwrecked and nearly drowned Simon into his home. Joe is a sad character who is unable to express his emotions appropriately. He has lost so much, his mother, father, pregnant wife, and son. All he has left is the unusual boy who cannot speak and continually gets into trouble. Joe feels that Simon's inability to function socially is partly caused by his own inability to raise a child. Joe feels like a failure, and these feelings drive him to beat Simon whenever he loses his patience with the boy.

Joe says that he would love to have Kerewin join his family, but it is not clear that he loves her. It seems more likely that Joe needs Kerewin. She is stronger than Joe in many ways, mentally, physically, and emotionally. Although Kerewin has her limitations, Joe's weaknesses are more incapacitating. Like Kerewin, Joe uses alcohol to numb his pain, and so he does not have to think about his problems. He encourages Kerewin to get drunk with him, as if this will bring them together.

Joe has more Maori blood in him than Kerewin has. It is through Joe's character that the author introduces some Maori myths and spiritual beliefs. Joe's transformation occurs in the midst of a myth: he meets an old, traditional Maori man, who has been waiting for Joe to appear. Joe is jailed for beating Simon. However, through the old Maori man, Joe is given the responsibility of living in an isolated place and protecting a sacred relic. This new role gives Joe the chance to think about his life and where he is headed.

Simon Gillayley

Simon uses the family name of Gillayley, but it is not clear if he is legally adopted by Joe Gillayley, the man who finds Simon on the beach after the young boy is shipwrecked.

Simon is badly hurt, both physically and emotionally. Although Simon is capable of talking, he remains mute throughout the story, except for a brief period when Simon realizes that he can sing. Simon has a lot of trouble dealing with others. He cannot find a place where he feels like he belongs. Kerewin appears to be the one who most understands Simon. The boy is amazed that she pays attention to him and seems to know what Simon means behind his words. She does not judge him and she does not punish or shun him, at least not until he pushes her beyond her limits.

Simon tests people to get their attention. He also acts out to release emotional tension. He often makes Joe angry, apparently in hopes that after Joe beats him, Joe will love him again.

Simon is frustrated by his inability to communicate. He stoically endures a lot of pain, both self-inflicted and imposed. The only time he really cries out is in his sleep.

Kerewin Holmes

Kerewin, the protagonist, lives in a tower on an isolated piece of land and does not encourage people to visit her. She is an artist who can no longer paint, and she sometimes drinks quite heavily in an attempt to forget her inability to create.

Something happened that caused her to leave her family and have no contact with them. She is closed emotionally and does not like being touched. At one time, she studied Aikido and is adept at the martial art. She uses this skill to get back at Joe after she discovers that Joe has beaten Simon.

Like the other two main characters, Kerewin is emotionally confused. She says she does not like company, yet she enjoys the company of Joe and Simon. She says she does not like to be kissed, and yet she is touched by Simon's affection for her. Her emotional conflict may be expressed by the pain that she endures during the second part of the novel. The independent Kerewin insists that she can heal herself, despite the doctor's suggestions that she may need surgery. She somehow pulls herself through the physical crisis, as well as the emotional challenges she faces. By the end of the novel, she appears to be the happiest character of the three. She has her health, family, and even her guitar restored to her.

Kerewin refers to herself as a "neuter," neither male nor female. Her neutrality expresses itself also in her not being committed to Simon and Joe. She wants to live alone but also greatly misses her family. She is an artist, but she cannot paint. She is not a mother, yet her motherly instincts drive her to embrace Simon.

Ben Tainui

Not much is said of Ben Tainui, the oldest son of Wherahiko and Marama, except that he has taken over the maintenance and day-to-day running of the family farm because his parents are no longer able to do so.

Luce Tainui

Luce, the youngest son of the Tainuis, makes a brief appearance in the story. He is the least liked by Joe, as Luce seems to enjoy spreading bad news. It is Luce who tells Joe that Simon has been over to see Binny Daniels. Then Luce taunts Joe with this information, stating that Simon is going to grow up to be just like Joe.

Marama Tainui

Marama, Wherahiko's wife, often acts as Simon's grandmother, taking care of him and even spoiling him, as Joe tells it. Marama loves intensely but is not physically strong. She has suffered a stroke and is in the hospital when Simon is sent there after the final beating that Joe gives him. Marama is viewed as the ideal wife and mother.

Piri Tainui

Piri, the second son of Wherahiko and Marama Tainui, is the most visible of the couple's three sons. He often takes charge of Simon when Joe is too drunk or too tired at the end of the day. Piri is also the most vocal of the Tainuis in telling Joe to stop hurting Simon and then threatening to take Simon away from him. Piri's wife has left him, which leads Piri to drink in excess.

Wherahiko Tainui

Wherahiko is Joe's uncle. He and his wife, Marama, are surrogate parents for Joe. They often take care of Simon when Joe is working. Wherahiko tries to counsel Joe on how to raise Simon. He also tries to tell Kerewin about Joe's beating of Simon, but at the last minute, Wherahiko decides to give Joe one more chance to tell Kerewin himself. Wherahiko has suffered a heart attack. Though he is old, he has a happy life with his wife.

Themes

Child Abuse

Hulme's *The Bone People* gives graphic descriptions of child abuse. The young boy, Simon, receives this abuse. He is abused by his peers because they do not understand his inability to speak and his frustration in not being able to communicate. In some ways, he is abused by the people who are responsible for his education because they quickly dismiss him, unwilling to penetrate Simon's self-protective façade. These educators see only a troubled little boy who does not fit their idea of a typical school child. They do not take the time to see his intelligence. They want to get Simon out of their sight; they do not want to be responsible for him or troubled by him.

The harshest abuse, however, comes from the hands of the one person who claims to love Simon. Joe, who has accepted the responsibility of raising the abandoned boy, beats Simon, almost to the point of death. Joe excuses the harsh punishment by claiming that it is the only way to communicate to the child. Simon makes trouble, or at least this is what almost everyone claims. The only way to curb that behavior, Joe insists, is to give Simon trouble in return.

Joe is not totally convincing in this assertion, however, not even to himself. He knows if Kerewin discovers that he beats Simon, the relationship he hopes to build with Kerewin will be destroyed. On some level, Joe seems to know that what he is doing to Simon is wrong.

The child abuse is presented in an unusual manner. In part, the abuse is looked upon in a negative light. Joe's family, as represented by the Tainuis, knows that Joe has often abused Simon. They threaten to take the boy away from him and to tell Kerewin about it if Joe does not curb his brutality. But the reader might wonder why the Tainuis have allowed this behavior to continue for so long. If they know about it, how many times are they going to allow it to happen before they actually intervene?

When Kerewin realizes that Simon is being beaten, she suspects that Joe is the one who is doing it. Though Joe denies it, it is fairly easy to figure out that Joe is the perpetrator. Who else would beat Simon with a belt? But Kerewin decides not to do anything about the abuse. She does not want the responsibility. Then, as the story develops, Kerewin promotes the abuse. She loses her patience with the boy. She once understood that Simon's behavior was an attempt to get attention (and thus love); however, when Simon acts out against her, Kerewin loses her temper. She hits Simon, and then she tells Joe that he has her permission to hit Simon some more.

Simon is a defenseless little boy, yet the adults use corporeal punishment as the sole means of

Topics For Further Study

- Watch the DVD *Whale Rider* (2003) and mark the places where Maori traditions are portrayed. Look for an example of hongi, or traditional Maori greeting. Also mark the places where Maori war arts are shown. Pay attention to Maori arts, language, and traditional dress, too. Then take the DVD to your class and skim through the movie to give your classmates a quick overview of how Maori culture is portrayed in this movie.
- At least two of the art pieces that Kerewin works on in this story are described in detail. One is a drawing of spider-like webbing, and the other is a sculpture of Kerewin, Simon, and Joe all interconnected. Create your own interpretation of what you think one of these works might look like. Use any medium you choose. Present your work to the class and discuss it.
- Compile statistics about the Maori people over the past half century. How has their standard of living changed? Consider statistics about their health, education, and economic status. Also include statistics on the population of Maori people in New Zealand. Look for statistics on alcoholism, marriage and divorce, and child abuse. Where do most Maori people live? In an urban settings? Or is that changing? Present your findings to your class.
- Both the author and her protagonist are interested in fishing. Research the sport of fishing in New Zealand. What are some of the favorite fish people like to catch? What kind of fish is New Zealand noted for? Find a map of New Zealand and plot the more popular places to go fishing. Note the seasons for each type of fish as well as what kind of bait is most successful. Present your findings to the class.

controlling him. Joe was beaten as a child, and this fact is used, in some ways, to explain his abuse of Simon. Kerewin, however, states that she was never abused. She was hurt emotionally in some way that is never revealed, and she confesses that she is emotionally unavailable to others and avoids intimacy. Despite her awareness, when sufficiently provoked, she resorts to committing and condoning child abuse. The story ends on a seemingly happy though inconclusive note, but the road that takes the characters to the final scene is full of pain, anger, and abuse.

Relationships

Characters attempt to create relationships, but these relationships are based on shaky terms, to say the least. Simon needs to be nurtured by a maternal figure, someone who will care for him and protect him. Joe needs help in handling the troubled boy and in compensating for the loss through death of his own son and pregnant wife. Kerewin denies that she needs others; however, by the end of the story, the reader realizes that family relationship is what she craves most.

The story explores the difficulties of building relationships. Simon is severely hampered in expressing his needs because he cannot speak. Kerewin resists being touched by other people, preferring to remain aloof. Joe wants to express himself and make connection, but when he expresses himself, he often does so violently, creating counterproductive effects. The three characters must undergo a change before they can enjoy the benefits of sharing and exploring personal relationships.

A Sense of Going Home as Cure

The three main characters spend most of their time trying to return home, which they finally appear to accomplish at the end of the novel. Kerewin, who has built a tower in which she hides and curses intruders who attempt to befriend her, has left her family behind. The home she has built serves as a barrier to the world. She hopes it will become her home, but even at the beginning of the story, she refers to her tower as a prison. At the beach hut, Kerewin feels happily connected to a place. At the beach, she welcomes Joe and Simon to what she refers to as her real home. When she returns to the tower, she becomes depressed and ill. When she goes back to the beach again and nearly dies from some illness (both physical and psychological), she is able to finally go home. She finds her cure with her family.

Joe has a parallel experience. Joe's rage over his wife's death, and his inability to make sense of Simon explodes in a bloody scene in which he almost loses his life (when Simon responds to Joe's brutality and stabs Joe). Joe is sent to prison, where he confronts his emotions and reflects upon his life. Upon release, Joe encounters an old man who figuratively takes Joe back to his Maori roots. This is Joe's return home. Through the old Maori mystic, Joe grounds himself. The Maori culture is Joe's home, in other words. After this experience, Joe is determined to find Kerewin and to create a family with her and Simon. He knows that this is his destiny.

Simon, who is beaten severely, is also driven by a sense of home. It is all that he asks about once he regains consciousness toward the end of the book. He wants to know when he can go home. At this point, Simon does not know where Joe and Kerewin are, but he is determined to find them. It may be that his urge to go home keeps Simon alive. He does what he must to get released from the public authorities who attempt to keep him under their care. He runs away and finds Joe and Kerewin. At the end of the book, the three characters are reunited with the circle of family and home. The novel ends with a sense of happiness, fulfillment, and cure.

Style

Shifts in Setting and Voice

In *The Bone People*, Hulme employs sudden shifts in setting without explanation and subtle movements from inner dialogue to dreams to narration; moreover, the story is told in a variety of different voices. This unusual style creates a dream reality, a mystical atmosphere. Hulme combines poems, short essay-like reflections, and journal entries in order to narrate the story in a non-traditional way.

For example, Hulme begins her story with three poems, each focusing on one of the three main characters: Kerewin, Joe, and Simon. Next comes three short introductions (each less than a page long), one each for the three characters. The introductions are not connected to one another. At the end of the novel, readers understand what these poems and passages mean. These parts comprise the prologue of the novel.

In the first chapter, readers note that the dialogue is not attributed to specific speakers. Readers do not know who speaks the lines. Before the end of the page, the protagonist, Kerewin, is described in third-person point of view, but the text simultaneously provides Kerewin's inner thoughts, conveyed in first-person point of view. Sometimes when the protagonist is speaking through interior dialogue, the text is completely indented, signaling that the passage is indeed interior dialogue. However, other passages written in first person are not indented. Rather, they are set the same as the narration, which is most often rendered in third person. Readers adjust to this fluctuation, and soon the flow of the narration from one point of view to another begins to matter less than the content that is being delivered. Thus, typical patterns of narration are broken. The form of the novel fits its characters and their stories.

For example, in the first chapter, Kerewin discusses fishing for flounder. This part of the story is told in third-person point of view then switches to non-attributed dialogue, then back to third-person narration that reflects on what was just spoken in the dialogue, then on to interior dialogue, which is then interrupted by third-person narration that is subsequently interrupted by interior dialogue.

> When the smoke is finished, she unscrews the top of the stick and draws out seven inches of barbed steel. It fits neatly into slots in the stick top.
>
> "Now, flounders are easy to spear, providing one minds the toes."
>
> Whose, hers or the fishes,' she has never bothered finding out. She rolls her jeans legs up as far as they'll go, and slips down into the cold water. She steps ankle deep, then knee deep, and stands, feeling for the moving of the tide. Then slowly, keeping the early morning sun in front of her, she begins to stalk, mind in her hands and eyes looking only for the puff of mud and swift silted skid of a disturbed flounder.
>
> All this attention for sneaking up on a fish? And they say we humans are intelligent? Sheeit . . .
>
> and with a darting levering jab, stabbed, and a flounder flaps bloodyholed at the end of the stick.
>
> Kerewin looks at it with slow smiled satisfaction.
>
> Goodbye soulwringing night. Good morning sinshine, and a fat happy day.

By switching between the various voices, whether it is the narrator observing the character's actions or the character herself revealing her thoughts, the reader gains multiple viewpoints regarding what is going on in the scene. This multiplicity provides more insight into the character and another dimension for viewing the action.

As the novel continues, readers are also privy to the inner thoughts of Joe and Simon. The information that is provided through inner dialogue explains, for example, why Joe acts the way he does toward Simon, how he feels about the abuse he perpetrates, and what contradictions exist in his emotions. Regarding Simon, inner dialogue conveys his fears, which he cannot articulate through hand signals and written notes. In these stylistic ways, Hulme distinguishes between what is known about external reality and what is the inner reality of a given character.

Ethnic References

Hulme's novel is filled with references to the Maori culture. To make the setting of the novel even more authentic, the author makes extensive use of the Maori language and customs. Hulme does so without providing references or explanations in the text. Translations are provided at the back of the book of Maori phrases, sentences, and dialogues. However, the text itself offers no support or explanation. The text has a jarring or disjointed quality. The author may have included the Maori language without explanation to give the reader the sense of being an outsider; the reader is a witness yet remains a cultural outsider.

Historical Context

New Zealand Maori History and Culture

New Zealand was inhabited by Polynesian people, who arrived by boat probably from southeastern Asian islands (referred to in mythology as Hawaiki), possibly as early as 800 A.D. What is referred to as the Great Fleet (arrival of masses of Polynesians on the islands of New Zealand) may have begun as late as 1350. However, this approximate date is questioned by some modern anthropologists and historians. Much of the early history of the Maori was transmitted through oral tradition, or story telling, rather than by written records.

The Maori first settled along the coastlines of the two major islands that make up New Zealand. Tribal ancestors are designated by the name of the large canoe that each group used to come to the island. Each tribe has its own special (and original) canoe that is honored in stories. The name Tainui (which is used by Hulme in her novel) designates one of the major, original canoes. Many early tribes settled on South Island, where a large, turkey-like flightless bird, called the moa, was plentiful and a good source of food. As the population increased with the arrival of more people and diverse tribes, wars broke out between groups that vied for power and control of land. One tactic of warfare was cannibalism, the victor of the battle consuming the vanquished. By the time Europeans arrived, all the land had been explored and claimed by the Maori people.

New Zealand, or Aotearoa as it was called in the Maori language, was a difficult place in which to live for many among the migrating people. They had come from more tropical climates and were not used to the cold weather or local crops. Their traditional foods, for example coconut and taro, did not adapt to New Zealand. The newcomers hunted many birds and seals to the point of extinction and were forced to turn to farming.

The Dutch man Abel Tasman, in 1642, became perhaps the first European to circumnavigate (but not set foot upon) what was later called New Zealand. James Cook, in 1769, went ashore, but little is known about his experience. Cook's explorations, however, led to the arrival of European immigrants, which began about 1800. Europeans added muskets to warfare between the various Maori tribes. In 1840, a controversial treaty, written in both English and Maori, was signed between the Europeans and several hundred Maori chieftains. Into the early 2000s, the interpretation of the Waitangi Treaty remained in dispute. The translations, reportedly, often do not match. The so-called Pakeha (descendants of European settlers) claimed British authority over the lands, while the Maori claimed authority for the tribal chiefs. Through conflicts with Europeans, the Maori lost large tracts of land.

During the twentieth century, the Maori population declined dramatically due to diseases introduced by Europeans. The Maori population fell from 800,000 to 50,000. This decrease cost the native people political influence in the developing nation. However, out of this loss rose several important individuals. One of them was Apirana Ngata, who formed a political party that eventually placed Maori members in the parliament, introduced widespread health reforms, and changed the land tenure arrangements. Ngata also promoted Maori culture by collecting and publishing traditional songs and creating traditional carved meeting houses for many of the tribes. In the 1960s and 1970s, urban Maori youths protested the loss of tribal land and breaches in the Waitangi Treaty. Long protest marches and other political activity brought attention to the protest movement, and in some cases, land was given back to tribes. In the

Compare & Contrast

- **1980s:** Research conducted at the University of Otago, New Zealand, suggests that four out of five children receive corporal punishment, with 6 percent of that group receiving what is considered extreme punishment, such as being hit with a belt or being repeatedly kicked.

  2000s: According to a report by the Family Help Trust, New Zealand has one of the worst child mortality rates worldwide due to child abuse. In New Zealand, twelve Maori children in every 1000 suffer abuse.

- **1980s:** According to New Zealand government statistics, the Maori population stands at approximately 400,000, almost 10 percent of the total population of New Zealand.

  2000s: The Maori population continues to increase and is anticipated to reach one million by the middle of the twenty-first century, which would make it almost 20 percent of the total population of New Zealand.

- **1980s:** According to the New Zealand Ministry of Health, alcohol consumption rises sharply in the 1980s to just under twelve liters per person annually.

  2000s: According to the Alcohol Advisory Council of New Zealand, over 1.2 million New Zealanders believe that regular bingeing of alcohol is an acceptable practice.

early 2000s, a Waitangi Tribunal hears cases and presides over land disputes. The Maori language is also taught. Maori radio and television stations have been established. Problems remain, however. Cases of diabetes and cancer are more frequent among Maori than among Pakeha populations. Unemployment is also higher. The Maori are known for being able to adapt, however, an ability that continues to serve them as they enter the twenty-first century.

Maori Language

Maori is a Polynesian language spoken by indigenous population in New Zealand. In 1800, the Maori language was a unifying factor among indigenous people. Though the language has dialects, it had one single source. As late as 1840, as Europeans were arriving in large numbers, the Maori language dominated. European scholars worked with the Maori to help them devise an alphabet and, therefore, a written language. Into the 1870s, missionaries and European settlers and their children learned to speak Maori, with the children becoming more fluent than the adults. This all began to change, however, as the twentieth century approached. Maori quickly became less used, and indigenous people were taught English. By the early twentieth century, speaking Maori was a punishable offense. Maori parents encouraged their children to learn English, as it was fast becoming the language of New Zealand industry. In order to succeed in an increasingly Eurocentric society, Maori children needed to be fluent in English. However, at home, the people continued to speak their native tongue. Maori remained the first language of Maori children, and the language was used exclusively in religious ceremonies.

As urbanization increasingly affected Maori people after World War II, the number of speakers of Maori fell, reaching a low point in the 1980s of an estimated 20 percent of the Maori population. Urban youths lost contact with their language and, as a consequence, often with their cultural heritage as well. A twentieth-century movement attempted to immerse preschool children in the Maori language. This effort halted the decline but did not significantly increase the numbers of Maori-speaking individuals.

Critical Overview

The Bone People received both positive and negative reviews. Neil Hanson, writing for the *Los Angeles Times*, reports on the opposing verdicts: "The unknown Hulme had been the rank outsider

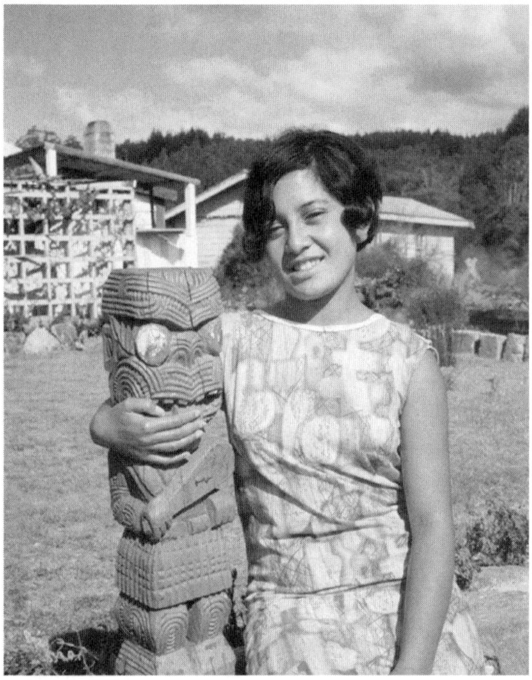

A young Maori woman sits on a rock wall with a wood sculpture at Whakarewarewa, New Zealand © Paul Almasy/Corbis

in an international field of literary heavyweights, and while those who loved her book did so with a passion, there was no middle ground; the rest absolutely hated it. She became one of the most controversial winners in the history of the Booker [Prize]." One of the critics who enjoyed Hulme's novel was Ursula Hegi, also writing for the *Los Angeles Times*. Hegi calls the novel "powerful and courageous." Hegi also stresses: "Hulme is a writer who trusts her voice and accepts her inner reality as valid. The result is a novel that is mysterious and violent, gentle and unsettling, compassionate and honest."

In his article for the *Seattle Times* called "Years of Rejection Didn't Stop Author's Quest to Publish," Andrew Moncur refers to Hulme's book as "the novel that nobody wanted." Moncur calls the novel "a prose-poem," a work remarkable "for the absence of anything resembling a sex scene." Moncur suggests that some people speculated that "the missing ingredient" contributed to the book's being turned down by commercial publishers.

Rebecca Brown, writing for the *Seattle Times*, praises Hulme's style: "Her prose, which sometimes reads like poetry, is gently self-mocking and full of puns and buoyant bawdy oaths." Brown adds: "Clearly, Hulme risks falling into bathos. Nonetheless, her scampering language and ironic wit ensure that the book never lapses into sentimentality. Indeed, the almost ridiculous action of the story renders the lessons the characters learn almost sublime."

Susan P. Willens, writing for *Belles Lettres*, is one of those critics who attacked the book, but with a qualifying note: "At its marrow," Willens writes, "this is a simple and compelling story—but it tries to do too much. With admirable ambition Hulme wants to blend together autobiography, sociology, anthropology, and Maori and Western literary styles. The mix becomes lumpy. Still, while the novel galumphs self-consciously along, it fascinates."

Writing for the *New York Times*, Claudia Tate labels Hulme's first novel "unforgettably rich and pungent." Tate explains further: "Miss Hulme's provocative novel summons power with words, as in a conjurer's spell." Offering a more negative view, critic Michiko Kakutani, also for the *New York Times*, writes that the "huge, ambitious work that aspires to portray the clash between Maori and European cultures . . . never quite lives up to its billing." Kakutani cites the continual inclusion of bits and pieces of dreams as well as the length of the story as detracting features. "The language employed by Miss Hulme's characters tends to range, back and forth, from the lyrical to the crude," Kakutani adds. However, Kakutani finds the ending of the story promising. In the final chapters, in which Hulme details the "spiritual rebirth" of each character, Kakutani locates the best of Hulme's writing. "Miss Hulme finally succeeds in finding a voice capable of welding together her inclinations toward the mythic and the naturalistic." These chapters demonstrate, according to Kakutani, Hulme's "considerable, if unfulfilled, gifts as a writer."

Criticism

Joyce Hart

Hart is a published writer and former teacher. In the following essay, she examines the silences in Hulme's novel The Bone People *and how the author uses them.*

There are many different kinds of silences in Hulme's *The Bone People*. There are the obvious silences of the characters as well as those that are embedded in the story. As many teachers, poets, mentors, and public speakers (just to name a few) know, silence can be a powerful tool. So-called pregnant pauses in a speech can subdue an audience as it awaits the next words to be spoken. Hulme, who has a collection of poems called *The Silence Between* (1982) evidently understands the capacity of silence and has used it throughout her novel.

Hulme's use of silence in her story and her characters is sometimes obvious, such as in Simon, a child who cannot speak. Simon's silence is not total, however, for he can sing. So his vocal chords clearly work. Simon's silence is more than physiological. He has been pushed into a world without audible words because he is so afraid of saying the wrong thing. He makes hand motions instead, signals that can be read by some people but not by all. He also writes notes, which express details but not necessarily his emotions, unless someone is paying particular attention. Kerewin suggests that Simon is silent in order to gain attention. "Is his face really that easy to read, or am I just looking harder because he can't talk?" Kerewin wonders. Getting people to notice him is both positive and negative; his silence works both for and against him. At one point in the story, Kerewin remains silent for part of a day while she wanders through the small town where she lives. After this little experiment, she comes home feeling strange. People stared at her, talked louder to her, and talked behind her back. Living in that kind of silence was not appealing to Kerewin, although she has silences of her own.

Simon is also silent about his pain. He barely whimpers when he is beaten. He does not tell anyone that he has been beaten, and when anyone discovers his sores or scars, he does not tell them who injured him. This silence of fear is tinged with other emotions as well. Simon's fear might be that he could lose Joe if he reports him as the perpetrator. Joe even tells Simon that if Simon tells Kerewin, they both will lose the chance of having Kerewin join them in a family. However, Simon may also be ashamed, believing that he has done wrong and deserves to be beaten. He learns that after the beatings, his relationship with Joe improves. Tensions are released, and Joe expresses some love for the boy. Simon is likely lost in a maze of confusion, too. He remembers things about his past, such as the name Clare, that he sometimes calls himself by. He does not share this detail with anyone. Simon's past is dark and terrifying. His silence then becomes a shield or protective armor that he wraps around himself, disallowing anyone to penetrate his thoughts. However, as Kerewin discovers, sometimes a protective shield can turn into a prison.

"This final silence for them might be likened to the silence of the womb. It is as if they have returned to the fetal stage, where they rebuild themselves and finally are reborn."

Kerewin's silence is in many ways similar to Simon's, although hers is more subtle. She has built a tower in which to hide from the world. She has created a silence through solitude. She refers to anyone who breaks this silence as an intruder. Although the tower is material and, therefore, protects her physically, it is symbolic of the tower she has built around her emotions. She does not want to be touched, physically or emotionally. Another kind of silence surrounds Kerewin's need to be protected. Neither the narrator nor the character Kerewin ever fully explains why Kerewin insists on her silence. She was not abused as a child, she tells Joe when he asks. All she knows (or all she says) is that she has never, even when she was very young, liked being touched. She describes herself as a neuter, neither female nor male; but neuter could also refer to being neutral emotionally. She has no feelings, she implies. However, if she truly had no feelings, it would not matter if she were touched, so one might deduce that Kerewin is hiding something. Indeed, she withholds information by using silence. She does not want to talk about why she acts the way she does; why she does not want to become involved with Joe; why she does not even want to take responsibility for Joe's senseless beatings of Simon.

Kerewin's silence about her own emotions is one thing. However, Kerewin's silence about Joe's beating Simon is a different matter completely. This silence facilitates the child abuse. The illness that Kerewin suffers toward the end of the story, whether one thinks of it as a physical cancer or a psychological one, may result from all the silences that are built up inside her. The illness begins, or at least becomes most noticeable, when she finally stands up to Joe and uses her physical and mental skills to defeat him at his own game—that of picking on (or beating up) someone much smaller than he is. Kerewin uses the skills that she has learned in Aikido to outsmart and outmaneuver Joe. She

What Do I Read Next?

- *Once Were Warriors*, published in 1990, is Alan Duff's reflections, in fictionalized form, on urbanized Maori people and the problems they have faced. One of the solutions that Duff provides is a return to the traditional Maori culture.
- Hulme's *Homeplaces: Three Coasts of the South Island of New Zealand* (1989) is a book of essays and photographs that vividly and beautifully capture some of Hulme's favorite places.
- Besides writing fiction, Hulme is a poet. *Bait* is her 1992 collection of poems, which covers topics of fishing, beaches, chants, and memories of her Maori culture.
- Carson McCullers, a twentieth-century American author, is most famous for her novel *The Heart Is a Lonely Hunter* (1940), which is about the residents of a small Southern town. One of the characters in the book is a deaf mute in whom many of the townspeople confide their problems.
- Describing another culture, Arundhati Roy's *The God of Small Things* (1996) is also a Booker Prize winner. The story follows the lives of twins as they grow up in India under the oppression of the caste system and the political system that supports it.

defeats him. But shortly afterward, she is in serious pain. This moment signals the beginning of her disintegration, which eventually leads her to the point of death and finally a rebirth. Kerewin's pain mounts as she returns to her usual life after a vacation with Joe and Simon at the beach. Coincidentally, Kerewin's pain also mounts as Joe's beatings of Simon increase in frequency and severity. This all culminates in an important upheaval when Joe almost kills Simon and Simon almost kills Joe. Kerewin, of course, is the catalyst for this eruption, and her guilt in playing that role creates a similar upsurge inside her. The silence Kerewin has kept concerning Joe's behavior toward Simon may cause Kerewin's pain to erupt.

Joe has silences, also. Unlike Simon or Kerewin, Joe loves to talk and to be sociable. He is quite gregarious. He shares stories with anyone around him who wants to listen. When the three of them, Joe, Kerewin, and Simon, go to the little village near the beach where they spend a vacation, Joe soon has a crowd of people around him, much like he does in his own home town, despite the fact that at the beach village Joe is a complete stranger. Joe has the gift of gab. However, Joe tells Kerewin that he has often wanted to cry but could not. This is Joe's emotional silence. Joe has suffered great losses. He lost his mother when she gave him to his grandmother. Shortly afterward, Joe's father died, and Joe felt his father's death was his fault. Joe studied to be a priest then lost his desire to be religious. When he met Hana, his first wife, Joe dropped out of the teacher's college he was attending and, therefore, lost a profession. Moreover, he also lost his son and his pregnant wife to the flu. Despite all these losses, Joe never expressed his emotions freely. He kept them locked inside of him, surrounded by silence. In this case, however, the pent up emotions came out in bursts of physical violence against Simon.

Another type of silence portrayed in the novel has to do with creativity. Kerewin's creative silence is the most obvious. She is a blocked artist. Where she could once paint with confidence and express her inner thoughts or feelings by depicting them on canvas, she can no longer do so. She makes attempts at it, but the images she has, at least in her mind, are all wrong. They no longer give her pleasure or satisfaction. The creative energy is misguided or stifled and does not translate adequately. So what she might have expressed in her paintings remains unarticulated.

Joe is an artist, too, a wood carver. But Joe keeps himself either too busy or too numb with alcohol to allow his creative energy to be expressed. He spends long hours on the job then slips on over to the local bar when he has time off and gets drunk. In this way, he can tell himself that he does not have time to be creative. So his intuitive (or creative) energies are muted.

In some ways, Simon is the most creatively expressive of the trio. He builds formations in the sand then listens to the music that comes from them. Kerewin appreciates and encourages these constructions, but Joe silences them. The forms that Simon creates scare Joe. Joe does not want anyone to know that he has heard the music (which might also be called the muse). So he goes out at night to listen in secret. Then, after hearing the sounds, Joe squashes the creations, or to put it another way, Joe silences Simon's creative expressions.

However, the three characters have one creative expression in common: music. Joe sings. Kerewin plays the guitar and sings, and Simon sings wordless melodies. But toward the end of the story, Simon destroys Kerewin's guitar. This destructive act triggers Kerewin's rage and retaliation. Kerewin punches Simon and then condemns him to Joe's brutal beating.

Kerewin, Joe, and Simon are ambivalent about having a relationship with one another. The silence in this case is like the two sides of a magnet, pulling together or pushing apart. The three characters all take steps forward and almost break through their own and each other's silences, but then one or the other takes a step back. To share love is to speak loudly to one another, both figuratively and physically. Although a lot can be said in silence, love needs expression and response.

At the end of the story, all three characters deepen the silence around them. Simon is beaten so badly, he loses his ability to hear. Simon's whole world thus grows silent. Meanwhile, Joe ends up taking care of an old Maori mystic's isolated land claim, living by himself at the edge of the sea, the only guardian of an ancient and sacred Maori secret. Kerewin also retreats from the world. She isolates herself in order to go into herself and find the source of her ailment and dissolve it. These characters find a way to heal themselves through the silence. They enter it as deeply as they can and emerge into new lives. This final silence for them might be likened to the silence of the womb. It is as if they have returned to the fetal stage, where they rebuild themselves and finally are reborn. This silence has been a potion for them, a potentially poisonous one, but they choose to use it to purge themselves of their impurities and resurface with new determination.

Silence can draw an audience in, as Hulme must realize. She does not offer many answers to the questions that her story poses. Readers are strung along the path of this story as they try to find the answers and finally realize that they must interpret the story's silences for themselves. However, Hulme might present these silences not as a technique but rather as an allegory of life itself, which is filled with different types of silences.

Source: Joyce Hart, Critical Essay on *The Bone People*, in *Novels for Students*, Thomson Gale, 2007.

Stephen D. Fox

In the following essay, Fox comments on the authors' "untraditional" treatment of disabled individuals in postcolonial New Zealand and Africa and how they "define the relationships of disability to each of the two cultures."

Two recent popular novels, Barbara Kingsolver's *The Poisonwood Bible* and Keri Hulme's *The Bone People,* explore postcolonial situations—in Africa and in New Zealand—and present pivotal characters with disabilities who eventually define the relationships of disability to each of the two cultures. Although the two novels have different perspectives, each appears to depart from traditional literary representations of disability that have been exploitative and highly limiting. But do they really break new ground?

Disability studies is an emerging field, still defining its theories and parameters and borrowing much of its methodology from gender, racial, postcolonial, and queer studies, which often derive from theorists such as Foucault and Derrida, but with an important difference. Whereas the other studies may overlap—lesbian writing in India could conceivably be studied by all four of the above methodologies—only disability studies is universal in its application. Disability is one of the most pervasive markers ("Body Criticism," Thomson 284–86). Anyone in any group could be, could have been, or could become a person with a disability, and everyone will experience some form of disability if he or she lives long enough. Yet critics in this new field find that authors have traditionally used, and abused, the concept of disability merely as a literary convenience, a handy metaphor for Otherness or for alternative social disturbance. David T. Mitchell and Sharon L. Snyder argue that alternatives in gender, race, and sexual orientation have often been demonized by marking those groups with physical or intellectual abnormalities. Martha Stoddard Holmes sees nondisabled

> "For Maoris, family is culture is cosmic spirituality, in a series of widening vibrations (Te Awekatuku 49). The three areas are not distinguishable or separable, and the link is intergenerational as well. A Maori cut off from his family, as are all three main characters in the story, becomes ontologically isolated and a self-divided."

individuals historically defining themselves as normal by using disability as a universal metaphor for abnormality. That is, if people with disabilities did not exist, non-disabled people would have to invent them. However, the situation for characters with disability differs from other frequently marginalized groups in that they have "a plethora of representation in visual and discursive works. Consequently, disabled people's marginalization has occurred in the midst of a perpetual circulation of their images" (Mitchell and Snyder 6). Although other groups may suffer a lack of literary exposure, people with disabilities get plenty of fictional press, usually of a negative kind.

Not surprisingly, characters in fiction with disabilities almost always are flat and static. Because they most often function as symbols, their perspectives are not developed and are unimportant to the development of the plot. Physical aberration in a literary character is indicative of mental, emotional, social, or spiritual aberration or any combination of those states. Physical difference marks the outsider or the monster, who rages or is isolated and dying inside unseen, for example, Ahab in *Moby-Dick* or the deaf narrator in *The Heart is a Lonely Hunter*. Dracula and his heirs, including the latest Anne Rice creation, are pigment deficient, dentally freakish, and daylight-challenged—in the best nineteenth-century tradition of the "freak" sideshow. These figures, in literature as in real life, allow nondisabled people to shiver with horror as they congratulate themselves on their own normality. Because of his or her convenient symbolism, a disabled character is given a foil voice and complex personality and subjective perspective is difficult to find.

Barbara Kingsolver and Keri Hulme, appearing to split from this exploitative tradition, offer realistic, complex disabled characters, not simply metaphors. Kingsolver has a highly politicized agenda in *The Poisonwood Bible*: She critiques European and American imperialist policies toward Africa, oppressive patriarchal attitudes toward women, racial oppression in the American South, and alienating cultural assumptions about disabled people. Nonetheless, she gives us full characterizations and complete subjective experiences. Her characters, including Adah, who is disabled, are not symbolic pawns. They live on their own.

In *The Poisonwood Bible,* Nathan Price, a Southern preacher, drags his wife and four daughters to the Congo to fulfill his messianic visions. He is the only one in the novel not granted a subjective voice. The result is that he appears to be a stock character, a wild-eyed religious fanatic. Eventually his motivation is revealed to be a hellish World War II experience that left him with an overwhelming sense of evil and guilt that now compel him to confront the world and remold it, a prime situation for displaying a series of major and minor oppressions and alienations, through complex flesh-and-blood people.

The overriding theme of alienated "Otherness" and the cultural rejection of it manifests in the issue of disability. Kingsolver is aware of recent scholarship in disability studies, and in *The Poisonwood Bible*, she dramatically uses disability to depict cultural fear of the Other and the necessity of having the Other to define normality. The twin sisters Leah and Adah Price are the novel's examples of physical otherness. Leah's fetus is supposed to have consumed half of the brain of Adah's fetus while the two were still in the womb, thus marking both as abnormal almost from conception. The two children are assumed to be retarded and are treated as such until a sympathetic educator discovers that, on the contrary, both are geniuses. Adah with her half-brain has an extraordinary talent for languages, one quirk of which is a preference for creating, thinking, and writing in palindromes. Suspension of disbelief is strained here because medical opinion finds the coupling of hemiplegia with high-end intelligence to be extremely unlikely. Kingsolver may be stretching probability, but she has a point to make. The pendulum in the story swings the other way, and the two are still seen as freaks, now for being too smart. The irony of their situation foregrounds the fact that retardation and genius are not simply facts of nature or of medical opinion, but are culturally defined. Society uses the extremes, the nonaverages, to define what is to be called normal. Suspicion of the disabled and the superabled provides an opposing cohesion that unifies the majority as standard. Unity comes from exclusion so society must mark some individuals for exclusion. Alienation by definition is a requirement for maintaining the social fabric.

Adah is also electively mute. She chooses not to speak because she accepts her role as outsider. That is, she will not communicate with a society that does not see her as a person. Later, when she chooses her own path in life (college and medical school), instead of acquiescing to social definition, she achieves selfhood and begins to talk. She discovers that her extreme lameness had been only a cultural marking, an unconscious manifestation of her acceptance of her social monstrosity. She begins to walk almost normally.

Her family also marks her. Like all the female Prices, her wishes count as nothing against the monomania of her father, who is so obsessive and unrelenting that, against the advice of the villagers, he refuses to stop pulling up poisonwood shrubs even when their sap causes his skin to erupt painfully. He must impose his will on nature and on humankind, no matter what the consequences. In fact, his insistent imposition of his will puts both the villagers and the women in his family in the position of the colonially oppressed. In the terms of postcolonial scholarship, Nathan Price is the "dominant discourse":

> The dominant discourse constructs Otherness in such a way that it always contains a trace of ambivalence or anxiety about its own authority. In order to maintain authority over the Other in a colonial situation, imperial discourse strives to delineate the other as radically different from the self [. . .]. The other can, of course, only be constructed out of the archive of "the self," yet the self must also articulate the other as inescapably different. [. . .] Of course, what such authority least likes, and what presents it with its greatest threat, is any reminder of such ambivalence (Ashcroft, Griffiths, and Tiffin, *Empire* 103)

Even Adah's mother Orleanna, faced with having to decide which child to save during a devastating invasion of army ants, hesitates, then chooses the nondisabled child, Ruth May, leaving slow-moving Adah to probable death. Adah's family marginalizes her; she is doubly oppressed, as a woman and as a disabled person.

Some feminist critics recommend considering Adah's situation from the perspectives of class and race. Nathan Price comes originally from the lowest level of Southern white society but gains some limited status through becoming a religious figure. He transports his Southern racism to the Congo and, at least in his own mind, translates the African villagers into another social stratum below himself. His attempts to impose his will on the villagers can be seen as efforts to manufacture and sustain his own classist and racial superiority, and from the angles of postcolonial studies and disability studies, he puts his daughters on the same inferior level as the Africans. In Price's hierarchy, African males, American females, and the disabled all occupy a lower social rung. His refusal to have any dealings with village women puts them on an even lower rung. The villagers, however, politely but firmly reject Nathan Price's constant assertions, seeing them as weirdly inappropriate. By their rejections they script their own selfhood and their equality to him. In the face of their assertions, he must continue to demand acquiescence or lose all pretense of superiority. Cora Kaplan notes the coordination in fiction and politics of feminine degradation with the oppression also of working classes and colonized cultures:

> The unfavourable symbiosis of reason and passion ascribed to women is also used to characterize both men and women in the labouring classes and in other races and cultures. [. . .] Through that chain of colonial associations, whole cultures became "feminized," "blackened" and "impoverished" each denigrating construction implying and invoking the others. (602)

Price's extreme obsession, which leads eventually to his abandoning his family, to insanity or at least insane behavior, and death, is the outcome of his desperate need to maintain his social, gendered, and nationalistic supremacy.

Fortunately, Adah slowly becomes aware that the African society would, on the contrary, not close the option of family to her: "I did know that many women in Kilanga were more seriously disfigured and had husbands notwithstanding" (*Poisonwood* 72). African culture, specifically the Congo's, liberates Adah and most of the Price women. The name "Price" is itself tempting: is it the price they pay as women, or the price—the death of youngest daughter Ruth May by snake bite, the self-destruction of their father—that African demands for freeing the others from their cultural chains? Rural Georgians see Adah, whether retarded or genius, as an atypical horror and reject her, and her physical difference identifies her alien nature. But in the Congo Adah finds that disability, in a sense, does not exist; it is so prevalent that it is seen as a normal, integrated part of life. Because disability is inevitable, people accept it and get on with their lives, like Mama Mwanza in the hut next door continues as an enthusiastic wife and mother despite a lack of legs. It is assumed that given the harshness of this life, everyone will be disabled in some way, sooner or later. Thus, disability is accented here as alternate ability. Adah is not marked as different, and her inclusion allows her to pursue selfhood when she returns home. This is a refreshing break with the long literary tradition in which the disabled individual remains pitiable because he or she functions as a symbol, not a person and either self-destructs as the abnormal should, or is destroyed by representatives of an enraged normality. True, Kingsolver plays with another stereotypical trap, the rescue by a nondisabled mentor. An older doctor persuades Adah that her lame leg is a psychosomatic reaction to social expectation. This mentor even becomes her lover, summoning up ghosts of other rescuers from *Johnny Belinda* to *Dark Victory* to *The Miracle Worker*. In all of those the caretaker receives most of the credit. However, Kingsolver is aware and astute. She has Adah recognize that no matter how many good intentions both parties have a relationship can never escape the trap of a patronizing pity. Adah drops her doctor-mentor and goes off to live life on her own terms.

We can, of course, regard this plot solution in two ways. The first, implied above, is to see Kingsolver's critique of attitudes toward disability. It is clear that Adah's dysfunctions are completely socially marked. When she redefines herself as unique and worthy, the stigma of her disability vanish. Just as European and American business and religious interests "colonized" (in the pejorative sense used in postcolonial critical methodology) the Congo—exploiting the country with the justification that its people were Other and inferior—so the cultural perceptions of the nondisabled people of Georgia colonized Adah. They expected a monster; so they created one. Their labels became part of her manifest flesh. In an ironic reversal, it is possible to say that the Congolese culture, by allowing Adah to reinvent herself, recolonizes her by its more appropriate physical expectations. The colonized become the colonizers, to the benefit of all.

It is wise to remember that "for Kingsolver, writing is a form of political activism." As Kingsolver's themes reject traditional cultural attitudes toward the disabled, so her literary structures deconstruct traditional exploitations of disabled characters.

Or do they? It would be possible to argue alternatively that this plot twist is a sellout that allows a relatively happy ending. Worse, we find that the disability never really existed except as a figment. Leslie Fiedler warned that certain kinds of fiction indicate a desire to erase disabled people—either "by kill or by cure"; that stories evoking pity for the handicapped also express "a wish that there were no handicapped, that they would all finally go away" (46, emphasis in original). Perhaps Kingsolver has had it both ways. Initially Adah is the weapon for ironizing American cultural attitudes—a useful metaphor once again. Then, after suffering Adah's disability with her for more than four hundred pages, we find our empathy and our growing critique of culture both unceremoniously dumped. We might say that this twist of events is only fair, for now we, as readers, can feel exploited by our own assumptions, just as Adah has always been. I doubt Kingsolver intends anything that devious. What saves the story from betrayal (of its themes or its characters or its readers) is the fully subjective perspective given to Adah throughout. She is a total personality and she evolves. As a person, she evades the role of metaphor because she does not simply erase her disability. Rather, she continues to acknowledge that, although she is no longer silent and limping, her past is still her: "Tall and straight I may appear, but I will always be Ada [the palindromic name that she used to identify her disabled self] inside. A crooked little person trying to tell truth. The power is in the balance: we are our injuries, as much as we are our successes" (*Poisonwood* 496). Here she offers a poignant recognition that we are all the totality of ourselves, present and past, and in so doing she transcends any suspicious machinations of plot.

That full characterization may help compensate for another regrettable aspect of the story as well. In her portrayal of happy, integrated, fully functioning disabled people in the Congolese village, Kingsolver is debunking one metaphor (the Otherness of disabled people) while promoting another one (the colonial romanticizing of Africa). As James Charlton's study of disability in developing countries indicates, whatever problems that Americans with disabilities may have, the situation is worse elsewhere. A real Mama Mwanza would be treated simultaneously as both pitiful and a pariah, forbidden to marry or work because she would bring bad luck and is an offense to gods and ancestors, economically oppressed and shunned, probably bereft of support services (Charlton 25, 59–60). One African word for "cripple" has even worse connotations than its English equivalent: chirema means someone, not only with mobility issues but also utterly useless, a complete failure in life (66). The rural nature of the village would make the circumstances not more bucolic as in the novel, but worse in all regards. The sense of oddity as ritual pollution and affront to the gods of natural forces would be even stronger, the shunning by family and tribe more certain and rigid, and practical assistance almost unknown (108).

We must ask if Charlton's sources can reliably speak for all African people with disabilities, and because, as postcolonial studies point out, the African continent is by no means homogeneous, we must also ask if Charlton's sources can be applied specifically to Kingsolver's Congolese culture. Charlton notes that data about the numbers and situations of individuals with disabilities in the various sectors of the planet Earth are not a problem; reliable sources such as the United Nations and independent agencies have had accurate numbers "for twenty years." On the other hand, he acknowledges that his study is limited in that it does not describe living conditions of all sectors or all disabilities. Specifically, he chooses to set AIDS aside: politics and difficulties with access have hampered his work. In fact, his African information depends on thorough interviews with numbers of people with disabilities who are also disability rights advocates, specifically in South Africa and Zimbabwe (xv). Clearly such people will emphasize problems, but Charlton's study has credibility nonetheless by constant reference to specific circumstances and facts, not just personal narratives.

The second question is trickier: can information from sources in formerly British South Africa and Zimbabwe be stretched to apply to the formerly Belgian Congo? Actually one of the consulted organizations, the Southern Africa Federation of the Disabled (SAFOD), is transnational and works in many other areas of Africa, including Botswana, Malawi, Mozambique, Namibia, Swaziland, Zambia, and others, albeit apparently not in the Congo. At a conference organized by SAFOD in 1991 in Harare, Zimbabwe, "forty delegates came from all over Africa to discuss disability issues" (Charlton 146–47, emphasis added). That fact suggests that individuals with disabilities share a similar fate in various African cultures. Current African thinking in most regions supports a general emphasis on political and social commitment and a common aesthetic despite local "ideological differences" (Ashcroft, Griffiths, and Tiffin, *Empire* 132).

Given the Africawide applicability of Charlton's information, it probably is fair to say that Kingsolver's liberal intentions have created an African Utopia for disability similar to how Europeans in earlier centuries fancied a New World El Dorado inhabited by Noble Savages. As a writer in the New World giving readers a romantic Africa where people are naturally compassionate and tolerant, Kingsolver has now partially reversed the earlier process. Kingsolver claims not to draw her characters from real life and has said that she does not remember her experience of Africa as a child seven, in 1963. The villagers she describes in her novel seem quite generalized, almost completely lacking in noteworthy or unique customs. For example, the issue of which Africa language they use never arises. Her credits at the end of the novel (perhaps intended to add political ballast to the story) include Nigerian fiction about the Ibo and Igbo people (Chinua Achebe's *Things Fall Apart*), Conrad's nineteenth-century *Heart of Darkness* (ostensibly about the Congo), other books on the Congo, as well as works on snakes in Southern Africa, ritual and magic from all over Africa, birds and east Africa, and folk tales from the entire continent. She also professes to have relied on friends' reports and on her own travel in other parts of Africa, but not in the Congo/Zaire (author's note ix–x). Clearly, although the history and politics in the story are Congolese, the indigenous people are (intentionally or by lack of information) generically sub-Saharan pan-Africa. Only the specifics about some rather vicious flora and fauna (crocodiles, poisonwood, army ants, asps) makes them African at all. Because of this fogging of ethnicity, applying Charlton's information about individuals with disabilities seems as reasonable for Kingsolver's villagers as for any real life African group.

In addition, unfortunately for Kingsolver, the task of portraying the feelings of real African village women may be, according to feminist critics such as Cora Kaplan, impossible from the beginning:

> The subjectivity of women of other classes and races and with different sexual orientations can never be "objectively" or "authentically" represented in literary texts by the white, heterosexual, middle-class woman writer, however sympathetically she invents or describes such women in her narrative. (602)

This criticism seems all too applicable to *The Poisonwood Bible*, as Kingsolver has projected a fantasy of her own libertarian ideals onto Mama Mwanza. Indeed, it might be fair to say that Mama Mwanza (and the fingerless Tata Zinsana, the goitered Mama Nguza, and others) reveal more about

Kingsolver's own liberal, middle-class desire for political intervention than about the true situation of rural, disabled Congolese.

The result in the novel is a mixed success. Kingsolver is able to humanize metaphors that elsewhere exploit people with disabilities, but she trades them for romantic (and romantic Marxian) metaphors about Africans. In the process she does a grave disservice to individuals with disability in developing countries by minimizing their actual plights. Is Kingsolver, in effect, establishing a Western humanistic ideal as a universal norm and then, after deriding its absence in the West, projecting it imperialistically onto African peoples? The entire process of colonial imposition required just such a sleight of hand as the one made by Kingsolver, involving a "naturalizing of constructed values" on "the unconscious level" that, instead of promoting the values of the colonized, actually makes them "peripheral" or "marginal" (Ashcroft, Griffiths, and Tiffin, *Empire* 3). Ironically, by idealizing the Congolese in her pursuit of particular humanistic goals, Kingsolver erases those people's true natures and actual needs.

The Bone People also has family and cultural concerns, but Keri Hulme goes far beyond those concerns to an infusion of culturally appropriate mythic spirituality. For Maoris, family is culture is cosmic spirituality, in a series of widening vibrations (Te Awekatuku 49). The three areas are not distinguishable or separable, and the link is intergenerational as well. A Maori cut off from his family, as are all three main characters in the story, becomes ontologically isolated and a self-divided. So the three characters, before they find salvation by fusing into a spiritual and psychological triad, are initially self-destructive. Kerewin extrudes horrific art that ingests the light like her Suneater or pours forth as nightmare images on paper. Joe reels under the impact of incessant drinking, his sense of his lost wife, and a constant teetering on the edge of violence. Simon, orphaned by storm and shipwreck and adopted by Joe, insists on his elective muteness and rebelliousness. In addition to their individual angst, the three form a dysfunctional family that is physically abusive, a parody of father-mother-child relationship. Joe regularly beats Simon and tries to beat Kerewin, who, to her horror, is eventually provoked into beating Simon. On one occasion, she thoroughly beats Joe as well, and Simon deliberately provokes the beatings. As a negative triad, they are a study in self-hate and mutual flagellation.

As the two try unsuccessfully to merge, they also manifest the divided culture, the disturbed coexistence of colonial European (Pakeha) societies with Maori ones. Kerewin is genetically and culturally half and half, Joe is almost completely Maori, and Simon is European, perhaps even Scottish nobility. The violence and alcoholism are seen as outgrowths of their mutual loss of roots, of having lost a source that they have not replaced. All the major characters in the novel, not just Simon, find verbal communication unacceptable or insufficient, preferring instead visual art, drunkenness, silence, and extreme physical action. Reaching across the boundaries between people requires an effort too strenuous to be borne by mere words. Hulme's rhetoric is a fractured pastiche of half-thoughts and flash descriptions, which befits the splintered relationships." The characters' individual, familial, and cultural lives are negative because each of them lacks the spiritual infusion necessary for unity and growth, a unity that they eventually achieve after much suffering and mythic revelation. Hulme indicates that the violence, especially Joe's, represents misdirected energy and aggressiveness now split apart from the "strongly hierarchical, strongly spiritual system" of the traditional Maori family:

> Once a rural and tribal people, Maoris have now become urban and divided into very small family groups. [. . .] In the cities, you are cut off from the life of the land, the sea, your family marae, from your ancestral roots." (Hulme, "Mauri" 293)

Reestablished convergence with "'the spiritual world,' or numinous world, which all of us are part of whether we will or not" is what Hulme hopes will reconcile Maori and Pakeha societies and render the violence obsolete (Hulme and Turcotte 140, 153).

The three characters eventually solve their problem, and Simon, the child with a disability, is the pivot. Disability here is a spiritual as well as a cultural wound. Simon has a special secret ability to see human auras, those natural spiritual energies that emanate from each individual but which partake of the whole nature. At one point he tries to explain this talent to Kerewin:

> ON PEOPLE? scratching his head with the pencil, frown still in place, writing again finally, ON PEOPLE.
>
> "I don't see anything on people. Do you?"
>
> He nods wearily. Then he keeps his head bent, apparently unwilling to look at her.
>
> Kerewin's turn to frown.
>
> What the hell would you see on people in the dark. Shadows in the daytime, yeah, but at night?
>
> It's the word shadows that gives her the answer.
>
> "Wait a minute . . . Sim, do you see lights on people?"

> Head up fast, and his bright smile flowering. O Yes.
>
> [. . .]
>
> In the library, the books spread round them,
>
> "Well, that's what they are. Soul-shadows. Coronas. Auras. Very few people can see them without using screens or Kirlian photography." [. . .]
>
> He touches by her eyes.
>
> "No, I can't see them. I'll bet Joe can't either."
>
> Right, says the boy, grinning wolfishly. He writes quickly, SCARED SAID NOT TO SAY.

Thus Simon is marked, not as a disabled mutant (although the local town folk see him as that), but as a young shaman, of European origin but in touch with the islands' energy and spirit. He does not communicate through speech because the situation is skewed and people are incapable of understanding each other. In such negative circumstances, violence is the only viable communication, people can only contact each other physically; and Simon is the self-appointed lightning rod for that violence. Forbidden to tell of his ability to see the souls of others, violence is his way of "speaking" and of allowing others also to "speak" through their violence toward him. His "disability" becomes a bridge between the two adults and between the two cultures. Simon is completely conscious of using violence for mediation. He chooses this role and becomes the agent that creates a new, united community to replace the fragmented old one:

> All morning the feeling had grown, start a fight and stop the illwill between his father and Kerewin. Get rid of the anger round the woman, stop the rift with blows, with pain, then pity, then repair, then good humour again. It works that way . . . it always did. There isn't much time left for anything to grow anymore. It must be in this place, or the break will come, and nothing will grow anymore.
>
> So start a fight.

Simon is sensitive to the precise status of the relationship, to its fractures and fault lines, and he knows just when to apply the ameliorating explosion.

Kerewin and Joe are first aware of each other in a bar. Joe is drunk and loud; Kerewin feels contempt for him, and they do not make contact. The two are brought together only when Simon invades Kerewin's isolated tower home, forcing Joe to come for him. Simon continues to be the agent that propels them out of their shells and into each other's lives. Like Kingsolver's Adah, Simon is supernormal and would generate fear in both cultural communities if knowledge of his talent were to be widespread. He must reach people, not through his divine gifts, which they would reject, but through physical action, the only means they are able to understand and to accept.

All the major characters in the novel are disabled in the sense that they are emotionally and psychologically crippled. Literally, the eponymous "bone people" are the displaced bones of the Maori ancestors, but more generally they signify all the displaced people "orphaned" by family schism (Tawake 330). Additionally the "bone people" can denote the totemic waima in the story: the mystical disfigured person Kerewin encounters; the old man, Tiaki Mira, who helps Joe; and Simon himself (Hulme and Turcotte 142). Because everyone has a wairua—"an unseen double, a soul-shadow, your own spirit"—these figures can be seen as extensions or doubles of Kerewin and Joe (Hulme, "Myth" 33). And everyone's invisible soul doubles, the auras, are seen as well, by Simon.

Thus Hulme seems to agree with the perspective of the African villagers in *The Poisonwood Bible* that sees disability, not as sinister Other, but as something positive. Both books direct attention to postcolonial situations and attitudes, and both seem to posit non-Western spiritualities, a cultural oneness with the land, as a rebuttal to Western fragmentation and compartmentalization. The village of Kilanga has a solid culture that both accepts and respects the laws of the surrounding jungle. The spiritual beliefs of the villagers accord with the natural forces around them. Nathan Price with his Christian fundamentalism is utterly at odds with those forces. His insistence, against local advice, on growing Western vegetables by Western farming methods leads only to humiliating failure. Perhaps the best example of his being at odds with African natural forces is his demand that all children be baptized in the local river, ignoring the very real problem of crocodiles. That idea is politely but firmly rebuffed, and the credibility of his Western god declines still further.

Adah's empathy for the truths of the village enables her to free herself of injurious Western definitions: "In the way of the body and other people's judgment I enjoy a benign approval in Kilanga that I have never, ever known in Bethlehem, Georgia" (*Poisonwood* 72). Later she adds, "In that other long-ago place, America, I was a failed combination of too-weak body and overstrong will. But in Congo I am those things perfectly united: Adah." Disability is natural—literally part of the spirit of nature. Adah is normal because her essence transcends her body:

> The Bantu speak of "self as a vision residing inside, peering out through the eyeholes of the body, waiting

for whatever happens next. Using the body as a mask, muntu [self] watches and waits without fear, because muntu itself cannot die. The transition from spirit to body and back to spirit again is merely a venture. (343)

These comments late in the book corroborate what her mother Orleanna had said to Nathan early after their arrival in Kilanga about the prevalence of disability among the villagers:

> Father said, "They are living in darkness. Broken in body and soul, and don't even see how they could be healed."
>
> Mama said, "Well, maybe they take a different view of their bodies."
>
> Father says the body is the temple. [. . .]
>
> She took the pins out and said to him, "Well, here in Africa that temple has to do a hateful lot of work in a day." She said, "Why, Nathan, here they have to use their bodies like we use things at home—like your clothes or your garden tools or something. Where you'd be wearing out the knees of your trousers, sir, they just have to go ahead and wear out their knees!" (53, emphasis in original)

Georgia Christian wrote shame onto Adah's existence: "Recently it has been decided, grudgingly, that dark skin or lameness may not be entirely one's fault, but one still ought to show good manners to act ashamed" (493, emphasis in original). The alternative African mystic vision of the eternal self beyond temporary physical aberration "abled" Adah.

Similarly in *The Bone People,* Kerewin and Joe move out of isolation—and the self-destructive behavior that goes with it—only after near-death visions that are accepted by the text as mystic. Kerewin's cancer goes away when she sequesters herself in a natural retreat appropriately owned by her estranged family, and Joe's vision of the underground water prepare them to join the Triad with Simon. They become the triple-headed figurine, created in a fire by Kerewin, with their three faces and hair entwined. The three people are shriven in preparation for rebirth: Kerewin's cancer is a diseased, false pregnancy that will be replaced by a true son, Simon, who is also the "sun child" who replaces the destructive Suneater, her artistic monstrosity. Joe must survive a belly wound, making him a kind of Fisher King whose renewal will be tied to that of the land itself. And Simon must transcend a near-fatal beating.

The Maori see themselves as one with the land, and, until the British arrived, they had no concept of land as commodity, as something to be owned:

> Papatuanuku is the Earth Mother, combining all elements of the planet; her immediate form is whenua, the land. Continuing the organic metaphor, whenua is also the Maori word for the placenta, which is promptly buried with simple ritual after birth. The practice is still observed today, even in cities; thus the word itself reflects the relationship between people and the land [. . .]. (Te Awekotuku 33)

Each character must reunite with the land before he or she can merge again with family and society, for "the Maori relationship to the land is intense" and "everything growing or moving on the land [. . .] has a relationship with humanity" (Hulme, "Mauri" 302–04).

It is appropriate that when she goes into retreat and cures herself Kerewin leaves the Triad sculpture buried in embers and takes a small bag of earth from near her tower. Her connection with the Earth Mother and with the concept of home will go with her, as the Triad is baked in what is both a funeral pyre and a phoenix's rebirth. Hulme's emphasis on place also suggests the general privileging of space over time noted by postcolonial scholars:

> Post-colonial literary theory, then, has begun to deal with the problems of transmuting time into space, with the present struggling out of the past, as it attempts to construct a future. [. . .] Place is extremely important in all models, and epistemologies have developed which privilege space over time as the most important ordering concept of reality. (Ashcroft, Griffiths, and Tilfin, *Empire* 36–37)

In the novel, Hulme's awareness of the Maori past evolves into the vision of a syncretic future that encompasses both Maori and European derivations. Because Kerewin considers entering the fire herself, it is both an image of death—the dissolution of self—and of necessary purgation. In fact, transformations occur for a number of properties connected with the three characters. All three have haircuts, and because hair is one of the oldest symbols of the life force, the loss of their hair suggests the shriving of their old lives. Meanwhile, the painful fishhook in Simon's thumb is supplanted by the jade hook Joe gives Kerewin, said by Kerewin to be set into her heart. A braid from Simon's hair is attached to the jade ("greenstone"), which is the color of his eyes and a substance the Maoris consider mystical (Hulme, "Mauri" 307). Clearly Simon is marked as transcendent.

After Kerewin returns, she destroys the tower in which she had lived in isolation and constructs instead a spiral house along the lines of the chambered nautilus. Here the shellfish theme that recurs in the novel is a superb symbol of inclusion. The concept of family in the larger Maori sense is thereby fulfilled: Kerewin is reconciled to her own family on all levels, from a nuclear family of parents and child to her whole tribe and to humanity

New Zealand Maori men perform a war dance using weapons © Anders Ryman/Corbis

and the entire Earth. Individual selves are preserved within the separate chambers, all within the unity of the society in accord with the natural, spiritual realm, the nautilus. Simon is the agent of this fruitful evolution, which unfortunately puts him squarely in the tradition that views people with disabilities in the other extreme, as links with the divine. Again, the norm is defined by contrast with the abnormal, only in *The Bone People,* it is the supernormal. Therefore, Hulme's treatment of disability is problematic as is Kingsolver's. Treating difference as heroic or mystical is in keeping with Maori beliefs as well as with those of many other peoples (for example, the Yoruba of Nigeria. But that treatment has the unfortunate side effect of placing people with disabilities above others and hence regarded as separate and abnormal. Hulme, like Kingsolver, allows her character with disability to emerge as a fully complex individual with a personal perspective on events and an evolution of self. These characters are saved from the traditional literary exploitation, but only by the implementation of yet another traditional metaphor, the disability as divinely linked. This problem with disability may be countered, however, by postcolonial benefits; Hulme is privileging precolonial beliefs and so subverting the European domination of her people.

In the process of this unification, Hulme also creates bridges across lines of class, race, and gender. The three main characters represent the three social strata: European aristocracy (Simon, probably of Scottish nobility), New Zealand middle class (Kerewin, who is educated, has traveled and has studied martial arts), and New Zealand working class (Joe). At the same time those three represent the two races, Pakeha and Maori (Simon and Joe) and the hybridization of the two (Kerewin, who at the close of the novel is also the fulcrum for the hybridization of all cultures and personalities in the new nautilus structure). Finally Kerewin completely subverts Joe's attempts at male domination, both physically and emotionally, attaining gender equality. The resulting synthesis is sweeping, encompassing all perspectives.

Hulme is in an excellent position to rescript the cultural concept of disability and other Western perspectives. As residents of a "settler colony," the Maori are "doubly marginalized," pushed to the psychic and political edge of societies [. . . they] have experienced the dilemma of colonial alienation. For this reason they demonstrate a capacity, far greater than that of white settler societies, to subvert received assumptions about literature [. . .]. (Ashcroft, Griffiths, and Tiffin, *Empire* 144)

We might add, "assumptions" about culture in general. Thus Hulme's hybridized, syncretic cultural solution is typical of the literature from her kind of postcolonial situation: "This is a strategy of subversion and appropriation" (Ashcroft, Griffiths, and Tiffin, *Empire* 154). In this case, disability provides the means.

Thus, Barbara Kingsolver and Keri Hulme are proceeding toward inclusiveness. Their novels reject past Western concepts of disability as their writings move beyond the traditional literary use of disabled figures as metaphors by which to define normal society. Adah and Simon are representational—symbolic, if you like—but no more so than other major characters. Their human complexity is as deeply portrayed as that of the non-disabled characters; they are allowed their own subjective viewpoints and development. Regrettably, Kingsolver romanticizes African disability; and, much more understandably given Maori tradition, Hulme associates disability with mysticism. Both attitudes are distortions. In sum, the portrayal of disability in the two novels may not be entirely naturalistic, but it displays a fullness and respect for the characters with disability not traditionally found in literature.

Source: Stephen D. Fox, "Barbara Kingsolver and Keri Hulme: Disability, Family, and Culture," in *Critique*, Vol. 45, No. 4, Summer 2004, pp. 405–20.

Thomas E. Benediktsson

In the following essay, Benediktsson examines the "ruptures in realisms" in Hulme's novel that are attempts to find alternatives to the Western ideology that supports "unhealthy realism."

Realism in the contemporary novel depends on two contradictory claims. The first one is that the narrative is not literally true. The familiar statement in the frontispiece that "the characters and incidents portrayed herein are entirely imaginary and bear no resemblance to real persons, living or dead" is not only a protection against lawsuit but also a statement of the conscious fictionality of realistic narrative. Of course, that statement is duplicitous if viewed in the light of realism's second claim, that the work bears a resemblance to social and psychological reality, that in important ways it tells us the truth about "the effect of experience on individuals" if not about "the nature of experience itself." The distinction is Edward Eigner's, who argues that the attempt in the nineteenth-century novel to reconcile scientific truth with metaphysical truth was initiated to discredit the empirical, not to validate it. In this paper I am taking a similar position: attempts to reconcile realism with the supernatural in the contemporary postcolonial novel are undertaken in an effort to undermine the ideological base that supports realism.

The act of reading a realist text, then, is based on the reader's conscious or unconscious assimilations of the text's incorporated contradictions: fictionality and mimesis. Like Chief Broom in *One Flew Over the Cuckoo's Nest,* readers (I should say readers innocent of literary theory) say to themselves "It's the truth, even if it didn't happen."

Increasingly, however, theory has focused our attention on realism's first claim by attacking the second. Defining mimesis as a set of conventions, structuralism analyzed its arbitrary, elaborated codes. Terry Eagleton discusses *S/Z,* Roland Barthes's classic structuralist study of mimesis as the "work of the break," which points the way toward poststructuralism by emphasizing the "irreducibly plural" nature of texts (138). Poststructuralism, asserting that language does not so much reflect reality as create the reality we know, had led in the 1970s and early 1980s to many discussions of the way realistic texts construct and deconstruct their own claims to representations.

The poststructuralist "death of the author" (Barthes) has led us in two directions: on the one hand into an emphasis on textuality and intertextuality, on the other to an exploration of the social and material conditions that generate literary texts. In this latter respect the text is "always charged by ideology—those unspoken collective understandings, conventions, stories and cultural practices that uphold systems of social power" (Kaplan 6). For some, then, realism engages in an active dialogue with a changing culture, creating and critiquing its meanings. In that sense realism is "one of the crucial symbolic forms through which collective sense is forged" (Pendergast 217). For other poststructuralist critics, the realist novel, born in the late eighteenth century and persisting in a conservative literary tradition into the present, is part of the vast project of bourgeois capitalism; its emphases on totalization and closure, in fact on the mimetic correspondence between narrative form and social reality, are hegemonic, or as Derrida puts it, "a matter for the police" (102). Ruptures in realism—violations of its codes—can be construed as acts of rebellion against this tyranny.

In this essay I would like to examine some "ruptures" in the realism of two postcolonial novels, each of which attempts to find alternatives to the Western rationalism, pragmatism, and linearity that support realism's codes. In the first, Leslie Silko's *Ceremony,* Tayo, half white and half Pueblo Indian, is a young World War II veteran who, as a prisoner of war, cursed the jungle monsoon that he felt was causing his step-brother's death. Having returned to the reservation after a time in a veteran's hospital, Tayo is convinced that his curse caused the drought that is now afflicting his reservation. Suffering from his guilt and from other forms of distress, Tayo learns that his illness is part of a larger pattern of evil—the "witchery" brought about by those who seek the world's destruction. Tayo is healed by a series of Pueblo and Navaho purification ceremonies and by a personal ceremony he performs for himself. During his quest he has an encounter with a mysterious young woman named Ts'eh, later identified as Spider Woman, a supernatural figure from Pueblo legend.

The second work I will discuss is Keri Hulme's *The Bone People,* a novel first published in 1984, by the Spiral Collective, an independent press formed in New Zealand to bring out the book after it had been rejected by the major publishers in that country. Kerewin Holmes, part white and part Maori, is a failed artist who lives alone in a stone tower by the ocean. Her alcoholic solitude is broken by the wayward mute orphan child Simon and by his stepfather Joe, a nearly full-blooded Maori. Kerewin's growing love for Joe is blighted by her discovery that he brutally beats Simon, and she decides tragically to intervene. When she gives Joe permission to beat Simon, and he beats the child nearly to death, he is imprisoned and Simon institutionalized. Kerewin, afflicted by stomach cancer, withdraws to a distant place to die; she is cured by the miraculous intervention of a supernatural figure. Joe, released from prison, is cured of his violence and guilt by the discovery of a sacred place, the landing-site of one of the original Great Canoes. Simon, escaping from his foster home, is reunited with Kerewin and Joe at the end, as his character blends with Maui, the Trickster figure of Maori myth.

These two novels share a plot that has become common in the postcolonial novel. In labelling novels by an American Indian and a New Zealand Maori "postcolonial," I am using the term in a fairly broad sense. My point is that the plot pattern I have identified here, common in postcolonial novelists as diverse as Achebe, Narayan, and Ousmene, is a literary representation of a deep cultural conflict among formerly colonized people. A member of an oppressed and marginalized people is suffering from a grave illness, a malady that seems simultaneously to be psychological, physical, and spiritual. Eventually this character is healed through traditional ritual and through a literal encounter with the supernatural, whose reawakening accompanies the main character's rebirth. At the end of the novel this powerless person has appropriated a source of transcendent power, and there is hope for a new society based on the values of the reborn traditional culture: as Silko puts it at the end of *Ceremony,* the witchery "is dead for now" (261).

"Tempted to deconstruct the text as we read it, we search for autobiographical clues that may or may not be present in a narrative that in other ways proclaims its fictionality. This double reading does subvert realism."

The form of both novels involves breaking the codes of realism, not only introducing romance elements and evoking the supernatural, but also disrupting the linearity of the narrative and altering its spatial and psychological geography. The stream-of-consciousness technique, used in both novels, alters rationalism through the nonrational flow of sensation, perception, and intuition. The introduction of myth layers the text further by juxtaposing the temporal with the timeless, the diachronic with the synchronic. These textual strategies not only force the Western reader to abandon empiricism, but they also create a fictive realm of possibility and power—the possibility of the awakening of the traditional gods, and the power of those reawakened gods to cure the postcolonial malaise . . .

Unlike *Ceremony*, *The Bone People* does not include traditional myths and stories that challenge realism's codes. Rich in physical and psychological detail, the novel's dialogue and indirect discourse employ a pungent New Zealand vernacular interspersed with Maori phrases, which are translated in an appendix. With considerable vividness and plenitude of detail, there is a strong impression of verisimilitude. The ruptures in realism occur in other ways.

The first is an issue that should in some ways reinforce rather than subvert the novel's claim of mimesis. The name "Kerewin Holmes" bears obvious similarity to that of the author Keri Hulme. We suspect that Joe, Simon, and other characters have living counterparts as well, and we are thus encouraged to read the text both as novel and as autobiography. Thus the novel may contain traces of an implied autobiographical text or texts. Tempted to deconstruct the text as we read it, we search for autobiographical clues that may or may not be present in a narrative that in other ways proclaims its fictionality. This double reading does subvert realism.

Traces of still other texts abound in *The Bone People*. The lonely woman living in a stone tower by the sea, visited by a mute child, a changeling who himself came from the sea—the plot is redolent of fairy tale, of Celtic romance. Further, since Kerewin is both eclectically well-read and verbally histrionic, her voice, which dominates the text, is filled with allusions and echoes. And finally, the technical influence of James Joyce is ubiquitous.

These intertextual elements, leading the reader to an encounter with the materiality of the text itself, comprise ruptures in realism. As in *Ceremony*, the linear flow of the narrative is altered through the introduction of a controlling metaphor or hermeneutic trope—not the spider web of Thought Woman's design, but the spiral, a design element in Maori art that has special meaning to Kerewin and ultimately to the narrative itself, which will move not only linearly but in a spiralling, concentric pattern, as Kerewin and Joe confront their innermost fears and desires. Like *Ceremony*, realism here is ruptured irrevocably by the introduction of the supernatural that accompanies the reawakening of the traditional gods.

Late in the novel, when Joe meets the kaumatua (old man) who has been guarding the sacred site of the landfall of one of the Great Canoes, he learns that he, Kerewin, and Simon are the foretold new guardians. He also learns that the spiritual power of the place emanates not from the site but from a stone that came on the canoe, a stone holding a mauriora (life-power) that has not yet departed from the world. After the kaumatua's death, when Joe takes the stone with him, there is hope that Kerewin, Joe, and Simon—reunited and cured of madness, illness, and violence—will create a new "marae" or site of community, inspired by the presence of the awakened mauriora. Like Tayo, they represent hope for a new world.

Both *Ceremony* and *The Bone People* portray characters who are at first trapped in narratives of victimization and oppression, narratives inscribed and supported by the codes of realism. It is the ideological task of realism to make its structures seem "natural" and "inevitable"—"natural" in the conviction that language offers a clear and undistorted view of social reality, and "inevitable" in the conviction that the social reality portrayed exercises a determining influence on the life of an individual. Tayo's plight is the *necessary* outcome of the oppression of the American Indian. Joe's abuse of Simon is the *necessary* behavior of a Maori who, brutally beaten himself as a child and deeply thwarted in his life, cannot cure himself of violence. For Tayo and Joe to evade their "fates" is for the novels in which those lives are inscribed to evade the structures of realism.

In that sense, we could argue that Silko and Hulme, in providing their characters with an escape from their narratives, may have devised sentimental evasions, fantasy solutions for problems that cannot be solved in "real life," but which can be solved literarily by disrupting mimesis, the correspondence of "fiction" to "life." Violating the reader's sense of verisimilitude and probability, attaching magical "happy endings" to otherwise tragically determined narratives, Silko and Hulme may be evading responsibility for their own plots; as one cynical student put it when my class finished *The Bone People,* "Well, roll the credits!"

The evasion might be not only sentimental but also political. *Ceremony* was written toward the end of a time of activism when American Indians, in an effort to call attention to their historic oppression, demonstrated at Wounded Knee Battlefield, occupied Alcatraz Island, and called for the restoration of traditional salmon fishing rights in the Columbia River. Hulme's novel, written a few years later, coincided with a Maori nationalist movement that led to some parliamentary reforms but has otherwise polarized New Zealand society. Both novels, by dramatizing the awakening of a traditional spirituality and by portraying characters who heal themselves by rejecting conflict, may be advocating quietism and avoiding the threatening but potentially more effective arena of political action, an arena avoided by both authors . . .

In *The Bone People,* as in *Ceremony*, the mixed ancestry of the protagonist is emphasized. Kerewin is only part Maori by blood, but like Tayo, the native part of her is the deepest:

> "It's very strange, but whereas by blood, flesh and inheritance, I am but an eighth Maori, by heart, spirit, and inclination, I feel all Maori." She looked down into the drink, "I used to. Now it feels like the best part of me has got lost in the way I live."

Though many New Zealanders can claim mixed ancestry, Hulme stresses Kerewin's marginality in other ways—her solitude, the tragic break with her family that has led to the failure of her art. Kerewin's sexuality is also marginal:

> ". . . I've never been attracted to men. Or women. Or anything else. It's difficult to explain, and nobody has ever believed it when I have tried to explain, but while I have an apparently normal female body, I don't have any sexual urge or appetite. I think I am a neuter."

Hulme stresses Kerewin's androgyny. Physically powerful, she smokes cigars, performs hard physical labor when the occasion warrants it, and dominates the few relationships she enters. Trained in the combat skills if not the spiritual discipline of aikido, she intervenes in Joe's violence toward Simon violently. She beats Joe to insensibility; and having thereby established her dominance over him, she makes him promise never to beat Simon again without her permission, a permission which, tragically, she gives.

At a public reading of her work at Montclair State College in May 1987, Hulme remarked that violence against children is a pervasive social problem in New Zealand, among Maoris and Pakeha (white New Zealanders) alike, and that she had written *The Bone People* in part to draw attention to it. In this culture of violence, the key to personal redemption for both Joe and Kerewin is the renunciation of violence. The Maori society discovered by the Europeans who colonized New Zealand was itself exceptionally violent, with ritual cannibalism and continual bloody warfare among rival clans and kingdoms. To heal her characters through a recovery of Maori spirituality, Hulme, like Silko, must create an alternative narrative of Maori culture.

The kaumatua, an old man with facial tattoos inscribed in a pattern not seen for hundreds of years, is, like Betonie in *Ceremony,* the key to Joe's healing and to the recovery of a lost spirituality. Known in his neighborhood as "the last of the cannibals," he tells Joe of his relationship with his grandmother, who urged him to eat of her flesh when she died. Unable to do that, he took over her life's work, the guardianship of the sacred stone. In describing to Joe the nature of the spirit he guards, he, like Betonie, is the spokesman for the author's revision of traditional history:

> I was taught that it was the old people's belief that this country, and our people, are different and special. That something very great had allied itself with some of us, had given itself to us. But we changed. We ceased to nurture the land. We fought among ourselves. We were overcome by those white people in their hordes. We were broken and diminished. We forgot what we could have been, that Aotearoa was the shining land. Maybe it will be again . . . be that as it will, that thing that allied itself to us is still here. I take care of it, because it sleeps now. It retired into itself when the world changed, when the people changed.

The "sleeping god" to whom the kaumatua has dedicated his life is the spirit of a powerful, nonviolent spirituality that was debased, not only by the Europeans but also by the original Polynesian settlers who became the Maoris. If this "mauriora" were to awaken, an entirely new society, constructed on principles even more ancient than those of the Maoris, would be formed.

When, after the kaumatua's death, Joe brings the stone that holds the mauriora to Kerewin's property in Whangaroa, it sinks deep into the earth. The spiral house Kerewin builds there, and the family relationship that is established among the white child and the two Maoris, represent not only their triumph over their own personal demons but also the germ of a new society, neither Pakeha nor Maori, whose spirituality is based on the mauriora life-energy, now grounded in the land and in its people. The people has awakened:

> They were nothing more than people, by themselves. Even paired, any pairing, they would have been nothing more than people by themselves. But all together, they have become the heart and muscles and mind of something perilous and new, something strange and growing and great.
>
> Together, all together, they are the instruments of change.

In both novels the central characters will become leaders of a revitalized society, one that embraces traditional spirituality but that does not seek the counter-Manicheanism of nationalism. The ideological project of the novels is not to overturn the white culture but to transform it. In the process, realism as a literary mode of representation has been transformed.

These speculations have led us from a consideration of the technical disruptions of realism into a discussion of the political stance of the novels. Yet we have not really digressed; realism is intrinsically ideological. Barthes argues that realism is "unhealthy" because it denies that language is socially constructed (Eagleton 135). Its claim that it is natural and that it offers the only way to view the world is totalitarian and hegemonic, an esthetic equivalent of colonialism. The gods reawaken: Silko and Hulme disrupt "unhealthy" realism in order to heal their characters, just as they challenge the narrative of colonial oppression in order to offer an alternative narrative of entitlement.

Source: Thomas E. Benediktsson, "The Reawakening of the Gods: Realism and the Supernatural in Silko and Hulme," in *Critique*, Vol. 33, No. 2, Winter 1992, pp. 121–31.

Randall D'Arcy

In the following review, D'Arcy notes the question of "national and international cultural politics" involved in the critical reception of The Bone People.

In her preface to *The Bone People*, Keri Hulme describes the novel's development from a short story, and its publishing history:

> "Simon Peter's Shell" began to warp into a novel. The characters wouldn't go away. They took 12 years to reach this shape. To me, it's a finished shape, so finished that I don't want to have anything to do with any alternation of it. Which is why I was to embalm the whole thing in a block of perspex when the first three publishers turned it down on the grounds, among others, that it was too large, too unwieldy, too different when compared with the normal shape of novel.
>
> Enter, to sound of trumpets and cowrieshell rattles, the Spiral Collective.

Yet in this preface, ironically, Hulme has indeed altered the "finished shape" of her published text by providing a blueprint for the imaginative expansion of its many myths. Four years after it was first published, the text is a character in another, ongoing series of legends and stories, all interwoven with the reception and interpretations of an international crowd of critics and readers.

One popular legends is that *The Bone People* was summarily rejected outright by commercial publishers (dominated by white, middle-class males) and was rescued only through the efforts of Spiral. It went on to dramatic sales and critical success in New Zealand, won the coveted Booker McConnell Prize, vindicating Hulme's talent and determination, the faith and efforts of Spiral, and feminist endeavour. Many critics included this legend, or another version of it, almost as an incantation, using it to support their particular position. Australian and New Zealand publishers look very stupid not to have recognized the novel's potential, and Elizabeth Webby wrote ruefully in 1975 that readers in Australia would now have to wait for the copies from London and New York.

A year after *The Bone People* was first published, C. K. Stead, in response to the text which he described as "touch[ing] a number or currently, or fashionably, sensitive nerves", tried to defuse the legend by arguing that one of the three rejecting publishers was a feminist, who found it "insufficiently feminist for her list", and the two others did not so much "turn it down" as ask for more work to be done on it.

One could argue that, from the point of view of the author, rejection is rejection, but in Sandi Hall's interview in *Broadsheet*, Keri Hulme herself tears away part of the towering legend by describing the early support of a male "commercial" publisher, David Elworthy at Collins (NZ), who tried to publish the novel but was prevented by Collin's London office. This makes sense in light of how critics and readers of both genders and different classes and cultures in New Zealand, from isolated Maori communities to post-modernist contributors to *Landfall*, embraced the novel in various ways, and to the difficulties in reception and understanding the novel encountered in the UK and, to a lesser degree, the USA.

The enthusiastic reception in New Zealand during 1984–85 was not, as far as I can tell, particularly "feminist" in its orientation; the relationship between Maori and Pakeha cultures appears to have been a more central focus. Miriama Evans preferred to discuss the novel in the context of politics and Maori literature rather than within "feminist perspectives". *The Listener* published two reviews, one Maori (Arapera Blank), one Pakeha (Joy Crowley), both profoundly supportive:

> Keri Hulme, tena koe, whanaunga o roto o Ngai-Tahu o Ngati-Mamoe! You have the nerve to leave the reader with the heart-acne of responding to the crying of many aching bones!

and

> We have known this book all our lives. . . . We are the bone people. Keri Hulme sat in our skulls while she wrote this work.

Peter Simpson, in a more conventionally "critical" review (published in 1984 in both New Zealand and Australia), like Crowley and others, claimed the work for Pakeha as well as Maori readers:

> *The Bone People* might be seen not only as a cultural document of immense significance to New Zealanders of all races and as a major novel in its own right, but also as an important advance in the development of New Zealand fiction, effecting a new synthesis of the previously distinct Maori and Pakeha fictional traditions.

Then, in 1985, the joint Spiral/Hodder and Stoughton edition was published in the UK. One of the earliest reviews there was by the New Zealander Fleur Adcock who, like Stead, was not prepared to be swayed by the novel's legendary status:

> Wary of hype, I approached it with caution. A few pages of arty prose at the beginning did nothing to reassure me; but once the narrative gets going the style settles down into something readable while still rich, varied and flexible, and the story becomes utterly compelling.

Adcock's review, taken in isolation, might be read as one of modified support, respectful of Hulme's achievement if not entirely won over by it. Unfortunately, this position was undercut at the start by her opening line: "It is hard to be sure whether this remarkable novel is a masterpiece or just a glorious mess." This phrase seems to have set the tone for what was to follow. In the following months, *The Bone People* was outspokenly "rejected" by most UK reviewers, and even the more balanced critics tended to use their most original lines for snide remarks.

This archipelago of hostility did not erupt until after the novel was short-listed for the Booker McConnell prize on 30 September, 1985. Most novels receive some unfavourable reviews, but an overwhelmingly 'negative' reception is usually a silent reception (at least in Australia) unless reviewers think a 'point' has to be made. It appears that if a prize as lucrative and prestigious as the Booker is at stake, the silent treatment cannot be considered. The power of the Booker shortlist alone in selling books and making author's reputations is enormous, and winning puts the author and title in a different category altogether.

In 1985, the members of the Booker judging panel were under some pressure. Claire Tomalin reported that the judges had been accused of selecting only "good reads for the public", but that "their spokesman . . . has just reaffirmed that the prize is meant to be for serious fiction, possibly risky or experimental fiction at that, fiction of lasting value—well, lasting enough to be 'still read in 20 years'." One judge, Norman St John Stevas, was reported as asserting that "he and his team [had] chosen their list not at all on the basis of the good read, but for being serious, major and well-written, even though they may be abnormal or upsetting books." The previous year's prize had gone to Anita Brookner's *Hotel du Lac*, a polished novel but an un-upsetting choice; in 1985 Brookner's *Family and Friends* (and Thomas Keneally's *A Family Madness*) were significant by their absence on the shortlist.

When it was not accused of being "abnormal or upsetting," *The Bone People* was considered a "dark horse" from the start in a contest the London papers treated as a horse-race, giving 'tips' and betting odds. "Not Hulme," wrote Tomalin, "because her book is more a prodigious curiosity than an achieved novel."

By 12 October, the media seemed to be grooming Peter Carey as the winner, and in the week before the announcement, *The Bone People* was ranked fairly low:

> No. No one could remember or even pronounce her name. . . . And moreover, the whole feel of her winning would be akin to J. M. Coetzee's *Life and Times of Michael Kin* 1983.
>
> (Joseph Connolly, *The Standard*, 24 Oct. 1985.)
>
> The language is rich and powerful. . . . The fly in the ointment is Kerewin, whose ability to fling a man over her shoulder while spouting tracts of poetry may do much for the spirit of New Zealand women but leaves the non-antipodean reader cold and not entirely convinced.
>
> (*The Economist*, 26 Oct.)
>
> *The Bone People* . . . is a very depressing book indeed . . . I was unable to finish, even in the course of duty.
>
> (Angela Huth, *Listener*, 24 Oct.)

Only a few days later, the *Mail* on Sunday gave Hulme the second-highest "score", and by the eve of the announcement, 31 October, W. L. Webb had narrowed the choice to the "antipodean odd couple". However, most Booker-watchers saw Hulme's win as a big surprise, and reactions were suspicious (Carey would have won, it was suggested in the *Standard*, if all the judges had been present), hostile and disappointed.

> The actual winner of the Booker McConnel Prize is a longer book, a longer yawn.
>
> (*London Review of Books*, 21 Nov.)
>
> The strangest novel ever to win the Booker. . . . That there is insight and some wild poetry in *The Bone People* . . . cannot be denied, but . . . Keri Hulme has hardly shaped it into a finished fiction in the way that . . . Peter Carey managed.
>
> (W. L. Webb, *The Guardian*, 1 Nov.)

Three weeks after the prize was announced, Lorna Sage in the *Times Literary Supplement* admitted that *The Bone People* had survived the

> **"The enthusiastic reception in New Zealand during 1984–85 was not, as far as I can tell, particularly 'feminist' in its orientation; the relationship between Maori and Pakeha cultures to have been a more central focus."**

critical assault; "proving more readable than some people feared. Publishers Hodder and Stoughton . . . report sales of 17,500 since the prize was announced, which makes 27,500 to date in this country, not to mention an extraordinary 35,000 copies in New Zealand." Last but not least, Alastair Niven finally gave the novel a strong positive review in *British Book News* in February 1986.

The main reception in the USA began shortly after the Booker Prize was announced. Early reviews by Claudia Tate in the *New York Times Book Review* and the Australian Elizabeth Ward in the *Washington Post* acknowledged the Booker Prize but not the controversy, and were very positive. Ward's incorporated the "legend", borrowed from the *Guardian*. More reserved and mixed reviews plus brief positive acknowledgments appeared later in journals. Although most US reviewers acknowledged the novel's importance in the context of New Zealand culture, its originality in language and form, the reception was disparate compared to those of New Zealand (and Australia) and the UK. Susan Willens's review, published in the context of other Australian/New Zealand fiction praised the "rich and strange" world, but admitted to being overwhelmed by the effort of reading so much unfamiliar text: "The effect of all the cultural education on the reader is too much, like being locked in the Natural History Museum overnight."

It is tempting to construct schematic patterns of extreme affection and violence in the reception of *The Bone People* and to blame this on Hulme's infectious storytelling. It is possible to take the 'evidence' of hastily compiled journal reviews too seriously but, read together, the UK response does form a pattern, almost a negative image of the predominant New Zealand acclaim. The dramatic circumstances of the novel's own history I think contribute to this. The UK responses to the Booker shortlist and prize bring out not so much an antidote to New Zealand's accolades than a concentrated expression of a hegemonic attitude to what constitutes literary value in the UK publishing/reviewing establishment. The different hegemony in New Zealand has recently been analysed by Simon During, and expatriate New Zealander.

> the book's rapturous reception owes more to the desire of New Zealand to see a reconciliation of its postcolonising and postcolonised discourses than it does to either close reading of the text itself, or an examination of the book's cultural political effects.

The reception of *The Bone People* raises a number of interesting questions of national and international cultural politics, and the production of literary value, that would merit a much lengthier investigation.

Source: Randall D'Arcy, "Keri Hulme's *The Bone People* and the Literary Lottery," in *Hecate*, Vol. 14, No. 1, May 31, 1988, p. 71.

Sources

Brown, Rebecca, "First-Rank Debut—Novel from New Zealand Masterfully Captures Spirit of Country's Native Culture," in *Seattle Times*, January 5, 1986, p. J10.

Hanson, Neil, "*Bone People*, Fishing and a Search for *Bait*," in *Los Angeles Times*, August 14, 2005, p. R12.

Hegi, Ursula, "Cracking Open the Shell of a Reclusive New Zealand Artist," in *Los Angeles Times*, November 18, 1985, p. 8.

Hulme, Keri, *The Bone People*, Penguin, 1984.

Kakutani, Michiko, Review of *The Bone People*, in *New York Times*, November 13, 1985, p. C23.

Moncur, Andrew, "Years of Rejection Didn't Stop Author's Quest to Publish," in *Seattle Times*, January 5, 1986, p. J10.

Tate, Claudia, "Triple-Forged Trinity," in *New York Times*, November 17, 1985, p. BR11.

Willens, Susan P., "At Home with the Maoris," in *Belles Lettres*, Vol. 2, No. 1, Fall 1986, p. 3.

Further Reading

Duffie, Mary Katharine, *Through the Eye of the Needle: A Maori Elder Remembers*, Wadsworth Publishing, 2000.

The history of the Maori people is told in this book through the voice of a Maori woman.

Harawira, K. T., *Beginner's Maori*, Hippocrene Books, 1997.

This book introduces readers to the basics of the Maori language.

Masson, Jeffrey Moussaieff, *Slipping into Paradise: Why I Live in New Zealand*, Ballantine Books, 2004.

When Masson, an American psychologist and author, moved to New Zealand, he decided to explore the local landscape, culture, and people, to discover what New Zealand was. This book gives an intelligent and entertaining view of what Masson found to love about his adopted home.

Smith, Philippa Mein, *A Concise History of New Zealand*, Cambridge University Press, 2005.

As of 2005, Smith is an associate professor of history at the University of Cambridge in the United Kingdom. In this extensive history of New Zealand, she covers the formation of the geography, the landing of the Maori people, and the relationships that have developed between the Maori and the European settlers up until the beginning of the twenty-first century.

The Bridge of San Luis Rey

Thornton Wilder

1927

The Bridge of San Luis Rey was Thornton Wilder's second novel, published when he was just thirty, and it won him the Pulitzer Prize in 1928. It tells the story of a religious man's spiritual quest to determine why God allows disasters to occur. Wilder sets the action in Lima, Peru, in 1714, where a Franciscan monk witnesses the collapse of a bridge that has stood for over a century, killing the five people on it. The priest becomes determined to develop a scientific method for calculating what personality characteristics the five might have shared that would make God ready to call them to him. In the novel, Brother Juniper spends years compiling data about each victim in order to draw his conclusions. Wilder fits their personal stories into a slender volume, told with a voice that resonates across years and cultures.

Almost since its first publication, *The Bridge of San Luis Rey* has been recognized as a literary masterpiece. Its unique mixture of the spiritual with the humane has given readers throughout the decades a point of reference when considering the apparent horrors that can occur in a world that is explained increasingly through cold scientific eyes. In his memorial tribute to the victims of the terrorist attacks in the United States on September 11, 2001, British prime minister Tony Blair quoted from the book, and since then it has become even more popular, as the world has struggled to reconcile faith with catastrophe.

Thornton Wilder © AP Images

Author Biography

Thornton Niven Wilder was born in Madison, Wisconsin, on April 17, 1897, along with a twin brother who did not survive childbirth. His father was a newspaper editor who joined the Foreign Service, eventually being named as the U.S. consul to Hong Kong in 1906. Wilder lived briefly in Hong Kong, returned to the United States, then went back to the Far East in 1911 when his father was reassigned to Shanghai. He returned to California once more. He attended an exclusive boarding school in Ojai, which he found to be a miserable experience, feeling isolated and being treated as an outcast for being a homosexual. Throughout his life, the isolation he felt during his high school days persisted. He returned home to attend school in Berkeley for two years, and there he started writing plays. During World War I, Wilder served two years in the Coast Guard.

Wilder attended college at Oberlin in Ohio and then transferred to Yale, where his first full-length play, *The Trumpet Shall Sound*, was published in the prestigious *Yale Literary Magazine* in 1920, later to be produced onstage in 1926. After graduation he studied archeology in Rome at the American Academy for a year then returned to the United States to attend Princeton, teaching French at a New Jersey high school while working on his master's degree in French, which he earned in 1926. That year, his first novel, *The Cabala*, was published. The following year saw publication of his second novel, *The Bridge of San Luis Rey*, which won him the Pulitzer Prize. He won a second Pulitzer in 1938 for his play *Our Town* and a third in 1942 for the play *The Skin of Our Teeth*. His second famous play was *The Matchmaker*, a 1955 Broadway production that was based on Wilder's 1939 play *The Merchant of Yonkers* and which itself became the basis for the musical *Hello, Dolly*. In all, he wrote seven novels and over a dozen plays and is credited for translating several foreign plays into English.

Wilder died in his sleep on December 7, 1975, in Hamden, Connecticut, of a heart attack.

Plot Summary

Part One: Perhaps an Accident

The first few pages of the first chapter of *The Bridge of San Luis Rey* explain the book's basic premise: this story centers on an event that happened in Lima, Peru, at noon of Friday, June 12, 1714. A bridge woven by the Incas a century earlier collapsed at that particular moment, while five people were crossing it. The collapse was witnessed by Brother Juniper, a Franciscan monk who was on his way to cross it. Curious about why God would allow such a tragedy, he decides to take a scientific approach to the question. He sets out to interview everyone he can find who knew the five victims. Over the course of six years, he compiles a huge book. Part One foretells the burning of the book that occurs at the end of the novel, but it also says that one copy of Brother Juniper's book survives and is at the library of the University of San Marco, where it sits neglected.

Part Two: The Marquesa de Montemayor

The second section focuses on one of the victims of the collapse: Doña María, the Marquesa de Montemayor. She was the daughter of a cloth merchant, an ugly child who eventually entered into an arranged marriage and bore a daughter, Clara, whom she loved dearly. Clara was indifferent to her mother, though, and married a Spanish man and moved across the ocean. Doña María visits her daughter, but when they cannot get along, she returns to Lima. The only way that they can communicate comfortably is by letter, and Doña María pours her heart into her writing, which becomes so polished that her letters will be read in schools for hundreds of years after her death.

Doña María takes as her companion Pepita, a girl raised at the Convent of Santa María Rosa de la Rosas. When she learns that her daughter in Spain is pregnant, Doña María decides to make a pilgrimage to the shrine of Santa María de Cluxambuqua. Pepita goes along as company and to supervise the staff. When Doña María is out at the shrine, Pepita stays at the inn and writes a letter to her patron, the Abbess, complaining about her misery and loneliness. Doña María sees the letter on the table when she gets back and reads it. Later, she asks Pepita about the letter, and Pepita says she burned it because it was not brave to write it. Doña María has new insight into the ways in which her own life has lacked bravery, but the next morning, returning to Lima, she and Pepita are on the bridge when it collapses.

Part Three: Esteban

Esteban and Manuel are twins who were left at the Convent of Santa María Rosa de la Rosas as infants. The Abbess of the convent, Madre María del Pilar, developed a fondness for them as they grew up. When they became older, they decided to be scribes. They are so close that they have developed a secret language that only they understand. Their closeness becomes strained when Manuel falls in love with Camila Perichole.

The Perichole flirts with Manuel and swears him to secrecy when she retains him to write letters to her lover, the Viceroy. Esteban has no idea of their relationship until she turns up at the twins' room one night in a hurry and has Manuel write to a bullfighter with whom she is having an affair. Esteban encourages his brother to follow her, but instead Manuel swears that he will never see her again.

Manuel cuts his knee on a piece of metal and it becomes infected. The surgeon instructs Esteban to put cold compresses on the injury: the compresses are so painful that Manuel curses Esteban, though he later remembers nothing of his curses. Esteban offers to send for the Perichole, but Manuel refuses. Soon after, Manuel dies.

When the Abbess comes to prepare the body, she asks Esteban his name, and he says he is Manuel. Gossip about his ensuing strange behavior spreads all over town. He goes to the theater but runs away before the Perichole can talk to him; the Abbess tries to talk to him, but he runs away, so she sends for Captain Alvarado.

Captain Alvarado goes to see Esteban in Cuzco and hires him to sail with him. Esteban agrees. He wants his pay in advance in order to buy a present for the Abbess. The Captain offers to take him back to Lima to buy the present, and at the ravine, the Captain goes down to a boat that is ferrying some materials across the water. Esteban goes to the bridge and is on it when it collapses.

Part Four: Uncle Pio

Uncle Pio acts as Camila Perichole's maid, and, in addition, "her singing-master, her coiffeur, her masseur, her reader, her errand-boy, her banker; rumor added: her father." The story tells of his background. He has traveled the world engaged in a variety of businesses, most related to the theater or politics, including conducting interrogations for the Inquisition. He came to realize that he had just three interests in the world: independence; the constant presence of beautiful women; and work with the masterpieces of Spanish literature, particularly in the theater.

He becomes rich working for the Viceroy. One day, he discovers a twelve-year-old café singer, Micaela Villegas, and takes her under his protection.

Media Adaptations

- The most recent film version of *The Bridge of San Luis Rey* was made in 2004, written and directed by Mary McGuckian. It stars Robert De Niro, Harvey Keitel, Kathy Bates, and Gabriel Byrne.
- The most familiar film version of *The Bridge of San Luis Rey* is the 1944 release starring Akim Tamiroff, Lynn Bari, and Francis Lederer. It was written by Howard Estabrook and directed by Rowland V. Lee.
- *The Bridge of San Luis Rey* was originally filmed in 1929 as a part-silent, part-sound production, starring Lili Damita, Ernest Torrence, and Raquel Torres. Charles Brabin directed. The only known surviving print of this version is held at the George Eastman House in Rochester, New York.
- The Thornton Wilder Society maintains a website at http://www.tcnj.edu/~wilder/ dedicated to preserving the memory of the author and his works.

Over the course of years, as they travel from country to country, she becomes beautiful and talented. She develops into Camila Perichole, the most honored actress in Lima.

After years of success, Perichole becomes bored with the stage. The Viceroy takes her as his mistress, and she and Uncle Pio and the Archbishop of Peru and, eventually, Captain Alvarado meet frequently at midnight for dinner at the Viceroy's mansion. Through it all, Uncle Pio is faithfully devoted, but as Camila ages and has three children by the Viceroy she focuses on becoming a lady, not an actress. She avoids Uncle Pio, and when he talks to her she tells him to not use her stage name.

When a small-pox epidemic sweeps through Lima, Camila is disfigured by it. She takes her son Jaime to the country. Uncle Pio sees her one night trying hopelessly to cover her pock-marked face with powder: ashamed, she refuses to ever see him again. He begs her to allow him to take her son and teach the boy as he taught her. They leave the next morning. Uncle Pio and Jaime are the fourth and fifth people on the bridge to Lima when it collapses.

Part Five: Perhaps an Intention

Brother Juniper works for six years on his book about the bridge collapse, trying various mathematical formulae to measure spiritual traits, with no results. He compiles his huge book of interviews, but a council pronounces his work heresy, and the book and Brother Juniper are burned in the town square.

The story shifts back in time to the day of a service for those who died in the bridge collapse. The Archbishop, the Viceroy, and Captain Alvarado are at the ceremony. At the Convent of Santa María Rosa de la Rosas, the Abbess feels, having lost Pepita and the twin brothers, that her work will die with her. Camila Perichole comes to ask how she can go on, having lost her son and Uncle Pio. Doña Clara comes: throughout the book she has been in Spain, and no one in Lima knows her. As she views the sick and poor being taken cared for at the convent, she is moved. The novel ends with the Abbess's observation: "There is a land of the living and a land of the dead and the bridge is love, the only survival, the only meaning."

Characters

Captain Alvarado

Captain Alvarado is a world traveler, known to many of the characters in the novel. Uncle Pio brings him into the group that has frequent midnight dinners at the estate of the Viceroy, and the Marquesa de Montemayor writes about him in a letter to her daughter. The Abbess of the Convent Santa María Rosa de la Rosas sends for him when she hears that Esteban is grieving the loss of his twin brother Manuel, knowing that both boys have sailed with the Captain before. The Captain goes to Esteban and convinces him to not commit suicide, consoling him, "It isn't for long, you know. Time keeps going by. You'll be surprised at the way time passes."

The force driving Captain Alvarado is that he once had a daughter, who died while he was away at sea. The Marquesa says about him in her letter, "You will laugh at me, but I think he goes about the hemispheres to pass the time between now and his old age."

Archbishop of Lima

The Archbishop is an epicure, more concerned with good food and good wine than with salvation. He is part of the group that meets at the Viceroy's mansion each evening for long, all-night dinners, to discuss politics and philosophy. He considers himself to be an amateur philologist, so when he hears about the secret language that Manuel and Esteban use for speaking to each other, he calls them to teach it to him, but when he sees how embarrassed they are about it he allows them to leave.

Doña Clara

Clara is the daughter of Doña María. Doña María loves her dearly and centers her life on her daughter, though Clara is, for the most part, disinterested in her mother and even somewhat embarrassed by her. When she is old enough to marry, Clara weds a Spanish nobleman and moves to Spain. Her mother visits her there once, but they do not get along, so their primary means of communication is through letters, which take six months in transit each way by ship.

Doña Clara makes her first appearance in the book at the very end, when she shows up at the Convent of Santa María Rosa de la Rosas on the day that there is to be a memorial for her mother and the other victims of the bridge collapse. Following the Abbess through the convent, she sees the sick and old people who are cared for there. The Abbess expects her to leave, but she stays, looking at the wretched people whom she has never been so near in her privileged life, learning about suffering that she never understood before.

Conde Vincente d'Abuirre

The husband of Doña Clara has little to do in this novel. At one point, his amusement at the letters written by his mother-in-law, the Marquesa de Montemayor, is mentioned. Also, the Viceroy forces his mistress, Camila Perichole, to apologize after she has made fun of the Marquesa because he has business in Spain and he knows that Conde Vincente is a very powerful figure there.

Marquesa de Montemayor

See Doña María

Don Andrés de Ribera

The Viceroy, Don Andrés, has had a hard life, and is a broken-down old man with a high title. He is crippled with gout, a widower without children. He hires Uncle Pio to look after secret affairs for him, and through Uncle Pio he meets Camila Perichole and takes her as his mistress. She adores him.

When she sings a song that insults the Marquesa de Montemayor, Don Andrés forces her to apologize for three reasons: to keep peace in Lima; to humble his mistress because he suspects her of cheating on him with a matador; and to curry favor with the Spanish court, to which the Marquesa's son-in-law belongs.

At the memorial service for the victims of the bridge collapse, the Viceroy is very conscious of people looking at him, expecting for him to grieve for his dead son Don Jaime. He wonders where the boy's mother, the Perichole, is, having no contact with her.

Abbess Madre María del Pilar

The Abbess, head of the Convent Santa María Rosa de la Rosas, is instrumental in the stories of two victims of the bridge collapse. In addition to being in charge of the orphanage, she runs a hospital for the old, sick, and infirm. The narrative refers to her as "that strange genius of Lima."

The Abbess raises the orphan Pepita and decides to give her a chance at a worldly education by sending her off to be the companion of the Marquesa de Montemayor. She also raises the twins, Manuel and Esteban, of whom she is very fond, even though she is not generally fond of men.

After the bridge collapse kills Pepita and Esteban, the Abbess is left forlorn. She has lost two of her favorite people, and she foresees that, once she herself is dead, there will be no one to run the convent and care for the poor. This conclusion becomes uncertain at the end, though, when the previously haughty actress Camila Perichole comes to her for consolation and the rich Doña Clara, who ignored her own mother most of her life, shows an interest in helping the poor. The Abbess sees how a tragedy can bring together people who would otherwise have no connection.

Esteban

Esteban and Manual are twins who were abandoned at the Convent of Santa María Rosa de la Rosas as infants. They are inseparable, traveling the world as sailors and developing a secret language that is understood only by them.

One day, when the Perichole comes to their house to request Manuel write a letter for her to her lover, Esteban notices that Manuel is in love with her. This drives a wedge through their close relationship, but Esteban tells his brother to follow her; instead, Manuel declares that his infatuation with her is over and that he will never see her again.

Later, an injury on Manuel's leg becomes infected. Manuel is in so much pain that he curses Esteban's efforts to heal the wound, damning him to hell. Manuel eventually dies, and Esteban acts crazy, shunning all people and giving his name as "Manuel" when asked.

An old friend, Captain Alvarado, finds Esteban drinking in a restaurant and invites him to sail the world with him. Esteban agrees, as long as he can be kept constantly busy, so that he will not be reminded with his brother. The next morning, he says that he has changed his mind and that he cannot leave Peru, but the Captain reminds him that he had expressed interest in buying a present for the Abbess of the orphanage who raised him. He goes to his room, and the Captain follows him there just in time to stop him from hanging himself. They leave, and while Esteban is on the bridge it collapses and he is killed.

Don Jaime

Don Jaime is the only son of the Perichole. He is a sickly child, which is the main reason that his mother remains at her villa in the mountains, away from Lima. He dies in the bridge collapse when Uncle Pio is taking the boy to Lima to live as his student for a year.

Brother Juniper

Brother Juniper is the focus of the first and last chapters of the novel. He can be considered the protagonist of the book, even though his appearances are few and brief. He is a Franciscan monk, in Peru to convert Indians to Catholicism when he witnesses the collapse of the bridge. Being a religious man, he wonders why God would make such a tragedy occur, and he sets about to explore the lives of the victims of the collapse so that he can better understand what standards God holds for humanity.

Brother Juniper has a scientific mind, and he believes that theology should be held to the same standards of inquiry as the other sciences. A talk with an old school friend who has become a hardened skeptic leads him to devise a chart that rates people according to goodness, piety, and usefulness, a system that he tries out during a plague at the town of Puerto, calibrating his scale by applying the same standards to people killed by the plague and people who have survived. He finds out that no such standard is helpful in measuring the moral attributes of those who die early.

After his inquiry into the bridge collapse has proven inconclusive, a panel of judges examines Brother Juniper's work and declares it to be heretical. The book is burned in the town square, and Brother Juniper is sentenced to be burned too. The night before his execution, he thinks about why he is being punished when all he wanted to do was to help the church. He finds no reason for his death, and the narrator says that there were many in the crowd who believed in him. He goes to his death thinking that St. Francis, at least, would support his work.

Manuel

Manuel and Esteban are twins who were abandoned as infants at the Convent of Santa María Rosa de la Rosas. In childhood they developed a secret language that no one but the other twin can understand. They are scribes. While copying a script at the theater, Manuel falls in love with Camila Perichole. She has him write letters for her to her lovers.

When his twin brother finds out that Manuel is in love with the Perichole, Manuel is so embarrassed that he swears he will not see her again. He proves good to his word when she sends a servant for him and he refuses to go.

Manuel cuts his knee and it becomes infected. The doctor tells Esteban to treat it with cold compresses. Every time Esteban puts a compress on the wound, the pain is so intense that Manuel curses at Esteban, damning him to hell, even though they have always been inseparable. Eventually, Manuel dies of the infection.

Doña María

Doña María is the first of the bridge collapse victims to have a section of the book dedicated to her. She is introduced as a legendary figure, famous for her letters, which now, two hundred years after her death, are well-known examples of the writing of her time. The grand obsession in her life is her daughter Clara who, as soon as she is old enough, marries and moves away to Spain.

Doña María is known around Lima as an eccentric. She is a secret drinker. The Abbess Madre María del Pilar looks at her and sees a "grotesque old woman." When the Perichole sings an insulting song about her at the theater and is forced to apologize, she initially thinks that Doña María is being gracious when she claims to know nothing of the incident, but, as the scene continues and Doña María makes a fool of herself, it becomes clear even to the Perichole that the old lady really is oblivious.

Doña María takes a girl from the orphanage, Pepita, as her companion. Pepita can see how the other servants take advantage of the Marquesa, mocking her behind her back and stealing from her, but Doña María remains ignorant of what they think of her until one day, when her entourage is at a shrine in the hills praying for the baby, which she has heard, almost casually, that her daughter had. There, Doña María happens upon a letter Pepita has written, explaining how unhappy she is. Doña María later offers to mail the letter for her, but Pepita says that she burned it because writing such a letter was not courageous: from this, Doña María receives sudden insight into courage, and she realizes just how much her own life has lacked courage. She decides to start living differently just as the bridge collapses beneath her and Pepita, killing them.

Pepita

Pepita was left as an orphan at the Convent Santa Maria Rosa de la Rosas. The Abbess grooms Pepita to be her successor, and in order to give her a broader education and introduce her into wealthy society the girl is sent to be a companion at the house of the Marquesa de Montemayor. Pepita hates it there. Not only is her mistress a vain, drunken, ignorant woman, but Pepita is left to deal with the household staff's dishonesty as they steal from the Marquesa, make fun of her behind her back, and use her house for their own pleasures. They pick on Pepita and make her the victim of practical jokes. Still, she remains faithful to her duty.

The day before her death, Pepita is so miserable about her life with the Marquesa that she writes a letter to the Abbess, detailing her complaints. She destroys the letter, but not before the Marquesa has seen it on the table. When the Marquesa asks why she did not send the letter, Pepita holds tight to her suffering and says that the letter betrayed a lack of courage in her.

Camila Perichole

Wilder bases this character on the title character of *La Perichole*, a Jacques Offenbach opera that opened in Paris in 1868 (more than a hundred years after *The Bridge of San Luis Rey* takes place). It concerns a Peruvian street singer who is brought to the palace to amuse the Viceroy. Her last name means "half-breed [b——]." Her first name is taken from the 1848 novel *Camille: The Lady of the Camellias* by Alexandre Dumas fils (the younger).

Throughout the story, the woman born Micaela Villegars is referred to as, alternately, "Camila" or "the Perichole." She is discovered by Uncle Pio at the age of twelve in a café, and he decides to make her a singing star. He trains her and takes her around the world, so she can sing in different countries while honing her craft. When they end up in Lima she is lauded as the best singer and actress in Peru. Through her relationship with him she meets the Viceroy, who is a much older man; she becomes his mistress and has three children, a boy and two girls, with him.

The Perichole is a vain social climber. During a break in a concert, she sings a song making fun of the Marquesa de Montemayor, a rich eccentric, mocking her for the drinking she thinks is secret and her devotion to her daughter. At age thirty, the Perichole decides to quit the stage and be a lady. She stops associating with Uncle Pio, and she makes up family members with classy social backgrounds.

Her vanity is assaulted when she contracts smallpox, which leaves her face pockmarked. She tries unsuccessfully to hide the scars with makeup. She agrees to allow Uncle Pio to take her son Jaime to Lima, to train the boy as he trained her, but they are killed in the bridge collapse.

In the end, the Perichole is humbled, arriving at the Convent Santa María Rosa de la Rosas without makeup, kneeling before the Abbess there to ask for religious counsel.

Uncle Pio

Uncle Pio is the subject of the fourth section of the book. He is a successful, self-made man, having been in a variety of businesses and traveled the world. He does secret work for the Viceroy. Still, nothing makes him happy until he takes young Micaela Villegas under his control and trains her to be the popular singer, Camila Perichole. His association with her allows him to follow his three interests: being a free and independent man; being surrounded by beautiful women; and working in or near the theater.

He brings the Perichole up in society, introducing her to his friends. Eventually, she decides to turn her back on her singing career, and she distances herself from Uncle Pio. He finds excuses to see her. Once, after her looks have been marred by smallpox, he comes upon her trying to cover up her scarred face with makeup, and she tells him that she does not want to ever see him again. He makes up elaborate schemes in order to see her, once hiding in her garden at night and crying like a little girl, hoping that it will affect her subconsciously and make her more compassionate. When that does not work, he asks to take her son Jaime to Lima and train the boy as he trained her. The bridge collapses as they cross it en route to Lima, and Uncle Pio and the boy die.

Viceroy

See Don Andrés

Micaela Villegas

See Camila Perichole

Themes

Search for Knowledge

After witnessing the collapse of the bridge, Brother Juniper does not embark on a quest to find the physical causes that would explain why a structure that has stood for a thousand years would give out at that particular time. He takes such tragedy as a part of life, like disease and old age. Instead of concerning himself with physics, which is not his field of expertise, Brother Juniper takes a theological approach. He is determined to use scientific methods to try to understand God's will. He creates a scale for measuring such abstract moral values as piety and goodness, and he applies his scale to people who have suffered from tragedy and those who have not, in order to find the proper relation between them. Because the bridge collapse is such a freak accident with a limited number of victims, he feels that the event poses a rare opportunity to conduct his study with a manageable sampling.

Even though the lives of five people represent a small group, Brother Juniper finds out that there are so many minute facets to their lives that nothing can be measured. He compiles thousands of pages of information but is not able to draw any satisfactory conclusions from them. He does not find commonality between the lives of those killed and

Topics For Further Study

- Read a history written by a person who was not involved in the event, but who found out about the background of the people through research. Report to your class on what happens in the book and also on what you think the author's attitude is toward the participants.
- Wilder uses the special language shared by Manuel and Esteban to represent the unique, exclusive bond between the twins. Do some research on scientific studies about the emotional connection between twins and make a chart showing how it differs from the ways that non-twin siblings relate.
- In the wake of the catastrophe, the people of Lima have a period of great soul-searching, looking at their misdeeds with repentance and defensiveness. Research some personal stories of how people felt in the week after the terrorist attacks in the United States on September 11, 2001, and report to your class the ones that you think sound most like the reactions of the people in Lima.
- Just before the bridge collapse, Brother Juniper hears "a twanging noise . . . as when a string of some musical instrument snaps in a disused room." Read about the physics of bridge collapses, and explain what the connection between this sound and the ensuing tragedy could be.
- Choose a religion, examine its theology, and write a report on how you think it would explain a catastrophe like the collapse of the Bridge of San Luis Rey.

so is not able to point to any particular characteristic that would mark these individuals for tragedy.

Though Brother Juniper's line of inquiry is fruitless, the book does not leave the search for knowledge completely unfulfilled. It ends with the suggestion that there is, after all, some reason for an otherwise senseless tragedy: the event brings together people such as Doña Clara, Camila Perichole, and the Abbess of the Convent of Santa María Rosa de la Rosas, who would otherwise not have any relationship to each other, and it gives hope that the Abbess's work with the poor and suffering will be continued. Though this knowledge gives meaning to an event after it has happened, it is no good for predicting, as science attempts, when a similar event is going to occur.

Parental Love

Another theme in *The Bridge of San Luis Rey*, the relationship between doting parents and ungrateful children, is established early in the novel, in the story of the Marquesa de Montemayor, who leads a lonesome life in Lima, pining away for attention from her daughter, Doña Clara, even though she receives no love in return. This parental devotion is reflected in the relationship between Camila Perichole and her son, Don Jaime, whom she treats kindly but holds at a distance. Wilder does not show her to be unloving, but she is more concerned with appearances than with expressing her affection.

The fathers in this novel present similar contrasts. Captain Alvarado is explained to be ruled by the memory of his dead daughter, so devoted to her that even in her absence she is the driving force behind his every moment. The Viceroy, on the other hand, is unmoved by the death of his son Don Jaime in the bridge collapse, concerning himself with public appearances at the memorial service, wondering how much sorrow to show.

The story is also filled with symbolic parent-child relationships. The Abbess, of course, since she is in charge of the orphanage, has a parental role in the upbringing of Pepita, Manuel, and Esteban. Uncle Pio behaves like a father to Camila and, at the end of his story, is ready to assume a similar role toward her son Don Jaime: ironically, Camila rejects him as strongly as Doña Clara rejects her own mother, also out of social embarrassment. The orphans attach themselves to parental figures when Esteban lets himself fall under the guidance of Captain Alvarado and Pepita becomes fiercely devoted to the Marquesa, although she treats Pepita badly.

Epiphany

In literature, an epiphany is a sudden realization that allows a character to view the world in a completely new way. Some of the characters in this book have epiphanies before their deaths, and some do not. For instance, just before going to the bridge, Doña María, the Marquesa de Montemayor, realizes that she has not been brave in the past, an insight that cuts through the self-delusions that allowed her to hide her embarrassing lifestyle from herself. Similarly, the novel hints that Captain Alvarado's explanation to Esteban that "Time keeps passing by" appears to have stopped Esteban's suicide and given him a reason to go on in spite of his grief for his brother Manuel, even though a catastrophe takes his life just minutes later. Madre María del Pilar, the Abbess, is falling into despair that her life's work will be for nothing before realizing, in a flash, that the appearances of Doña Clara and Camila Perichole at the convent constitute a sign that there is a connection between all people dead and living.

The one notable exception in this book is Brother Juniper, who devotes his life to the search for understanding and, in the end, receives none. Though he compiles his book with good intention, the accusations of the religious tribunal that finds against him make him doubt his own motives. He prays for someone to believe in him, but dies without knowing that a delegation supporting his views has come. Upon his death, he is even afraid to call out to God, being too unsure of his right to do so because he might be evil.

Style

First Person Narrator

For the most part, this novel is told through the third person omniscient point of view. It is third person because it is told about other people, referring to them as "she" and "he." The narrative is omniscient because it does not limit itself to any one person's perspective: it can shift from one person's thoughts to another's in one line, and then back, as when it goes from Manuel's infatuation with Camila Perichole to Esteban's reaction to his brother or shifts from one perspective to another during the ceremony for those killed in the collapse. It is also able to give readers information that no one in the novel would be able to know, such as the inadequacy of the word "resignation" to describe what the Marquesa felt at the inn in Cluxambuqua.

Technically, though, this is a first-person account. The narrator refers to himself or herself several times as "I," particularly at the end of Book One, with the line, "And I, who claim to know so much more, isn't it possible that even I have missed the very spring within the spring?" There is some effort to explain how a modern-day narrator would have been able to gain information about the people described in the book, primarily through the one remaining copy of Brother Juniper's work and the letters of the Marquesa, which have been saved for centuries. Still, Wilder gives more information than what any first-person narrator, years removed from the event, could know. Drawing attention to a narrator who is trying to reconstruct their lives invites a parallel to Brother Juniper's quest to understand them through his research.

Multiple Protagonists

In the first section, it seems as if Brother Juniper is going to be the protagonist, or main character, of this story. The tragedy occurs on page one, and the book focuses right away on Brother Juniper's response to it; furthermore, Brother Juniper is a compelling character, searching for an answer to an essential question about human existence. At the end of Part One, though, Brother Juniper disappears from the novel, and he does not come back until the last part.

The book then goes through a series of protagonists, each identified by the title of a chapter: the Marquesa de Montemayor, Esteban, and Uncle Pio. These chapter titles are helpful because it is not always easy to tell who is the main character. Part Three, for instance, focuses on Manuel and his growing love for the Perichole before it settles on Esteban, and Part Four gives a detailed background of Camila Perichole, leaving Uncle Pio out of the story for dozens of pages. The final part starts with Brother Juniper and his intellectual quest, but after his death shifts to the Abbess, Madre María del Pilar, who up to that point has been a relatively minor character.

Epistolary Narrative

Wilder uses the letters of the Marquesa de Montemayor to tell significant parts of the story, quoting from them liberally. He does not just do this in her section of the story but refers back to the Marquesa's writings in order to introduce new characters, such as Uncle Pio and Captain Alvaraz. In addition, he includes a large passage of Pepita's letter to the Abbess, and he uses Manuel's occupation as a scribe to include sections of love letters dictated by Perichole. A story that is told through people's letters is called an epistolary narrative.

Compare & Contrast

- **1714:** The Catholic Church supports a formal Inquisition board in Peru. An offshoot of the dreaded Spanish Inquisition, it has the ability to execute those found guilty of heresy.

  1927: As Peru becomes more internationally oriented, the people are exposed to a wider variety of worldviews: still, Catholicism is strongly entrenched.

  Today: About three-fourths of the population of Peru are Catholic.

- **1714:** The basic means of transportation over a mountain pass is by foot or in an animal-drawn cart.

  1927: Rail lines are constructed to connect dangerous mountain areas.

  Today: Roads and bridges for cars make most locations accessible.

- **1714:** Peru is a colony, under the control of Spain.

  1927: Freed of Spain's rule a century before, Peru is controlled by a series of powerful dictators, who exploit the country for its rich mineral holdings. It has been ruled by Augusto Bernadino Leguia y Salcedo since 1908.

  Today: Peru's democratic government has been challenged in recent years by, on one side, the violent Maoist guerilla movement Shining Path and, on the other, by the government's authoritarian measures to fight the insurgents.

- **1714:** In Peru, as in much of the world, professional scribes (like Manuel and Esteban in the novel) are needed to write and read letters for the mostly illiterate population.

  1927: Peru is still an agrarian society. The literacy rate is between 30 and 40 percent.

  Today: Over 90 percent of Peruvians are literate. Education is required between the ages of six and fifteen, and it is free.

- **1714:** Spain's viceregal capital of colonial Peru, Lima is isolated from Europe. News takes six months or more to travel across the sea.

  1927: Telephone connections between New York and London are first established (at a rate of $75 for a three-minute call). Telephone service between Peru and Europe is decades away.

  Today: Thanks to satellite technology, a person walking down the street in Lima can contact any phone anywhere.

Referring to letters gives the novel a sense of being in direct contact with characters who are supposed to have died hundreds of years ago. As opposed to a first-person narrative, which could have the character talking directly to the reader or musing privately, the use of letters shows the character's formal side, the personality that is conveyed to the public or at least to one other person.

Historical Context

The Inquisition

The Inquisition was a judicial process instituted by the Papacy to investigate and try those charged with opposing the teachings of the Roman Catholic Church. It was prevalent in Europe from 1184 on, in one form or another until 1836, and was enacted in some European colonies such as Peru.

The point of the Inquisition was to investigate and prosecute charges of heresy. Throughout the late 1400s and early 1500s, a number of secular governments helped the church in persecuting people deemed to be insufficiently pious. The church established a formal Inquisition in Rome in the 1500s, under the control of a board of cardinals answering to the pope. The Italian Inquisition followed court process, allowing defendants to answer charges against them and to appeal convictions. Sentences were often fines or brief imprisonment.

The most brutal phase of the Inquisition occurred in the late 1400s in Spain. There, the burden of proof shifted to the accused. Panels of inquisitors went from town to town and heard cases, often convicting people in their absence, or for failure to confess the crime of which they were accused. To extract confessions, torture was used. The Spanish Inquisition had the authority to try, sentence, and execute citizens who were assumed to pose a threat to the teachings of the Roman Catholic Church. These tribunals had the authority to confiscate the estates of those who were convicted, creating an immediate conflict of interests.

Conquered by Spain in 1533, Peru remained under Spanish domination until 1824. Subject to Spanish law, it was also subject to the religious decrees of the Catholic Church and, therefore, to the rules of the Spanish Inquisition. Lima, a small, conservative town, was made the seat of the Peruvian Inquisition, which was most active during the 1500s and 1600s. By the time of this story in 1714, the Inquisition was seldom enacted. The court was formally closed by the church in 1836.

The Lost Generation

Though Thornton Wilder is not frequently associated with their ideals and concerns, the literary scene at the time when he was writing this novel was dominated by a group of writers referred to, collectively, as the Lost Generation. The name comes from a quotation by Gertrude Stein, which was used as an epigraph to Ernest Hemingway's 1926 novel *The Sun Also Rises*, which is considered a key text of his generation.

The label, Lost Generation, is used to describe the writers who came to prominence after World War I ended in 1918 and their disillusionment caused by the horrors they experienced during that first great global conflict. After the war, many American writers, such as Hemingway, F. Scott Fitzgerald, John Dos Passos, Kay Boyle, e. e. cummings (who chose to print his name in lower case), William Faulkner, Archibald MacLeish, and Thomas Wolfe, moved to Paris for two main reasons: first, the monetary exchange rate was favorable and Americans could live there cheaply if supported by U.S. dollars; second, the city was a gathering place for intellectuals from across Europe, including the Irish James Joyce and the Spanish Pablo Picasso.

The works of the writers of the Lost Generation expressed a sense of nihilism, betrayal, and spiritual abandon. These writers, many of whom had been raised in wealthy, well-established families, realized the pre–WW II social order, which supported previous generations, had come to an end. If they started life thinking that they would follow in their fathers' footsteps or grow old and die in the towns where their families had lived for generations, their participation in the Great War taught them the impermanence of life. Their works often express a search for moral values not based on tradition, an inquiry into truth that rejects the conclusions of previous generations.

Wilder is often categorized as a member of the Lost Generation, and chronologically he fits right into it, having been born in 1897, right between its two most prominent members—Fitzgerald (1896) and Hemingway (1899). He lived only briefly in Paris, though, and his writing lacks the sense of loss that characterizes most Lost Generation literature.

Critical Overview

Thornton Wilder's literary reputation is primarily based on his work as a playwright, not as a novelist. Of the few works of fiction he did produce, *The Bridge of San Luis Rey* is by far the most celebrated. It won the Pulitzer Prize in 1928, though he won two Pulitzers for drama, for *Our Town* and *The Skin of Our Teeth*. Bernard Grebanier, in his 1964 pamphlet about Wilder for the University of Minnesota Press, explained why: "In an era overrun by naturalistic novels, against which James Branch Cabell was almost the only challenger, Wilder calmly took his place as a leading storyteller who could not be satisfied with a documentation of the externalities of life, yet without adopting Cabell's deliberate escape from the realities of experience." In other words, Wilder's writing straddles the fine line between faith and rationality.

While not fitting into the category of "naturalistic" fiction, the book avoids "such deficiencies in taste and wisdom as are evident in most American religious fiction," according to Martin Goldstein. "*The Bridge* is not sentimental; it offers no promises of earthly rewards and no overestimation of the worth of the characters. Nor does it speak out against active participation in this life in favor of patient waiting for the life to come."

Wilder himself noted that many readers found the book inspirational reading, ignoring the darker implications of death erasing entire existences from the face of the earth. Still, readers over the decades have proven savvy enough to accept the complexity of his worldview and to appreciate the clarity of his prose. The book has stayed in print continuously

Kathy Bates as the Marquesa in the 2004 film version of The Bridge of San Luis Rey © The Kobal Collection

since its first publication, and in 2001 the editorial board of the American Modern Library selected it as one of the hundred best novels written in the twentieth century.

Criticism

David Kelly

Kelly is an instructor of creative writing and literature. In this essay, Kelly explains how looking at the novel as a religious work might produce too narrow an interpretation.

Since its initial publication in 1927, Thornton Wilder's novel *The Bridge of San Luis Rey* has been praised as a religious statement, examined for its theological implications, and categorized as Christian literature. To a large extent, this judgment is valid. The story takes place in Lima, Peru, in 1714, a time when the hegemony of the Roman Catholic Church was nearly absolute—when there was no real secular authority, only the religious hierarchy. It concerns a Franciscan monk, Brother Juniper, who witnesses the collapse of the bridge and sets about to understand the will of God. Brother Juniper is deeply faithful, and unable to accept the idea that a loving God would cause the deaths of five unrelated people, he becomes determined to understand the reasoning behind the event by understanding the lives of the victims. Before its end, however, the novel drops Brother Juniper's quest—he is executed for heresy by the Inquisition—and brings together some of the survivors among those connected to the dead, who inspire the Abbess of the Convent to think the book's often-quoted closing line: "There is a land of the living and a land of the dead and the bridge is love, the only survival, the only meaning."

It makes sense, then, to read this novel as a religious story. In reality, though, religion is not so much a guiding factor in this story as is its rural setting. The book's Lima is a frontier town, an oasis of Western culture in the middle of the Peruvian jungle. Unlike towns in the early 2000s, which sprawl in all available directions, Lima in 1714 is isolated from the world beyond it, having more in common with Spain across the ocean, than with the people a mile or two outside the city limits. For all of its talk about the will of God, the novel is more interested in presenting ways for people to break out of their isolation.

Early in the novel, Brother Juniper considers how the bridge collapse offers him an ideal opportunity to explore the variations of life that would be subject to such calamity because there are only five people killed, and five seems a manageable number to explore. For the same reason, the limited number of victims is useful to Wilder, giving him more chance to explain his characters in depth than he could have if there were a larger group. In fact, he only really focuses on three of the dead—the Marquesa de Montemayor, Esteban, and Uncle Pio. Two of the dead are auxiliary characters, traveling with the others. He also includes significant biographies of several important characters among the living, including Manuel, the Viceroy, the Archbishop of Lima, the Abbess of the Convent of Santa María Rosa de las Rosas, and Camila Perichole.

The fact that this event takes place two hundred years before he wrote it, in a remote, unknown region, made it possible for Wilder to present his characters as isolated. They are specimens, floating in the liquid of his distant, dreamy prose. They are also all stereotypes, though in some cases fleshed out with more details than in others. He presents the ingénue and the faded beauty (both Camila Perichole); the abandoned sibling; the hard-working orphan girl; the neglected parent (Doña María, literally, and Uncle Pio figuratively); and a chorus of corrupt government officials. Usually, the charge of stereotyping is leveled as a criticism of the author, implying a failure of imagination and an inability to come up with characters true to life, but in this case, the fact that Wilder is using basic types works to the story's advantage. If his point is that people are isolated from each other, then making each character an overly familiar stereotype enforces that isolation by sealing them each off from their surroundings.

To test this hypothesis, one only needs to look at the last half of the final chapter, in which the Abbess Madre María del Pilar becomes the book's focus. She has been mentioned before, interwoven in the stories of other characters, just as others (such as Captain Alvarado and Camila Perichole) play roles in a few different stories. Readers know her as an efficient administrator, working behind the scenes to provide a decent education for Pepita in one place and sending the Captain to console grief-stricken Esteban in another. It is not until the end, however, that readers see her deep concern that the work to which she has devoted her life might fade away after her death. The officious personality that seemed obvious from the outside turns out to be hiding a worried human being inside. The Abbess plays her social role, which is a minor one throughout the novel, but Wilder shows in the end that even bit players have human concerns, a fact that he punctuates by

"It could be said that the novel is still primarily religious, because breaking through isolation is the point of religion, but such a reading relies on stretching the definition of religion a bit, blurring the line between organized religion and piety."

having Doña Clara, who has been conspicuously absent from the novel, show up at the end, grieving.

It could be said that the novel is still primarily religious, because breaking through isolation is the point of religion, but such a reading relies on stretching the definition of religion a bit, blurring the line between organized religion and piety. Brother Juniper, for instance, might be driven by his devotion to God, but his quest is something that he and possibly he alone would consider religious. The idea of devising a calculation that can measure God's intent is basically flawed. If divine agency in the world could be understood by rational means, as mechanical as the trajectory of a moving object, then there would be no need for faith at all. If the universe were as predictable as Brother Juniper would like it to be, God would be irrelevant. Brother Juniper seems, shortsightedly, to be on a quest to defend God, not worship him. His goal is really irrelevant to religion.

The church in the story is clearly political, not spiritual. The Archbishop of Lima is discussed only in terms of his refined, epicurean appetite; his appreciation of fine European music; and his hobby of dabbling in linguistics. The church's most active role in the story comes when an anonymous panel of judges sentences Brother Juniper to death so callously that it is expressed as almost an afterthought, once his book is condemned. As with the stereotypical personalities that form boundaries around the characters, the rules and regulations of the church serve to isolate people from each other. The fear of heresy expressed by the church is a fear of infiltration by outside knowledge, which would contaminate the system that is already established.

Wilder fills the novel with attempts to break through isolation, to bridge the gaps between one

What Do I Read Next?

- Though Wilder never won another Pulitzer Prize for his fiction, his other novels are considered just as powerful and moving as this one. In particular, readers who like *The Bridge of San Luis Rey* tend to find the same lingering tone and spiritual presence in *The Eighth Day*, about a coal miner in a southern Illinois town who, sentenced to death, escapes and hides out with a family. Published in 1967, it won the National Book Award for that year.
- Like Wilder's novel, Willa Cather's *Death Comes for the Archbishop*, also published in 1927, is an historic story that deals with a cleric traveling in frontier territory, trying to reconcile faith and wonder. It tells the story of two French Catholic priests traveling among the Native Americans and Mexicans in the American Southwest in the 1850s.
- The most prominent Peruvian writer of modern times is Mario Varga Llosa. His novel *Death in the Andes*, published in 1997, gives a good view of what Peru was like at the end of the twentieth century, from the mountain life in the Andes to political machinations in the capital, Lima.
- For an insider's look at Wilder's life and career, readers may enjoy *Thornton Wilder and His Public*, written by his older brother, Amos Niven Wilder. It was published by Fortress Press in 1980.
- The main character of Orhan Pamuk's 2005 novel *Snow* faces a spiritual quest similar to Brother Juniper's, but with a decidedly modern theme: when he returns to his home in Istanbul for his mother's funeral, he is drawn into investigating a rash of suicides by girls who are forbidden to express their religious beliefs freely, finding himself contemplating corruption and the will of God in the process.
- Readers interested in Wilder's life can see his warmth and wit on display in his correspondences with the author Gertrude Stein, the matriarch of many writers of the postwar generation and a good friend of his for many years. *The Letters of Gertrude Stein and Thornton Wilder*, published in 1996 by Yale University Press, is insightful and candid.

person and another, but something, usually social position, stands in the way. The bond between Doña María and her daughter never really gels because the Marquesa does not really believe in motherhood, just the idea of it; the bond between Manuel and Esteban that seems natural proves unable to stand when looked at through the spectrum of pain and romantic love; the bond that Uncle Pio works hard to establish with Camila Perichole is severed when she decides he is an obstacle to her social-climbing ambitions; the bond that Pepita thinks she has with the Abbess is left unstated because neither party feels it would be proper to express it. All of the characters play their assigned roles, but none is happy about it.

The only character who manages any type of human contact in this novel is the Abbess, though there is hope in the end for the other two, Camila and Doña Clara, who go to her with their grief. The Abbess is forced to rein in her affection for Pepita and for the twins, but she does have outlets for her caring that involve her in humanity. She finds a bridge between her spiritual rigidity and the spiritual wilderness. Her part in the structured hierarchy cannot be denied: she is, at heart, a bureaucrat, looking after the day-to-day functions of several institutions. Yet she is also on the outskirts of the social order, dealing with outcasts from their birth at the orphanage through their deaths at her hospital. As Wilder says, "Madre María del Pilar . . . was able to divine the poor human heart behind all the masks of folly and defiance." This quotation leads to the observation that she found herself unable to see the heart in the Marquesa de Montemayor, a situation that is resolved in the novel's final pages when she consoles the woman's grieving daughter.

It may seem just a matter of semantics to shift the focus of The Bridge of San Luis Rey from religion to isolation: the "love" that is invoked at the end of the book is a key element in religion every bit as much as it is a part of humanism. But readers should always view a novel carefully and with skepticism: they are not always about what seems most obvious. In this case, the story is steeped in a religious tradition that fits the setting, but even more significant is the fact that the story is set in a remote time and place. This is a story about people, and the ways they work to break through their isolation. It is the story of a bridge.

Source: David Kelly, Critical Essay on *The Bridge of San Luis Rey*, in *Novels for Students*, Thomson Gale, 2007.

Lincoln Konkle

In the following essay excerpt, Konkle discusses how Wilder examines "issues of this life that have ultimate ramifications in the next life," and how the worldview in The Bridge of San Luis Rey *is similar to Puritan doctrine.*

The Bridge of San Luis Rey (1927), Wilder's second and most popular novel which also won him his first Pulitzer Prize, is neither an allegory of Judgment Day, nor does it allude to Judgment Day explicitly; yet, it is centrally concerned with judgment of the principal characters. Indeed, the effect and meaning of "the sometimes obtrusive presence of the omniscient author, who judges and interprets as he narrates the histories and inner lives of the main characters" (Burbank 48) is quite similar to Act Four of Wilder's Judgment Day play *The Trumpet Shall Sound.* However, it is not only the author—or the narrator, to be more precise—but also the Franciscan priest Brother Juniper who judges the characters. In fact, he devises a system of evaluating the victims of "acts of God" to detect the hand of Providence at work. Like Peter Magnus in *Trumpet,* Brother Juniper, though for different and disinterested reasons, has conducted his own "trial of all flesh." Thus *The Bridge of San Luis Rey* (hereafter *Bridge*) examines ontological and epistemological issues of this life that have ultimate ramifications in the next life, making it kin to the other literary descendants of *The Day of Doom* already discussed above, despite the non-New England and non-Protestant milieu—eighteenth-century Peru in predominantly Catholic South America.

With regard to setting *Bridge* in Peru, scholars have noted that it was only a defamiliarizing technique. In an interview Wilder himself said, "It merely supplied the background of the story. It could have been placed in any other country just as well. Peruvian scenery and manners were not essential" (Bryer 6). In the text of the novel, too, there are hints that Wilder was thinking of the story as closer to home. In referring to the Marquesa coming back to Peru from Spain, the narrator says that she "took ship and returned to America," even though, properly speaking, it is *South* America. Later the narrator identifies South America—or Peru, at least—as "the New World."

> **"The dominant interpretative issue in *Bridge* is Providence . . . ."**

As for the Catholic context of the theological issues raised in the novel, as Haberman says, "[T]he meaning of life of the novel's characters is closer to old-fashioned Protestant individual will." But though we do not have Protestant characters counterpoised to Catholic characters, as in Wilder's other 1920s works, there are still vestiges of Puritan prejudice toward Catholics, as in the following passage: "*I am told that in the convent the silly sisters inhale it so diligently that one cannot smell the incense at Mass.*" Does the following description mock just the Marquessa or Catholic devotion in general: "She hysterically hugged the alter-rails trying to rend from the gaudy statuettes a sign, only a sign, the ghost of a smile, the furtive nod of a waxen head." Idolatry was one of the charges the iconoclastic Puritans made against Catholics; even the Abbess is said to have "torn an idol from her heart." Except for Brother Juniper, priests are not much regarded in the book, even by their superior: "The Archbishop knew that most of the priests of Peru were scoundrels." Furthermore, the Archbishop is portrayed in terms hardly respectful.

Yet the novel's respect for Brother Juniper and especially for the Abbess makes up for any unflattering descriptions of Catholicism elsewhere; furthermore, the theological issues are framed more in Puritan terms than Catholic. The dominant interpretative issue in *Bridge* is Providence; as the narrator says in his description of Brother Juniper's investigation, "Either we live by accident and die by accident, or we live by plan and die by plan." The hermeneutic Brother Juniper applies to experience is almost identical with that of Edward Johnson, the author of a seventeenth-century Puritan history of the settlement of America entitled *Wonder-Working Providence:* "If there were any plan in the universe at all, if there were any pattern in a human life, surely it could be discovered mysteriously latent in those lives so suddenly cut off. . . . This collapse of the bridge of San Luis Rey was a sheer act of God. It afforded a perfect laboratory. Here at last one could surprise His intentions in a pure state."

The claim that Brother Juniper, a Catholic priest, expresses a theology closer to Puritanism than to Catholicism may seen less radical in view of the response his project elicits from his superiors: he is burnt at the stake as a heretic. Another indication that the version of Christianity *Bridge* represents is closer to Puritanism than it is to Catholicism occurs when the narrator describes Brother Juniper's purpose with an allusion to a rather famous Puritan poet's intention in retelling the story of the garden of Eden: "He would fall to dreaming of experiments that would justify the ways of God to man"—Milton's *Paradise Lost.*

Despite the apparent indeterminacy suggested by Brother Juniper's failure to prove God's intentions and the titling of the frame chapters "Perhaps an Accident" and "Perhaps an Intention" ("perhaps" is one of the most repeated words in the novel), Wilder provides enough information about each of the characters for the hand of Providence to be seen in the bridge falling: "He [Brother Juniper] thought he saw in the same accident the wicked visited by destruction and the good called early to Heaven." Kuner concludes, "Pepita was a good child, so was Jaime. Therefore the accident called the young to Heaven while they were still pure. On the other hand, Uncle Pio had led a dissolute life and the Marquesa was an avaricious drunkard. Therefore the accident punished the wicked." Besides, for all his skeptical commentary on Brother Juniper's quest, the narrator expresses the alternatives to the question of Providence in such a way that neither version denies a Calvinistic universe ruled by a sovereign God: "Some say that we shall never know and that to the gods we are like flies that the boys kill on a summer day, and some say, on the contrary, that the very sparrows do not lose a feather that has not been brushed away by the finger of God." Borrowing from Shakespeare (Lear) and the Bible (Matthew), the point is the same: the gods or God controls history; the difference lies in the point of view—tragic or comic (in Calvinistic terms, reprobate or elect). While the narrator's own stance would not allow a glib, "All's for the best in this best of all possible worlds," he does admit near the end, "But where are sufficient books to contain the events that would not have been the same without the fall of the bridge?" From one perspective, then, the accident was a fortunate fall.

The belief that Providence operates on a larger historical level is also affirmed in *The Bridge,* as seen in the Abbess' feminism and her care of the mentally ill: "She was one of those persons who have allowed their lives to be gnawed away because they have fallen in love with an idea several centuries before its *appointed* appearance in the history of civilization" (emphasis added). For the Puritans, everything had its appointed appearance in God's plot, especially the establishment of a colony in New England. Clearly, Wilder—or his narrator—is affirming the belief that "there's a divinity that shapes our ends, rough-hew them how we will."

Of course the problem with deterministic explanations of history, at least when the Determiner is believed to be good, is the existence of evil in the world, in events, and in people. As demonstrated in Wigglesworth's *The Day of Doom,* it was possible for the Puritans to rationalize that the doctrine of predestination did not absolve individual souls of responsibility for their reprobate nature or behavior. Compared to Wigglesworth's hard-line Calvinism, Edward Taylor's consideration of evil in his Puritan morality play *Gods Determinations Touching His Elect* seems much more humanistic. In this Puritan answer to *Everyman* the blame for the failure or delay of the allegorical character named "Soul" to come into assurance of election is laid upon Satan, whose temptations Taylor vividly dramatizes. In the theological tradition which extends in the United States from Wigglesworth and Taylor to the present, Wilder addresses in *Bridge* the theodicy problem with a providential world view by including in his anatomy of souls an allegorical representation of the devil—Uncle Pio.

In *The Trumpet Shall Sound* Wilder's allegorical representation of Satan went awry, perhaps, because Flora's crime was too insignificant and her punishment too harsh on the literal level of the narrative; in *Bridge* Wilder creates a more appropriate Satanic character to represent the devil in an attempt to address the problem of evil within a providential universe. Although other characters in *Bridge* exhibit attitudes and behaviors considered sinful in a Christian context, what distinguishes Uncle Pio is his manipulation, temptation, and destruction of others. That is, Uncle Pio is a representative of the category of souls in Brother Juniper's Judgment scheme which "was not . . . merely bad: [but] was a propagandist for badness."

That there will be no mistaking what or who Uncle Pio represents, the summary of his life includes descriptions that are traditionally associated with the devil or Satan. For example, the narrator says that he can be seen on a street in a typical posture as he "*whispers, his lips laid against his victim's ear*"; he is to be left to "*his underworld. . . . He is like a soiled pack of cards* [and the Marquesa] *doubt*[s] *whether the whole Pacific could wash him sweet and fragrant again*"; "He possessed . . . that *freedom from conscience* that springs from a contempt for the dozing rich he *preyed upon*"; "He spread *slanders* at so much a slander . . . was sent out by the government to inspirit some half-hearted *rebellions* in the mountains so that the government could presently arrive and wholeheartedly crush them"; "His *pretensions to omniscience* became more and more plausible" and "was perpetually astonished that a prince should make so little use of his position, for power, or for fantasy, or for *sheer delight in the manipulation of other men's destinies*"; he watches Camila give a performance, "standing at the back of the auditorium, bent double with joy and *malice*" (emphasis added in all of the above). When brother Juniper conducts his research on Uncle Pio, only Camila speaks well of him: "Her characterization of Uncle Pio flatly contradicted the stores of unsavory testimonies that he had acquired elsewhere." (She was, of course, greatly indebted to him for her own success in life; therefore, she could not be considered an unbiased source.) If this were not enough, even Uncle Pio's physical appearance resembles the traditional portrait of the devil: "With his whisp [sic] of a mustache and his whisp of a beard and his big ridiculous sad eyes."

As a deceiver of great subtlety and invention, Uncle Pio is a pretender to and a parody of God. Thus his name—Uncle Pio, suggesting pious—is ironic. The ostensibly affectionate title of "uncle" should not necessarily be taken at face value either. In the 1943 film *Shadow of a Doubt,* for which Wilder was hired by Alfred Hitchcock to write the screenplay, Uncle Charlie turns out to be a serial killer. Furthermore, Wilder follows Milton's portrayal of Satan as one who would rather rule in hell than to serve in heaven: "Even in this kingdom he [Uncle Pio] was lonely, and proud in his loneliness, as though there resided a certain superiority in such a solitude." This allegorical Satan even has his own version of Calvinistic predestination:

> He divided the inhabitants of this world into *two groups,* into those who had loved and those who had not. It was a *horrible aristocracy,* for those who had no capacity for love (or rather for suffering in love) could not be said to be alive and certainly *would not live again after their death.* They were a kind of straw population, filling the world with their meaningless laughter and tears and chatter and disappearing still lovable and vain into thin air. . . . He regarded love as a sort of cruel malady through which *the elect* are required to pass in their late youth and from which they emerge, pale and wrung, but ready for the business of living. (emphasis added)

From a Puritan perspective, then, on the literal level of the narrative Uncle Pio's untimely death would not seem to bode well for a blissful afterlife since he has not made progress during his life on earth, as Camila tells him: "You don't seem to learn as you grow older, Uncle Pio." That Uncle Pio is categorically different from Camila in the state of his soul is evident in the narrator's comment that "One day an accident befell that lost him his share in *her progress*" (emphasis added). Camila's slow conversion from her former selfish life is confirmed by the implication (though it is fairly oblique) that it will be she who takes over the charitable work of the Abbess (caring for the mentally ill and other unfortunates): "She [the Abbess] disappeared a moment to return with one of her helpers, one who had likewise been involved in the affair of the bridge and who had formerly been an *actress.* 'She is leaving me,' said the Abbess, 'for some work across the city'" (emphasis added). For Camila to have gone from cafe singer, to honored actress, to member of the social Cabala in Lima, to comforter of the poor and sick, attests to the progress of grace in her life. Uncle Pio was responsible for her ascension in the world, but her spiritual growth was solely the result of the accident of the bridge, an act of God which, as we have seen, had fortuitous as well as tragic effects. For the Puritans, the proof was in the progressive manifestation of their election. Wilder plots such a trajectory for Camila, but not for Uncle Pio.

Bridge also affirms progress on the historical level, as is evident when the narrator or Wilder employs dramatic irony (relying on the reader's knowledge of the advances made in the twentieth century for the care of the mentally ill, the physically handicapped, and so forth) in the Abbess' hopeful musing on what could be done for the suffering of those she cares for as best she can:

> The Abbess would stop in a passageway and say suddenly: "I can't help thinking that something could

Robert de Niro as the Archbishop in the 2004 film version of The Bridge of San Luis Rey

> be done for the deaf-and-dumb. It seems to me that some patient person could, . . . could study out a language for them. You know there are hundreds and hundreds in Peru. Do you remember whether anyone in Spain has found a way for them? Well, some day they will." Or a little later: "Do you know, I keep thinking that something can be done for the insane. I am old, you know, and I cannot go where these things are talked about, but I watch them sometimes and it seems to me. . . . In Spain, now, they are gentle with them? It seems to me that there is a secret about it, just hidden from us, just around the corner."

Of course she is right; sign language, Braille, psychoanalysis and other theories and methods of psychiatry are just around the corner by a century or so. In some ways, then, things do get better: the kind of charity people like the Abbess used to do as a matter of their religious beliefs becomes institutionalized; society itself becomes more charitable. Thus *Bridge* shows us a world in which there are no real accidents, nor the free reign of evil; a Judgment Day awaits us all within the providence that presides over the events of our lives; progress is made on the historical and personal levels (at least for the elect); and all of this is discernible—even provable, though Brother Juniper paid with his life for trying to provide the proof that each soul must find for him- or herself. As the Abbess tells herself near the end of *Bridge* when all loose ends have been tied up, all plot lines resolved, "'Learn at last that anywhere you may expect grace.' And she was filled with happiness like a girl at this new *proof* that the traits she lived for were everywhere, that the world was ready" (emphasis added). The very last lines of *Bridge* are more bittersweet in tone as they remind us of the deaths of the five on the bridge, and allude to the death and being forgotten predestined for us all; yet the narrator allows the Abbess to pronounce an acceptance of this aspect of the human condition: "But the love will have been enough; all those impulses of love return to the love that made them. Even memory is not necessary for love. There is a land of the living and a land of the dead and the bridge is love, the only survival, the only meaning."

That this world view is as affirmative as the cosmic optimism of the Puritans is evident. The similarity of particular aspects of this world view in *Bridge* to Puritan doctrine and Puritan writers' ways of expressing their beliefs in narrative works is no coincidence. In this last work of the 1920s and Wilder's own twenties, we see the young author finding the combination of theme and form, shaped in part by the Puritan legacy in his familial and American heritage, that would later bring him his greatest artistic and popular success in *Our Town,* which along with *The Skin of Our Teeth,* again dramatized a Puritan expectancy of the prophesied end of human history in an American context. Thornton Wilder may not have believed in Judgment Day by that time, but the belief in Judgment Day was in him, and thus, as we have seen, was also in his early drama and fiction written in the moral wilderness of the Jazz Age.

Source: Lincoln Konkle, "Judgment Day in the Jazz Age . . .," in *Thornton Wilder: New Essays*, edited by Martin Blank, Dalma Hunyadi Brunauer, and David Garrett Izzo, Locust Hill Press, 1999, pp. 81–89.

Rex Burbank

In the following essay excerpt, Burbank describes how Wilder affirms "the moral nature and value of love" courageously in The Bridge of San Luis Rey.

II The Bridge of San Luis Rey

Like *The Cabala, The Bridge of San Luis Rey* (1927) is a romance. Although the fantasy of *The Cabala* is missing, *The Bridge* has the remoteness of setting, the symbolism, the yoking together of past and present, the moral and religious themes, and the episodic structure of the earlier book; and in it Wilder attempts, as he did in *The Cabala,* to capture not only surface realism but the complex workings of the inner life as well. He had stated his conviction that the purely realistic fiction of the day had run the course of its usefulness and effectiveness when he told Harry Salpeter in 1928 that he felt that America was turning away from the rule of realism to the introspective novel. "Until about ten years ago," he told Salpeter, "experience was very valuable as a preparation toward the writing of novels. Authors who had been stokers and barhands did bring something valuable to America in the process of discovering itself. But now the notation of things has been done so well through such men as Sinclair Lewis that from now on the profounder assimilation of a little experience rather than a rapid view of a great deal is the more desirable. Literature, now that America has discovered itself, could spring from solitude and reflection, with less emphasis on observation and more on intuition."

Nevertheless, in both *The Cabala* and *The Bridge* the characters are portrayed with considerable realism and clarity as individuals; and, from the standpoint of response to the promptings of the flesh and susceptibility to forces of environment and heredity, they are conceived with enough naturalism to allay any charges that Wilder ignores the observable and unpleasant facts of life. Marcantonio's losing struggle with his "lower nature," for instance, is as compulsive and has a pathetic consequence similar to that of Clyde Griffith in Dreiser's naturalistic *American Tragedy*; and Camila Perichole in *The Bridge* feels the same physical attraction to bullfighters that Hemingway's Lady Brett Ashley does in *The Sun Also Rises.* The Cabalists and the victims of the disaster at San Luis Rey, moreover, are as subject to the forces of history and circumstance as any characters of Dos Passos or Stephen Crane.

But Wilder's humanism precludes what he regards as the one-sidedness of philosophical naturalism and realism. The characteristic feature of these two novels and of *The Woman of Andros* is the inclusion of the inner as well as the outer facts of life with the intent of reaffirming the sense of the mystery of life which realistic and naturalistic writers had tended to ignore in their concern with external, observable data and with the power of heredity and environment. Wilder gives full scope to the claims of scientific, observable, objective knowledge (as manifested in literature by naturalism); but he insists that the inner life—the passions, the intellect, the hope and the aspirations—is a

"Having thus defined love and the abstract qualities that give it moral significance, Wilder concludes the book with the theme of love as a moral responsibility."

mystery whose workings and purposes defy rationalization. The life of the mind is one of constant struggle between the lower and the higher qualities in man. Moreover, the inner struggle has a metaphysical parallel in the universal tension between change and purpose. This view of course is not original, but the achievement of it in a literary work is difficult. If the work is original, the ideas take on fresh meaning.

Wilder revealed that it had been his intention in these early works to try to restore the aura of mystery to life when he told Walther Tritsch in a Berlin interview in 1931 that "It is the magic unity of purpose and chance, of destiny and accident, that I have tried to describe in my books." The superiority of *The Bridge* over *The Cabala* consists in large part in its more successful achievement of the "magic unity" through dialectic. The action of *The Bridge* begins when Brother Juniper, a Franciscan monk, sees the bridge fall and the five victims plunge to their deaths in the canyon below. "Why did this happen to *those* five?" he asks. "If there were any plan in the universe at all, if there were any pattern in a human life, surely it could be discovered mysteriously latent in those lives so suddenly cut off. Either we live by accident and die by accident, or we live by plan and die by plan."

Convinced the incident is an act of God, he sees in it an opportunity to observe God's intentions "in a pure state"; but, when his investigation of the lives of the victims shows no pattern of cause and effect, he concludes that the "discrepancy between faith and the facts is greater than is generally assumed." Juniper's mistake is that he never learned the "central passion" of the lives of the three adult victims—the Marquesa de Montemayor, Pio, and Esteban. So the omniscient author steps in to recount these intimate facts although he admits that it is "possible that even I have missed the very spring within the spring." We move, then, from the extrinsic motivations revealed by Juniper's investigation to the intrinsic motivations in the minds and hearts of the victims.

Wilder borrowed some of his material for *The Bridge* from Prosper Mérimée's *La Carosse Du Saint Sacrement.* In the Perichole, he combined Mérimée's Perichole with the parrot that taunts her; and he drew the Marquesa de Montemayor after Mérimée's marquise d'Altamire. But it is with Conrad's *Chance,* rather than Mérimée's work, that the book can most profitably be compared. Like *Chance, The Bridge* explores the themes of moral isolation and love and raises the question of whether events occur by accident or design. The title of Conrad's novel is ironic: Life is not a matter of chance or accident. Even where chance appears to govern men's lives—as it does in the events involving Flora de Barral and young Powell—there are causal factors at work. Conrad took as the epigraph for *Chance* a quotation from Sir Thomas Browne: "Those who hold that all things are governed by fortune had not erred, had they not persisted there." While Browne believed that all events have a divine cause, Conrad showed them in *Chance* to be governed by human motivation. He presented a series of incidents that seemed to be the result of sheer chance, but then showed that behind the appearance of accident was an intricate network of human causes. Flora's suicide attempt, for instance, appears to have been caused by a chain of misfortunes that began with her father's financial disaster; but it actually can be explained by her abusive treatment at the hands of the disgruntled Eliza, whose actions can also be explained in terms of clear-cut traits of character.

Wilder's strategy is to set forth the two alternatives by means of external and internal evidence—that which Brother Juniper adduces to prove the presence of the hand of God in the fall of the bridge, and that which he cannot see because it is in the minds and hearts of the characters. Juniper combines the two extreme and dogmatic interpretations of the incident: the scientific, which sees the fall as something that can be explained in physical terms; and the orthodox Christian, which sees in all events the operation of Providence. Both of these views are based upon externals, and Juniper's collection of data in the scientific manner in order to settle a theological question is a *reductio ad absurdum* of both positions, since his investigations lead to no conclusion at all.

Attention is thus directed to the inner sources of evidence when the omniscient author points to the "central passion" in each of the major characters. Beyond this purely human explanation lies the suggestion that there is a divine cause in the "central passion," love, in the victims. The fall of the bridge of San Luis Rey symbolizes the force of circumstance or of the meaningless workings of nature, but the passions of the victims act as the primary human cause leading them to the bridge. Fusion of these two factors brings about the "magic unity" of purpose and chance that provides the element of mystery which is the essence of mysticism. The applicability of the Browne epigraph to *The Bridge* is thus apparent: Those who hold that the fall of the bridge was an accident would not err in the position if they did not insist upon its being the whole truth. To this Wilder adds: Those who believe would not err if they did not insist, like Juniper, upon proving God's presence in all the events of life.

Between the first chapter ("Perhaps an Accident") and the last ("Perhaps an Intention"), three flashback chapter recount the lives of the three chief victims up to the time of the disaster. Each of them, it turns out, is a person with deep spiritual attachments whose "central passion" is thwarted either by emotional coldness or selfishness or by natural circumstance. But each is also governed to such an extent by his consuming passion that the conflict it generates and the disaster that follows it have the earmarks of fate. Yet each one is a free spirit and has an opportunity, just before the fall of the bridge, to make a compromise with the circumstances of his situation and rebuild his moral life. The vision is a tragic one: Their deaths are an inescapable fact, regardless of the interpretation one makes of their lives; but their deaths are not entirely futile, since they generate a love in the survivors that did not exist before.

The sense of mystery is achieved in the episodes dealing with the individual victims, whose complexity demonstrates why Juniper's investigation is futile. The Marquesa de Montemayor has fixed her whole spiritual being upon her daughter, Dona Clara, who has married a Spanish nobleman to escape her mother's extreme affection. Cold and intellectual like her father (and like Blair in *The Cabala*), Dona Clara is the opposite of the Marquesa, whose love for her daughter is the chief factor in her life. Dona Clara sails from Peru to Spain "with the most admirable composure, leaving her mother to gaze after the bright ship, her hand pressing now her heart and now her mouth."

The object of her life gone, the Marquesa turns in upon herself and lives a mental drama in which she and her daughter live as she, the Marquesa, would have them live. "On that stage were performed endless dialogues with her daughter, impossible reconciliations, scenes eternally recommenced of remorse and forgiveness," the Marquesa always being the one who forgave and the daughter feeling remorse. To the people of Lima there was no indication that the Marquesa was suffering the agonies of the unloved. They knew her as a slovenly, drunken old woman who talked to herself; at one time there was a petition circulated to have her locked up, and she had been denounced by the Inquisition. They were unaware, when interviewed by Juniper, that she read widely and that she wrote letters to her daughter (letters Wilder patterned after those of Madame de Sévigne) which "in an astonishing world have become the textbook of schoolboys and the anthill of grammarians." These letters, like all great literature, reflected "the notation of the heart."

But while genius was concealed by outward ugliness and kindled by suffering, the Marquesa had moral weaknesses that were a part of the love that generated the great letters. For one thing, her devotion to her daughter was "not without a shade of tyranny: she loved her daughter not for her daughter's sake, but for her own." And even the great letters, in their sophisticated tone of detached amusement at the people and events in Lima, concealed the lack of humility and courage in the love that produced them. The Marquesa learns the lessons of humility and courage from the orphan girl Pepita, who also dies in the disaster.

Pepita, whose devotion to the Abbess, Madre Maria, is as strong as the Marquesa's for Dona Clara, is sent by the Abbess to serve the Marquesa. Feeling as strongly about her separation from the Abbess as the Marquesa does about hers from her daughter, Pepita writes a letter to the Abbess asking to return to the convent. She does not send the letter, however, because she feels it "wasn't brave." The Marquesa, having read the letter, discovers in it the humility and willingness to sacrifice that she herself lacks. The night before the fall of the bridge, watching Pepita as she sleeps, the Marquesa whispers to herself, "Let me live now . . . Let me begin again."

The Marquesa's "central passion" gains an added dimension by her apparent victory over circumstance. Like Pepita, she has had an unfortunate beginning in life, Pepita being an orphan, the Marquesa having had an unhappy childhood. Pepita, however, since coming under the guardianship of the Abbess, has lived in an atmosphere of love and sacrifice that has enabled her to withstand the affliction of separation with courage, which the Marquesa was not able to do without losing her religion and seeking escape in drinking. The Marquesa's life has been directed by circumstance up to the time she reads Pepita's letter, since, in addition to having a daughter who is colds towards her, her selfishness and lack of courage both stem from an unhappy childhood and a marriage she was forced into against her will. When she decides to "begin again," therefore, she affirms the triumph of her will over circumstance. Yet, ironically, she seems to lose to circumstance finally when the bridge falls.

The complex development of the Marquesa's character and the interplay between the forces of will and circumstance preclude any easy metaphysical or theological affirmations. The episode ends in mystery, as do those involving Esteban and Pio. But the moral imperative of love is clear enough; and the highest love is the kind of disinterested love shown by Pepita and by the Abbess, whose life is devoted to the care of the suffering. The levels of love are worked out in a somewhat broader fashion in the Esteban chapter and represent Wilder's humanistic answer to the contention that love is a purely human contrivance.

At the lowest level are Camila's shabby, clandestine affairs with various men of Lima. She hires Manuel to write letters to her lovers, all of whom she quarrels with and almost casually abandons. In contrast to her animal-like passion, vulgarity, and absence of profound feeling is Manuel's brief but intense love for her. Manuel himself is not inexperienced sexually; for both he and Esteban "had possessed women, and often, especially during their years at the waterfront; but simply, Latinly." His love for Camila, however, represents a departure from purely physical pleasure: ". . . it was the first time that his will and imagination had been thus overwhelmed." That is, he rose for the first time to a human level in love and above the mere promptings of nature. He "had lost that privilege of simple nature, the dissociation of love and pleasure." Understanding nothing higher than physical pleasure, Camila is cynical about love. "There is no such thing as that kind of love," she tells Pio. "It's in the theater you find such things." But Manuel, without art or learning, has no such cynicism. Love is as natural to him as pleasure, but more intense, and in it one undergoes a "crazy loss of one's self." He represents an affirmation that love may spring from a higher source than sexual desire.

He shows an even higher type of love than this love for Camila in giving her up for the sake of

Esteban. Again, there is no intellectual analysis, no reflection, in his sacrifice. He intuitively feels the isolation of Esteban; and, while his attachment to him is not so complete as Esteban's for him, it is strong enough to make Manuel willing to sacrifice to save his brother from misery.

Yet profound as Manuel's devotion to Esteban is, it falls below Esteban's for him. If Manuel's love is characterized by sacrifice, Esteban's is characterized, after Manuel's death by blood poisoning, by the complete identity of himself with his brother. But Esteban discovers in Manuel's attraction to Camila "that secret from which one never quite recovers, that even in the most perfect love one person loves less profoundly than the other. There may be two equally good, equally beautiful, but there may never be two that love one another equally well." Esteban's love attains the level of the tragic, for it is a part of the human condition that "the most perfect love" is never quite perfect.

This ascending scale of types of love, culminating in Esteban's devotion to his brother, sets the stage for Captain Alvarado, who has also suffered a loss, that of a daughter. The cause of the girl's death is not mentioned, but it is implied that there is no more "reason" for it than for Manuel's. The captain's grief is as profound as Esteban's, but they react in opposite ways. The captain travels "about the hemispheres," as the Marquesa writes to Dona Clara, "to pass the time between now and his old age." Yet he is reconciled to life, is determined to live it out to its end, and even hopes to see the girl again. Esteban cannot, however, face life or reconcile himself to it without Manuel. His identification with Manuel is so complete that he buries himself, figuratively, and assumes Manuel's name; and the night before the bridge falls, he attempts suicide. The inability of Esteban to face life without his brother symbolizes the pathos of man before circumstance. Endowed with a profound capacity for love and for pain, Esteban is unable either to comprehend or to accept a world which cares for neither. When the captain asks him to sail aboard his ship, he accepts in the hope that he can escape from his hopelessness in ceaseless activity. But this hope is short-lived: He cannot leave Peru, where Manuel is buried.

By the end of the Esteban episode, the moral qualities that comprise the highest form of human love appear in the acts of courage, humility, and sacrifice performed by the victims prior to the fall of the bridge. In the Pio episode, love is seen in terms of its highest and most concrete expression in art. The theme of artistic beauty being wrested from ugliness through the agency of love, a minor theme in the Marquesa episode, is developed fully in the Pio chapter. When Pio decides to "play Pygmalion" with Camila, his three great passions—"his passion for overseeing the lives of others, his worship of beautiful women, and his admiration for the treasures of Spanish literature"—assume moral significance. Until he meets Camila, Pio is totally unscrupulous. The conflict that develops when he begins to train her for the stage is the conflict between the artist (it is he, more than Camila, who is the artist) and his recalcitrant materials, the raw life from which the artist creates. Camila is Pio's "great secret and reason for his life"; but she is "quite incapable of establishing any harmony between the claims of her art, of her appetites, of her dreams, and of her crowded daily routine." Each of these is "a world in itself, and the warfare between them would soon have reduced to idiocy (or triviality) a less tenacious physique." Lack of a profound love to integrate the various claims upon her leaves Camila without any real meaning in her life. She leaves almost at random, the theatre at times capturing her enthusiasm, love at others; but nothing lasts for long, including her love for the Viceroy, whose mistress she becomes. Once during the twenty years she and Pio are associated love comes into her life—when she first meets the Viceroy—and then her acting reaches its perfection.

Pio's attempts to bring art and life together in a perfect union in Camila are successful only when love is present to bridge the gap between the two. This would be a platitude if it were not for the fact that the love that informs both is accompanied by suffering. This profoundest love, Pio believes, is a "cruel malady through which the elect are required to pass in their late youth and from which they emerge, pale and wrung, but ready for the business of living." He has the humility and compassion that come from the "illness" of love—the "rich wisdom" of the heart that Camila does not find until she has lost her beauty (by smallpox), Pio, and her son Jaime.

Having thus defined love and the abstract qualities that give it moral significance, Wilder concludes the book with the theme of love as a moral responsibility. All the survivors realize their failure to respond to the love directed toward them, imperfect though it was in the cases of Pio and the Marquesa. The full impact of love as a first condition to meaningful living comes to all the survivors after the disaster; and the Abbess, the only character in the book whose life has fulfilled itself in love (although even she, as she confesses to herself, has been too busy to appreciate fully the devotion of Pepita) expresses the significance of love in a world meaningless and purposeless without it: "Even now . . . almost no one remembers Esteban and Pepita, but myself. Camila alone remembers her Uncle Pio and her son; this woman [Dona Clara], her mother. But soon we shall die and all memory of those five will have left the earth, and we ourselves shall be loved for a while and forgotten. But the love will have been enough; all those impulses of love return to the love that made them. Even memory is not necessary for love. There is a land of the living and a land of the dead and the bridge is love, the only survival, the only meaning."

Limited as it is to the human level, this proposition is directed to believers and skeptics alike; it warns both that, whatever their beliefs about God, love is indispensable if life is to have any meaning. The question raised by Juniper remains a mystery; the "perhapses" in the titles of the first and last chapters remain. At one level, human motivation brought the victims to the bridge at the same time—and in this *The Bridge* resembles *Chance*—but these motives have been shown to be so bound up with circumstance that the two are hardly separable. Moreover, as Juniper's investigation shows, the "good" died with the "bad"; there was no discernible relationship between desert and reward. Moral behavior, Wilder maintains, is, therefore, a purely human responsibility and has clear-cut human consequences: Whatever the interpretation of the disaster, it generated in the survivors a love that had not previously existed.

The theological and metaphysical question remains, however, in the "magic unity" achieved in the mysterious synthesis of circumstance and human motivation; and the sense of mystery in the lives and deaths of the characters provides an option for both believer and non-believer; at the same time the mysterious is in itself, paradoxically, the basis for a mystical interpretation. With regard to the persuasive effect of "magic unity"—which it was Wilder's declared aim to achieve—Kenneth Burke has remarked: "Mystery is a major resource of persuasion. Endow a person, an institution, a thing with the glow or resonance of the Mystical, and you have set up a motivational appeal to which people spontaneously ('instinctively,' 'intuitively') respond. In this respect, an ounce of 'Mystery' is worth a ton of argument." This mystery in the lives of the characters convinces rather than the "arguments" set against one another by Juniper. Thus, while Wilder doesn't say it in *The Bridge,* the "spring within the spring"—the love that bridges the land of the living and the land of the dead—has mystical significance. . . .

The Bridge has become a classic of American fiction, and it will likely continue to hold a high place among that very august company of novels written during the twenties by such men as Lewis, Hemingway, Fitzgerald, and Dos Passos—different as it is from their works. Despite its technical weaknesses, it has all the intellectual scope, depth of feeling, and complexity of character that make a mature and aesthetically satisfying vision. It was an unusual, courageous act in the twenties for a serious writer to affirm the moral nature and value of love—a subject most serious writers were associating in one way or another with sex. The almost inherently banal and sentimental "higher" manifestations of love were being abandoned to the hack writers or rejected as "genteel." But as he defines love in *The Bridge,* it is a most difficult thing; for it is accompanied by selfishness, confronted by human coldness, and loss upon a universe that does not seem to know or care that it exists. Considering the critical climate that prevailed in the twenties, it might fairly be said of Wilder himself what he says in *The Bridge:* "There are times when it requires high courage to speak the banal." *The Bridge* shows that not only courage but also the touch of the poet is there. The familiar takes on new life and meaning in art.

Source: Rex Burbank, "Three Romance Novels," in *Thornton Wilder*, Twayne Publishers, 1978, pp. 44–56.

Malcolm Goldstein

In the following essay excerpt, Goldstein discusses various misinterpretations by both readers and critics of The Bridge of San Luis Rey.

In review, the victims of the bridge are these: an old woman whose daughter spurns her affection, an adolescent girl who lives only for the affection of an older woman, a young man whose sole object of love is dead, an old man whose sole object of love has rejected him, and a child whose mother is too self-involved to give him the affection he requires. For one reason or another, each stands apart from human society: two because they are old and unkempt; two because they are orphans; and the fifth because he is chronically ill. And with the exception of Don Jaime, each has added to the barrier between himself and society by failing to respond to any activity which does not involve his beloved. Pepita is at only slightly greater odds with the rest of humanity than Don Jaime, but even she

> **"Unhappily, Wilder's latter-day critics have served him no better than his most naive readers."**

must think constantly of the one person she loves in order to sustain herself, and it is not until she begins to recognize the selfishness inherent in her distress in the Marquesa's household that she is allowed to escape through death. Perhaps it is a flaw in the novel that Don Jaime's life so poorly fits the pattern set by the other characters; yet he resembles them in part by agreeing to leave his mother, the only person whom he adores, and to go down to Lima with Uncle Pio. But, for that matter, Wilder flatly asserts that it is difficult, if not impossible, to find patterns in existence, and Brother Juniper is burned as a heretic for trying to do so.

Although *The Bridge of San Luis Rey* is imperfect, its faults are not ruinous. Whatever they may be, they are not caused by such deficiencies in taste and wisdom as are evident in most American religious fiction—the novels of Lloyd C. Douglas provide suitable examples for comparison. *The Bridge* is not sentimental; it offers no promises of earthly rewards and no overestimation of the worth of the characters. Nor does it speak out against active participation in this life in favor of patient waiting for the life to come. Yet, noting that many persons have misunderstood his intention, Wilder has himself remarked: "Only one reader in a thousand notices that I have asserted a denial of the survival of identity after death." While it is true, as this comment suggests, that many find the book "inspirational" and read it precisely as they read Bishop Fulton J. Sheen's *Peace of Soul* or Rabbi Joshua Loth Liebmann's *Peace of Mind,* it is difficult to understand how they could be misled. For, far from recommending a narcotic contemplation of the afterlife, Wilder speaks out for the vigorous pursuit of purely human relationships. If the five characters are tragic, they are so not because they die suddenly, or simply because they die, but because they have not truly lived, and at no point are we led to think that they will win the reward of an eventual reunion in heaven with the recipients of the love that for so many years enchained them. Threading through the narrative is the career of the Abbess, whose closeness to the life of Lima and attentiveness to everyday events are a reminder of the indifference of the others to such matters in their pursuit of a single goal. None of the victims escapes the measurement of his personality against that of this very vital woman. The consecration of her life to a program of work for the good of all humanity, involving her in the sacrifice of Pepita, Manuel, and Esteban, puts to shame the selfishness of the others as it is reflected in their indulgence in the anguish of love. In *The Bridge,* as in *The Cabala* and the major works which followed, Wilder insists that the life that is a rush of unanalyzed activity is as nothing when compared to the life in which the participant allows himself to become fully aware of the meaning of each experience.

Unhappily, Wilder's latter-day critics have served him no better than his most naive readers. Impatient with the slow-moving, aphoristic style and the historical setting, they have looked back on *The Bridge* as a kind of sport among the popular novels of the 1920's and mention it as such if they mention it at all. It is true that this work contrasts bleakly with the naturalistic novels which now seem to be the sum of the literature of the decade, but to admit that fact is not to deny its quality. However much it may differ in technique from the fiction of, say, Hemingway, Fitzgerald, or John Dos Passos, it does not display a soft attitude toward the human condition. At the time of its publication it offered a considerable change in tone from the fast-paced novels of the age, and obviously a welcome change in view of the sales record, but it did not offer easy lessons in contentment.

Source: Malcolm Goldstein, "Voyages into History," in *The Art of Thornton Wilder*, University of Nebraska Press, 1965, pp. 60–62.

Sources

Goldstein, Martin, *The Art of Thornton Wilder*, University of Nebraska Press, 1965, pp. 60–61.

Grebanier, Bernard, *Thornton Wilder*, University of Minnesota Pamphlets on American Writers, No. 14, University of Minnesota Press, 1964, p. 15.

Further Reading

Bunge, Nancy, "'New Modalities of the True and Beautiful': Point of View in Thornton Wilder's Novels," in *Thornton Wilder: New Essays*, edited by Martin Blank, Dalma

Hunyadi Brunauer, and David Garrett Izzo, Locust Hill Press, 1999, pp. 157–68.
Bunge examines Wilder's aesthetic philosophy and applies it to his fiction.

Cowley, Malcolm, "The Man Who Abolished Time," in *Critical Essays on Thornton Wilder*, edited by Martin Blank, G. K. Hall, 1996, pp. 32–38.
This essay, by one of the great literary critics of the twentieth century, explains ways that Wilder toyed with the concept of time in this and other novels.

Harrison, Gilbert, *The Enthusiast: A Life of Thornton Wilder*, Ticknor & Fields, 1983.
This comprehensive biography by a writer who knew Wilder for several decades is one of the best books available on the writer's life.

Kuner, M.C., *Thornton Wilder: The Bright and the Dark*, Thomas Y. Crowell Co., 1972.
Kuner considers Wilder's major works in terms of the author's two conflicting moods.

Walsh, Claudette, *Thornton Wilder: A Reference Guide, 1926–1990*, G. K. Hall, 1993.
This reference work is an indispensable, comprehensive guide for finding articles by and about Wilder.

Wescott, Glenway, "Talks with Thornton Wilder," in his *Images of Truth: Remembrances and Criticism*, Books for Libraries Press, 1972, pp. 242–308.
Wescott, a social observer and lively, personal writer, captures Wilder's personality in this essay on his long relationship with the author.

Foreign Affairs

Alison Lurie

1984

Foreign Affairs (1984) is a Pulitzer-Prize-winning novel by American author Alison Lurie. Set mostly in London, it is the story of two American professors of English from an Ivy League university who spend several months in the capital city of England. Ostensibly, Vinnie Miner, an unmarried woman in her fifties who specializes in children's literature, and Fred Turner, a twenty-nine-year-old eighteenth-century specialist who has just separated from his wife, are in London to work on their academic research projects. However, during their stay, both are drawn into unexpected romantic relationships—Vinnie with an American tourist from Oklahoma and Fred with a glamorous English actress—that have very different consequences for each character. Lurie's witty comedy of manners plays with some of the cultural differences between England and America while spinning a tale that explores the illusions of love as well as the wisdom, joy, and sadness it may bring.

Author Biography

Alison Lurie was born in Chicago on September 3, 1926, the older of two daughters born to Harry and Bernice (Stewart) Lurie. Her father was a teacher of social work and her mother a journalist. When Lurie was four, the family moved to New York City and soon after that to the rural suburb of White Plains in Westchester County.

From early in Lurie's childhood, her parents and teachers encouraged Lurie to believe that she was good at storytelling, but at first Lurie wanted to be a painter. It was not until she was in high school that she decided to try her hand at writing. After she graduated from a boarding school in Connecticut in 1943, she entered Radcliffe College, graduating in 1946 with a bachelor's degree in history and literature. In 1947, she worked as an editorial assistant at Oxford University Press in New York City, and in the following year, she married Jonathan Peel Bishop, a graduate student in English at Harvard University.

During the period from 1953 to 1960, Lurie gave birth to three sons. She stayed at home to raise them while her husband pursued his career at Amherst College, Massachusetts; University of California in Los Angeles; and then Cornell University in 1961. Lurie thus moved house three times during this period. She did not like caring for small children and was restless and ambitious. She had had two short stories published in magazines in 1947 and had continued writing, but during the 1950s she had no success in getting her work, which included two novels, published.

This situation changed in 1962, when her first novel, *Love and Friendship*, was published. In 1963, 1964, and 1966, she received Yaddo Foundation Fellowships, and in 1965, she was a Guggenheim Fellow. Her second novel, *The Nowhere City*, was published in 1965, followed by *Imaginary Friends* (1967) and *Real People* (1969).

In 1969, Lurie began her teaching career at Cornell University, where her husband also taught. In 1973, she was promoted to associate professor, and she became a professor in 1976. Her specialty was children's literature. By this time, she had separated from her husband, and they were divorced in 1985.

Lurie's fifth novel, *The War between the Tates* (1974), about a disintegrating marriage, was her first commercially successful book. It was made into a movie for television in 1977. In 1979, Lurie published her sixth novel, *Only Children*, a story told through the eyes of two eight-year-old girls; her seventh novel, *Foreign Affairs*, followed in 1984. It was nominated for an American Book Award and won the Pulitzer Prize in 1985. It was also filmed for television.

Lurie wrote two more novels: *The Truth about Lorin Jones* (1988) and *The Last Resort* (1998). As of 2006, she was the Frederic J. Whiton Professor of American Literature Emerita at Cornell University.

Alison Lurie

Plot Summary

Chapter 1

Foreign Affairs begins as Vinnie Miner, a small, plain-looking professor of children's literature at an Ivy League university, boards a flight to London. In her imagination, she is accompanied by a small dog called Fido, who represents self-pity, a fault to which Vinnie is prone.

Vinnie, who is unmarried, is to stay for six months in England. She has received a grant to study the folk-rhymes of schoolchildren, a subject on which she is an expert. But she is unhappy because she has just read an attack on her work by L. D. Zimmern, an American professor, in a national magazine. Zimmern thinks her work is trivial and a waste of public funds.

On the plane, Vinnie reluctantly gets drawn into a conversation with Charles (Chuck) Mumpson, a sanitation engineer from Oklahoma who is starting on a two-week package tour of England. Vinnie finds him ignorant and crass.

After the plane lands at midnight at Heathrow Airport, Vinnie is unable to find a taxi. Mumpson arranges for her to ride on the tourist bus to downtown London. When the bus drops her off, she takes a taxi to the flat she is renting on Regent's

Media Adaptations

- *Foreign Affairs* was adapted for television in 1993, and as of 2006, it was commercially available on VHS. It was directed by Jim O'Brien, with Joanne Woodward as Vinnie, Brian Dennehy as Chuck, Eric Stolz as Fred Turner, and Stephanie Beacham as Rosemary.

Park Road. She feels relieved that she has finally arrived.

Chapter 2

At six in the evening, Fred Turner waits for a train in the Underground station at Notting Hill Gate in London. He is an assistant professor of English at Corinth University, where Vinnie teaches. Fred is over twenty-five years younger than Vinnie and much more attractive—tall, dark, and handsome, in fact. He is in London for five months doing research on John Gay, an eighteenth-century English writer. Fred is not happy, however, because he has just split up with his wife, Ruth. He is also frustrated because he is not getting an authentic experience of London; he attributes this in part to the disorientation that comes with being a tourist. He is also short of money.

Fred arrives for supper at the flat of his American friends, Joe and Debby Vogeler. The Vogelers, who teach at colleges in Southern California, are on leave in London and are disillusioned with it. They do not like the weather or the people, and they are unimpressed by all the tourist spots. The Vogelers commiserate with Fred over his failed marriage.

As Fred returns home, he thinks back gloomily over how he met Ruth, an attractive, dark-haired photographer. Ruth is an outspoken radical feminist, and Fred's friends were not entirely comfortable with his choice of bride.

Fred plans to attend a party given by Vinnie later that week. He does not know Vinnie well, but she will have a say in whether he gets tenure at Corinth University, so he does not wish to offend her by turning down her invitation.

Chapter 3

Several weeks later, in March, Vinnie meets her friend, the editor Edwin Francis, at a restaurant. Edwin tells her that Fred Turner has become romantically involved with the famous English actress Rosemary Radley, whom he met at Vinnie's party. Vinnie is surprised by this news and tells Edwin that the relationship cannot last for long, since Fred has to return to Corinth in June to teach summer school. Edwin worries that if Rosemary gets too smitten with Fred, she may start skipping her professional commitments, and he asks Vinnie to persuade Fred to break off the relationship. Vinnie refuses.

The next day, Vinnie studies in the London Library Reading Room. She regrets that she asked Fred to her party, since she normally tries to keep her English friends and her American colleagues apart. She does not quite trust Rosemary Radley, and even though they meet fairly often because they get invited to the same parties, they do not like each other much.

After she leaves the library, she unexpectedly encounters Chuck Mumpson in a department store. Vinnie is not pleased to see him again, but she lets him buy her tea. She is surprised that he is still in London, but he tells her he has been laid off at work and has plenty of time. He is searching for information about an ancestor of his, a great lord who lived in the southwest of England and later became a hermit, living in a cave in the woods and becoming known as a kind of wise man. Vinnie begins to feel a professional interest in Chuck, and she advises him about how to proceed in his search.

Chapter 4

Fred, who is in love with Rosemary partly because she is the opposite of his wife, has arranged to meet her at a theater. Rosemary is usually late, and this time she keeps him waiting for over forty minutes. They quarrel over Fred's desire to pay for his own dinner later that evening. He does not like her always paying for him.

Fred and Rosemary are weekend guests at the country house of Rosemary's aristocratic friends, Penelope (Posy) Billings and her husband, Sir James (Jimbo), who is out of the country. Other guests are Edwin Francis, Nico (a young male friend of Edwin's, with whom he has a sexual relationship), and a nondescript middle-aged man named William Just, who at first appears to be a cousin of Posy. Fred feels provincial and out of place in this sophisticated English company.

After dinner, the group plays charades, but the game is interrupted by the unexpected return of Jimbo from his business trip abroad. Posy does not want him to find them playing charades, so she orders everyone out and greets Jimbo as if nothing were going on. She orders William to the boathouse and orders Fred and Nico to pack up everything in William's room. Fred wonders why William has to be banished, until Nico informs him that William is, in fact, Posy's lover. Nico knows this because Edwin told him. As Fred learns more about the goings-on in this English house, he develops distaste for the situation, but he stays on because of Rosemary.

Chapter 5

Vinnie visits an elementary school playground and watches some little girls skipping rope. She is continuing to collect material about schoolyard rhymes. She consults with the children, and as she is leaving she is accosted by Mary Maloney, a rough, poorly dressed girl of about thirteen, who says she knows some rhymes. Mary persuades Vinnie to pay her a small sum for reciting them. Vinnie does not like the rhymes, one of which is racist and the other obscene. She hurries away.

That night Vinnie attends a performance of a Mozart opera. During the interval, she encounters Fred and Rosemary. Fred tries to get Vinnie to back him up in persuading Rosemary to hire a housekeeper for her notoriously messy house, but Vinnie does not wish to take sides in their argument.

That night, as she is lying in bed, Vinnie receives a surprise visit from Chuck. He is downhearted because he has discovered that his ancestors were not members of the aristocracy. They were farmers, mostly. He has spent several days in southwest England finding this out and now he is full of self-pity. He also tells Vinnie about his recent life back home: his fruitless search for a job, his unhappy marriage, his drinking, and his arrest for driving while intoxicated (DWI). He stayed on in England after the package tour ended because he could not bear to go back to his family. Vinnie rebukes him for feeling sorry for himself; he takes offense and leaves abruptly. But later he calls her, acknowledges she was right and offers to take her out. Vinnie is of two minds but accepts his invitation.

Chapter 6

In May, Fred is on his way to a party at Rosemary's. He is happier than he was before he met Rosemary but is worried that his work on John Gay is not progressing well. He is also not sure how to respond to a conciliatory letter he has received from his wife. He has put off answering for nearly two weeks.

Rosemary has hired a housemaid named Mrs. Harris, and the house looks unusually clean. At the party, Fred meets Chuck and Vinnie, and Daphne Vane, an elderly actress. Debby and Joe Vogeler also arrive with their baby son, Jakie. Jakie knocks over a vase that sends water and foliage streaming over a famous drama critic and notable bore named Oswald. After the party, Fred apologizes to Rosemary over the incident, but she says she found it amusing, since Oswald has in the past written unpleasant things about her and her friends. Then Fred tells her that he must return to Corinth University within a month. Rosemary at first refuses to believe him but then takes the news badly and throws him out of the house.

Chapter 7

Vinnie is sick with a cold. She is also depressed because her grant to study in England has not been extended because of the opposition of Professor Zimmern, who sits on the committee. She is consoled by a telephone conversation with Chuck, who is in Wiltshire, in southwest England, still learning about his ancestors. Vinnie has in recent weeks gotten to know him better, and he has told her his life story. He grew up in a dysfunctional family and was a juvenile delinquent but straightened himself out following his military service in World War II. It also transpires that Vinnie's English friends, who met Chuck at Rosemary's party, find him entertaining and likable, regarding him as an example of a real American cowboy.

Vinnie has also recently encountered Fred, who is miserable following his break-up with Rosemary. Fred asks Vinnie to have a word with Rosemary on his behalf. Vinnie agrees reluctantly.

That evening, Chuck arrives at Vinnie's, bringing with him an Indian takeout supper. He tells her about his latest research into his ancestors. He now feels he should be more proud of Old Mumpson, the hermit. He has discovered that the old man's illiteracy was no disgrace, since a lot of country people were illiterate in those days. Chuck has also been spending time observing an archeological dig and because of his knowledge of geology has been asked to join it. He has been offered a house and is planning to stay in Wiltshire for the summer.

After dinner, Vinnie and Chuck collide in the kitchen and are drenched with soup and coffee.

Their efforts to clean each other up generate some sexual tension. Vinnie sends Chuck into the bathroom to change, and he returns draped in one of her bedspreads. He kisses her, and soon they are making love.

Chapter 8

The narrative returns to a little while before Vinnie last saw Fred. Fred is anxious to see Rosemary following their quarrel. He goes to Holland Park, where Rosemary is being filmed in a television role. As they talk afterwards, Rosemary tells him that they have been invited to Wales at the end of June, but he reminds her that he must return to Corinth. Rosemary does not understand his insistence that he must honor his commitments. She rejects him, and they part unreconciled.

As the days pass and he cannot get to see Rosemary again, Fred becomes desperate. He goes to her home in Chelsea, but only Mrs. Harris is there, and she will neither let him in nor take a message. He fills in time by seeing the Vogelers. They walk alongside a canal with the baby, Jakie, who manages to speak his long-delayed first word.

Fred tries to see Rosemary by going to the BBC building where she is taking part in a radio program. But after the program is over, he waits outside the wrong door and fails to meet her. He is angry with Rosemary and with himself. He thinks of his wife and decides that he must answer the letter she wrote him. Realizing that will be too slow, he decides to send a telegram.

Chapter 9

Vinnie sits watching the polar bears at London Zoo, happier than she has been in months. In recent weeks, she has been seeing a lot of Chuck, and he stays overnight at her flat frequently. He has been gone for a week in Wiltshire, and Vinnie misses him. However, she does not want her friends to know that she has become romantically involved with him.

Vinnie attends Daphne's party but finds it noisy and crowded. Since Vinnie prepares to leave at the same time as Rosemary, Rosemary invites her to share a cab, and Vinnie tries to put in a good word for Fred, as she promised she would do. Rosemary, however, is drunk and hostile. She denounces Fred and insults Vinnie. Vinnie gets out of the cab in a hurry and takes a bus for the remainder of the journey home. Chuck calls and invites her to Wiltshire to stay with him for the summer. Vinnie cannot go for the whole summer but thinks she will go for a short visit.

Chapter 10

In a bitter mood, Fred packs and prepares to return to the United States. He has not heard from his wife, and his academic work is going badly. He still has a key to Rosemary's house, and he decides to go there to reclaim his possessions. He lets himself into the house, goes downstairs, and finds Mrs. Harris in the basement kitchen. Her head is covered in a headscarf, and she does not look up as she speaks to him in an insulting way. Fred returns to the hall and then goes up to Rosemary's bedroom, which is untidy and unclean. He is angry at Mrs. Harris for not clearing up and even thinks she may be using Rosemary's room in her absence. The drunken Mrs. Harris follows him into the room. He stands in the closet as she approaches him, and to his astonishment she seems to want to seduce him, taunting him with phrases that Rosemary uses. Fred is furious at this evidence that Mrs. Harris must have been listening in on their conversations. He pushes her away and rushes out of the house. In bed later that evening, he realizes with horror that the woman he thought was Mrs. Harris was, in fact, Rosemary. He realizes that he has never had a good view of Mrs. Harris, having met her only once, for a fleeting moment. He wonders whether there ever was a Mrs. Harris. He is angry and realizes that Rosemary has played a trick on him; she has never really loved him. Then the thought occurs to him that Rosemary may not have been merely acting; she may be having a nervous breakdown. He decides he must get someone to look out for her welfare before he leaves.

Chapter 11

Vinnie attends a symposium on children's literature but is bored. She also gets a shock when she discovers that her academic nemesis, Professor L. D. Zimmern, has just published a collection of essays that is almost certain to include the hostile piece he wrote about her. She knows that she would be able to complain about it to Chuck, but she still cannot make the decision to visit him. She does not much like living with anyone. She knows she will go to Wiltshire eventually, but she keeps trying to put it off.

Vinnie gets a telephone call from Ruth, Fred's estranged wife. She wants her to pass on a message to Fred that she will not be in Corinth when he returns the following day. She has no way of reaching him other than by leaving a message with Vinnie. Ruth also lets slip that her father is none other than L. D. Zimmern. Vinnie realizes she has a chance to revenge herself on him by failing to pass on the message, but she listens to the better side of her nature and decides to find Fred that evening. She knows he is going to watch the Druids perform midsummer solstice rites on Parliament Hill, a location on Hampstead Heath. Even though it is about eleven o'clock at night, she takes a train to Hampstead. She finds Fred, who is with the Vogelers on the Heath, and passes on the message.

Early next morning, Fred arranges to meet Edwin Francis outside Rosemary's house. Rosemary is home, but Edwin advises Fred that although she is all right, she is in no condition to see him. Fred makes his way to the airport to catch his flight home.

Chapter 12

Vinnie wonders why she has not heard from Chuck in over a week. She fears that his affection for her may have cooled. Then she receives a call from Barbie Mumpson, Chuck's daughter, who says that her father died a few days ago. Barbie is in London, and she visits Vinnie in the afternoon, informing her that Chuck had a history of heart problems and died of a heart attack. His body has already been cremated and the ashes scattered in the English countryside. Barbie presents Vinnie with an engraving of Old Mumpson, that Chuck wanted her to have. After Barbie leaves, Vinnie weeps over her loss.

A week later, Vinnie has lunch with Edwin Francis. Edwin tells her that Rosemary is fine now and that she has had a history of odd behavior when she is not working steadily. He also offers the opinion that there never was a Mrs. Harris. The talk turns to Chuck's death, and Vinnie admits that she loved him. As Vinnie returns to her flat, she is happy that she has now loved and been loved, but she is also sad that the man who loved her is dead, and she allows herself to become self-pitying again.

Characters

Sir James Billings

Sir James Billings, known as Jimbo, is the husband of Posy Billings. He is a businessman specializing in high-risk investments.

Lady Posy Billings

Lady Posy Billings (Posy is short for Penelope) is an attractive, aristocratic English lady, a friend of Rosemary Radley. She has two young children. Posy likes to entertain at her country home, where she invites her lover, William Just, when her husband is out of town. Jimbo is fully aware of his wife's infidelity and accepts it in exchange for his own freedom.

Edwin Francis

Edwin Francis is a children's book editor, writer, and critic. He is small and rather overweight, with an off-hand, self-deprecating manner that hides the fact that he is a powerful figure in the children's book world. He is a friend of Vinnie and Rosemary and also something of a gossip. Edwin is a homosexual who has a succession of young lovers. His latest friend is Nico.

Professor Mike Gibson

Mike Gibson is an Oxford University professor who leads the archeological dig in Wiltshire to which Chuck Mumpson becomes attached.

Mrs. Harris

Mrs. Harris is purportedly the cleaning woman hired by Rosemary Radley to clean up her messy house. At first, Mrs. Harris gets a reputation for being efficient, but she also acts strangely, refusing to answer the telephone or the door when she is at work. Rosemary takes a liking to her and frequently quotes her jaundiced pronouncements on current events and people in the news. Mrs. Harris also comes up with little bits of folklore that Rosemary delights in repeating, such as "Mrs. Harris believes that looking at the full moon through glass makes you loony, unless it's over your left shoulder." Later, however, it transpires that Mrs. Harris does not, in fact, exist. No one has ever seen her for more than a moment; she is merely a character that Rosemary, the actress, has invented.

William Just

William Just is a man of about fifty with a mild, self-effacing manner. He works for the BBC. William is a houseguest at Posy Billing's home and attends Posy's party. Although he is referred to as a cousin of Posy, it transpires that he and Posy are, in fact, lovers.

Mary Maloney

Mary Maloney is a skinny, badly dressed girl of about thirteen with a bad complexion. She accosts Vinnie in the school playground and offers to recite some rhymes for her, while insisting that Vinnie pay her for the privilege.

Ruth March

Ruth March is the wife of Fred Turner. He gives her the nickname, Roo. Ruth, a photographer by profession, is dark, sturdy, earthy, sensual, coarse, and passionate. She is a feminist and much more unconventional than her husband. When they married, Ruth would not take Fred's last name, preferring to adopt a new name altogether rather than retain her maiden name of Zimmern. (She is the daughter of Professor Zimmern.) Fred's friends Debby and Joe think, although they do not say it in as many words, that Ruth is "too emotional, too political, too arty, too noisy, and too Jewish," but Fred's parents like her. Fred and Ruth had been married for only a few years when Ruth had a one-woman exhibition of her photographs at Corinth, but she included photographs that offended her husband (not surprisingly, since they were of his genitals). She also included photos of the body parts of other men, although she denied to Fred that these men were her lovers. The long quarrel that followed the exhibition eventually led to the breakup of their marriage, although at the end of the novel, it is clear that they are likely to be reconciled.

Vinnie Miner

Vinnie Miner is an unmarried fifty-four-year-old professor of children's literature at Corinth University, a fictional Ivy League university. She is small and plain in appearance, "the sort of person that no one ever notices." At the beginning of the novel, Vinnie is on her way to England to further her research on the play-rhymes of British and American children. She loves England and entertains a dream of becoming an English lady and living permanently in that country. She tends to overdo her Anglophilia, and her English friends regard her as something of a comic turn, with her passion for "everything British that is quaint and out-of-date."

Vinnie has been successful professionally, having published several books and established a reputation in her field. But she has not been successful in love. She was married once, when she was young, but the marriage was brief and unhappy. The men she has been involved with sexually since have tended to regard her more as a friend than a lover and choose her as a temporary distraction from the effort of pursuing other, more glamorous females. Vinnie, who has a strong tendency towards self-pity, no longer expects much from men, and she certainly does not expect to be loved. She still has sexual desires, however, and spends some mental energy creating imaginary erotic dalliances with literary critics whom she admires.

Vinnie has some small vices, also. She regularly pilfers small items, such as the toiletries available in the airplane's washroom, as well as flowers from nearby front gardens. She also enjoys inventing imaginary torments and deaths for those she perceives as her enemies, especially Professor L. D. Zimmern. She is not especially kind or generous, and she does not go out of her way to do things for other people.

When she first meets Chuck Mumpson, she looks down on him as an ignoramus, but later she discovers his virtues. After they unexpectedly become lovers, she becomes happier than she has been for months, perhaps for years. He finds her attractive, and she is able to respond to him as well. She finds out that even though she regards herself as elderly, if not downright old, life can still produce pleasant surprises, even love.

Barbie Mumpson

Barbie Mumpson, Chuck Mumpson's daughter, is in her mid-twenties, tanned and somewhat overweight. She brings Vinnie the news that Chuck has died of a heart attack.

Chuck Mumpson

Chuck Mumpson is a fifty-seven-year-old sanitation engineer from Tulsa, Oklahoma. He is married with two children. Chuck meets Vinnie on the plane to London, where he is going on a two-week package tour. Judging by his manner and his appearance, Vinnie thinks he is uninteresting. She pegs him as a Midwest businessman or rancher and as a typical American tourist, barely worth talking to. But after they meet by chance again in London, she gradually gets to know him. Chuck reveals that he was a delinquent in his teenage years, and he has had a drinking problem. Once when he was driving while intoxicated, he caused the death of a young man. He is in a loveless marriage and suffers from low self-esteem. When his company laid him off, he was unable to find alternative employment, and this did nothing for his self-confidence. In London, he is lonely and bored. However, despite his ignorance and his personal problems, Chuck has an engaging, bluff, friendly manner, and he is genuinely interested in and admires Vinnie. Because of his attitude toward her, Vinnie gets drawn into a sexual and romantic relationship with him. Chuck turns out to be a kind and generous lover and a good friend who listens to Vinnie's problems and cheers her up.

Myrna Mumpson

Myrna Mumpson, Chuck's wife, appears in the novel only through Chuck's comments about her. She is a real estate agent, and according to Chuck, she no longer has any affection for her husband.

Nico

Nico, a young Greek Cypriot, is Edwin Francis's lover. He is well educated, fluent in English, and has ambitions to work in television or cinema. His interest in others is in direct proportion to how much he thinks they will be able to help him achieve his goals.

Rosemary Radley

Rosemary Radley, an aristocratic English actress, stars in a British television program *Tallyhoo Castle*, a comedy-drama series about upper-class country life. She is an accomplished actress on television and in films. Officially, Rosemary is thirty-seven years old, but she is probably older than that, although she does not look it. She has been married twice, unhappily, and has no children. She lives alone and has a history of short, tempestuous love affairs. As an actress, Rosemary specializes in portraying highborn women from every period in history, but she is frustrated because she is never asked to take on the big tragic roles, such as Lady Macbeth, for which she lacks the necessary gravitas. "Her voice is too high and sweet, and she doesn't project that kind of dark energy," says her friend, Edwin Francis. Rosemary is very attractive and charming, "with a teasing, impulsive intimacy which yet holds its victims at arm's length." She is graceful, sophisticated, and witty, but also impulsive and contradictory. She is flirtatious and on social occasions is always the center of attention. This suits her because she has a narcissistic personality; from her point of view, the world ought to revolve entirely around her. Rosemary enters into a romance with Fred Turner but spurns him when he tells her he must shortly return to the United States. She also reveals a nasty side of her personality when, drunk, she insults Vinnie. Eventually, her personality is revealed to be brittle and unstable, and she comes close to having a nervous breakdown.

Fred Turner

Fred Turner is a twenty-nine-year-old American who, like Vinnie Miner, teaches literature at Corinth University. He specializes in the eighteenth century and is in London to do research on the English writer, John Gay. A handsome man, Fred is often mistaken on the street for a movie or television star. He is athletic, energetic, self-confident, and outgoing, yet with a serious manner. However, he is unhappy in London because he has just split up with his wife, Ruth, who was to have accompanied him on his trip. Fred's fortunes improve, however, when he begins a romance with Rosemary Radley, an aristocratic English actress. He falls in love with her and for a few months enjoys a pleasant social life meeting Rosemary's wide circle of upper-class English friends. But when he informs Rosemary that he must return to Corinth in June to teach summer school, she breaks up with him and refuses to see or talk to him. Angry and disillusioned with Rosemary, he effects reconciliation with his wife and recovers all his optimism as he prepares to return to the United States. He feels that he is "striding toward his future with a supernatural speed and confidence."

Daphne Vane

Daphne Vane is an elderly actress who has starred with Rosemary Radley in the television program, *Tallyhoo Castle*. She attends Rosemary's party.

Debby Vogeler

Debby Vogeler is Joe's wife and the mother of the baby, Jakie. Dumpy and not very pretty, she teaches at a college in southern California, and she and her husband are spending some leave in London. Debby and Joe are old friends of Fred Turner. When they were students, Debby had a romantic interest in Fred, but he was unaware of it. She now thinks him immature and resents his professional success.

Jakie Vogeler

Jakie Vogeler is the Vogelers' one-year-old son. He is a difficult baby and causes quite a stir at Rosemary's party, when he knocks over a vase and drenches one of the guests.

Joe Vogeler

Joe Vogeler is Debby Vogeler's husband. Like his wife, he teaches at a college in southern California. His discipline is philosophy. Joe is a native Californian, and the damp English climate does not agree with him, but he bears his frequent sickness stoically.

Professor L. D. Zimmern

Professor L. D. Zimmern is an American academic who writes an article in the *Atlantic Monthly*, attacking as trivial Vinnie Miner's research in comparative folklore.

Themes

Appearance and Reality

Both of the main protagonists, Vinnie and Fred, are initially deceived by outward appearances. Vinnie eventually learns not to judge by appearances, and

Fred learns to value what he already has. Vinnie's personal growth is probably the more interesting of the two, because when she is compared to Fred—a plain, unmarried woman in her fifties, as opposed to a tall, dark, handsome young man—the odds seem so much stacked against her. Because Vinnie is an intellectual and professor of English, her expectations of life have been scripted by books. Since she was a little child, classic English fiction has "suggested to her what she might do, think, feel, desire, and become." Sadly, the older woman does not fare well in traditional English novels. As Vinnie notes, people over fifty "are usually portrayed as comic, pathetic, or disagreeable." Nothing exciting ever happens to them. True to form, Vinnie does not expect to find love at her age. After all, she believes that she has never really been loved by a man, so why should that change now? She also realizes that contemporary culture reinforces this belief. As portrayed in the media, only the young have sex. That older people might also have satisfying, even passionate sexual relationships is passed over in embarrassed silence. Vinnie is quite prepared to accept this situation, telling herself that even though she still has erotic impulses, it is time "to steer past . . . elderly sexual farce and sexual tragedy into the wide, calm sunset sea of abstinence."

When Vinnie first meets Chuck, she cannot see beyond the surface of the man. She thinks of him as a cartoon American tourist who wears a cowboy costume and is loaded up with cameras, maps, and tour guides. He appears to lack everything she values, including an education in the humanities. Education to Vinnie means being well read; it does not mean gaining the knowledge to become a sanitation engineer and earning enough to retire comfortably in one's late fifties.

However, when circumstances conspire to throw her and Chuck together, she realizes that Chuck has some substance to him that she has hitherto overlooked. He has the capacity to appreciate her, to make her feel like a woman, and he is, as she puts it, "wonderful in bed." This gives her a new perspective on what it means to participate fully in life. She is ready to cast away the predetermined script handed down to her by her beloved books and embrace what life brings her. She starts to write her own life script rather than act out someone else's. She learns, to use a cliché, that just as all that glitters is not gold, all that does not glitter is not trash. Behind Chuck's almost comic appearance and Midwestern drawl—which is also all her English friends observe in him—is a solid human being with something to offer her that she desperately needs. In her acceptance of the unexpected, her whole outlook changes. She realizes that "this world . . . is not English literature . . . [there is] plenty of time for adventure and change, even for heroism and transformation."

Vinnie's new openness to life carries over into her attitude toward her profession. Now that for the first time she has found value in a man who is completely nonintellectual, she shows some impatience with the ponderous rituals of her chosen academic profession. This shift in attitude is apparent when she becomes bored at the conference on children's literature. She is impatient with an English professor who drones on about some abstraction he calls "The Child." Vinnie wants to shout at him that "There is no Child . . . there are only children, each one different, unique, as we here in this room are unique." She has discovered that it is an error to pigeon-hole people, whether they are children, people over fifty, or people who happen to go around in cowboy outfits.

The unlikely romance that comes to plain, fifty-four-year-old Vinnie suggests that youth and beauty to do not have all the triumphs in love. Fred, for example, is much younger than Vinnie and is the epitome of a sexually attractive man. But while Vinnie's fortunes rise, Fred's fall. His infatuation with Rosemary almost brings him to disaster. He is so attracted to the image that Rosemary presents that he cannot bear to think of her as embodying any other qualities. He thinks of her as a heroine from a novel by Henry James, not only beautiful and delicate but also "too generous . . . lighthearted and trusting" to see that her friends Posy and Edwin are not true friends. Rosemary does not, in Fred's eyes, "see them as they are." In reality, however, it is Fred who does not see Rosemary as she is. He is blind to the reality that Rosemary is all appearance and little substance. Only finally, after going through all the agonies that a spurned lover endures, does Fred learn Vinnie's lesson about seeing through surface appearances. Then he realizes that whatever the faults of his wife, who is in every way Rosemary's opposite, she could never be false in the way that Rosemary has been. Once he is free of the spell cast on him by Rosemary, he assesses his life and his conduct in a more objective way. He realizes that he was foolish to allow his quarrel with his wife to get out of hand, and he also accepts that the fiasco with Rosemary was in part his fault, since he encouraged her to love him even when he knew he would be returning to America in a short while. With greater self-knowledge, free

Topics For Further Study

- To what extent is the United States still an Anglo culture with a special relationship to England? Using Internet research, analyze how immigration patterns to the United States have changed over the last century. From what countries do most immigrants now come? How does this compare to the nineteenth century? How are changing immigration patterns changing America? Write an essay on your findings.
- Write a short essay in which you analyze the technique by which Lurie builds up to the revelation that Mrs. Harris and Rosemary are the same person. How do the narrator's comments about Rosemary's character, her acting ability, etc. ensure that the revelation is believable while at the same time a huge surprise for the reader?
- Chuck says in *Foreign Affairs* that the English talk funny, and sometimes he has difficulty understanding them. Form a group with three or four other students and listen to one another talk. What accents do you hear? Are they all the same or are they different? In what way? How does a Brooklyn, New York, accent differ from, say, a Midwestern accent? Do you think that the prevalence of a national mass media is reducing the variety of regional accents? If it is, is this a good trend or something to be deplored?
- Select a British show from PBS, BBC America, or any other source. What image of England does it present? Is it romantic and idealized, or does it seem realistic? What are the main differences that strike you between the culture as presented in this program and the American culture with which you are familiar? Make a class presentation to illustrate your points, using clips from the program, if possible.

of the dream of the appearance of love, Fred places his feet on the firmer ground of reality.

Style

Fairy Tales and Folklore

Lurie uses elements from fairy tales to enhance the theme of transformation. People are not always quite what they appear, and they can change. The most fully developed allusion is to the classic fairy tale of the frog prince, a tale that has existed, its first author unknown, for hundreds of years in Europe. It was published by Jacob and Wilhelm Grimm in Germany in 1812. The basic story is that a young princess encounters a frog at a stream after the ball she is playing with falls into the water. The frog says he will retrieve the ball for her if she will love him and let him live with her. She agrees and allows him to get the ball, but then she goes home and forgets the frog. The next day, just as the princess is sitting down to dinner, the frog knocks on her door and reminds her of her promise. The princess's father tells her she must keep her word, so she allows him to eat and then sleep the night on her bed. Then he leaves in the morning. This goes on for three nights. When the princess awakes on the fourth morning she is astonished to see that the frog has turned into a handsome prince. They live happily ever after.

In *Foreign Affairs*, the frog is Chuck Mumpson, the princess Vinnie. When Vinnie first speaks to Chuck on the airplane, she notices that he blinks slowly. When she next encounters him, unexpectedly, she notices that "he blinks at her in the slow way she recalls from the flight," thus identifying him with the small reptile in question. Moreover, Chuck wears a "semitransparent greenish plastic raincoat," a kind of reptilian skin which Vinnie dislikes. This raincoat later acquires symbolic importance.

On their first meeting, like the princess in the tale, Vinnie allows Chuck to do her a favor (arranging for her to get to downtown London on the tourist bus) and then, like the princess, promptly forgets all about him. Again like the princess, Vinnie then has three encounters with her "frog." On her first two encounters, she is indifferent to him, even contemptuous. On her second encounter, for example, when Chuck comes to her flat for the first time (chapter 5), she chides him for his self-pity, and he leaves. But her third encounter is different. This is the meeting in which the "frog" undergoes a process of transformation. Accidentally, his clumsiness gets the two of them covered with avocado-and-watercress soup, a green mixture that might resemble pond slime. But when he emerges from the bathroom comically wrapped in Vinnie's bedspread, it is as if he has shed his frog's loathsome skin, and the prince has started to emerge. Vinnie discovers that she likes being the object of his attentions and that he is a sensitive and generous lover, which is exactly what she needs. The theme of the frog losing its skin and becoming something else is emphasized by Vinnie's tossing of his plastic raincoat into the trash can. When she picks it up, she does so with distaste, "observing how the greenish-gray plastic managed to feel stiff and slimy at the same time." She likens it to a "dead fish," which is the author's thinly disguised reference to the underlying frog-prince theme.

This being a worldly-wise novel, however, it comes as no surprise that the happy ending of the fairy tale is subverted. Vinnie and Chuck, princess and frog/prince, do not live happily ever after.

Lurie uses more folklore elements in the Rosemary Radley/Fred Turner plot. The lovely Rosemary, who holds everyone in thrall but is fully known by no one, is like an enchantress who bewitches Fred. This pattern echoes a fairy tale found in various literary works, including John Keats's poem "La Belle Dame Sans Merci." In his poem, a beautiful lady tells a knight that she loves him; he falls under her spell (just as Fred falls under the spell of Rosemary's irresistible charm), and she takes him into, what Keats calls, "her elfin grot" (Rosemary's house in Chelsea). Then he is cast out and ends up miserable and alone. Similarly, after Rosemary rejects him, Fred endures long empty days and nights and wanders the streets of London alone. Again, however, in *Foreign Affairs*, there is a reversal of the fairy tale motif, since Fred, after his initial distress, is able to come to his senses and return to his wife.

Lurie adds yet another fairy tale allusion when Rosemary is presented as a beautiful enchantress who turns into an ugly old hag (Mrs. Harris). This is both the equivalent of a comic reversal of the frog-into-prince motif and a reversal of the more common theme in folklore, of the ugly hag who turns out to be a beautiful princess. (Keats's poem "Lamia," in which a beautiful woman seduces a young man but is then transformed into a serpent, suggests the variant theme.)

On two occasions, Lurie directly mentions fairy tales, as if hinting to the reader about the subtext of her novel. The first occurs when Vinnie, who is trying to educate Chuck, sends him down to Wiltshire with a book of English fairy tales to read. The second occurs when Vinnie is shown at her typewriter, writing a review of four books of folktales.

Historical Context

The History of the Academic Novel

Foreign Affairs is a variant of the genre known as the academic novel, which satirizes life on the college campus. One of the earliest and most amusing of all academic novels is *Lucky Jim* (1954) by British writer Kingsley Amis, in which Jim Dixon, a young working-class lecturer in history, attains a position at a provincial university where he has to deal not only with his own dislike of the job but also with the upper-class fool who heads the department. In addition to being extremely witty, Amis also makes insightful points about the attempts of the post-World War II generation to break through England's traditional class structure. Following in Amis's footsteps were other British writers, including Malcolm Bradbury, who wrote *Eating People Is Wrong* (1959), *Stepping Westward* (1965), and *The History Man* (1975), and David Lodge, whose novels *Changing Places* (1975) and *Small World* (1984) manage to satirize both British and American academic life. Barbara Pym's *An Academic Question* (1986), which focuses on academic rivalry between two professors of sociology at a provincial university, is also a notable contribution to the genre.

In the United States, Randall Jarrell's *Pictures from an Institution* (1954), set in the fictional Benton College, a women's college resembling Bryn Mawr, is the first post-World War II academic novel. Lurie continued the tradition with her *The War of the Tates* (1974). *Foreign Affairs* might be considered a variant of the genre, since it is not set on a college campus, but it does feature academics in major and minor roles and has much to say about the frustrations and perils of the academic enterprise.

Compare & Contrast

- **1980s:** Americans appreciate the high quality of British television programs and the charming picture of British life and culture these programs present. British serial dramas such as *Upstairs, Downstairs* and comedies such as *Monty Python's Flying Circus*, shown on Public Broadcasting Service (PBS), gain a wide following.

  Today: PBS reduces its British-based programming in favor of more American programming. But American lovers of British television can still watch British imports on BBC America, the Arts and Entertainment Channel (A&E), and Bravo.

- **1980s:** The so-called special relationship between the United States and Great Britain flourishes. President Ronald Reagan and British prime minister Margaret Thatcher, who are both political conservatives, develop a strong rapport and pursue similar economic and foreign policies.

  Today: Britain remains the closest European ally of the United States in the war against terrorism. Britain sends more troops to aid the U.S.-led invasion of Iraq than any other country.

- **1980s:** Tourism is one of the largest industries in Britain, contributing about 3.6 percent of its gross domestic product. In 1980, Britain receives two million visitors from North America. However, during the 1970s and 1980s, revenue in London from tourism is adversely affected by fears of terrorist attacks by the Irish Republican Army (IRA).

  Today: The number of tourists visiting Britain from North America doubles, when compared to the 1980s, to about 4.5 million per year. This number includes 3,616,000 visitors from the United States (in 2003). In 2004, the United Kingdom (Great Britain and Northern Ireland) ranks sixth in the international earnings league from tourism. Tourism provides an estimated 1.4 million jobs in the United Kingdom, which amounts to about 5 percent of all people in employment.

Academic Study of Children's Literature

One of Lurie's specialties as a professor of English during the 1970s and 1980s was children's literature. She also made her heroine, Vinnie Miner, a professor who "has a well-established reputation in the expanding field of children's literature." As an academic discipline, the study of children's literature established itself only in the 1970s. In the novel, Vinnie complains "that children's literature is a poor relation in her department—indeed, in most English departments: a stepdaughter grudgingly tolerated." During the 1980s and afterward, however, the study of children's literature grew quite rapidly, with many colleges and universities starting to offer courses, and even entire degree programs, in children's literature. Children's literature began to be studied with the same critical theories that were applied to other forms of literature, such as structuralism, reader-response criticism, and feminism. Scholars explored issues of ideology, class, and gender, and argued that children's literature is important because it shapes how children see the world and the attitudes they are encouraged to adopt. Lurie herself made a contribution to the field in her book, *Don't Tell the Grown-ups: Subversive Children's Literature* (1991). In Lurie's view, the best children's literature is as good as, and even more influential than, the best adult literature.

Critical Overview

Reviewers were quick to praise *Foreign Affairs.* The general opinion was that it was Lurie's best novel up to that time. In *Newsweek*, Walter Clemons calls it "ingenious" and "touching" and praises Lurie's skill in characterization: "Vinnie is an entirely successful creation, Chuck almost as

The Reading Room at the British Museum would provide an atmosphere similar to that experienced by Vinnie doing her research

© Andy Kingsbury/Corbis

good." Clemons had some trouble believing what eventually happens to Rosemary and had a few other quibbles, but he acknowledges that "Vinnie Miner is granted a moving acknowledgement of love."

Like Clemons, Christopher Lehmann-Haupt in the *New York Times* comments favorably on the author's handling of her characters, who are "so securely fixed . . . at just the right distance between the pathetic and the ridiculous—that we can both like them and laugh at them." Lehmann-Haupt also comments on the novel's structure:

> I couldn't help visualizing a diagram with the rise of Vinnie's fortunes superimposed on the decline of Fred Turner's. There's something almost musical in the way the two plots interplay, like two bands marching toward each other playing consonant music.

The reviewer for the *New Yorker*, November 5, 1984, comments on "the originality of Alison Lurie's comic vision, which has a sharp edge and a dark side," while *People Weekly* emphasizes the character development that the two protagonists undergo: "Vinnie is transformed by love from a mean-spirited old lady into someone who makes a difficult romantic gesture. Turner is changed from a prudish postadolescent into an appreciative husband."

Over twenty years after its publication, *Foreign Affairs* had retained its position as Lurie's finest novel.

Criticism

Bryan Aubrey

Aubrey holds a Ph.D. in English and has published many articles on twentieth century literature. In this essay, he analyzes the interaction between British and American culture in Foreign Affairs.

Placing American characters in a London setting gave Lurie the opportunity to show, just as Henry James had done nearly a century earlier in *The Ambassadors*, the interaction between two cultures. But where James had contrasted American provincialism with European culture and sophistication, Lurie's contrasts are not so easily categorized. If *Foreign Affairs* is seen as a clash between different cultures, the naturalness and sincerity of American culture eventually proves itself equal if not superior to the present condition of English upper-class society.

Perhaps the best case for England rests not with the English but with the classic example of the American Anglophile, Vinnie Miner, who sits in her "flat" (i.e., apartment) with a "pot of Twining's Queen Mary tea" and sometimes entertains the notion that one day she might even be able to become a citizen of the country she has loved since childhood. For Vinnie, England has always been "the imagined and desired country," formed in her understanding by all the English literature she read, long before she ever visited the country in person. London seems like home to her, a welcome change to "billboards, used-car lots, ice storms and tornadoes," as well as "sensational and horrible news events," not to mention political demonstrations and drunken student brawls at Corinth University. Such is Vinnie's jaundiced view of American culture, to which she seems a complete stranger. Indeed, Vinnie acts in such an English manner, outdoing even the English, that it is not surprising that on the airplane Chuck Mumpson, the engineer from Oklahoma, mistakes her for an Englishwoman. A sub-theme here is the clash between two Americas; Vinnie's New England-inspired tact and refinement is set against Chuck's hearty directness and vulgarity, which earns him and his ilk Vinnie's sneer at "half-literate middle Americans." She and Chuck may be from the same country, but they are from different worlds.

Vinnie's Anglophilia is juxtaposed with the disillusionment of the Vogelers. The narrator points out that they are like many American teachers of English literature who fall in love with England based on its literature but then are disappointed when the reality fails to match their idealized expectations. Thus, the Vogelers complain that London is cold and wet, the people are unfriendly, and the tourist attractions are all disappointingly small, as if they are imitations of something grander. For the Vogelers, Britain's long and illustrious past may rise up in the imagination like an impressive mountain range, but its present reality is a collection of very ordinary foothills. Even when they start to mix with real upper middle-class English people, at Rosemary's party, they are not impressed. Joe Vogeler considers them "kind of phony-baloney" and tells Fred, "That's how the English are, especially the middle-class types . . . You never really know where you are with them."

Chuck also has a rather negative impression of London, complaining to Vinnie about the lumpy bed in his hotel and that English food "tastes like boiled hay; if you want a half-decent meal, you have to go to some foreign restaurant." Chuck is a practical, curious type, and he finds some evidence that backs up the Vogelers' disappointment in tourist attractions when he discovers that at the Tower of London, the crown jewels he has just paid good money to see are, in fact, copies; the real crown jewels are locked up somewhere else, inaccessible to the likes of him and other tourists. This little piece of fakery suggests indeed that London is, at least for tourists, not all that it might seem to be in the glossy travel brochures back home that seduce them into making the trip.

The English setting gives the American author plenty of opportunities for observations about the differences between the two cultures. On the airplane to England, Vinnie takes note of the excessive friendliness of Americans when traveling, and how detailed personal information is so readily divulged. Vinnie, like the true Englishwoman she is in spirit, finds this off-putting, noting that in England, "the anonymity of travelers" is preserved, and conversations between strangers are limited to topics of general interest. For his part, Chuck, who is a lot more observant and intelligent than Vinnie at first gives him credit for, notices the self-deprecating quality that is so much a part of the English character; the English have the ability to make fun of themselves, and he notes how different things are in Tulsa, Oklahoma, where the rule is "Smile, accentuate the positive, keep your eye on the doughnut, that kind of thing." Anyone who is familiar with both cultures will recognize the accuracy of Chuck's and Vinnie's observations.

"Vinnie's friends might not understand, but she now acknowledges that the smooth, polished exterior—as embodied in Rosemary and her aristocratic friends—may not be the ultimate arbiter of value."

Fred Turner, who like Vinnie is steeped in English literature but unlike her is on his first trip to England, also observes some cultural differences, especially when he stays for the weekend at Posy Billings's country house and takes part in a game of charades. He notes that unlike the American version of the game, which is competitive and rewards individualism and speed, the British version is more leisurely and cooperative; there are no winners, and the game is not much more than an excuse for dressing up and behaving in a silly fashion.

Lurie also calls attention, as one might expect, to some of the more obvious differences in language that an American visitor to England could hardly fail to note: the English use "lorry," for example, for truck, and "ring" someone on the telephone rather than call them, as an American would say. Only once does Lurie's ear let her down, and that is when she has an English girl who is employed as Rosemary's answering service tell Fred that Rosemary is "out of town." This phrase is not used in England; more likely the girl would have said something like "He's away at the moment," which in characteristic English fashion conveys unavailability while divulging as little information as possible.

It might be argued that all these differences, while no doubt accurately recorded, are unremarkable, little more than common knowledge for the transatlantic traveler. Just occasionally, however, in *Foreign Affairs*, the stereotypical ideas about each culture prove unsatisfactory and have to be revised. Vinnie, for example, believes that British playground rhymes are older and more poetic than

What Do I Read Next?

- Lurie's novel *The War between the Tates* (1974) is an academic novel that takes place on the campus of the fictional Corinth University, which is based on Cornell University, where Lurie teaches. The novel treats in satiric fashion the collapsing marriage of Brian Tate, a professor of political science, and his wife, Erica.
- British author David Lodge writes exceedingly funny academic novels. In *Changing Places: A Tale of Two Campuses* (1975), English and American academic life are subjected to hilarious satire when English academic Philip Swallow of the University of Rummidge swaps places for half a year with American scholar Morris Zapp of State University of Euphoria.
- Henry James's novel *The Ambassadors* (1903) shows the interaction of American innocence with sophisticated European society. Lambert Strether is sent by a rich widow to Paris to persuade the woman's son, who has taken up with an aristocratic Frenchwoman, to return home to the family business in Woollett, Massachusetts.
- Richard Russo's *Straight Man* (1997) is a hilarious adventure in the neurotic weekend of an interim chairman of English at a struggling U.S. university, at which administrators are laying off tenured faculty and shifting curriculum from traditional subjects, such as English literature, to more marketable applied subjects, such as technical and computer courses.

their American counterparts, which she thinks are newer and cruder. But this is apparently disproved by Vinnie's jarring encounter with the scruffy young girl, Mary Maloney, whose obscene rhymes shock the staid professor. There are some ironies, too, relating to the two cultures, as when Chuck Mumpson, whilst declaring himself unimpressed by London, shows also, in his aspiration to find in his ancestry an English lord, that he is not immune to the lure of the older culture.

What does all this playing with cultural differences amount to? In short, by the end of the novel, honest American virtues have demonstrated their usefulness, even when matched against a society that has been shaped by hundreds of years of civilization. This can be seen first in English-in-spirit Vinnie, who overcomes her prejudice against a man who happens to come from what dwellers on the coasts of the United States are said to refer to as "flyover country." She learns to value the Midwestern virtues of sincerity, openness, and friendliness, as embodied in Chuck, even though he is so far removed from her idea of what a cultured man should be that until she makes her confession to Edwin Francis, she conceals her relationship with him from her English friends. Vinnie's friends might not understand, but she now acknowledges that the smooth, polished exterior—as embodied in Rosemary and her aristocratic friends—may not be the ultimate arbiter of value.

This is the lesson also learned, even more profoundly, by Fred Turner. A comparison with James's *The Ambassadors* illumines the point. In that story, Chad Newsome, the twenty-eight-year-old provincial American in Paris has been educated in the social graces by an older, aristocratic Frenchwoman. In *Foreign Affairs* , another American in his late twenties forms a relationship with an aristocratic Englishwoman at least eight years his senior, who introduces him to her upper-class circle of friends. But unlike Chad Newsome, Fred Turner is not an uncultivated provincial. He is a professor at an Ivy League university and is as intellectually sophisticated as any of the British people he meets, and he is not in the least overawed by them. In fact, after his weekend at the country house of the Billings, he is hardly enamored of the morals or lifestyles of England's rich and famous. Then when he discovers that Rosemary is, to say the least, not all she appears, with some relief he repairs his relationship with Ruth, his estranged American wife.

Rosemary and Ruth (known as Roo) emerge almost as symbols of their respective cultures. Roo is earthy, lusty, robust; she is associated with the freedom of nature and the outdoors. She likes to make love in the open air, and when Fred thinks of her, he visualizes her exposing her naked, tanned body to the sun and the air or wandering nude around the house, as was her habit. Roo is in this respect a true child of nature, not of art or civilization. The white-skinned Englishwoman Rosemary, on the other hand, is all art. She conceals rather than reveals, both physically and psychologically. She tells Fred nothing of her past, and she bathes and dresses alone. Although they are lovers, Fred has never seen her completely naked, and she makes her clothes part of her mystery and her elusiveness. Her art is the art of illusion. Fred's return to Roo, therefore, represents his flight from the mannered, artificial world of London high society—behind its genteel politeness, what secrets may lie?—to the virtues of American naturalness, which may be crude but is not false.

Source: Bryan Aubrey, Critical Essay on *Foreign Affairs*, in *Novels for Students*, Thomson Gale, 2007.

Liz Lear

In the following interview, Lear talks with Lurie about writing, the author's works and characters, and the people and places that inspire her.

[*Liz Lear*:] *I am interested in the idea that creative people are attracted to certain places in the world. Some of these places are said by some to have a cosmic quality or energy. Do you think Key West is one of those places?*

[Alison Lurie:] I don't know that I believe in cosmic vibrations. I think that for a variety of reasons there are places that are particularly hospitable to artists and writers. First and foremost would be a relaxed and permissive atmosphere; writers are not comfortable in the typical small town because they would stand out like freaks and misfits. Secondly, the place should have life and vitality without certain standards of behavior or appearance. Climate, accessibility and beauty are other important factors. Key West certainly fits that criterion. It's a multi-cultured society living together in comparative harmony. Eccentric or original ideas, dress or behavior won't bring down disapproval. It's a sunny charming resort and there's something very seductive about living somewhere that other people pay to go to. Writers attract other writers who are friends. Once a critical mass of creative people establish themselves in a certain spot, more energy is created. There are more people to talk to, more ideas. There are people around who have read your books, who are even eager to discuss them with you. Writers have been coming to Key West for 60 years. So many writers come here now that, in fact, a critical mass does exist. Obviously it's a good time to be a writer in Key West.

"Anna was the headmistress of the little progressive day-school that I attended. She was a very important influence in my life. In those days professional women were thought to be spinsterish and oppressive. She wasn't like that all. She was very much in charge of her own life, yet always warm and kind."

Do you find this an easy place to work? Or do you find the underlying sensuality distracting?

I would find it boring to lie in the sun all day. I suppose some writers need a grey, regimented, puritanical atmosphere to keep their noses to the grindstone. I'm not one of those.

Did you always want to write? And when did you start?

I always thought it would be nice. I was encouraged as a child to think that I was good at inventing stories, so writing was always in the back of my mind as a fantasy. First I thought I'd be a painter. Then I realized that I'd become abstract and I wasn't interested in that because I was more interested in imitating nature than in playing with paint. I was in high school when I decided to try to write.

Do you write every day?

When I'm in the middle of something, I do. Sometimes I don't write at all. And sometimes I get stuck in the middle of something and have to stop and work on something else.

Who are your favorite writers?

Oh, that's difficult! From the past, I would say Dickens, Jane Austen, George Eliot, and many of the other Victorian novelists. In the 20th century, the ones who influenced me the most were people like Christopher Isherwood and Mary McCarthy. I also admire many writers that I don't have much in common with, like Bellow and Updike in America, and Waugh and Greene in England.

Have other writers been supportive of your work, and is there one in particular to whom you owe a debt of gratitude?

Many writers have been very good to me. I would say initially that my friend, Edward Hower, an excellent writer, is very important to me. I would say that I owe the most to my friend, Diane Johnson. She and I exchange manuscripts as soon as we have finished. We have been doing this for many years—actually, since she started to write and my books started to be published. Philip Roth has also been most helpful. He read a number of my earlier books and his constructive criticism was invaluable.

Of all your books, which is your favorite?

That's like asking a mother which is her favorite child. I would say that I like them all equally. When I go back to them I'm as glad to see them as I am to see my rather far-flung children when they return for a visit.

You teach at Cornell, and university life has played a large part in your books. Has this in any way affected your relationships with other faculty members?

I don't think so. I am always careful not to write about people I know, or create characters and situations that might be recognizable.

In Real People, *which I presume takes place at Yaddo, the writer's retreat, you say that there's a rule that those who accept their hospitality must never write about it; if that rule is broken, they will never be allowed to return. Since you have broken this rule, are you now persona non grata at Yaddo?*

I haven't asked to go back, so I really can't say. The old director who felt so strongly about this is no longer there. Possibly the new one feels differently. They try to avoid publicity as a whole simply to avoid being inundated with applications and tourists. I haven't asked to go back there because I don't need it anymore. When I first went there, I had children and no money of my own. Now I can afford my own writer's retreat.

Continuing with Real People, *there is a paragraph that says, "The worst industrial hazard of literature is the poisonous gas of reputation that is discharged around a writer in direct proportion to his success." Do you feel that success and celebrity corrupt everyone to a degree?*

I certainly don't. As I remember, I was talking about what happens to writers living in conventional society, which is certainly something to be avoided. I think that it's very important to know who and where you are in life at the time you attain success. If you come to it quietly and relatively late, as I did, then it isn't damaging. If you're young—say, in your twenties—suddenly you're famous for writing something very autobiographical and you're a celebrity for being the kind of person you have written about, then this can be very destructive. Truman Capote and Erica Jong are good examples of this. If you're constantly surrounded by people who tell you that you're a certain kind of person, it's very hard to go beyond that point and grow.

One of the characters in Only Children, *which takes place in 1935, says, "The women we grew up with before the 19th Amendment are usually pretty irrational, like children really, because that's how they were brought up to be. When they got the vote and short skirts, it was too late for them." Did you find this true of your mother's generation?*

I don't think the character in my book was right about all women. My mother and her friends were privileged not to be in that situation, even though they grew up before the 19th Amendment. They went to college, they had jobs after marriage, or did serious volunteer work. I and my friends were lucky that our mothers were not that kind of woman. As I grew older, I met a lot of women whose mothers were not in that privileged position. I think it's true that the majority of women don't know how to cope with the new freedom.

Does the character, Mary Ann, stem from your own childhood recollections? She would have been about the same age.

I tried to remember as much as I could about my own childhood in terms of what the world looked like or how I felt. The family situation in the book had a resemblance to mine, but was also similar to that of two little girls who were friends of mine at that time. I think that Mary Ann and Lolly are exaggerations of myself as a child. Mary Ann in the book is more sensible and down-to-earth than I was, and Lolly more drifty, dreamy and wrapped up in her imagination. I guess I stood somewhere between the two.

I liked your character, Anna, tremendously. Is her philosophical view of life and love similar to yours?

One can never make one character spokesperson for everything one thinks. Anna was a very real person and an exception to my rule of not putting real people in my books. She was long dead by the time I thought of this book. Also, there were no descendants to be disturbed. Besides, my view of her was so positive. Anna was the headmistress of the little progressive day-school that I attended. She was a very important influence in my life. In those days professional women were thought to be spinsterish and oppressive. She wasn't like that all. She was very much in charge of her own life, yet always warm and kind. She was very good to me and encouraged me to write and draw, and impressed upon my parents the importance of taking me seriously.

Would that we all had someone in our lives like Anna!

I was lucky in both my parents and my school in that I didn't have to go through what so many women of my generation went through—that fight to get out of the mind-set idea that women were only good enough to take second place to men.

Is War Between the Tates *particularly biographical? It seems to have chronologically coincided with some important changes in your life.*

No. You feel that way because of the lag between the book's conception and the publication date. *War Between the Tates* was conceived while my marriage was all right. It was based on the cases of a handful of women I knew or had heard of, whose husbands had left them for younger women. My marriage broke up about six years after *War Between the Tates* was conceived, and for quite different reasons.

Do you still believe that there's a rule that we get what we want in life, but not our second choices?

I think that unless you're very lucky, you don't get your second choice. Anyway, your second choice usually contradicts your first.

In one of your books you comment that college campuses are filled with tired words. Was this a momentary cry from the heart?

When I first started to teach, it was on a year-round basis. This can be very oppressive. Now, at Cornell, I only teach four months out of the year, so I enjoy it very much. I think there's still a lot of tired words around because when you teach there is a continuing flood of student papers on literature and most of them aren't very inspiring.

Things are very tight in the publishing business, and it's almost impossible for anyone but an established writer to get published. As a teacher of writing, do you see much hope in the future for your students, and what advice do you give them?

It's true that things are tight, but there are some hopeful signs. For instance: there's said to be 14,000 small-press publishing houses in operation. If you have a success with one of them, you stand a good chance of getting published by a major company. Another hopeful thing is that there are many opportunities in journalism. When I was a graduate student, journalism was rather cut-and-dried, impersonal stuff. The new journalism allows you to write in an interesting, individual way, about things that take your fancy. Among my students, only a handful have published books, but many of them have gone into journalism. Some have gone into television, and get their ideas across that way.

It's rare for a book to become a bestseller. Occasionally, it happens. Most of the writers I know have at least one unpublished novel in a desk drawer. When their first book is published, it's only after having been sent around to a great many places.

Do you take an active part in politics, or support a particular political party?

I wouldn't say so. Occasionally, I give a little financial support, or sign things I approve of both locally and on the national level, but it's no big thing in my life.

What prompted you to write Imaginary Friends, *and did it require a great deal of research?*

I have always found sociology fascinating, and my father was a sociologist. I was reading a book one day called, *When Prophecy Fails.* The book was about a team of sociologists who infiltrate a midwestern cult which thinks that the world is coming to an end. I was interested in the question of cults and believers, and at the time there was an abundance of them. People were seeing flying saucers and claiming to see each others' auras and meditation was the big thing. I was fascinated with all of these things that were happening. I wondered what kind of people were susceptible and what was necessary to have that kind of belief. I thought it would make a good story, so I invented a couple of sociologists and wrote the book.

I noticed that a character named Zimmer appears in all of your novels. What is the significance of this?

Leonard Zimmer was the hero of my first unpublished novel. I felt sorry for him because he was never able to publicly express himself. Later on I started to mention him in my books and it became

Big Ben and the Parliament buildings, prominent landmarks of London, setting for Foreign Affairs

Photograph by Susan D. Rock. Reproduced by permission

sort of a joke. Now I introduce him peripherally into all my books.

Your characters are real people to you then?

Yes, I suppose, in a way, they are real people.

You live in Ithaca, New York, where you teach. Key West is home part of the year and you also spend time in London. Why London?

I usually go to London for a month each year. My books are all published there and I have had relatively more success in England than I have had over here. Over the years I've got to know a lot of English people. I have friends that I want to see each year, so I do.

The publishing business has long been and still is dominated by men. The women's movement has accelerated the emergence of more women writers than ever before. Men's literature seems to be in need of a new theme, a new road to adventure and a new kind of hero. Much that is new and innovative today seems to be coming from women writers. Do you foresee a more favorable balance in the world of publishing because of this?

Since the early 19th century there have been a great many women writers. It was one of the few careers open to intelligent women of that time. Statistically, there were probably as many books written by women as by men. They just didn't achieve the same sort of reputation, except in a very few cases. In Victorian England there were famous male novelists like Dickens, Trollope, and Thackeray. Their female equivalents were the Brontës, Jane Austen, and George Eliot. The problem, as I see it, isn't a lack of women writers, but that their work hasn't been taken as seriously. A woman has to work harder and publish more before she gets the same kind of professional recognition even though her sales might be as good. For example, it took me four published novels to get a low-level teaching position at Cornell. Had I been a man, with published novels of equal quality and success as far as sales and reviews were concerned, I would have got the job much faster.

I do think that women are moving into more positions of power and it will be easier for women to get serious consideration in times to come. Unfortunately, there seems to be some back-sliding on the equality issue.

I was reading the Mellon Fellowship Award list the other day. I was pleased to note that there were 61 female awardees and 56 males. Some of them will be at Cornell.

A healthy sign. We always try to take people into our graduate program who have been out in the world for a while. We find that people who have been in school since kindergarten just haven't experienced enough to write about. Though they might write charmingly, they just aren't worldly enough. I think one can be a wonderful poet at twenty, but not a great novelist.

Your new book, Foreign Affairs, *was nominated for the American Book Award, the prestigious Critics Circle Award, and received the 1984 Pulitzer Prize. Do you think this is your best book to date?*

It's always nice to know that people are reading your book. It's all so arbitrary because I don't think that this book is any better than my other books. So much depends on timing, publicity, or whether or not your editor has another book he wants to push. Does your editor and publisher think that what you have to say is going to appeal to a larger audience? In this instance they do because the book says that it's possible for a not particularly attractive woman over fifty to have a romantic love affair. The publisher thinks that a great many women, forty and over, are going to want to read this book. When they guess something is going to be a success they spend a great deal of money on advertising and promotion and like a self-fulfilling prophecy the book becomes successful.

One last question. Do you think there is hope for continuing life as we know it on this planet? Or do you think we will annihilate ourselves?

I'm hoping we won't annihilate ourselves. I'm a little more optimistic than some of my friends because I remember my father saying, after the bomb was dropped on Hiroshima, that the world would end in ten years. Well, it didn't. So I think we might muddle through for a while yet.

Source: Liz Lear, "Alison Lurie: An Interview," in *Key West Review*, Vol. 1, No. 1, Spring 1988, pp. 42–52.

Dorothy Wickenden

In the following review, Wickenden describes Lurie's novel as an "exercise in verbal and structural ingenuity" and argues that her characters are unappealing with secrets "no longer enticing."

Alison Lurie's world, for all its domestic discord, has always been snug. She draws us inside the sheltered environs of academe and marriage with homely scenes and limpid prose, and then regales us with indiscreet confidences about her characters' lives. We are made to feel a privileged acquaintance, with whom she can share her exasperation about the blunders, the neuroses, and the self-indulgences of the others. In her early fiction, and in her widely admired fifth novel, *The War Between the Tates,* Lurie submitted her characters to all of the indignities of the post-'50s social and sexual revolution, and left them battered and dazed. In her last novel, *Only Children,* a clever though rather cloying pastoral comedy which takes place at a summer house over the Fourth of July weekend in 1932, she examined the sexual antics of two couples and their hostess largely through the eyes of two 8-year-old-girls. Underlying all of this disorder was the sardonic voice and steady hand of Lurie herself, deftly putting the pieces back in place.

"Still simplicities and stereotypes aside, Lurie is as deft as ever when she turns to the mortifications of romance. She is an uncannily accurate observer of the ambivalent emotions that enter into unconventional sexual alliances. . . ."

In *Foreign Affairs,* although Lurie leaves her American setting behind and ventures into the bowels of the British Museum and the drawing rooms of country estates, she carries along many of her old belongings. The two characters at the center of the story, Vinnie Miner and Fred Turner, are by now familiar types in her fiction: professors from Corinth University who are painfully aware of their own provincialism, but seemingly incapable of overcoming it. Vinnie is a jaded, unattractive middle-aged specialist in children's folklore with "no significant identity outside her career"; Fred, a dashing but priggish and dim-witted young colleague who is writing a book about John Gay and pinning over his estranged wife, Roo (who has grown from the animal-loving child in *The War Between the Tates* into a defiantly feminist photographer). They are on leave to pursue projects in London of equally dubious scholarly merit, and to indulge in unrestrained Anglophilia.

Unexpectedly, however, sexual adventures beckon for both of them. In an effort to forget Roo, Fred impulsively takes up with a stunning British aristocrat and actress named Lady Rosemary Radley; and Vinnie, who is nursing her rage over a vicious reference in *The Atlantic* to her life's work as "a scholarly study of playground doggerel," is slowly won over, to her chagrin, by the man who sat next to her on the flight to London, a retired waste disposal engineer from Tulsa named Chuck Mumpson. As Vinnie is making her startling discovery of the true Chuck (he's a lovable—even witty—oaf, not a boorish one), Fred is slowly uncovering the sordid truth about Lady Rosemary (her refined Boucher-like features mask dissipation, just as his own Edwardian looks and manners disguise an empty soul). In the process each stumbles across the rotting underbelly of Britain's upper class, and both briefly reckon with their own neglected consciences.

There is potential here for the kind of sharp social satire Lurie excels in, and the novel contains flashes of her distinctive wit and style. But *Foreign Affairs,* like its two protagonists, is hampered by an inability to surmount its own pettiness. The plot is mechanical and cluttered with unpolished jottings on everything from tourist disorientation to the ways in which specialists in Vinnie's field relate to real children; and the characters are both overwrought and undeveloped. Even Lurie's keen ear for colloquial speech and her eye for revealing mannerisms frequently fail her: in characterizing Chuck and Rosemary, Lurie vacillates between joining Vinnie and Fred in their crude typecasting—Chuck talks in an exaggerated Western twang; Rosemary flutters and giggles and pouts—and taking them to task for it.

All of Lurie's novels are programmatic: like most comic writers she relies upon formal contrivances to heighten irony, to create startling juxtapositions, to make a larger point about the individual's accommodations to the demands of society. In *The War Between the Tates* Erica and Brian's marital battles were punctuated by a sonorous voice-over narration which compared them to the social and political upheavals accompanying the Vietnam War. In *Only Children* Lurie failed in her occasional attempts to blend the naïveté of two little girls with her own stinging cynicism. But Erica and Brian were energetically and realistically drawn; and Lolly and Mary Ann, if somewhat limited as narrators, brought a fresh glimpse into the old themes of marital boredom and infidelity. In both novels Lurie credibly evoked a chapter in American social history. Alas, in *Foreign Affairs* the characters are so unappealing and the contrivances of plot so labored that the ironies are leaden rather than leavening. And, its title notwithstanding, the only affairs she addresses here are carnal.

As for the lessons Lurie lays out, they are of the most rudimentary sociopsychological sort. Yet these two reputable professors are maddeningly slow learners. Fred, filled with self-love, can't find happiness until his obsession with what Lady Rosemary represents is replaced by a clear-eyed recognition of what she is. (Even his lovers assume the shape of academic equations in his mind: "She is small, soft, and fair; Roo large, sturdy, and dark. . . . In manner and speech Rosemary is grateful, melodious; Roo by comparison clumsy and loud—in fact, coarse. Just as, compared with England, America is large, naïve, noisy, crude, etc.") It is during a game of charades—what else?—that he has his first vague glimmerings that Rosemary is not quite the fragile English flower she seems. Suddenly she and her cultivated friends appear raucous, even depraved: Rosemary "is not only vulgarly made up and loaded with costume jewelry, but is wearing the lace butterfly nightgown in which, just a few hours ago. . . . He wants to protest, but makes himself laugh along with the rest; after all, it's only a game." Vinnie, for her part, filled with self-hate, must not only cease to see Chuck Mumpson as a source of revulsion and pity, but herself as well. "Vinnie doesn't want her London friends to confuse her with Chuck, to think of her as after all rather simple, vulgar, and amusing—a typical American." In the end, of course, it becomes clear to Fred that Lady Rosemary, far from representing "the best of England," actually embodies the destructive self-indulgence of a decadent class society; and to Vinnie that Chuck, who reminds her of all that's shameful and ugly in America, in fact personifies American openness and stolid decency.

Still simplicities and stereotypes aside, Lurie is as deft as ever when she turns to the mortifications of romance. She is an uncannily accurate observer of the ambivalent emotions that enter into unconventional sexual alliances, and when she abandons her gimmicky plot devices and moral posturing, *Foreign Affairs* is funny, touching, and even suspenseful. As Fred's affair with Lady Rosemary is being consumed in horror (the final revelation scene is a weirdly appropriate combination of Hitchcock suspense and Lurie humor), Vinnie's affair with Chuck is being consummated in a moment of poignant farce. This odd couple is finally brought together thanks to a suitably ludicrous matchmaker: Chuck's plastic fold-up raincoat.

At last, a character with integrity. This homely garment not only has a perverse charm of its own, it also helps to transform Vinnie, the perpetually peevish man-hating snob, into a flustered, touchingly vulnerable woman. When Vinnie and Chuck first bump into each other in London, she disdainfully notes that he is wearing "a semi-transparent greenish plastic raincoat of the most repellent American sort," and registers it as an emblem of his personality: coarse, tasteless. Yet the raincoat comes to show Vinnie more about her own shortcomings than it does about Chuck's. Her hatred of it festers over the weeks, and she turns on it in furious embarrassment after Chuck's first bumbling embrace in her tiny kitchen, in which he knocks a bowl of watercress and avocado soup over them both: "If he only had a decent raincoat instead of that awful transparent plastic thing—she gives it a nasty look as it hangs in the hall—then he could wear that while his clothes dried, or even go home in it." In several quick scenes the raincoat explains Vinnie's social pretensions and fragile dignity; and in the scenes that follow, it gives credence to the evolution of her contempt for Chuck into tolerance, affection, and—most remarkably of all—hearty sexual appetite.

In *Foreign Affairs* Lurie shows once again that she is a farsighted observer of human fallibilities, but an odd kind of moralist. Hers is a particularly brutal form of mockery: she forces her characters into compromising positions and then denies them any real escape. The end of the novel superficially follows the traditional comic pattern—the characters are sent back home; the social order resumes—but Lurie doesn't think much of spiritual regeneration. In the departure lounge at Heathrow, Fred begins to berate himself for behaving like a cad toward both Roo (who has forgiven him) and Rosemary (who has not), and to reflect on his shattering experiences in London. "Well, if he's learned one thing this year, it's that everyone is vulnerable, no matter how strong and independent they look. . . . Fred feels worse about himself than he has ever felt in his adult life." Even this elementary insight, however, is quickly supplanted: "he is, after all, a young, well-educated, good-looking American, an assistant professor in a major university; and he is on his way home to a beautiful woman who loves him." Vinnie, whose affair has ended no less disastrously, is courageous enough to confess to her gossipy British friend Edwin, who makes a slighting remark about Chuck, that she loved him. "Something has changed, she thinks. She isn't the same person she was; she has loved and been loved." An hour later she's telling herself, "It's not her nature, not her fate to be loved . . . her fate is to be always single, unloved, alone."

Of course, neither Fred nor Vinnie has essentially changed at all: he is still impossibly obtuse, she has reverted to whining self-pity. This elaborate novel is more of an exercise in verbal and structural ingenuity than it is a full-fledged comedy or melodrama. The snugness has become oppressive, and the secrets Lurie invites us to share, no longer enticing, are for the most part trivial, sordid, and sad.

Source: Dorothy Wickenden, "Love in London," in the *New Republic*, Vol. 191, No. 15, October 8, 1984, pp. 34–36.

Sources

Clemons, Walter, "Lovers and Other Strangers," in *Newsweek*, September 24, 1984, p. 80.

Keats, John, *Keats: Poetical Works*, edited by H. W. Garrod, Oxford University Press, 1973, p. 351.

Lehmann-Haupt, Christopher, Review of *Foreign Affairs*, in *New York Times*, September 13, 1984, p. C21.

Lurie, Alison, *Foreign Affairs*, Random House, 1984.

Review of *Foreign Affairs*, in *New Yorker*, November 5, 1984, p. 170.

Review of *Foreign Affairs*, in *People Weekly*, Vol. 22, November 5, 1984, pp. 18–19.

Further Reading

Costa, Richard Hauer, *Alison Lurie*, Twayne, 1992, pp. 55–60.
Costa offers a reading of *Foreign Affairs* that emphasizes Lurie's debt to Henry James, especially to James's novel, *The Ambassadors* (1903).

Lear, Liz, "Alison Lurie: An Interview," *Key West Review*, Vol. 1, No. 1, Spring 1988, pp. 42–52.
Lurie talks about living in Key West, Florida, where she spent the winter months; her writing practices; her favorite authors, and other topics.

Newman, Judie, "Paleface into Redskin: Cultural Transformations in Alison Lurie's *Foreign Affairs*," in *Forked Tongues? Comparing Twentieth-Century British and American Literature*, edited by Ann Massa and Alistair Stead, Longman, 1994, pp. 188–205.
Newman discusses the interactions in the novel between American and British culture.

Rogers, Katharine M., "Alison Lurie: The Uses of Adultery," in *American Women Writing Fiction: Memory, Identity, Family, Space*, edited by Mickey Pearlman, University of Kentucky Press, 1989, pp. 114–34.
This article covers Lurie's fiction up to and including *Foreign Affairs*. Rogers's analysis focuses on how the protagonists in these novels learn to look critically at their own lives.

Showalter, Elaine, *Faculty Towers: The Academic Novel and Its Discontents*, University of Pennsylvania Press, 2005.
Elaine Showalter's study is a decade-by-decade survey by a leading American feminist scholar of the history of the academic novel. Showalter discusses Lurie's work as well as books by David Lodge, Philip Roth, Jonathan Franzen, Francine Prose, Mary McCarthy, Malcolm Bradbury, and others. Showalter argues that academic novels provide a comprehensive social history of the university as well as a guide to the academic profession

Forever . . .

Judy Blume

1975

Forever . . . , published in 1975, is Judy Blume's eleventh book and in some ways has remained a troublesome publication for the author. Despite the fact that it is one of the most popular with her readers, it is also one of the most controversial of Blume's books, with some librarians and county officials having banned it shortly after it appeared and as recently as 2005. The book even has made it on the American Library Association's (ALA) top one hundred banned books list.

The controversy revolves around the candid discussion of teenage sex that *Forever . . .* provides. Some parents have complained that they could understand why the book might have been banned when they were teens in the 1970s, but they do not understand why it is banned in the early 2000s. Despite their arguments, however, Blume's book still stirs the emotions and not just of those who read it for enjoyment.

The story is about young love, the first sexual encounter of a high school girl. Katherine, the protagonist, wants to make her first experience mean something. She does not want to lose her virginity merely for the sake of physical satisfaction or curiosity. She wants her relationship with her boyfriend Michael to have emotions attached to it. Her and Michael's relationship deepens, and finally she relents to his gentle suggestions.

Katherine learns more than just what it means to have a sexual relationship. She matures through the process, gains confidence, and discovers that

Judy Blume © AP Images

when one is young, sometimes "forever" does not mean the same thing as "everlasting."

Author Biography

Judy Blume was born February 12, 1938, in Elizabeth, New Jersey. She attended New York University and was married before she earned her degree in education in 1961. By 1970, Blume had two children and had published two somewhat traditional children's books, but neither of them exhibited what would become the author's trademark: frank subject matter aimed at an adolescent audience. Blume's *Are You There God? It's Me, Margaret* (1970) was the first book to draw notice, not all of it positive. In the 1970s, placing frank discussion about first bras, menstruation, and breasts in a novel was not considered proper. But of course, Blume's young readers loved it. Libraries, however, had trouble with it. According to Karen Holt, in an article written for *Publishers Weekly*, *Are You There God? It's Me, Margaret* "is one of five books by Blume that appear on the American Library Association's list of most frequently challenged books of the 1990s." The other four, according to Holt, are Blume's *Deenie* (1973), *Blubber* (1974), *Forever . . .* (1975), and *Tiger Eyes* (1981).

Between 1970 and the early 1990s, Blume wrote eighteen more young adult novels and three novels for adult readers. One of her most loveable characters, Farley Drexel Hatcher (called "Fudge") was first brought to life in Blume's *Tales of a Fourth Grade Nothing* (1972). Blume's son Larry inspired this character. Fudge was so loved by readers that Blume created *Superfudge* (1980) and *Fudge-a-mania* (1990). Blume's grandson Elliot, according to an interview with Blume conducted by Mary Ann Grossman for the *St. Paul Pioneer Press* (October 4, 2002), encouraged the author to bring Fudge up to the twenty-first century. In 2003, *Double Fudge* was published.

As of 2006, Blume lived in New York City, in Key West, Florida, and on Martha's Vineyard in Massachusetts, with her husband George Cooper, a law professor and also a writer.

Plot Summary

Chapters 1–4

At the beginning of *Forever . . .*, the protagonist, Katherine, and her best friend Erica, (both seniors in high school) attend a New Year's Eve party. The party is given by Erica's cousin Sybil, who is described as having a poor self-image because she is overweight and tends to be sexually promiscuous in order to feel loved. At the party, Katherine meets Michael, a friend of Sybil. The next day, Michael asks Katherine to go for a drive with him. Afterward, he kisses Katherine before saying good-bye and tells Katherine that she is delicious.

Katherine is at home, telling her mother that she has met a nice boy and that she has a date with him that weekend. Katherine describes her mother, whose name is Diana and who works in the children's room at the local library, as thin and tall and not necessarily athletic. Jamie, Katherine's younger sister, is also introduced. Jamie is in the seventh grade and is artistic, unlike Katherine. Jamie and Katherine, despite their age difference, appear to be friends. They respect one another's talents and are supportive of one another. Jamie volunteers, for example, to embroider a design on Katherine's jeans to wear on her first official date with Michael.

Katherine then talks about Tommy Aronson, the boy whom she dated before she met Michael. Her relationship with Tommy was not good. Tommy dated Katherine, she finally discovered, only to have sex with her. When Katherine made it clear that she did not want to have sex with him, Tommy dropped her for another girl, presumably one who would. Unlike Tommy, Michael makes Katherine feel good about herself. He is attentive and caring.

Katherine invites Michael to come back to her house after their date. She takes him to a private room downstairs that has a lock on the door. They start to kiss, but Katherine stops Michael when he goes a little too fast for her. He asks if she is a virgin, to which Katherine answers yes.

Katherine introduces her father, who is a pharmacist. Later, Katherine invites Michael and Erica over to the house. Michael brings Artie with him. Erica and Artie play backgammon in the kitchen, while Michael and Katherine retreat to the downstairs room. They kiss, but Katherine stops Michael again because he is moving too fast for her. Michael and Artie leave, and Erica spends the night. Erica says that Artie seems shy because he did not even try to kiss her. Then Katherine and Erica discuss their feelings about sex. Erica says that girls do not have to be in love to have sex, but Katherine disagrees.

Chapters 5–7

Jamie plans a big dinner with her grandmother, who has come to stay with the girls while their parents are away. Michael picks Katherine up one night at the hospital where she works as a candy striper. Michael invites Katherine to his school's play. Artie has the lead role, so Katherine then invites Erica to come along. When they get home, Katherine introduces Michael to her grandmother, who later warns Katherine to be careful about pregnancy and venereal diseases. Katherine is a little embarrassed and disturbed that her grandmother assumes that Katherine will have sex.

After Michael leaves, Jamie tells Katherine that she wishes Michael had a younger brother. When Jamie asks if Katherine and Michael are having sex, Katherine becomes upset. Jamie tells her that Katherine's generation is too hung up on sex.

By chapter six, Erica is frustrated in her relationship with Artie. He still has not kissed her, so she tells Katherine that she plans on doing something about it. The two girls then go to see Artie in the school play. Sybil and Elizabeth are also in it. When Katherine sees Elizabeth, her jealousy begins to swell. By the time the play is over and everyone has gone to Elizabeth's house for a party, Katherine has trouble controlling her emotions. Everyone congratulates Artie for his wonderful performance, but this is not a sufficient distraction for Katherine, who can barely talk because she is so emotional.

Michael and Katherine leave the party early and end up at Katherine's house. They make out for awhile, but once again Katherine stops Michael when she thinks he is going too far. She tells him that she might be physically ready to have sex, but she also wants to be mentally ready, too. Later, when she is alone, she realizes that the thought of sex frightens her.

In the next chapter, Michael invites Katherine to go skiing with him and his sister and her husband in Vermont. Katherine would be away from home for three nights, so her parents want to think it over before giving Katherine an answer. As Katherine waits for her parents' answer, she talks to Erica about the tension she is feeling. Erica informs Katherine that Artie has told her that he might be gay. He is in the process of trying to find out what his sexual feelings are. Erica has told Artie that she will help him find out. Later, Katherine finds out that her parents have agreed to let her go.

Chapters 8–9

The next two chapters are set in Vermont. Katherine and Michael have adjoining bedrooms and before Katherine falls asleep, Michael comes in and asks if he can be with her. Katherine tells him not to get too physically aroused because she does not want to have sex. That is when Michael tells Katherine that he loves her. Katherine is not ready to say this back to Michael, although she feels she loves him. They fall asleep in one another's arms.

Before they go skiing the next day, Sharon and Katherine have a talk. Sharon tells Katherine that Michael is a good boy and is also very vulnerable; and she does not want to see Michael get hurt. This comment concerns Katherine, who wonders if Sharon thinks that Katherine is just using Michael.

Michael teaches Katherine to ski. They are on the slopes all day. At night, they return to the apartment to find Ike and Sharon smoking marijuana. Both Katherine and Michael have tried it before, but they pass on the invitation to join the other two. Instead, they go to bed. Michael climbs into bed with Katherine, and they make out. This time, they both reach climaxes without having full intercourse. Before going to sleep, Katherine tells Michael that she loves him.

Chapters 10–13

When Katherine returns from Vermont, her father confesses that he is concerned that Katherine is getting too involved with Michael. He does not want to see her tied down to one boy, he tells her. The next morning, Katherine's mother explains that Katherine's father just wants to see her spending time with more people. On the way to school, Katherine asks if her mom was a virgin when she married Katherine's father. Her mother says she was until they were engaged. Katherine's father was not a virgin, however. But Katherine's mother explains that there were different standards for girls and boys back then. It was all right for boys to have sex. But girls were supposed to be virgins when they got married. Katherine's mom then warns Katherine that having sex with someone can make her more vulnerable. She also tells Katherine that she is not going to tell Katherine what to do. It is up to her, but Katherine should make sure that she is ready for it.

Later, Erica says she cannot believe that Katherine is still a virgin, although Katherine has not admitted whether she is. Erica says that she can tell, however, that Katherine has not yet had sex. Katherine then tells Erica that what she does with Michael is private, and she does not want to share it. She also confesses to Erica that she really loves Michael. Erica tells Katherine that she believes that Artie is not gay but rather impotent.

On a double date, Erica announces that Artie has been accepted at the American Academy of Dramatic Arts, a school that Artie would love to attend. Artie's father, however, refuses to let him go. When Erica tells Artie that he should stand up to his father, Michael tells Erica to leave it alone. Later, Katherine tells Michael that she has never seen Artie so depressed.

Michael goes away for ten days with his sister. It is a ski trip, one that will help Michael get his instructor's certificate. Katherine stays busy, but she misses him a lot. Katherine's father again makes the statement that he wishes Katherine would see someone in addition to Michael. Katherine's mother makes the point that Katherine will have to learn to live without Michael when she goes away to college in the fall. This comment makes Katherine go to her counselor to try to apply to the University of Vermont. She wants to go to school wherever Michael goes. When Katherine is told that she will need her parents' permission to apply, Katherine assumes they will support her change of mind. But they do not.

Michael comes back from the ski trip early and surprises Katherine. They go on a date, and Katherine cracks a joke about venereal disease (VD), but Michael does not find it funny. Then he confesses that he once had what he refers to as the clap.

Katherine and Michael end up at Michael's sister's apartment. Sharon and Ike are out of town. Katherine and Michael spend time in bed together, but it is not until the next night that Katherine finally loses her virginity. The experience is a little disappointing, and Katherine wonders why everyone makes such a big deal about it.

Katherine's old boyfriend, Tommy Aronson, calls at the beginning of chapter 13. He is back in town and wants to see Katherine. She sees right through him, knowing that all he wants is sex. She turns him down for that reason and the fact that she has no interest in him any more.

Chapters 14–16

Katherine receives a package from her grandmother. It is filled with Planned Parenthood pamphlets. Katherine calls her grandmother and sets a date with her. Katherine then telephones Planned Parenthood and makes an appointment with them. In chapter fifteen, one of the clinicians at Planned Parenthood asks Katherine some personal questions about her relationship with Michael. They then discuss various birth control devices. Katherine is also tested for gonorrhea, a sexually transmitted disease. By the end of the chapter, Katherine has chosen a birth control pill to use.

Both Michael and Katherine come down with the flu. They must stay apart from one another for several days. When Michael takes Katherine out on her birthday, he gives her a present. It is a necklace that holds a small silver disk with "Katherine" engraved on one side and "Forever . . . Michael" on the other. Katherine tells Michael that she has a surprise for him, too. She tells him that she is now on the pill.

Katherine and Michael go to Michael's house. His parents will be gone until midnight. They make love in Michael's bed and afterward take their first shower together.

Chapters 17–19

Katherine mentions that her sister, Jamie, is going back to a summer camp in New Hampshire, but Katherine does not yet know what she will be doing for the summer. She has been job hunting without success. Michael is looking for a summer job also.

Erica, in the meantime, has found a position on the local newspaper. Erica tells Katherine that her cousin Sybil is pregnant. Sybil has been able to hide her pregnancy from everyone because she wore large-sized dresses, as she always had. Sybil is planning on giving the baby up for adoption.

Because Katherine's parents will not give her permission to apply to another college just to be with Michael, Katherine and Michael develop a plan of their own. Michael will take off one semester and work as a ski instructor in Colorado.

Katherine's father announces that he has talked to Sam Fox, the director of the summer camp that Jamie will attend. Sam tells Katherine's father that he needs a tennis counselor, since one of the counselors he had hired is sick. Katherine's father tells Sam that he is sure Katherine would love to work there. Katherine balks at the idea. It would mean being away from Michael. Katherine's father insists that Katherine take the job. She has no choice. Katherine is very upset.

Erica invites Katherine, Michael, and Artie to her house, while her parents are away. They celebrate Michael's birthday, but this depresses Artie, who sees no future for himself. Later, the couples go their separate ways to different rooms. Katherine tells Michael that she has to go to New Hampshire for the summer. Michael announces then that he accepted a summer job in North Carolina. Michael's parents wanted him to take it. Katherine and Michael resolve not to let the separation change their relationship as their parents are hoping it will.

After the boys leave, Katherine finds Erica crying in her bedroom. She has told Artie that she cannot take it anymore. She cannot help him any further. Artie then locked himself in her bathroom and threatened to kill himself. Artie later calms down, as if he were acting out a role, and tells Erica that he does not blame her.

At the beginning of chapter 19, Artie has tried to hang himself from the shower curtain rod in his bathroom. The attempt failed because the rod broke. He has been taken to a private psychiatric hospital. Both Michael and Erica feel guilty about not having done more for Artie. The chapter ends with Michael and Erica going out with Katherine to a bar and getting very drunk.

Chapters 20–26

Sybil has her baby. Erica and Katherine visit Sybil in the hospital. Sybil will miss her graduation but has decided to lose weight and to accept Smith's offer for college. She is also going to be fitted for an intrauterine device (IUD), a birth control device. She poses a strong front in giving away her baby, but both Erica and Katherine are near tears.

Katherine attends Michael's graduation. It is sad for her when both Sybil's and Artie's names are called and no one appears on stage. Katherine's graduation is held next. Shortly afterward, Erica invites Katherine and Michael to her parents' summer home on Long Beach Island. Four days after that, Katherine and her sister, Jamie, are at the New Hampshire camp.

Chapter twenty-two consists of a series of letters. Katherine and Michael exchange news and details of their lives and write about how much they are missing each other. In a letter to her parents, Katherine first mentions Theo, the head of the tennis program at the camp. She also mentions Theo to Erica. Katherine writes a quick note to Artie who is still hospitalized.

In chapter twenty-three, Katherine narrates a typical day at camp. Readers can tell that she is becoming somewhat attracted to Theo. She describes in detail what he looks like. The two of them play tennis together and go swimming. One night, Theo asks Katherine about the necklace she wears, the one that Michael gave her for her birthday. When he sees the word "Forever" engraved on one side, Theo tells her that he thinks forever is a very long time for someone as young as Katherine. Later, Katherine dreams she is making love to Theo and feels ashamed. One night, Theo asks her to slow dance with him. After the dance, Katherine runs away and cries because she does not understand her mixed emotions. When Katherine's parents come to visit, she shows them a box stuffed with letters from Michael. She confronts them by saying she bets they thought the separation would stop them from communicating. The box of letters is proof that the separation has not affected their relationship, Katherine half-heartedly believes.

Chapter twenty-four brings the news that Katherine's grandfather has died. Katherine's parents believe that it is best that neither Katherine nor Jamie come home. Grandpa did not want a funeral, and their grandmother will appreciate the solitude for a couple weeks.

Theo comforts Katherine when she tells him why she is crying. When Theo walks Katherine back to her cabin, he kisses her on the forehead. Katherine then pulls him into her and kisses him on the mouth. However, Theo gently untangles himself from her arms and tells her that he does not want her like this, implying in her time of weakness. Katherine stops writing to Michael, as she needs time to think. Finally, she writes him a letter, trying to be as honest as she can. She tells Michael that she has met someone else, but she is not sure what her emotions are. She cannot finish the letter and decides that she could never send it.

Michael surprises Katherine with a visit at the camp. He catches Katherine holding hands with Theo. Later, when Katherine and Michael are in Michael's motel room, Michael wants to make love, but Katherine cannot do it. Michael guesses that there is some other guy in her life. Michael refers to the necklace and the word "Forever." He wants to know what that means now. Michael decides that their relationship can never be the same again, although Katherine holds onto the hope that it can. Michael tells Katherine that he is not about to share her with anyone. He says she cannot have it both ways. Katherine asks if that means it is all over between them. Michael says that he thinks it is. Katherine takes off the necklace and gives it to Michael. But Michael drops it into Katherine's purse.

Katherine returns home. She accidentally bumps into Michael while she is out with Erica. Michael tells them that Artie is home. He also tells Katherine that he was offered the ski instructor position at Vail, which means he could be in Colorado during the winter. But he is not certain he will take it. He says that it all depends on, and then he does not finish his sentence. Katherine tries to explain to Michael that she will always love him. And they part.

The book ends with Katherine at home. She has just been told that Theo has called.

Characters

Tommy Aronson

Tommy is the boy whom Katherine, the protagonist, liked before she met Michael. Katherine had a crush on Tommy and thought she loved him. But she soon discovered that all Tommy wanted her for was to have sex. When she turned him down, he dropped her and found another girl. Tommy is one year older than Katherine and goes away to college in Katherine's senior year. When he comes back to town, he calls Katherine up and asks her to go out with him. By this time, Katherine is over him and turns him down. Tommy represents the negative side of boys who attach no emotions to a sexual relationship. He was barely interested in friendship. All he wanted to experience was the pleasure of having sex.

Diana Danziger

Diana is Katherine's mother. She is a librarian, specializing in children's literature. Diana is very supportive of her daughter and fairly open minded for the timeframe of this novel. She speaks rather candidly to Katherine about boyfriends and relationships. She allows Katherine to go on trips with Michael. She is not as candid as her mother, Hallie Gross, however. Diana stops short of helping Katherine to find a method of birth control. Rather, Diana talks in generalities and hopes that Katherine is smart enough to take care of the details. Although Diana approves of Katherine's relationship with Michael, she supports her husband when it comes time to separate Katherine from Michael during the summer after high school graduation. The separation, the parents hope, will cool the bond between Katherine and Michael, which it does. Diana is aware that Katherine has much more time ahead of her to become serious with some boy. She wants her daughter to explore more possibilities before making a final decision. Since Diana is also a professional woman, she does not want her daughter to be so focused on a love relationship that she forgets, or loses interesting in, her studies and other activities. In other words, Diana wants her daughter to have more options. Diana is a woman of the world. But when it comes to her daughter, she clamps down a bit, falling back into the influences of the 1950s when silence about certain topics seemed the best practice.

Jamie Danziger

Jamie is Katherine's younger sister. She is everything that Katherine is not. Jamie is very artistic. She creates designs that her family then turns into rugs. She sews artistic patterns on clothes; she paints; and she plays the piano. She is not athletic like her sister, Katherine, but Jamie wishes that she were. She is supportive of her sister and cooks a delicious meal for Katherine and Michael to celebrate their relationship. She has a slight crush on Michael but not in a competitive manner. She merely likes him and wishes he had a younger brother. She is much the admiring younger sister. The author uses Jamie and a few generic younger teenagers to help reflect on Katherine's slightly more mature perceptions of life and love.

Katherine Danziger

Katherine is the protagonist of this story. It is through her perception that the story is told. She is a senior in high school and a virgin when the story opens. She is very rational and must think things through before she acts on them. This habit has protected her from having sex with Tommy Aronson, who was merely interested in her body. Katherine is attracted to Michael as soon as she meets him, although she does not admit it to herself immediately. As the relationship develops, she thinks she wants to have sex with him, but she is a bit frightened by the situation. She keeps pulling back, wanting to sort through her feelings. Eventually she gives in and feels herself falling in love with Michael. She wants to be with him all the time.

Katherine begins to rearrange her life so that she can spend more time with Michael, and she becomes angered when her parents try to thwart her efforts. Her parents insist that she take a job at a summer camp, away from Michael, the summer after her graduation from high school. While at the camp, she finds that she is attracted to another boy, Theo. She does not quite understand why. She has trouble explaining her lack of loyalty to Michael, even to herself.

Katherine is often confused by her mixed emotions. Even by the end of the book, Katherine does not really come to any clear conclusions. She does sense, however, that she is ready to travel down some roads (such as losing her virginity) but not others (such as committing herself to Michael forever). She is portrayed, in some ways, as a typical teenager, who fights her parents' attempts to completely dominate and define her. This difficult struggle must take place in order for a teen to mature into an adult. Hopefully, as this process is portrayed through Katherine, the struggle does not damage the teen's relationship with the parents.

Although it is not explained, apparently by the end of the story Katherine realizes that the love she feels for Michael was developed through the experience of having lost her virginity with him. Though that experience is memorable, it does not warrant her making a permanent commitment to Michael. Theo makes her realize that she has many other emotions to explore and many more experiences to have before she is ready to settle down with one person. Katherine's parents have led her in the right direction, but she must choose for herself whether to walk down that path.

Mr. Danziger

Katherine's father is a pharmacist and owns two drug stores. He is an athlete, like Katherine, and is also good at tennis as Katherine is. He is a little more protective of Katherine than Katherine's mother and usually argues against Katherine's going away with Michael. He insists that Katherine take the job as tennis instructor at the summer camp. He is more rigid or maybe old fashioned in his ways. And the fact that his first name is never offered, could reflect some of the older generation's attitudes about the roles for men and women. Katherine's mother (whose first name is provided), on the other hand, is a little more progressive, but not by much.

Sybil Davison

It is Sybil's New Year's Eve party that opens this story. Sybil is Erica's cousin. She is sexually promiscuous, behavior the narrator links to low self-esteem. Her self-image is also suggested in the fact that she is overweight. She equates sexual attention with love. In the end, Sybil gets pregnant. She decides to give her baby up for adoption, to lose weight, and to be fitted with an IUD, a birth control device. She also accepts the offer to attend Smith College. In the story, Sybil dramatizes all the wrong reasons to experiment with sex, and she suffers the consequences of not protecting herself. By the end of the story, however, Sybil attempts to turn her life around.

Grandpa Gross

Grandpa Gross is Hallie's husband and Katherine's maternal grandfather. As with Katherine's father, Grandpa's first name is never provided. Like Hallie, his wife, Grandpa is a lawyer. He has suffered a stroke, however, and no longer works. Toward the end of the story, Grandpa dies. Since he has told his family that he does not want a funeral, Katherine's mother decides that it is not necessary for Katherine and Jamie to come home from summer camp. Katherine must mourn the loss while still at camp, which draws her to Theo.

Hallie Gross

Hallie Gross, Katherine's maternal grandmother, is a politically active lawyer who once ran for the U.S. Congress. She is involved with Planned Parenthood and suggests that Katherine go to the clinic for some kind of birth control. Almost seventy years old, she comes over in January to baby sit Katherine and Jamie when Katherine's parents take a winter vacation. Hallie is a progressive woman for her generation. She is more liberal than her own daughter, Katherine's mother. Whereas Katherine's mother only hints at sexuality in her conversations with Katherine, Hallie is blunt and forthcoming. Because of Hallie, Katherine starts taking an oral contraceptive pill.

Elizabeth Hailey

Elizabeth is Michael's friend. She is his date in the opening scene at Sybil's New Year's Eve party. Katherine sees Michael kiss Elizabeth, and later Katherine is jealous of her. Katherine holds a party after the school play in which Artie is a star. Elizabeth's role in the novel seems mostly to stimulate Katherine's insecurity.

Ike

Ike is married to Michael's sister. Katherine's mother is impressed by the fact that Ike is a resident in internal medicine, which makes her feel more secure about Katherine's safety when Katherine goes to Vermont on the ski trip. Although he is a doctor, Ike smokes marijuana, which surprises Katherine. Her response suggests that Katherine is more mature or more rational than Ike. Katherine thinks before she acts. The suggestion is Ike has not really thought through the consequences of using an illegal drug.

Artie Lewin

Artie is Michael's friend. He is somewhat shy, but when he is up on stage he becomes self-confident. Acting comes naturally to him, and he wants to pursue an acting career. However, his father is against it. Artie is not sure of his sexual orientation. He hides a lot of his feelings behind games that he likes to play when he is in a social setting. Erica tries to help him and discovers that Artie is not gay but rather impotent. Erica finally gives up on Artie, and in the end, Artie has a mental breakdown and tries to commit suicide, which makes Erica and Michael feel guilty, as if they did not help Artie enough. After Artie's attempt, he spends some time in a psychiatric ward and misses his graduation. At the end of the story, Artie is back home.

Sharon

Sharon is Michael's married sister. Katherine meets her on the ski trip to Vermont. Sharon is an anthropologist who works for some museum. She represents (for the 1970s) an independent woman with a career and no children. Sharon, at one point in the story, asks Katherine to be careful with Michael because he is vulnerable emotionally. While this shows Sharon's concern for her brother, it also flips the table on the focus of sexual roles. Typically, concern is expressed for girls because they can become pregnant. Boys, too, this story points out, have emotions and can be hurt, which is what happens when Katherine breaks up with Michael. These are the consequences of early sexual experiences, the story appears to say.

Erica Small

Erica is Katherine's best friend. She is said to be a good analyzer of people and she thinks Katherine is insecure. That is why Katherine tends to be sarcastic when someone exposes her feelings, according to Erica. Erica becomes involved with Artie. Erica wants to have sex with Artie, but he shies away from her. Erica feels responsible for Artie's breakdown after she tells him that she no longer wants to have anything to do with him. She feels guilty when Artie attempts suicide. She believes it is all her fault.

In many ways, Erica represents the opposite of Katherine. However, toward the end of the story, the two girls appear to be fairly similar. Erica is lucky in school, having been accepted at Radcliffe, although Katherine suspects it is not for Erica's grades, which are not as good as Katherine's. But Katherine is more successful in relationships, and apparently Erica is a little jealous of that.

Juliette Small

Juliette Small, Erica's mother, is a famous film critic, and it is through her fame that Erica hopes to be accepted at Radcliffe.

Theo

Theo is the head of the tennis program at the New Hampshire camp where Katherine and Jamie spend the summer after Katherine's graduation from high school. Theo is attracted to Katherine, and she to him. Theo is twenty-one and a senior at Northwestern University, and it could be his maturity that is partially responsible for Katherine's attraction to him. He teases Katherine about the necklace that Katherine wears, the one that says "forever" on it. He counsels Katherine that she is too young to commit herself to anyone. Eventually, it is because of her feelings for Theo that Katherine and Michael break up. Theo represents other experiences Katherine will have, experiences she would miss out on if she continued her exclusive relationship with Michael.

Michael Wagner

Michael is an old friend of Sybil. He returns to Sybil's house the morning after a party just to have a chance to get to know Katherine. A relationship grows between him and Katherine, and he eventually persuades her into having sex with him. Michael is gentle and caring in his relationship with Katherine. Although he prompts Katherine to have sex with him, he does so out of true affection. The relationship appears to be building into something special until Michael takes a job in North Carolina, moving away from Katherine the summer after she graduates from high school. He is caught off guard when Katherine stops writing to him; he arrives at the summer camp where Katherine is working and senses that she might be interested in someone else. Michael is hurt when he discovers that Katherine is not committed to him. He also demonstrates that once two people have sex, they cannot go back to just being friends. Michael cannot handle the idea of Katherine being with any other boy. He tells her that she cannot have it both ways.

Themes

Teenage Sexuality

The major subject of this novel is teenage sexuality. The sexual language of the novel is graphic. The sexual scenes are slightly vague about details, but they are nonetheless realistic. The sexual act is described in open terms. The book was written in the midst of the so-called sexual revolution of the 1970s, when young people were attempting to throw off limiting social rules that, on the surface, demanded that girls remain virgins, while they gave boys permission to act out sexually. As Katherine's mother suggests, there were two types of girls: those who remained virgins were the ones the boys wanted to marry; those who had sex were dated for fun but did not get married. That was the dichotomy that dominated Katherine's mother's time, but it was not necessarily the reality, and the sexual revolution of the 1970s generation brought the truth closer to the surface, as does Blume's book.

There are different attitudes toward sex in this novel. Sybil, who is described as having a poor self-concept, uses sexuality to feel loved and to gain affection from boys. She does so unwisely, and this, Blume points out, is not a good idea no matter what generation a person belongs to. Sybil does not think highly enough of herself to protect herself, and she ends up pregnant.

Erica, a friend of the protagonist, does not believe that people have to be emotionally invested in order to have sex. Sex, to Erica, is a dramatic experience. Erica is eager to gain the knowledge that a sexual encounter affords. Her relationship with Artie, however, is too challenging for her. The topic of male impotence is discussed in connection to Artie. Erica mistakenly believes that if she can attract him, she can cure him. Artie's problem goes too deep, though, and Erica's attempts only make the matter worse. She does not understand the psychological implications in Artie's inability to have an erection.

Michael is more experienced than Erica or Katherine, but not by much. He had one other sexual partner before he met Katherine. Michael did not even know the girl's last name, so apparently he felt no particular commitment to his first partner. Michael wanted to have a sexual encounter, and the unnamed girl was available. But she was a bit too available as the story implies, and Michael receives a sexually transmitted disease in the process.

Katherine is a virgin like Erica. It is through Katherine's relationship with Michael that the story develops. Katherine is rational about engaging in sexual intercourse. At one point, she is so rational that she understands that despite the fact that her body physically longs for the sexual act, her mind is not ready. Katherine also wants the experience to amount to more than just physical satisfaction. She wants to feel something exceptional on an emotional level, too. She wants her first sexual experience to be with a special person. She could have had a sexual (or physical) experience with her previous boyfriend, Tommy Aronson, but she knew that he did not really care about her as a person.

Blume carefully orchestrates the pressures that Katherine feels as a teenage girl moving toward sexual intercourse. Little by little, Katherine weighs the consequences of each of her steps. Blume discusses not only the fear that teenage sexuality can cause but also the joy and pleasure. The author even uses humor by having Michael introduce his penis to Katherine by giving it a name.

Birth Control and Venereal Disease

Blume's novel offers a reminder that teenagers need to protect themselves when they are having sex. Sybil, who is referred to as a genius at the beginning of the book and is smart enough to be accepted by prestigious Smith College, finds herself pregnant. Michael, who was engaged in unprotected sex with a girl he hardly knew, contracts a venereal disease. In the 1970s, when this book was written, there was not as much open discussion of birth control and venereal diseases as there is in the early 2000s. The birth control pill became available in the 1960s. Various IUDs had been used for awhile, but some, such as the Dalkon shield, which was pulled off the market due to its causing serious side effects, caused widespread concern. The most common form of birth control was the prophylactic, or condom.

Topics For Further Study

- Pretend that you have been asked to go before your board of education to argue for censoring this book or for including it in the school library. Prepare a statement, using examples for the book itself and from other research you conduct on censorship. Read your statement to your class.
- Choose a partner and write a dialogue between two of the characters, covering an area of the story that was not fully detailed. For instance, you could write a dialogue between Katherine and Erica that takes place after Katherine returns home and has broken up with Michael. What would the two friends say? Or you could write a dialogue between Michael and Artie, after Artie has been released from the hospital. Choose a portion of the book you are comfortable with. Then act out your dialogue (with a classmate) in front of your class.
- Jamie is portrayed as an artist who creates designs that her parents then make into rugs. Imagine that a play based on *Forever . . .* is going to be staged at your school. You are in charge of set designs, and you need to reproduce the scene in Katherine's house in which Katherine introduces Michael to her family. Create a rug design that the family is working on. Make it as imaginative as you can to reflect Jamie's creativity.
- Gather as much information as you can about teenage pregnancies in your city or state. Compare them to national averages. Then go back a couple of decades. Has the rate decreased or increased since then? What are the experts saying has made a difference? Present your findings to your class.

With the advent of the AIDS crisis in the 1980s, open discussion of venereal disease and other sexually transmitted diseases (STDs) led to widespread public awareness. Although in the 1970s teens knew there were certain diseases that one could catch, the fear of those diseases usually remained in the background. The first fear was becoming pregnant. The inclusion of the character Hallie Gross (the protagonist's grandmother), therefore, was a rather bold choice on Blume's part. The author's decision to send Katherine to Planned Parenthood to learn about birth control and venereal disease shows Blume to have been well ahead of her time. By focusing on both the emotional factors that surround the sexual act and by providing factual information about taking precautions, Blume presents a balanced story. She also provides lessons about sexuality without appearing to preach.

Developing Emotions

Teenage sexual development and activity cause intense emotional reactions. Blume is explicit about the sex act, and she also discusses the emotions that are aroused in intimate relationships.

The protagonist's emotional battles as she confronts her fears of having sex are juxtaposed with her desires for sexual gratification. Added to this conflict are Katherine's concerns about getting pregnant and about contracting a sexually transmitted disease. Moreover, Katherine is confused by the various messages she receives from the adults around her. Katherine becomes annoyed when her grandmother assumes that she is having sex, when Katherine is not. She is likewise annoyed when she is enjoying sex with Michael, yet at the same time, she must hide her feelings from her parents. There are many pressures on young people, Blume is saying through her story, that parents (and teens alike) may not fully realize.

Erica and Artie have different experiences they must try to figure out. Artie feels impotent in various ways. He does not do well academically in school but is a master on stage. However, his father does not appreciate acting as a profession and insists that his son conform to the father's wishes. The parental domination makes Artie feel powerless. He is caught in a no-win situation. This impotence is carried through to his sexuality. Erica believes that her caring and loving caresses as well as her own physical attractiveness are enough to cure Artie's problem. When she discovers they are not, she takes it personally and feels that Artie is draining her emotionally. One thing leads to another, and the emotional storm intensifies. Artie does not understand his impotence any more than Erica does; eventually he tries to kill himself. Erica is then left with a sense of guilt because she believes she has failed Artie. All these emotions are powerful enough to completely devastate a vulnerable teenager. Through this aspect of her story, Blume points out that sexuality is not as simple as some people might believe. Emotional reactions are part of sexuality and are challenging to handle.

Meanwhile, Katherine is thrown into conflict with her parents who force her to take a leave of absence from Michael. Sexual intimacy has made their relationship intense. It is very difficult for Katherine to imagine being without Michael. Yet not too long after the separation, she finds that she enjoys the attention that Theo gives her. She does not understand how this could be possible. How can she love two boys at the same time, she wonders.

The title of Blume's novel points ironically to the emotional fluctuation which the protagonist experiences. Through Theo's words, the author speaks her thematic phrase: "forever" is an inappropriately permanent concept for teenagers. The word implies too much; a "forever" commitment is beyond most young people's scope. Yet when many teenagers engage in sex, they assume the intensity of their emotions means they will always feel this way toward the present partner. They are disillusioned or confused when such intense emotions subside and others take their place. Sexual relationships are not as simple as inexperienced teens may assume.

Style

Romance Novel

In romance novels the main plot concerns falling in love and courtship. There are challenges along the way for the couple, but these are generally overcome. Some secondary characters are not quite as lucky as the two main characters, which provides other views of courtship and distinguishes the main couple's experience from the experiences of others. The romance novel often ends on a happy note. In this case, Blume uses the romance novel as a venue for examining what is different when teenagers become sexually active, so the problems that arise here are connected to the characters' ages, inexperience, and parental strictures or absence. Blume's novel ends with the female protagonist soon to be off to school and onto new adventures. Katherine has made it through her first, quite temporary sexual relationship, not unaffected, but mostly unscathed.

The romance novels of Jane Austen end in appropriate coupling and marriages in which each character gets a suitable mate: good protagonists win equally good mates; self-interested or materialistic characters end up with mates equally limited in virtue. But in Blume's handling, the point is, at least in part, that for teenagers sexual relationships are temporary and their adult lives lie ahead of them, years of experiencing relationships before they enter marriage.

Sexual Education

Although this novel tells a story, its purpose is to educate. The tone is never preachy, but lessons are presented about sexual initiation, birth control methods and how to obtain them, sexually transmitted diseases, and the emotional impact of being sexually active. Through the experiences of the main characters, sensitive topics such as impotence, pregnancy, and the fear that can sometimes precede the sexual act are all presented. Having read the novel, some people may make different decisions regarding sexual choices. Readers never feel, however, that the author is pointing a finger or shaking her head in disapproval. Blume treats her characters sympathetically and without judgment. She allows her readers to witness how a few teenagers deal with their introduction to sexual relationships. She explores the challenges they have to face and the decisions that they make. Blume uses the storyline to present information for young readers who may have questions they hesitate to ask.

Explicit Diction

Diction is word choice, and Blume's language employes the correct term for subjects that may elsewhere be described euphemistically. For example, Blume refers to the male sexual organ as a penis rather than using a slang term. When the two main characters have sex, she describes the scene explicitly. She describes what happens both physically and emotionally. She is equally candid about Artie's impotence and his attempted suicide. She never backs away from a topic that other authors might have avoided, fearing that their audience

Compare & Contrast

- **1970s:** Acquired immunodeficiency syndrome (AIDS) virus (HIV-1) is not yet recognized by the U.S. Centers for Disease Control and Prevention.

  2000s: Over 40 million people in the world are living with human immunodeficiency virus (HIV) and AIDS. By 2005, over 25 million have died from AIDS.

- **1970s:** Approximately 60 out of every 1000 unmarried teenage females give birth.

  2000s: By 2000, these numbers have dropped. Now, fewer than 50 out of every 1000 unmarried teenage females give birth.

- **1970s:** The rate of suicide among teenagers is 5.9 per 100,000.

  2000s: Suicide is the third leading cause of death among young adults at a rate of 7.9 per 100,000.

- **1970s:** According to the American Diabetes Association, 5 percent of American adolescents are considered obese (are 25 percent over their correct body weight).

  2000s: According to the American Diabetes Association, adolescent obesity approaches 20 percent of the U.S. teenage population.

(or their audience's parents) might not understand or might object. She does not condone drugs, but she knows that drugs are often a part of the teenage social scene. She even mentions that her protagonist, Katherine, hears her parents engaging in sexual intercourse, hears her mother, in particular, making funny noises while doing so. Blume's frankness is both the draw for many readers and a reason why others have objected to the novel. Blume's frank treatment of the subject set the book apart from others of its time. The book was controversial, yet it became a classic.

Historical Context

Censorship

Blume's *Forever . . .* was not the author's first novel to be banned. Her *Are You There, God? It's Me, Margaret* (1970) was banned for its discussion of bras and budding breasts. Over the years as an author who was censored, Blume became involved politically, promoting freedom of the press. The impulse to censor and the resistance to censorship is not new. Indeed, as early as 1660, Sir William Avenant in Britain censored seven of Shakespeare's plays because he considered them too bawdy, or vulgar. Hitler burned books that were perceived to threaten or contradict ideas promoted by the Third Reich. In the United States, many books have been banned that were later widely accepted as classics: *Winesburg, Ohio* (1919) by Sherwood Anderson; *Catcher in the Rye* (1951) by J. D. Salinger; *Portnoy's Complaint* (1969) by Philip Roth; and *I Know Why the Caged Bird Sings* (1970) by Maya Angelou.

The American Library Association celebrates the reading of banned books each year during the month of September. This program comes with an endorsement from the U.S. Library of Congress. The association points out that what one era condemns may be applauded in a subsequent period, and it promotes the concept that everyone should have the right to choose what they read. The matter is complicated, however, when the publications fall in the category of pornography and obscenity, and some works have had their content evaluated in a court of law to determine what, if any, cultural benefit the work serves. Such an incident occurred regarding D. H. Lawrence's *Lady Chatterley's Lover*, which was published privately in 1928, published in an expurgated version in London in 1932, and did not appear in a full text version until 1960.

Planned Parenthood

As of the early 2000s, the Planned Parenthood Federation operated about nine hundred facilities across the United States. People at the clinics provide information concerning sexually transmitted diseases (STDs) and birth control measures, and physicians in these centers perform abortions, vasectomies, and breast and cervical exams, to name a few of their services.

Planned Parenthood began in 1916 in Brooklyn, New York, as the National Birth Control League. Margaret Sanger (1883–1966), her sister, Ethel Byrne, and Fania Mindell were in charge of the small office where they handed out information about birth control to the poor people who lived in that community. All three women were arrested for breaking the Comstock Law of 1873, which prohibited the dissemination of birth control information.

In 1922, Sanger formed the American Birth Control League. In 1936, Sanger and her group won a victory when a U.S. court of appeals judge made it legal to ship contraceptives by mail in the United States and ordered liberalization of the Comstock Law. In 1952, the International Planned Parenthood Federation was founded, which as of 2006 included clinics in India, Hong Kong, Singapore, and various European countries.

Controversy has surrounded Planned Parenthood. The services that are provided, especially abortions, go against the tenets of some religions. But this is not the only point of contention. The founder of Planned Parenthood, Margaret Sanger, was criticized for supporting eugenics—a movement that professed the benefits of social intervention in human evolution. Sanger has been criticized for offering birth control methods to the poor to reduce their population, while encouraging the rich and elite to have more babies.

Critical Overview

Judy Blume's novel *Forever . . .* has not received much literary attention over the years. But this book has drawn considerable social criticism, and as a result, it is often banned. The frank discussion of sex in this novel has made it controversial. Jennifer Frey, writing for the *Los Angeles Times*, comments on Blume's wide readership: "Blume's work may be better known for popular appeal than critical acclaim; she's had mixed reviews, but her 23 books have sold more than 75 million copies worldwide." Frey adds: "'Forever' was the book passed around among friends in their teens, each reading it surreptitiously under the bedcovers, sure that its subject matter—a girl's first experience with love and sex—was something parents would label contraband." The reason for Blume's popularity, according to Frey is that "Blume made sense of things in simple, familiar terms. The world she wrote about felt real."

Cautioning regarding the age appropriateness of this novel, a parent in Illinois, according to Rick Margolis, writing for *School Library Journal*, "believed the book's sexual content, obscene language, and drug references to be inappropriate for middle schoolers." A tenth-grader in favor of Blume's *Forever . . .*, according to Beverly Goldberg, writing for *American Libraries*, declared: "Judy Blume did not write the book to be a dirty piece of smut." The book appears on library shelves or disappears from those shelves, depending on the numbers either in favor or against it and concerns about the age of its readers.

In 2004, Blume was honored for her life's work with the National Book Foundation's Medal for Distinguished Contribution to American Letters. Affirming that contribution, Jennifer Goldblatt, writing for the *New York Times* states: "Judy Blume is one of those stealth cultural icons. She has been writing, mainly for children, for more than 30 years. And while the Roths, Rushdies, Updikes and their like grabbed the bulk of bookish headlines, all Ms. Blume did was win the hearts and minds of millions of teenage and pre-teenage readers." Goldblatt adds that Blume's books "have been widely adored and scrutinized for their candid treatment of coming-of-age themes." Goldblatt mentions that Blume's "ability to capture the complexity of growing up and her willingness to tackle subjects such as menstruation and masturbation have earned her legions of loyal fans." Then Goldblatt quotes Seth Lerer as having made the following evaluation of Blume's influence on children's literature: "Blume's impact has been in making it possible to write for young people of all ages about things that young people are concerned about."

Criticism

Joyce Hart

Hart is a published author and former teacher. In the following essay, she examines what Blume's readers seem to cherish most about the author's novels—her frankness.

Judy Blume's novel *Forever . . .* has been criticized and banned for its sexual content. Her fans, however, praise the author's frankness. In many ways, both Blume's critics and fans say the same thing. Blume writes with complete honesty. She is forthright about her characters, presenting them realistically as people who make mistakes and talk about subjects that, in 1975 when the book was published, were not frequently discussed in stories written for teens. This essay explores how Judy Blume presents her material. Just what makes Blume's writing so frank? How does the author make her characters feel so real?

There are little things about Blume's writing that make her characters endearing. Take the opening of chapter three, in which the protagonist, Katherine, talks to her mother about having just met a new boy. While she talks, Katherine's mother is cutting her toenails. This is a rather intimate moment. The setting is the bathroom—a small room not often used as a scene for a conversation between two characters in a novel. Katherine's mother is performing a fairly personal act and an unusual one to be included in fiction. Readers get a glimpse behind the characters' public faces, as if readers were eavesdropping on a private conversation. Now that readers have witnessed this scene, they have the feeling that they know the characters better, although they hardly know anything about them at all. It is only after setting up this scene in the bathroom that the narrator begins to fill in details about her mother and other members of her family. But in giving that one personal peek, a view of the mother that no other "public" character would see of her, readers feel as if they belong, as if they are trusted guests, invited in to share a personal story. Readers immediately feel a part of Blume's fictional family.

Soon after the bathroom scene, still in chapter three, Blume adds a specific detail that is a so true to life that readers cannot ignore the author's honesty. The narrator is discussing how people often park in their cars when on dates. They do so, coincidentally, in Erica's neighborhood. Erica has told Katherine that she knows people park there to have sex because she is always finding used rubbers that have been thrown out of cars and left on the street or on the sidewalks. The mention of the discarded condoms sets the stage for other events, a foreshadowing of sexual activity as well as the discussion of birth control and prevention of venereal disease.

Like the author, Katherine's parents are open-minded. Although they do not come right out and tell Katherine that she can have sex in the house with her boyfriends, they do tell her that it is unsafe to do so in a car, parked on a street. This frankness may be objectionable to some parents who read Blume's books. But this is just the beginning. Blume's openness has just begun to go to work.

"... Blume is saying, this is life. This is what really happens. Nothing can be counted on. This is not the movies."

Next comes the beginning of the discussion of sex or, rather, the exposure of the young couple (Katherine and Michael) as they fumble their way toward having sex. Michael fumbles physically as Katherine fumbles with her emotions and the thoughts in her head. The descriptions of Michael's first attempts to arouse Katherine sexually are not erotic. This book was not meant to excite readers but rather to inform them. There are references to Michael's hands and to Katherine's clothing, but these are only briefly mentioned, unveiling the characters' intended actions but not glorifying them. Readers who have had sexual experiences can assume what is happening, but inexperienced readers may need to guess. The passages might be titillating for young readers, but they are not erotic. Blume writes statements, such as "I felt his body against mine," "He reached under my sweater," and "He touched me," which suggest that the two characters are engaging in foreplay. The statements are frank, describing the couple's actions, but they are not prurient.

Later, Katherine admits that she is no prude when it comes to sex, and through this admission, Blume suggest her character is realistic. Katherine has doubts about whether she is ready for sex but admits that she would like to experience it. She is honest enough with herself to realize that had circumstances been different, she might have had sex with Michael during one of the first times they made out. "If Artie and Erica hadn't been there I doubt that I'd have stopped Michael from unbuttoning my jeans," Katherine states. In other words, Katherine is not angry at Michael for trying or for encouraging her to give in to him. She understands his physical urges because she feels them, too. Blume has created a protagonist who is real, someone who is challenged by the thoughts of being sexually active. Blume examines the complexities of teen sexual

What Do I Read Next?

- *Are You There God? It's Me, Margaret*, published in 1970, was Blume's first controversial novel. One of the major concerns of the protagonist of this story, a concern commonly shared by teenage girls, pertains to when she is going to fill out her first bra. Before Blume, teenage girls had talked among themselves about this subject, but no one had ever written about it.
- Published a little more than ten years after Blume's *Forever . . .*, Maureen Daly's *Acts of Love* (1987) similarly portrays a young girl in love and the challenges that she must face. The author describes a daughter's first love as similar to experiences the teen's mother had.
- Judith Caseley's novel *Kisses* (1990) tells the story of a young violinist who finds love where she never suspected she would. This is another romance about a teenager who is looking for love but cannot seem to find it.
- With a little more dramatic tension, Mary Downing Hahn turns a would-be romance into something of a thriller as the protagonist's boyfriend rides his motorcycle carelessly at the climax of this young love story in an attempt to kill himself. The novel is called *The Wind Blows Backwards* (1993).

impulse and activity. She is not afraid of creating a character that is complex. That is what makes Katherine seem so authentic. In observing Katherine's thoughts, readers know that this story is going to be more than a simple exposition of what some teens do when they are on a date. This story explores many of the issues that surround sexuality; maybe even some topics which readers, for one reason or another, have never encountered before.

Grandma Gross is one step removed from parenting and can, therefore, be a bit more objective than a mother or a father. Grandma Gross senses that Katherine and Michael are getting closer to one another. The logical next step would be for them to have intercourse, and Grandma Gross wants to make sure that Katherine is at least physically prepared. It is through Grandma Gross's promptings that Katherine seeks advice about birth control and protection from venereal diseases. It is also through Grandma Gross that Blume's readers receive this wise advice. The pertinent information, especially back in the 1970s when *Forever . . .* was first published, pertained to contraception and venereal disease. Sex education in schools was not as fully developed as it later became after the AIDS epidemic hit in the 1980s. Parents, as a general rule, often had trouble talking about sex, in particular, with their daughters. Most parents want their teenage children to be protected, but they do not want to encourage their children to be sexually active. While teens in the 1970s experienced a sexual revolution, their parents experienced a very different climate when they were themselves teenagers. Discussions of sex were typically evasive and vague, as Blume demonstrates in the dialogues between Katherine and her parents. Grandma Gross, a liberated, free thinker, a woman well ahead of her own times, could be frank, whereas Katherine's mother, whose values were more shaped by the 1950s, could not be.

Blume also presents male impotence. Artie feels impotent in various ways. Whether this is played out through his sexuality is for a professional to determine. But Artie definitely has problems. Given the details Blume provides about Artie's life, readers can assume that at best Artie is confused and troubled. What was Blume trying to say? There is a hint of homosexuality, but that does not seem to be the author's main point. Rather, it appears that the topic has more to do with the relationship between Artie and Erica. Could Blume have wanted to focus on Erica's mistaken notion that she could help Artie? Was Blume trying to state that sexual activity cannot in itself solve problems? Whatever the author's reasons, the character of Artie brings the serious matter of dysfunction to the novel. His impotence, mixed with Erica's failed attempts to help Artie, and Artie's depression and attempted suicide are all very real problems that teenagers sometimes face. In her desire to be honest, Blume might be saying that in the real world, life is not always about fun and physical pleasures. As Blume's fans know, Blume is all about representing what is real.

Finally, there is Katherine's sexual initiation. For all the passion that is hinted at as Katherine and Michael move toward experiencing sexual intercourse, at the moment when Katherine actually allows Michael to enter her, the passion is nowhere to be found. There is more discussion about Michael's using a condom than there is about the act itself. Katherine and Michael talk about pregnancy and venereal disease and about Katherine's period instead. Then there is more talk about Michael's sexual actions, for which he apologizes, because he has an orgasm before penetration. Michael continues to apologize. Katherine repeatedly tells him that everything is all right. It does not really matter. So what is going on here?

Blume appears committed to not idealizing the first sexual experience. Even at the height of what should be physical pleasure, things can (and do) go wrong. Katherine's and Michael's experience serves as an illustration. The big moment develops in an unanticipated direction. Again, Blume is saying, this is life. This is what really happens. Nothing can be counted on. This is not the movies. This is real; or this is at least as real as a novel can put it.

So the teenagers try once again. In the second attempt, Michael is successful, but Katherine is unimpressed. She tries to comfort Michael who senses Katherine's disappointment. "Everybody says the first time is no good for a virgin. I'm not disappointed," she tells Michael. But she is. Katherine is honest, at least to herself. "I'd wanted it to be perfect," Katherine announces to the readers.

It is as if Blume is saying that life is not perfect. The dreams and fantasies attached to some of the subjects Blume explores in her book are often glossed over with imagined perfection. When adults are not willing or unable to have frank discussions about all the elements of sexuality, those fantasies can grow. Blume does not allow that to happen. She makes a point of telling a story with all its imperfections and disappointments. "I can't help feeling let down," Katherine says. "Everybody makes such a big thing out of actually doing it." Too bad Katherine does not have a book like this one to read. Thanks to Katherine's story, however, and Blume's frank telling of it, maybe other teens will know beforehand that there is a lot to love and life, and not all of it is like what they may have imagined. Life and love, as Michael states, takes practice. It is nice to be reminded of this from time to time. Maybe that is why Blume's fans are so attracted to the author's frankness.

Source: Joyce Hart, Critical Essay on *Forever . . .*, in *Novels for Students*, Thomson Gale, 2007.

Laura Pryor

Pryor has a B.A. from the University of Michigan and twenty years experience in professional and creative writing with special interest in fiction. In this essay, she examines the influence of the feminist movement on this novel, the many pressures placed upon the teens in Forever . . ., *and how the story would be different if it were told in the early 2000s.*

While *Forever . . .* could be briefly summarized as the tale of one teenager's first love affair and sexual experience, the story illustrates not just adolescent attitudes and difficulties with sex, but the pressures and problems they face in many other areas as well. The characters deal with these pressures in their own ways, making their own inevitable mistakes, though some mistakes have more serious consequences than others.

The central character, Katherine, is a responsible, cautious achiever, who handles the pressures and desires of being seventeen (later in the story, eighteen) and in love in an almost ideal manner. Her liberated yet responsible behavior could have been scripted by the staff of Planned Parenthood. She refuses to be pressed into sex, she insists on using birth control, and then, after her first sexual encounter, she makes an appointment at Planned Parenthood for a complete gynecological exam and a prescription for the Pill. It is no wonder her behavior is so exemplary; her parents are understanding and communicative; her grandmother is a lawyer who once ran for Congress, works for NOW, and sends Katherine pamphlets on birth control, abortion, and venereal disease. For the feminist movement in the 1970s, Katherine is an idealized vision of how young women (and their families) should handle sex. Two years before this novel was first published, feminist tennis great Billie Jean King beat Bobby Riggs in the much-hyped "Battle of the Sexes"; not surprisingly, the one sport at which Katherine excels is tennis.

Even Blume's symbolism makes the point that Katherine is heir to the feminist movement, an equal partner in any relationship. In the apartment where she loses her virginity, Michael looks in the refrigerator and offers, "How about an apple . . . or a grapefruit?" Katherine replies, "I'll have an apple." Unlike Eve, Katherine has the power to choose—she is not seduced or coerced in any way.

Fortunately, Blume does not portray Katherine as strident or militant in her feminist attitudes, and the author gives her most of the same insecurities about sex that an average teenage girl experiences. She worries that it will hurt, that she will bleed; at one point, she muses, "Sometimes I want to so much—but other times I'm afraid." After eating the apple she gets from Michael at the apartment, she

> **"Despite the negative aspects of teen sex, Blume treats the subject as a natural and inevitable part of growing up."**

wraps the core in toilet paper and hides it in her purse, afraid to leave any evidence behind. To further emphasize her representative status, she is even the same age as the average girl having her first sexual encounter in the 1970s.

If Katherine exemplifies the right way for a teenage girl to handle sex, then her friend Sybil represents the opposite, the downside of teens living in a sexually liberated environment. Here, Blume acknowledges that for teens without the maturity to handle it, becoming sexually active too soon is playing with fire. Overweight and insecure, Sybil uses sex to prove her desirability and ends up missing graduation to give birth to a baby girl she must put up for adoption. Ironically, Sybil is described as having "a genius IQ," and is accepted at every Ivy League school to which she applies. Clearly, Sybil is searching for a different kind of acceptance.

Despite the negative aspects of teen sex, Blume treats the subject as a natural and inevitable part of growing up. To emphasize this, she juxtaposes Katherine's sexual awakening with the gradual deterioration and death of her grandfather, the birth of Sybil's baby girl, and her younger sister Jamie getting her first boyfriend. When Katherine reaches out to Theo and kisses him after hearing of her grandfather's death, Theo links the two events with his own amateur psychology: "it's a very common reaction . . . somebody dies . . . you need to prove you're alive . . . and what better way is there?"

No sexual issue facing teens is left unexplored by Blume. Michael admits that he contracted gonorrhea after a casual encounter with a girl at the beach the summer before he met Katherine. Good girl Katherine admonishes him, "You should never take chances." Sybil becomes pregnant and chooses to have the baby; ever the feminist, Katherine tells her friend Erica, "I'd have an abortion . . . wouldn't you?" Blume even tackles the issue of impotence with the character of Artie Lewin, who, with the help of Erica, determines that he is not gay but is still unable to have sex. In this case, however, impotence is not just a sexual issue. It symbolizes the lack of autonomy the male characters experience in other parts of their lives. Artie's case is the most serious, as his father has denied him the opportunity to pursue his one great passion, acting. In addition, Artie appears to suffer from manic depression. In one scene, Katherine says that "Artie was in one of his high moods," but seconds later his mood plummets, and he tells everyone that "From now on it's all downhill." Just as his father has robbed him of the power to choose his future, the illness has made him powerless to even regulate his own emotions. Impotence, for Artie, has become a way of life. Similarly, the one time Michael is unable to get an erection, it is just after he has admitted to Katherine that his parents are forcing him to take a job in North Carolina for the summer. The adults in this story urge responsibility, but they sometimes deny the teens the autonomy to make the decisions for which they will bear the responsibility. This paradox plagues the characters throughout the story. As high school seniors, they deal with decisions regarding their future occupations, choice of college (which in turn affects where they will live for the next four years), and financial issues (both Katherine and Michael feel pressure to get summer jobs to help fund their educations). An encounter Katherine has with Michael's uncle illustrates this pressure clearly:

> "So tell me," he said, "What do you want to do with your life?"
>
> "Do?" I repeated.
>
> "Yes . . . you've thought about it, haven't you?"
>
> "Sure."
>
> "So?"
>
> "I want to be happy," I told him. "And make other people happy too."
>
> "Very nice . . . but not enough."
>
> "That's all I know right now." I turned and walked away from him.

None of the adults seems to realize that this pressure is at complete odds with a more realistic view of the teens' love lives. Both Katherine and Michael's parents urge them to slow down, not become tied down. Katherine's parents talk about relationships they had in high school, trying to drive home the point that "forever" is an unrealistic goal at age eighteen. Katherine herself demonstrates her own inability to comprehend what "forever" means, when her parents insist that she take a job as a camp tennis instructor for seven weeks: "Seven weeks may not be a lot to you but to me it's forever!" While the parents are quick to acknowledge this inability in regards to love and sex, they somehow feel these same teens should be able to accurately predict their future occupations and the education they will need to prepare for them.

Though most of the emotions and dilemmas facing the teens remain valid in the early 2000s, echoes of the 1960s and early 1970s are heard throughout the novel. For instance, when Katherine's younger sister Jamie uses the word "f——" in reference to Katherine and Michael's relationship, Katherine is taken aback, but Jamie reminds her, "hate and war are bad words but f—— isn't." Michael's older sister, Sharon, and her husband casually smoke marijuana in front of Michael and Katherine and offer some to them as well. The bed where Katherine and Michael first have sex sits beneath the iconic "LOVE" poster, and Katherine's mother "never wears a bra." In addition, the main concern of Katherine's parents is not whether she is having sex with Michael but that the relationship is getting too serious. In the era of AIDS, such a relaxed attitude is less common.

If Judy Blume wrote *Forever . . .* in the early 2000s, how would the story change? First of all, for Katherine to be the "Everygirl," she would be about sixteen, the average age for a first sexual experience in the early 2000s, and so she would not be dealing at the same time with the pressures of first-time sex and an impending college education. As Blume acknowledges in a note added at the beginning of the novel, if Katherine went to Planned Parenthood for the Pill in 2006, "she would be told it is essential to use a latex condom, along with any other method of contraception," for the prevention of AIDS. Responsible Katherine would probably insist that Michael have an AIDS test as well. She would have a wider array of contraceptive methods available to her, including lower-dose pills, injections, implants, and the patch, to name a few. Other factors—cable TV, earlier sex education in the schools, the Internet—would probably make the twenty-first century Katherine just as knowledgeable at sixteen as the 1975 Katherine at eighteen, and maybe even more so. However, would a sixteen-year-old Katherine handle the affair with the same maturity? If she did, would the reader find her believable?

Also, a teenage girl coming of age in the early 2000s faces new dangers unimagined in 1975. Sexual predators on the Internet lure young girls by preying on their idealistic, romantic views of love, the same views that Katherine has about her relationship with Michael. Katherine's oversexed former boyfriend, Tommy Aronson, who left her because she would not have sex with him, might in the early 2000s decide to slip her a date-rape drug to make her more pliable.

On the positive side, public awareness of mental illnesses is so much greater than in 1975 that Artie's apparent manic depression probably would have been diagnosed earlier and treated with medication.

Overall, despite the obvious differences between 1975 and the early 2000s, the story holds up because the central conflicts are emotional ones, and the questions asked by Katherine still plague every teenage girl: should I have sex now or wait? If now, is this the right boy? Am I doing it right? What if I get pregnant? And the question that Katherine reads in a pamphlet and is unwilling to consider: "Have you thought about how this relationship will end?"

What teens may find irksome is that even though Blume is so sympathetic in her portrayal of teen life and love, in the end, it turns out (once again) that the adults were right all along. The young reader cannot help but wish that Katherine and Michael could buck the odds and make it last, showing those meddlesome parents once and for all that they do not know everything. Teen readers everywhere can take some solace in the fact that, with nearly half of all marriages ending in divorce, adults are having their own problems with the idea of "forever."

Source: Laura Pryor, Critical Essay on *Forever . . .*, in *Novels for Students*, Thomson Gale, 2007.

Sarah Crown

In the following interview, Crown discusses censorship, the "current climate of sexual fear" and the popularity of Forever . . . .

My copy lived under the mattress; my sister kept hers in a locked desk drawer; my best friend's was buried under a pile of too-small clothes at the back of her wardrobe. I was 13 or so when overnight it became de rigueur for every girl in my year to have—and hide—a copy of Judy Blume's teenage classic, *Forever.* As unforgettable as a first kiss for the generation of young women who grew up with it, Forever tells the story of Katherine and Michael, two teenagers who meet, fall in love and, once they've decided their relationship is serious, have sex. Owning, reading and conducting whispered, and occasionally baffled, conversations

> **"While the shadow of HIV has created a far chillier sexual climate for today's teenagers, the book's appeal has in no way diminished. 'What I hear from my readers,' Blume says, 'is that the story itself is timeless. There will always be first love, first sexual feelings, first sexual relationships.'"**

about the book was a mark of maturity, a step on the road to adulthood. We'd giggled through sex education classes and blushed through awkward parental conversations, but none of us had ever come across anything like this: a book that discussed sex frankly, but placed it in the context of normal teenage life—school, friends, family, a loving relationship. A book that talked, in short, about the sort of sex we could one day dimly see ourselves having. It was revolutionary stuff.

In the 30 years since *Forever* was published, it has sold over 3.5m copies worldwide; an anniversary edition, complete with a new foreword from Blume, hit the shelves last week. In addition to the forthright descriptions of sex that lead teenage girls the world over to squirrel their copies away—no doubt to the great amusement of their mothers—it is a deeply likeable book, a tender, intelligent exploration of the intensity of first love and the difficulty of accepting that it might end. Despite the seismic changes to the sexual landscape brought about by the advent of AIDS in the intervening years, it remains just as in demand today as it was in 1975. Girls who grow up with Blume's enduringly popular novels for younger children (*Are You There God? It's Me Margaret; Tales of a Fourth Grade Nothing*) come to trust her sensitive, insightful treatment of the issues—love, death, divorce, appearance, periods—that make up the fabric of their lives. When they pick up *Forever,* her hallmark folksy, first-person voice eases their transition into the book's more adult world, conveying subliminally the idea that sex is not something "other"—and therefore to be feared—but something "more"; the logical next step on the ladder to adulthood.

But while her candid, nonjudgmental treatment of teenage sexual relations is at the root of the book's perennial appeal, Blume's matter-of-fact approach is not always viewed positively. *Forever* provoked a storm of controversy when it was first published. Despite the laudable responsibility which Katherine and Michael display (discussing their feelings carefully before deciding to have sex, and visiting a family planning clinic to obtain contraception), moves to ban the book from schools and public libraries began then and continue to this day; a Texan librarian is currently campaigning to have *Forever* taken off the shelves of every school library in the state. Blume now finds herself in the rather curious position of being, as she herself puts it, "one of the most banned writers in America", and the recipient, in 2004, of a National Book Award for her services to American literature.

Her sanguine reaction to the criticism levelled at *Forever* may have its roots in the fact that when the book was first published it was, conversely, the last thing on her mind. "At the time, I was going through a divorce and preparing to move to London with my kids," she says. "Looking back, my personal life was a mess: controversy over the publication of *Forever* was not my number one priority." One incident, however, does stick in her mind. "I remember the review Margaret Drabble wrote for the *Times*—I think it was the *Times*," she recollects. "It talked about what American teens did in their cars—though Katherine and Michael never made love in a car. She also talked about "insies" and "outsies", mistakenly thinking the words had to do with genitalia, when really they were Katherine's descriptions of belly buttons. I was a huge fan of Margaret Drabble's—I read everything she'd written—so I was fascinated though, ultimately, disappointed by her review. And who knows if I'm even remembering what she wrote accurately . . ."

Fortunately, not even Margaret Drabble's poor grasp of belly button jargon has been enough to put the book-buying public off. While the shadow of HIV has created a far chillier sexual climate for today's teenagers, the book's appeal has in no way diminished. "What I hear from my readers," Blume says, "is that the story itself is timeless. There will always be first love, first sexual feelings, first sexual relationships. Here we are, 30 years later, and just as many young people are reading the book today as when it was published."

Blume acknowledges and addresses the threat posed by AIDS in her foreword to the new edition of *Forever*, but a heightened awareness of risk is just one of the sea changes in that has occurred since 1975. When Katherine and her mother discuss sex in *Forever,* it is clear that attitudes have relaxed considerably between the 1950s, when Katherine's mother grew up, and the present-day of the 1970s. "In the old days girls were divided into two groups—those who did and those who didn't," says Katherine. "My mother told me that. Nice girls didn't, naturally." The expectation in late 1970s America was that this process of liberalisation would continue. If anything, the reverse has been true. The rise of the religious right wing is evident today in the ubiquity of pressure groups such as True Love Waits, who preach sexual abstinence until marriage; President Bush's administration has doubled federal funding for abstinence education programmes and introduced the partial birth abortion bill, seen by the pro-choice lobby as a move to limit the control women gained over their bodies following the landmark *Roe v. Wade* case in 1973. Blume is clearly dismayed by the lurch away from the more latitudinarian attitudes of the time of *Forever*'s publication.

"The 70s was a much more open decade in America," she says. *Forever* was used in several school programmes then, helping to spur discussions of sexual responsibility. This would never happen today. How are young people supposed to make thoughtful decisions if they don't have information and no one is willing to talk with them? Girls and boys have to learn to say 'no' or 'not without a condom' without fear. I hear from too many young people who give in because they're afraid if they don't, their partner will find someone else.

"How have things changed since I wrote the book?" she muses. "Of course it was always seen as taboo by some. But from the 1980s onwards, the religious fundamentalists have grown in power. Fear is contagious and those who wish America to become a faith-based society are doing their best to spread it."

Does she regard the present situation as irretrievable? Not quite, perhaps. "In the 80s and early 90s this fear affected what a publisher was willing to take a chance on," she says, turning to the subject of censorship which has been central to her working life. "Fascinatingly, that tide appears to have turned. Even in this fanatically religious political climate, publishers are choosing 'young adult' novels that deal frankly with sex and other topics of interest to teens. I've read some very good books lately. In one [*A Bad Boy Can Be Good for a Girl* by Tanya Lee Stone]" she says, with a note of pride, "*Forever* plays a major role."

That Forever should play a central part in another author's take on the issues it tackled for the first time 30 years ago is a fitting homage to what was, and still is, a groundbreaking book. Without Forever, authors such as Melvin Burgess and Anne Cassidy would not be entrancing and challenging new readerships today.

But for those of us who grew up with it, its significance can perhaps best be measured by one odd and lasting side-effect of its popularity: the consigning of the name Ralph—which is what Michael memorably decides to name his penis—to the dustbin of history. "I've heard from several young men who say: 'Judy, how could you do this to me?'" Blume admits. "I apologise to all of them. It's nothing personal."

Source: Sarah Crown, "Interview: Judy Blume," in *Financial Times, Ltd.*, June 8, 2005.

Roger Sutton

In the following interview, Sutton talks with Blume about writing and the impact Forever . . . *has on young adults.*

Judy Blume is the 1996 recipient of the Margaret A. Edwards Award, given annually by ALA's Young Adult Library Services Association and sponsored by *School Library Journal.* The award honors an author who has made an outstanding contribution to literature for young adults. Blume is being cited for her novel *Forever* (Bradbury, 1975). The award will be presented next month during ALA's Annual Conference in New York City. (For Carolyn Caywood's thoughts on *Forever*'s significance to young adult literature, see "Teens and Libraries," p. 62.) In anticipation of the award presentation, I met with Blume to talk about her writing and the impact of *Forever* on young adults.

[Judy Blume:] As I tell the kids, you can ask me anything.

[*Roger Sutton*:] *Well, I was told I had to ask you whether you married the man on the motorcycle [in* Wifey].

No way. That came from a little story I heard from a friend of my husband's who was picked up by the police just after he got out of the army. A sheet was found with his military ID on it and they

> "She really yells at me. *Forever* is about people. It is about feelings. It is not a sex manual."

brought him in for questioning. A woman had seen some guy drive up on a motorcycle, throw off a bedsheet, masturbate, and then drive away. It was 20 years later that I used that [incident as a catalyst for sexual awakening] in *Wifey*.

I was working in a public library when Wifey *came out, and the kids were coming in looking for "Judy Blume's new book." We had 10-year-olds asking for it.*

Oh, well, I hope they stopped reading soon. It's like *Forever*. I've had letters from kids as young as 10 who said, "I have read this book and I understood everything in it and everything about it." When kids at a book signing ask me, "How old do I have to be before I read *Forever*?," I say, "I think you should be at least 12 and then you should have somebody to talk to about it." I think you get more out of a book when you are closer to the protagonist's age. I've also had letters from kids that said, "I started *Forever* and I don't think I'm ready. So I'm going to wait."

Would you keep younger kids away from Forever, *if you could?*

No, but I was bothered when I saw it—more than once—on a bookstore shelf right next to *Tales of a Fourth Grade Nothing*. I said to the manager, "This makes me uncomfortable. This book doesn't really belong here. It's a whole other group of readers, and I would feel much better if you had it with the mass market paperbacks." She said, "Oh, we did, but it just wasn't moving, and as soon as we put it in the children's section it flew off the shelf."

The hardcover edition of Forever *states very prominently on both jacket flaps that the book is "Judy Blume's first novel for adults."*

It wasn't. Bradbury Press did that to protect themselves. It was a shock to me when I saw on the inside flap, "her first book for adults," because it wasn't. I never said it was. I didn't want anybody to be told that it was. But Bradbury was young then. [Bradbury's founders] Dick Jackson, [the late] Bob Verrone, and I were all young. I think that they just wanted to say that so they could say to angry parents or teachers or whomever, "But look, this says clearly. . . ." When *Wifey* was published, I insisted it say right on the cover An Adult Novel because it is. *Forever* isn't. There really weren't any YA books at that time.

Well . . .

There were no YA books. This was 1975. When did YA books happen?

Well, there was The Outsiders *in '67,* The Pigman *in '68.*

But they weren't called YA books. We were writing for "young people." *Forever* was for an older audience than the younger kids I had written for. I wrote it because my daughter Randy was then 14. It's the only book of mine that came that way. She was reading what a librarian friend called the "pregnant books." They were books about teenaged girls getting pregnant. And the girls had sex because there was something terribly wrong in their lives. They did this terrible thing with a guy not because it felt good, not because they were turned on, not because they loved him, but because something bad was happening in their family. And when they inevitably got pregnant, the pregnancy was linked with punishment. Always. If you had sex you were going to be punished. Now the guys, they were never punished, only the girls.

Randy was reading a lot of these, and she said to me, "Couldn't there ever be a book about two really nice kids in high school who love each other and they do it and nothing bad happens?" That's how I got the idea for *Forever*: I wrote it because it really bothered me that the message being sent to kids—and primarily to young women—was that sex was being linked with punishment, rather than with pleasure and responsibility. It's the only book I've written because somebody asked me to, and I'm not sure that's how the best books are written. I had a letter last week from the director of a national Down Syndrome organization, and she asked me to write a book for kids who may meet Down Syndrome kids in their classes. I wrote back the letter that I always do, saying that the best books come from someplace deep inside.

A good writer doesn't write what somebody else needs to read.

Sometimes it turns out to be what somebody else needs to read, but you don't write it for that reason. When Marilee Foglesong, chair of the

Edwards Award committee, called to tell me I had won, she said "We're giving you this award for *Forever*." I said, "Really? That's not my best book. For the same age group, I think *Tiger Eyes* (S. & S., 1982) is a much better book." And she said, "Oh." So then I said, "But, you know, that's very nice if you want to do this."

You know this was a very controversial award.

I'm sure it was. It's been 26 years since I published *Are You There God? It's Me, Margaret,* and I've never had an award from the library world. I've enjoyed that. I never felt accepted and that was ok. The kids like the books and I don't even remember how *SLJ* reviewed *Forever.*

They hated it, but noted—presciently—that it would be very popular.

Did they?

I also had a student in a YA lit class who felt that Forever *should be pulled from the shelves because Katherine and Michael don't practice safe sex.*

In all the new reprints of the book there is a letter from me about sexual responsibility, which has a different meaning in 1996 than it did in 1975.

The student said that Forever *should be removed from libraries—although she liked the book a lot—because it is presented as contemporary fiction yet does not address AIDS, not to mention the more complicated understanding we have of the Pill's benefits and drawbacks. Can you expect fiction to fulfill the need for nonfiction information about sex?*

No. My very dear friend Leanne Katz, who heads the National Coalition Against Censorship, has had this very discussion with me. Sometimes I feel, Oh dear, is it responsible, is it okay to have *Forever* in the library? She really yells at me. *Forever* is about people. It is about feelings. It is not a sex manual. Does it mean we shouldn't be allowed to read [John O'Hara's] *A Rage to Live* or [Saul Bellow's] *The Adventures of Augie March*—two of the "forbiddens" from my youth—because they don't address AIDS? Just because the rules have changed? You can't do that.

I wonder how today's kids read Forever.

I think they read it as an absolutely contemporary novel.

Do they wonder why the characters don't practice safe sex?

You know, there are still so many kids who are not practicing safe sex at all, who feel invulnerable. And so many girls who still say, "He doesn't like condoms, and he says if I won't do it without one then he'll find someone who will." I say to them, "Good, tell him to find somebody else. You tell him that if he's not willing to use a condom, you're not willing to have sex." Of course I couldn't write the same book today. I'm different. The times are different. *Forever* was published in 1975, and obviously I have to look at where I was, too. I was on the brink of divorce. I had never rebelled as a teenager. I was a very good girl, married very young, and felt that at 35, 36, which was the age I was when writing *Forever,* that I had missed out on a lot. And yet, while writing the book, I didn't identify so much with Katherine as I did with her mother.

She's a really good mother.

She's a nice mother—she's a librarian.

I don't think Forever *is so much a sex manual as it is an introduction to what having sex "is like."*

If you're lucky. When that book came out 20 years ago, I really got it for allowing a young woman to enjoy her first sexual experiences. I can remember an angry letter from a librarian who said, "How dare you? Women don't enjoy their first sexual experiences. It takes years and years." Well, not always. Granted, this girl has a very gentle and loving boyfriend, and not everyone is so lucky.

You know, people said you broke a taboo in Forever *and changed the rules for YA literature, doing for adolescent sex what Robert Cormier did for downbeat endings in* The Chocolate War. *Yet YA books, by and large, still have optimistic conclusions, and I think I could count on one hand those that feature on-the-page sex the way* Forever *does.*

I don't think you'd call *Forever* erotic.

If I were 16, I might. What about those ellipses, starting right in the title? I think that has something to do with it.

That's just the way I write. That's just me.

There's hardly a sentence in there that comes to a full stop.

That's how people talk. Maybe I do it too much. Even when I write letters, it's always dot, dot, dot. People rarely talk in full sentences.

I think it gives an atmosphere of expectancy to the book. There's more to come, there's something left out, there's something not on the page. It sort of heats the book up because you keep thinking, What would happen if that sentence got finished?

It would be nice if I could tell you I did it on purpose, but I didn't. When I read things that other people have written about my books, I'm always surprised. I wonder, Is that what I meant? Or, oh, that's what I meant. I never analyze. Norma Klein, a wonderful friend and writer, once decided that book by book, she was going to analyze what I wrote. She started with *Forever* and sent me pages on it. It was a very generous and loving analysis, and I wrote back and said, "Don't ever do this to me again. If you want to analyze my books, fine, but don't send the results to me." I don't want to know. It's too scary. We're all scared enough, those of us who write: will it ever happen again? Will I get another idea? How did I do this? When I pick up a book of mine that I wrote even a few years ago, I wonder, How did I do this? I think the more you understand something the worse off you are. It's taken me 20 years to figure this out. I suppose everybody else already knows this, but it's been news to me. When you're writing, you're operating out of some different part of the brain. When it's happening, you're not aware of it, you don't know where what you write is coming from. And when you read it later, you think, Wow. I did that? It's like a surprise.

Source: Roger Sutton, "An Interview with Judy Blume: *Forever* . . . Yours," in *School Library Journal*, Vol. 42, No. 6, June 1996, pp. 24–26.

Sources

Blume, Judy, *Forever . . .*, Pocket Books, 1975.

Frey, Jennifer, "Otherwise Known as Judy Blume the Great," in *Los Angeles Times*, December 1, 2004, p. E10.

Goldberg, Beverly, "The *Forever* Challenge," in *American Libraries*, Vol. 33, No. 2, February 2002, p. 21.

Goldblatt, Jennifer, "Blume's Day," in *New York Times*, November 14, 2004, p. 14NJ1.

Holt, Karen, "Judy Blume Wins NBF Lifetime Achievement Prize," in *Publishers Weekly*, Vol. 251, No. 38, September 20, 2004, p. 10.

Margolis, Rick, "Illinois Librarian Fights On," in *School Library Journal*, Vol. 47, No. 11, November 2001, p. 14.

Further Reading

Bell, Ruth, *Changing Bodies, Changing Lives: Expanded Third Edition: A Book for Teens on Sex and Relationships*, Three Rivers Press, 1998.

This book covers most topics readers may want to know about sexuality and teen relationships, including AIDS, STDs, pregnancy, gay sex, and sexual technique. It includes expert essays, teen interviews, and illustrations.

Connell, Elizabeth, *The Contraception Sourcebook*, McGraw-Hill, 2001.

Connell discusses contraception practices for contemporary couples, ranging from abstinence to the pill. The historical background for each form plus its advantages and disadvantages are provided.

Hernandez, Roger E., *Teens and Relationships*, Gallup Youth Survey: Major Issues and Trends, Mason Crest Publishers, 2005.

Hernandez has compiled information from a survey taken between 1985 and 2005 to determine what teenagers think about parents, the effects of divorce, family relationships, dating, and friendships.

Sanger, Margaret, *The Autobiography of Margaret Sanger*, Dover Publications, 2004.

First published in 1938, this book tells the story of Margaret Sanger, founder of Planned Parenthood, who dedicated her life to making sure birth control was understood to be a basic human right.

Wheeler, Jill C., *Judy Blume*, Abdo Publishing Company, 2004.

This book explores the professional challenges that faced Judy Blume as she pursued publication and fought censorship.

Gilead

Marilynne Robinson

2004

Gilead by Marilynne Robinson was published in 2004 and won the Pulitzer Prize for Fiction in 2005, amid widespread acclaim. This epistolary novel presents a sympathetic portrait of Reverend John Ames, who writes about his life and his beliefs ever mindful of the fact that he has only a short time to live. Reverend Ames takes up the task of writing in the hopes that his little boy will read this book when he is an adult and thus become acquainted with the father he may barely remember otherwise.

This is a story of fathers and sons. John Ames, the narrator, tells a story of three generations of fathers named John Ames, addressing it to the single direct descendent, the unnamed son readers may assume is the fourth John Ames. The story of the Ames family includes the story of the narrator's best friend, Robert Boughton, and his son who was named after the narrator, John Ames Boughton. In order to reduce confusion, these characters are referred to here in terms of their relationship to the narrator, that is, the narrator's grandfather, the narrator's father, and the narrator's son, to whom the narrator addresses himself in this text. As in the novel, Reverend Boughton's son is referred to by his nickname, Jack.

Author Biography

Source material providing biographical information on Marilynne Robinson is scant and all too often conflicting in its facts, focusing on her publications

Marilynne Robinson Photograph by Adam Rountree. AP Images

and the host of awards she has won, rather than on biographical details. Robinson was born in Sandpoint, Idaho, probably in 1944 (though 1943 and 1947 are also reported), where she grew up and there attended Coeur d'Alene High School, from which she graduated in 1962. She graduated in 1966 with a B.A. in history and religion from Pembroke College in Warren, Rhode Island, an institution which became affiliated with Brown University in 1971. In 1977, Robinson received her Ph.D. from the University of Washington.

Robinson's first novel, *Housekeeping*, was published in 1980. The work, which is dedicated to Robinson's husband and "four wonderful boys," was nominated for the Pulitzer Prize and won the PEN/Hemingway Award for best first novel. In the 1980s, Robinson wrote essays for such publications as *Paris Review*, *New York Book Times Review of Books*, and *Harper's*. She also began teaching and was a writer-in-residence at various colleges and universities, including the University of Massachusetts, Amherst College, and the University of Kent.

As of 2006, Robinson has published two works of nonfiction. The first was the controversial *Mother Country: Britain, the Welfare State, and Nuclear Pollution* (1989), a thoroughly researched exposé of the Sellafield Nuclear Processing Plant, exploring the nuclear energy industry, its environmental impact, and its opponents, specifically Greenpeace, an organization that successfully sued the British publisher of this book for libel and got the book banned in England. Nonetheless, *Mother Country* was a National Book Award finalist in the United States.

Sometime after that publication, Robinson and her husband divorced, and she eventually joined the faculty of the Writers' Workshop at the University of Iowa, where she remained through the 1990s and into the first decade of the twenty-first century. In 1998, she published *The Death of Adam: Essays on Modern Thought*, a collection of prose pieces that mostly had appeared originally as articles or speeches. This collection, in part, traces the legacy of what Robinson calls the idea of "continuous cull," as it appears in Thomas Malthus, emerges in Darwin's theory of the survival of the fittest, and recurs in the economic theory of Karl Marx and the racist ideologies of Friedrich Nietzsche and Adolf Hitler. As with her two previous books, this collection displays Robinson's erudite, theoretical mind and exceptionally fine prose style. Like *Mother Country*, *The Death of Adam* challenges beliefs that define modern Western culture with arguments enlightened by deep learning and wide reading.

In 2004, Robinson published her second novel, the 2005 Pulitzer Prize winner for fiction, *Gilead*, which immediately garnered universal acclaim. As of 2006, Robinson was on the faculty of the Writers' Workshop at the University of Iowa.

Plot Summary

This novel is not divided into chapters, and the events are not presented in chronological order. Rather, in the letters to his son, the narrator describes events that transpire in the immediate present, while he is writing this journal, and he narrates old family stories as they occur to him, along with other subjects that matter to him. Certain dominant memories that span his seventy-five years in Gilead, between 1882 and 1956, are referred to repeatedly, and the narrator also tells important stories that stretch back through his father's and grandfather's lives.

The Present Year: 1956

The immediate present spans the late spring, summer, and fall of 1956 in the fictional plains village of Gilead, Iowa. Through these months, the narrator, Reverend John Ames, who turns seventy-seven in early fall, keeps a journal in which he writes a series of letters to his son, who is not yet seven. The narrator hopes that as a grownup, the son will read this book and come to know the man his father was. The narrator is dying of heart disease, and while he is able, he wants to commit this personal history to paper as a legacy for his son.

Writing about himself causes the narrator to examine his private feelings, his religious beliefs, the role sermon writing has played in his life as a minister, his study of the Bible and various philosophical and psychological questions he has been unable to resolve. As the narrator records the events of 1956 and summarizes a family history that covers 120 years, he digresses frequently into topics connected to his ministry, to his congregation, and his lifelong friendship with Robert Boughton. These parts inter-rupt the plot line but effectively reveal the narrator's mind and his personal challenges, his grief and regrets. Through the journal, the narrator hopes to present himself to his son with a candor quite different from his day-to-day reserve.

The narrator begins writing by reporting a conversation the previous night between him and his son in which the narrator broached the subject of his illness and possible death. The son refused to believe the narrator may die. The narrator assures the son that "there are many ways to live a good life"; this journal relates one of them, a minister's life in service to others.

The son struggles with his school work, needs prodding to get to bed at night, and tolerates the concentrated attention of both his mother and the narrator in morning preparation for school. During this spring, the narrator feels pretty good, though on some nights he has difficulty sleeping and goes to his upstairs study to write or read or doze in his chair. Some nights he leaves the parsonage and walks through the neighborhood to his church; he sits in the sanctuary awaiting the dawn. On some afternoons, he walks to the home of his friend, Reverend Boughton, the father of eight children and now a widower, who is cared for by his daughter Glory. Their good news is the expected arrival of Reverend Boughton's son, John Ames Boughton, whom everyone calls Jack.

The narrator's son plays with the family cat, spends an afternoon blowing bubbles with his mother, and draws airplanes while lying in a square of sunlight in the narrator's study. The son also plays with his Lutheran friend Tobias Schmidt. On pleasant evenings, the narrator, his wife Lila, and the son sit on the front porch. On Sunday afternoons, the wife and son study their lessons, the wife reads her western novel, and Reverend Ames falls asleep over his books.

Slight hints appear that through the summer the narrator's health declines. He reports having trouble breathing, lifting his son, and going upstairs. Jack Boughton arrives in town, much to his father's delight, but he is an irritation to the narrator. Jack visits the Ames family at the parsonage, and once he attends service at the narrator's church. During the summer months, Jack plays catch with the narrator's son. Jack also helps Lila move some of the narrator's belongings from his upstairs study to the ground floor parlor, in the process handling the journal, which the narrator takes as an affront to his privacy. On hot days, the son and Tobias play in the sprinkler; once they attempt to camp out in Tobias's backyard, but noises frighten them, and they end up coming to the parsonage for some late-night sandwiches and a safer sleep indoors. As the narrator's health declines, members of the congregation send in casseroles and donate a television so Reverend Ames can watch his baseball games.

The narrator confesses in his journal to being troubled by Jack Boughton's presence. At forty-three years of age, Jack is only a couple years older than the narrator's wife, and he is physically able to play catch with the narrator's son. Jack may seem benign and well-intentioned, but he arouses jealousy and fear in the narrator, which the narrator tries to hide. These feelings are triggered, in part, by what the narrator knows about Jack's past and what he envisions about his future in Gilead. The narrator wonders if Jack may take his place as Lila's husband once the narrator has died. After all, Jack seems to be a more appropriate partner for the narrator's wife and a more age-appropriate father for the narrator's son. Reverend Ames is angry about being old and dying when he loves his wife and son so much and wants to remain with them.

In a short time, the narrator discovers Jack has his own problems, and he has returned to Gilead hoping to find resolution and forgiveness. Jack feels he can talk to the narrator but not to his own father. Speaking privately to the narrator, Jack reveals that he has a black common-law wife and a son by her. Anti-miscegenation laws in Missouri prevented their marrying when they became committed to each other, and her family has as of this summer effectively separated them. Troubled and not knowing where to turn, Jack leaves Gilead. But just as he departs, he accepts the narrator's blessing. This act of benediction seems reflexively to resolve the internal conflict which has tormented the narrator and somehow brings him to a point of peace where he can leave off writing.

Years in Gilead: 1882 to 1956

Born in Kansas in 1880 and having moved to Gilead when he was two years old, the narrator has really known only this one town as his home. He was virtually an only child in a family of five children. Edward, the first son, studied abroad and settled into a teaching career at the state college (later University of Kansas) in Lawrence. There he married and had six children. After Edward, who was born in 1870, the narrator's father and mother had three children, two daughters and a son, all of whom died of diphtheria. Then John was born and reared practically alone.

John recalls fondly his early years in Gilead, walking on stilts with his friend Robert Boughton, whom he called Bobby; trying to be friends with a little girl, Louise, who would allow nothing to interrupt her rope skipping and who then stopped long enough to marry the narrator during his last year in seminary. Louise died giving birth to their premature daughter, Angeline, who died shortly after birth. The now ailing narrator refers several times to this primary double loss. After all these years and now happily married with a son, the narrator continues to grieve for his first wife, and thinks repeatedly of the moments he held their daughter, of how she opened her eyes right before dying, to look at him. He envisions that after dying himself he will meet Louise and their baby in heaven.

The narrator was a widower at age twenty-five. A new minister, he tended his congregation, sat by the dying, gave his sermons, and alone in the parsonage ate his fried egg sandwiches and listened to baseball games broadcast over the radio. He continued his friendship with Robert Boughton, who married happily and had eight children, all of whom grew into adulthood. The narrator thinks about the luck Boughton has had, living in a lively household full of children, being able to see his children mature and marry, being able to see his wife age along with him. The narrator loves Boughton, admired him so much when he was a young man, now so appreciates his theological and Biblical insights, and yet he is bitterly jealous of him. The narrator admits failing in the commandment against covetise.

However, twenty or so years into Boughton's life as a family man, difficult times came to this family which the narrator envies. The son called Jack got involved with a very young woman and impregnated her. A daughter was born. Jack went away to college, leaving his parents to cope with the realization that their granddaughter was living in abject poverty. They tried in vain to help her, but the child died at age three and the child's mother ran off to Chicago. Looking back on that scenario, the narrator concludes that Jack "squander[ed] his fatherhood as if it were nothing." This sequence of events haunts John Ames in his final year: Jack denied his paternity while John Ames had his paternity stolen from him by death. Now, as he faces his own failing health and Jack's return, Reverend Ames envisions a replay of the earlier events; he imagines that when he dies, Jack may get too close to Lila and their son and then do them harm. The working out of this problem constitutes the main action recorded in the journal during the year in which it is written, 1956.

Before Gilead: 1830 to 1882

Of the previous generations of family members, the narrator writes most about his eccentric, radical grandfather. This first John Ames at age sixteen in Maine had a vision in which Jesus appeared to him cuffed in chains that cut his wrists to the bone. The vision urged the boy to liberate the captive, directions that prompted him to leave Maine in the 1830s and head for Kansas. There in the 1850s conflict between Free Soilers and abolitionists, on the one side, and proslavery forces, on the other, was waged. The grandfather participated in that conflict. He also knew John Brown, an historical figure who led the attack on Harpers Ferry and, thus, in part, precipitated the Civil War. When the Civil War began, the grandfather wanted to fight in the Union Army, though his age disqualified him. Still, he went as a clergyman and was injured at the Battle of Wilson's Creek in Missouri on August 10, 1861, during which Brigadier General Nathaniel Lyon was killed. In the battle, Grandfather Ames lost an eye. After the war, he married, had a family, and later moved with his son, daughter-in-law, and grandson, the narrator, to Iowa, where Grandfather Ames became one of the founders of the town of Gilead.

As he aged, Grandfather Ames became eccentric and even more radical in his beliefs. He took a militant stand for liberty and supported the World War I enlistment of local boys. Taking charity to an extreme, he would steal laundry from the wash, including his own bedding, and coins from the pantry lard can, all to give to vagrants and ne'er-do-wells who happened by asking for a hand-out. He impoverished his son and daughter-in-law and took belongings from other members of their congregation. All these were charitable acts to his mind. He also had repeated visions in which Jesus spoke to him.

The narrator's father was a pacifist, completely set against the militancy of the grandfather. When the grandfather advocated war, the father temporarily left the church and went among the Quakers to worship. Shortly after this defection, the grandfather left Gilead for Kansas, never to return. Years later, when the narrator was twelve, the father received a package containing the grandfather's belongings and set out with the narrator to find the grandfather's grave. In 1892, this journey was dangerous, given the drought and scarcity of food, and the narrator recounts several stories associated with it. The most important of these pertains to how he and his father tended the grandfather's long-neglected grave before heading home to Gilead.

The narrator's father sees his own defection from the grandfather's brand of religion differently when he must deal with his son, Edward. The narrator's brother, Edward, returns briefly to Gilead after college study abroad, and the father learns that Edward is now an atheist. The narrator is in awe of his older brother, is persuaded to read the atheist philosopher Ludwig Feuerbach as he has, and to socialize with Edward despite his extraordinary refusal to say grace over the family meal. The church (the denomination of the church the Ames family attends and in which the male members serve as ministers is not specified) paid for Edward's education, and on the first of each year, Edward habitually sent back a check to the congregation by way of thanks. The narrator sees the good in Edward, and yet he struggles with ambivalence, loyalty to his parents and love for his brother. Edward lived out his life a few hundred miles away in Lawrence where he had a wife and six children. The narrator's parents in time leave Gilead, too.

In his sixty-seventh year, the narrator falls in love with a young woman who begins attending his church. Her past is a mystery and she is completely without family. She immediately captures the narrator's attention when she enters the church for the first time on a rainy Pentecost Sunday. Later, she takes lessons in the faith from Reverend Ames, and he baptizes her. She helps around the parsonage and then surprisingly proposes marriage to him. This emotional upheaval and sudden devotion transforms the narrator's lonely existence. They marry and have a son. As he writes the journal, the narrator repeatedly tells the story of Lila's arriving at the church and of her proposing marriage. In him, Lila found the settled life she had never known; in her, the narrator found the magnetic, romantic chemistry he had never before experienced.

Characters

Angeline Ames

Daughter of narrator John Ames and his first wife, Louisa, baby Angeline, named by Robert Boughton and baptized by him, died shortly after her birth. The narrator, who refers to her as Rebecca, the name he would have given her, had a moment in which to hold the baby. She opened her eyes and looked at him shortly before she died. Her loss, along with her mother's death in childbirth, is a grief that hounds the narrator, one to which he returns in his letter to his son.

Edward Ames

Ten years older than the narrator and his brother, Edward Ames left Gilead as a young man to study philosophy in Germany where his own beliefs were shaped by the work of Ludwig Andreas Feuerbach (1804–1872), a materialist who challenged orthodox religion, for example attacking the Christian belief in immortality. Feuerbach believed that the idea of God is a projection of the inner nature of man. When Edward returned to the United States, he married a young woman from Indianapolis, and the couple had six children. He taught at the state college (later University of Kansas) in Lawrence until his death. For Edward, leaving Gilead was "like waking from a trance"; he lived out his years only a few hundred miles away, rarely visiting his parents or brother John in Gilead.

Reverend John Ames

Reverend John Ames, the narrator, son and grandson of Protestant ministers with the same name, turns seventy-seven in the early fall of 1956. Throughout most of 1956, he writes a journal addressed to his son. The narrator was born in 1880 in Kansas, the son of John and Martha Turner Ames, and grandson of John and Margaret Todd Ames. He has lived all but two years in Gilead, Iowa. Ames has been a widower most of his adult life, having married his childhood sweetheart, Louise, who died giving birth to their only child,

Angeline, when Ames was twenty-five. The baby died shortly after birth. For the next forty-two years, the narrator lived a solitary, contemplative life as a small town minister.

When he was sixty-seven, John Ames married Lila, who shortly thereafter bore him a son. Because of his age and failing health, the narrator has no hope of seeing his son, now nearly seven years old, grow into manhood. To account for himself, Reverend Ames writes of his "own dark time," during which he got by on "books and baseball and fried-egg sandwiches." He looks at the present moments with wife and son and neighbors; his memories of his birth family and grandparents; and his future both on earth and in heaven, all through the lens of his approaching death. A person habitually aware of the world's beauty, he now sees his life with a sharp tenderness, knowing he is soon to leave it. This novel purports to be the journal John writes in his final year in the hope that his son will read it when he is an adult.

Lila Ames

Second wife of Reverend John Ames and mother of his son, Lila is forty-one in 1956 as her husband writes his journal letter to their son. John says of his wife, he "never knew anyone . . . with a smaller acquaintance with religion." Lila appeared in Ames's church in May 1947 on Pentecost Sunday, when the narrator was sixty-seven and she was thirty-two. She had a difficult past, arriving in the small Iowa town with a face full of "settled, habitual sadness." She has no family. She admires the book knowledge of John Ames, who eventually baptizes her. She helps out around the parsonage, and when Reverend Ames admits not knowing how to thank her, she suggests marriage to him. She loves her husband and is devoted to their son, and she wants to improve her book learning so she can assist in the education of their son. Lila loves the western novel, *The Trail of the Lonesome Pine*, a romantic story of a May-December marriage. She is mindful of her role as the minister's wife and tries to speak correctly and act appropriately.

Louisa Ames

Louisa Ames, childhood playmate and then teenage sweetheart and first wife of Reverend John Ames, dies in childbirth. John Ames continues to grieve for her, remembering her as a child skipping rope, her braids flopping on her shoulder, and anticipating with pleasure seeing her and baby Angeline in heaven after he dies.

Margaret Todd Ames

Margaret Ames, the narrator's paternal grandmother, does not get much attention in the novel. She is eclipsed by her husband, the narrator's eccentric grandfather. But the narrator does provide one story. After the narrator's father walked out on the grandfather's sermon, Margaret Ames, who was suffering from cancer, had her daughter carry her to the church to attend the service. In this dramatic way, she communicated her loyalty to her husband, in the face of the disrespect shown him by their son.

Martha Turner Ames

Martha Ames, the narrator's mother, is strong enough to stand between her husband and her father-in-law when they begin to fight. She is committed to the family, hard-working and prudent, and saves what she can by hiding some coins in the pantry and some in a handkerchief under her blouse. She chaffs at the grandfather's so-called charity, an "endless pillaging" of the family's goods, for the sake of giving to beggars and vagrants, yet she respects the old man for his tenacity and religious vigor.

When a storm blows through, soiling the day's wash on the line and destroying the hen house and her chickens, Martha Ames has the resilience to make a joke of the disaster: she closes one eye and uses the one-eyed grandfather's favorite line, "I know there is a blessing in this somewhere." Remembering the scene years later, John Ames remarks about his mother, "She always did like to make me laugh." Martha Ames drank whiskey to dull her rheumatism and slept poorly at night. Then during the day she would doze by the kitchen fire. The narrator remarks: "She'd wake up if the cat sneezed . . . then she'd sleep through the immolation of an entire Sunday dinner two feet away from her."

John Ames Boughton

Called Jack, John Ames Boughton is named after his father's best friend, Reverend John Ames, who was widowed and childless at the time Jack was born. Now forty-three, Jack returns to Gilead in the summer of 1956. He is the most beloved of Boughton's sons, but he is also described as "the lost sheep, the lost coin." He misbehaved as a teenager, pulled pranks, and was a nuisance. Then as a young man, he brought shame on his family when he fathered a child out of wedlock and left town, leaving the young mother and baby in poverty. Away from Gilead and unknown to his family, he establishes a long-term loving relationship with "a colored woman" and has a son by her. He would marry her, but anti-miscegenation laws prevent it. Now back in Gilead Jack seeks connection with John Ames, "father of his soul," across their troubled past relationship, and hopes briefly that Gilead may provide a place in which he and his common-law wife and son can live.

Robert Boughton

Robert Boughton, "a staunch Presbyterian" minister and the narrator's best friend, whom the narrator called Bobby when they were children, is now bent double with arthritis and in frail health. Robert was best man at the marriage of John and Louisa Ames; he named and baptized their daughter, Angeline, shortly before the baby died; and he married John and Lila Ames forty-two years later. Living near one another, Boughton and the narrator visit regularly, discussing theology and scripture.

Boughton and his wife had eight children, four of each sex, and their house was lively and crowded, quite a contrast to John's parsonage during the decades in which he was alone. Thinking John would never have a son of his own, Boughton named one of his sons, John Ames, as a tribute to their lifelong friendship. Boughton grew old with his wife, who died in 1951. Once a lively, handsome man, Boughton is in 1956 in even poorer health than the narrator. He is cared for by his daughter, Glory, at home now after her own marriage has failed. The narrator loves his friend but has over the years also been jealous of him. Widowed for decades, John saw Boughton's family life as "blindingly beautiful."

Father

The pacifist father of the narrator and husband of Martha Todd Ames, John Ames was born in Kansas and moved to Iowa in 1882. Reverend John Ames and his wife Martha had five children: Edward, the oldest; then two daughters and a son who died of diphtheria; and then, ten years younger than Edward, their last child, John, named after his father and grandfather before him, the narrator of this novel. The youngest child, John, did not know the three middle children who died. The narrator's father, a Protestant minister, recoiled from the violence of the Civil War, became a pacifist and preached the doctrine of love. He was angry with his own father, the narrator's grandfather, for being a militant abolitionist and in the pre-Civil War violence in Kansas for being willing to kill if need be to assure Kansas would be a free state. When the United States entered World War I in 1917 and American men enlisted, the narrator's father became ill and nearly died. The narrator describes his father as Abel, covering up "the guilt of his father," the narrator's grandfather.

Glory

Glory, daughter of Robert Boughton, has returned home to care for her father in his final illness after her own marriage has failed. She maintains the family home and garden, cooking for her father and extending herself to her brother Jack when he visits and to their neighbors. Glory is devoted to her father and to the family and criticizes Jack for leaving just as their siblings and spouses circle around their father on his deathbed.

Grandfather

The militant grandfather of the narrator and husband of Margaret Todd Ames, John Ames was born in Maine and went west in the 1830s. As a youth of sixteen, he had a vision in which Jesus, bound in chains, laid his hands on him, and thereafter John felt called to be a militant abolitionist. As a young man he participated in the Free Soilers violence in Kansas led by John Brown. Later, too old to enlist as a soldier, he served with the Union forces as a clergyman, and lost an eye at the Battle of Wilson's Creek in Missouri (1861). After the Civil War ended and now living in Gilead, Iowa, and serving the community as a minister, the grandfather preached the righteousness of war to a congregation of women whose men and sons were away at war or already casualties of it. This act enraged his son, the narrator's father, who walked out of the church and went to worship with the pacifist Quakers. Shortly thereafter, the grandfather left Gilead for Kansas where he was an itinerant preacher until his death. When the narrator was twelve he accompanied his father on a life-threatening journey into drought-afflicted Kansas. They found the grandfather's neglected grave, attended to it, and prayed over it.

Jack

See John Ames Boughton

Tobias Schmidt

The narrator's son's best friend, Tobias Schmidt, lives across the street and is a Lutheran. The two boys play together throughout the summer of 1956. Tobias has a strict father who prohibits his son from watching television at the Ames's parsonage and talks to Reverend Ames about the bad language the boys use. This conversation becomes a joke between the narrator and Robert Boughton.

The boys take to spelling the alphabet in such a way that they speak the letter "L" with "worldliness and scorn," making it sound like a swear word. Tobias's father thinks Reverend Ames must be a lax Unitarian because he is amused by the boys' conduct. Later Boughton pretends to agree with Mr. Schmidt, saying, "I have ong fet that etter ought to be excuded from the aphabet."

Son

John Ames's six-year-old son is not named in the novel. The narrator addresses his son directly in the journal as "you." The old men in town call the boy "Deacon," which suggests a natural seriousness and may also convey others' belief that he will grow up to be a minister just like his great-grandfather, grandfather, and father were. But the son also resembles his mother. In fact, the narrator says that the son's face has a look of "half sadness and half fury" in it, very much like his mother's. The son plays with his friend Tobias, draws pictures of airplanes while lying on the floor in his father's study, and enjoys the family cat, Soapy. In one scene the son and his mother blow soap bubbles. When Jack Boughton comes to visit, he plays catch with the boy. There are tender moments too between the son and his father, John Ames; in fact, the novel begins with one. However, as the months progress, the father's illness prevents his engaging in a lively way with his son.

Themes

Father and Son Relationships

The most important theme in *Gilead* pertains to the difficulty in making connection across the generations, particularly between fathers and sons. In some places in the novel, this difficulty is explored in terms of the parable of the Prodigal Son. Indeed, in several cases in the novel, the son's decision to leave (leave the family home town, leave the faith) is understood by the father as a "defection," (the military term suggests both cowardice and disloyalty). The father and son feel rejection, and anger simmers between the two.

The grandfather left Maine to fight for abolition in Kansas, to join the Union Army in the Civil War; as he aged and perhaps even more so after he was wounded in battle (losing his eye, losing his depth perception), he became all the more radical and eccentric. He gave sermons with a gun in his belt, urging people to fight for what is right, and continued doing so, even when he was mostly addressing widows and mothers whose husbands and sons had died in the war. This stance enraged his son, the narrator's father, also a minister in the same Protestant sect, causing him to walk out on the grandfather's sermon and worship with the Quakers. This defection by the father angered the grandfather so much he decided to leave Gilead and return to Kansas, where he remained until his death. The irony is that the breach between generations is a snag that holds the two connected, even against their will; the father received the grandfather's personal belongings, buried and unburied them, and finally took the narrator, then only twelve years old, in search of the grandfather's grave. They found the grave, cleaned it, and prayed over it, but what a struggle it was to get to that place and what a struggle it was to return from it.

The father "grieved . . . bitterly that the last words he said to his father were very angry words and there could never be any reconciliation between them in this life," and yet that breach recurred between the father and his firstborn son, Edward, the narrator's brother. Edward left Gilead to study in Germany, came home an atheist, and refused to say grace in his father's parsonage. He could quote the Bible still, but he preferred the works of the atheist Feuerbach to his own father's sermons. Scholarly Edward lived out his life in Lawrence, Kansas, at the state college (later University of Kansas), just a few hundred miles away, believing that in leaving Gilead and in leaving the narrows of his father's Protestantism, he awoke as if from a "trance."

Robert Boughton's son, John Ames Boughton, called Jack, defected in more than one sense. In his early twenties, he left Gilead, abandoning a young woman whom he had impregnated and their child who, in neglect and poverty, died at age three. The narrator, now twenty some years later, accuses Jack of having "squander[ed] his fatherhood" and further suspects Jack of perhaps intending to move into a relationship with Lila, once the narrator has died. In fact, when Jack returns in the summer of 1956, ostensibly to see his dying father and privately in hopes that Gilead will provide haven, the narrator scorns him. The narrator sees Jack in terms of his earlier abandonment, even in terms of his childhood misdemeanors. This attitude contrasts with old Boughton who rejoices in his son's return, the one "whom he has favored as one does a wound" and seems to rally in his presence. Repeatedly the narrator considers "warning" his wife and son about Jack, a person who seems so friendly and yet may

Topics For Further Study

- Write a letter to a relative of yours or to your child or a child you envision having one day. For a week write in the letter every day both about memories you have, about what is happening in the immediate moment as you write, and about what you imagine the future holds for yourself and for the person to whom you are writing. You may decide to keep the letter for a child or for a child not yet born. Or you may decide to mail the letter to the relative to whom it is addressed.
- Get the full names of your parents, your grandparents, and your great-grandparents. For all of these ancestors, see if you can determine the year and place of their births, and if they are deceased, the year and place of their deaths. Now interview family members, asking for stories the family has passed down about these ancestors. When you have the genealogical information and a couple stories, write an essay about what you have learned. If you wish, you may include in the essay some of the stories.
- Get a blank map of the United States and draw on it the migration route of Grandfather Ames from his birthplace to Gilead. Since Gilead is a fictional town you can choose its location in Iowa, based on what you learn about the narrator's journey into Kansas by horse and on foot and how long that takes. Draw a route the narrator and his father may have taken on their trip into Kansas. Last, locate St. Louis, Missouri, and Lawrence, Kansas, on the map, writing a few words next to each, telling what happens according to the novel in these cities. How does making a map clarify the plot of this novel?
- Define miscegenation and do some research on this topic in order to better understand the problem Jack Boughton has and what his options are in the 1950s. Then write an essay explaining the term and the legal issues associated with it. Explain any relevant laws of the 1950s or earlier which might affect Jack's situation. Conclude your essay by explaining what you think might have happened to Jack, his wife, and child.
- Look through old letters, journals, or albums your family has. Select some document or photograph of a time the predates your earliest memories and write a story based on the document or photograph.

hide evil intentions. Like Edward in this one respect, Jack has also abandoned the faith of his father. While Edward has succeeded professionally and had a good marriage which produced six children, Jack has been a loner and a ne'er-do-well; a professional liar by his own admission, he has charmed his way through life without finding a calling or purpose. In a sense, though Jack returns to Gilead for a visit, he remains lost. The seed for healing, however, lies in the secret Jack carries home and confides in the narrator, the man whom he calls "Papa."

The parable of the Prodigal Son is about the breach between a father and the son who leaves him and about the father's great joy in this son's return. It equally pertains, however, to the relationship between the father and the other son, the one who remains at home, steadfast and working, while his sibling is off spending his inheritance. This devoted son is the one with whom the narrator identifies. Though he believes himself to have been a disappointment to his father, the narrator recognizes that he fulfilled the role of "the good son . . . the one who never left his father's house." The narrator's intention in the journal is to make connection with his own son, despite that most final of defections, death. He writes his sermons imagining his baby daughter, walking into church some Sunday, all grown up. He writes this journal to communicate, as if from the grave, that his son has "been God's grace to [him], a miracle."

The departure of the son may be as natural as the decision by another son to remain behind in the father's house, but as in "the Parable of the Lost Sheep," the father focuses on the lost one. In this novel, an increasing focus is on Boughton's son Jack who returns for the summer. While the narrator is writing to his own son, creating this time capsule the boy may read when he is an adult, the narrator is approached by his godson and namesake, John Ames Boughton, who repeatedly attempts to engage the narrator in conversation. When the narrator realizes Jack's predicament, that Jack has lost his common-law wife and child, he sees Jack differently, sees his "beauty" and blesses him. With a fine symmetry, he blesses his friend's son as Jack leaves Gilead for the last time, just as Boughton blessed Reverend Ames's premature baby daughter before she died.

Forgiveness

This novel presents a minister who struggles to learn the lessons he preaches, a man who seeks scriptural insights to help him live a moral life. The humanity of John Ames is fully conveyed in so many ways, and not least of these is his admission of his own failings. Of these perhaps the one that hounds him most is his covetousness, that he envies his beloved friend Robert Boughton. Reverend Ames also struggles with anger, the family trait which characterized the father's feelings about the grandfather and the grandfather's feelings about almost everything.

John Ames envies Reverend Boughton for his long marriage and for having so many children, all of whom Boughton saw grow up. Boughton had the opportunity to grow old with his wife, and John Ames envies him that. Reverend Ames found the lively Boughton household "blindingly beautiful," a beauty that over the decades while he was widowed seemed to eclipse the fact the Ames had once had a wife, too, and a daughter. Also, the beauty in Boughton's family life seemed to negate what Reverend Ames found beautiful in his own solitude. Regarding his preference for visiting with Boughton, just the two of them, in the narrator's own kitchen, John Ames explains: "I don't think it was resentment I felt then. It was some sort of loyalty to my own life." In facing his grief over the untimely death in childbirth of his first wife and the neonatal death of their daughter, Reverend Ames still appreciates the beauty in those forty-two years of solitude before he met Lila, his second wife. Imagining their son as an adult reading this journal, Reverend Ames states: "I hope you will understand that when I speak of the long night that preceded these days of my happiness, I do not remember grief and loneliness so much as I do peace and comfort—grief, but never without comfort; loneliness, but never without peace. Almost never." While insisting on the positive aspects of his solitary life, the narrator also admits how he feels about seeing Boughton with his grown son, Jack: "It has been one of the great irritations of my life, seeing the two of them together." The point in all of this for Reverend Ames is that while he savors the good in his own life, he struggles with the grief in it, the loss of his first wife and their daughter and also the recognition that he will not live to see his own little boy grow up. So, yes, there is comfort and peace, and great joy in the son's presence but also a gnawing grief, which expresses itself as irritation, anger, envy, covetousness.

Reverend Ames sees Jack in a new way once he knows Jack has also lost a wife and child. Realizing they share a common grief, Reverend Ames stops judging Jack by wrongs he committed, both in childhood and adulthood, and stops seeing Jack as a sneaky culprit and potential threat. Face to face with Jack's loss, Reverend Ames softens. He offers money, but more, he offers benediction. In blessing Jack, Reverend Ames soothes his own irritation, appeases his own covetousness.

Details about the characters' ages may be a subtle hint at the theme of forgiveness. One of these details is that in early fall, John Ames turns seventy-seven. His son is not quite seven. Jack Boughton is forty-three (four and three add up to seven). These specific ages, taken together, may echo the law of forgiveness taught by Jesus in Matthew 18:22: "I say not unto thee, until seven times: but, Until seventy times seven." Reverend Ames seems satisfied after he blesses Jack. He has forgiven Jack and seen "the beauty" in him. It is as if in identifying with Jack, John Ames is able to find the balm he seeks in Gilead.

Style

The Novel as Journal or Letter

As it is used in literary criticism, the word, genre, according to *A Handbook to Literature* designates "the distinct types or categories into which literary works are grouped according to FORM or technique or, sometimes, subject matter." But the distinctions between genres may not always be absolute, since a given work can draw from various types or categories of writing to achieve the desired effect. *Gilead* is a work of fiction, a novel, yet it clearly has features of other kinds or types of writing. The novel reads as though it is a collection of private letters or one long private letter to one person, written piecemeal over time, a text intended for only one reader, the writer's son. This feature makes the work sound like a private document, one never intended to be published and read by a wide audience. The sense readers have that they are reading someone else's private letter increases the impression of intimacy in the text; the device brings readers closer to the narrator's most inner self. The strategy deepens and narrows point of view. Using the letter device makes the work akin to a subcategory of the novel genre called the epistolary novel, which is a novel comprised of letters instead of chapters.

Moreover, since the text presents itself as one that was written over the course of several months, with brief entries added on an almost-daily basis, it also appears to be a journal or diary. It is worth noting that the novel as a genre tends to present itself not as fiction but as a historical account, a history (Leo Tolstoy's *War and Peace*), a collection of letters (Daniel Keyes' *Flowers for Algernon*), a journal (Daniel Defoe's *Journal of the Plague Year*), an autobiography (Margaret George's *The Autobiography of Henry VIII*). Clearly, even if a work of literature falls in one category, as Robinson's is definitely a novel, it can blend characteristics from various types or categories. What does an author stand to gain in giving a work these features? In this case, Robinson gains depth of insight into the single point of view; she can scroll back into American history for her themes within the family history this narrator wants to record, and yet she is not obliged to write a conventional conclusion. She can also omit how and when the narrator dies and how the narrator's son receives the journal left for him as his legacy.

Setting: The Balm in Gilead

The balm, or soothing element (literally the honey-like resin from certain trees thought to have medicinal properties) in the fictional town of Gilead, Iowa, lies in part in its historically having served as "a place John Brown and Jim Lane could fall back on when they needed to heal and rest." Iowa, "the shining star of radicalism," the state without anti-miscegenation laws, lay just beyond Kansas. It served as a safety zone for abolitionists and Free Soilers who fought to make sure that Kansas was admitted to the Union as a free state. Before the Civil War, Gilead and other towns like it served as havens for runaway slaves. Many houses in town have "hidden cellars or cabinets where people could be put out of sight for a day or two." These houses testify to a time when Gilead was a stop on the Underground Railroad, with townspeople hiding escaped slaves who were headed north. The militant grandfather was one of the town's founders, a man who counted it a blessing to have known John Brown personally and to have lost an eye supporting the Union effort in the Civil War. This historical role of Gilead in accepting and aiding blacks waned in subsequent generations. The black church closed and its congregation moved to Chicago after someone started a fire next to the building, and when Jack returns in hopes that Gilead might provide a haven for him and his common-law wife and biracial child, he realizes there is no racial diversity in the town.

Plot

A plot summary describes the action of the novel, generally using divisions of chapters or sections. This novel, however, is not divided into chapters. It reads like a journal. Entries are separated by space breaks: some spaces are blank, and some are marked with a horizontal line. Toward the end of the novel, one space break is so large it suggests the conclusion of the body of the book and the beginning of a final section, something like an epilogue. Given these characteristics of the text, the plot contains both immediate events that transpire as the narrator writes during the summer of 1956 and reaches into the past of the narrator and further back into the lives of his father and grandfather. Dominant memories of the narrator are related, such as the trip he made at age twelve with his father in 1892 when they went to Kansas in search of the grandfather's grave. An important earlier trip is one the narrator made with the grandfather to Des Moines to see a baseball game in which Bud Fowler, the first African American to play professional baseball, participated. The narrator tells childhood stories about the ongoing disagreement between his father and grandfather, about how his mother stared down the old man who wanted to give her household savings to beggars, and about how the narrator's grandmother suffered from cancer and yet directed her daughter to carry her to church to show her support for her husband. Going further back, the narrator reports the grandfather's visions of Jesus and his adamant, militant stance against slavery.

The discursive prose slides from event to reflection to theological question to immediate scene, following the movement of the narrator's thought and focus. Behind this natural, shifting movement across subjects occur tiny hints strategically placed to reveal indirectly what lies beyond the narrator's focus. For example, while the narrator is away from the parsonage, Jack Boughton, at Lila's request, moves furniture and personal articles from the minister's upstairs study to the main floor parlor; the narrator returns to discover that his journal has been placed where he never keeps it. Also, the congregation's awareness of the narrator's failing health is conveyed indirectly by the casseroles that show up in the parsonage kitchen and by the women in the church beginning to cry immediately when, in his sermon, Ames alludes to how an old minister may worry about the congregation he must soon leave.

The entries in the journal are not dated, but hints are given of time passing. In the present, the narrator refers to the previous night or this morning; he plans a sermon, thinking about the Bible stories he wants to mention, then later he mentions having given the sermon. Also, clues appear regarding his physical decline. He reports feeling all right then not being able to lift his son as he used to do and not finding the steps as easy as they were once. He complains about not sleeping and having trouble breathing while lying down. In one scene, Jack Boughton helps the narrator out of his porch seat, and the narrator is humiliated by the fact that he needs the assistance. In these ways, indirectly, his failing health is conveyed. In all, the handling of plot in this novel works to reveal the mind of John Ames, the way he associates ideas, the way he holds onto regret. In this way, the plot serves to reveal his character.

Allusion

An allusion is an indirect reference to a literary or historical figure or event; its effectiveness depends on the shared knowledge of the author and the reader. The more well-read the reader, the more likely it is that allusions will be recognized and the meaning of the work thereby enriched. Allusions can occur in tiny details or take up considerable text. In telling the story of their trip to Kansas in search of the grandfather's grave, the narrator reports that his father had said they "were like Abraham and Isaac on the way to Mount Moriah." In this reference, Robinson makes use of the Old Testament story and also draws upon historical fact, for in 1892, a severe drought in Kansas made food extremely scarce. The narrator's father proved his love for the grandfather by going to this extreme trouble to locate and care for his grave, yet in proving that love, he put himself and his own son, the narrator, at risk. The father was at risk of starvation or being shot for gleaning from gardens, and the narrator admits if his father had died on this trip, the narrator himself would have been stranded in Kansas, just a boy of twelve. This allusion is amplified later in the novel when the narrator dwells on stories about Abraham and his two sons and gives a sermon on that subject.

Other allusions serve to anchor the setting historically; for example, the narrator refers to Woodrow Wilson in his discussion of World War I (1914–1918), and he also states that he will vote for Eisenhower and then in the fall alludes to the election. Dwight Eisenhower was re-elected to the presidency in the fall of 1956. One literary allusion suggests Lila's unwavering devotion to her husband. Lila loves reading *The Trail of the Lonesome Pine*, a novel by John Fox published first in 1908, which was made into a film in 1936. Fox's novel tells the story of a May-December romance and marriage in which the wife remains faithful to her much older husband. While the narrator entertains ideas about Jack Boughton's intentions regarding Lila and she is friendly and open to Jack, her love for Fox's novel is a hint that she is in truth devoted to her husband.

Historical Context

Nineteenth-Century Kansas, Missouri, and Iowa

Gilead spans 126 years of American history, from 1830 to late 1956. Major historical events, most of which occur in Kansas, Missouri, and Iowa, create a backdrop for the first two generations in the Ames family. The grandfather heads west in 1830 and participates in the 1850s violence in Kansas over the slavery question. A strict abolitionist and totally opposed to the spread of slavery to the territories or to having any state join the Union as a slave state, the militant grandfather knew John Brown (1800–1859) and was willing to engage in gunfights and may have even killed one or more men, all in the name of freedom.

In the decades leading up to the Civil War, people had opposing opinions about whether territories in the West should be allowed to enter the Union as slave or free states. Southerners wanted new states to permit slavery; northerners in general wanted slavery contained in the South. Some antislavery advocates opposed the practice on economic grounds; they feared that if new areas permitted slavery, plantation-style farming would occupy large tracts of land, eliminating the possibility of ordinary people having small farms. Other abolitionists were more thoroughgoing in their opposition and were prepared to fight against slavery wherever it was promoted. These included individuals who called themselves Free Soilers, who were willing to settle in new territories and fight if necessary to prevent slavery from occurring in the new area. The conflict was brought to a head by the Kansas-Nebraska Act of 1854, which divided the Kansas territory into northern and southern parts and allowed a local referendum to decide if slavery was to be legal in either section. Violent outbreaks, some of which were led by abolitionist John Brown, were so bloody that they came to be collectively referred to as Bleeding Kansas, and many saw what happened in Kansas as a preview of the Civil War.

When the Civil War erupted in 1861, the grandfather wanted to enlist; refused because of his age, he served with the Union forces as a clergyman. He was seriously wounded and lost one eye at the Battle of Wilson's Creek, Missouri, which was fought on August 10, 1861. Brigadier General Nathaniel Lyon died in this battle; he was the first Union general to be killed in the Civil War. The grandfather felt his own injuries, including the loss of an eye, were inconsequential compared to the loss of Lyon.

In 1892, the narrator, then age twelve, and his father, left Gilead, Iowa, and returned to Kansas, in search of the grandfather's grave. A terrible drought gripped the southwestern third of the state, a drought that engulfed half of the state in 1893. The parched farmland gave rise to dust storms like those that recurred in the late nineteenth century and in the 1930s, the latter exacerbating the economic depression of that period.

In the last half of the nineteenth century, Iowa was known as "the shining star of radicalism." Glory talks about "towns like ours," which were "a conspiracy," because "Lots of people were only there to be antislavery by any means that came to hand," including building houses that had "hidden cellars or cabinets." Runaway slaves, if they got across into Iowa, might well find refuge in these small towns en route to Canada. Moreover, unlike Kansas, Iowa never had anti-miscegenation laws, which explains why Jack hopes briefly to find a place for himself, his common-law wife, and their biracial son to live in the town of Gilead.

Spanish Influenza

The novel mentions a 1916 outbreak of influenza. In fact, in December of 1915 and throughout 1916, there was a major respiratory disease epidemic in the United States. This disease was often referred to as Spanish influenza because its origins were traced to Spanish-speaking Central America. By the spring of 1918, just as World War I was slowly drawing to a close, the pandemic influenza began, a disease so deadly it took about fifty million lives worldwide, more than died in total in the war. The one sermon Reverend Ames recalls never giving pertained to the sudden outbreak of deadly influenza in 1916 at Fort Riley. He stated: "They drafted all the boys at the college, and influenza swept through there so bad the place had to be closed down and the building filled with cots." In his sermon, Ames stated that the boys' "deaths were a sign and a warning to the rest of us that the desire for war would bring the consequences of war, because there is no ocean big enough to protect us from the Lord's judgment when we decide to hammer our plowshares into swords." His pacifist father would have been pleased with that sermon, but Reverend Ames decided not to give the sermon, knowing the few women attending church were apprehensive enough without it.

Critical Overview

Gilead was widely and wonderfully well received. Stacy Carson Hubbard in her review entitled, "The Balm in Gilead," writes that the story of John Ames "unfolds in a ruminative style, full of pithy vernacularism and homiletic wisdom." Hubbard stresses that "Ames's tale is not so much a celebration of goodness as it is a celebration of complexity and ambiguity." The novel, she writes, is "a meditation on the meaning of fatherhood, both literal and figurative. . . . Every father here is as much a mystery to his child as God is to humanity, and every son is in need of that 'boundless compassion' which Karl Barth—our narrator's favorite theologian—identifies with the radical otherness of God." Hubbard concludes that Robinson's novel is "remarkable and redemptive," a work that "invites us, with a kind of understated ecstasy, to contemplate the mysteries of being in the world."

Thomas Meaney, in his review entitled "In God's Creation," praises the "masterly control" of *Gilead*'s narrative. He also points out that John Ames is a sympathetic character, "a wise old Iowa minister," so unlike many ministers evoked in novels who "come outfitted in the vestments of their own unraveling." Meaney explores Robinson's handling of the concept of predestination, and he concludes that her "Heaven . . . may afford an extraordinary amnesty for sinners. But *Gilead* also argues that, in this world, moral responsibility lies squarely on the individual's shoulders." Gerald T. Cobb, writing for the journal *America*, concludes

A prairie scene showing a landscape similar to the setting in Gilead © Annie Griffiths Belt/Corbis

that "Robinson deftly combines the elegiac and the eulogistic into a compelling sense that this minister of a small town has a privileged view of life's horizons and depths."

Among so many positive assessments perhaps the last word should belong to Scott A. Kaukonen who evaluated the novel for *The Missouri Review*. Comparing Robinson's *Gilead* to other contemporary writing, Kaukonen writes: "In a culture where bombast passes for insight and where theological nuance suffers amid sound bites and power politics, *Gilead* refreshes like water from a deep, cold spring. . . . It reminds us that grace and mercy can be more than planks in a political platform."

Criticism

Melodie Monahan

Monahan has a Ph.D. in English and operates an editing service, The Inkwell Works. In this essay, Monahan examines the healing role journal writing plays in the life of John Ames, the narrator of Marilynne Robinson's Gilead.

In *Gilead* (2004), the central action, it might be argued, is the habitual daily writing Reverend John Ames does during what he anticipates will be his final year. Robinson's protagonist is a man writing a journal, a "letter" to the "grown man" his son will be. At the outset his purpose in writing this journal is clear: John Ames is dying of heart disease, and he wants to leave a message for his little boy to read when he grows up. The novel is that message, a year-long journal or extended letter. On the surface, this task is transparent: Ames, who has written fifty sermons a year for forty-five years, sets out to do some different writing now. He intends to create a personal account of himself, write something intimate. Someday his son, who stands to inherit precious little, will at least have this book, written by his dad in the last year of his life, quite an inheritance in its own right. What Reverend Ames does not realize, however, is that unlike a sermon that gets tied up neatly in thirty pages or so, ongoing daily writing can lead away from the initial subject into unexpected terrain, and it can affect the writer in ways he does not anticipate. Writing the journal, Reverend Ames fulfills his original intention, but he also accomplishes other work: he learns more deeply about what makes him heart-sick, his grief, his anger, and envy; he even engages at one point in a dialogue with himself, part of a valiant effort to sort through his feelings and find the balm his heart requires. Equally important, he extends himself to his namesake, his best friend's son, repairing that longstanding troubled relationship. These unexpected developments in his journal writing may be facilitated by Reverend Ames's resolve to make the journal "an experiment with candor." The novel traces, then, how the writing process itself transforms the writer's thinking and over time may bring healing to chronic, hidden wounds. *Gilead* provides an opportunity to observe how journal writing draws the writer toward the meaning he implicitly seeks and how that meaning affects his actions. In short, journal writing is shown to be a catalyst for personal transformation and action.

Insomniac John Ames has lived his life awake in more than the literal sense. A poet, a philosopher, and man without pretense who searches for the truth and admits harboring unanswered questions, Ames writes deliberately. In the early pages of the journal, he notes his attention to words. He loves the word "susurrus" (full of whispering sounds) and describes himself as having "a certain crepuscular quality" (resembling twilight). He is self-conscious as he writes, trying to do a good job. He comments on "the care it costs [him] not to use certain words more than [he] ought to." He talks about the word "just," as an ordinary intensifier. He remarks on using the word "'old'" too often but explains that, for him, it "has less to do with age . . . than it does with familiarity. . . . with a modest, habitual affection." He calls his lifelong friend, "'old Boughton'"; he refers to Gilead as "'this shabby old town,'" meaning in both instances "very near" his heart. In frequent passages, his word choice reveals his aesthetic eye for detail. He describes soap bubbles, for example, that "ripen toward that dragonfly blue . . . before they burst." He describes his son standing on the swing, with the "planted stance of a sailor on a billowy sea"; the son swings so high "the ropes bow like cobwebs, laggardly, indolent." He wants to save experience by anchoring it in text. He regrets Boughton's remarkable sermons were never written down: "So that is all gone." About his own sermons saved in boxes, they may "seem foolish or dull," but he wrote them with "the deepest hope and conviction. Sifting [his] thoughts and choosing [his] words. Trying to say what was true." Reverend Ames sets out to write the journal with the same deliberate care he used to compose his sermons. However, as he continues writing in his journal, his self-consciousness recedes somewhat; he becomes more engaged with his own ideas and feelings, sorting these out, wondering about them.

Reverend Ames ponders scripture; the stories in both Testaments having to do with fathers and sons and with parents and children recur in his thinking. These stories resonate with his circumstances, and he finds comfort in the way some stories conclude. He reports in his journal how "the story of Hagar and Ishmael" came to him while he was praying. As he worries about how his wife and child will manage without him (once he is dead, they will have to leave the parsonage and find somewhere else to live), he refers to this Biblical story and takes heart: "That is how life goes—we send our children into the wilderness. . . . Even that wilderness, the very habitation of jackals, is the Lord's. I need to bear this in mind." He imagines that without him his wife and child will be thrust into a wilderness of vulnerability. He specifies what in the parsonage belongs to him, things they should take with them, and he cautions his son to accept any help parishioners offer since during his service to the church he has generously helped its members. He repeatedly regrets having so little to leave his wife and son by way of an inheritance.

"... in the darkness of his suffering and longing, quite surprisingly, Ames undergoes a jolting change of heart."

Full of love and concern for his wife and boy, he nonetheless admits a mean-spirited irritation with John Ames Boughton (called Jack by everyone), the son of his lifelong best friend, Robert Boughton. The emotion stems, perhaps, from an initial event intended as a kindness. Eight years after Reverend Ames's first wife died along with their premature baby daughter, Reverend Boughton had yet another child, a son. Reverend Ames baptized this baby, and when he asked what it was to be called, he was shocked to learn it would bear his own name. In that baptismal moment, Reverend Ames rejected the baby, feeling that this child somehow denied his own little daughter's existence. Remembering this moment late in the journal, Ames writes: "my heart froze in me and I thought, This is *not* my child." In the same passage, he explains envy as it applies to himself: "covetise is . . . in my experience . . . not so much desiring someone else's virtue or happiness as rejecting it, taking offense at the beauty of it." As he writes now about it, he sees a sermon topic in this line of thinking, and he also ponders whether the baby John Ames Boughton "felt how

What Do I Read Next?

- Robinson's first novel, *Housekeeping* (1980), which was nominated for a Pulitzer Prize, is a work of remarkable metaphoric richness, full of American literary allusion. The novel is set in a small western town situated on the edge of a lake and tells the story of three generations of women, coping in various ways with the task of going on despite traumatic losses.
- Robinson's *The Death of Adam: Essays on Modern Thought* (1998) is "contrarian in method and spirit," as she states in her "Introduction." Of the included essays, "McGuffey and the Abolitionists" and "Puritans and Prigs" cover topics that surface in *Gilead.*
- Gloria Naylor's novel *The Women of Brewster Place* (1989) follows the lives of seven women living in Brewster Place, a ghetto housing project in a northern U.S. city. The poignancy of these women's lives and their hopes and challenges clearly depict the difficulty that poor African American women face living in poverty and coping with racial and sexual prejudice.
- Ursula Hegi's *Sacred Time* (2003) tells the story from three different points of view of an extended Italian family living in the Bronx in the 1950s. The accidental death of one of the children traumatizes parents, aunts and uncles, and cousins, and becomes the shaping event in the lives of that child's generation.
- Against the backdrop of the American Civil War, *The Glory Cloak* (2004), by Patricia O'Brien, tells the story of an orphan girl who travels to Concord, Massachusetts, in 1858 to live with her cousin, Louisa May Alcott. Susan Gray goes with the Alcott family to Washington, D.C., to volunteer in helping Union casualties.
- Norman Maclean's collection *A River Runs Through It and Other Stories* (1976), containing two novellas and one short story, tells the story of a young man and his family, set in rural western Montana.
- *March* (2004), by Geraldine Brooks, is a novel which draws from personal journals and letters of Louisa May Alcott's father. Brooks based the main character on the father in *Little Women.* In this novel, a father leaves his family to fight in the Civil War and in the process discovers what he believes.
- *Letters from an Age of Reason* (2001), by Nora Hague, tells a Civil War story of an interracial and cross-class relationship between the rich white daughter of a New York family and the black house servant in a family of French American slave holders.

coldly I went about his christening, how far my thoughts were from blessing him." Jack grew up during the years in which Ames remained widowed and childless, and Reverend Ames confesses that seeing Jack with his father was "one of the great irritations" of his life.

Reverend Ames continues to think of what happened to the Biblical Abraham's sons; as he writes in his journal, he makes plans for a sermon on the subject. He focuses on the idea of wilderness and what can soothe it: "My point was that Abraham is in effect called upon to sacrifice both his sons, and that the Lord in both instances sends angels to intervene at the critical moment to save the child." He concludes, taking Abraham's fate for his own, that the father must "trust to the providence of God." Even more, he realizes that each person is destined for the wilderness, that Abraham "himself had been sent into the wilderness . . . this was the narrative of all generations." As he writes, applying these stories to his own situation, Ames begins to realize that he is called upon to have faith regarding his wife and son (Hagar and Ishmael) and himself (Abraham). Normally in his sermons Reverend Ames would not refer to personal matters, but in writing later in his journal about how he delivered this sermon, he reports digressing to mention how an old pastor may worry about what might become of his congregation after his death; the pastor is called upon to believe that God is in charge. The Old Testament stories are paradigms: no matter what manner the abandonment, Reverend Ames comes to understand in his journal writing, his faith is called upon to recognize that God is in charge in the wilderness. As he soon realizes, the wilderness has both a physiological and a psychological dimension.

As he broods about what he calls his "sin of covetise," Reverend Ames chaffs at the smiling presence of Jack Boughton. He resents Jack's having helped move Reverend Ames's study to the main floor parlor and is offended by Jack's placing the journal in a drawer where Reverend Ames never puts it. He knows he is unreasonable, but with candor he writes out his feelings. Gnawing him is the suspicion that Jack will get close to Lila and their son after Ames dies and may do them harm. This thought torments Ames. These present feelings are triggered by his age-old envy of Boughton, who had four sons, all of whom he saw grow up; Boughton loved Jack the most, the one who since childhood irritated Reverend Ames. Ames defines covetise as "that pang of resentment you may feel when even the people you love best have what you want and don't have." In order to steer clear of breaking the "Commandment, Thou shall not covet," Ames has avoided the Boughton household, despite his love of Reverend Boughton. In 1956, when Jack comes home, he wants to talk privately with Reverend Ames on a matter he cannot discuss with his father; Jack repeatedly approaches, and Reverend Ames recoils, irritated and guarded, tempted repeatedly to warn his wife and son about Jack's potential to harm them, in all feeling increased physical and emotional agitation.

As Ames struggles with this issue, he juxtaposes in the journal different types of writing. In one instance, Ames uses his journal to sort out his feelings about Jack, especially in the face of Jack's request for consultation. Ames engages in a dialogue with himself. He imagines a scene in which he, Ames, calling himself Moriturus, comes to Reverend Ames for consultation, and the dialogue he writes out surprises him:

> Question: What is it you fear most, Moriturus?
>
> Answer: I, Moriturus, fear leaving my wife and child unknowingly in the sway of a man of extremely questionable character.
>
> Question: What makes you think his contact with them or his influence upon them will be considerable enough to be damaging to them?
>
> Now, that really is an excellent question, and one I would not have thought to put to myself. The answer would be, he has come by the house a few times, he has come to church once. Not an impressive reply.

This dialogue shows Ames that he does not have evidence to prove Jack's alleged culpability. Ames realizes that his fear is directly connected to the envy he feels when he sees Jack sitting in the pew with Lila and their son: "I stood there in the pulpit, looking down on the three of you, you looked to me like a handsome young family, and my evil old heart rose within me . . . I felt as if I were looking back from the grave." This turmoil is not about Jack but about Reverend Ames, and the journal writing allows Ames to realize it. It makes perfect sense: "The fact is," he concludes, "I don't want to be old. And I certainly don't want to be dead." Even Jesus "wept in the Garden," knowing he was to die; Reverend Ames can feel some compassion for himself; he knows himself to be "failing." Sleep becomes "elusive" and "grueling," and prayer has not quieted him. Then, in the darkness of his suffering, quite surprisingly, Ames undergoes a jolting change of heart.

He reflects again in his journal upon the baptism of Jack Boughton, considering how Reverend Boughton had given John Ames this baby "to compensate for [his] own childlessness." Reverend Ames realizes that his rejecting the baby, in a way, seems like Jack's rejection of his own baby daughter born out of wedlock. He prays now "for the wisdom to do well by John Ames Boughton" yet acknowledges that his "sullen old reptilian self would have handed him over to the Philistines." His conflict heightens: he reports being unable to sleep: "My heart is greatly disquieted. It is a strange thing to feel illness and grief in the same organ." An "old weight in the chest" informs him that he knows more than he knows, and he "must learn it" from himself. He goes back over what he knows about Jack, about his pranks in childhood, particularly how the boy stole a photograph Ames had of his first wife, Louise, and then how the child smiled innocently at him afterward, seeming to mock him while calling him "Papa." Now he thinks the child Jack was "'lonely,' though 'weary' and 'angry'" also describe him. Curiously, he depicts the young Jack in terms that apply to himself now as he writes. Remembering how the child galled him, Ames reports, just writing about it "is not doing me any good at all." He says elsewhere in the journal that transformations can be "abrupt" (as the change in him when he first saw Lila in church on "that blessed, rainy Pentecost"). Suddenly, Ames feels connected to Jack: "John Ames Boughton is my son. If there is any truth at all in anything I believe, that is true also. . . . That language isn't sufficient, but for the moment it is the best I can do." Concern for writing style is less important than this realization: "it is a rejection of the reality of grace to hold our enemy at fault."

In these journal passages, as he seeks both psychological and theological clarification of his feelings about Jack, Ames is fully self-referential. He is no longer writing to his little boy; now he is sorting through his own feelings, outlining his own blind spots. He rereads his journal. He is troubled. In the moment, he concludes, "Oh, I am a limited man, and old, and [Jack] will still be his inexplicable mortal self when I am dust." Because Ames is freighted with these feelings, it is not surprising that the first two private conversations between him and Jack fail. Ames is antagonized by Jack's pleasantries; he reports in his journal, "I am angry as I write this. My heart is up to something that is alarming the rest of my body."

Shortly after this entry, a blank page appears in the journal, not unlike the kind that signals the end of a chapter. When the text begins again, it is on the facing (recto) side of the next page, with a large first letter, matching the format used on the novel's first page. This new section of the journal appears almost to be an epilogue. It begins with the secret Jack confides in Reverend Ames: Jack has a wife and child, "a colored woman, and a light-skinned colored boy." Here all the time Reverend Ames has been mucking around in his own grief, examining his private wounds, interpreting Jack and everything else in terms of his own problems, Jack has been preoccupied with a quite different, but equally weighty problem. Jack cannot speak to his own father about his cross-racial relationship or about his biracial son. He returned to Gilead to see his ailing father, to be sure, but he cherished the hope that Gilead, a place that once harbored runaway slaves, would be a haven beyond anti-miscegenation laws, one in which he could live with his family. While he is in Gilead, however, Jack learns that his common-law wife and their son have been removed from him permanently by her family. He tells Reverend Ames about all of this. Reverend Ames quotes Jack at length, admitting that in doing so he violates "pastoral discretion." He excuses himself to his son: "I just don't know another way to let you see the beauty there is in him." How interesting that here Ames uses that word "just," which in the early pages he says conveys "something ordinary in kind but exceptional in degree." Facing Jack's pain in losing his family, seeing no "grounds for [his] own dread," Reverend Ames admits, "I felt as if I'd have bequeathed him wife and child if I could to supply the loss of his own." This is transformation, indeed.

In the journal's closing pages, Reverend Ames expresses his gratitude "for the splendor" of the world, which he found also in Lila and in their son's "sweetly ordinary face." He knows that "old Boughton," if he could, would rise out of his "decrepitude" and follow Jack into the world to bless him, that son "he has favored as one does a wound." Reverend Ames longs to witness such "extravagant" blessing as Boughton would bestow in Jack, this "prodigal son" who leaves Gilead while Boughton lies on his deathbed. In the consummate scene, Reverend Ames enacts what Boughton cannot physically accomplish: Ames blesses Jack. Jack thinks he is leaving Gilead forever, and Reverend Ames understands. They wait at the bus stop; Reverend Ames has "to sit down on the bench beside him on account of [his] heart." Reverend Ames places his hand on Jack's forehead and pronounces "the benediction from Numbers . . . 'The Lord make his face to shine upon thee.'" All the roles a man may play coalesce in the blessing Reverend Ames adds: "Lord, bless John Ames Boughton, this beloved son and brother and husband and father."

In this moment of benediction, face to face with Jack, as in the journal consultation he faces himself, Reverend Ames evokes what elsewhere he calls "incandescence." In seeing the beauty in John Ames Boughton, John Ames sees the beauty in himself. He resolves to "put an end to all this writing." The first snow arrives. Ames concludes his journal with the best of his faith: "the Lord loves each of us as an only child." Then addressing his son again, he assesses the legacy: "What have I to leave you but the ruins of old courage, and the lore of old gallantry and hope? Well, as I have said, it is all an ember now, and the good Lord will surely someday breathe it into flame again." The journal which began as a letter to this son, grown into manhood after the father's death, has become a journey into the writer's self. Uncovering the "bewilderments" of that "new territory," that wilderness of soul, became the process by which this journal writer made himself known, first to himself, next to his son. Late in his journal writing, Reverend Ames realizes that he set out to do one thing and the writing took him in an unanticipated direction:

> I have been looking through these pages, and I realize that for some time I have mainly been worrying to myself, when my intention from the beginning was

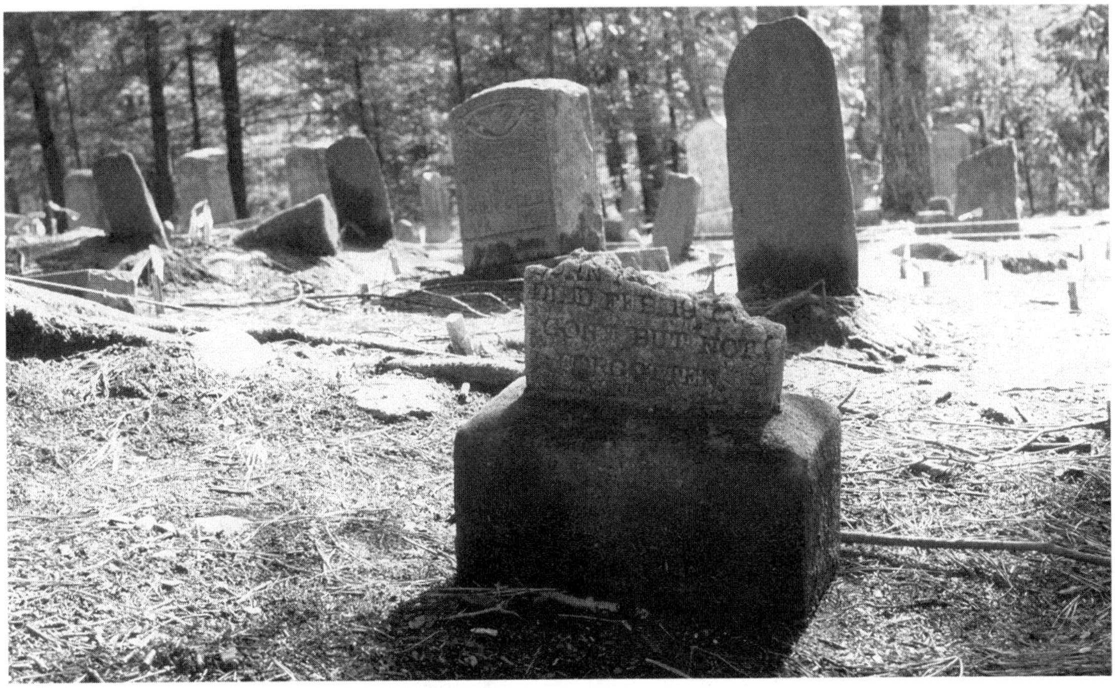

An abandoned graveyard, perhaps similar to the grandfather's neglected grave mentioned in the novel Photograph by Robert J. Huffman/Field Mark Publications. Reproduced by permission

> to speak to you. I meant to leave you a reasonably candid testament to my better self, and it seems to me now that what you must see here is just an old man struggling with the difficulty of understanding what it is he's struggling with.

Journal writing invited this disclosure. This text promises to touch Reverend Ames's beloved son because it depicts with candor the writer's struggle and its resolution.

Source: Melodie Monahan, Critical Essay on *Gilead*, in *Novels for Students*, Thomson Gale, 2007.

J. A. Gray

In the following review, Gray expounds on Robinson's exploration of the father/son relationship involving a preacher on the "familiar American prairie."

Marilynne Robinson's *Housekeeping,* published in 1981, is an extraordinary work of art, and many readers have waited impatiently for Robinson to publish a second novel. I'm among them, although I've waited more in dread than in anticipation. Robinson describes American landscapes as superbly as Willa Cather and peers into the American soul as relentlessly as Herman Melville—and in *Housekeeping* she combined these talents to frighten me badly.

Housekeeping takes place in a waterlogged little town in the northwest, where two adolescent sisters, orphaned when their mother drowns herself, become the wards of their aunt, a drifter who leaves off riding the rails in order to come live with them. In the house left them by their dead grandmother, the girls wage a quietly epic struggle against the pull of their aunt's transient ways, against the intrusive lake and its implacable tides, against the grief that becomes a universal solvent. Can the girls avoid the dissolution of their home, their futures, their very souls? Is there any ground on which they can plant an intimacy or nurture an ambition that will not be swamped by sorrow?

Robinson tells their story in a prose that embodies perfectly the entropic sadness that she finds lapping at all foundations and saturating every good intention. Her watery symbolism accumulates a depressing power, as everything begins to fall of its own sodden weight. Love reaches out only for what is out of reach, and eros provides no countervailing warmth, as the men of the family

"Into Ames' apparent ramblings Robinson has carefully built many omissions, suppressions, and avoidances. Unobtrusive and only dimly sensed, they contribute to one's uneasiness and a sense of buried intrigue. Never does Ames address his son by name or even report his name."

have long since slipped beneath life's surface. Nor is there any prospect of spiritual rescue. Robinson finds among the flotsam some scraps of pagan myth and some pages from the Judaic testaments, old and new, but these wisdoms are themselves orphans, uprooted and adrift. There is no sign of an ark, of a Moses who might part the waters, of a savior who can walk upon the flood without sinking.

In this diluvian world the little church where grandmother used to sing in the choir is a source merely of unwelcome and finally fatal intrusions. The ladies of the congregation bring to the girls' crumbling home not the good news of salvation but only casseroles and coffeecakes that are left untouched and uneaten. Their well-meant meddling incites the book's climax, when the young women set fire to their house and flee across the lake into a life of endless wandering. The people of the church and the town suppose them to be drowned—as indeed they are, spiritually. In the contest of life and grief, grief has won.

Housekeeping bears repeated rereading, if one can stand the chill and the damp, and if one can surrender one's secret hope (well, my secret hope) that next time it will turn out differently. It never does. Thus I approached *Gilead* with cautious alacrity. In *Housekeeping* Robinson had demonstrated the futility of any attempt to make a home; would she persuade me in *Gilead* that there is no balm for the sin-sick soul? To my relief, her project in *Gilead* seems to be not to tear down but to build up, or at least to restore to this world much of what she washed away in *Housekeeping.*

As narrator we have not a rootless and unchurched young woman but an elderly Congregationalist minister who has lived all his life in the same parsonage in the town of Gilead, Iowa. When this preacher ("preacher" is what he prefers to call himself) says things like, "I remember walking out into the dark and feeling as if the dark were a great, cool sea and the houses and sheds and the woods were all adrift in it, just about to ease off their moorings," we know we are still on Planet Robinson, but these prove to be the sunnier latitudes of that melancholy globe. The prairies of Iowa and Kansas offer dry land aplenty, and water here is not a carrier of paralyzing sorrow but a healing substance, lustral and often luminous. Male figures, so conspicuously absent in *Housekeeping,* dominate the foreground. The preacher, John Ames, is writing out for his son an account of his life and the lives of his forebears, father and grandfather, who were also ministers of the gospel, dating back to before the Civil War. Thus the church, so dismissible in *Housekeeping,* is central to *Gilead.* Even those Christian casseroles are redeemed: Ames lived in his parsonage as a widower for some forty years, and he dined contentedly on the very dishes, donated by the ladies of his congregation, that the women of *Housekeeping* could not stomach.

The novel is a single long letter, written over the course of half a year or so in the mid-1950s. Reverend Ames, aged seventy-six, has been medical diagnosis: angina pectoris could kill him at any time. His son, his only child, is seven years old; the letter will be given to the boy's mother, Ames' forty-one-year-old wife, to keep for the boy to read when he is grown. The letter is the preacher's sole legacy ("I do regret that I have almost nothing to leave you and your mother") and in it he attempts to enact the love that he will not be present to give the boy, offering advice, sharing memories, discussing life's meaning—and occasionally (such is the force of professional habit) making notes for new sermons as they occur to him.

Ames writes of his grandfather, an abolitionist preacher and Free Soiler in the Kansas territory in the 1850s, and of his father, a young soldier in the Union army and later a preacher in Gilead, and of his own brief first marriage, which ended with his wife and daughter dead in a premature childbirth. He lived alone for decades—"I didn't feel very much at home in the world, that was a fact. Now I do"—until the boy's mother, a stranger in town, walked into his church one Pentecost Sunday: "She makes a very unlikely preacher's wife. She says so herself. But she never flinches from any of it. Mary

Magdalene probably made an occasional casserole, whatever the ancient equivalent may have been. A mess of pottage, I suppose."

Ames has tried always to live as the Lord wants him to live, which for him entails ceaseless prayer, constant self-questioning, and a startlingly ferocious pacifism. He takes a certain modest pride in the fifty years' worth of sermons he has stored in boxes in his attic, noting that he is "up there with Augustine and Calvin for quantity." Impatient with apologetics and uninterested in doctrine ("It was Coleridge who said Christianity is a life, not a doctrine, words to that effect"), he never tires of thinking on the loveliness of creation and the goodness of God ("Augustine says the Lord loves each of us as an only child, and that has to be true.") Occasionally he offers an insight from one of his favorite theologians: John Calvin, Karl Barth, and (yes) Ludwig Feuerbach.

Robinson skillfully impersonates this sober, righteous, progressive parson with a hint of poesy in his voice as she interweaves the three themes—his family history, the abolition of slavery, and his practice of the Christian faith—that dominate his seemingly discursive jottings. Suddenly, however, a new event intrudes upon Ames' autumnal reflections: the ne'er-do-well son of Ames' neighbor Boughton, the Presbyterian minister, unexpectedly returns to Gilead. Pastor Boughton is Ames' best friend, and the returning prodigal, now a middle-aged man and still mysteriously erratic, is Ames' godson. Why is he back after so long away? And why does he show such interest in Ames' wife and child?

This matter is resolved, though not wholly to the benefit of the book's integrity, for in concentrating on it Robinson veers away from the carefully crafted illusion of a digressive letter and begins to write scenes straight from, well, a novel. When Robinson's wrap-up of important themes is done, John Ames finds, coincidentally, that he has written enough to his son, and he brings his letter to an elegiac close.

Reviews of *Gilead* have been numerous—ranging from rapturous to respectful—but uniformly superficial. Ames is taken to be a reliable old fellow who imparts his nuggets of gospel-tinged wisdom and his small-town epiphanies with Robinson's unequivocal approval. Robinson is commended for daring to employ so unpromising a mouthpiece and is praised for the artistry with which she (mostly) keeps the loquacious minister from being a bore.

Such readings underestimate both Robinson and Ames. As with the emblematic casserole on the parsonage table, the presentation is homely but the dish is not simple: there are layers upon layers, and it has been simmering a long time. Ames the facile sermonizer finds candor elusive; he steels himself to speak but often draws back; he acknowledges that he is skilled at concealing from himself his own motivations, and he worries repeatedly about people who can "see through" him. Some reviewers have said that Robinson skimps on "plot." But there is no shortage of fraught and suspenseful episodes, including murder, religious terrorism, apostasy, fornication, child abandonment, and secret miscegenation. Of these Ames is the most reluctant of chroniclers, generally proving to say most where he says least. So obliquely and unemphatically are the deepest wounds divulged—his grandfather's commission of a gratuitous and monstrous sin against Ames' ten-year-old father, and Ames' father's loss of his religious faith (abetted, unhappily, by Ames himself)—that a reader who blinks may miss them.

Into Ames' apparent ramblings Robinson has carefully built many omissions, suppressions, and avoidances. Unobtrusive and only dimly sensed, they contribute to one's uneasiness and a sense of buried intrigue. Never does Ames address his son by name or even report his name. (Would not a father writing such a valedictory naturally chant, sing, caress the beloved name of the son of his late age?) Never does he speak the name of his wife, and about her past he is mute, though the single clue of "Mary Magdalene" posted here by the author reads like an unsubtle semaphore. Also questionable are Ames' repeated self-exculpating apologies for his family's looming poverty ("There was no way for me to make any changes to provide for the two of you"). Indications are that his congregation has the money to build a new and bigger church—after he is gone. So is Ames tacitly conveying the congregation's rejection of his new wife?

All in all, Ames' reticent revelations give an impression not so much of mellow wisdom securely possessed as of a pitiable impactedness bravery struggled against. His erotic-domestic resurrection by a wayward young woman late in life has rolled back the stone behind which he had buried his heart. In this new access of feeling, he is dimly aware that some of the warmth of his pastoral compassion derives from the old, banked fires of anger toward his father and grandfather that lie within. Newly alive to so much, he expresses keen regret that he will not be present as a father to help his boy grow up. But is there also, perhaps, a certain relief that he will not be there to wound his son or to suffer the wounds that sons can inflict on fathers? His demanding but beneficent creator, Marilynne Robinson, seems to know about this deeper layer, but she has taken care to keep the good old man from suspecting it himself.

Robinson is far too fine an artist to offer us the sort of univocal and easily mastered fiction that some have taken this book to be. She is both persistent and brave. In her superb first novel she gave voice to the griefs and losses of the mother-daughter relationship, placing them in a near-mythic world of flux and darkness. Here she attempts a harder thing, imagining her way into the conflicts and joys of the father-son relationship and staging them more terrestrially, on the familiar American prairie, in the prosaic Midwestern light, along the arc of some of the most impassioned episodes in American history.

It is brave of her, too, to try to body forth, in John Ames, some version of what the church has to offer in response to the ever-fresh and never-less-than-bitter news that we have here no lasting home. The novel may prove to be of less interest as a vehicle of Christian wisdom than as a portrait of fathers and sons—indeed, not all readers will agree that what Ames preaches and practices is (doctrinally, theologically, ecclesiologically) Christianity. But the preacher, damaged as he is and elusive as he may be with other people, is admirably assiduous in trying to turn his face always toward his Lord. With his Bible in one hand and his Feuerbach in the other, he tries to understand the world as God's gift and to offer back unceasingly his thanks and praise. "Wherever you turn your eyes the world can shine like transfiguration," he says in closing his letter to the son he must leave behind. "You don't have to bring a thing to it except a little willingness to see. Only, who could have the courage to see it?"

Source: J. A. Gray, "Christ and Casserole," in *First Things: A Monthly Journal of Religion and Public Life*, March 2005, pp. 37–40.

Sources

Cobb, Gerald T., "The Way It Was, Son," in *America*, Vol. 192, No. 14, April 25, 2005, pp. 27–30.

Holman, C. Hugh, and William Harmon, eds., *A Handbook to Literature*, Macmillan, 1986, p. 220.

Holy Bible, King James Version, Matthew 19:22.

Hubbard, Stacy Carson, "The Balm in Gilead," in *Michigan Quarterly Review*, Vol. 44, No. 3, Summer 2005, pp. 541–45.

Kaukonen, Scott A., Review of *Gilead*, in *Missouri Review*, Vol. 28, No. 1, 2005, pp. 226–28.

Meaney, Thomas, "In God's Creation," in *Commentary*, Vol. 119, No. 6, June 2005, pp. 81–84.

Robinson, Marilynne, *The Death of Adam: Essays on Modern Thought*, Houghton Mifflin, 1998. pp. 1, 41.

———, *Gilead*, Farrar, Straus, Giroux, 2004.

Further Reading

DeCaro, Louis A., *Fire in the Midst of You: A Religious Life of John Brown*, New York University Press, 2005.

To understand the militant abolitionism of Grandfather Ames, readers may enjoy this biography of the great abolitionist John Brown. This study places Brown in his nineteenth-century social and religious context and explains his brand of Puritanism. DeCaro portrays John Brown as a Protestant saint, a man ahead of his time, seeking to fulfill divine providence by acting on his radical faith.

Frost, Karolyn Smardz, *I've Got a Home in Glory Land: The True Story of Two Runaway Slaves Whose Flight to Freedom Changed History*, Farrar, Straus, and Giroux, 2006.

This book tells the true story of slave couple Lucie and Thornton Blackburn and their 1831 escape from Louisville, Kentucky, to Canada. Efforts were made to have them extradited to the United States, but the Blackburns made it to Toronto where they began the city's first taxi business. Canada's lieutenant governor came to their assistance, and their case set a precedent for those of subsequent fugitive slaves.

Gosse, Edmund, *Father and Son: A Study of Two Temperaments*, Nonsuch Publishing, 2006.

First published in 1907, Edmund Gosse's autobiography is about growing up in the strict Victorian household of his parents who belonged to the Protestant sect called Plymouth Brethren. As a little boy, Gosse was taught the imagination is evil, and instead of reading children's stories, he was expected to read stories about missionaries. As he developed into adulthood, he became interested in the outside world and questioned his father's rigid beliefs. This autobiography is an important portrait of an exceptional Victorian family.

Lubin, Alex, *Romance and Rights: The Politics of Interracial Intimacy, 1945–1954*, University Press of Mississippi, 2006.

This book studies how interracial sexual relationships were treated in U.S. culture in the ten years following World War II, in the decade leading up to the civil rights movement. Lubin explains that the federal government wanted interracial relationships to be treated as private matters so that the contradictions between a post-war atmosphere of cultural freedom and the realities of Jim Crow policies and anti-miscegenation laws would go unnoticed. Lubin's primary sources include African American literature, NAACP documents, and segregationist protest letters, among other writings.

Stellingwerff, Johan, *Iowa Letters: Dutch Immigrants on the American Frontier*, William B. Eerdmans, 2004.

These nineteenth-century immigrant letters, first published in Dutch, were written by religious dissenters from the Netherlands Reform Church and cover the period from 1840 to 1870. The letters consist of the correspondence between the settlers in Iowa and their family members back home.

Light in August

William Faulkner

1932

While William Faulkner's complex novels drew mixed critical responses in the 1930s, two events in the 1940s helped inspire a fresh look at his work and a subsequent reevaluation of his literary talent: the appearance of Malcolm Cowley's edition of *The Portable Faulkner* in 1946, which included Cowley's astute analysis of Faulkner's work, and the awarding of the Nobel Prize in Literature in 1949 to Faulkner, followed by his stirring acceptance speech. As of 2006, more scholarly work was being done on Faulkner than on any other American author, which attests to his work's relevance to modern readers. In the early 2000s, he was considered one of America's finest authors.

Light in August, published in 1932, is one of his most highly acclaimed works. The novel traces the experiences of three main characters: Lena Grove, who is searching for the father of her unborn child; Gail Hightower, an elderly minister who seeks a measure of peace in his troubled existence; and Joe Christmas, who spends his life struggling to deal with his belief that he is part black. As Faulkner weaves together the stories of these three characters, he explores the devastating effects of racism and religious fanaticism. Inevitably, however, the novel's tragic elements are juxtaposed with resilience and optimism, especially in its closing pages. *Light in August* thus becomes an apt illustration of this famous passage from Faulkner's Nobel Prize address: "I believe that man will not merely endure: he will prevail. He is immortal, not because he alone among creatures has an inexhaustible voice, but because he has a soul, a spirit capable of compassion and sacrifice and endurance."

Author Biography

William Faulkner was born in New Albany, Mississippi, on September 25, 1897 to Murry Falkner, and Maud Butler Falkner. His father held various positions, including a railroad worker, factory owner, and business manager.

William Faulkner's great-grandfather, William Clark Falkner, (Faulkner added the "u" in 1918) was an accomplished author, lawyer, and Confederate army officer who became the inspiration for Colonel John Sartoris in *Sartoris* (1929) and *The Unvanquished* (1938). Faulkner modeled Sartoris's son, Bayard, who appears in these two novels as well as *The Town* (1957), after his grandfather, John Wesley Thompson Falkner. Faulkner also fictionalized in his stories the events surrounding his great-grandfather's murder on a street in Ripley, Mississippi. Faulkner's immediate family was much less eccentric and notorious than his ancestors.

After showing academic promise in his early years, Faulkner soon lost interest in his studies and developed a passion for football, writing, and drawing. He dropped out of Oxford High School in Mississippi and began working as a bookkeeper in his grandfather's bank. During this time, he continued writing and began to read and study avant-garde literature. He tried to enlist in the U.S. Air Force at the onset of World War I but was rejected due to his short stature.

After returning to Oxford, Faulkner began working at a post office where he spent most of his time writing poetry. In 1919, he enrolled at the University of Mississippi and subsequently had several poems and a short story published by the student newspaper. He dropped out, however, before obtaining a degree but after winning the university's annual prize for the best poem. On August 6, 1919, his first poem, "L'Apres-midi d'un faune," was published in *The New Republic*. Later that year, his short story "Landing in Luck" appeared in the *Mississippian*.

Soon after, Faulkner met author Sherwood Anderson, who encouraged his artistic endeavors. Faulkner did not get much response to his first book, *The Marble Faun*, a collection of verse published in 1924. Anderson helped him find a publisher for his first novel, *Soldier's Pay* (1926), which earned some critical but no popular success.

William Faulkner © Getty Images

On June 20, 1929, Faulkner married his childhood sweetheart, Estelle, who was married before and had two children when she returned to Oxford. The couple had two children of their own, one of whom died in infancy. By the early 1930s, after the publication of *The Sound and the Fury* (1929), *As I Lay Dying* (1930), and *Light in August* (1932), Faulkner was heralded as a brilliant author. Yet the general public found his work too dark and complex. Struggling financially, he agreed to write Hollywood screenplays, including *To Have and Have Not* (1945) and *The Big Sleep* (1946). He continued writing lucrative screenplays along with his fiction for the next few decades.

While scholarly appreciation for his work remained high, by the mid-1940s, all of Faulkner's books were out of print. The publication of *The Portable Faulkner* in 1946, however, which included editor Malcolm Cowley's study of Faulkner's mythical Yoknapatawpha County, sparked new and intensified interest in Faulkner, which led to his reputation in the early 2000s as one of the most important writers of the twentieth century.

Faulkner died of a heart attack on July 6, 1962, in Byhalia, Mississippi. His major awards include the O. Henry Memorial Short Story Award in 1939, 1940, and 1949, the Nobel Prize for Literature in

1949, the National Book Award in 1951 for *Collected Stories*, the Legion of Honor of the Republic of France in 1951, the National Book Award and Pulitzer Prize in 1955 for *A Fable*, and the Pulitzer Prize in 1963 for *The Reivers, a Reminiscence*.

Plot Summary

Chapters 1–2

When *Light in August* opens, Lena Grove has been walking for four weeks from Alabama to Jefferson, farther from her home than she has ever traveled. After living in a tiny room in her brother's house in the small town of Doane's Mill for eight years after her parents died, she began to sneak out of the bedroom window at night until she found herself pregnant. Even though Lucas Burch had left town six months before her brother found out, Lena refused to reveal his name.

Deciding not to wait for him to come for her, Lena sets out to find Lucas. On the road, Mr. Armstid, a farmer, decides to bring her home for the night. She later admits to him and his wife that she is not married but makes excuses for Lucas, insisting that such a good natured fellow as he needs some time to settle down. The next morning Armstid drives her to the town store and informs the men there that she needs a ride to Jefferson.

Byron Bunch thinks about the time three years earlier when he first met Joe Christmas at the lumber mill where he works in Jefferson. Joe did not speak to anyone, and no one spoke to him for months. Another stranger who came to the mill named Brown revealed that Joe lived in the woods on Joanna Burden's estate. After three years, Joe suddenly quits his job at the mill. Rumors circulate that he and Brown are selling whiskey and that they both are living in the cabin on Miss Burden's place.

One Saturday afternoon, Byron is alone at the mill since the others have gone to watch the fire that is consuming Miss Burden's house. Lena appears looking for Burch, and Byron falls in love with her. Byron soon realizes that the man she is looking for is Brown and, in order to prevent her disappointment, provides her with only a few minor details about him.

Chapters 3–5

The narrative shifts to Reverend Gail Hightower, a defrocked minister who now struggles to make a living by selling greeting cards. He had been the town's Presbyterian minister but lost his church after "his wife went bad on him." She was killed in Memphis one night after either jumping or falling from a hotel window. The townspeople heard rumors that there was a man in the room with her and that they both were drunk.

Believing that Hightower drove his wife to commit suicide, the townspeople refused to come back to his church, so he was forced to resign. After he did not fire his housekeeper when he was warned about being alone in his home with a black woman, he was severely beaten by members of the Ku Klux Klan. Eventually, the townspeople began to ignore him and left him alone.

Byron tells Hightower about Lena, whom he has just set up at the boarding house, and they wonder who started the fire at the Burden house. A man passing by saw the fire and found Brown drunk inside the house. Upstairs, he discovered Miss Burden, almost decapitated. Byron informs Hightower that Brown and Joe have been selling whiskey from her property and that Joe is part black.

That night, Brown appears in town claiming Joe killed Miss Burden and demands the reward that has been promised for information about the murder. He tells the sheriff that she and Joe had been living "like man and wife" and that Joe is of mixed race. Byron believes that Brown set the house on fire and hopes that if he gets the money, he will marry Lena.

The narrative then goes back to the night before the murder, as Joe thinks about his complex and brutal two-year relationship with Joanna Burden. He is angry that she lied about her age and never told him that women can lose their sexual desire after going through menopause. He is also incensed that she tried to pray over him. Filled with the desire to "smell horses . . . because they are not women," and hearing strange voices in his head, he walks the next day to the black community on the outskirts of town and confronts some residents with a razor in his hand. Later, that night, he kills Joanna.

Chapters 6–7

The narrative flashes back to when Joe was five and living in an orphanage "like a shadow . . . sober and quiet." One day, he sneaks into the washroom and eats some toothpaste that belongs to the young dietician who works at the orphanage. As the dietician enters the room with a man, he hides behind a curtain and begins to feel ill from the toothpaste. When the couple begins to have sex, Joe throws up and so is discovered. Thinking that he had been spying on her, the woman screams, "you little n——bastard!"

Over the next few days, she becomes desperate as she waits for him to tell the matron about what she was doing in the washroom. Determining that the janitor, who readers later discover is Joe's grandfather, hates Joe as well, the dietician tells him what happened. The janitor snatches him the next morning, afraid that he will be sent to a black orphanage. The police catch him, however, and bring Joe back.

The woman who runs the orphanage determines that Joe needs to be placed at once and finds a farming couple, Mr. and Mrs. McEachern, who agree to adopt him. Mr. McEachern, who is characterized by his cold eyes, vows to make Joe "grow up to fear God and abhor idleness and vanity."

Three years later, the battle of wills between Joe and Mr. McEachern has intensified, as evinced in an incident when the latter tries to force the boy to learn his catechism. When Joe refuses, Mr. McEachern beats him. Feeling pity for the boy, Mrs. McEachern brings him a tray of food that evening but he dumps it in the corner. An hour later, he eats the food alone in his room, "like a savage, like a dog."

When Joe is fourteen, a group of friends and he gather one afternoon at a sawmill where they take sexual turns with a black girl who sits in the shadows. When it is Joe's turn, he begins to beat her and the others pull him off. At home, McEachern whips him for fighting.

Chapters 8–9

One night, when Joe is eighteen, he climbs out his window using a rope. He wears the new suit that he had hidden in the barn, bought with the money he gained from selling his calf. McEachern had given the calf to Joe to teach him responsibility. Joe sneaks out that night to meet Bobbie, a waitress he met in town, and to take her to a dance at the local schoolhouse. He wishes that McEachern would try to stop him.

Joe's relationship with Bobbie began a year earlier when he and his father went to the restaurant one day. Joe was immediately drawn to her, but his father determined that the place was disreputable and so never went there again. When Joe turned eighteen, he returned with a dime in his pocket. After ordering pie and coffee, he discovers that he does not have enough to pay for both. Bobbie covers for him, insisting that she had made the mistake in the order. Out on the street, "his spirit [is] wrung with abasement and regret."

Joe returns to the farm where he works hard, almost feverishly. His father notices and decides to reward him with the calf, although he insists that he probably would regret his action when Joe falls back "into sloth and idleness again." One month later, Joe goes to town with a half dollar that his mother gave him. When he tries to leave the coin for Bobbie to repay her for her kindness, the men in the restaurant make fun of him. On the street, however, Bobbie shows him her appreciation for his thoughtfulness.

A week later, he meets her after climbing out of his window at night. She tells him that she is "sick," and at first, he does not understand that she is trying to explain that she is menstruating. When he finally understands, he strikes her and runs away into the woods where he vomits. A few days later, he meets her again and drags her into the woods where they have sex.

Joe soon begins to steal money from his mother that he uses to buy presents for Bobbie. One night, when they are lying together in her bed, he tells her that he thinks that he is part black, but she refuses to believe him. One night Joe catches her with another man, strikes her, and then breaks down. Bobbie tells him that she thought he knew she is a prostitute.

Mr. McEachern sees Joe slip out the window the evening of the dance and follows him. When he spots Joe dancing with Bobbie, he approaches them and demands, "away, Jezebel! . . . Away harlot!" He turns to Joe and begins hitting him, convinced that the face he hits belongs to Satan. After Joe crashes a chair over his head, Mr. McEachern falls unconscious to the floor. Bobbie, enraged by Mr. McEachern's words, turns on Joe, blaming him for putting her in this situation.

Joe leaves for home, exalting in the thought that he has killed his stepfather, which he had sworn to do. He takes the money Mrs. McEachern has

Media Adaptations

- Random House produced an audio version of the novel, read by Scott Brick, in 2005. As of 2006, no film versions had been made.

been saving so that he can marry Bobbie. When he goes to her house, though, Bobbie is still livid, screaming at him, "Getting me into a jam, that always treated you like you were a white man." Joe is amazed that she turns on him after he has committed murder and stolen for her. After Bobbie tells the others in the house that Joe is part black, one of the men beats him, and they all leave him there on the floor.

Chapters 10–12

For the next fifteen years, Joe travels across the country, working as a laborer, miner, prospector, gambler, and soldier. After a prostitute tells him that she does not mind sleeping with blacks, he practically beats her to death. He then relocates to Chicago where he lives in a black community. At thirty-three, he ends up in Mississippi and spots Miss Burden's house. After discovering that she lives alone, one night, half starved, he breaks into her kitchen where she discovers him.

As they begin their relationship, they talk very little. Even after a year, he still feels like a robber when he comes to her at night, "to despoil her virginity each time anew." He takes her violently, but she does not resist. One night she opens up to him, telling him of her own mixed-race ancestors. Her brother and grandfather had been killed in town by an ex-slaveholder and a Confederate soldier over a dispute concerning black voting rights. As a result of that incident, coupled with the fact that they were from New England, the town hated her and her remaining family members, seeing them always as outsiders, or worse, carpetbaggers. Joe responds, "Just when do men that have different blood in them stop hating one another?"

Joanna's fanatically religious father told her that her brother and grandfather were "murdered not by one white man but by the curse which God put on a whole race before" any of them was born. He insisted that blacks were "a race doomed and cursed to be forever and ever a part of the white race's doom and curse for its sins." She tells Joe, "None can escape" this curse, and she admits, "I seemed to see [blacks] for the first time not as people, but as a thing, a shadow in which I lived, we lived, all white people." Joe admits that he does not know for sure if he is black but concludes, "If I'm not, damned if I haven't wasted a lot of time."

Soon after, Joe feels as if he is in "the second phase" of their relationship, "as though he had fallen into a sewer." She experiences a "fierce urgency that concealed an actual despair at frustrate and irrevocable years," which produces in her extreme emotions of rage and lust. He determines that he is in danger of being corrupted by her. As "if she knew somehow that time was short," she begins to talk about wanting a child and a few months later, she tells Joe that she is pregnant.

In the last phase, Joanna tells Joe that she wants him to get a degree from a black school and then to take charge of her finances. At this point, she has lost her sexual desire and so will not let him touch her. Joe stops coming to the house for a few months, and when he returns, she appears to have become an old woman. When he realizes that she is not pregnant, that she has begun menopause instead, he strikes her and tells her that she is "not any good anymore." Joanna responds, "Maybe it would be better if we both were dead." One night three months later, she asks Joe to pray with her, but he refuses. She pulls out a revolver, intending to shoot him and then herself, but he grabs the gun and then slices her throat. Afterwards, he escapes by stopping a car and demanding a ride.

Chapters 13–14

The townspeople, along with the sheriff, come out to watch the fire burn out. After seeing evidence that someone has been living in the cabin on the estate, the sheriff interviews a local black man. When the man insists that he does not know who lives there, the sheriff's deputy whips him until he admits that he has seen two white men there but does not know who they are. Another man on the scene reveals that everyone in town knows that Joe and Brown live there.

Brown soon finds the sheriff back in town and demands the thousand dollar reward for the information he has about the murder. The sheriff tells him that if he catches Joe, he can have the reward and takes him to jail "for safekeeping." The sheriff then arranges for dogs to track Joe. That night, the boy who gave Joe a ride after the murder tells his story to the sheriff. His father wants to claim the reward.

Byron discusses Lena's situation with Hightower, noting that Brown has changed his name to keep her from finding him. Hightower says that she should go back to her people, but Byron disagrees and notes that she wants to go out to the cabin and wait for Brown. Byron knows that if he tells Brown that Lena is there, he will run. Hightower suggests that is what Byron wants Brown to do and chides him for it, insisting that the devil is influencing his behavior.

Later, Byron takes Lena out to the cabin and pitches a tent near it so he can help her when the baby comes. Hightower tries to convince him to leave, arguing that he will be sinning if he tries to interfere with Lena and Brown and claiming, "It's not fair that you should sacrifice yourself to a woman who has chosen once and now wishes to renege that choice. It's not right. . . . God didn't intend it so when He made marriage." Byron, however, does not listen to him.

The sheriff discovers Lena living in the cabin on the Burden estate but decides to leave her and Byron alone, claiming, "I reckon they won't do no harm out there." A few days later, a black man tells the sheriff that the night before at a revival meeting in a church twenty miles away, a white man interrupted the service by attacking the preacher and cursing God. Some of the church members tried to restrain him but were not successful, and the man fled. The next morning the sheriff arrives at the church with bloodhounds and finds an "unprintable" note addressed to him, stuck into a plank on one of the walls. Joe is able to elude the trackers and catches a ride to neighboring Mottstown.

Chapters 15–16

A poor, elderly couple named Hines had lived in Mottstown for thirty years when Joe was captured there. Mr. Hines, who came to be known as Uncle Doc, was secretive, "with something in his glance coldly and violently fanatical and a little crazed," which kept people away from him. He and his wife lived off of the little money he earned, working at odd jobs in town and the food that black women would bring to them. Every Sunday he traveled around the county, holding revival services in black churches where he would at times "with violent obscenity, preach to them humility before all skins lighter than theirs." The black members believed that he had gone crazy after being touched by God.

On the afternoon that Joe is captured, Doc is in town and witnesses the frenzy surrounding the incident. At one point, when he comes face to face with Joe, Doc strikes him and rages, "Kill the bastard!" Later, he declares that he has a right to kill him himself. Mrs. Hines, who witnesses her husband's outbursts, becomes increasingly suspicious about Joe and asks her husband what he did with their daughter's baby. She insists that she be brought to Joe so that she can get a good look at him. Afterward, she and Doc go to Jefferson where Joe has been sent—Doc to lynch him and Mrs. Hines to prevent him.

Byron tells Hightower that Joe has been captured and that his grandparents have been found. Later, he brings them to see Hightower, and Mrs. Hines admits that Doc took Joe to an orphanage after he was born because their daughter was not married. She did not see Joe for the next thirty years. Hines also murdered Joe's father when he caught his daughter trying to run away with him before the baby came. He would not let his wife go for the doctor when his daughter was in labor, and as a result, she died.

Mrs. Hines thinks that Joe's father was Mexican, but Hines insists that he had black blood. Hines explains that he became a janitor at the orphanage to keep an eye on Joe. Byron asks Hightower to say that Joe was with him on the night of the murder, but Hightower refuses.

Chapters 17–18

The next morning, Lena's child is born, and Byron realizes that he must tell Brown. When Hightower instructs Lena to send Byron away because her child is not his, she admits that she has already refused Byron's marriage proposal and she would still do so.

Byron decides that he will leave as soon as Lena and Brown reunite. He convinces the sheriff to send Brown out to the cabin without telling him that Lena is there. Brown goes, thinking that is where he will pick up his reward money. When he sees Lena, his face registers "shock, astonishment, outrage, and then downright terror." Byron watches the cabin after Brown goes in and soon sees him running out the back. In an effort to defend Lena's honor, Byron catches up with him and challenges him to a fight, even though he admits, "now I'm going to get the hell beat out of me." Two minutes later, Byron is on the ground bleeding, and Brown is gone. On his way back to Lena, he hears that Joe has been killed.

Chapters 19–21

Joe escapes and flees to Hightower's house. After knocking Hightower out with a pistol he has stolen, he crouches behind a table, waiting for the sheriff to come for him. Percy Grimm, a local, patriotic zealot, insists that it is his responsibility to preserve order and so recruits some men to go after Joe. He finds Joe at Hightower's. Hightower tries to convince Grimm that Joe was with him the night of the murder, but Grimm refuses to listen and shoots Joe. While Joe is clinging to life, Grimm castrates him, and Joe dies.

Soon after, a traveler picks up Lena, her child, and Byron, who insist that they are looking for Brown but do not seem to know or care where they are going. When Byron tries to join Lena under the blanket in the back of the truck, Lena wakes up and declares, "aint you ashamed." Mortified, Byron gets off the truck and does not catch up with them until the next day. At the end of the book, the two continue on as Lena expresses her amazement over how far she has traveled.

Characters

Bobbie Allen

Bobbie Allen, Joe's first girlfriend, is a waitress and a prostitute. She is small, "almost childlike," looking much younger than her years, which makes her seem approachable to Joe. Yet, a closer look would reveal that her size was due to "some inner corruption of the spirit itself: a slenderness which had never been young."

At first, she is patient with Joe as she gently educates him about women and sexuality. The corruption of her spirit, however, emerges during the dance when Mr. McEachern accuses her of being a harlot. Her wounded pride causes her to lash out at Joe and to betray his trust in her and their future together.

Martha Armstid

Lena stays the night in Martha Armstid's home on her way to Jefferson. Martha's appearance and the work she does in her kitchen are described as savage. She has "a cold, harsh, irascible face," which is "like those of generals who have been defeated in battle." She is a bitter woman who tells her husband that he "never lifted no hand" raising their kids, but she is kind enough to give Lena some money. Her presence at the beginning of the novel illustrates the harsh reality of a woman's life in the South during the first part of the twentieth century, a reality that Lena eventually has to face.

Mr. Armstid

Armstid picks up Lena along the road and, pitying her, takes her back to his home for the night.

Miss Atkins

Twenty-seven-year-old Miss Atkins is the dietician at Joe's orphanage. Willing to do anything to save her position, she turns against Joe, who she thinks saw her having sex with a man in the washroom. Her guilt and fears of retribution cloud her judgment, causing her to misread Joe's intentions. Convinced that Joe is torturing her by waiting to tell about the incident, she tries to malign him to the janitor, convinced that others are as racist as she. As a result, Joe is eventually forced to leave the orphanage.

Lucas Brown

Lucas Brown, also known as Lucas Burch, is notorious for his tendency to tell stories, and so the people of Jefferson "put no more belief in what he said that he had done than in what he said his name was." Unfortunately, Lena does not see this quality in him and so he is able to con her into believing that he would marry her and provide for their family. Lucas "liv[ed] on the country, like a locust," waiting to land on any opportunity that he could work to his advantage. Others knew that "he'd be bad fast enough . . . if he just had somebody to show him how." He is loyal to no one, including Lena, whom he deserts, and Joe, whom he turns in for the reward money.

Byron Bunch

Unassuming Byron Bunch is "the kind of fellow you wouldn't see the first glance if he was alone by himself in the bottom of an empty concrete swimming pool." He is a hard worker who has little in his life except for his six-days-a-week job at the mill and the choir he directs on Sundays until Lena comes to Jefferson. Hightower, whom he visits two or three nights a week, is his only friend in town. Lena initially mistakes Byron for Brown. The juxtaposition of the two characters in this way highlights their differences.

After Lena comes to town, Bunch proves himself to be an honest and decent man. Initially, he tries to think of ways that he can keep Lena and Brown apart, but his conscience, along with some prodding from Hightower, forces him to place Lena's needs above his own. Even though he is in love with Lena, he tries to reunite her with Brown because Brown is the father of her child. When Brown deserts her again, Byron's protective nature emerges as he demands justice for Lena and challenges Brown to a fight that he knows he will lose. By the end of the novel, he leaves with Lena, taking an active role in plotting the direction of his life.

Lucas Burch

See Lucas Brown

Joanna Burden

Although Joanna Burden was born in Jefferson and has lived there all of her life, she is considered an outsider because her family came from New

England during Reconstruction. The townspeople label her a Yankee and a "n——lover," and they all gossip about the improper relationships she has with blacks. Her brother and father were killed in town during an argument about voting rights for blacks, and she has continued their legacy of helping blacks, most notably through her financial support of black schools and colleges.

She remains aloof in her isolated existence on the edge of town. Her personality has a certain duality, one side feminine and "the other the mantrained muscles and the mantrained habit of thinking . . . [with] no feminine vacillation." Her attitude toward blacks is based on the fanatical notions about race that have been passed down by her grandfather. Like him, she sees the black race as the white man's curse, her "burden," and so feels responsible for their welfare.

The rigid strictures of her faith have caused her to repress her sexuality until Joe appears. She then indulges in her passions with a sense of wild abandon. As Joe notes, she experiences "the abject fury of the New England glacier exposed suddenly to the fire of the New England biblical hell." When she loses her sexual desire during menopause, her religious beliefs become intensified. In effort to absolve herself and Joe for their promiscuity, and perhaps in response to her inability to have children, she tries to kill them both.

Joe Christmas

In the orphanage, Joe is a lonely child, shunned by the other children who think him strange and of mixed blood. Never knowing who his parents are or whether he is part black, Joe is consumed with a life-long search for a sense of identity and place but is never able to alleviate his profound sense of loneliness or self-hatred. "Doomed in motion, driven by the courage of flagged and spurred despair," Joe is never able to establish sustaining connections. He continually feels as if there is a "black abyss which had been waiting, trying, for thirty years to drown him."

After he leaves the orphanage, Joe is influenced by McEachern, who fills his head with visions of sin and retribution and little tolerance for the weakness of others. McEachern also passes on his sexism and his propensity for violent outbursts. Mrs. McEachern tries to temper her husband's harsh treatment of Joe, but Joe rejects her offers of comfort. His fear of becoming weak prevents him from acknowledging her kindness, "which he believed himself doomed to be forever victim of and which he hated worse than he did the hard and ruthless justice of men." Misreading her intentions, Joe declares, "she is trying to make me cry," and he continually rejects her overtures toward him.

He develops a thick skin and a menacing air while living with his adoptive parents and after Bobbie's betrayal. The others at the mill notice that "he carried with him his own inescapable warning, like . . . a rattlesnake his rattle" and worked with a "brooding and savage steadiness." His father has taught him that the world is brutal and harsh; Bobbie has taught him that feelings of love are a sign of weakness and can be deceptive.

He tries to live in both white and black worlds but is not comfortable in either. His confused sense of himself emerges in his relationships with both races, illustrated when he moves to Chicago and lives with blacks: "he had once tricked or teased white men into calling him a negro in order to fight them, to beat them or be beaten; now he fought the negro who called him white." In Chicago, he tries "to breathe into himself the dark odor, the dark and inscrutable thinking and being of negroes, with each suspiration trying to expel from himself the white blood and the white thinking and being." Yet, he becomes enraged when Joanna gives him the opportunity to get a law degree from a black college and to carry on her work in the black community.

By the end of the novel, he appears to be tired of searching; he passively commits suicide when he runs to Hightower's home and is killed, holding a gun that he never fires.

Percy Grimm

Percy Grimm, born and raised in Jefferson, is a patriotic zealot, who was too young to serve in World War I and always regretted it. His guilt and his need to prove himself spur him to fight anyone he perceives shows any disloyalty toward his country. He harbors "a sublime and implicit faith in physical courage and blind obedience," and along with his belief in the superiority of Americans, he is convinced that "the white race is superior to any and all other races." When Joe escapes jail, Grimm insists on taking a lead role in preserving order in the town, and he convinces the sheriff to deputize him. His monomaniacal beliefs cause him to think he has the right to kill Joe, but not before he castrates him.

Lena Grove

Byron insists that Lena has "eyes that a man could not have lied to if he had wanted," although Brown does so on more than one occasion. Like

Byron, Lena is trusting and sympathetic. She refuses to believe that Brown has deserted her and is willing to give him several chances to make good on his promises. She also shows a remarkable resiliency and adaptability. When she eventually recognizes that Brown will never acknowledge his responsibilities toward her and their child, she accepts Byron's offer of companionship and support and suggests that they might be able to share a future together.

Lena's experiences contrast with Joe's. In contrast to Joe's circle of violence and eventual tragic death, Lena becomes a life force in the novel through her optimism and resilience as well as through the birth of her child. She overcomes her hardships with her ability to adapt to her circumstances without regret or bitterness.

McKinley Grove

McKinley Grove, Lena's brother, is a hard man whose character, "except a kind of stubborn and despairing fortitude and the bleak heritage of his bloodpride had been sweated out of him." When he discovers Lena's pregnancy, he calls her a whore.

Reverend Gail Hightower

Fifty-two-year-old Gail Hightower was minister in one of Jefferson's principle churches. Twenty-five years ago, he was defrocked, due to a scandal involving his wife, and he has been an outcast in the town ever since. His only friend and confident is Byron. His present philosophy is that "all that any man can hope for is to be permitted to live quietly among his fellows." His fear of change is recognized by Byron when he notes that Hightower stays in town "because a fellow is more afraid of the trouble he might have than he ever is of the trouble he's already got." He concludes that "it's the dead folks that do him the damage. . . . that he can't escape from."

Hightower had failed his wife, the main "dead folk" whom Byron mentions, because of his overweening self-interest and inability to live in the present. Like many of the main characters in the novel, Hightower was damaged by his strict religious upbringing, specifically his father's stern refusal of affection or kindness. As a result, he turned to the church and immersed himself in a fictional past with his grandfather, a Confederate raider. His self-absorption causes him to ignore the needs of his wife who eventually, after a series of affairs, commits suicide.

After the scandal forced his resignation from the ministry, Hightower is resilient and tenacious as he refuses to allow the townspeople to drive him away from his home. Yet, he becomes self-satisfied in this position, living as a martyr until Byron forces him back to the present and an involvement with humanity through a connection to Joe and Lena. Through his relationships with them, he is able to regain a measure of pride and dignity, and he becomes a kind of moral touchstone for Byron.

Eupheus Hines

At the end of the book, Faulkner reveals that Eupheus Hines is Joe's grandfather and also the janitor who kidnapped him from the orphanage. The people of Mottstown, who consider him quite mad, call him Uncle Doc and determine that he has "a face which had once been either courageous or violent—either a visionary or a supreme egoist." After his history is revealed, however, he proves himself to be the latter in each category. Another one of Yoknapatawpha County's religious fanatics, he considers his daughter to be a whore and so will not send for the doctor when she goes into labor. He also uses his beliefs to justify murder and kidnapping, insisting that Joe is God's abomination and that he, Hines, is the instrument of God's will.

Mrs. Hines

Mrs. Hines has allowed herself to be dominated by her husband throughout their marriage, refusing even to rebel against his authority as her daughter lay dying because he would not allow a doctor to care for her during childbirth. When she discovers that Joe is her grandson, however, she defies her husband and does everything she can to prevent him from harming Joe. Her profound grief over the loss of her daughter and her grandson causes her mind to break after the birth of Lena's child. In a delusional state, she believes that Lena's child is her own lost grandson, Joe.

Mrs. McEachern

Mrs. McEachern, Joe's stepmother, has "a beaten face" and "looked fifteen years older than the rugged and vigorous husband." Under her husband's strict hand, "she had been hammered stubbornly thinner and thinner like some passive and dully malleable metal, into an attenuation of dumb hopes and frustrated desires now faint and pale as dead ashes." She does, however, try to gain a measure of power regarding the treatment of Joe. She would never openly defy her husband, but after he doles out his harsh punishment to Joe, she often tries to ease her son's suffering.

Simon McEachern

Simon McEachern, Joe's adopted father, tries to justify his sexism and authoritarianism through the tenets of his faith, specifically his belief in divine retribution. Insisting his actions are the result of God's direction, he promotes a "rigid abnegation of all compromise," and so he beats Joe when he does not obey him. McEachern is a ruthless man who has never known either pity or doubt. Joe learns to match his father's stubbornness with his own. Simon's wife, however, has been broken by his iron will and his lack of sympathy or charity.

Themes

Destructive Righteousness

The community of Jefferson is predominantly Presbyterian or Calvinist, following the strict doctrines of predestination and of original sin, which become its excuse for the persecution of others. Characters in the novel who adopt this puritanical point of view refuse to forgive human frailty or to act with charity. The stern and implacable Eupheus Hines and Simon McEachern, extreme versions of this type of righteousness, insist that they are the representatives of the wrathful God, and so they take it upon themselves to determine Joe's fate. When these two men are disobeyed or thwarted on their path to redemption, they become violent, using Old Testament scriptures as justification. One of the great ironies of the novel is the fact that Joe is named "Christmas" and becomes the character most pursued and ultimately destroyed by Christian faith.

Joanna Burden's faith is just as fanatical but has a different focus. She has been taught through her strict religious upbringing that blacks are God's cursed race and so their torment can never be eased. As her name suggests, she becomes obsessed with the "burden" this ideology places on whites who suffer from the resulting guilt. Her relationship with Joe reflects this sense of righteousness as she struggles to redeem him. Her own guilt over her masochistic sexual relationship with Joe, coupled with his refusal to allow her to impose her spiritual vision on him, eventually results in her death.

Percy Grimm displays a patriotic righteousness as he envisions himself not as God's representative but as America's. Due to their promotion of their own rigid rules of conduct, the people of Jefferson "accepted Grimm with respect and perhaps a little awe . . . as though somehow his vision and patriotism and pride in the town, the occasion, had been quicker and truer than theirs." Grimm's patriotism, like the others' religious righteousness, convinces him that he has the right and obligation to persecute Joe for breaking the rules of a racist white society.

When she discovers that she is pregnant, Lena Grove faces the consequences of religious righteousness when her brother throws her out of the house, but later she is able to exist outside the strict boundaries of its doctrine. She is accepted in Jefferson as an unmarried, pregnant woman, most likely because she has been abandoned by Brown and she tries to convince him to marry her. When she cannot accomplish that goal, she leaves with Byron, moving beyond the reach of the town's rigid views of sexuality.

Misogyny

Misogyny, or the hatred of women, is generated by religious fanaticism and male insecurity, and it often results in violence. Hines allows his daughter to die in childbirth because he spurns her as a whore. When her mother tries to go for a doctor, he aims his shotgun at her and warns, "get back into that house, whore's dam."

Topics for Further Study

- Choose one of the themes discussed in the fiction section and write a poem or a short story that explores that theme in a different way.
- Read another one of Faulkner's works, like *Sanctuary*, that is set in Jefferson and prepare a PowerPoint presentation about how the setting in each becomes an important part of the work.
- Research and write a report analyzing attitudes toward blacks in the South during the time that the novel was written.
- The novel has never been filmed, probably due to the complexity of its narrative. How would you depict the novel's disrupted chronology and the intertwined stories in a film? Write a screenplay of a portion of the novel that cuts back and forth between at least two characters.

McEachern teaches Joe a similar view of women, which is evident in his response to his discovery of menstruation. Like Hines who regards this biological function as "God's abomination of womanflesh," Joe, when told about it by his friends, becomes outraged that women's "smooth and superior shape in which volition dwelled [was] doomed to be at stated and inescapable intervals victims of periodical filth." His obsession with this function turns to outrage. A few weeks later, he shoots a sheep and covers his hands with its blood as it is dying.

Joe's belief that women's biology and sexuality are an abomination results in his attacks on a young black girl and on Bobbie. He savagely beats the black girl with whom his friends encourage him to have sex, and he strikes Bobbie when she tells him that she is menstruating. His attitude toward sex becomes evident when his retreat into the woods after hitting Bobbie becomes a phallic landscape: "he entered, among the hard trunks . . . hardfeeling, hardsmelling," where he envisions "a diminishing row of suavely shaped urns in moonlight, blanched. And not one was perfect. Each one was cracked and from each crack there issued something liquid, deathcolored, and foul." This image of female sexuality causes him to vomit. Ironically, the cessation of menstruation, with its accompanying reduction of sexual desire, is one of the factors that prompt him to kill Joanna.

Joe also rejects feminine compassion as evident in his treatment of Mrs. McEachern, whom he considers an enemy. He refuses to accept her offers of comfort in response to her husband's cruel treatment of him, as when she brings him food after a severe beating, insisting that she wants to weaken him with her pity. As a result, he feels no remorse when he steals money from her.

His self-hatred becomes evident when he beats almost fatally a white prostitute who is not upset when he tells her that he is part black. The thought of a white woman agreeing to have sex with a black man sickens him so much that he stays ill for two years. Joe's misogyny appears to stem from his own victimization by a society that values neither blacks nor women.

Racism

The characters' failure to recognize the humanity and rights of blacks, coupled with their sense of righteousness, leads to Joe's persecution and ultimate destruction. The people of Jefferson have been able to ignore successfully the blacks who live on the margins of their town as long as they keep their distance from the white population. Joe becomes dangerous to them when he crosses this line, so he must be destroyed. Their fear of any black encroachment into white territory is illustrated in their response to Joanna and her ancestors' civil rights activities when they ostracize the former and kill the latter.

The town accepts Eupheus Hines's involvement with the black community because they determine him to be "an old man" whose behavior is "harmless"; however, if a young man acted similarly, he would have been "crucified." As a result, "the town [blinded] its collective eye" to the black women who brought food to Hines and his wife, probably from the white homes in which they cleaned and cooked. The town will not look away, though, when they are told that Joe is black and has murdered the white woman with whom he had a sexual relationship.

Style

Disruption of Chronology

The events in this plot are not presented in chronological order. Many of the characters are glimpsed through extended flashbacks, which disrupt the sequential order of events. This technique conveys to what extent the past is present in and continues to affect the characters' lives. Most of the characters are revealed through flashback or stories they tell about their past and about their ancestors' lives. This structure emphasizes the point that the current state of affairs is shaped by past events, and it highlights the novel's insistence on determinism, a philosophy that asserts that acts that appear to be freely chosen are actually determined by forces that lie beyond the individual's control, such as the will of God or natural or social laws.

Faulkner provides glimpses of Joe Christmas, Gail Hightower, Joanna Burden, Percy Grimm, and Eupheus Hines in present time but then flashes back to important parts of their pasts that explain their behavior. Readers see the effect of the past most clearly in the character of Joe, who cannot escape the influence of his time in the orphanage or of his life with the McEacherns. His experiences during these two periods shape his character and propel him toward his tragic destiny. Gail Hightower is also negatively affected by the past as he endlessly relives the glory of his grandfather's cavalry charge. This obsession prevents him from living in the present, effectively destroying his marriage and eventually his reputation and branding him an outcast. Joanna Burden's upbringing in a rigid Calvinist environment influences her relationship with Joe and ultimately leads to her murder.

The stories of two main characters, Lena and Byron, however, are not told through flashbacks, except for Lena's very brief one that names Brown as the baby's father and notes her departure from her hometown. B. R. McElderry Jr., in his article on the novel's narrative structure in *College English*, insists: "It is important that the Lena-Byron story is told in chronological sequence, just as it developed. This is the simple narrative thread that gives a recurrent sense of forward motion." The two main story lines of the novel, involving Lena and Byron and Joe and Joanna, fuse when Lena appears at the top of the hill overlooking Jefferson and watches Joanna's house burn. Lena and Byron escape from the destruction symbolized by that fire, while Joe and Joanna are consumed by it.

Setting

Yoknapatawpha County and its seat, Jefferson, comprise a fictional setting that Faulkner used in fifteen novels and several short stories. The county is bordered by the Tallahatchie River on the north and the Yoknapatawpha River on the south. Frenchman's Bend, a poverty-stricken village, is nearby as well as plantations, farms, and tenant farmer shacks in the countryside surrounding it. Its citizens, past and present, include Indians, wealthy landowners, farmers, poor whites and blacks, and carpetbaggers. For inclusion in the first edition of *Absalom, Absalom!* (1936), Faulkner created a map of the county, identifying himself as sole owner and proprietor. Giving these works a shared setting creates a rich geographical and ancestral framework, which emphasizes to what degree these separate publications are related to each other. The construct also reinforces Faulkner's own sense of how individuals' lives are determined by their ancestors and by the geography within which they live.

Light in August focuses on four main settings: the town, the mill, the Burden estate, and the Hightower home. The two homes, where most of the action takes place, are set on the outskirts of Jefferson, and their remoteness highlights Joanna's and Hightower's separation from the community. The juxtaposition of the Burden home and the estate's slave shack where Joe lives reinforces the novel's class and racial divisions.

Historical Context

Modernism

American literature written in the 1920s and early 1930s was dominated by a group of writers who were disillusioned by World War I (1914–1918). This group, which would come to be known as the modernists, reflected the *zeitgeist*, or spirit, of their age—a time when, in the aftermath of war, many Americans had lost faith in traditional institutions such as the government, social institutions, established religions, and even in humanity itself.

Modernism became one of the most fruitful periods in American letters. Modernist authors such as Ernest Hemingway, F. Scott Fitzgerald, and John Dos Passos became part of what Gertrude Stein called the Lost Generation, creative people who witnessed the horrors of war and who struggled to survive despite having lost their values and ideals. The spirit of the Roaring Twenties, or the Jazz Age as F. Scott Fitzgerald called this period, was reflected in Modernist themes. On the surface, the characters in many of these works lived in the rarified atmosphere of the upper class. They drank, partied, and had sexual adventures, but underneath the glamorous surface there persisted a sense of the meaninglessness at the heart of their existence. Other modernists such as William Faulkner and playwright Eugene O'Neill focused on lower-class Americans whose sense of meaninglessness was compounded by their economic limitations.

Each modernist writer focused on separate ways to cope with the loss: some characters tried to drown a sense of emptiness in the fast-paced, alcohol-steeped life of the 1920s; some tried to overcome a profound sense of isolation through relationships; and some attempted to overcome meaninglessness through personal acts of courage. Hemingway's men and women faced a meaningless world with courage and dignity, exhibiting grace under pressure, while Fitzgerald's sought the redemptive power of love in a world driven by materialism. Faulkner's characters tried to establish a sense of identity as well as ties to family, all the while pressed by the social burden of Southern history. All ultimately had difficulty sustaining any sense of fulfillment and completion in the modern age.

Modernists experimented with different narrative styles to convey their themes. They abandoned traditional notions of narrative structure that suggest that stories have a specific beginning,

Compare & Contrast

- **1930s:** After a decade of buying on credit, Americans find themselves in the grips of a severe economic depression. African Americans are hardest hit by the Depression, which leaves half of their population out of work.

  Today: Economic policies, such as unemployment compensation, are designed in part to prevent the country from falling into a severe depression that would yield the kind of national devastation Americans experienced in the 1930s.

- **1930s:** Racial violence increases in the South during the Depression (1929–1940). For example, lynchings increase from eight in 1932 to twenty-eight in 1933. Some lynching results as blacks challenge the racially prejudicial Jim Crow laws, which are designed to deny African Americans their legal rights. These laws mandate segregation, make it difficult for blacks to vote, and stall efforts by blacks to gain economic, political, and social equality.

  Today: Racial discrimination is against the law. Many African Americans hold positions of power and prestige in the United States. Yet more subtle forms of discrimination persist, involving housing, employment, and promotion.

middle, and end. Instead, they often started their stories in the middle, jumped back and forth in time, and left their endings ambiguous, suggesting that this structure more closely resembles reality. They felt that human interaction rarely started at the beginning of the story and rarely achieved closure at the ending of the story.

Influenced by the theories of Sigmund Freud, modernists pondered the psychology of their characters, often articulating both subconscious and conscious motivations. To accurately reflect these levels of consciousness, modernists employed stream-of-consciousness narratives (a way of telling a story by presenting the associative sequence of thought in consciousness) and replaced traditional omniscient narrators with subjective points of view that allowed often a narrow and distorted or multiple vision of reality.

Oxford, Mississippi

Faulkner's Yoknapatawpha County, with Jefferson City as its county seat, is based on his hometown, Oxford, Mississippi, and Lafayette County, where he observed the region's people, architecture, typography and geography, and incorporated these into his fictional landscape. The region in which Faulkner lived had a long history similar to that of Yoknapatawpha County; it was steeped in the legacies of the Civil War and in racism.

Some specific details in *Light in August* are taken from actual sites in Oxford, including the southward-looking statue of a Confederate soldier, the stores located on the square, the hill on which Lena stands when she first sees Jefferson, the ditch in which Joe hides from Percy Grimm, and most of the route Joe travels from the barbershop through Freedman Town. The cabin on Joanna Burden's property in which Joe lives and Lena gives birth is a pre-Civil War slave cabin. Yet, Jefferson does not have the University of Mississippi, and it has a higher percentage of Presbyterians than did Oxford, which enabled Faulkner to explore in more detail his religious themes.

Critical Overview

In the decades after *Light in August* was published, the novel suffered from the same critical response as did much of Faulkner's works. Scholars were split over Faulkner's literary merit: some praised him for his compelling vision and artistry while others condemned him for his obscurity and bleak vision of humanity. Warren Beck, in a 1941 article for *College English*, argues that condemnation of Faulkner "seems based chiefly on two erroneous propositions—first, that Faulkner has no ideas, no point of view, and second, that consequently he is melodramatic, a mere sensationalist." He cites one example of this type of criticism when he quotes a reviewer who claims that in *Light in August*, "nothing is omitted, except virtue."

After Malcolm Cowley's publication of *The Portable Faulkner* in 1946 and Faulkner's winning the Nobel Prize in Literature in 1949, Faulkner's popularity increased, and scholars again found much to praise in his works. During the late 1940s and early 1950s, Faulkner began to be regarded as one of the twentieth century's most important authors and *Light in August* as one of the best novels of the American South.

B. R. McElderry Jr, in his *College English* article on the novel's narrative structure, writes, "it is doubtful if any of the [other major novels] combines so richly the easy natural comedy and the violent tragedy of which Faulkner at his best is a master." McElderry concludes that there are problems with the novel's structure, especially with the characterization of Joanna Burden and Hightower. "Yet when the difficulties of the structural problems are fairly confronted, the achievement overshadows such defects."

Harold Bloom, in his study of Faulkner in *Genius*, insists that the novel is one of Faulkner's greatest works, arguing that the relationship between Joe and Joanna "is the most harrowing, and yet testifies to what most typifies Faulkner's uncompromising genius for characterization."

Criticism

Wendy Perkins

Perkins is a professor of American and English literature and film. In this essay, she examines the tensions between community and individual in the novel.

Byron Bunch, the inconspicuous mill worker in William Faulkner's *Light in August*, becomes the moral conscience of the novel as he observes the townspeople of Jefferson City and declares, "people everywhere are about the same." Byron not only offers astute judgments of the citizens of the city; he also notes their harsh, even brutal treatment of individuals who do not fit into their notions of community. Revealing his understanding of group dynamics, he insists that for those who live in a small town like Jefferson "evil is harder to accomplish." As a result, "people can invent more of it in other people's names. Because that was all it required: that idea, that single idle word blown from mind to mind." This type of group response becomes an important agency in *Light in August* as Faulkner explores the disastrous effects the community can have on the individual who tries to establish a sense of independence.

"Joe's exclusion from the community begins as a result of a combination of racism and righteousness when his grandfather takes him to the orphanage."

Donald M. Kartiganer, in an article on Faulkner for *The Columbia Literary History of the United States*, concludes that in the community of Jefferson, which is the setting for *Light in August* as well as that of many of Faulkner's works, "the codes of honor and courage, the respect for an old frontier individualism, give way . . . to rules of propriety and a crushing conformity." This conformity, he argues causes "a fundamental split within Jefferson's social fabric between white and black, group and individual . . . The violence that inevitably ensues, [claims] its nonconformist victims." The victims of this intolerance in *Light in August* are Joe Christmas, Joanna Burden, and Gail Hightower.

An ideal community could create a sense of wholeness by recognizing and sustaining each individual's separate identity. Jefferson, however, with its seemingly inescapable ties to its southern past, is far from that ideal. The tensions that arise between the individual and the community in this city are the result of deep-seated racism and Calvinistic righteousness. These factors cause the townspeople to view those who do not conform to their values and rules as members of another group, either of blacks or of sinners. The townspeople see Joe as a black man and a sinner. This otherness convicts the nonconformist, who must be marginalized and/or punished.

Joe's exclusion from the community begins as a result of a combination of racism and righteousness when his grandfather takes him to the

What Do I Read Next?

- Joseph Blotner's *Faulkner: A Biography* (1974) presents a fascinating chronicle of Faulkner's life and an insightful analysis of his work.
- Faulkner's *Sanctuary* (1932) also takes place in the fictional Jefferson City.
- Faulkner's novel *The Sound and the Fury* (1929), which focuses on the lives of members of a southern family, is considered to be Faulkner's most complex and successful work.
- F. Scott Fitzgerald's celebrated novel, *The Great Gatsby* (1925), employs similar stylistic techniques to those of *Light in August*, most notably a disruption in chronology that reveals the importance of the past and reinforces the focus on a search for identity.
- Joel Williamson's *The Crucible of Race: Black-White Relations in the American South since Emancipation* (1984) examines the interaction between blacks and whites in the South and the resulting tensions between the two races.
- Flannery O'Connor's short story "Revelation," which can be found in *Flannery O'Connor: The Complete Stories* (1971), explores the question of racism in a religious context.

orphanage. Eupheus Hines's refusal to accept a grandson born out of wedlock and fathered by a dark-skinned man initiates a pattern of isolation that Joe is forced to endure for the rest of his life.

The sense of separation he experiences as an orphan is heightened in the orphanage where the other children shun and taunt him with racial epithets, believing him to be of mixed blood. In order to save her reputation after Joe discovers her sexual indiscretion, Miss Atkins plays on the communal racism when she spreads the rumor that he is black and thus effectively precipitates his removal from the orphanage and into the hands of the brutally self-righteous Simon McEachern.

After he kills McEachern and is rejected by Bobbie, Joe tries unsuccessfully to become a part of white and black communities, but after he arrives in Jefferson, he appears to have accepted his role as an outsider. Prior to Joanna Burden's murder, the townspeople regard Joe as a stranger but leave him alone because they assume he is white and they are put off by his imperious and often menacing demeanor. After Brown insists that Joe is of mixed race and has killed Joanna, however, their attitude changes dramatically. The fact that a murder has been committed, heightened by rumors of the crime of a black man engaging in a sexual relationship with a white woman and his arrogant disregard of his socially abhorrent behavior, all convince local people that Joe must be destroyed.

Faulkner illustrates the townspeople's attitude when Joe is captured after walking in plain sight in the center of Mottstown. The community is appalled that he is "all dressed up and walking the town like he dared them to touch him, when he ought to have been skulking and hiding in the woods, muddy and dirty and running." Joe acts, they argue, "like he never even knew he was a murderer, let alone a n—— too." Jefferson's rampant racism fosters a hatred in Percy Grimm so intense that he feels justified in castrating the dying Joe.

Joanna Burden, another marginalized citizen of Jefferson, is not the victim of violent intolerance, but her ancestors were when they stood up for black voting rights in town. As a result of her grandfather and brother's actions and her own work with blacks in the area, she has become an outcast. Joanna understands that the community feared her family's and her own support of black rights would stir up "the negroes to murder and rape" and threaten "white supremacy." As a result, they call her "N——lover" in town and refuse to "[allow] their wives to call on her." Joanna, like Byron, understands group dynamics and so is more generous toward her neighbors, insisting that her father "respect[ed] anybody's love for the land where he and his people were born and [understood] that a man would have to act as the land where he was born had trained him to act."

The intensity of their animosity toward Joanna, however, emerges after her murder when the townspeople swarm to the site of the fire: they "knew, believed, and hoped that she had been ravished too: at least once before her throat was cut and at least once afterward." Yet, "even though she had supplied them at last with an emotional barbecue, a Roman holiday almost, they would never forgive her and let her be dead in peace and quiet." And so, hearing rumors that a black man had killed her, "some of them with pistols already in their pockets began to canvass about for someone to crucify."

Ironically, Joanna's fate is sealed by her own participation in group mentality. Like the members of her community, she sees blacks not as individuals but as a group. Influenced by the religious dogma of her ancestors, Joanna regards Joe only as one of a doomed race and ultimately as a sinner who refuses to kneel down with her and pray for absolution. As a result of this limited view, and her own belief that she too has sinned, she tries to kill them both. In a violent reaction to her attempts to control him, Joe kills her.

In another observation of group dynamics, Byron suggests that often "what folks tells on other folks aint true to begin with." The town's treatment of Reverend Gail Hightower proves his point. After Hightower's wife returned from the sanatorium, the righteous women in Jefferson began to spread disparaging rumors concerning Hightower's relationship with his wife and "the town believed that the ladies knew the truth."

The rumors intensify after Hightower's wife dies under suspicious circumstances to the point that no one in town attends his Sunday sermons, which eventually forces him to give up his ministry. The town's response to Hightower turns violent when he determines to keep his black cook. After stories spread about the two, the community agrees that Hightower "had made his wife go bad and commit suicide because he was not a natural husband . . . and that the negro woman was the reason." As a result, Hightower was viciously beaten.

After Hightower refuses to leave Jefferson, eventually "the whole thing seemed to blow away, like an evil wind," and the community decided to let him be: "it was as though the town realized at last that he would be a part of its life until he died, and that they might as well become reconciled." Byron analyzes the community's treatment of Hightower when he likens the situation to "a lot of people performing a play and that now and at last they had all played out the parts which had been allotted them and now they could live quietly with one another."

While the narrow-minded bigotry and righteousness of the community of Jefferson damages or destroys the lives of many of the novel's central characters, the townspeople do offer some support to Lena as she searches for the father of her unborn child. They do not try to ostracize her for her illegitimate pregnancy, most likely because she is trying, in their view, to rectify her sin by marrying Brown. However, she and Byron eventually leave Jefferson, more perhaps to get away from the restrictive values of the community than to find Brown.

Joe's violent death at the end of the novel appears to force the community to recognize the effects of its rigid codes. As the people who have followed Joe to Hightower's home witness his last breath, Joe "seemed to rise soaring into their memories forever and ever." The narrator insists, "They are not to lose it, in whatever peaceful valleys, beside whatever placid and reassuring streams of old age, in the mirroring faces of whatever children they will contemplate old disasters and newer hopes." In this sense then, Joe becomes a Christ-like figure, who begins the process of redemption for a community that has allowed its prejudices and fears to repress its sense of humanity.

Source: Wendy Perkins, Critical Essay on *Light in August*, in *Novels for Students*, Thomson Gale, 2007.

C. Hugh Holman

In the following excerpt, Holman proposes that unity is manifest in Faulkner's novel through the "paralleling of character traits" and "actions" of Joe Christmas and Christ.

The nature of the unity in William Faulkner's *Light in August*, in fact, even the existence of such unity, has been seriously disputed by his critics. The debate has ranged from Malcolm Cowley's insistence that the work combines "two or more themes having little relation to each other" to Richard Chase's elaborate theory of "images of the curve" opposed to "images of linear discreteness." Those critics who see a unity in the novel find its organizing principle in theme or philosophical statement—"a successful metaphysical conceit," a concern with Southern religion, the tragedy

"The central fact in this story of the suffering servant Joe Christmas is his belief that he bears an imperceptibly faint strain of Negro blood, an ineradicable touch of evil in the eyes of the society of which he is a part and in his own eyes as well."

of human isolation, man's lonely search for community—but they fail to find a common ground for the unity they perceive because they neglect properly to evaluate the objective device which Faulkner employs in the novel as an expression of theme. That device is the pervasive paralleling of character traits, actions, and larger structural shapes to the story of Christ. Viewed in terms of this device the novel becomes the story of the life and death of a man peculiarly like Christ in many particulars, an account of what Ilse D. Lind has called "the path to Gethsemane which is reserved for the Joe Christmases of this world." However, that account is in itself perverse, "a monstrous and grotesque irony," unless the other strands of action in the book—the Hightower story and the Lena Grove story—are seen as being contrasting portions of a thematic statement also made suggestively by analogies to the Christ story. This essay is an attempt to demonstrate that such, indeed, is the basic nature of the novel and that it has a unity which is a function of its uses of the Christ story.

I

The parallels between Christ and Joe Christmas, the leading character in the novel, have not gone unnoticed. However, although many critics have commented in passing on their presence, they have usually been dismissed as casual or irresponsible. But the publication of *A Fable,* with its very obvious and self-conscious use of Christian parallels in highly complex patterns, forces us to accept Faulkner's concern with the Christ story as profoundly serious, and recent criticism has also shown us that such a concern is not a late occurrence in his work. Furthermore, in a recent interview, Faulkner has talked very directly about the use of Christian materials in *A Fable* and the function that he feels that such material has in a novel. He said:

> In *A Fable* the Christian allegory was the right allegory to use.
>
> Whatever its [Christianity's] symbol—cross or crescent or whatever—that symbol is man's reminder of his duty inside the human race. Its various allegories are the charts against which he measures himself and learns to know what he is. . . . It shows him how to discover himself, evolve for himself a moral code and standard within his capacities and aspirations. . . . Writers have always drawn, and always will, of the allegories of moral consciousness, for the reason that the allegories are matchless.

Apparently Faulkner intends to use parallels to Christ as devices to invest modern stories with timeless meanings; and Christian allegory, when it appears in his work, may justifiably be viewed as a means of stating theme. Dayton Kohler correctly says, "Faulkner's treatment of Hebraic-Christian myth is like Joyce's use of the Homeric story in *Ulysses* and Mann's adaptation of Faustian legend in *Doctor Faustus*." It is a pervasive and enriching aspect of the total book, and we expect to see it bodied forth, not only in fragments and parts, but in the complete design.

Light in August consists of three major and largely separate story strands, what Irving Howe has called "a triad of actions." These strands are the story of Joe Christmas, his murder of Joanna Burden, and his death, together with long retrospective sections that trace his life in considerable detail from his birth to the night of Joanna's death; the story of Gail Hightower, his reintroduction into life through Lena Grove and Joe Christmas, and his death, together with retrospective and narrative sections on his marriage and his ministry; and the story of Byron Bunch and Lena Grove, of her search for the father of her illegitimate child, and of its birth. These strands are tied loosely together by the accident of time, some interchange of dramatis personae, and by the almost mechanical device of having characters in one strand narrate events in another. Lucas Burch, the father of Lena Grove's bastard child, is Joe Christmas' helper and would-be betrayer. Byron Bunch, Lena's loving slave, is a friend of Hightower, narrates much of the Joe Christmas story to Hightower and is himself the retrospective narrator for a good deal of Hightower's early story. Joe Christmas' grandmother attempts, with Bunch's assistance, to persuade Hightower to save her grandson, and Joe turns to Hightower in the last moments of his life. Hightower assists at the birth of Lena's child, and Joe's grandmother confuses Lena with her daughter Milly and Lena's child with Joe as a baby. However, these links are not sufficient to tie the triad of actions into "a single action that is complete and whole."

A certain mechanical unity is imposed upon the novel through Faulkner's establishing the action of the story in the ten days between Joe Christmas' killing Joanna Burden and his being killed by Percy Grimm. However, the significance of these present actions is to be found in the past, and the bulk of the novel actually consists of retrospective accounts of that antecedent action. Faulkner attempts to preserve a sense of present action as opposed to antecedent action by the device of telling in the present tense all events that are imagined to be occurring in a forward motion during these ten days, and in the past tense all retrospective and antecedent events.

Also there are three distinct bodies of material in the book: formal Protestant religion, sex, and the Negro in Southern society. Each of the story strands deals predominantly with one of these matters but contains the other two in some degree. The story of Joe Christmas is centered on the problem of the Negro in Southern society; the Gail Hightower story is centered in the Protestant church; and the sex element is the controlling factor in the story of Lena Grove, her search for the father of her child, and Byron Bunch's love for her. The interplays of these materials among these separate story strands help to knit the parts of the novel into a whole, but these bodies of material and the stories constructed from them find their most meaningful thematic expression as contrasting analogues of the Christ story.

II

The most obvious of the Christ analogues is in the story of Joe Christmas. Faulkner establishes numerous parallels between Joe Christmas and Christ, some of which are direct and emphatic and some of which are nebulous, fleeting, almost wayward. Strange dislocations in time occur; events in Christ's life have multiple analogies and are sometimes distributed over long periods of time. The parallels often seem perverse and almost mocking, yet they all seem to invite us to look at Joe Christmas as a person *somehow like Christ in certain aspects.* Around his birth and his death events are closely parallel to those in Christ's life; in the middle period of his life the analogies grow shadowy and uncertain.

Joe is the son of an unmarried mother, and the identity of his father is hidden from him and from the world. He is found on Christmas day on the steps of an orphans' home, and he is named Joseph Christmas, giving him the initials JC. His grandfather says that God "chose His own Son's sacred anniversary to set [His will] a-working on." When he is five, his grandfather spirits him away by night to Little Rock to save him from the orphanage authorities who have discovered that he has Negro blood. After he is returned, he is adopted by the Simon McEacherns, and upon his first entering their home Mrs. McEachern ceremoniously washes his feet. The stern Calvinism of Simon McEachern represents the accepted religious order of Joe's world, an equivalent of the Pharisaic order of Christ's, and Joe achieves what he later senses to be manhood and maturity when at the age of eight he sets himself against the formal codification of that order by refusing to learn the Presbyterian catechism. He rejects three temptations: Mrs. McEachern's food and the feminine pity which it represents; the Negro girl whom he refuses when he is fourteen; and McEachern's attempt by means of a heifer to purchase Joe's allegiance to his orthodox conventions. He also rejects food three times, as Robert D. Jacobs has pointed out. Once, when he is taken into Mottstown at the age of eighteen by his foster father, Joe goes to a restaurant where he meets Bobbie Allen and begins to learn about the larger world of which he is a part, the restaurant being a kind of carnal temple and Bobbie and its owners being priests of that world.

His middle years are cloaked in obscurity, but at the age of thirty he comes to Jefferson, and there he is first introduced to us as a man with a name that is "somehow an augur of what he will do." He is rootless, homeless, "no street, no walls, no square of earth his home." For three years he works in Jefferson. At first he works in the sawmill with Brown who is later to betray him, and Faulkner refers to them as "master" and "disciple." He becomes the lover of a nymphomaniac, Joanna Burden, who, after reveling for a while in depravity, when sex is no longer interesting to her, tries to convert him to the Pharisaic religious order.

Then one Friday night he kills her, striking in self-defense against her use of a pistol to force him to subscribe through prayer to her religion. He flees, and he is betrayed, although ineffectually, by his "disciple" Brown for $1000. On the Tuesday of his week of flight, the day of Holy Week on which Christ cleansed the temple, he enters a Negro church and, using a table leg, drives out the worshippers. On Thursday night, the night of the Last Supper, he finds himself in the cabin of what he calls a "brother" and a meal mysteriously appears before him. Jacobs observes that "this Christ has no disciple except himself and always must eat alone." Faulkner says, "It was as though now and at last he had an actual and urgent need to strike off the accomplished days toward some purpose, some definite day or act." The next morning he frantically questions to learn the day of the week, and, finding it to be Friday, sets his face steadfastly toward Mottstown. Although up to this time he has been walking, he now enters the village riding with a Negro in a wagon drawn by mules. First he gets a shave and a haircut; then a man named Halliday recognizes him and asks, "Aint your name Christmas?" Faulkner reports, "He never denied it. He never did anything." Halliday hits him twice in the face, so that his forehead bleeds. His grandfather, who, being a stern Calvinist, speaks for the Pharisees, tries to incite the crowd to violence, shouting, "Kill him. Kill him." The mob, however, leaves him to the "law." He is moved from Mottstown to Jefferson, another legal jurisdiction, and the Mottstown sheriff yields his responsibility happily. In Jefferson he is guarded by volunteer National Guardsmen, who spend their time gambling. He escapes from the sheriff in the town square, runs to a Negro cabin where he steals a pistol, and then runs to the home of the ex-minister Hightower, where he is shot by the leader of the Guardsmen, a self-important soldier. As he is dying, the Guardsman takes a knife and mutilates him, so that "from out the slashed garments about his hips and loins the pent black blood seemed to rush like a released breath." And Joe Christmas, at thirty-three, as Gail Hightower had earlier prophesied that he would, becomes "the doomed man . . . in whose crucifixion [the churches] will raise a cross."

These parallels have been dismissed as insignificant, I believe, because critics have looked for a theological Saviour, whose death becomes an effective expiation for man's guilt, and viewed in these terms Joe Christmas is a cruel and irreverent travesty on Christ. However, Faulkner has defined the function of allegory to be a chart against which man can measure himself and learn "to know what he is." And Christian allegory uses Christ as "a matchless example of suffering and sacrifice and the promise of hope" (*Paris Rev.*, p. 42). The Christ to whom Faulkner parallels Joe Christmas is not the Messiah of St. Paul's epistles but the suffering servant of Isaiah, who is described thus:

> he hath no form nor comeliness; and when we shall see him, there is no beauty that we should desire him.
>
> He is despised and rejected of men; a man of sorrows, and acquainted with grief: and we hid as it were our faces from him; he was despised, and we esteemed him not. . . .
>
> He was oppressed, and he was afflicted, yet he opened not his mouth: he is brought as a lamb to the slaughter, and as a sheep before her shearers is dumb, so he openeth not his mouth.
>
> He has taken from prison and from judgment: and who shall declare his generation: for he was cut off out of the land of the living: for the transgression of my people was he stricken. (Isaiah liii.2–3, 7–8)

III

The central fact in this story of the suffering servant Joe Christmas is his belief that he bears an imperceptibly faint strain of Negro blood, an ineradicable touch of evil in the eyes of the society of which he is a part and in his own eyes as well. This Negro blood exists for him as a condition of innate and predetermined darkness, a touch of inexorable original sin, a burden he bears neither through his own volition nor because of his own acts. In the lost central years of his life his sense of this innate damnation leads him to shock his many women with confessions of his Negro blood. At last he finds a woman who is not shocked.

> She said, "What about it? . . . Say, what do you think this dump is, anyhow? The Ritz hotel?" Then she quit talking. She was watching his face and she began to move backward slowly before him, staring at him, her face draining, her mouth open to scream. Then she did scream. It took two policemen to subdue him. At first they thought that the woman was dead.
>
> He was sick after that. He did not know until then that there were white women who would take a man with a black skin. He stayed sick for two years.

It is from this aspect of himself that Joe runs in such fatal and precipitant flight down "the street which was to run for fifteen years."

Hightower equates this Negro blood in Joe to "poor mankind"; and Joe, running from the Negro quarter of the town, sees it as the "black pit," and thinks, "It just lay there, black, impenetrable. . . . It might have been the original quarry, abyss itself." It is this black blood that stands between Joe and a natural life. It is his own knowledge of it that stands between him and his becoming "one with loneliness and quiet that has never known fury or despair." And it is this black blood which, in Joanna Burden's impassioned view of the "doom and curse" of the Negro, casts a "black shadow in the shape of a cross."

Gavin Stevens believes that Joe Christmas' actions, after he escapes in the town square, were the results of a series of conflicts between his black blood, which is a form of evil, and his white blood, which represents his humane and good impulses. This conflict reaches its climax when the black blood leads him to strike the minister to whom he had run for help, but, Stevens says:

> And then the black blood failed him again, as it must have in crises all his life. He did not kill the minister. He merely struck him with the pistol and ran on and crouched behind that table and defied the black blood for the last time, as he had been defying it for thirty years. He crouched behind that overturned table and let them shoot him to death, with that loaded and unfired pistol in his hand.

After Percy Grimm shoots Joe down, he mutilates him, and then, with the crowd watching, "the pent black blood" rushes from him. Faulkner says:

> It seemed to rush out of his pale body like the rush of sparks from a rising rocket; upon that black blast the man seemed to rise soaring into their memories forever and ever. They are not to lose it, in whatever peaceful valleys, beside whatever placid and reassuring streams of old age, in the mirroring faces of whatever children they will contemplate old disasters and newer hopes. It will be there, musing, quiet, steadfast, not fading and not particularly threatful, but of itself alone serene, of itself alone triumphant.

This is Joe Christmas' crucifixion and his ascension, and this outrushing and ascending stream of black blood becomes his only successful act of communion with his fellowmen. Through it, a symbol of his Negro qualities shed for sexual reasons in the house of a man of religion, Joe Christmas becomes one of "the charts against which [man] measures himself and learns to know what he is . . . a matchless example of suffering and sacrifice . . ." (*Paris Rev.*, p. 42).

Joe's life is also shaped by sexual distortions, perversions, and irregularities. His mother was unmarried; his grandfather's righteous anger at her impurity and at what he believes to be the Negro blood in Joe's father makes him kill Joe's father and refuse his mother the medical assistance which would have prevented her death at his birth. Thus this anger sends Joe into the world an orphan. His accidental witnessing of the illicit relations between an orphanage dietician and an interne results in the dietician's learning of his Negro blood and in his being adopted by the McEacherns. At fourteen, when Joe's turn comes in a group assignation with a Negro girl, he is repelled by the "womanshenegro" and it is against "She" that he struggles and fights, until "There was no She at all." Significantly this early sexual experience is allied in Joe's mind with the Negro.

The menstrual period becomes for him a symbol of darkness and evil. Learning about it from boys' conversation, "he shot a sheep. . . . Then he knelt, his hands in the yet warm blood of the dying beast, trembling. . . . He did not forget what the boy had told him. He just accepted it. He found that he could live with it, side by side with it." This blood sacrifice he is to duplicate himself in his death. But three years after killing the sheep, when he confronts the idea again in connection with Bobbie Allen, it fills him with horror. "In the notseeing and the hardknowing as though in a cave he seemed to see a diminishing row of suavely shaped urns in moonlight, blanched. And not one was perfect. Each one was cracked and from each crack there issued something liquid, deathcolored, and foul." This image of the urn is to appear crucially in each of the major story strands.

Woman thus becomes for Joe a symbol and source of darkness and sin, the dark temptress who is viewed with revulsion alternating with attraction. Joseph Campbell expresses such a duality in attitudes toward women in terms that might have been designed to define Joe's feeling when in his study of religion and mythology he says:

> Generally we refuse to admit within ourselves or within our friends, the fullness of that pushing, self-protective, malodorous, carnivorous, lecherous fever which is the very nature of the organic cell. . . .
>
> But when it suddenly dawns upon us, or is forced to our attention, that everything we think or do is necessarily tainted with the odor of the flesh, then, not uncommonly, there is experienced a moment of revulsion: life, the acts of life, the organs of life, woman in particular as the great symbol of life, become intolerable.

Simon McEachern's harsh and grimly puritan ideal of chastity drives Joe to the prostitute Bobbie Allen, appropriately named for the hard-hearted heroine of the Southern folk version of the Scotch ballad "Barbara Allen." And this cheap and cruel woman is Joe's closest approach to love and acceptance, and she at last turns upon him, screaming against his Negro blood.

This pattern of unhappy if not unnatural sex reaches its climax for Joe Christmas with the puritanical nymphomaniac Joanna Burden. In a sense, the ministry that Joe performs during his three years in Jefferson is to call to life in this cold, barren woman the primitive sex urge; as he expresses it, "At least I have made a woman of her at last." But what he awakens in her is not a natural urge, but an unnatural and perverted one, for she was too old to bear children, too old to serve the purposes of nature. Faulkner says, "Christmas watched her pass through every avatar of a woman in love. . . . He was aware of . . . the imperious and fierce urgency that concealed an actual despair at frustrate and irrevocable years. . . . It was as though he had fallen into a sewer." Having perverted his "ministry," she finally denies it and attempts to force him into her sterile religious patterns. It is then that he kills her in an act of self-defense, for she had tried to shoot him; and in an act of spiritual self-preservation, for he could live only by refusing to pray with her; but in an act of suicide, for he could not himself long survive her killing.

It is in the Joanna Burden episode that the sex material of the Joe Christmas story reaches its fullest statement. It is in her episode, too, that the union of this material with the idea of Joe's Negro blood is most clearly stated, for Joanna is the daughter of a Northern father in a Southern town. From her childhood she had been taught that the Negroes were "A race doomed and cursed to be forever and ever a part of the white race's doom and curse for it sins" and that "in order to rise, you must raise the shadow with you . . . the curse of the white race is the black man who will be forever God's chosen own because He once cursed Him!" She first befriends Joe because he is a Negro. And when the flames of her sexual desires die out she wishes to send him to law school and to have him administer her numerous charities for Negro people, but this involves an acceptance of his Negro status, and such acceptance is intolerable to Joe.

Joanna serves adequately to link these two matters, sex and the Negro, to religion, for she is a conventionally devout person, and when she attempts to shoot Joe, thus forcing him to kill her, it is because he refuses to join her in her return to religion through prayer.

The formal Protestant religion, an aspect of which Joanna represents, has been haunting Joe from before his birth. His grandfather Eupheus Hines is a half-made religious zealot with a special and spiteful hatred of women, of what he calls "abomination and bitchery." He believes that God speaks directly to him, telling him how to execute His vengeance on earth. In the narrow, vindictive, cruel God to whom Eupheus listens may be seen the primitive Protestant Old Testament Jehovah of anger and jealousy. The Negro has been singled out for the special wrath of this God, and Hines goes about as a quasi minister to Negro congregations preaching to them of God's disfavor. He becomes a kind of perverted and evil divine father for Joe, and he pursues passionately his desire to destroy his grandson. Although his religion is unorganized and brutally primitive, he seems to speak on the lowest level of the religious order and attitudes of Joe's world.

Simon McEachern, Christmas' foster father, into whose hands he is committed when he passes from the orphanage and Hine's control, is a Presbyterian elder. He attempts to instill through grim authority the cheerless pattern of Calvinistic conduct and belief. His only weapon is the flail, and to him love is a deplorable weakness. The crucial occurrence in Joe's relationship with him comes when McEachern attempts unsuccessfully to force Joe to learn the Presbyterian catechism. Finally Joe strikes McEachern down in murderous rage when his foster father comes between him and the closest thing he has known to love, Bobbie Allen.

When Joe is running away after killing Joanna, he re-enacts Christ's cleansing of the temple by interrupting a Negro church service and driving out the worshippers with a table leg. His grandmother, anxious to give him a respite from the punishment he is to suffer, turns to the disgraced Presbyterian minister Hightower and asks him to give Christmas an alibi for the time of Joanna's murder. She tells Joe to go to the minister. When he escapes in the town square, he turns first to a Negro cabin and then to Hightower, but he strikes the minister down, as he has struck down the others who have symbolized church to him.

Significantly, organized religion is represented by the Presbyterian Church rather than the Baptist or the Methodist, both of which are numerically superior to the Presbyterian in Faulkner's country. Yet Faulkner is remarkably ignorant of the government and instruction of that church. He gives it an episcopal government quite contrary to the government by elders from which it gains its name. He seems naïvely ignorant of how the catechism is learned, for he has Joe Christmas standing silent with the book in his hands, as though the catechism were a litany to be recited rather than a group of answers to be repeated to questions. However, the Presbyterian Church is the doctrinal church of the Protestant sects, the church of unrelenting Calvinism. As such, it represents the Pharisaic order and is an example of what man does in codifying into cold ritual and inhumane form the warm and living heart of religion.

It is against the dead order of his world as it is defined by this formal religion that much of Joe's rebellion is directed. He defines himself by rebellion against McEachern's catechism and grim and inhumane morality, against Joanna Burden's attempt to force him into her religious patterns, against a symbol of the organized church when he strikes out in flailing anger against the Negro congregation, and against the ex-minister Hightower when he strikes him down. He is pursued and harried by the organized church of his day in a way suggestive of that in which Christ was pursued and harried by the Pharisees.

Joe Christmas is like Christ, so many of whose characteristics his creator has given him, in that he bears our common guilt, symbolized by his Negro blood, that he is denied by the world, and that he is ultimately offered as a blood sacrifice because of the "original sin" he bears. But he is not Christ; he is a rebelling and suffering creature, embittered, angry, and almost totally lacking in love. In his ineffectual death is no salvation. He is a futile and meaningless expiation of his "guilt."

Source: C. Hugh Holman, "The Unity of Faulkner's *Light in August*," in *PMLA*, Vol. 73, No. 1, March 1958, pp. 155–66.

B. R. McElderry Jr.

In the following essay, McElderry argues that the importance of narrative structure in Light in August *is often overshadowed by a focus on Faulkner's symbolism.*

Light in August is now regarded as one of Faulkner's major novels, and it is doubtful if any of the others combines so richly the easy natural comedy and the violent tragedy of which Faulkner at his best is a master. Consider the perfection of the brief dialogue early in the novel when Lena Grove confronts Byron Bunch at the lumber mill, expecting to find her pseudo-husband:

> "You ain't him," she says behind her fading smile, with the grave astonishment of a child.
>
> "No ma'am," Byron says. He pauses, half turning with the balanced staves. "I don't reckon I am. Who is it I ain't?"

Or consider the terrible scene in Hightower's kitchen, when Joe Christmas, the escaped murderer, is cornered and castrated by that incipient storm-trooper, Percy Grimm:

> When the others reached the kitchen they saw the table flung aside now and Grimm stooping over the body. When they approached to see what he was about, they saw that the man was not dead yet, and when they saw what Grimm was doing one of the men gave a choked cry and stumbled back into the wall and began to vomit. Then Grimm too sprang back, flinging behind him the bloody butcher knife.

Light in August was first published in 1932, and it is interesting to speculate on how differently Faulkner's reputation might have developed if this novel had been quickly reprinted in the Modern Library—instead of *Sanctuary*, included in that series the same year, and thus for a long time the most easily accessible of Faulkner's novels. Not until 1950 was *Light in August* added to the Modern Library, and most of the serious discussion of the novel has appeared within the past ten years. Interpretation has frequently been concerned with symbolical implications. Thus Richard Chase wishes to persuade us that "linear discrete images," such as a picket fence, the identical windows in a streetcar, and rows of identical houses "stand for modernism, rationalism, applied science, capitalism, progressivism, emasculation, the atomized consciousness and its pathological extensions" (*KR*, X, Autumn 1948, 540). Meanwhile, too little attention has been given to the extraordinary structural problems which Faulkner solved in *Light in August*.

What, essentially, is the story of the novel? How does Faulkner tell it? And why did he tell it the way he did? If we look at the beginning and ending, usually positions of great emphasis, we might say that this is the story of Lena and Byron. They meet, Byron at first sight falls in love with Lena, he helps her, she refuses him, he arranges for her seducer Brown (or Burch) to see her again, and he vainly fights the escaping Brown. In the last chapter, which has the quality of an epilogue, Byron is doggedly faithful to Lena, and her eventual acceptance of him is implied. In essence, this is a simple small-town idyll, with a touch of comic irony. Lena never deceives Byron, for when they meet it is obvious that Lena is pregnant and deserted by her lover. Yet for Byron there is no meanness or cheapness in her. His help to her is a gift. He never shows any resentment at her reluctance to allow him to take the place of the vanished and worthless Brown. The comic tone of the last chapter is the contribution of the furniture dealer, the rank outsider ignorant of previous episodes, merely trying to make a good story for the amusement of his wife. It is important that the Lena-Byron story is told in chronological sequence, just as it developed. This is the simple narrative thread that gives a recurrent sense of forward motion.

The word *recurrent* is deliberate, for during most of the novel (Chs. 3–19) we are chiefly occupied with the Joe Christmas story, which is told in violently

"Since Faulkner shows that he can tell a story simply, it is reasonable to suppose that the complexity of the Joe Christmas story is deliberate and accountable. And since the author demonstrates a strong liking for complexity, it is natural to accept his simple episodes as genuinely simple, not artificially simplified."

non-chronological order. Clustered about the Joe Christmas story are the four stories or sub-stories of (1) Joe's partner Brown (or Burch), of (2) Joanna Burden, the benefactress and mistress murdered by Joe Christmas, of (3) the Hineses, grandparents of Joe, and of (4) Hightower, the unemployed, discredited preacher. Three levels of time are used. There is the present, which begins with the report of Joanna Burden's murder (Ch. 4). This present action is continued by the sheriff's investigation of the crime, Christmas's arrest, escape and death (Chs. 13–19). By time and coincidence the major action concerning Christmas is related to the Lena-Byron action, through Byron's friend Hightower. The second time level is the immediate past in which Christmas committed the crime: part of Ch. 2 explains Brown's (or Burch's) association with Christmas; Ch. 5 tells the quarrel between Brown and Christmas on the night of the murder; Chs. 10, 11, and 12 tell the story of Christmas's relationship with Joanna over a period of three years, including the murder and Christmas's flight. The third level of time is the remote past, which gives distance and perspective to our knowledge of three characters. The early life of Hightower, the unfrocked preacher, is given in Chs. 3 and 20, the boyhood of Christmas in Chs. 6–9; and the story of Joanna Burden's abolitionist family is interjected into Christmas's early acquaintance with her in Ch. 11. Through the Hineses the circumstances of Christmas's birth are brought out in Chs. 15–16.

Deprived of the vitalizing force of description and dialogue, such a structural synopsis seems more confusing than the novel itself, but the elements of the structure are at least underlined: the contrast of major and minor action; the intertwining of present, immediate past, and remote past. How are these elements combined and made to function? What advantages accrue from this structure to set over against the loss in clarity involved in departure from a straight chronological sequence?

An important consideration is the relation between the enveloping—though minor—Lena-Byron story and the central Joe Christmas story. It is a chronological accident that they come together at all, for Lena arrives in Jefferson on the very day that the murder is discovered. There is a startling contrast between the simplicity of the one action and the devious complexity of the other that is appropriate to the characters involved. Each story helps to make the other more acceptable. Since Faulkner shows that he can tell a story simply, it is reasonable to suppose that the complexity of the Joe Christmas story is deliberate and accountable. And since the author demonstrates a strong liking for complexity, it is natural to accept his simple episodes as genuinely simple, not artificially simplified. There is, too, the obvious contrast of love and hate. Joe Christmas is a loveless person. In youth he distrusts the kindness of Mrs. McEachern as he later does that of Joanna. He is not at home with whites or Negroes, with men or women. Lena and Byron, on the contrary, are lovers. They supply the circle of humanity which Christmas stands outside of. Both stories are, if you like, implausible, but their implausibility is minimized by their contrast.

The first link between the two actions is an incidental mention in Ch. 1 of the fire at the Burden place. The next link is in Ch. 4, when Brown's confused story, retold to Hightower by Byron, and from this we learn what the town first finds out about the murder. This leads backward in Ch. 5 to the day and evening Christmas spent preceding the murder, with his concluding thought: "Something is going to happen. Something is going to happen to me." Now at this point we already know what is going to happen. We know that Joe is going to murder Joanna Burden. But we do not know why he will, and this is a spring of interest powerful enough to carry us through five chapters of Joe's early life and one of Joanna's before we come back to the night of the murder in Ch. 12. Ch. 13 then begins on the morning after the murder and the fire. With our own superior knowledge we watch the sheriff struggling to piece together the bits of evidence. The spring of interest now is in wondering how long it will take the Sheriff to catch up to the understanding of the crime which we as readers already possess. The flight and capture of Joe Christmas is next suggested in a series of scenes. Then in Ch. 15 the Hineses are catapulted into the action. The spring of interest now becomes surprise rather than suspense. We the readers, who felt we knew the whole story of Christmas now learn that his grandfather took him to the orphanage because of his supposed Negro blood, a "fact" Christmas later came to suspect. But the Hineses do not merely support the idea that Christmas has Negro blood. Their own conflict creates a new suspense about Christmas, now prisoner in the county jail. Hines tries to incite the lynching of his own grandson. and his wife tries to prevent him. Next there is the desperate proposal that Hightower give a false alibi for Christmas, Hightower's refusal, Christmas's unexpected and hopeless break away from the Sheriff, and his violent death in Hightower's kitchen.

The slow shift from minor to major action, the strategic use of the reader's responses, and the solid delineation of Joe Christmas are triumphs of narrative structure. Yet two important characters seem insufficiently developed: Joanna Burden and Hightower. The full focus of attention is turned on Joanna in only two chapters; elsewhere she is incidental. In these chapters Faulkner tells first of the seduction of Joanna, then the tangled earlier history of the spinster, the last of a New England abolitionist line, perversely settled in the South. After Colonel Sartoris killed her half-brother and grandfather, Joanna lived in isolation, using her income to support Negro schools. At forty-one, after Joe possesses her, she turns into a nymphomaniac, determined to possess him completely by adding religious sanction to their relationship. The climax of Ch. 12 is Joanna's melodramatic attempt to compel Joe to pray with her at the point of a gun. It is this gesture which precipitates the murder, though the murder itself is implied rather than described at this point. Joanna's behavior seems to me convenient to Faulkner's purpose of accounting for Joe Christmas's action, but not sufficiently developed to be acceptable in itself as a convincing portrayal of Joanna.

The objection to Hightower is of a different kind. Like Joanna, it is true, Hightower is a character isolated by a peculiar family history, and in fiction as in life, an isolated character is harder to judge than one in close and familiar association with other people. The episodes of his life fit into no ordinary pattern. If the fictional character is vivid we tend to accept him as at least an interesting possibility. Years before our story opens, the scandal regarding Hightower's wife had lost him his church and had ostracized him from the community, yet he refused to leave it. Living on without purpose, he is nevertheless represented as developing an attitude of intense compassion. "Poor man, Poor mankind," he says when he first hears the story of the murder. His assistance at the birth of the Negro baby, and later at the birth of Lena's child, illustrates this idea. He listens with compassion to the strange story of the Hineses, even though he vigorously refuses to give the false alibi for Christmas. (Ironically, when Percy Grimm has cornered Christmas, Hightower vainly shouts the alibi he had earlier refused to give.) Like Joanna, the unfrocked preacher is convenient to Faulkner's action, but unlike her, Hightower sometimes seems the mouthpiece of the author. Before the Hineses come in, Hightower is represented as thinking:

> Listening [to Protestant music], he seems to hear within it the apotheosis of his own history, his own land, his own environed blood: that people from which he sprang and among whom he lives who can never take either pleasure or catastrophe or escape from either, without brawling over it. Pleasure, ecstasy, they cannot seem to bear: their escape from it is in violence, in drinking and fighting and praying; catastrophe too, the violence identical and apparently inescapable. *And so why should not their religion drive them to crucifixion of themselves and one another?* he thinks.

In this and many other passages, the design of the author seems too palpable, to use Keats's adjective. Finally, in Ch. 20, there seems to be an attempt to magnify the importance of Hightower beyond his significance in the action. Before discussing this chapter further, however, I wish to set it in its context.

The peculiar structure adopted by Faulkner permits the maximum of variety in tone and texture in the last three chapters of the novel. At the very end of Ch. 18 the news of Joe Christmas's death comes to Byron Bunch in the flattest and least circumstantial tone of country gossip. "What excitement in town this evening?" says Byron, and the countryman, still disappointed that he himself had missed the excitement, replies: "I thought maybe you hadn't heard. About an hour ago. That nigger, Christmas. They killed him." Ch. 19, which follows immediately, is a typical Faulknerian time complication. Instead of taking us at once to the murder, Faulkner begins with various opinions on why Christmas had taken refuge in Hightower's house. This leads into the scene at the railroad station, where Lawyer Stevens is putting Christmas's grandparents on the train for Mottstown and promising to send the grandson's body to them for burial. As it happens, a friend of Stevens, a college professor, alights from this very train, and it is to the professor that Stevens gives four pages of his own theory that Mrs. Hines saw an irrational hope in the preacher and confided it to Christmas when she visited him in the jail, just before his escape. Stevens theorizes shrewdly:

> And he believed her. I think that is what gave him not courage so much as the passive patience to endure and recognize and accept the one opportunity which he had to break in the middle of that crowded square, manacled, and run. But there was too much running with him, stride for stride with him. Not pursuers: but himself: years, acts, deeds omitted and committed, keeping pace with him, stride for stride, breath for breath, thud for thud of the heart, using a single heart. It was not alone all those thirty years which she [Mrs. Hines] did not know, but all those successions of thirty years before that which had put that stain either on his white blood or his black blood, whichever you will, and which killed him. But he must have run with believing for a while; anyway, with hope. But his blood would not be quiet, let him save it.

This passage illustrates Faulkner's remarkable capacity to reveal the complexity just beneath the seeming simplicity of the surface. It is the revelation of complexity that generates a strange yet believable intensity. Concreteness and abstraction are cunningly blended. There is the picture of the manacled man making the sudden break in the crowded square, there is the sense of his running in "stride," "breath," and "thud of the heart." But running with him are "years, acts, deeds committed or omitted," abstractions not bare for us, but richly prepared for in the previous accounts of the orphanage, the McEacherns, Barbara Allen, and Joanna Burden. The structure of the narrative has placed us inside these abstractions. We understand the difference between belief in freedom and mere hope of it.

At the end of Stevens's account there is a break in the chapter and a shift in tone to a straightforward account of Percy Grimm, born too late for World War I, but now the young captain of the National Guard company. Percy seems the personification of civic responsibility, of law and order, forcing the sheriff to permit Legionnaires to act as special guards over the weekend. On Monday afternoon Percy instantly interprets the deputy's shots as announcing Christmas's escape. Then follow four pages of as sharply told pursuit as I know. Minutes later—seconds, perhaps—Percy follows Christmas into Hightower's house. Hightower's protest and false alibi enrage him, and the disciplined intelligence by which Percy pursued gives way to blood lust. Shooting through the overturned kitchen table behind which Christmas cowers, Percy mortally wounds him. Then seizing a butcher knife, he castrates the living man. For many writers this crude act of violence would be the ultimate effect, but not for Faulkner. In the sentences which picture the dying Christmas an inner tension is created which surpasses the physical violence.

> He just lay there, with his eyes open and empty of everything save consciousness, and with something, a shadow, about his mouth. For a long moment he looked up at them with peaceful and unfathomable and unbearable eyes. Then his face, body, all, seemed to collapse, to fall in upon itself, and from out the slashed garments about his hips and loins the pent black blood seemed to rush like a released breath. It seemed to rush out of his pale body like the rush of sparks from a rising rocket; upon that black blast the man seemed to rise soaring into their memories forever and ever. They are not to lose it, in whatever peaceful valleys, beside whatever placid and reassuring streams of old age, in the mirroring faces of whatever children they will contemplate old disasters and newer hopes. It will be there, musing, quiet, steadfast, not fading and not particularly threatful, but of itself alone serene, of itself alone triumphant. Again from the town, deadened a little by the walls, the scream of the siren mounted toward its unbelievable crescendo, passing out of the realm of hearing.

The seemingly disjointed organization of this chapter has justified itself. Every necessary explanation has been made earlier. When the shattering climax comes, the print on the page renders the concentrated experience.

Ch. 20, with its long account of Hightower's early life, is structurally much less effective. Miss Hirshleifer, whose analysis of this novel (*Perspective*, II, Summer 1949) has been much praised, says that it "is not anticlimactic after Christmas's death, but the vital philosophical counterpart of it" (p. 233). I agree that this was probably Faulkner's intention, but I think the chapter fails for most readers to overcome this sense of anticlimax. First, as to the intention. Hightower though discredited and isolated, is the conscience that broods over the action of the novel. He is also the link between the Lena-Byron and the Joe Christmas action. Through his suffering, Hightower has learned compassion: "Poor man. Poor mankind," he says, and when Christmas takes refuge in his house, Hightower instinctively shouts the false alibi he had earlier refused to give. As this action illustrates, Hightower's compassion came too late in life to be effective.

Even as a boy, he idealized not the earnest peace-loving father, but the swashbuckling grandfather. Hightower's religion was thus corrupted from the beginning by his dreams of a past military glory, so corrupted that even his marriage was poisoned—though Hightower's wife was certainly frustrated and neurotic before her marriage. It is the corruptness of Hightower's religion, the pitiful lateness of his mature compassion, that represents the sickness in the spiritual life of Jefferson. Needing a religion of wisdom and compassion, the community gets all too often, even from a "good" minister like Hightower, a religion of dynamic hatred, intolerance, and frustration. And thus the brutalities of the Joe Christmas story can occur.

The foregoing statement is doubtless too simple. But I think that it gives the general direction of Ch. 20, and justifies Miss Hirshleifer's insistence that it is not anticlimactic. Yet in my first reading of the novel I missed this meaning, or at any rate found it obscured by a great deal of elaboration that did not seem pertinent. The reason, I think, is that in trying to avoid the obvious ways of registering this idea, Faulkner has overreached the reader (this one, anyway) as, in a sense, Shakespeare never overreaches the reader or spectator. With the tremendous climax of Ch. 19, the reader is almost literally in a state of shock. As he turns the page to begin the next chapter, I think he expects to find out what happened next—at least what happens to Hightower, for he already knows that Lawyer Stevens put the Hineses on the train for Mottstown that very evening, promising to send the body of Joe Christmas to them for burial. Ch. 20 begins:

> Now the final copper light of afternoon fades; now the street beyond the low maples and the low signboard is prepared and empty, framed by the study window like a stage.
>
> He can remember how when he was young, after he first came to Jefferson from the seminary, how that fading copper light would seem almost audible, like a dying yellow fall of trumpets dying into an interval of silence and waiting, out of which they would presently come. Already, even before the falling horns had ceased, it would seem to him that he could hear the beginning thunder not yet louder than a whisper, a rumor, in the air.

This leads into Hightower's memories of his childhood, his father, his grandfather, his mother, and the old Negro slave. Now I can very well believe that being involved in an event like the killing of Joe Christmas would cause a man, particularly an isolated and introspective man like Hightower, to remember his early life, to reconstruct and search for a meaning in the whole pattern of his being. But for me the transition is too abrupt, the long chapter digresses too much from natural reminders of the immediate past. There are one or two references to Hightower's bandaged head. That is all. There is no answer even to the obvious question: When Byron returned to town for Lena, did he go to see Hightower? It seems to me that Faulkner's narrative judgment is less sound in Ch. 20 than in Ch. 19. Nevertheless, this may be a defect in the reader rather than in Faulkner. Once the intention of the Hightower chapter becomes clear, or when the chapter is read as an episode partially detached from its structural context (that is, as an account of Hightower's youth) it is memorable. The little boy fingering the coat his father wore in the army is a fine detail, and so is the remark of the old slave: "No suh. . . . Not Marse Gail. Not him. Dey wouldn't *dare* to kill a Hightower." And I would not want to sacrifice the wonderful vision of the wheel merging the faces that represent Hightower's experience in a swirling confusion that announces his death as he looks out the window. Whether Ch. 20 is satisfactory or not in the general strategy of the novel, it offers a remarkable contrast in tone and texture to the violence of Ch. 19.

The final chapter strikes still another note, the unexpected one of comedy. In the Lena-Byron action, which must now be concluded in harmony with the opening of the novel, and with the characters of Lena and Byron, all the elements of a conventional ending are present. Now that Brown has run out on her a second time, there is really nothing for Lena to do but reward the patient and devoted Byron. Granted her easy acceptance of what life brings her—a lover, a baby, a ride in a wagon—we may doubt whether she would ever have shown any reluctance or delay in taking such an obviously good mate as Byron. But regardless of when she accepts him, the prospect is that the last chapter will be a conventional footnote, with an intimation of happy wedded bliss. Faulkner is not the man to be trapped into any such tame conclusion. Instead of winding up the Lena-Byron story himself, that is in his own voice, he invents a traveling furniture dealer, a rank outsider who knows nothing of the previous history of this strange pair—or trio, if you count the baby. The furniture dealer, telling the story to his wife, doesn't really have to explain the story he tells, because he can't be expected to understand it. He simply tells what he saw and what he heard, with a few shrewd guesses. Within these limits he is so good a storyteller that he entertains the reader as well as his wife. Lena's persistence in the search for the worthless Brown, and her reluctance to take Byron may in fact be implausible. Seen through the furniture dealer's eyes, they seem merely comical illustrations of the unfathomable perversity of women. The furniture dealer sets down Lena's reluctance to her childlike interest in travel, and Lena's final comment bears him out: "My, my. A body does get around. Here we aint been coming from Alabama but two months, and now it's already Tennessee."

In this paper I have not tried to show that the narrative structure of *Light in August* is perfect. Joanna Burden remains convenient rather than convincing, Hightower is too obtrusive, and the fusion of major and minor actions may be called ingenious rather than inspired. Yet when the difficulties of the structural problems are fairly confronted, the achievement overshadows such defects. In 1939 George M. O'Donnell called the novel "confused" and "malproportioned." Richard Rovere (1950) and Irving Howe (1951) both found it loose in structure. These judgments do not take into account the difficulty of the problems Faulkner faced, and the resourcefulness of his solutions. If the structure of the novel is firmly grasped, we may find that the story itself is more interesting than paraphrases of its supposed symbolic meaning.

Source: B. R. McElderry Jr., "The Narrative Structure of *Light in August*," in *College English*, Vol. 19, No. 5, February 1958, pp. 200–07.

Sources

Beck, Warren, "Faulkner's Point of View," in *College English*, Vol. 2, No. 8, May 1941, pp. 736–49.

Bloom, Harold, "William Faulkner," in *Genius: A Mosaic of One Hundred Exemplary Creative Minds*, Warner Books, pp. 565–68.

Faulkner, William, *Light in August*, Vintage, 1987.

Kartiganer, Donald M., "William Faulkner," in *Columbia Literary History of the United States*, edited by Emory Elliott, Columbia University Press, 1988, pp. 887–909.

McElderry, B. R., Jr., "The Narrative Structure of *Light in August*," in *College English*, Vol. 19, No. 5, February 1958, pp. 200–207.

Further Reading

Martin, Timothy P., "The Art and Rhetoric of Chronology in Faulkner's *Light in August*," in *College Literature*, Vol. 7, No. 2, Spring 1980, pp. 125–35.

Martin analyzes Faulkner's use of time in the novel and compares it to other modernist works.

McMillen, Neil R., *Dark Journey: Black Mississippians in the Age of Jim Crow*, University of Illinois Press, 1990.

McMillen studies the treatment of blacks in Mississippi between 1890 and 1940 and chronicles their response to the segregation and racism they experienced during this period.

Toomey, David M., "The Human Heart in Conflict: *Light in August*'s Schizophrenic Narrator," in *Studies in the Novel*, Vol. 23, No. 4, Winter 1991, pp. 452–69.

In this study, Toomey argues that the narrative could be read as Hightower's interior thoughts.

Volpe, Edmond L., *A Reader's Guide to William Faulkner*, Farrar, Straus & Giroux, 1964.

Volpe divides his study of Faulkner's major works and style into three sections. The first traces thematic and stylistic patterns, the second contains close readings of Faulkner's nineteen novels, and the third traces the actual chronology of events within some of the more difficult works.

Williamson, Joel, *William Faulkner and Southern History*, Oxford University Press, 1993.

Williamson places Faulkner's texts along with Yoknapatawpha County in a cultural and historical context, focusing on the presentation of race, class, sex, and violence in the works. Williamson also includes biographical details that reveal Faulkner's own philosophy and experience with these subjects.

The Lion, the Witch and the Wardrobe

C. S. Lewis

1950

The Lion, the Witch and the Wardrobe by C. S. Lewis is the first—although sequentially the second—of seven books Lewis wrote about the imaginary world of Narnia. It is set during World War II, at the time when London was being bombed by Nazi Germany, and was inspired by Lewis's life with refugee children who came from London to stay at his country home during the bombings. One of the children, fascinated by the black oak wardrobe standing in the Lewis's hall, wanted to know if there was a way out of the back of the wardrobe, and if so, what was on the other side. Lewis's response was *The Lion, the Witch and the Wardrobe*, the story of a world under siege by the powers of darkness, only it is not Hitler who leads the attack but the White Witch. *The Lion, the Witch and the Wardrobe* marked a return to a familiar Lewis theme: the battle between good and evil. As a Christian author living in a grim age, Lewis felt he could not avoid this theme.

When Lewis decided to write children's fiction, his publisher, as well as some of his friends, were less than enthusiastic. They thought producing such stories would hurt his reputation as a serious writer. Nonetheless, Lewis went ahead, helping to begin a renaissance in children's literature. Since their initial publication, the Chronicles of Narnia have sold more than 100 million copies and are beloved by readers all over the world.

C.S. Lewis © UPI-Corbis-Bettmann

Author Biography

C. S. Lewis was born November 29, 1898 in a suburb of Belfast, Ireland. His father, Albert, was a successful lawyer. The family house, called Little Lea, had long corridors, empty rooms, and secret nooks in which Lewis and his brother, Warren, played. In the attic, the boys spent many rainy days writing and illustrating stories about imaginary worlds. Sometimes, when their cousin came to visit, the three of them would climb into a black oak wardrobe, hand-carved by Lewis and Warren's grandfather, and sit in the dark while Lewis told stories.

In 1908, Lewis's mother died of cancer. Lewis spent the next six years in and out of boarding schools, and during that time, he grew increasingly antagonistic towards the idea of a benevolent God. Then his father placed him with the private tutor W. T. Kirkpatrick, who provided an education that challenged Lewis's intellect and stimulated his imagination. In 1917, Lewis earned a scholarship to Oxford University, but with England in the midst of World War I, Lewis felt it his duty to enlist. The following year, he was wounded at the Battle of Arras; after that, he returned to Oxford to pursue his studies.

As an Oxford student and eventual fellow of Magdalen College, Lewis became close friends with writers and scholars who altered his worldview and encouraged him to write. This circle of friends, whom Lewis later dubbed the "Inklings," included J. R. R. Tolkien, Charles Williams, Neville Coghill, and Owen Barfield. Each man was instrumental in showing Lewis the reasonableness of Christianity, but more than anything else, it was Tolkien's views on the relevance of myth to the Christian faith that moved him. Lewis became a Christian at the age of thirty-two.

For fifteen years, the Inklings met regularly in Lewis's sitting room to read aloud from and discuss their own work. In these friendly gatherings, Tolkien first read *The Hobbit* and *The Lord of the Rings*. Lewis, in turn, presented his listeners with *The Allegory of Love* (1936), *The Problem of Pain* (1944), *The Screwtape Letters* (1944), and his science fiction trilogy: *Out of the Silent Planet* (1938), *Perelandra* (1943), and *That Hideous Strength* (1945). In the late 1940s, Lewis began writing children's stories, but the Inklings no longer provided much creative support. Charles Williams's death in 1945 struck them all very hard, and afterward they met less regularly. Lewis published *The Lion, the Witch and the Wardrobe* in 1950 and went on to write six more Narnia books over the next six years. The final installment of the series, *The Last Battle* (1956), won the Carnegie Medal. Letters from fans poured onto his desk by the thousands, and Lewis answered every one.

After completing his Narnia series, Lewis wrote *Surprised by Joy* (1956), an account of his conversion to Christianity. During this time, he married Joy Davidman, a good friend who had recently been diagnosed with terminal cancer. The wedding took place in Joy's hospital room, after which Lewis took her home with him to die. Instead of dying, however, she got better, and the two of them had three years together before her death in 1960. Shortly thereafter, Lewis wrote *A Grief Observed* (1961). Troubled by declining health himself, Lewis resigned in the summer of 1963. He died on November 22, 1963, one week short of his sixty-fifth birthday.

Plot Summary

Chapter One: Lucy Looks into a Wardrobe

It is wartime, and four siblings (Peter, Susan, Edmund, and Lucy) are sent away from their home in London to escape the air-raids. They go to stay at a large house in the country, where live a funny-looking old Professor (to whom they take an instant

Media Adaptations

- *The Lion, the Witch and the Wardrobe* was adapted as a radio dramatization by Focus on the Family in April 1999. The full-cast production features realistic sound effects and notable actors. Paul Scofield is the storyteller, and David Suchet is the voice of Aslan. As of 2006, it was available on audio CD.
- *The Lion, the Witch and the Wardrobe* was first adapted as a television series (nine twenty-minute episodes) in 1967 by the ABC Television Network and was directed by Helen Standage from a screenplay by Trevor Preston. As of 2006, it was unavailable for home viewing.
- *The Lion, the Witch and the Wardrobe* was produced as an animated television special in 1979 by the Episcopal Radio-TV Foundation and the Children's Television Workshop. This production's animators were Steve and Bill Melendez; the screenwriter was David D. Connell. It aired on CBS, was watched by thirty-seven million viewers, and won an Emmy for Outstanding Animated Program. As of 2006, it was available on DVD.
- The BBC produced *The Lion, the Witch and the Wardrobe* as a television miniseries (in a combination of live action and animation) in 1988, adapted by Alan Seymour and directed by Marilyn Fox. Over the next two years, the BBC filmed *Prince Caspian*, *The Voyage of the "Dawn Treader,"* and *The Silver Chair*. The four miniseries were nominated for a total of fourteen awards, including an Emmy for Outstanding Children's Program. They were later edited into three feature-length films, and as of 2006, they were available on DVD.
- Buena Vista Pictures released *The Chronicles of Narnia: The Lion, the Witch and the Wardrobe* as a major motion picture in December 2005. This Walt Disney and Walden Media production, a combination of live action and computer animation, was directed by Andrew Adamson. As of 2006, it was available on DVD.
- *The Lion, the Witch and the Wardrobe* was adapted as a musical in 1985, with music, book, and lyrics by Irita Kutchmy. As of 2006, it was available from Joseph Weinberger Ltd.
- *Narnia*, another musical adaptation of *The Lion, the Witch and the Wardrobe*, was written by Jules Tasca with lyrics by Ted Drachman and music by Thomas Tierney. It was first published by the Dramatic Publishing Company in 1987, and as of 2006, it was available.
- *The Lion, the Witch and the Wardrobe* was adapted as a stage play by Joseph Robinette in 1989. As of 2006, it was available from the Dramatic Publishing Company.

liking), a housekeeper named Mrs. Macready, and three servants. At the first opportunity the children explore the house, and after walking through a labyrinth of stairs, corridors, and rooms, they come to a spare room that is empty save for a big wardrobe. Uninterested, Peter, Susan, and Edmund move on, but Lucy stays behind to check out the wardrobe. She gets inside, moves through rows of fur coats and, to her amazement, walks right into the middle of a snow-covered forest at night. A light shining in the distance catches Lucy's eye and she goes toward it: it is a lamppost. As Lucy is wondering how a lamppost got to be in the middle of a forest, a Faun carrying brown-paper parcels steps out of the trees. The Faun is so startled at the sight of Lucy that he drops all his parcels.

Chapter Two: What Lucy Found There

The Faun introduces himself as Tumnus and invites Lucy back to his cave for tea. He serves lots of food, tells delightful stories, and plays a tune on an odd little flute that puts Lucy to sleep. When she wakes up, Mr. Tumnus starts crying uncontrollably and confesses to being in the pay of the White Witch, an evil queen who makes it always winter but never Christmas in Narnia. Her orders to him were that if ever he was to see a Son of Adam or Daughter of Eve in the forest, he must capture and deliver them to her. Mr. Tumnus explains that he was just pretending to be her friend so that he could lure her to his house, wait until she fell asleep, then sneak out and tell the witch, but now that he has gotten to know Lucy, he cannot bring himself to turn her over. Lucy thanks him, and he leads her back to the lamppost. She returns through the wardrobe and runs to tell her sister and brothers all that has happened.

Chapter Three: Edmund and the Wardrobe

Lucy's siblings do not believe her story, and when she tries to prove it by showing them the inside of the wardrobe, nothing is there except coats. Lucy is very upset, and Edmund makes matters worse by teasing her. A few days later, however, Edmund follows Lucy into the wardrobe during a game of hide-and-seek, and he too discovers Narnia. Edmund walks alone through the strange, dark wood, thinking that Lucy ran off because she is angry with him. Presently, he is met by a sledge pulled by two white reindeer and driven by a fat Dwarf. A very tall lady with pale white skin and bright red lips, sporting a white fur coat, golden crown, and golden wand, sits high up in the sledge. She does not recognize the sort of creature Edmund is, so she asks him. He has no idea what she means, so he says his name. The lady does not like the way Edmund is addressing her and asks him how he could talk to the Queen in such a manner. She is astounded to discover he did not know she was the Queen.

Chapter Four: Turkish Delight

The Queen soon finds out that Edmund is a Son of Adam, and she is about to do something terrible to him when another idea crosses her mind. She invites Edmund into her sledge and offers him a hot drink and several pounds of enchanted Turkish Delight, the kind that keeps one begging for more. She tells Edmund that he can be King of Narnia and eat all the Turkish Delight he wants if he brings his brother and sisters to her. The Queen leaves him with directions to her house and instructions not to tell anyone of their meeting. As Edmund watches the sledge disappear, Susan runs up and expresses her happiness that he got in, too. She says she just had lunch with Mr. Tumnus and found out all kinds of terrible things about the White Witch. Lucy cannot wait to tell everyone they have both been to Narnia, but Edmund is not excited about it. His stomach is hurting from the Turkish Delight, and his pride is hurt as well.

Chapter Five: Back on This Side of the Door

When Lucy tells Peter and Susan what happened, Edmund denies it and says Lucy is making it all up. Hurt and dejected, Lucy runs from the room, and Peter chastises Edmund for being "perfectly beastly" to her. The next morning, Peter and Susan go to the Professor for advice about what to do with Lucy. He surprises them by saying that since Lucy is a very truthful girl and obviously not insane, they must believe she is telling the truth. The subject of the wardrobe is dropped for some time; nobody talks about it or goes near it, that is, until the day the children run into the spare room to keep away from Mrs. Macready and a group of sightseers she is leading through the house. They think surely no one will follow them into that room, but then they hear someone fumbling at the door, and they all jump into the wardrobe.

Chapter Six: Into the Forest

The cramped, dark wardrobe opens up into the snowy wood. Peter apologizes to Lucy for not believing her, and then all eyes are on Edmund because of his lie. Peter suggests they go exploring with Lucy as the leader. She takes them to Mr. Tumnus's cave, which they find abandoned and in shambles. They also find a piece of paper with a message from Maugrim, the Captain of the Secret Police, explaining that Mr. Tumnus has been arrested on a charge of high treason. Lucy insists they go looking for him, since it was on account of his befriending her that he was arrested. Peter and Susan consent, although they have no idea how to begin looking. A bright red Robin appears, and Lucy gets the impression that the bird wants them to follow it. The Robin leads them through the forest, and all the time they are walking, Edmund questions whether they are doing the right thing.

Chapter Seven: A Day with the Beavers

The children follow the Robin to a place where they meet a Beaver, who has been cautiously observing them from behind the trees. It turns out he is a friend of Mr. Tumnus, and he tells the children they must speak quietly because the Witch's spies are everywhere. Assuming that they know more than they do, the Beaver whispers, "Aslan is on the move." The children, of course, have no idea who Aslan is, yet they all derive a certain comfort from the name. That is, all except Edmund, who is horrified by it. Lucy, who is very concerned about Mr. Tumnus, wants to know where he has been taken. The Beaver (called Mr. Beaver from now on) invites them back to his place for dinner where they can talk in secret. There they meet Mrs. Beaver, who graciously welcomes them, and they share a sumptuous meal of fish and potatoes. Mr. Beaver cocks an eye toward the window and remarks with satisfaction that it is snowing: the snow will cover their tracks and thereby prevent unwanted visitors.

Chapter Eight: What Happened after Dinner

After dinner, Mr. Beaver tells the children that Mr. Tumnus has probably been taken to the Witch's castle and turned into stone. He says they can do nothing for him without Aslan, the great lion and King of the wood, whom they are to meet the very next day at a place called the Stone Table. Mr. Beaver relates the prophecies that speak of how the White Witch's reign will come to an end when Aslan returns and two Sons of Adam and two Daughters of Eve sit on Cair Paravel's thrones. He explains that the White Witch will want to kill the children out of fear that they are the fulfillment to the prophecy. When Mr. Beaver finishes speaking, everyone notices Edmund is missing. They rush outside and call for him, but it is no use: he has gone to the White Witch. Mr. Beaver's biggest concern is that Edmund heard everything about Aslan and the meeting at the Stone Table and is going to tell the Witch; she will then try to stop them before reaching Aslan. Mrs. Beaver suggests they leave at once.

Chapter Nine: In the Witch's House

Edmund, who left the Beavers' house soon after Mr. Beaver spoke of the meeting with Aslan, stumbles over rocky and icy terrain to get to the Witch's house. As he walks, he dreams about everything he will do as King, including getting even with Peter. The Witch's house, a creepy little castle with towers, pointed spires, and shadows, has a courtyard filled with stone statues of all manner of creatures. Edmund climbs some steps to the threshold of a doorway where Maugrim the wolf lies quietly. Thinking Maugrim to be a statue like all the others, Edmund begins to step over him, but the huge wolf rises to block his way. Terrified, Edmund identifies himself and states his business. Maugrim fetches the White Witch, who is angry to see Edmund without his brother and sisters. Edmund explains that they are nearby, and he relates everything Mr. Beaver said about Aslan. The news about Aslan greatly startles the Witch. She orders her fat Dwarf to prepare the sledge.

Chapter Ten: The Spell Begins to Break

The children and Mr. Beaver impatiently wait for Mrs. Beaver as she packs food, matches, and handkerchiefs for the journey. After much fussing over what they should take, they finally set off and travel a great distance over ice and snow. Lucy is practically asleep on her feet when Mr. Beaver leads them to a secret hiding place in the ground where they rest for the night. They awake to the sound of sleigh bells. Up above, Father Christmas waits in his sledge with presents for everybody: Mrs. Beaver gets a new sewing machine delivered straight to her house, and Mr. Beaver gets a finished and fully repaired dam. Peter receives a sword and a shield, and Susan gets a bow, a quiver full of arrows, and an ivory horn that summons help whenever blown. Lucy receives a dagger (although Father Christmas tells her she is not to fight in the battle) and a cordial of special healing juice. Before leaving, Father Christmas breaks out one final present: hot tea for everyone. The children and the Beavers share an enjoyable breakfast before moving on.

Chapter Eleven: Aslan Is Nearer

Edmund could not be more miserable. He asks for Turkish Delight and the fat Dwarf brings him dry bread and water instead. Then, after ordering Maugrim and his swiftest wolves to hunt down the Beavers and humans, the Witch forces Edmund to go with her in her sledge on a long, cold journey to the Stone Table. En route, they pass a merry party of creatures feasting in the wood. This sight of such happiness angers the Witch, and when they tell her Father Christmas gave them the food, she becomes enraged. Despite Edmund's pleas, the Witch turns them all to stone then smacks Edmund hard on the face for asking favors for spies and traitors. They continue on, but their journey is slowed by a sudden thaw: the sledge keeps getting stuck in the mud. The Dwarf binds Edmund's hands, and they begin to walk. Trees bud, flowers bloom, and birds sing all around them. Spring has arrived, and, the Dwarf exclaims, it is Aslan's doing. The Witch responds, "If either of you mentions that name again . . . he shall instantly be killed."

Chapter Twelve: Peter's First Battle

The children and the Beavers travel across the greening countryside and up a hill to an open space where stands the Stone Table, a giant grey slab with strange lines and figures carved on it. Music heralds the approach of Aslan, who enters a pavilion surrounded by many forest animals and mythological creatures. Aslan welcomes the children and Beavers and says that all will be done to save Edmund, though it will not be easy. As a feast is being prepared, Aslan leads Peter to the eastern edge of the hilltop and shows him Cair Paravel, the far-off castle where Peter is to be king. Suddenly, the sound of Susan's horn summons Peter to battle. Maugrim and another wolf have infiltrated the camp, and to his horror, Peter sees Maugrim chase Susan up a tree. Peter kills Maugrim with his sword, and the other wolf darts away. Aslan orders his swiftest creatures after it, announcing that it will lead them to Edmund and the Witch. After Peter cleans his sword, Aslan knights him, "Sir Peter Wolf's—Bane."

Chapter Thirteen: Deep Magic from the Dawn of Time

After walking for what seems an eternity to Edmund, the Witch and the Dwarf hatch a plan to kill Edmund before he can be rescued. But just as the Witch is sharpening her stone knife, Aslan's rescue party arrives. Edmund is saved, but the Witch and the Dwarf escape using her magic. The next morning Edmund has a private conversation with Aslan that Edmund always remembers. Aslan then delivers Edmund to his siblings, telling them there is no need to speak of what has passed. Later, the Witch arrives and pronounces Edmund a traitor. She further proclaims that, according to the Law of the Deep Magic, she has the right to kill all traitors. Aslan requests a private conference with the Witch, during which they arrive at an agreement that will spare Edmund's life. The Queen, with "a look of fierce joy on her face," asks Aslan how she knows he will keep his promise. Aslan responds with a terrible half laugh, half roar.

Chapter Fourteen: The Triumph of the Witch

Aslan leads his forces from the hilltop to the Fords of Beruna, where they set up camp. He then discusses battle plans with Peter, telling him that he will be the one to lead the campaign. That night, Susan and Lucy find Aslan walking forlornly through the moonlit woods. He is sad but tells the girls he would be grateful if they walked with him for a while with their hands on his mane. They presently arrive at the hill leading up to the Stone Table, and Aslan says they must here part company. The girls cry uncontrollably as Aslan leaves and heads for the Stone Table, where the White Witch and her evil minions await. They bind, shave, and torture Aslan before dragging him onto the Stone Table. Susan and Lucy, watching from a safe distance, expect Aslan to fight back at any moment, but he never does. The Witch tells Aslan that his death accomplishes nothing because she is going to kill Edmund anyway. Susan and Lucy cannot bear to watch as the Witch drives her knife into Aslan's heart.

Chapter Fifteen: Deeper Magic from Before the Dawn of Time

The Witch charges off with her minions, and Susan and Lucy approach the Stone Table. They remove Aslan's muzzle but cannot unbind him because the knots are too tight. Suddenly, hundreds of little field mice appear and chew through the cords. The girls sit with Aslan all night, holding him and crying. At dawn they go for a walk to warm themselves and are startled by a thunderous cracking sound. They turn to see the Stone Table split and Aslan's body gone. Just as they wonder what it all means, Aslan, alive and well and standing behind them in the sunlight, explains: the Witch did not account for the Deeper Magic, which states that death will work backward when a willing victim who committed no crime is sacrificed in a traitor's stead. Overjoyed, Susan and Lucy shower Aslan with kisses, and they run and play all around the hilltop. Aslan lets out an earth-shaking roar, tells the girls to hop on his back, and off they go to the Witch's castle. When they arrive, Aslan makes a flying leap over the wall into the courtyard filled with stone statues.

Chapter Sixteen: What Happened about the Statues

Aslan frees the statues, one by one, by breathing on them. Before long, the whole courtyard erupts in joy. Susan gets a bit nervous when Aslan breathes on the Giant Rumblebuffin's feet, thinking it may not be safe, but Rumblebuffin turns out to be a friendly giant. One of the last statues to be freed is Mr. Tumnus, and he and Lucy dance for joy at their reuniting. Giant Rumblebuffin knocks down the gates with his giant club so they can get out, and Aslan leads the charge to the battlefront. They arrive to discover Peter's army badly depleted and fighting desperately. Stone statues dot the battlefield, so it is obvious the Witch has been using her wand, but at that moment, she is fighting Peter with her stone knife. Aslan erupts with another earth-shaking roar and hurls himself on the White Witch. Peter's tired army cheers, and the newcomers join in the fight.

Chapter Seventeen: The Hunting of the White Stag

Aslan kills the Witch, and the rest of his companions wipe out the Witch's forces. Peter says Edmund saved the day by smashing the Witch's wand to prevent her from turning any more of their army into stone, but in so doing Edmund was badly wounded. Lucy pours a few drops from her cordial into Edmund's mouth, he recovers fully, and Aslan knights him on the spot. The next day, Aslan crowns Peter, Susan, Edmund, and Lucy kings and queens of Narnia at Cair Paravel. The Pevensies reign for many years, until one day they go on a hunt for the White Stag, believing that the White Stag will grant wishes to anyone who can catch him. They chase him into a thicket, where they discover a vaguely familiar lamppost. Thinking some new adventure or unexpected treasure awaits, they venture past it. Within moments, the children tumble out of the wardrobe into the spare room. Mrs. Macready and the guests are still out in the corridor. The children run to tell the Professor all that has happened, and he says that someday they will return to Narnia, but it will be when they least expect it.

Characters

Aslan

Aslan is the Great Lion, King of Beasts, King of the land of Narnia, Lord of the wood, and son of the great Emperor-beyond-the-Sea. His purpose is clear the moment he returns to Narnia: to overthrow evil by serving others. The thawing of the witch's winter and renewing of spring comprise the first phase of Aslan's service, followed by the giving of gifts to the Pevensie children and the creatures of the wood through Father Christmas. After the children arrive at the Stone Table, Aslan serves them all with his hospitality, but Peter he serves more specifically by teaching him how to think and act like a military leader. Aslan's service to Edmund is threefold: he sends his forces to rescue Edmund from the White Witch, has a talk with Edmund that changes Edmund's life for the better, and, in the ultimate selfless act, sacrifices his life so that Edmund may live. At the same time, Aslan is saving all of Narnia from destruction in accordance with the Deep Magic, which states that unless life is forfeit in payment for the crime of treachery, Narnia will be destroyed by fire and water. While the witch thinks she has won the final victory and taken control of Narnia forever, Aslan knows that victory will be his because of the Deeper Magic, which states that death will work backward when a willing victim who committed no crime is sacrificed in a traitor's stead. In performing the ultimate service for Edmund and for Narnia, Aslan is able to return to life and complete his purpose. His next two acts of service bring a speedy end to evil's reign: He breathes life back into the stone statues and kills the White Witch in his jaws. The final phase of Aslan's service is to crown the Pevensie children kings and queens of Narnia, after which he leaves to tend to his other countries.

Mr. Beaver

Mr. Beaver is a wise, hardworking, and practical creature dedicated to the cause of good in the battle against evil in Narnia, and due to his unwavering faith in Aslan and belief in the fulfillment of the ancient prophecies, he takes it upon himself to lead the Sons of Adam and Daughters of Eve to Aslan. When he hears they have entered Narnia, he springs into action. At great risk to his life, Mr. Beaver befriends the Pevensie children in the wood, warns them that the witch's spies are everywhere, and invites them into his home. From there, he leads his wife and three of the children on a dangerous journey to meet Aslan, the one who will save Edmund and all of Narnia from the White Witch. At the children's coronation, Mr. Beaver is rewarded and honored for his faith and service.

Mrs. Beaver

Mrs. Beaver, the kind wife of Mr. Beaver, is dedicated to helping, comforting, and providing for others. The fact that her sewing machine is her most valuable possession reveals the extent of her dedication. With the help of her husband, she cooks a sumptuous meal for the Pevensie children, then, with little help from her husband, packs food for their journey to the Stone Table. Mr. Beaver and the children are in a great hurry to leave and feel that Mrs. Beaver is wasting valuable time by packing a dinner. During the arduous journey, however, they are grateful for her foresight. She comforts and nurses the wounded Edmund, and she sweetly takes her husband's hand while awaiting the outcome of the private talk between Aslan and the White Witch. Mrs. Beaver is dearly loved by the children, and they bestow gifts and honors upon her at their coronation.

Emperor-beyond-the-Sea

The Emperor-beyond-the-Sea is Aslan's father and author of Narnia's laws. He is never seen, but his presence is felt in the discussions about the Deep and Deeper Magic. His "hangman," as Mr. Beaver calls her, is the White Witch, who delights in being able to bring about death, but as it was written in the Deeper Magic, death is not final, and the Emperor sends Aslan to Narnia to reveal this truth.

Father Christmas

Unlike the jolly Santa Claus depicted on the other side of the wardrobe, Father Christmas is big, glad, and most significantly, real. (They do, however, have the white beard and bright red robe in common.) To see him makes the children both glad and solemn at the same time. His arrival is a sign that the Witch's spell is weakening and that Aslan has returned. He is Aslan's helper and gives the Pevensie children—as well as all the creatures of the wood—gifts to help them continue in their fight against evil.

The Lion

The lion was turned to stone by White Witch in her courtyard, and his statue terrifies Edmund at first glance. When Edmund realizes that the lion is made of stone, he mocks this king of beasts by drawing a moustache and a pair of glasses on his face. Aslan, however, shows that he holds lions in highest regard among creatures by breathing on the stone lion first. A bit later, Aslan astounds this relatively simple-minded lion when he refers to the two of them together as "*Us Lions*: "Those who are good with their noses must come in the front with us lions to smell out where the battle is." In using this pronoun, Aslan treats the lion as his equal, thereby bestowing dignity and honor upon him and bringing him great joy. The children further honor and reward the lion at their coronation.

Mrs. Macready

Mrs. Macready, the Professor's housekeeper, is not particularly fond of children. It is her job to take visitors on guided tours of the house, and she gives the children strict instructions to stay out of her way when she is bringing visitors through the house. The children's adventure in Narnia begins and ends on a day when Macready is leading a tour; in order to stay out her way, the children hide in the wardrobe and make their way into Narnia. When they return, Mrs. Macready is still with the visitors.

Maugrim

Maugrim, or *Fenris Ulf* as he is known in British editions, is an evil grey wolf and Captain of the White Witch's Secret Police. He is quite crafty, as is evident when he pretends to be one of the Witch's statues in order to take Edmund by surprise, but his inability to manage his anger proves to be his downfall. After Maugrim chases Susan up a tree, Peter lashes out at him with his sword. Peter misses, but the audacity of the action enrages Maugrim so much that he has to howl, giving Peter just enough time to plunge his sword into Maugrim's heart.

Edmund Pevensie

Edmund, the second youngest of the Pevensie children and the bad one of the bunch, despises the high-minded superiority of his older brother, Peter, and the maternal control of his sister Susan. The only sibling he is older than is Lucy, and he takes his discontent out on her with a vengeance. He mocks and teases endlessly after she tells of her experience through the wardrobe and maliciously betrays her by denying her story about Narnia to Peter and Susan even after having been there himself. The moment they all get through to Narnia, Edmund slips up and says something to reveal that he has been there before, which results in Peter calling him a "poisonous little beast." Edmund resolves that he will get revenge on his brother and sisters.

The primary inducement for Edmund's revenge, however, is neither his unfortunate position in the sibling rivalry nor simply an innate badness. Rather, he is driven by his excessive appetite for food and power as brought on by the Witch's evil magic. The enchantment resulting from eating the Witch's Turkish Delight does not suppress Edmund's ability to distinguish right from wrong; it makes right and wrong appear inconsequential in contrast to his craving. As Edmund walks to the Witch's castle, the narrator says that deep down Edmund knew the Witch was evil and Aslan was good, but thoughts of power kept him from turning around and making peace with his brothers and sisters. Not until he makes the journey with the Witch does he realize the extent to which he has misjudged her and begins to have a change of heart. This change is revealed when he begs the Witch not to turn the merry little party of woodland creatures into stone. Edmund's compassion is genuine, and as the narrator states, it was "the first time in this story [Edmund] felt sorry for someone besides himself."

After Edmund is rescued by Aslan's forces and has a private conversation with Aslan, he is a new person. He apologizes to his brother and sisters, then distinguishes himself in battle by destroying the Witch's wand. Aslan knights him for his valor and later crowns him a king of Narnia. The difficult lessons Edmund learns in his early life lead him to become "a graver and quieter man than Peter, and great in council and judgment." He is lauded as "King Edmund the Just."

Lucy Pevensie

Although Lucy is the youngest of the Pevensie children, she is the most observant and perceptive, and it is through her eyes that Lewis tells the story. The moment the children first see the Robin, Lucy senses that the bird wants them to follow it, and on the night Lucy and Susan cannot get to sleep, Lucy tells Susan she feels something is wrong with Aslan and suggests they go looking for him. (In both of these instances, her intuition proves to be correct.) But it is Lucy's smaller observations that give her character depth: When Aslan claps his paws together, Lucy observes, "Terrible paws . . . if he didn't know how to velvet them!"; and in the moment before Aslan's death, Lucy thinks he looks "braver, and more beautiful, and more patient than ever."

Lucy also serves as a foil to Edmund: while Edmund is dishonest and selfish, Lucy is truthful and generous. She wants to help those in need and puts the best interests of others ahead of her own. Her first thought upon discovering Mr. Tumnus has been captured is that she and sister and brothers must try to rescue him, and up to the moment Mr. Beaver says Aslan is the only one who can save him, all Lucy can do is think about his safety. Similarly, the first thing Lucy wants to know from Aslan is if anything can be done to save Edmund. In accordance with her selfless and compassionate nature, Father Christmas gives Lucy a cordial made of healing juice from fire-flowers that grow on the sun, a gift she can use in service to others. Interestingly, Lucy's only mistake comes in using this gift. She administers the juice to a wounded Edmund, then waits for it to have an effect while other wounded are suffering around her. When Aslan lets Lucy know that what she is doing is wrong, she snaps at him, and he responds with a subtle yet stern reminder: "Must *more* people die for Edmund?" Lucy is instantly repentant and immediately goes about the task of healing the others.

Lucy is known as "Queen Lucy the Valiant" after she assumes the throne. She continues to be happy and golden-haired throughout her reign, and many local princes want her to be their queen.

Peter Pevensie

The Lion, the Witch and the Wardrobe traces how Peter Pevensie, the oldest of the children, develops from a thirteen-year-old boy into the High King of Narnia. From early on, Peter seems to have the makings of a king: his choice of animals (eagles, stags, and hawks) he hopes to see on the grounds of the estate reveals a regal temperament; his willingness to suspend judgment on the veracity of Lucy's story until all the evidence is in reveals the kind of wisdom necessary for good leadership; and his decision to make Lucy the leader after they arrive in Narnia shows sound judgment. Peter shows more leadership ability as the story progresses. When the beavers and the children arrive at the Stone Table, Susan and Lucy are too nervous to step forward and meet Aslan, so Peter goes first. He then has the courage and honor to assume part of the responsibility for his brother's actions, telling Aslan that by getting mad at Edmund he "helped him to go wrong."

There is one leadership characteristic, however, that Peter must develop before earning the title of High King: courage in the face of battle. Aslan knows this, so at the sound of Susan's horn, he sends Edmund out to fight Maugrim alone. Peter is terrified, but realizing that both his and his sister's life are in jeopardy if he does not act, he swallows his fear and slays Maugrim. As result of this display of courage, Aslan gives Peter command of his army. Peter is, understandably, uncomfortable at the thought of having to fight a battle without Aslan by his side, but he does not back down. Instead, he rises to the challenge, and the next day he courageously leads the charge against the White Witch's evil forces. The battle itself is Peter's final preparation for high kingship because it is the ultimate test of his leadership, and in the end he prevails. Afterwards, in the ultimate noble gesture, Peter credits Edmund for the victory, and it is then that Lucy comments on Peter's changed appearance: "His face was so pale and stern and he seemed so much older." Lucy's observation reveals just how far Peter has come since the beginning of the story and indicates that he is now ready to be High King.

The courage Peter once lacked is, by the end of the story, his greatest strength. He becomes "a great warrior" with a deep chest and is known as "Peter the Magnificent."

Susan Pevensie

Susan Pevensie, the second oldest of the children and elder sister, exerts a motherly control over her siblings. Unlike Peter and Lucy, she possesses neither leadership qualities nor intuitive ability; rather, she is practical, extremely cautious, and a bit self-centered. Their discovery of Mr. Tumnus's arrest leads Susan to the conclusion that Narnia "doesn't seem particularly safe," and along with concerns over the dropping temperature and not having any food, she recommends they go home. Only after Lucy makes her arguments for rescuing Mr. Tumnus does Susan get the sense that this is the right thing to do, although she does not "want to go a step further" and "wishes [they]'d never come." After the children follow the robin, Susan's first inclination, again, is to do the most cautious and practical thing: go home where it is safe.

Susan's cautious nature stems from her propensity to see the bad in difficult situations and to expect the worst possible outcomes. Her myopia contrasts with Lucy's acuity and results in judgment errors that Lucy is always on hand to counter. For example, on the night she and Lucy discuss Aslan's strange behavior, Susan says she suspects Aslan of "stealing away and leaving" before the battle, but Lucy, who has faith in Aslan and is concerned about him personally, correctly asserts that "some dreadful thing is going to happen to him." Furthermore, when the two of them see the mice crawling over Aslan's body, Susan is instantly repulsed and tries to shoo them away. Lucy, however, notices that the mice are really nibbling at the ropes in order to free Aslan, and she points this out to Susan. Lastly, Susan takes issue with Lucy's suggestion that Edmund be told what Aslan did for him: "It would be much too awful for him." Lucy, on the other hand, thinks "he ought to know."

As Susan watches in horror as Aslan suffers cruel torture and death, she undergoes a transformation: she changes from being self-centered to having compassion for others. She cries all night with Lucy, holding Aslan in her arms, and even suggests trying to untie him. During her reign as Queen she is called "Susan the Gentle," known for her graciousness and long black hair.

The Professor

The wise and generous Professor opens his large country home to the Pevensie children during the London air raids. The children take an instant liking to him, due in part to his funny appearance. Peter and Susan turn to him for advice on what to do about Lucy, and he surprises them by saying that, if they use logic, they will conclude that Lucy's story is true. Of course, Peter and Susan soon discover the Professor is right, and when all the children run to him at the end to tell of their adventures in Narnia, he is not in the least bit surprised. In fact, he believes every word and responds by saying that they will surely return to Narnia someday.

Giant Rumblebuffin

Giant Rumblebuffin is a good giant who was turned to stone by the White Witch and is restored to life by Aslan's breath. Because of Rumblebuffin's great size and strength, Aslan enlists his help in letting everyone out of the Witch's castle. Happy to be able to serve his King and little comrades, he bashes in the gate with his huge club and wrestles down the towers. He works up such a sweat that he asks if either Susan or Lucy has a handkerchief he can use to wipe his brow. When Lucy gladly offers hers up, Rumblebuffin reaches down and mistakenly picks her up instead, thinking she is the handkerchief. This action prompts Mr. Tumnus's comment to Lucy that although the Rumblebuffins are "one of the most respected of all the giant families in Narnia" they are "not very clever." Giant Rumblebuffin receives rewards and honors at the children's coronation.

Mr. Tumnus

Mr. Tumnus is the first creature Lucy meets in Narnia. He invites Lucy to his cave under the pretense of hospitality, while his true intention is to kidnap her and take her to the White Witch. He is, however, a good Faun at heart, and he cannot bring himself to turn her over to the Witch. The Witch arrests him for High Treason and turns him to stone, but he is eventually restored to life by Aslan's breath. At the children's coronation, he is the first friend to receive honors and rewards. Many years later, he informs the Pevensies of the White Stag's return.

The White Stag

The White Stag is an enchanted creature who grants wishes to those who can catch him. Mr. Tumnus tells the four rulers that the White Stag had been seen in the Western Woods, and a royal hunt ensues. The Pevensies chase the animal through the woods and into a thicket, where they decide to dismount their horses and follow it. Their search leads them past the lamppost and back through the wardrobe.

The White Witch

The White Witch is the evil, self-proclaimed Queen of Narnia. The narrator does not say how she assumed power, but the reader knows her claim to the throne is illegitimate by way of Mr. Tumnus through Lucy: "She calls herself the Queen of Narnia though she has no right to be queen at all, and all the Fauns and Dryads and Naiads and Dwarfs and Animals—at least all the good ones—simply hate her." The good creatures hate her because of her ruthlessness and cruelty: she has cast a spell over the land so that it is always winter but never Christmas, and she indiscriminately uses her magic wand to turn her enemies to stone. The White Witch bases her claim to be Queen on the assertion that she is human, but Mr. Beaver says that although she looks human, "there isn't a drop of real human blood in [her]."

The White Witch lives in fear of the prophecy that both her life and her reign will end when two Sons of Adam and two Daughters of Eve sit on the thrones at Cair Paravel, and she does whatever she can to stay in power. When her plans to capture and kill the Pevensie children fail, she confronts Aslan and accuses Edmund of treachery, audaciously invoking the Deep Magic, which gives her the right to kill traitors. Aslan, however, offers his own life as a substitute for Edmund's, and the Witch gladly accepts, thinking that her victory is assured with Aslan out of the way. She tortures, mocks, and kills the rightful King of Narnia. Her immorality and incapacity to love prevent her from knowing the Deeper Magic—which has the power to overcome death—and secure her destruction in the end.

Themes

The Triumph of Good over Evil

Lewis's view of good and evil is predicated on the biblical doctrine of the Fall (the corruption of man's perfect state as a result of Adam and Eve's disobedience to God), to which the only remedy is God's redemption through Jesus Christ. According to Genesis, when Satan entered God's unfallen creation in the form of a serpent, he tempted Adam and Eve by saying that if they were to eat from the forbidden tree, they would become like God and have knowledge of all things. Adam and Eve succumb, or fall, and thereby introduce sin/evil into the world. Lewis shows the nature of sin and evil through the character of the White Witch in *The Lion, the Witch and the Wardrobe*. (In *The Magician's Nephew*, evil is introduced into the delightful and uncorrupted world of Narnia through the actions of characters who, like Adam and Eve, cannot resist temptation.) The nature of goodness is embodied in the character of Aslan, and its characteristics are manifested through the actions of many other characters in *The Lion, the Witch and the Wardrobe* as well.

In the chapter "The Invasion" in *Mere Christianity*, Lewis explains that he does not see good and evil as opposites; rather, he sees evil as a perversion of good. Money, sex, and power, for example, are good things unless they are pursued for the wrong reasons. One good thing that cannot be perverted, however, is love, because as John reveals in his gospel, God is love (and God cannot be perverted). Love, therefore, is the ultimate good. If a man pursues wealth and power for selfish purposes, he is not acting out of love and, therefore, his actions are evil. Such are the actions of the White Witch. She does all she can to ensure her control over Narnia, even to the point of hurting and killing. Aslan, on the other hand, performs selfless acts for the benefit of others, sacrificing his life so that Edmund may live and breathing on the stone statues so that they may return to life. Characters such as the Beavers and the Pevensie children act out of love by showing hospitality: the Beavers serve a good meal to the children, and the children later have a feast served to their coronation guests.

Because evil is a perversion of good, Lewis reasons, it is subordinate to it. In his essay, "Evil and God," published in *God in the Dock: Essays on Theology and Ethics*, Lewis likens evil to a parasite living off a tree, explaining that good "exists[s] on its own while evil requires the good on which it is parasitic in order to continue its parasitic existence." The idea that evil is subordinate to good accords with Christian theology, according to which Christ defeated Satan/death by dying on the cross and rising from the dead, and one day Christ will return and put an end to evil once and for all. Although Christians differ in their eschatology (beliefs about the end times), many agree that the end will be accompanied by the destruction of evil and the triumph of good. This doctrine fuels the climax and resolution of *The Lion, the Witch and the Wardrobe*, as Leland Ryken and Marjorie Lamp Mead point out in *A Reader's Guide through the Wardrobe*: "The turning of the statues back into people, a gigantic and decisive last battle, coronations at a great hall, living 'in great joy' and remembering 'life in this world . . . only as one remembers a dream'—all of these have an eschatological feel to them."

Awakening to New Life

The theme of awakening to new life functions in both physical and spiritual ways. On a physical

Topics For Further Study

- An allegory is a composition, whether pictorial or literary, in which immaterial or spiritual realities are directly represented by material objects. Write a short story that is an allegory. Take an abstract concept or a virtue, such as honesty or patience or courage, and write a story in which the main character in human or animal form conveys the characteristics of your chosen abstract concept.
- Watch the 2005 film adaptation *The Chronicles of Narnia: The Lion, the Witch and the Wardrobe*, noting where the film follows Lewis's book and where it differs. Consider elements such as theme, plot, dialogue, and characterization. Why do you think the filmmakers decided to make these changes? Prepare a class presentation in which you discuss the differences, but be sure to highlight some similarities as well. Use clips (DVD or VHS) from the movie to support your conclusions.
- The morning after Edmund's rescue from the White Witch, Aslan and Edmund have a private conversation apart from everyone else, even the reader. The narrator says, "There is no need to tell you (and no one ever heard) what Aslan was saying, but it was a conversation which Edmund never forgot." Based on your knowledge of the characters, what do you suppose Aslan said to Edmund? How do you think Edmund responded? Imagine the conversation and then write it out as a dialogue between the two characters.
- Music plays an important part in *The Lion, the Witch and the Wardrobe* and occurs at four different times. Mr. Tumnus plays a tune for Lucy on his strange little flute that makes her "want to cry and laugh and dance and go to sleep all at the same time." When Mr. Beaver first mentions Aslan's name, the narrator says, "Susan felt as if some . . . delightful strain of music had just floated by her." Stringed music accompanies Aslan's heraldic entrance at the Stone Table. At the coronation of the four Pevensie children, the music inside the castle Cair Paravel is answered by "the voices of the mermen and mermaids swimming close to castle steps and singing in honor of the new Kings and Queens." The narrator describes these voices as being "stranger, sweeter, and more piercing" than the music inside. Choose two or more of these four occasions and locate pieces of music that you feel fit the respective occasions. Music pieces could be classical (Beethoven, Wagner, etc.), modern (Gershwin, Bernstein, etc.), or otherwise (The Beatles, Led Zeppelin, etc.). Present your findings to the class: play the recordings and explain why you feel they are suitable.

level, the children's entry through the wardrobe into Narnia is an awakening to a new life: a new world is revealed to them that they never knew existed. Their ensuing adventures leading to the overthrow of the White Witch are just the beginning of a new life for them. They become kings and queens in Narnia and reign for many happy years, and the narrator says, "if ever they remembered their life in this world it was only as one remembers a dream." Springtime in Narnia, a result of Aslan's return, is nature's awakening to new life from one hundred years of winter. After the White Witch kills Aslan, he awakens to new life because of the Deeper Magic; he rushes to the witch's castle and awakens the stone statues to new life by breathing on them. The subsequent defeat of the White Witch and the crowning of the Pevensie children as kings and queens awakens Narnia to a new life free from tyranny.

The Giving of Great Gifts

Unlike honors or rewards, gifts are given out of love and not because the recipients have done anything to deserve them. Aslan, the embodiment of love, is the great gift giver in *The Lion, the Witch and the Wardrobe*, and the gifts he bestows all aid in the overthrow of evil in Narnia. Through the character of Father Christmas, Aslan gives tools for battle to Peter, Susan, and Lucy; to the Beavers, he gives gifts to help improve their everyday lives; and to them all, he gives a pot of hot tea along with cups and saucers to drink it with. To Edmund and the stone statues, Aslan gives the gift of life.

All the gifts, beginning with those given through Father Christmas, aid in the overthrow of evil in Narnia. Susan's horn summons help from Aslan's subjects when Maugrim and his pack of wolves first attack. Peter kills Maugrim, a key member of the White Witch's evil forces, with his sword. This sword, along with Susan's bow and arrow, are used in the final battle against the witch's army and figure prominently in their destruction. Susan uses her cordial containing supernatural restorative powers to heal Edmund of a fatal wound, thus allowing for the fulfillment of the prophecy that evil in Narnia will end when four children sit on Cair Paravel's thrones. Susan also uses her vial to restore many other wounded to health, bringing to an end the physical suffering that results from evil. The tea service allows the children and the Beavers needed refreshment and relaxation so they can continue their journey, which ultimately ends with the witch's downfall. Mrs. Beaver's new sewing machine and Mr. Beaver's repaired dam help make their lives easier and serve as encouragements to carry on in a discouraging time. Only by carrying on without being discouraged can they defeat evil.

Next are the gifts of life given by Aslan himself. First, Aslan sacrifices his own life for Edmund's so that Edmund may live. This allows for the fulfillment of the prophecy mentioned in the previous paragraph and also directly results in evil's destruction because it is Edmund who, while fighting on the battlefield, comes up with the brilliant idea of breaking the witch's wand with his sword. The witch is unable to turn her opponents into stone with a broken wand, and Edmund's action buys his army more time before Aslan's reinforcements arrive. Had it not been for Aslan's self-sacrifice, Edmund would not have been alive to stop the witch. Furthermore, Aslan's gift of life to the stone statues enables him to form the reinforcement army that helps destroy the forces of evil in Narnia.

Hospitality

This theme extends the good versus evil and gift giving themes. Hospitality is, in essence, gift giving. When people express hospitality, they give the gifts of their food and the shelter of their home; quite simply, they give their guest the best of all they have to offer. Hospitality makes room for the stranger at one's own hearth, creating relationship by lovingly welcoming the outsider to one's own home. Prime examples of hospitality in *The Lion, the Witch and the Wardrobe* occur when Mr. and Mrs. Beaver welcome the Pevensie children and serve them in a meal; when Aslan has a feast prepared for Peter, Susan, and Lucy upon their arrival at the Stone Table. Finally, the newly crowned kings and queens show hospitality to their guests at Cair Paravel: "And that night there was a great feast in Cair Paravel, and revelry and dancing, and gold flashed and wine flowed."

Yet the story also shows how good things can be perverted for evil purposes. Mr. Tumnus uses hospitality in order to trick Lucy: he pretends to be her friend, lures her back to his cave, serves her tea and tries to lull her to sleep with his flute, so he can kidnap her and take her to the White Witch. But because Mr. Tumnus is really a good Faun, he is unable to commit such an evil deed, so he confesses everything to Lucy and helps her escape. In similar fashion, the White Witch feigns hospitality to Edmund: she invites him into her sledge, wraps her warm mantle around him, and serves him a hot drink and the best Turkish Delight he has ever tasted. She hopes he will one day return to her with his brother and sisters, so she can kill them, thus protecting her reign in Narnia.

Style

Biblical Allusion

Lewis makes many references to the Bible in *The Lion, the Witch and the Wardrobe.* (Allusions are references to other works of literature, ideas, persons, or events, which are designed to lend additional meaning to the work at hand.) Lewis uses biblical references to imbue the story with Christian meaning. (For a comprehensive compilation of allusions in the Chronicles of Narnia, see Paul F. Ford's *Companion to Narnia.*) The way Aslan's death is handled, for example, illustrates how Lewis draws parallels between the children's story and the story of Christ. When Susan and Lucy meet Aslan in the wood before his capture, Aslan says, "I should be glad of company tonight," and "I am sad and lonely." Lewis is probably deliberately echoing here the biblical story of the scene in the Garden of Gethsemane when Christ made similar comments to his disciples not long before his arrest (Matthew 26:38). Furthermore, before killing Aslan, his captors shave him, spit on him, and jeer at him, an allusion probably to the torments Christ endured before being led to the cross (Matthew 27:31). The moment before the White Witch plunges the stone dagger into Aslan, she says, "In that knowledge, despair and die," another Christian reference to Christ's words on the cross about being forsaken and feeling despair before dying (Matthew 27:46).

Aslan's self-sacrifice so that Edmund may live suggests Christ's self-sacrifice so that others may live (John 3:16; Matthew 20:28). By sacrificing himself, Aslan satisfies the Deep Magic, which states that the penalty for the crime of treachery is death, an allusion perhaps to the penalty for sin under the Old Testament covenant (Romans 6:23; Hebrews 9:17–22). But his sacrifice also satisfies the Deeper Magic, an incantation which causes Death to work backward when an innocent victim is sacrificed in a traitor's stead; the reference here seems to be to the remission of sins by Christ Jesus under the New Testament covenant (Romans 6:23; Hebrews 9:12–15). In these and countless other ways, Lewis elevates the children's story to the level of Christian teaching or parable.

Point of View

Lewis weaves first, second, and third person points of view throughout the telling of *The Lion, the Witch and the Wardrobe*. Sometimes he expresses his personal opinions (first person), sometimes he addresses the reader directly (second person), and sometimes he relays the action in the voice of a third-person narrator. When done well, this style can be very effective in children's stories because it emotionally engages readers and makes them feel as if they are part of the action. For example, when the narrator relates how the Pevensie children feel when they hear the name of Aslan for the first time, he conveys their sense of wonderment and excitement directly to the reader by suggesting the reader has perhaps experienced something as mysterious in a dream:

> And now a very curious thing happened. None of the children knew who Aslan was any more than you do; but the moment the Beaver had spoken these words everyone felt quite different. Perhaps it has sometimes happened to you in a dream that someone says something which you don't understand but in the dream it feels as if it had some enormous meaning—either a terrifying one which turns the whole dream into a nightmare or else a lovely meaning too lovely to put into words, which makes the dream so beautiful that you remember it all your life and you are always wishing you could get into that dream again. It was like that now.

Another example occurs when the narrator describes the sadness Susan and Lucy feel after Aslan's death. He comforts the reader, too, as a person who also knows what grief is: "I hope no one who reads this book has been quite as miserable as Susan and Lucy were that night; but if you have been—if you've been up all night and cried till you have no more tears left in you—you will know that there comes in the end a sort of quietness." In this case, Lewis draws in the reader by referring to grief experienced by the reader that may help the reader identify with the children's reaction.

What makes this style even more effective is Lewis's familiar and friendly tone. The narrator does not feign omniscience (to be all-knowing) and is never condescending or patronizing. In fact, using direct address, Lewis puts himself on the same level as his readers, apparently addressing each one of them personally. This intimate tone may contribute to the book's popularity. *The Lion, the Witch and the Wardrobe* lends itself to being read aloud, which is suitable for a children's book.

Historical Context

The Battle of Britain

The backdrop of the novel is Germany's World War II bombing attacks on London, which began in the summer or 1940 and stretched through the winter months into 1941. Britain had recently withdrawn 224,000 of its troops from France and had no remaining allies on the European continent, yet Winston Churchill refused to seek terms with Hitler. Hitler prepared a landing operation against England, called Operation Sea-Lion. German High Command realized, however, that such an operation could not be successfully carried out unless they had gained air superiority over the English Channel, and in August of 1940 German bombers began daily and nightly attacks on British factories, ports, and airfields. Then, Britain launched its own night bombing raids on Berlin. Furious, Hitler ordered his air force to focus less on military targets and more on the city of London itself. In the ensuing months, parents evacuated their children from the city and many London residents spent their nights in underground (subway) stations as Nazi bombers shelled the city. But the Germans were unable to break the spirit of the British people: civilian morale remained high, industrial production continued, and the British air-fighter command put up a heroic and inspired resistance in the night skies over London. These factors, combined with the sinking of numerous German invasion transports docked in their port in France, forced Hitler to continually postpone Operation Sea-Lion. The Battle of Britain may not have defeated Hitler in the short term, but it was a defensive victory that strengthened England's resolve to continue fighting until Hitler's defeat in 1945.

Compare & Contrast

- **1950:** The end of World War II against Germany and Japan results in a worldwide shortage of food and raw materials badly needed in Great Britain. Unable to export at high enough levels to meet the international balance of payments, England becomes a debtor country.

  Today: England is the world's fourth largest creditor country, with the highest percentage of this money being poured into German industry. Japan is the world's largest creditor country, while the United States, by contrast, is the world's largest debtor country.

- **1950:** The cold war is underway, and Great Britain cooperates with the United States in a military campaign in Korea to drive invading North Korean forces out of South Korea. The stated U.S. goal is to stop the spread of communism and make the world safe for democracy.

  Today: The cold war concludes in the early 1990s, but the U.S. war on terror is ongoing. Great Britain cooperates with the U.S.-led invasion of Iraq, which ousts dictator Saddam Hussein.

- **1950:** A golden age in children's literature begins in Great Britain, a period of intense creative outpouring on the part of children's authors. Unlike pre-war children's literature, which according to Peter Hollindale and Zen Sutherland in *Children's Literature: An Illustrated History* expressed British imperialism and "domestic norms of social class and sexual roles," the post-war literature is "singularly free of prescriptive ideologies."

  Today: Children's literature, while still imaginative, is restricted by fashionable ideologies of political correctness. As Hollindale and Sutherland state in *Children's Literature: An Illustrated History*, "From the 1970s onwards another rulebook gain[s] authority, prescribing a new agenda of political correctness in matters of sex and gender, class and race, faithfully reflecting tensions and divisions in the adult political world."

The post-war years in which Lewis wrote *The Lion, the Witch and the Wardrobe* witnessed great economic instability in Great Britain. The newly elected Labor government of 1945 implemented an austerity program due to worldwide shortages of food and raw materials that Britain needed to import. Food, clothing, and sources of energy were severely rationed; in 1947, food rations were cut to well below wartime levels, and the use of gasoline by civilians was prohibited. Only when financial aid started funneling in from the Marshall Plan (the U.S. assistance program to help rebuild European economies), to the tune of $2.7 billion between 1948 and 1951, did Britain's economic situation begin to improve.

But beyond the economic and political forces at work in post-war Britain, a more sinister spiritual force was starting to take hold: moral uncertainty. Belief in a moral universe of absolutes and faith in a benevolent God were shaken by awareness of war atrocities led many to the conclusion that theirs was not a culture of moral progress and development but a culture of death. Moreover, the future prospect of living under the cold war's dark cloud of nuclear threat did nothing to strengthen a belief in mankind's capacity for goodness. As a result, church attendance in Great Britain steadily declined, and faith in a deity was replaced by faith in one's own ability to succeed in a world devoid of God. In response to this climate of skepticism and cynicism, Lewis wrote *The Lion, the Witch and the Wardrobe*, a story which asserts that even in a universe corrupted by evil, there still exist beauty, truth (standards of right and wrong), joy, and the presence of a benevolent creator who will eventually make all things right.

Critical Overview

Surprisingly, *The Lion, the Witch and the Wardrobe* received very little critical attention when first published in 1950 considering the renown Lewis had

Tilda Swinton as the White Witch in the 2005 film version of The Chronicles of Narnia: The Lion, the Witch, and the Wardrobe © Walt Disney Pictures/Walden Media/The Kobal Collection

achieved from his previous writings. Perhaps the fact that it was a children's book, and a fairy tale at that, caused it to be overlooked by many critics and not taken seriously by others. *Prince Caspian* (1951), the second book to be published in the Chronicles of Narnia, was more widely reviewed, probably due to the sales success of *The Lion, the Witch and the Wardrobe* and the fact that Lewis was beginning to stake his claim as a legitimate children's writer. Lack of critical attention aside, the reviews received by *The Lion, the Witch and the Wardrobe* were generally favorable, albeit not particularly analytical.

One reviewer who had mixed opinions about the book was Chad Walsh, whose review of *The Lion, the Witch and the Wardrobe* appeared in the November 12, 1950, edition of the *New York Times*. He says he thought the book "well-written," adding that "one would expect that of the author of *The Screwtape Letters*," but found it lacked the "sense of the uncanny and magical that one finds in *The Wind in the Willows* and the writings of George MacDonald." Nonetheless, Walsh's children would not let him stop as he read it to them, leading Walsh to make a rather hasty generalization about children enjoying the story more than adults: "I made the mistake of reading them the first chapter, and since then it has been two chapters a night, sometimes followed by tears when a third chapter is not forthcoming. I see that children like their fairy land folk matter of fact, whereas adults prefer them whimsical or numinous."

Mary Gould Davis, in her December 9, 1950, *Saturday Review of Literature* review, also refers to a George MacDonald story, but not in order to show how Lewis's book is lacking; rather, she simply says *The Lion, the Witch and the Wardrobe* compares to *The Princess and the Goblin* in that "[it] has an underlying meaning in its theme." As regards the book's visual effectiveness, Davis compliments Lewis on his "beautifully drawn" word pictures and credits Pauline Baynes's drawings for "effectively bring[ing] out the children, Aslan, and the wood creatures of Narnia." She concludes with the praise, "It is an exceptionally good new 'fairy tale.'"

The 2000 unabridged audio release of *The Lion, the Witch and the Wardrobe*, celebrating the book's fiftieth anniversary, was reviewed in *Publishers Weekly* on November 20, 2000. With the reputation of *The Lion, the Witch and the Wardrobe* as a children's classic already well established, this review's focus is on the reading of British actor Michael York, calling it "a nimble, enchanting performance." The reviewer also says York "conveys an unflagging sense of wonder and excitement, certain to captivate a broad range of listeners."

> **"Only by applying logic, carefully analyzing the text, and looking to scripture can Father Christmas's place in *The Lion, the Witch and the Wardrobe* be properly understood."**

Criticism

Timothy Dunham

Dunham has a master's degree in communication and a bachelor's degree in English literature. In the following essay, he analyzes common critical misconceptions of Father Christmas's place in The Lion, the Witch and the Wardrobe *and offers an alternative perspective.*

The presence of Father Christmas in the land of Narnia has long been a source of puzzlement and consternation for critics and admirers of *The Lion, the Witch and the Wardrobe* and has resulted in a variety of conjectures as to his appropriateness and significance in the story. Unlike the character of Aslan, whose role is generally interpreted one way, Father Christmas remains an enigma. Some insist that Father Christmas is a jarring incongruity in this fairy tale world of nymphs, fauns, and talking animals. Others, who are made uncomfortable by his presence yet hesitate to dismiss him entirely, try to explain him away as a literary device. Still others, in an attempt to defend his presence, imbue him with meaning by reducing him and his gifts to biblical allusions. Sifting through these discordant views reveals nuggets of truth, but on the whole, most of this scholarship seems to lack careful thoughtful analysis.

J. R. R. Tolkien registered the first negative reaction to Father Christmas as a Narnian character in 1948, two years before *The Lion, the Witch and the Wardrobe* was published. Tolkien disapproved of Lewis's mixing of creatures with distinct mythological origins in a single setting; he thought it was artistically inappropriate and especially disliked Father Christmas's attendance among the creatures. On this point of contention (not taking into account the animosity he harbored toward Lewis), Tolkien dismissed the story entirely and pronounced it so bad that it was it beyond saving. Such scathing criticism from his longtime friend and colleague hurt Lewis deeply and further weakened his confidence in a story he already feared had little merit. Lewis might not have finished the book had it not been for the encouragement of Roger Green, a former pupil and friend who shared Lewis's love of fairy tales. Green greeted *The Lion, the Witch and the Wardrobe* with great enthusiasm and, unlike Tolkien, offered praise as well as helpful criticism. But he too reacted against the appearance of Father Christmas, seeing it as an artistic liability that worked to the story's detriment. Although not unlike Tolkien's opinion, Green's reason was more objective and less based on personal taste. He viewed Father Christmas as a kind of earthly intruder whose appearance in Narnia breaks the spell of this magical world, and Green urged Lewis to take out the character. But Lewis refused both Green's suggestion and Tolkien's opinion that mythologies should not be mixed. Narnia was his own imaginary world, and he was determined to fashion it according to his own imagination. He made it his artistic prerogative to borrow from many myths and to populate Narnia with any creature he deemed necessary to fulfill his creative vision. Father Christmas fit in perfectly. The purpose of this essay is to argue how Father Christmas, given the nature of his seemingly incongruous role in *The Lion, the Witch and the Wardrobe*, is a completely logical choice which provides an added spiritual dimension Lewis could not have achieved with any other character.

The assertions by Tolkien and Green regarding Father Christmas's being out of place in Narnia are peculiar given the fact that Father Christmas is as much a mythical character as others in the book. Then, too, he is the figure most frequently associated with gift giving in Western culture. It makes perfect sense to some readers that Lewis should chose Father Christmas for the role of gift giver in *The Lion, the Witch and the Wardrobe*. If Father Christmas fits in for Narnia, why is his

What Do I Read Next?

- Readers who enjoy *The Lion, the Witch and the Wardrobe* may want to read the rest of the books in the Chronicles of Narnia: *Prince Caspian* (1951), *The Voyage of the "Dawn Treader"* (1952), *The Silver Chair* (1953), *The Horse and His Boy* (1954), *The Magician's Nephew* (1955), and *The Last Battle* (1956). If the reader is eager to discover how Narnia began and how the lamppost and the White Witch first got into Narnia, then *The Magician's Nephew* (1955) is the book to read.
- *Beowulf*, one of Lewis's favorite epic poems, was instrumental—along with J. R. R. Tolkien—in shaping Lewis's ideas about faith and mythmaking. This Anglo-Saxon poem narrates the adventures of the Scandinavian hero-warrior. *Tales of Beowulf: Champion of Middle Earth* (2006), edited by Brian M. Thomson, is available from Avalon Publishing Group.
- Published by Ballantine Books in 1970, *Phantastes*, by George MacDonald, is a must-read for anyone who wants to experience the book that made a significant impact on Lewis's creative and spiritual life. It is the story of a young man's journey through Fairy Land in search of life's meaning. *Phantastes* is an enchanting work from the author considered to be the innovator of the modern fantasy.
- Alan Jacobs's 2005 book *The Narnian: The Life and Imagination of C. S. Lewis* is an eminently readable biography that examines how the people and events in Lewis's life helped to shape his imagination. Unlike other, more conventional Lewis biographies, this one focuses on the reasons behind Lewis's decision to start writing for children.

---

appearance so jarring to certain readers, namely adults? The reason, Lewis may have believed, lies in his being so familiar. Father Christmas is a prominent, indeed ubiquitous, cultural figure; like an icon, he assumes less of a mythical and more of a religious status, and for him to take on a role in a fairy tale somehow comes across to some as scandalous. In removing Father Christmas from his iconic position in Western culture and locating him in a fantasy world, Lewis makes an important point about how far Christian societies have come in supplanting the meaning of Christmas with a myth: the real incongruity is not that Father Christmas is out of place in Narnia but that he is not more out of place in Christian societies. Consequently, to view Father Christmas's incongruous presence in Narnia as some kind of error in Lewis's artistic judgment is to miss the point entirely. Arguably, Lewis knew what he was doing when he selected Father Christmas to be the Narnian bearer of gifts. Father Christmas is incongruity with intent: By drawing attention to Father Christmas as a mythical figure, Lewis points to the spiritual reality Father Christmas has replaced. Apart from acting as a kind of spiritual indicator through his incongruity, Father Christmas serves another spiritual function through his role as a gift giver.

Taking a different position, Leland Ryken and Marjorie Lamp Mead, in their book *A Reader's Guide through the Wardrobe*, see Father Christmas as a device to foreshadow future events. At first, it appears, they do not know quite know what to do with him and would like to dismiss him entirely, but without going so far as Tolkien or Green in deeming him inappropriate and out of place, Ryken and Mead make the following criticism:

> Surely on a first reading his appearance is totally unexpected. He seems stuck into the action. He makes an appearance and then disappears from the story, as though he were some sort of phantom figure. The whole episode is interpolated into the main story, and nothing would be missing from the main action if this episode were omitted.

Ryken and Mead see the character's purpose as both symbolic and prophetic. They explain that his appearance and "distributing of gifts are the first proof that a great reversal is just around the corner" and that "the particular gifts Father Christmas gives, along with the specific person whom he designates as the recipient of each present, foreshadow future action." This is all well and good, but nonetheless a misunderstanding of Father Christmas's role. The real significance of Father Christmas is as a helper who performs a similar function in Narnia as Christians believe the Holy Spirit performs in their world.

It is important to keep in mind, however, that Father Christmas is not an allegory for the Holy Spirit, but rather what Lewis thought of as a supposition. The difference between the two may be described as follows: an allegory shares a direct one-to-one relationship with the thing signified, whereas a supposed figure shares only certain characteristics with the thing signified. Lewis used the latter concept for describing the relationship between Aslan and Christ. In *C. S. Lewis: Letters to Children*, Lewis says his intent was not to recreate the scriptural Jesus in the form of a lion in Narnia, but something quite different: "I said 'Let us *suppose* that there were a land like Narnia and that the Son of God, as He became a Man in our world, became a Lion there, and then imagine what would have happened.'" If Aslan were an allegory, he would possess all the divine attributes of Christ, which he does not, and his life would parallel that of Christ's in every detail, which it does not. Because Aslan is what Lewis called a supposal (a supposed or imagined figure), he possesses only some attributed to Christ; for example, he is good, just, compassionate, self-sacrificing; he is treated as a deity, the King of creation and conqueror of death. Father Christmas is a supposal in a similar way. Unlike the Holy Spirit, Father Christmas is not a deity, nor is he a spirit who dwells within the King's followers; but like the Holy Spirit. Father Christmas bestows gifts on the faithful to help them fight the good fight while awaiting the King's triumphal return.

While some critics recognize the correlation between Father Christmas and the Holy Spirit, they tend to gloss over shared character attributes and focus on the individual gifts. In so doing, they end up over-spiritualizing the gifts and forcing parallels where they may not exist. Both Paul F. Ford, in *Companion to Narnia*, and Marvin D. Hinten, in his essay "'Deeper Magic': Allusions in *The Lion, the Witch and the Wardrobe*," consider Father Christmas's combat gifts to be an allusion to the "whole armor of God" found in Ephesians 6:11–17, in which the shield represents faith, and the sword stands for the Word of God. But there are too many discrepancies between the armor given by Father Christmas and that found in the Bible for this theory to be convincing. There are, for example, no armor of God equivalencies for Susan's horn and bow and arrow or for Lucy's cordial and dagger. Similarly, none of the children is given a belt, breastplate, shoes, or helmet, all of which are part of the spiritual armor in Ephesians 6. Another problem with this view is that spiritual armor is not, biblically speaking, a gift, nor is the outfitting of believers with spiritual armor an activity of the Holy Spirit. Quite simply, Ford and Hinten do not provide enough evidence in order to draw a convincing parallel between the combat gifts and scriptural idea of the armor of God.

With regard to Susan's horn and Lucy's cordial, Hinten suggests these gifts have other spiritual overtones: the horn is "analogous to prayer" while the cordial represents the gift of healing. Such a reading may be valid, but because Hinton does not or cannot point out individual analogical functions for all of the gifts, it is difficult to accept. Critics such as Hinton who analyze Father Christmas's gifts in an attempt to discover Christian meanings may be missing the bigger picture. The significance of the gifts may be better understood if Father Christmas is seen to function as a supposal or supposed figure representing the Holy Spirit.

As mentioned earlier, Father Christmas is a helper who performs a function in Narnia that is similar to the scriptural description of the Holy Spirit's function. In John 14:16, Jesus tells his disciples that after He departs, the Heavenly Father will send "another Helper," namely, the Holy Spirit. The New Testament Greek word for "Helper" is "Parakletos," a word associated also with the idea of "encouragement." According to Lewis's religious beliefs, the Holy Spirit's primary activity, then, is to encourage Christ's followers, and one of ways the Spirit accomplishes this is by giving "perfect" gifts (James 1:17) to meet their needs (Philippians 4:19) and the needs of the body of believers (I Corinthians 12:7). Father Christmas's primary activity is exactly the same and so is the means by which he accomplishes it. The gifts he gives, however, have no correlation to gifts given by the Holy Spirit; they are not supposed to. Each gift is uniquely tailored to meet the needs of the individual receiving it for the collective good of Narnia. With this reading in mind, one may see Peter's sword and shield are perfect gifts for him because, at the time he receives them, he lacks the necessary courage to fight in the upcoming battles. The gifts encourage Peter to step forward in battle, become the great leader he is meant to be, and help overthrow the forces of evil in Narnia.

Land of Narnia by Brian Sibley includes a photograph of Lewis at three years of age, holding a favorite toy—Father Christmas riding a donkey. The image is striking because of the way it conjoins the myth of Father Christmas with imagery associated with Jesus. The toy evokes Jesus's entry into Jerusalem on a donkey, and it most certainly brings to mind Father Christmas's role as Helper in *The Lion, the Witch and the Wardrobe.* Years before the book's publication, Father Christmas's function in Narnia was misunderstood and misinterpreted by critics and scholars who, for whatever reason, failed to grasp the supposal. Only by applying logic, carefully analyzing the text, and looking to scripture can Father Christmas's place in *The Lion, the Witch and the Wardrobe* be properly understood.

Source: Timothy Dunham, Critical Essay on *The Lion, the Witch and the Wardrobe*, in *Novels for Students*, Thomson Gale, 2007.

Wayne Martindale with Kathryn Welch

In the following essay, the authors explore the permeating theme of eating in the Narnia books and the use of hunger as a metaphor, indicating self-centeredness or theocentric devotion.

Generations of readers hungry for the truth have found food for their souls in Lewis's Chronicles of Narnia. Fittingly, of all the image patterns weaving in and out of the Narnia books, eating ranks among the most striking. From the first book to the last, as well as in many of Lewis's other works, we are never long without food. Lewis invites us to partake of not only the domestic meal but also the kingly feast. He tantalizes our taste buds with vividly described spreads of food but also gives us many symbolic scenes ranging from devouring demons to sacramental moments echoing the Lord's Supper, addressing the gamut of spiritual significance. Spiritually, imaginatively, and intellectually, all are invited to the high table: Narnia is food for the soul.

To dwell on the metaphor for a moment, Lewis's first gift is often to whet our appetites for spiritual nourishment. David Fagerberg ponders, "Why are we not naturally conformed to God's love? Our appetites have been misdirected, leading us to believe that there is a contradiction between God's glory and our own happiness, that we cannot submit our lives to God and still have what we really want. The 'original' sin is not primarily that man has 'disobeyed' God; the sin is that he ceased to be hungry for God and God alone." Here at once we have the root of human sin, its consequence in our dysfunctional relation to God, and, serendipitously, in the word "hungry" an entrée into one of Lewis's major metaphors for the spiritual life.

As humans, we need food—and the right food; we can't eat just anything. Only certain plants and animals constitute what we know to be "people food." In *The Magician's Nephew,* Digory and Polly look at each other in dismay when their horse, Fledge, enthusiastically suggests that they satiate their hunger with mouthfuls of grass. "But we can't eat grass," Digory insists. It's a simple but crucial point. Our bodies require specific nutrients, as is often reflected by our cravings. Likewise, we were created to be sustained by only certain spiritual food. But occasionally we need to be reminded, "No, that's not for eating." Good food is available, but not all food is good. What we eat can spell the difference between growth and stagnation or even life and death. One of the most moving uses of food as a metaphor for spiritual nourishment comes in *The Problem of Pain.* "God is the only good of all creatures; . . . that there ever could be any other good, is an atheistic dream. . . . God gives us what He has, not what He has not: He gives the happiness that there is, not the happiness that is not. To be God—to be like God and to share His goodness in creaturely response—to be miserable—these are the only three alternatives. If we will not learn to eat the only food that the universe grows—the only food that any possible universe ever can grow—then we must starve eternally." Our souls must be nourished by the bread of heaven.

The fact of human hunger is inescapable and is often the occasion of God's miraculous provision. When the Pevensie children are again whisked unsuspectingly off to Narnia in *Prince Caspian,* the first order of business is to provide for their basic needs of food and water. Susan insightfully observes, "I suppose we'll have to make some plans. We shall want something to eat before long." In his divine goodness God provides for their hunger. The children find a freshwater pool and apple trees—apple trees amidst the now ancient ruins of Cair Paravel where they had once feasted as royalty. Aslan, while providing for their needs, was intentionally leading them to a place prophetic of Narnia's return to right rule. Returning to the plight of Digory and

Polly, we find the youngsters resting in the assurance that Aslan will supply them with food. Polly does indeed find some toffee in her pocket, but it's hardly enough to sustain them through their journey. They plant a piece, in faith, hoping to repeat the miracle of the lamppost grown from an iron bar. Sure enough, they awake the following morning to the sight of a toffee tree. The supply of "daily bread" is occasion enough for the miraculous as God supplies the needs he created us with, needs which demonstrate our dependence on him.

Lewis's application of eating imagery ranges from the ordinary and natural to the extraordinary and supernatural. As we have seen in these first examples, he deals extensively with food and drink realistically as an important part of everyday life. It is crucial not to overlook the realm of the ordinary, where we should not be surprised to find deep significance from a man who cherished routine and championed domesticity. What to most would be ordinary is to Lewis extraordinary: "There are no ordinary people," he says so memorably in "The Weight of Glory," "you have never talked to a mere mortal." His sense of God's immanence extends to all creation and all human acts, asserting that "there is no neutral ground in the universe: every square inch, every split second, is claimed by God and counterclaimed by Satan." The same is true of such mundane human activity as making and eating meals and entertaining guests.

In fact, such domestic activities are, in Lewis's view, the very thing governments exist to protect, as he maintains in *Mere Christianity*: "The State exists simply to promote and to protect the ordinary happiness of human beings in this life. A husband and wife chatting over a fire, a couple of friends having a game of darts in a pub, a man reading a book in his own room or digging in his own garden—that is what the State is there for." If they are not aspiring to this end, Lewis continues, all of the laws and institutions of the State are "a waste of time." Lewis held quiet domesticity in such high esteem that it effectively legitimizes the state as its protector. One such encounter with the domestic comes early on in *The Lion, the Witch and the Wardrobe*. Mr. and Mrs. Beaver host the Pevensie children in their home and generously spread before them a home-cooked meal.

The meal is not simply filler. Not only does it provide a touch of realism; it espouses the value of hospitality. Each aspect of the scene, including Mr. Beaver's fetching of the fresh fish, the generous supply of butter, Mrs. Beaver's preparing of the sticky marmalade roll, the special allotment of milk for the children, and the intimate nature of the group sitting on wooden stools around a common table demonstrates the warmth and welcome inherent in hospitality. Clearly it is a grace. Hospitality certainly wasn't a foreign concept to Lewis, who treasured the ancient epics, reading them in the original languages. Homer's writings, for example, are saturated with the practice of hospitality. Upon the appearance of a stranger, the host must meet the guest's need for food, a bath, oil for the body, and rest before inquiring about the visitor's business. Such caretaking was necessary for survival in ancient travels. The prospect of a stranger being in actuality a god or goddess in disguise added extra incentive.

"As in the book of Revelation, Aslan brings joy and feasting, a common motif in Narnia, when he finishes some great work. It draws on the chivalric elements that thread through the stories and parallel Jesus' ministry."

Biblical injunctions to hospitality provide a parallel in the caution that we may be entertaining angels unaware (Heb. 13:2). The apostle Peter gives an even more stunning context, instructing followers of Christ on how to live, knowing that "the heavens will pass away with a roar, and the heavenly bodies will be burned up and dissolved" (2 Pet. 3:10 ESV): "The end of all things is near; therefore . . . be hospitable." (1 Pet. 4:7, 9). Since hospitality to friends and strangers ranks as a high virtue in both the biblical and classical sources Lewis esteemed, it does not surprise us to find Lewis emphasizing them in The Chronicles of Narnia. The domestic scene at Mr. and Mrs. Beaver's, which must soon be lost in the battle with usurping evil, is among the very things to be recovered by the victory—both in Narnia and on earth. The peace and intimacy of the shared meal has been threatened by forces of evil and must therefore be reclaimed in the name of the king.

Eating in Narnia often assumes a deeper theological significance, as illustrated in the plight of young Edmund in *The Lion, the Witch and the Wardrobe.* Edmund, as yet the very type of the spiteful and emotionally bullying older brother, has come into Narnia with egg on his face. Lucy is right; he is wrong. Enter Jadis, the white witch, with an offer he can't refuse. First, here's a chance to lord it over the others by becoming king of Narnia, knowing a secret they don't know, and tapping a power source unavailable to them. The apparent earnest on this promise is the magical appearance of his first wish, which is for the candy called Turkish delight—not for nourishment but for pleasure. Edmund assumes, since the witch came through on the Turkish delight, that she will come through on her promise to make him king. This is a case of wishful thinking, the sort that we all engage in when rationalizing some attractive indulgence we know deep down is sin.

It is no mere coincidence that, as with Adam and Eve, sin often takes the form of eating in The Chronicles. Here, abandoned to the dictates of his stomach, Edmund falls prey to the sin of gluttony. Gerard Reed remarks that "gluttony is a deadly sin because it so easily leads us to exchange essentially good things for things that superficially taste good." Edmund is later unable to appreciate the simple fare provided by the Beavers; rather, he fantasizes about Turkish delight. Gluttony necessarily excludes gratitude—the former wholly concerned with the filling of self; the latter centered on the subordination of self. Consequently gluttony focuses on the gift rather than the giver. Edmund's gorging on sweets contrasts starkly with the selfless hospitality of the Beavers and the other Pevensie children's enjoyment of their food and company. Edmund never gets enough, which is always the way with sin—it never satisfies—and, on top of that, it ruins his appetite for healthy food. So obsessed does Edmund become with the memory of Turkish delight that he is impelled to slip away from the small band at supper and seek out the white witch. Jadis recognizes the children as a threat to her claim on Narnia, so she entices this "son of Adam" by appealing to his baser nature. Like his original, Edmund is not long in Narnia before he succumbs to the tempter. Lulled into a fantasy world of endless Turkish delight and kingly command, Edmund unwittingly conspires to bring about even his own ruin. Edmund's indulgence of his appetite to a sinful degree leads him to betray his friends and family.

That gluttony is a serious sin with serious consequences we need not doubt, and Edmund is not the only one to learn this lesson. The demon Screwtape, who knows it from the other side, berates his nephew Wormwood in *The Screwtape Letters* upon the latter's dismissal of gluttony as inconsequential. Screwtape explains that desensitizing humans to gluttony's damning potential is one of Satan's greatest advances. In Screwtape's hands the temptation is far more subtle, and we learn that it is possible not only to partake of the wrong foods but to partake of food wrongly. Reed explains, "Too often limited to discussions of specific acts—overeating or drunkenness—gluttony actually refers to the abuse of good things. It's more an attitude than an act, more evident in the priorities by which we live than the portions of meat and potatoes we place on our plates." Gluttony is a deeply rooted sin that, while exercised on the physical level, ultimately involves the heart.

The church has traditionally understood the "vice of gluttony" as the act of eating "hastily, sumptuously, too much, greedily, daintily." Traditionally, gluttony doesn't necessarily presuppose the consumption of large portions of food. *The Screwtape Letters* offers a poignant example of what Lewis termed "gluttony of Delicacy, not gluttony of Excess." We make the acquaintance of a woman gluttonous in her demands on people, always wanting something other than what is offered, just a little, of course, if it is not too much trouble—but it always is. She loudly insists that her food be prepared in just such a manner as she indicates. Lewis observes that, as is true of all gluttons, this woman's "belly now dominates her whole life." Accordingly, gluttony is a sin that dictates lifestyle and mind-set alike. The main focus is self and fulfilling of selfish desires.

Eustace Scrubb, in *The Voyage of the Dawn Treader* and in one of the most dramatic episodes of The Chronicles, awakes to find himself in the form of a dragon. The sin of greed is at the root of his metamorphosis; and greed, of course, is rooted in self. He emerges from the dragon cave in search of food and, finding a dragon carcass nearby, devours it. He is, in fact, eating a fellow dragon in the same way that the demons (followers of "that old serpent, the Devil") see even one another as food. There is, then, some truth to the saying that "you are what you eat." Reed aptly observes that "whatever we ingest—physically, intellectually, or spiritually—we digest." In the most literal sense possible, Eustace becomes the sin that he indulges. Eustace has a dragonish greed that lures him to desert his tried shipmates and then enter a dragon's cave where he finds and dons a gold bracelet, then becomes a dragon. His greedy, dragonish thoughts precipitate his transformation into a dragon, even to the point of eating dragon's food—other dragons.

The Silver Chair, which recounts the travels of Eustace Scrubb, Jill Pole, and Puddleglum the Marshwiggle, explores the danger of selfishly focusing on personal comfort, feasting when they should be fasting. Having sought shelter at the castle of Harfang, home to a family of giants, the trio of Narnians is hosted generously. What would be a virtue in a different setting with different motives is here a treacherous trap. The queen orders comforts to be supplied to her guests, including a lavish meal and toys. One giant whispers to the weepy Jill, "Don't cry, little girl, or you won't be good for anything when the feast comes." Lulled in the lap of luxury, Jill readily yields to sleep in her soft bed. She forgets Aslan's directive to daily repeat the "signs." The danger of gluttony in this case is much more subtle and ironic: the Narnians are intended to *be* the feast! Only Aslan's dramatic appearance to Jill enables the Narnians to escape with their lives. As the episode of Harfang illustrates, we must take not only the right food but at the right time and in the right circumstances.

As in the book of Revelation, Aslan brings joy and feasting, a common motif in Narnia, when he finishes some great work. It draws on the chivalric elements that thread through the stories and parallel Jesus' ministry. On more than one occasion, Jesus fed multitudes miraculously, and he promises the grandest feast of all when he gathers us in heaven for the wedding feast of the Lamb. Feasting is associated both with life, as a necessity, and with joyful celebration in peace and plenty. Still there is a degree of trust involved in feasting: you must trust the host. We read that Ramandu's feast in *The Voyage of the Dawn Treader* is "such a banquet as had never been seen." However, the comrades are reluctant to taste the spread because it seems that magic is afoot. Edmund inquires of the young woman who invites them to eat how they can know it's safe. Her reply is simply, "You can't know.... You can only believe—or not." The party is aware that the table is set and sustained by Aslan's decree, but they are faced with risk regardless. Implicit here is the truth that eating at God's table requires an element of trust.

This feast is appropriately situated in the chapter entitled. "The Beginning of the End of the World." This reminds us that the destination of the *Dawn Treader* is Aslan's country. Couched in sacramental imagery and classical elements of hospitality, Ramandu's table serves a dual purpose. First, it refreshes the weary travelers on the way to their true destination. Food is provided to give strength and allow the journey to continue. Second, it prepares the travelers for what is to come. This daily-renewed feast gives a foretaste of what lies at the end of the world for those who are seeking it.

As they sail nearer to Aslan's country, references to Christ and our heavenly home accumulate quickly. Reepicheep discovers that the water is sweet! Caspian describes the phenomenon with synesthesia, using the terms of one sense experience to describe another: "It—it's like light more than anything else." The water is also filling, such that the Narnians no longer have to eat. This echoes Jesus' words to the woman at the well that one drinking of the water he gives never will thirst again. Then at the world's end the children see a lamb cooking fish on the shore, a lamb that turns into Aslan the lion. This episode is meant to recall Jesus' cooking fish for his disciples, which he eats to prove that he has risen from the dead. His appearance as lamb reminds that he is the Lamb of God, the perfect sacrifice for our sins.

Like the Narnians at Ramandu's table, Jill Pole struggles with trust as a necessity for obtaining living water in *The Silver Chair.* She is intensely thirsty, but the lion Aslan is between her and the stream. When Jill prevails upon him to "go away" so she can drink without perceived threat, Aslan responds with a low growl of disapproval. Since he won't move, Jill tries to exact assurances from him:

> *"Will you promise not to—do anything to me, if I do come?" said Jill.*
>
> *"I make no promise," said the Lion. Jill was so thirsty now that, without noticing it, she had come a step nearer.*
>
> *"Do you eat girls?" she said.*
>
> *"I have swallowed up girls and boys, women and men, kings and emperors, cities and realms," said the Lion. It didn't say this as if it were boasting, nor as if it were sorry, nor as if it were angry. It just said it.*
>
> *"I daren't come and drink," said Jill.*
>
> *"Then you will die of thirst," said the Lion.*
>
> *"Oh dear!" said Jill, coming another step nearer. "I suppose I must go and look for another stream then."*
>
> *"There is no other stream," said the Lion.*

This passage is loaded with theological significance and biblical echoes. Most immediately it evokes the account in John 4 of Jesus with a Samaritan woman at a well. Jesus implies, as he straightforwardly claims elsewhere, that he is the living water and anyone who drinks this water "will never be thirsty forever" (John 4:14 ESV). When Jill Pole decides she must risk all and drink from the stream, she finds it "the most refreshing water she had ever

Skandar Keynes as Edmund Pevensie in the 2005 film version of The Chronicles of Narnia: The Lion, the Witch, and the Wardrobe © Walt Disney Pictures/Walden Media/The Kobal Collection

tasted" and that "you didn't need to drink much of it, for it quenched your thirst at once." The drinking in both events also suggests Holy Communion, in which we drink of Jesus. And Lewis often uses the metaphors of eating and drinking to suggest total commitment and hence total blessing. First the total necessity: "He claims all because He is love and must bless. He cannot bless us unless He has us. . . . Therefore, in love He claims all. There is no bargaining with Him."

In *The Horse and His Boy,* Bree the Narnian-talking war horse, like most of us, likes to be in charge and has his full quotient of pride and must, predictably, be humbled. Like Jill he wants to command his own destiny and is fearful of Aslan. Unlike either of these two, Hwin, a Narnian mare, is so trusting, so simply in love with Aslan, that she wholly submits in this poignantly metaphorical language (we read it as metaphor, but she really means it): "Please, you're so beautiful. You may eat me if you like. I'd sooner be eaten by you than fed by anyone else." This contrasts with Jill's fear of being eaten by Aslan and with eating as a selfish act of dominance, as in *The Screwtape Letters* with Screwtape threatening to consume Wormwood, the demons threatening to dine on every human they can dupe, and Tash gobbling up Shift in *The Last Battle.* Hwin's submission to be eaten by Aslan is a desire to be consumed by him, a metaphor for complete union, which is our heart's deepest desire, the consummation of all desires. It contrasts directly with hell's aim, which is to consume and enlarge the self at others' expense. Screwtape, in his "Toast," views all humans won to hell as food. Hwin's submission to be eaten by Aslan overflows with love and trust; Screwtape's with hatred, double cross, and the gluttony of the persistently asserted self.

It is evident by this point that we have transitioned from the ordinary to the extraordinary: from the Beavers' mealtime hospitality to miraculous provisions at Ramandu's table; from raw dragon, as Eustace feeds upon his scaly counterpart, to devouring demons contrasted by the total submission of Hwin, as she literally offers herself to be eaten by Aslan. Finally we have seen episodes of eating rich with biblical allusion to Christ, from his earthly use of food to teach about himself and his kingdom to the communion meal, all with overtones of the supernatural. We have seen that every example of eating in The Chronicles, including the most ordinary, is imbued with spiritual significance of the highest degree.

We feed on the spoiled fruits of sin when we are self-centered, but our palates are ultimately satisfied by the bread of heaven and water of life when we yield ourselves to God to taste of him and see that he is good (Ps. 34:8). Thus, a dichotomy is established: the unrighteous live to eat, while the righteous eat to live. The biblical model of eating, as embodied perfectly in the person of Jesus Christ, engenders an entirely self-sacrificial devotion to God. Shortly after his conversation with the woman at the well, Jesus' disciples join him, urging him to eat something. "But he said to them, 'I have food to eat that you do not know about'" Bewildered, the disciples wonder if someone could have brought him food. "Jesus said to them, 'My food is to do the will of him who sent me and to accomplish his work.'" (John 4:32, 34 ESV). This is a picture of ultimate communion, where life is totally Christ centered and therefore food in and of itself. The feasting is continuous as long as we are hungry for God.

Lewis says the "joys of Heaven are, for most of us in our present condition, 'an acquired taste'—and certain ways of life may render the taste impossible of acquisition." This truth is all too apparent in *The Last Battle.* The dwarfs are utterly incapable of appreciating the feast spread before them by Aslan. They mistake the pies and meats for hay and turnips, and each one suspecting that his neighbor has received a better dish than he, they begin to brawl. Their prideful proclamation. "The dwarfs are for the dwarfs," amply summarizes their constriction into the self. The bread of heaven is an acquired taste. We don't have all the time in the world to acquire that taste. We have only our time in the world. In Jesus, the feast is before us, and all are invited. Let us heed Aslan's warning, for "there is no other."

Source: Wayne Martindale with Kathryn Welch, "Food for the Soul: Eating in Narnia," in *Narnia Beckons*, edited by Ted Baehr and James Baehr, Broadman & Holman Publishers, 2005, pp. 103–111.

Colin Manlove

In the following essay, Manlove describes The Lion, the Witch and the Wardrobe *as the most complete volume in the Narnia series and states that it comes closest to the innocence of a fantastic world. He also explores the themes of "good" and "evil" and growth and expansion pervasive in all the Narnia books.*

The Lion, the Witch and the Wardrobe, probably the best known of the Narnia books, stands alone perhaps more than any other book of the *Chronicles*. It is true that several of the other stories are "finished" in the sense of being self-contained: a rightful king or prince is restored in *Prince Caspian*, *The Silver Chair*, and *The Horse and His Boy*; a voyage to the end of the world is completed in *The Voyage of the "Dawn Treader."* Yet we know that these narratives are excerpts from the history of Narnia, with a before and after, where the first book is our first account of the country. (We know too that Lewis originally wrote it with no thought to a sequel.) Lewis struck in *The Lion, the Witch and the Wardrobe* a blend of fantasy and the everyday that he was not again to match. The book is an extraordinary mixture of diverse things, from a lion who is a Narnian Christ to a witch out of fairy tale, from a Father Christmas out of myth to a female beaver with a sewing machine drawn from Beatrix Potter, from a society of articulate beasts and animate trees to a group of strongly characterized children partly derived from Edith Nesbit. This is the only book in which the children themselves become kings and queens of Narnia. In all the others they are relative outsiders, and in all but *The Magician's Nephew* the rulers of Narnia come from within the fantastic realm. This separation adds to the sense of a Narnia that goes on without them. The "proximity" of the children to Narnia in *The Lion*, their close involvement in its transformation from deathly winter to the spring of new life, gives that book a special poignancy: the children do not come so close to the innocence of a fantastic world again, not even in *The Magician's Nephew*, where the Narnia is created by Aslan. In *The Voyage of the "Dawn Treader,"* the image of spiritual longing realized in the risen life of Aslan, and the victory and enthronement of the children as Sons of Adam and Daughters of Eve, is found only by going out of the world, by journeying across the seas to its end and beyond: what was "immanent" in *The Lion* is there found only by a process of transcendence. Narnia in *The Lion* is increasingly and uniquely shot through with holiness, embodied in the coming and eventual victory of Aslan. In the later books it is a much more secular world, with Aslan's presence more limited. *The Lion* seems to contain a pattern of spiritual renewal sufficient to itself: the winter of the White Witch is turned to spring, the cold laws of the Stone Table are transcended by the grace of Aslan's sacrifice, the sin of man is washed away in the restoration of Adam and Eve's lineage to their rightful thrones, the devil in the shape of the White Witch is finally slain, the paradise that was lost is regained. The whole seems to encapsulate something of the primal rhythm of Christian history, within the idiom of another world.

> **But the story as a whole can be seen as a spiritual journey through a landscape of the soul, from the frost of original sin to the flowers of the redeemed spirit. . . .”**

Lewis's method of introducing us to the realm of Narnia is, perhaps naturally, much more gradual in *The Lion* than in the later books, where the children are suddenly whisked away from a railway station where they are waiting to go their several ways to boarding school (*Prince Caspian*), or fall into a picture of an ancient sailing ship (*The Voyage of the "Dawn Treader"*), or are transported to Narnia via their deaths in a railway crash (*The Last Battle*). *The Lion, the Witch and the Wardrobe* portrays the gradual joining of two worlds. The emphasis in this novel, as in *The Magician's Nephew* and *The Last Battle*, which respectively describe the creation and eventual "uncreation" of Narnia, is on the permeability of Narnia (there through its fragility of being, here as part of a divine plan): it is entered, variously, by the children (on three different occasions), by Father Christmas, and by Aslan himself. It is of course a place that needs stimulus from the outside if it is to regain life at all, for it is a world frozen to perpetual winter by an evil witch, and nothing will change so long as she and her ice have power over it. But more than this, the book describes a gradual *incarnating:* not only Aslan's actions but the children's presence, long prophesied, in making themselves part of this world, will overthrow the witch and restore Narnia to its true nature.

For the moment let us deal with the first point, the gradualness of the approach. First the children are withdrawn from society by being sent away from the London air raids in wartime to their uncle's house in the remote country, "ten miles from the nearest railway station and two miles from the nearest post office." This uncle is odd-looking; he has so much white hair that it "grew over most of his face as well as on his head." The servants of the house are mentioned only to be dismissed as of no consequence to the story. The children are left free to do as they wish. All the time, identity and boundaries are melting away. The house is vast and uncharted. The world outside it seems a wilderness of mountains and woods, with the possibility of eagles, stags, and hawks among them, as well as the more domestic badgers, foxes, and rabbits. There is a hint here of likeness to the landscape of the world the children are to enter.

The discovery of Narnia, too, is gradual. One rainy day the children set out to explore the house, and one of them, Lucy (from *lux* meaning "light" or "perception"), investigates the inside of an old wardrobe in an otherwise empty room. It is a casual-seeming occurrence that turns to something quite other. Beyond one line of fur coats in the wardrobe Lucy finds another, and then as she pushes through that and feels the ground begin to crunch under her feet, fur turns to fir and she finds herself in a pine forest with the snow falling. The gradualism here is a marvelous tapering of everyday world into fantastic realm.

Once in this strange new world, Lucy meets a faun, Mr. Tumnus, in the forest, and it emerges, as she takes tea with him in his home, that he is a spy for the wicked White Witch. Having remorsefully confessed this, he ushers Lucy back through the wardrobe into her own world. Lucy is amazed to find that no time has passed in her absence—which could make her experience seem a dream. She tells the others of her adventure but they do not believe her, least of all the scoffing Edmund; and the wardrobe when examined by the children is now obstinately nothing but a wardrobe. Aslan's purposes transcend human wish and will. After some days, during a game of hide-and-seek on another wet day, Lucy has hidden in the wardrobe and Edmund pursues her there, only to find himself in Narnia. He then meets the White Witch herself, and she, mindful of the menace to her if the prophecy should come true and four humans become rightful kings and queens of Narnia, bribes Edmund to bring his brother and sisters to her castle. Edmund find Lucy on his way back to the wardrobe in the Narnian woods (she has been with Mr. Tumnus again), but when they return to their uncle's house and Lucy looks to Edmund for support, he tells the others that he has only been humoring Lucy's delusion. The next move occurs one day when all four children are trying to escape a group of visitors who are being given a tour through the house. They are eventually driven to the room with the wardrobe and through the wardrobe itself into Narnia. Now *all* believe, and what is believed *in* has shifted from an indefinite place to another world in which they are set. First one, then two, then four children have entered Narnia.

Once there, there are further gradations. At first visitors, the children are brought to realize that they are in part the focus of the hopes of the Narnian creatures. What seemed accident is part of a larger pattern, if they will play their part, and if Aslan comes to help. Initially guests of the Beavers, the three children (Edmund having sneaked away to the witch) are soon active agents in the cause of Narnia. And what Narnia is and means continually deepens. At first perhaps a fairy-tale world, it does not stop being that while also being a landscape of the spirit frozen in primal sin; and the witch, who seems something straight out of Hans Christian Andersen, retains something of this fairy-tale "lightness" while at the same time becoming an agent of ultimate evil, daughter of Lilith and the giants, and ancient enemy of Aslan. Then, too, we have what seem to be layers of magic, with the witch's evil wand that turns creatures to stone at one level, and the "Deep Magic" by which Aslan may through sacrificial death rise again, at quite another. Aslan himself is lion and much more than lion. As for the children, they do not till the end stop being themselves even when accomplishing heroic deeds. The Peter who slays Maugrim, the witch's great wolf, is still a frightened but resolute boy, and the Edmund who, reformed, hinders the witch from final victory in the battle by breaking her wand, is awarded plaudits which make him at once heroic and the brightest boy in the class.

But by this point the children are very "far in" (to use one of Lewis's favorite phrases). Just as the story has taken them to a world inside a wardrobe inside a room in a house within the heart of beleaguered England, so they have penetrated to the center of Narnia and in the end become its cynosures, as they sit dispensing justice and largess on the four thrones at the castle of Cair Paravel. They are the sovereign human element long missing from the hierarchy of rational or "Talking Beasts" of Narnia, and in that sense they belong most fully to that world. At that point things have changed: they are no longer children but young adults, they have forgotten their own world, and they speak the elevated language of medieval romance. That loss of former self, and the length of sojourn in Narnia, is found with no other of the children of the *Chronicles*: Lewis has steadily moved the children away from their old selves and understandings until they become wholly part of another world. Even the style that describes them has changed: "And they entered into friendship and alliance with countries beyond the sea and paid them visits of state and received visits of state from them. And they themselves grew and changed as the years passed over them"; "So they lived in great joy and if ever they remembered their life in this world it was only as one remembers a dream." And then having accomplished this, Lewis briskly returns the children to their own world through their pursuit of a white stag that leads them to a thicket wherein is the wardrobe; through which they return to England, abruptly restored to child form and their present-day clothes, having been absent, by the time of this world, for not one moment. This perhaps serves as an exercise in humility and a reminder that nothing that is mortal is permanent (a point to be made much more openly concerning Narnia itself in *The Last Battle*).

To some extent what is portrayed in this process is a form of spiritual development on the part of the children. They are asked to develop out of an old awareness into a new. They must show faith, trust, compassion, perception, and courage in transforming Narnia. It may be mistaken to see what happens too much from Narnia's point of view, with the children its promised saviors. It might be better to recall also that Lewis was steeped in allegory, and particularly in Spenser's *The Faerie Queene*, in which the landscape of Fairy Land is that of the soul. Narnia is, in one sense at least, a country within a wardrobe; a wardrobe seems an appropriate conveyance to Narnia, as it is a place for different clothes. If, too, we were to think of the children not just as four individuals, but also potentially as four parts of the one spirit, we might not always be wide of the mark. When the children first see Mr. Beaver surreptitiously beckoning to them from among the Narnian trees, the following exchange ensues:

> "It wants us to go to it," said Susan, "and it is warning us not to make a noise."
>
> "I know," said Peter. "The question is, are we to go to it or not? What do you think, Lu?"
>
> "I think it's a nice beaver," said Lucy.
>
> "Yes, but how do we *know*?" said Edmund.
>
> "Shan't we have to risk it?" said Susan. "I mean, it's no good just standing here and I feel I want some dinner."

It is possible to see Susan as "the body" here, simply observing and registering physical needs, with Peter as "reason," Lucy as the enlightened soul, and Edmund as the evil side of the self. Such a reading is certainly too stark, and the characters do play other roles elsewhere in the narrative. But the story as a whole can be seen as a spiritual journey through a landscape of the soul, from the frost of original sin to the flowers of the redeemed spirit; one in which the kingship and queenship reached at the end, and the completion of the hierarchy of creation in Narnia by the humans, suggest the integration and potential perfection of the soul in Christ. Such a reading might explain why in this book, the children are frequently isolated from one another (just as, say, Una and Redcrosse are divided in the first book of *The Faerie Queene*): Lucy alone, then Edmund alone, then Edmund away from the other three, then the girls absent from their brothers, and finally all four united. It is as though the spirit is broken up to be reconstituted. This reading at the very least shows how no single understanding of Narnia or the characters in it is adequate—there are multiple possibilities.

Either way, literally or allegorically, what is portrayed in *The Lion, the Witch and the Wardrobe* is growth away from the old self. Growth out of death is a theme central to the book, as Aslan dies to bring new life and winter turns to spring: that is the allegorical and anagogical level of the book (to use Dante's terms), where with the children the development is at the moral or tropological level. The antitype here is of course the witch. She is concerned only with maintaining her power over Narnia. She does nothing with it, exists for no other reason than to keep it (in contrast to the multiple activities of the children when they are kings and queens of Narnia). And Narnia expresses the nature of her spirit: frozen, uniform, static. For all life that thinks to exist independently of her will she has one answer: turn it to stone. Her castle seems to have nothing in it, and she herself in the end *is* nothing. That was the course Edmund would have gone. Drawn to her by his own self-conceit (where Lucy meets Mr. Tumnus, he "happens" upon the witch), he is tempted to bring his brother and sisters into her power to satisfy his appetites in the form of the Turkish Delight she offers him.

Where those whose allegiance is to the witch take, those whose allegiance is to Aslan give. The children are the long-awaited gift to Narnia. Aslan is a gift beyond telling, his coming turning winter to spring. He gives his life for Edmund's. Even Narnia itself, as a place of recovered innocence, is a gift of high adventure to the children. Right at the center of the narrative, not the anomaly he has sometimes been seen, is the arrival of Father Christmas, with a sackful of gifts for everyone. And *The Lion, the Witch and the Wardrobe* as a whole is a "box of delights" full for the reader of the most wonderful creatures and events, which become still richer as one "opens" them. The book, as a progressive revelation of Aslan's nature and of the deepest potential of the children, is like a gift gradually arrived at.

The narrowness of the self is "answered" in the character of the narrative of the book. Its title, *The Lion, the Witch and the Wardrobe*, suggests its creation out of at least three separate acts of the imagination. But all come together to make a pattern long foreseen: each "separate" item is part of a larger unity. So it is with the plot itself, which is really a series of "microplots." At first there is the issue of whether or not Narnia is real. Then there is the plan of the witch to seize the children and their escape from her. With Aslan's arrival, and spring's, the witch seems defeated, especially when Edmund is rescued from death at her hands. But then there is a new plot begun by her claim to Edmund's life through an old law that makes traitors forfeit to her. The later stages of conflict with the witch involve two plots: in one Peter, Edmund, and the Narnians fight her and her forces, while in the other Aslan breathes new life into the Narnians who were made statues at the witch's castle so that they may come to the aid of the others. All these little plots amalgamate to bring about the realization of the grand design, like little selves cooperating with others. And this idea of cooperation, of society, is central. The children themselves are constituents of Narnian society, to which we are progressively introduced throughout. This particular use of microplots is unique to *The Lion, the Witch and the Wardrobe.* Other books (apart from *The Magician's Nephew*) have a much more clear-cut quest or objective from the outset, but here a series of apparently local and unconnected doings together provide the key to unlock Narnia. In a sense, too, these isolated doings might in some cases suggest the benightedness of the soul amid evil: conditions under the witch in Narnia are such that incoherence is inevitable. Then the nighttime setting of many of the scenes in Narnia is also significant; and that Father Christmas arrives, Aslan rises again, and final victory over the witch is won in the morning.

Other features of the book seem to belong to this rejection of narrowness. For one thing, there is, as already partly seen, the theme of growing and of expansion. Growth is inherent in the story itself, which from apparently small beginnings involving a girl and a faun becomes an epic on which the fate of an entire world depends. Narnia is wakened from its sleep, the talking animals from their hiding-places, the spellbound creatures from stone, Aslan from death itself. The adventure begins through a "narrow" wardrobe that turns out to open onto a whole world. Inside Narnia the perspective gradually expands.

At first the omnipresence of the snow makes the adventures relatively local: Mr. Tumnus here, the Beavers there, the White Witch beyond. Gradually creatures congregate, and we begin to get a sense of Narnia as a whole and of the issues at stake. The Stone Table commands a view of all Narnia. Cair Paravel, the ultimate destination of the children, is in an open place by the shore of a sea that stretches to the world's end. The witch's castle however, is set in a hollow among hills, shut in on itself. She lives alone, but for the children the whole story involves an increase of friends: they themselves become the centers of a whole society.

We might extrapolate from the way that the White Witch has converted Narnia to a mirror image of herself in the form of one monotonous dead white, the mode by which Lewis refuses to let us settle to one view of a thing. Throughout, the children continually have their assumptions displaced. Mr. Tumnus is not just the jolly domestic host he appears to be; the wardrobe is more than a wardrobe; Narnia is not an illusion; Edmund is not rewarded by the witch; Edmund's rescue from the witch is not final; Aslan is not dead, but even more alive than before; they who were kings and queens of Narnia are in an instant returned to being modern children. Reality is not to be appropriated; its richness and depth elude ready absorption by mind. Our idea of Narnia is continually altered: at first apparently a little "play" world, it becomes more threatening with the witch, more metaphysical with Aslan, more holy in its ultimate foundation through Aslan's journey. Even then we are not to know the true and further realities until the afterworlds of *The Last Battle* are revealed, and Narnia upon Narnia lead us "farther up and farther in." Nothing is "mere": Lewis chose children as heroic protagonists to demonstrate that fact.

The object of the witch is to reduce all things to one dead level, to draw them back into herself. But the object of the story is in part to show how different, how "other" from one another things can be. To our minds Narnia may suggest the world of Andersen's "Snow Queen," of Kenneth Grahame or of traditional Christmas, but such a stereotype is swiftly dispelled as we find that this is a world in which the struggle between good and evil is between God and the devil. And if we then proceed to see similarities between Aslan's sacrifice and that of Christ in our world, we at once see that they are also quite different. Aslan is a lion in another world called Narnia. His voluntary death as a substitute for Edmund is not the same as Christ's less-chosen Crucifixion, nor His effective death on behalf of all men. Even the special sordid intimacy of Aslan's stabbing by the witch is quite different from Christ's more solitary and drawn-out bodily pain on the cross. Nor is it Aslan alone who saves Narnia: he does that through the mortal agency of the children and the Narnians themselves. The Deep Magic ordained by the "Emperor," whereby all traitors are forfeit to the witch or else all Narnia will be destroyed, is quite different in form from the "magic" that binds our world. Of course there are similarities. The process whereby Aslan dies only to rise again transfigured, is like Christ's death and resurrection. The breaking of the great Stone Table on which he is sacrificed is perhaps like the breaking of the power of the grave: as he tells the children, the witch did not know the "Deeper Magic" that "when a willing victim who had committed no treachery was killed in a traitor's stead, the Table would crack and Death itself would start working backwards." In terms of ultimate metaphysics, this is what Christ's death brought about in our world: though in Narnia the idea of death working backward has much more immediate and absolute import, in the sense that the deathlike winter of the witch's power over Narnia is now destroyed, and with the children enthroned Narnia will for the time become a recovered paradise. The basic pattern of the magic that Aslan enacts, because it is a spiritual rhythm based on divine reality, will be the same in all worlds; but in all worlds it will also be uniquely manifested.

The Lion, the Witch and the Wardrobe, then, dramatizes the difference between good and evil. There is more attention to the good, because it is more real. The witch as yet has no name, nor has her dwarf; she and her agents are present much less than the Narnians, Aslan, and the children. Where she is separate from Narnia, the children become progressively more involved, "farther in." She can only reduce things—Narnia to stasis, the rational creatures of Narnia to stone, Aslan to a shorn cat—even herself, at Edmund's rescue, to a mere formless boulder. In opposition to her the book is full of selves and "things." In no other of the Narnia books are the children so distinguished from one another: the impetuous, loving and perceptive Lucy, the rather more stolid and self-regarding Susan, the cynical and jealous Edmund, the rational and brave Peter. In themselves they are complex, a varying compound of good and evil that the witch can never be; and as a group they form a multiple nature. Further, they all change and develop through the narrative. Then there is the variety of creatures in Narnia, and of the objects that surround them.

There are a faun, a pair of beavers, Father Christmas, a great lion who is more than lion, and a group of modern children. The variety is heightened by juxtapositions—fur coats and fir trees, a lamppost in a wood, a faun with an umbrella, a female beaver with a sewing machine. The book conveys a gradual increase of population—first one faun, then two beavers, then a party of Narnians at a table; by the time the children and the beavers reach the hill of the Stone table where a pavilion is pitched, the pace of creation seems suddenly to leap, as they find Aslan surrounded by a whole group of Narnians as though they had been begotten by him—which, since he has released them from the Narnian winter, is in part true. Still more it is true later when he recreates more of the Narnians out of the stone to which the witch has turned them by the even more deadly winter of her wand. For Aslan death "is only more life." Everything that is good grows, and grows still more like its true nature.

At the center is Aslan. We see the witch early, but he is long heralded before his appearance. When first we see him the first words are, "Aslan stood." He is the creator, not the created; he is supreme being, *Yahweh,* "I am" (Exodus 3:14), to the witch's negativity. He radiates being to all about him. In him oppositions are not at war, as in most mortals, but are brought into energetic unity: he is both god and lion, both lovable and fearful. "People who have not been in Narnia sometimes think that a thing cannot be good and terrible at the same time. If the children had ever thought so, they were cured of it now. For when they tried to look at Aslan's face they just caught a glimpse of the golden mane and the great, royal, solemn, overwhelming eyes; and then they found they couldn't look at him and went all trembly." In the wake of the shame and humiliation of his death he can still play with the children in a romp at which "whether it was more like playing with a thunderstorm or playing with a kitten Lucy could never make up her mind."

. . .

The theme of growth and expansion that we have seen in this story is one that will be found throughout the *Chronicles of Narnia*; the enemy will always be that which shuts in, isolates or immobilizes. Every story will have a variation on the idea of no time at all passing in our world while the children have their adventures in Narnia, so that they return to waiting at a railway station, looking at a picture in a bedroom, or to a school where they are being pursued by bullies, at exactly the moment they left. Every book will show a gradual increase in society, from more or less isolated figures at the start, to gathering groups and then often meetings with whole peoples. Space, too, will grow, just as in *The Lion* a wardrobe opened into a forest, and that forest was found to be part of a whole country, and that country of a world. . . . There will be a similar process in *Prince Caspian.* In *The Voyage of the "Dawn Treader"* a picture of a ship will turn into an actual ship on a wide ocean, and a voyage to the east will extend through realm after realm until it reaches the truest realm of all. In *The Silver Chair* we will begin to explore the lands to the west of Narnia. In *The Horse and His Boy* we will be outside Narnia, in the land of Calormen, travelling back. In *The Magician's Nephew* we will enter three different worlds by magic. And in *The Last Battle* the Narnia we know will give way to larger and ever more real Narnias beyond it. And all this enlargement will be preparing us for the final journey to Aslan's country at the end of *The Last Battle,* a place of living paradox where the smaller contains the greater, where true progression is found where there is no time, where to go "farther up and farther in" is to go farther out, and where one's true identity exists beyond the loss of self in death. Meanwhile, throughout, the *Chronicles of Narnia* will be telling a story, a chronicle, of the birth, life, and death of Narnia: but they will also passingly embody, through paradox, reversals of narrative and often-felt Divine Providence behind the action, a sense within each "net of successive moments" of "something that is not successive," the eternity that is Aslan ablaze about the coiled filament of Narnian time.

Source: Colin Manlove, *"The Lion, The Witch and the Wardrobe,"* in *"The Chronicles of Narnia": The Patterning of a Fantastic World,* Twayne Publishers, 1993, pp. 30–42.

Sources

Davis, Mary Gould, Review of *The Lion, the Witch and the Wardrobe,* in *Saturday Review of Literature,* Vol. 33, No. 49, December 9, 1950, p. 42.

Ford, Paul F., *Companion to Narnia,* Collier Books, 1986, p. 230.

Hinten, Marvin D., "'Deeper Magic': Allusions in *The Lion, the Witch and the Wardrobe,*" in *Narnia Beckons: C. S. Lewis's The Lion, the Witch and the Wardrobe and Beyond,* edited by Ted Baehr and James Baehr, Broadman and Holman Publishers, 2005, p. 133.

Hollindale, Peter, and Zena Sutherland, "Internationalism, Fantasy, and Realism 1945–1970," in *Children's Literature: An Illustrated History,* edited by Peter Hunt, Oxford University Press, 1995, p. 259.

Lewis, C. S., *C. S. Lewis: Letters to Children*, edited by Lyle W. Dorsett and Marjorie Lamp Mead, Macmillan, 1985, pp. 44–45.

———, *God in the Dock: Essays on Theology and Ethics*, edited by Walter Hooper, William B. Eerdmans Publishing, 1970, p. 23.

———, *The Lion, the Witch and the Wardrobe*, HarperCollins, 1978.

———, *Mere Christianity*, Macmillan Publishing, 1978, pp. 32–36.

Review of *The Lion, the Witch and the Wardrobe*, in *Publishers Weekly*, Vol. 247, No. 47, November 20, 2000, p. 32.

Ryken, Leland, and Marjorie Lamp Mead, *A Reader's Guide through the Wardrobe: Exploring C. S. Lewis's Classic Story*, InterVarsity Press, 2005, pp. 74–75, 166.

Walsh, Chad, "Earthbound Fairyland," in *New York Times*, November 12, 1950, p. 222.

Further Reading

Caughey, Shanna, ed., *Revisiting Narnia: Fantasy, Myth and Religion in C. S. Lewis's Chronicles*, BenBella Books, 2005.
This book is a collection of twenty-five essays by writers of various disciplines and faiths, revealing a refreshingly diverse assortment of insights and interpretations on the mythological and theological nature of Lewis's Narnia stories.

Deighton, Len, *Fighter: The True Story of the Battle of Britain*, Castle Books, 2000.
This book gives a detailed account of the conflict, analyzing the strategies, weapons, and tactics employed by both the Germans and the British.

Hooper, Walter, *C. S. Lewis: A Companion and Guide*, HarperSanFrancisco, 1996.
This book, written by a well-known Lewis scholar, is an invaluable resource for those who wish to have an exhaustive biographical, textual, and historical study of Lewis's legacy at their fingertips.

Ryken, Leland, and Marjorie Lamp Mead, *A Reader's Guide through the Wardrobe: Exploring C. S. Lewis's Classic Story*, InterVarsity Press, 2005.
This book is a comprehensive literary and historical overview of *The Lion, the Witch and the Wardrobe*, which helps readers better understand both the story and its author.

Schakel, Peter J., *Imagination and the Arts in C. S. Lewis: Journeying to Narnia and Other Worlds*, University of Missouri Press, 2002.
This book provides in-depth analysis of Lewis's theory of imagination and demonstrates how Lewis teaches his readers, through the Chronicles and other works, the value of imagination as demonstrated in the various arts.

Middlesex

Jeffrey Eugenides

2002

Jeffrey Eugenides's novel *Middlesex* (2002) focuses on the chronicle of forty-one-year-old, hermaphroditic Calliope Stephanides, which presents her multigenerational Greek-American family and her struggle to establish a clear sense of self. After opening with the story of her grandparents, Desdemona and Lefty, and their subsequent union, Cal traces the damaged gene that this brother and sister passed down through the generations to Cal, which causes her gender irregularity.

Cal weaves together the story of her grandparents and their descendents with her own, comparing the problems they faced in their efforts to reconcile their Greek heritage with their adopted U.S. culture to Cal's attempts to find balance between her female and male halves. She sets her epic story, which moves from 1922 to 2001, against a historical backdrop of change, from the Turkish invasion of Greece, through Prohibition, the Depression, World War II, the civil rights movement, and the Vietnam War. As her family gradually adapts to their new world, Cal is also able to find a way to accept the duality of her own experience. Eugenides's ability to find the humor as well as the tragedy in their stories creates a compelling work that celebrates difference as well as community.

To avoid confusion, the narrator and main character in *Middlesex* is referred to here as "Cal" and the pronoun "she."

Author Biography

Jeffrey Eugenides was born in the affluent Detroit suburb, Grosse Pointe, Michigan, to Constantine and Wanda Eugenides on March 8, 1960. Despite the family's Greek heritage, his parents wanted to assimilate mainstream American society. He was so influenced by the world of his childhood that his first two novels are set there. His Greek parents' assimilation serves as part of the backdrop for *Middlesex* (2002).

Eugenides attended and graduated from the prestigious University Liggett School, in Grosse Pointe. After high school, he attended Brown University, from which he graduated magna cum laude in 1983. He continued his education at Stanford University where he received his master's degree in creative writing in 1986.

Until his first novel, *The Virgin Suicides*, was published in 1993, Eugenides worked at various jobs such as taking photos and writing for *Yachtsman* magazine, bussing tables in restaurants, and working as a newsletter editor at the American Academy of Poets in New York City. Eugenides also had some rather unusual jobs such as driving a cab in downtown Detroit and serving as a volunteer with Mother Teresa in Calcutta, India.

Eugenides won the Aga Khan Prize for fiction when he submitted an excerpt of *The Virgin Suicides* to the *Paris Review* in 1991. He completed the novel in 1993, and after its publication, it gained great critical acclaim and commercial success. In 2000, Sophia Coppola wrote the screenplay and directed the film version, which was also well received. Eugenides did not publish another novel for nine years. His second novel, *Middlesex*, won him the 2003 Pulitzer Prize for Fiction and a nomination for the National Book Critics Circle Award.

Besides his two novels, Eugenides has also written for such publications as the *New Yorker*, *Yale Review* and *Gettysburg Review*. He has received the Writers' Award, Whiting Foundation; Henry D. Vursell Memorial Award, American Academy of Arts and Letters; fellowships from the Guggenheim Foundation, National Endowment for the Arts, and Academy of Motion Picture Arts and Sciences; a Berlin Prize fellowship, American Academy in Berlin (2000–2001), and been made a fellow of the Berliner Kuenstlerprogramm of the DAAD. As of 2006, Eugenides lived in Berlin, Germany, with his wife, Karen, and their daughter.

Jeffrey Eugenides © Jerry Bauer. Reproduced by permission

Plot Summary

Book One

To avoid confusion, the narrator and main character in *Middlesex* is referred to here as "Cal" and by the pronoun "she." The novel opens noting two birthdates, the first when Cal was born as a baby girl in Detroit in 1960 and the second when she was born again as a teenage boy in a hospital in Michigan in 1974. She notes that she was written up in a gender study in 1975 and discussed in a medical journal, and she gives a brief history of her life, listing her various jobs and experiences. The novel's title refers to the name of the street where she lives in Grosse Point, a suburb of Detroit, and it is also an allusion to her sexual location between the polarities of male and female and incorporating some traits of each.

Cal, who is now forty-one, says that she feels "another birth coming on." As a result, she has determined to write down the history of "the recessive mutation on [her] fifth chromosome" that "polluted" her family's genetic pool and eventually caused her to be born a hermaphrodite.

Cal notes that three months before she was born, her grandmother, Desdemona, tried to divine her gender by dangling a spoon over her mother's

Media Adaptations

- In 2002, Audio Renaissance produced an audio version of the novel, read by Kristoffer Tabori. As of 2006, no film version had been made.

pregnant belly. She predicted a boy, which turns out was only half right. On the night Cal was born, her grandfather, Lefty, had the first of his thirteen strokes and lost the ability to speak.

Cal's narrative turns to the story of her grandparents' union, which begins in 1922 in Bithynios, a village on Mount Olympus in Asia Minor, later part of Greece. Twenty-one-year-old Desdemona lived there with her brother, Lefty. The two had always been close, but lately, he had been going into town looking for women. Desdemona tries to find a mate for him, but Lefty rejects them all. One night, in their village where "everyone was somehow related," the siblings admit and consummate their love for each other.

Cal shifts the narrative to the present when she lives in Berlin, working for the Foreign Service. She notes that she has "all the secondary sex characteristics of a normal man" except for her immunity to baldness. While she has lived as a man for half of her life, at times her feminine side emerges. She explains that she needs to go back to her grandparents' story to explain her own.

As the Turkish army advances, Lefty and Desdemona decide to immigrate to the United States, where their cousin Sourmelina lives. They set off for Smyrna where they hope to find a ship to carry them across the Atlantic. Desperate to get out before the Turkish troops arrive, they wait one week amid the chaos of the city's evacuation. A physician, Dr. Nishan Philobosian, treats a wound on Lefty's hand and gives him bread. As the Turks advance, they set fire to the city, forcing all of the residents to the wharf where Lefty convinces Desdemona to marry him. Posing as French citizens, they eventually gain entry on a ship bound for the United States. After Dr. Philobosian's family is brutally murdered by Turkish soldiers, Lefty claims he is his cousin and gains him passage as well.

Desdemona and Lefty pretend to meet and fall in love on the ship where they are soon married. Cal claims that they both carried a single mutated gene that they subsequently passed on to her. Lefty assures Desdemona that Sourmelina, called Lina, will keep quiet about their true identities because she has a secret as well: her lesbianism.

Book Two

Desdemona and Lefty move in with Lina and her husband, Jimmy Zizmo, in Detroit, and Lefty takes a job with the Ford Motor Company. When the management discovers Jimmy's criminal record, Lefty is fired.

Desdemona and Lina become pregnant with Cal's parents, and Lefty starts to work with Jimmy smuggling alcohol from Canada. Desdemona is convinced that the intermarriage will cause their child to be deformed. One night as they cross the lake into Canada, Jimmy accuses Lefty of having an affair with Lina. In a jealous rage, Jimmy races the car across the lake and cracks through the ice just after Lefty jumps clear. Desdemona gives birth to Milton, Cal's father, soon after Tessie, Cal's mother, is born to Lina. Everyone assumes that Jimmy has drowned in the river.

After Milton's baptism, Desdemona determines never to have any more children so her "sin" will not be passed on. Lefty opens an illegal bar, the Zebra Room, where he spends most of his time. A few years later, Desdemona gives birth to Zoë, Cal's Aunt Zo, and Lina and Tessie move out.

Desdemona gets a job during the Depression making silk clothing for the Nation of Islam in Detroit's Black Bottom ghetto. She discovers that Prophet Fard, who is credited with forming the Nation, is really Jimmy Zizmo. He is soon arrested for conducting illegal activities using the Nation as a cover. After he is released, he disappears and is never seen again. Lefty begins a lucrative business selling suggestive pictures of women lounging in cars. Determined not to pass on her sin to a child, Desdemona gets sterilized.

In the present time, Cal goes out on a date with Julie Kikuchi, an Asian-American woman Cal met in Berlin. In 1944, Germany is engaged in World War II. Milton serenades Tessie out his back window. Desdemona has been trying to fix him up with a Greek girl, not wanting any more intermarrying in the family. Milton, however, is in love with Tessie. Sometimes when they are alone together in the house, she lets him play his clarinet on her body.

Inexplicably, Tessie soon becomes engaged to Michael Antoniou, who is a seminarian at the Greek Orthodox church they attend. Milton is so upset at the news that he enlists in the navy. Stationed in San Diego, Milton begins to realize the dangers he will face when he is shipped overseas. Back in Detroit, Tessie thinks she sees him in a newsreel and immediately breaks off her engagement to Father Mike and determines to marry Milton. After receiving a ninety-eight on an application to the Naval Academy, Milton is immediately transferred to Annapolis. Within a year, he and Tessie marry.

By 1950, Aunt Zo has married Father Mike and Malcolm X has taken over the Nation of Islam. Whites start moving out of Detroit to the suburbs and the business in Lefty's bar drops off. When Milton comes home from the academy, he remodels the bar into a successful diner. With a lot of time on his hands, Lefty begins to gamble and soon loses all of his retirement savings. As a result, he and Desdemona have to move in with Milton, Tessie, and their son, whom Cal calls Chapter Eleven.

Book Three

Dr. Philobosian delivers Cal, but because he is distracted by his nurse, he does not closely examine Cal's genitalia. Subsequently, he pronounces her a healthy girl. When Cal urinates like a fountain on Father Mike during her baptism, "no one wondered about the engineering involved." Cal explains that she had no doubts she was a girl as she was growing up. Dr. Phil, who has faulty eyesight, never saw anything out of the ordinary during Cal's yearly examinations. Milton's diner begins to lose business as the neighborhood deteriorates. By the 1960s, it is worth less than when Lefty bought the bar in 1933.

In the present, Cal takes Julie away for the weekend to the sea. When she sees nudists on the beach, Cal complains, "What is it like to feel free like that? I mean, my body is so much better than theirs." In 1967, the diner is failing as racial tension increases in Detroit. One night after the police start making arrests in a local strip club, bottles and stones are thrown, and the Detroit race riots begin. Milton holes up in his diner for three days, trying to protect it from looters. Eventually, though, it is burned down. After Milton cashes in the insurance money, they are able to move out to Grosse Point, a small, elite Detroit suburb.

There Cal makes her first friend, Clementine Stark, who teaches her the right way to kiss. Cal admits, "there was something improper about theway I felt about Clementine." When her grandfather has another stroke while she and Clementine are playing naked in the bathhouse, Cal blames herself, thinking that she shocked him. The stroke affects Lefty's memory. Soon after, when Lefty dies, Desdemona takes to her bed where she spends the next ten years.

In the present, Cal and Julie end their weekend together. Cal thinks of the "very real possibility of shock, horror, withdrawal, rebuff. The usual reactions" and so decides to stop seeing her. Back in the past, Milton opens a successful chain of hot dog stands. After Detroit begins a busing program, Milton sends Cal to a private girls' school. She feels like an outcast there, especially when her features turn more ethnic, and she does not begin to develop as the other girls do.

When Chapter Eleven waits nervously for his number to be picked in the Vietnam War draft lottery, he and Cal grow closer. His high number ensures that he will escape the draft, and so he goes east to college. When he comes home for a visit with his girlfriend, he and Milton get into a nasty argument about his anti-war, anti-establishment views, and Chapter Eleven storms out.

Cal falls in love with the Object of Desire, one of the Charm Bracelets, the popular clique at school. During this time, Cal feels sexual urges and changes in her genitalia. She plays Tiresias in her school's production of *Antigone*, and Object plays Antigone. The two become friends as they rehearse, away from the pressures of school. During the opening performance, one of the girls has an aneurism and dies. Cal comforts Object, which is observed by Tessie.

That summer Cal spends every day with the Object at her swim club, and the latter declares that the two are best friends. Cal is despondent over an upcoming trip to Greece with her family, but it gets canceled after the Turks invade the country. After Milton renounces his heritage in response to the U.S. government's support of the invasion, the relatives stop coming over for their Sunday visits.

Cal is invited to the Object's summer home. One night Cal, the Object, the Object's brother Jerome, and a male friend of the Object's go to a cabin in the woods where they drink and smoke marijuana. As she watches the Object and her friend kissing, the inebriated Cal mentally slips into his body. Cal admits "*how right it felt*" to imagine herself caressing the Object. Jerome begins to have sex with Cal, which she allows. For the first time, she understands that she is not "a girl but something in between" and is sure that Jerome realizes it, too. Jerome, however, "hadn't noticed a thing."

The next morning, the Object calls Cal "a total slut." When Jerome tries to have sex with her again, Cal stops him, insisting that she does not like him "like that." The rest of the day the Object avoids Cal. During the night, Cal slowly begins to caress the Object as they lay together in her bed. This develops into a nightly pattern. One afternoon, Jerome catches them caressing each other on the porch swing and calls them "carpet munchers," a derogatory term for a lesbian. In response, Cal tackles Jerome and spits on him. Enraged, Jerome chases her. She runs head first into a tractor and is taken to the emergency room. The doctor who examines her tells her parents to take her to New York City to see a specialist. Cal finally confronts the fact that she "was no longer a girl like other girls."

Book Four

Dr. Luce conducts medical and psychological exams to determine Cal's sexuality. Cal lies on some parts of the psychological exam when he asks about her attraction to boys and girls. After two weeks of tests, Dr. Luce calls Cal's anguished parents in for a consultation while Cal waits in the library. He diagnoses her as "a girl who has a little too much male hormone" and tells them, "we want to correct that" through hormone therapy and cosmetic surgery. He also tells them that Cal can never have children. Although the last news upsets Tessie, she and Milton are relieved that "no one would ever know" about Cal's condition.

While in the library, Cal finds under the definition of "hermaphrodite" the synonym "MONSTER" and decides that is what she must be. Later, her parents tell her Dr. Luce's conclusions and assure her that her situation is "no big deal." She understands that her parents want her to remain a girl.

While waiting for Dr. Luce in his office, she reads her file, which shows that the doctor's assessment is based in part on his assumption that she is sexually attracted to boys. That conclusion, along with the possibility that the cosmetic surgery will prevent her from experiencing sexual pleasure, prompts Cal to write her parents a note declaring "I am not a girl. I'm a boy" and to run away.

Before she heads west, Cal gets her hair cut and tries to adopt more masculine mannerisms. She is not sure what to do next. Lonely and scared, she starts hitchhiking and eventually is picked up by a man who tries to seduce her. Later, Bob Presto, the owner of a strip club, picks her up and suggests that she go to San Francisco. He asks if she is gay or a transvestite and then insists that she call him if she gets in trouble. Back in Detroit, Milton and Tessie are despondent. Milton posts pictures of Cal in local stores and in his hotdog restaurants as the family gathers around. Tessie grows increasingly depressed.

Chapter Eleven comes home and joins Milton in the hot dog business. Cal arrives in San Francisco where she makes friends with other homeless teenagers. One night, while guarding their camp site in the park, two homeless people steal her money. After stripping her, they call her a freak and beat her up. . . . With nowhere else to turn, she calls Bob Presto.

Cal takes a job in his sex club where she works in a water tank as Hermaphrodites. She meets Zora Khyber there, another hermaphrodite who performs with her. Zora, who has done extensive research on hermaphrodites, talks to Cal about their gender issues, making Cal feel "less alone in the world." After the police raid the club, Cal calls Chapter Eleven, who says Milton has just been killed in an accident.

In the present, Cal attends an art opening and sees Julie. Cal tells her about herself, and the two go back to Cal's apartment. Back in Detroit, Cal learns about Milton's death. Milton had gotten a phone call from a man who insisted that he had kidnapped Cal and who demanded money for her release. Milton arrived at a train station where he dropped money they had agreed upon as ransom. After he saw Father Mike pick up the money, he chased him to the Canadian border. On the bridge to Canada, Milton died in a car crash.

Father Mike, who confessed that he was trying to get back at Milton for stealing Tessie from him, was sent to jail. Cal jumps ahead into the future and notes that Chapter Eleven ruins his father's business, and Aunt Zo, Desdemona, and Tessie move to Florida.

After Cal comes home for Milton's traditional Greek funeral, the family gradually adjusts to Cal as a male. Desdemona admits that Lefty was her brother and blames herself for Cal's situation. Cal tells her that Cal likes his life and that he is okay. The novel ends with Cal at the door, happy to be home, and "thinking about what was next."

Characters

Michael Antoniou

Father Mike, assistant priest at the Greek Orthodox church the family attends, married Zoë, Milton's sister, after Tessie broke off her engagement with him. He is sweet-natured before he marries Zoë, but her constant nagging about how successful her brother is compared to him wears him down and turns him bitter. In a desperate attempt to get enough money to leave Zoë and to get even with Milton for his success in business and in marriage, Father Mike tries to blackmail him.

Chapter Eleven

Chapter Eleven is the only name that Cal gives to her older brother. As a child, he likes to shoot, hammer, and smash things. He becomes geeky and nerdy as a teenager but turns into a "John Lennon look-alike" at college where he adopts anti-war and anti-establishment views. He ignores Cal for most of her life since they are far apart in age, but the two become closer when Chapter Eleven faces the Vietnam draft. He ultimately shows his loyalty when he rescues Cal from jail in California. His lack of business sense, however, causes him to ruin his father's hot dog franchise.

Jerome

Jerome, the Object's brother, is the first boy with whom Cal has sex. He seems to want to have a relationship with Cal, but after Cal rebuffs him, he turns on her and his sister with cruel epithets when he catches them together.

Zora Khyber

Zora Khyber, a hermaphrodite that works at the sex club, is sympathetic to Cal's gender confusion and so spends a lot of time sharing her extensive research with her. She has a marked violent streak, however, that frightens Cal.

Julie Kikuchi

Cal's relationship with Julie Kikuchi, a thirty-six-year-old Asian-American living in Berlin, appears in brief glimpses throughout the text. She is straightforward, asking Cal as soon as she meets her if she is gay. Julie's open-mindedness is evident when she is willing to begin a relationship with Cal after Cal admits that she is a hermaphrodite.

Peter Luce

Dr. Luce diagnoses Cal in New York and writes up her case and publishes it. Although he is considered the world's leading authority on hermaphroditism, he misdiagnoses the causes of the condition. Extremely confident in his medical theories, the "brilliant, charming, work-obsessed" Luce, nevertheless "prayed," Cal assumes, that she "would never show up to refute them."

Object of Desire

Cal names the Object of Desire after a famous European film. The Object is part of the popular clique in Cal's private school, whose members ordinarily shun ethnic girls like Cal. But the Object's loneliness, caused by parents who pay little attention to her, encourages her to begin a friendship with Cal that eventually turns sexual. The Object gives into her feelings for Cal but expresses her insecurities and frustration about her lesbian tendencies when she declares, "You understand everything I say. . . . Why can't you be a guy?"

Bob Presto

Bob Presto runs the sex club where Cal works. He appears to be sympathetic and kind-hearted when he rescues Cal after she is beaten up by the homeless men, but his ultimate goal is financial.

Clementine Stark

Clementine, Cal's first friend in Grosse Point, teaches her how to kiss properly and causes Cal's first feelings of gender confusion.

Calliope Stephanides

Calliope, who changes her name to Cal when she assumes a male identity, is the narrator of the story. She claims that she has a male brain but was assumed to be female at birth. Cal establishes a connection between herself and her family when she admits, "my grandparents had fled their home because of a war. Now, some fifty-two years later, I was fleeing myself." She joins the foreign service because she cannot have children and because she does not want to stay in one place for too long, fearing that her gender will be discovered.

Cal insists that from the beginning of her life she had "the ability to communicate between the genders, to see not with the monovision of one sex but in the stereoscope of both." Yet her hermaphroditism causes her great shame. As a result, she admits, "when I meet someone I like and who seems to like me, I retreat." Her humor helps her cope with her loneliness and enables her to take an honest look at her situation. By the end of the novel, she gains the courage, through a careful examination of the connection between her experiences and those of her family, to open herself up to a relationship with Julie.

Desdemona Stephanides

Cal's grandmother, Desdemona, is "perfectly designed for blocking people's paths" as she tries to maintain her family's ties to the old world. She reveals a sense of the dramatic whenever she is crossed by fanning herself with her "six atrocity fans" that list crimes committed against Greece. Cal notes: "the ominous, storm-gathering quality" of her fanning becomes "her secret weapon" in this battle.

Cal notes the difference between Desdemona and her cousin: "in the course of her life Sourmelina had become an American. Almost nothing of the village remained in her. Her self-entombed cousin, on the other hand, had never left it." Desdemona is superstitious, believing that her marriage to her brother dooms the family. As a result, she is consumed by guilt, which causes her to withdraw from her husband and eventually the world. When Desdemona spends the last ten years of her life in bed after Lefty dies, Cal calls her "a sick person imprisoned in a healthy body."

Eleutherios Stephanides

Eleutherios, or Lefty as he was known, is Cal's grandfather and Desdemona's husband. His nonconformist nature becomes evident when he frequents gambling and prostitution houses in Greece and convinces his sister to marry him. After he gambles away his money, he and Desdemona live in the attic of Cal's house; he spends his mornings translating Greek poems, while at night he smokes hash in a hookah. Cal develops a close relationship with her "Chaplinesque *papou*," with his elegant clothes and playful nature.

Milton Stephanides

Milton is Cal's father and Desdemona's son. He possesses "a flinty self-confidence that protected him like a shell from the world's assaults." Of the family members, he assimilates most successfully: he learns American jazz and business sense. He distances himself further from his homeland when he adopts right-wing politics, identifies with Nixon, and supports the United States so much that he denounces his Greek heritage. His obsession with the American dream distances him from his family as he becomes more preoccupied with his business worries. Cal notes "he began to leave a little more of himself at the diner each day" until he "wasn't really there at all."

Sourmelina Stephanides

Sourmelina, called Lina, is Desdemona's and Lefty's cousin. Her parents send her to the United States when they discover that she is a lesbian. She successfully assimilates American culture yet retains some ties to her heritage. When she thinks her husband, Jimmy, is dead, she grieves in the Greek style.

Tessie Stephanides

Tessie Stephanides, born Tessie Zizmo, is Cal's mother. Milton is attracted to her "all-American looks." She is quiet and, like Cal, enjoys watching people. After building her world around her family, she starts to feel useless when Chapter Eleven goes off to college and Cal matures. After Cal leaves, Tessie becomes depressed because her intense motherly devotion is frustrated. That same devotion, however, causes her to accept Cal's sex change from female to male, from a daughter to a son.

Zoë Stephanides

Zoë Stephanides, called Aunt Zo, is Desdemona's and Lefty's daughter, and Cal's aunt. She marries Father Mike by default when Tessie breaks off her engagement with him. Characterized by her good sense of humor and loud talk, she is uncomfortable with the prospect of being a role model as Father Mike's wife. Her jealousy over her brother's good fortune and Mike's obvious affection for Tessie turns Aunt Zo into a nag who constantly berates Mike for his shortcomings. She "never missed a chance to lament her marriage" to him.

Jimmy Zizmo

Jimmy, who is of unknown ethnic origin, is married to Lina. He is an ex-con, drug dealer, and scam artist whose adaptability becomes evident when he turns quickly from rum-running to proselytizing as the head prophet of the Nation of Islam in Detroit.

Themes

Fate and Free Will

Cal questions the primacy of fate over free will as she examines her and her family's experiences. She begins with the silk worm analogy, tracing the thread to the past that has determined her hermaphroditism. "The thread," she insists, "began on a day two hundred and fifty years ago, when the biology gods, for their own amusement, monkeyed with a gene on a baby's fifth chromosome. . . . and my destiny fell into place."

James Wood, in his review of the novel for the *New Republic*, comments that "Eugenides wishes to use his three-generational structure to suggest something about fate, the bequeathments of genetics, and the possibility of revolt once fate has displayed its cards." Eugenides refuses to privilege one force over the other, insisting that both can

Topics For Further Study

- Prepare a genealogical chart that traces your family's history as far back as you can. Interview relatives about personality or physical traits that were passed down through the generations. Add these bits of information to your chart.
- Read *The Virgin Suicides* and compare its coming-of-age theme with that of *Middlesex* in an essay.
- Conduct some research on hermaphrodites, reading if possible some firsthand reports by hermaphrodites. Make a presentation to your class on your findings and lead a discussion on how realistic Cal's experiences are as a hermaphrodite.
- Identify a place that you would like to visit and imagine living there for one year. Do some research on the place. Then write a short story or narrative about the experiences you imagine having while trying to adapt to a foreign culture.

affect human experience. Wood concludes, "the book clearly turns on this idea of destiny, and of destiny resisted, both by free will and by helpless action." While, for example, the damaged gene passed on by Desdemona and Lefty has left a clear mark on Cal, her grandparents had the freedom to choose to come to the United States, just as Cal chooses whether she will live as a man or a woman.

The tension between fate and free will also are evident in Cal's contradictory statements on the two forces. She claims at one point that tragedy "is something determined before you're born, something you can't escape or do anything about, no matter how hard you try." Yet by the end of the novel, she admits, "free will is making a comeback. Biology gives you a brain. Life turns it into a mind."

Coming of Age

One important focus in the novel is Cal's coming of age, a process that is complicated by her genetic irregularities. Initially, her maturation follows a familiar path. Her girlhood beauty makes her feel accepted by her peers. However, her lack of development during puberty makes her worry "about being left behind, left out," which in turn makes her feel "gypped" and "cheated." Her status as outsider is reinforced by her ethnicity.

Her growing awareness of her difference and her attraction to girls makes her feel even more ostracized from her peers. She is able to hide her sexual yearnings to a degree in a private girls' school where "school rituals reinforced an intimate atmosphere." But outside the classroom, her peers focus exclusively on boys. Cal admits that her "school remained militantly heterosexual." Her acknowledgement of her difference produces overwhelming bouts of shame. Yet, she is strong enough to reject Dr. Luce's determination to make her more what might be called normal.

Style

Mythological Allusions

The several mythological allusions in the novel reinforce Cal's sense of her Greek heritage and become important symbolically. Calliope, the goddess of epic poetry, is an appropriate name for the narrator as she tells her and her family's own epic story. In the opening pages, Cal plays Tiresias in her school's production of *Antigone*. She notes the similarities between the two, insisting that like him, she "was first one thing and then the other." The blind prophet Tiresias, who had lived as both a woman and a man, also becomes symbolic of Cal as a seer. Eugenides adds a touch of irony in this allusion, which correlates Tiresias, who can see into the future, with Cal, who can see into the past.

Cal also adopts a comic Homeric tone in the novel, characterized by its elevated, dramatic style of speech typical of epic poems like the *Iliad* and the *Odyssey*. This tone reflects her Greek heritage as well as her gently comic view of her family and its history. As she begins her story, she sets this tone when she writes, "Sing now, O Muse, of the recessive mutation on my fifth chromosome! Sing how it bloomed two and a half centuries ago on the slopes of Mount Olympus, while the goats bleated and the olives dropped."

Self-Reflexivity

Self-reflexivity is a term applied to texts that call attention to the creative process. At different points in the novel, Cal notes that she is fabricating some of her memories or altering them for literary purposes. One such example occurs in her description of her grandfather and Jimmy Zizmo driving past an amusement park. Cal admits that the park should be closed at 3 a.m., but she claims, "for my own purposes, tonight Electric Park is open all night, and the fog suddenly lifts, all so that my grandfather can look out the window and see a roller coaster streaking down the track." This is, she suggests, "a moment of cheap symbolism only." To be truthful, however, she must "bow to the strict rules of realism, which is to say: they can't see a thing." In this fabricated moment, Cal suggests that her story moves between fiction and reality, calling readers' attention to one of her main points in the novel: the difficulty in determining what is real and what is a fictional construct in people's assessment of who they are.

Historical Context

World War II in the Pacific

Two incidents in 1940 exacerbated the tension between the United States and Japan that resulted in the Japanese attack on Pearl Harbor and the U.S. declaration of war against Japan. Japan invaded Indochina and signed the Tripartite Pact, which created an alliance between Japan, Germany, and Italy against Great Britain and France. As a result, the U.S. government drastically increased economic sanctions by withholding oil and freezing all Japanese assets. In retaliation, Japan bombed Pearl Harbor, and the United States entered the war.

The United States battled Japan on the sea (most notably at Midway in 1942) and on Japanese-held islands and through a bombing campaign on the Japanese mainland. In 1942, Japan's forces occupied much of the southeastern Pacific: the Philippine Islands, Indonesia, and New Guinea. Also in 1942, the Americans launched their counterattack. The Coral Sea naval battle prevented the Japanese from gaining access to Australia and the U.S. Marines regained Guadalcanal.

U.S. forces took control of the Solomon Islands in 1943 and New Guinea in 1944. They advanced on Japanese-held island groups: the Philippines, the Marianas Islands, Okinawa, and Iwo Jima. After protracted fighting, the Allies took Birmania in October of 1944, Manila and Iwo Jima in March of 1945, and Okinawa in June of 1945. Japan resisted, however, until 1945. After the United States dropped atomic bombs on Hiroshima and Nagasaki in August of that year, Japan accepted the terms of an unconditional surrender: the dissolution of the Japanese Empire and the release of all seized territories.

Vietnam War

The Vietnam War was fought in South Vietnam and surrounding areas between U.S. forces and insurgents supported by North Vietnam. The war started in 1954 soon after the provisions of the Geneva Conference divided Vietnam into the Democratic Republic of Vietnam (North) and the Republic of Vietnam (South). Conflict initially broke out as a civil war between the North and the South but escalated as the United States threw its support to the South, initially by sending money and advisors and later by sending troops.

After the Tonkin Gulf Resolution was passed in August of 1964, the United States increased its military aid to South Vietnam. By the end of that decade, there were 550,000 U.S. troops involved in the conflict. North Vietnam gained armaments and technical support from the Soviet Union and other communist countries. Despite massive bombing attacks, the United States and South Vietnam failed to push back the insurgency.

Progress was made with peace talks after President Johnson decided not to seek reelection in 1968. After his election that year, President Nixon began troop withdrawals along with intensified bombing campaigns. In 1970, Nixon ordered the invasion of communist strongholds in Cambodia.

Public opinion in the United States turned against the war as the number of casualties grew and reports of war crimes such as the massacre at My Lai surfaced. Huge demonstrations took place in Washington D.C., as well as in other cities and on college campuses. A peace agreement was finally reached in January of 1973, but fighting between the North and the South did not abate.

On April 30, 1975, the South Vietnamese president Duong Van Minh surrendered to the communists. Saigon fell as the last U.S. troops left the country. More than 50,000 U.S. soldiers died in the conflict along with approximately 400,000 South Vietnamese and over 900,000 North Vietnamese.

Cal includes details about these two wars to reveal the historical and cultural context of her family's saga. Two members of her family, her father, Milton, and her brother, Chapter Eleven, must face the prospect of serving in these wars since they are American citizens. Fortunately for them and for the rest of the family, neither is sent overseas.

Critical Overview

Reviews for the novel have been decidedly positive. Many critics praise Eugenides's characterization of Cal. Max Watman, in *New Criterion*, writes that in this "first-rate" novel, "Eugenides normalizes the experience of a hermaphrodite and turns Cal into something other than a freak." James Wood, in the *New Republic* agrees, insisting, "Eugenides makes Calliope credible: she is not merely a theme." Joanne Wilkinson, in her review for *Booklist*, concludes that Eugenides "proves himself to be a wildly imaginative writer" and finds "perhaps what is most surprising about [his] offbeat but engrossing book is how he establishes, seemingly effortlessly, the credibility of his narrator." He is, she claims, "likely to hold readers in thrall" with "a sure yet light-handed touch" in his "affecting characterization of a brave and lonely soul and [his] vivid depiction of exactly what it means to be both male and female." In her review of the novel in the *Library Journal*, Rachel Collins concurs: "The author's eloquent writing captures the essence of Cal."

Praising the tone and style of the novel, Collins argues, "his confidence in the story, combined with his sure prose, helps readers overcome their initial surprise and focus on the emotional revelation of the characters and beyond." She concludes, "Eugenides proves that he is not only a unique voice in modern literature but also well versed in the nature of the human heart." A review in *Publishers Weekly* echoes Collins's claims, declaring the novel "beautifully written" with an "extraordinary sensitivity to the mores of our leafier suburbs" as it "effortlessly transcend[s] the stereotypes of gender."

Some readers, however, have found fault with the narrative. Wilkinson insists that "at times the novel reads like a medical text." Wood writes that the "novel is blemished by elements of didacticism and prolixity, and [Eugenides] is not without the postmodern urge to turn clouds of suggestion into storms of fact." He also criticizes Eugenides tendency to "[remind] us just how neatly he has planted everything."

Yet Wood finds much also to praise in the novel's voice and tone: "[the novel] is an often affecting, funny, and deeply human book. For all its scope and its size, for all the data that crowds this novel, Eugenides seems a charmingly ingenuous writer." Woods praises the "verve" and the "exactness" of the author's storytelling skills and his "simple confidence in his Greek material that disarms his vices." Wood concludes, "The result is . . . a descriptive immediacy, vividly comic, often precisely realistic, but with that tilt of the real the narrative needs." Ultimately, "Eugenides's charm, his life-jammed comedy, rescues the novel from its occasional didacticism." Wood adds, "Paradoxically, Eugenides's boldness, his decision to risk an emblem as obvious as a hermaphrodite narrator . . . is what steers the novel away, finally, from the temptation of editorial writing."

Wood reserves his highest praise for Eugenides's dual narrative structure, claiming that he has "accomplished one of the most difficult novelistic tricks" by combining "an adult voice using the full resources of the language and the proper prestiges of adulthood" with "a child's voice, representing an excited, receptive, and bolting response to the world." He concludes, "In our day, this achievement of a mature uncorruptedness represents something of a triumph."

Criticism

Wendy Perkins

Perkins is a professor of American and English literature and film. In this essay, she examines the tensions between integration and displacement in the novel.

Jeffrey Eugenides's *Middlesex* presents two narrative plot lines: the three-generational epic story of the Greek-American Stephanides family and a poignant coming-of-age tale of one member of that family. Cal's controlling voice integrates the two storylines that wind through the novel like Desdemona's silk threads, forming an intricate thematic fabric that illustrates the tensions between integration and displacement. As Cal recounts her

> "When Cal discovers that she is a hermaphrodite, she also finds herself caught between two worlds. Her position, however, is more complex and disturbing."

family's struggle to establish a clear sense of themselves in their new world, she eventually comes to a cautious recognition and acceptance of her own uniqueness as well as her connection to the human community.

In the beginning of the book, Cal immediately identifies herself as a hermaphrodite, noting that she has lived first as a girl and then as a boy. She explains, "After I started living as a male, my mother and I moved away from Michigan and I've been moving ever since." Berlin, formerly a divided city, is an appropriate local for Cal at the point when she is "hopeful" that she will be able to unite the two halves of herself.

In an effort to establish a more stable or cohesive sense of identity, Cal explores her genetic link to her family back through three generations to her Greek grandparents, Desdemona and Lefty. As she chronicles the tension they and their descendents' faced between their Greek heritage and the culture of their adopted country, the United States, Cal integrates her own story of a divided self and explores the struggle they all endured in their efforts to establish a measure of balance and wholeness.

After their immigration, Lefty and Desdemona respond to the United States in opposite ways: Desdemona fights against assimilation while Lefty embraces it. Desdemona's devotion to her ethnicity becomes immediately evident as she passes through Ellis Island. After her "immigrant braids" are cut off, she vows to regrow them, insisting that she does not "want to look like an *Amerikanidha*." For the rest of her life, she retains as much of her heritage as she can, while Lefty integrates American society.

Lefty quickly learns English while working at the Ford Motor Company and becomes an apt pupil as Jimmy teaches him how to be financially successful in his new world. Jimmy's wife, Lina, Lefty's and Desdemona's cousin, becomes a model of assimilation. Cal explains, "In the five years since leaving Turkey, Sourmelina had managed to erase just about everything identifiably Greek about her."

Lefty advances his adoption of a new identity through his role as an American business owner and supporter of equal rights, which becomes evident when a customer makes a racist slur in Lefty's bar and Lefty refuses to serve him. After the customer tells him to go back to his own country, Lefty insists, "This is my country" and pulls out a gun, which, Cal notes, is "a very American thing" to do. Lefty's and Desdemona's divergent responses to the United States, however, create tension and distance between them.

They both try to promote their own points of view in their children. Desdemona, however, has little success at trying to prevent her children from becoming Americanized. Zoë adopts the loudness of Americans while Milton inherits his father's capitalistic business acumen. Desdemona grimly recognizes how far her family is removed from its heritage when she mistakenly predicts Cal's sex while Milton, using more progressive methods, gets it right: "Her American-born son had been proven right and, with this fresh defeat, the old country, in which she still tried to live despite its being four thousand miles and thirty-eight years away, receded one more notch."

When the family moves out of the city where they enjoyed the company of other Greek immigrants into a mostly WASP (white Anglo-Saxon Protestant) suburb of Detroit, they experience both an increased pressure to assimilate and a sense of their own ethnicity. Cal notes this tension when she writes, "Everything about Middlesex [their street] spoke of forgetting and everything about Desdemona made plain the inescapability of remembering."

As he adapts to his Grosse Point neighborhood, Milton expresses strong support for the Republican agenda, becoming so Americanized that he denounces his heritage when the U.S. government backs the Turkish invasion of Greece. Cal explains, "Forced to choose between his native land and his ancestral one, he didn't hesitate." This response alienates his family and friends who stop coming over for Sunday visits.

Cal's family, however, eventually comes to a degree of balance between the old and new. Milton, the staunch Republican, who decries the anti-establishment activities of his son, displays his connections to both worlds in his Hercules hot dog stands. Lefty decorates his diner with American and Greek iconic figures: Mickey Mouse and Paul

Bunyan are posed next to Zeus and Aphrodite. Even Desdemona allows a certain duality. As Cal notes her grandmother's addiction to American soap operas, she explains, "Though she had lived in America as an eternal exile, a visitor for forty years, certain bits of her adopted country had been seeping under the locked doors of her disapproval." In a final note of ironic balance, Cal concedes that Desdemona's hair was used for one of Betty Ford's wigs.

When Cal discovers that she is a hermaphrodite, she also finds herself caught between two worlds. Her position, however, is more complex and disturbing. While her family members were never able to resolve all of the tensions involved in the assimilation process, they enjoy a sense of community with their relatives and other Greek immigrants. Cal's relatively unique situation offers her no such opportunities for commiseration or support.

She experiences the same feelings of ethnic displacement, especially after her father sends her to a private girls' school. Prior to their admittance to the school, she and her friends "had always felt completely American. But now the Bracelets' upturned noses suggested that there was another America to which we could never gain admittance." This ostracism, however, cannot compare to the complete sense of isolation Cal experiences as she confronts the realities of her genetic nature. When she discovers that she is a hermaphrodite, she becomes convinced that she fits the definition she finds in the dictionary—"MONSTER"—and the homeless men's epithet—"freak." Even the counterculture or the beaches of San Francisco could not offer solace, since, as she explains, "Nature brought no relief. . . . There was nowhere to go that wouldn't be me."

Cal begins to feel "less alone in the world" through her friendship with Zora who insists that "the original person was two halves, one male, one female. Then these got separated." She and Cal, she argues, should be content since they do not need to search "for their other half." They have "both halves already."

When she returns for Milton's funeral, Cal is also able to gain a measure of acceptance from her family who discovers "gender was not all that important." Cal eventually comes to the realization that she has learned to strike a balance between her two selves since, as she notes, "Even now, though I live as a man, I remain in essential ways Tessie's daughter." In the final scene, she establishes a connection with her family through her recognition of their and her own duality. As she stands in the doorway of the house on Middlesex, she describes her "Byzantine face, which was the face of [her] grandfather and of the American girl [she] had once been."

During the process of recounting the story of her family and herself to Julie, Cal is able to recognize her uniqueness as well as the universality of her experience. This understanding allows her to trust Julie and thus open herself to the possibility that she can now stop running from herself and establish a "last stop," finally able to accept her difference as well as her connection to her world.

Source: Wendy Perkins, Critical Essay on *Middlesex*, in *Novels for Students*, Thomson Gale, 2007.

James Wood

In the following review, Wood praises Eugenides's talent at "conjuring" an adult voice, with all its language and resource, that is simultaneously that of a child's "excited, receptive, and bolting response to the world."

In his memoir *The Noise of Time*, Mandelstam recalls a haughty friend who used to say,

What Do I Read Next?

- *The Virgin Suicides* (1993), Eugenides's first novel, chronicles the lives of five teenaged sisters living in suburban Detroit who all commit suicide.
- Augusten Burroughs, in his autobiographical *Running with Scissors* (2002), traces his harrowing childhood and his growing awareness of his homosexuality with an adept comic touch.
- The narrator in Jonathan Franzen's bestselling novel, *The Corrections*, published in 2001, explores the lives of his offbeat family members as he tells of his struggle to make peace with them.
- J. D. Salinger's classic coming-of-age story, *Catcher in the Rye* (1951), is narrated by Holden Caulfield, who tells the cynical but compelling story of a particular weekend in New York during his troubled teenaged years.

disdainfully, that "some men are books, others—newspapers." The remark might be adapted. Some books are books, others—newspapers. In recent years, the large American novel has frequently aspired to the condition of journalism. The great quarry of the last decade, and sometimes the great cemetery, has been the social novel, the vast report on the way we live now, the stuffed dossier, the thriving broadsheet streaming with contemporary brightnesses. Tom Wolfe's barely literate plea for more of just this kind of fiction has always seemed nonsensical in the age of Joyce Carol Oates, Philip Roth, Don DeLillo, Richard Powers, and most recently Jonathan Franzen. We have too much socially and politically obsessed fiction, not too little. Mimesis deserves a holiday. The bright book of life need not include *all* of life.

Jeffrey Eugenides's second novel seems, at first glance, a victim of this journalistic ambition to cover the twentieth-century American news. It is about three generations of a Greek-American family, and it moves from 1922 to the 1970s. We pass, as you would expect, through Prohibition, the Depression, World War 11, and the civil rights movement, and we end with the OPEC oil crisis. There is even an opportunistic "update," in which the narrator glancingly mentions September 11, as if the failure to include that catastrophe would make the novel untimely or in some way obsolete.

In addition to this reportorial urge, *Middlesex* is a child of its moment in its occasional recourse to those excitements, patternings, and implausibilities that lie on the soft side of magical realism and should be called hysterical realism: two cousins conceive their children on the same night and at the same moment, and these two children later marry each other; a character is named Chapter Eleven and seems never to have been given any other name; the Greek lady who flees Smyrna in 1922 later retires to Smyrna Beach, Florida; the novel's hermaphrodite narrator, Calliope Stephanides, who is born a girl but later decides to be a boy (hence "middlesex"), conveniently moves to a house on Middlesex Street, in Grosse Pointe, Michigan, in the 1960s, and conveniently narrates his story from present-day Berlin, formerly a city of two halves or sexes (which, of course, he remarks upon)—and so on.

It seems hard to convince contemporary novelists that true aesthetic patterning has little to do with such gunning symmetries, but is more akin to the ghostlier ideal of musical motif and repetition. Still, these deformities notwithstanding, *Middlesex* is certainly a novel and not a newspaper; and it is an often affecting, funny, and deeply human book. For all its scope and its size, for all the data that crowds this novel, Eugenides seems a charmingly ingenuous writer. A comparison might be made with that other big American novel, *The Corrections.* Despite his considerable powers as a dramatist, Franzen rarely leaves himself at the door. He is an intensely knowing novelist, and his many essaylets and op-ed riffs are written in a high-journalistic prose, and clearly by Franzen himself; they could be broken off the main stem of the book and crumbled into *The New Yorker* without much amendment. Eugenides, too, enjoys his authorial jags, and some are better than others, but he generally avoids knowingness. His prosy riffs are his narrator's, and they belong jealously to his novel. They are more likable than Franzen's, if less obviously smart. Above all, they partake of his narrator's curious innocence.

This is a way of saying that Eugenides at his best is a storyteller. Innocence in storytelling is a kind of learned cognitive naïveté, whereby the writer seems to discover each new detail synchronously with the reader. The narrator's revelation poses as self-revelation. This talent, actually very rare in contemporary novelists, is inseparable from a quality of epistemological delight, a joy in knowing. (Knowingness, by contrast, is joyless.) On the third page of the novel, the narrator's brother is sent upstairs to the attic where his grandparents live in the family home. The attic of Desdemona and "Lefty" Stephanides, grandparents of Chapter Eleven and Calliope Stephanides, is a curious one, stuffed as it is with they physical reminders of the old Greek world they left behind in 1922. But the reader does not know this yet. And so he must follow the novelist:

> In sneakers he passed beneath the twelve, damply newspapered birdcages suspended from the rafters. With a brave face he immersed himself in the sour odor of the parakeets, and in my grandparents' own particular aroma, a mixture of mothballs and hashish. He negotiated his way past my grandfather's book-piled desk and his collection of rebetika records. Finally, bumping into the leather ottoman and the circular coffee table made of brass, he found my grandparents' bed and, under it, the silkworm box. Carved from olivewood, a little bigger than a shoe box, it had a tin lid perforated by tiny airholes and inset with the icon of an unrecognizable saint. The saint's face had been rubbed off, but the fingers of his right hand were raised to bless a short, purple, terrifically self-confident-looking mulberry tree. After gazing awhile at this vivid botanical presence, Chapter Eleven pulled the box from under the bed and opened it. Inside were the two wedding crowns made from rope and, coiled like snakes, the two long braids

of hair, each tied with a crumbling black ribbon. He poked one of the braids with his index finger. Just then a parakeet squawked, making my brother jump, and he closed the box, tucked it under his arm, and carried it downstairs to Desdemona.

The reader instantly recognizes that he is in the presence of a real storyteller, whose admirable desire is to goad our tactilities. There is much confidence, dash, and charm in this little passage. First, the oddity of the objects themselves: the parakeets, the silkworm box, the wedding crowns of rope, the braids of hair. Next, the precision of the writing: exactly "twelve" birdcages, which are "damply newspapered"; the odor of "mothballs and hashish"; the box of olivewood and its perforated tin lid. And finally, the passage's charm: the little boy's domestic terror, the thick gloom or hideous mess of the room nicely suggested by that comical verb "found" ("he found my grandparents' bed"), and the delighted smirk that runs beneath the description of the priest on the box blessing the "short, purple, terrifically self-confident-looking mulberry tree." (The mulberry tree, remember, provides the silkworm with its home.)

Much of Eugenides's comic charm resides in, and flows from, his loyalty to his Greek-American background. If he has a curiosity that seems sweeter than the average postmodern writer, the run-of-the-mill I.Q.-with-an-iBook, it may have something to do with a willingness to let his ethnic material speak for itself. Certainly, although his novel is blemished by elements of didacticism and prolixity, and he is not without the postmodern urge to turn clouds of suggestion into storms of fact, Eugenides has a simple confidence in his Greek material that disarms his vices. He approaches his Greek-American immigrants without overweening mediation, as if these people have not been described very much until now. The result is usually a descriptive immediacy, vividly comic, often precisely realistic, but with that tilt of the real that narrative needs.

Thus we meet Desdemona Stephanides, who with her husband flees the Turks in Smyrna in 1922 and arrives in Detroit, where she has cousins. Desdemona, a formidable creature, has the habit of fanning herself when she gets angry or excited. "To anyone who never personally experienced it, it's difficult to describe the ominous, storm-gathering quality of my grandmother's fanning," says Calliope, her granddaughter and the book's narrator. And Desdemona's fans, it should be said, are eccentric: "the front of the fan was emblazoned with the words 'Turkish Atrocities.' Below, in smaller print, were the specifics: the 1955 pogrom in Istanbul in which 15 Greeks were killed, 200 Greek women raped, 4,348 stores looted, 59 Orthodox churches destroyed, and even the graves of the Patriarchs desecrated." Again, it is not only the verve of the writing that appeals, but its exactness. The idea of an "atrocity fan" is wonderful enough, but Eugenides's real talent lies in the detailed coda to this passage: "Desdemona had six atrocity fans. They were a collector's set. Each year she sent a contribution to the Patriarchate in Constantinople, and a few weeks later a new fan arrived, making claims of genocide and, in one case, bearing a photograph of Patriarch Athenagoras in the ruins of a looted cathedral." This is the kind of detail that *makes* narrative.

"Paradoxically, Eugenides's boldness, his decision to risk an emblem as obvious as a hermaphrodite narrator (an emblem, that is, of helpless destiny), is what steers the novel away, finally, from the temptation of editorial writing."

In addition to Desdemona, there is her husband Eleutherios, or "Lefty," who opens a speakeasy (later a diner) called The Zebra Room, and whose son Milton (Calliope's father) becomes a successful businessman, as the founder of Hercules Hot Dogs. Milton is a limited fellow, an instinctive American patriot and a Nixon supporter. Unlike his wife Tessie, he does not go to the local church, the Assumption Greek Orthodox, "having become an apostate at the age of eight over the exorbitant price of votive candles." Calliope often mocks her father, for the reader's benefit: "The only way my father could think of to instill in me a sense of my heritage was to take me to dubbed Italian versions of the ancient Greek myths." And there is Peter Tatakis, "Uncle Pete" as he is known, a proponent of the Great Books series, a collection of one hundred fifty world masterpieces (he has read them all twice). In the old country Uncle Pete has wanted to be a doctor, but the "catastrophe"—the flight from the Turks—ended that. "In the United States, he'd put himself through two years of chiropractic school, and now ran a small office in Birmingham with a human skeleton he was still paying for in installments."

In general, Eugenides's gift is for summation, for gargoyles rather than architecture. His characters tend to be introduced in blocks of description, which turn out to house their somewhat stable essences. It might be said that most of his Greek characters resemble each other—namely, that they all partake of the same kind of voluble Greekness, an ethnic robustness that skirts caricature. When Calliope tells us that throughout her childhood the slightest mention of the Depression would set Desdemona off "into a full cycle of wailing and breast-clutching," and that even the phrase "manic depression" once had this effect, we are being handed, too liberally and easily, a melodramatic essence, the fat wailing granny from the old country. In such cases, as so often in melodrama (in Babel's Cossacks, for instance), the complexities of characters are sacrificed on the altar of "vividness," and are simplified into mere appetite, which then becomes those characters' supposedly signal, but actually quite generic, attribute.

Eugenides often coaxes his Greek material; but in this regard he only coasts on it, as in a rather glib line like "every Greek drama needs a deus ex machina." Indeed, there are times when he comes close to the comedian's one-liner: "Easter Sunday, 1959. Our religion's adherence to the Julian calendar has once again left us out of sync with the neighborhood." The ecclesiastical reliably brings out the joker in Eugenides: "As far as I could tell, what happened every Sunday at Assumption Greek Orthodox Church was that the priests got together and read the Bible out loud. They started with Genesis and kept going straight through Numbers and Deuteronomy. Then on through Psalms and Proverbs, Ecclesiastes, Isaiah, Jeremiah, and Ezekiel, all the way up to the New Testament. Then they read that. Given the length of our services, I saw no other possibility."

If his people sound a little alike, they are ably diversified by the many lanes of the novel's effluviating plot. *Middlesex* is an enormously ambitious book, whose many stories do indeed gather to present a broad swath of Greek-American life. More, Eugenides wishes to use his three-generational structure to suggest something about fate, the bequeathments of genetics, and the possibility of revolt once fate has displayed its cards. To carry this thematic weight, he has chosen a very peculiar vehicle: his narrator's hermaphroditism. Desdemona and Lefty, we quickly learn, are brother and sister. Back in Bithynios, their tiny village in Asia Minor on the slopes of Mount Olympus, the parentless siblings began their incestuous affair on the crooked logic that although they were brother and sister, they were also third cousins, and cousins marry all the time. The relationship is jolted into hasty marriage by world events: suddenly the Turks are at their door and they must flee Smyrna, which is on fire. They marry on the boat to America, and pledge to keep their secret a secret.

It is hard not to admire the vigor with which Eugenides writes about Bithynios, and then about the sack of Smyrna. (It also allows him cheekily to quote from *The Waste Land*: "Mr. Eugenides, the Smyrna merchant/unshaven, with a pocketful of currants . . .") As Smyrna burns, the huddled citizens wait on the harborfront to be collected by anyone who will have them. A British frigate, anchored just offshore, makes no charitable gesture. Desdemona and Lefty, along with an Armenian doctor named Nishan Philobosian, are rescued by the French. A stirring epic froths forward. But what Eugenides gains in scope he loses in precision. A scene set on the British ship, in which fatuous officers scan the harborfront with binoculars and calmly say to each other. "Jolly crowded, what?" and "Nice cigar, what?" is cartoonish, an impression hardly helped by Eugenides's odd decision to have a "Major" (an army rank) on a naval boat, and to call the Royal Navy "His Majesty's Marines," whoever they are.

But once the novel arrives in America, it gains authenticity from the community in which Desdemona and Lefty live. They share a house in Detroit with another cousin, Sourmelina Zizmo. Lefty briefly works in the local Ford factory, then as a bootlegger for Sourmelina's husband, Jimmy. Sourmelina and Desdemona become pregnant on the same night, and give birth, respectively, to a daughter, Theodora (Tessie), and a son, Miltiades (Milton). When Jimmy dies, Lefty opens The Zebra Room, which in time will become a successful diner, until it falls victim to the Detroit riots of 1967. (Detroit's fires repeat, in American guise, the blazes of Smyrna.)

Meanwhile heredity advances with silent footfall. Desdemona is terrified that her incestuously conceived son Milton will be retarded or handicapped. He is neither, but he is carrying an invisible flaw, a mutation of the fifth chromosome—that is, hermaphroditism, a genetic oddity common in Bithynios, where for centuries families had intermarried. It is dormant until Milton marries Tessie, Sourmelina's daughter, also his cousin, who is carrying the same genetic flaw. Milton and Tessie's first child, Chapter Eleven, is unblemished. But their second, Calliope Stephanides, born in 1960, is a hermaphrodite, or more exactly a little girl who possesses recessed and barely visible male genitals, a victim of "5-alpha-reductase deficiency syndrome." An alert obstetrician might have noticed the tiny deformity, but Calliope was delivered by Dr. Philobosian, the Armenian refugee from Smyrna, now seventy-four and a little dithery.

Calliope maps the entanglements of her family inheritance with characteristic jollity. "So, to recap," begins one chapter. "Sourmelina Zizmo (née Pappasdiamondopoulis) wasn't only my first cousin twice removed. She was also my grandmother. My father was his own mother's (and father's) nephew. In addition to being my grandparents, Desdemona and Lefty were my great-aunt and -uncle. My parents were my second cousins and Chapter Eleven was my third cousin as well as my brother." Eugenides uses this genetic spaghetti as a way to embody, literally, the sentence of a family fate, Calliope, who in the magical realist mode is able to recount not only her birth but also her pre-history back to Bithynios, cannily ponders this burden, how to outwit it. At times too cannily: we hear about how "in the twentieth century, genetics brought the Ancient Greek notion of fate into our very cells," but that in the twenty-first century we have discovered that a surprisingly small number of genes actually determine our behavior. "And so a strange new possibility is arising. Compromised, indefinite, sketchy, but not entirely obliterated: free will is making a comeback."

The book clearly turns on this idea of destiny, and of destiny resisted, both by free will and by helpless action: first when Desdemona and Lefty have their lives changed and in turn change their lives by coming to America, and then when their granddaughter chooses, at the age of thirteen, to become a boy. Calliope, we are supposed to believe, is the synthesis that unites the restless dialectic of eros, and perhaps of history: a character neatly informs us that "Plato said that the original human being was a hermaphrodite. Did you know that? The original person was two halves, one male, one female. Then these got separated. That's why everybody's always searching for their other half. Except for us. We've got both halves already."

Whenever Eugenides presses on his themes this way, he bruises them; he stops trusting in his tale, apparently unaware that its very form incarnates its theme better than can any commentary. Alas, we are in a journalistically essayistic age, when a necessary component of a serious novel is thought to be a theoretical discussion of what the book is about. It is easy to forget that in fiction themes ideally mature like aloes, losing their stems as soon as they blossom; that is to say, themes need to forget themselves in the mind of the novel, need to break free of their beginnings. Eugenides is rather fond of reminding us just how neatly he has planted everything.

Yet once again Eugenides's charm, his life-jammed comedy, rescues the novel from its occasional didacticism. One can put it this way: a novel narrated by a hermaphrodite comes to seem largely routine, as if Calliope were simply rather fat or tall. A fact that might scream its oddity, and that might have been used again and again heavily to explore fashionable questions of identity and gender, is here blissfully domesticated. This Eugenides achieves by a patient and often funny adherence to the ordinary, which was exactly how he made the peculiar material of his last novel, *The Virgin Suicides,* seem just regularly suburban, Cheever-stamped fare. In short, Eugenides makes Calliope credible: she is not merely a theme (though she may sometimes be thematically used and abused, poor girl), but a high-spirited high school girl growing up in Grosse Pointe, Michigan. Paradoxically, Eugenides's boldness, his decision to risk an emblem as obvious as a hermaphrodite narrator (an emblem, that is, of helpless destiny), is what steers the novel away, finally, from the temptation of editorial writing.

Calliope may well be emblematic; but she is above all a hermaphrodite. One is reminded of Eudora Welty's crack that Melville needed a symbol so large and so real that it really had to be a whale. In some similar way, Eugenides's narrator, the product of many confused historical threads, had to be very, very confused. But the novel is helped enormously by Calliope's likability. Long before she is born and appears properly in the novel, we know her voice, because she has been telling us the history of her parents and her grandparents. So once she is installed in the book we are happy to follow her, from her baptism (she urinates on the priest) to her familial removal to the house on Middlesex Street and her enrollment at the fancy Baker and Inglis School for Girls at the age of twelve.

At school she falls in love with another girl: Eugenides has an interesting skill for evoking the love-thick air of teenage schoolrooms. In the math teacher's room, for instance, we are told that "a picture of the great mathematician Ramanujan (whom we girls at first took to be Miss Grotowski's boyfriend) hangs on the wall." A trip with the Love Object (as Calliope refers to her) to a bayside house yields some very good writing, though always strict and precise: "Out in front of us the bay flashed silver. The bay had scales, like the fish beneath." And so Calliope grows up—until the moment when, in part because of her affair with the Love Object, she discovers that she is not a girl, or not only one.

And then the skies come down, in Greek fashion. Her parents take her to New York to a specialist called Dr. Luce, a marvelously trendy, early-1970s figure, a slightly shady pioneer just breaking the newly fertile crust of "sexology." Calliope runs away and has many adventures, and while she is missing, her father Milton, founder of Hercules Hot Dogs, dies in very strange circumstances that involve the local priest, Father Mike. The novel ends with his funeral, somberly. But the book's merriness cannot be suppressed, and the residue that the comic spirit leaves behind gleams with energy. Perhaps the funniest of many delightful episodes in the novel involves the visit of Dr. Müller, a nutritionist, to the Stephanides home. Dr. Müller is doing a longevity study, and is writing an article on "The Mediterranean Diet." He is impressed by Desdemona's great age, and "to that end, he plied her with questions about the cuisine of her homeland.

> German by blood, he renounced his race when it came to its cooking. With post-war guilt, he decried bratwurst, sauer-braten, and Königsberger Klopse as dishes verging on poison. They were the Hitler of foods. Instead he looked to our own Greek diet . . . as potential curatives, as life-giving, artery-cleansing, skin-smoothing wonder drugs. And what Dr. Müller said seemed to be true: though he was only forty-two, his face was wrinkled, burdened with jowls. Gray hair prickled up on the sides of his head; whereas my father, at forty-eight, despite the coffee stains beneath his eyes, was still the possessor of an unlined olive complexion and a rich, glossy, black head of hair. They didn't call it Grecian Formula for nothing. It was in our food!

The doctor shows the family the graphs that he has made, listing names and birthdates of Italians, Greeks, and a single Bulgarian living in the Detroit area. The doctor thinks that Desdemona is ninety-one. The family does not mention that "Desdemona was actually seventy-one, not ninety-one, and that she always confused sevens with nines. . . . We couldn't. We didn't want to lose out to the Italians or even that one Bulgarian."

This is characteristic of the novel's high-spirited, Greek-obsessed, ethnically competitive clan. And it is characteristic, too, of Eugenides's conjuring of childish innocence. He has accomplished one of the most difficult novelistic tricks: an adult voice using the full resources of the language and the proper prestiges of adulthood (Calliope is recalling his story as a middle-aged man now living in Berlin) that is simultaneously a child's voice, representing an excited, receptive, and bolting response to the world. Eugenides successfully combines the two visions, and so the book is joyously Calliope's. In our day, this achievement of a mature uncorruptedness represents something of a triumph.

Source: James Wood, "Unions," in the *New Republic*, October 7, 2002, pp. 31–34.

Sources

Collins, Rachel, Review of *Middlesex*, in *Library Journal*, July 2002, p. 116.

Eugenides, Jeffrey, *Middlesex*, Picador, 2002.

Review of *Middlesex*, in *Publishers Weekly*, July 1, 2002, p. 46.

Watman, Max, "Suffer the Children," in *New Criterion*, November 2002, pp. 65–71.

Wilkinson, Joanne, Review of *Middlesex*, in *Booklist*, June 1 & 15, 2002, p. 1644.

Wood, James, "Unions," in *New Republic*, October 7, 2002, pp. 31–34.

Further Reading

Colapinto, John, *As Nature Made Him: The Boy Who Was Raised as a Girl*, Harper Collins, 2000.
Journalist Colapinto tells the true story of a boy who was raised a girl after he survived a botched circumcision.

Fausto-Sterling, Anne, *Sexing the Body: Gender Politics and the Construction of Sexuality*, Basic Books, 2000.
Fausto-Sterling examines the biological and environmental influences that determine sexuality.

Sowerby, Robin, *The Greeks: An Introduction to Their Culture*, Routledge, 1995.
This work presents a concise but comprehensive view of ancient Greek culture.

Woodhouse, C. M., *Modern Greece: A Short History*, Faber and Faber, 2000.
Woodhouse presents an overview of the history and culture of Greece from 324 to 1990.

The Poisonwood Bible

Barbara Kingsolver

1998

When *The Poisonwood Bible* was published in 1998, Barbara Kingsolver was already a well-established and respected author. Her fourth novel, however, became an overwhelming critical and popular success, especially after Oprah Winfrey chose it for her book club. The novel sold more hardcover copies than all of Kingsolver's previous works put together, including three novels, short story collections, a poetry collection, and two nonfiction works.

As in many of her other stories, Kingsolver in *The Poisonwood Bible* focuses on the complexities of family relationships and communities in which people experience a clash of cultures. Yet here, she widens her scope to include three decades in the second half of the twentieth century during a time of political upheaval in the Congo. The novel focuses on the experiences of the Price family, who arrive in the Congo in 1959, emissaries of the Southern Baptist Mission League. Orleanna Price, along with her four daughters, struggles to adapt to and to survive the harsh conditions there while her husband, Nathan Price, descends into madness as he tries and fails to force the villagers to adopt his rigid Christian doctrines.

The family's troubles become life-threatening as the Congolese fight for their independence from Belgium and from U.S. interference in their political and social affairs. Kingsolver's intermingling of politics and human drama results in a satisfying tale of betrayal and forgiveness. Reviewers have applauded the novel's compelling characters, its

Barbara Kingsolver © AP Images

political themes, and Kingsolver's insight into the complex dynamics of the family.

Author Biography

Celebrated author, journalist, and human rights and environmental activist, Barbara Kingsolver was born in Annapolis, Maryland, on April 8, 1955, but she grew up in rural Kentucky. As she watched her country doctor father serve the poor and working class, she developed a sense of social responsibility and devotion to community that was later expressed in her writing.

When she was in the second grade, her father accepted a medical position in the Congo and moved his family there. At that time, Kingsolver began her life-long habit of writing in a journal. During her junior year at DePauw University where she was studying biology, she took time off to work in Europe as an archaeologist's assistant. After eventually earning a degree at DePauw, Kingsolver lived for periods of time in Europe and the United States, supporting herself with an array of occupations, including typesetter, x-ray technician, copy editor, biological researcher, and translator. In 1981, she earned a master's degree in ecology and evolutionary biology from the University of Arizona and soon began working as a technical writer and freelance journalist.

By 1987, she decided to devote her time to writing fiction, and in the following year, her first novel, *The Bean Trees*, was published and gained national acclaim. The novel focuses on a young Anglo woman who moves to Arizona after adopting a Cherokee girl. Many of Kingsolver's later works are set in the American southwest and address the culture clash between Native Americans and Anglos. With *The Poisonwood Bible* (1998), Kingsolver broadened her scope to the landscape and politics of Africa.

Awards that followed for her other work include the Feature-writing Award, Arizona Press Club, 1986; American Library Association Award in 1988 for *The Bean Trees* and in 1990 for *Homeland*; citation of accomplishment from United Nations National Council of Women, 1989; PEN Fiction Prize and Edward Abbey Ecofiction Award, both 1991, for *Animal Dreams* (1990); Woodrow Wilson Foundation/Lila Wallace fellowship (1992–1993); an honorary doctorate from DePauw University, 1994; and the Book Sense Book of the Year Award, for *The Poisonwood Bible*, 2000. Also in 2000, Kingsolver received the National Humanities Medal, the highest U.S. award for service through the arts. Her devotion to her craft and to her progressive political sensibility prompted her to establish and fund the Bellwether Prize, awarded to previously unpublished authors who address themes involving social and political injustice.

As of 2006, Barbara Kingsolver was married to Steven Hopp, and the couple lived with their two daughters in Tucson, Arizona, and on a farm in Appalachia. Hopp and Kingsolver co-author essays and articles, some of which are included in her collection of essays, *Small Wonder* (2002).

Plot Summary

Book One: Genesis

The narrative presents multiple points of view as Orleanna Price and her four daughters each tell their own story of their family's experience in the Congo. Orleanna Price opens *The Poisonwood Bible* from Sanderling Island, Georgia, where she lives decades after her family left the Congo. While she thinks of Africa, she speaks to her dead child who is unidentified at this point. She remembers one afternoon when they went on a picnic. Even though she admits that the child she is speaking to was her favorite, she begs her daughter to leave her alone.

Fourteen-year-old Leah begins the story of the family's life in Kilanga, Congo, in 1959. The Price family came from Bethlehem, Georgia, bringing as many of the comforts of home as they could carry. Five-year-old Ruth May talks about segregation back home and insists that her sisters will not be going to school with the village children. She admits that she is bad sometimes and explains that Adah, Leah's twin, is brain damaged and hates all of them.

Fifteen-year-old Rachel takes stock of the situation when they land and realizes that they will have no control over their lives in the Congo. She immediately misses the comforts of home more than the others. The village men, bare-chested women, and naked children welcome them, singing their own versions of Christian hymns. After Nathan delivers a brief sermon about God punishing "sinners" for their nakedness, the villagers turn away dismayed, some women covering their breasts. When the Prices begin to eat food prepared by the villagers, Orleanna warns her daughters not to spit it out. That night, Rachel cries herself to sleep.

Adah describes the village with its little mud houses inhabited by "tired thin women." She remains mute because doctors who determined that she has hemiplegia, or the inability to move one side of her body, insisted that only half of her brain worked and that she would never speak. Leah explains that during their first days in Congo, the girls were all afraid to leave the house. They took bitter quinine tablets to ward off malaria, their greatest fear. Leah vows to work hard with her father in growing crops for the village to help them and to gain his recognition, which she desperately craves.

The children are in awe of Mama Bekwa Tataba, a village woman who becomes their servant and teaches them how to survive in the Congo. Leah is shocked that she is contemptuous of her father's planting skills, but Mama Tataba shows them the proper way to plant crops. When the rainy season comes, his crops are washed away.

On Easter Sunday, Nathan stages a pageant to encourage baptism, but the villagers, whose attendance at church has been sparse, refuse. Orleanna fries up chicken and passes it out to the village, winning them over. The family has inherited from Brother Fowles, the previous missionary, a parrot named Methuselah who has picked up his previous owner's earthy language, which vexes Nathan. He punishes Leah, Ruth May, and Rachel, thinking that they have taught the bird to swear, by forcing them to write out biblical verses. None tells him that Methuselah had overheard Orleanna swearing over the seemingly impossible task of keeping the family fed.

Nathan sets off dynamite in the river to kill fish for the villagers and so inspire them to join the church. So many fish are killed, however, that the day of abundance becomes a day of waste since there is no way to preserve the fish that are not eaten. They soon realize that their garden will never provide food because there are no insects to pollinate the plants. One day the family suffers two losses: Mama Tataba leaves after Nathan gives a long sermon on baptism, and Nathan releases Methuselah into the wild. Nathan later discovers that the villagers refuse to allow him to baptize them because a girl was eaten the previous year by a crocodile when she was swimming in the river.

Book Two: The Revelation

The narrative shifts back to Orleanna on Sanderling Island, reflecting on how Nathan hardened his will during their time in Kilanga and grew more distant from the children and from her.

Back in the Congo, Leah is fascinated by the new sights of the jungle and claims it to be a heavenly paradise. Ruth May makes friends with many of the village children, and Leah makes her first friend, Pascal, who teaches her the names of everything she sees as well as important survival skills. When Ruth May breaks her arm after falling out of a tree, Eeben Axelroot, a bush pilot and mercenary, flies her and Nathan to the doctor in nearby Stanleyville.

Later, Anatole, the village schoolteacher and interpreter of Nathan's sermons, warns Nathan that

Media Adaptations

- Brilliance Audio produced an unabridged audio version of the novel, read by Dean Robertson, in 2004. As of 2006, no film version had been made.

their chief, Tata Ndu is concerned that his people will turn their backs on their own customs and traditions. Anatole explains that the only villagers who are attending his services are those who feel that their gods have abandoned them. Tata Ndu fears that if Nathan lures too many people to his church, the gods will become angry and punish the village. Nathan tries to force Anatole to support him, but Anatole remains neutral. He also warns Nathan that he must respect the village's spiritual leader, Tata Kuvundundu, and notes that the previous missionary, Brother Fowles, had gained the trust of the villagers and so had been able to bring most of them to church. This comparison angers Nathan, who later takes it out on Orleanna.

Nelson, an orphan boy in the village, comes to help out the Prices in return for a place to live. Adah, who sometimes spies on the villagers, notices that Anatole supports the movement for independence in the Congo. One day, the chief mistakenly thinks that she has been killed by a lion that was tracking her. As a result, more villagers come to Nathan's church, thinking that Jesus must have saved her. Their response pleases Nathan, who turns his attention briefly to Adah, which makes Leah jealous. After Nathan strikes Leah "hard for the sin of pride," she runs off into the jungle and does not return until nighttime.

In January, the Underdowns, who finance the Mission League, come to warn the Prices to leave before the conflict over the country's independence gets worse. They remind Nathan that his mission there was never sanctioned by the league. When the Underdowns tell him that no one is coming to replace him, Nathan refuses to go, believing that God will protect them.

When the rainy season comes, many villagers die from disease. Orleanna continually pleads with Nathan to leave, but he refuses to listen to her. Patrice Lumumba becomes prime minister of the newly independent Republic of the Congo. After the Underdowns evacuate, the Prices' monthly stipend, which they used to buy food, stops. Orleanna becomes despondent, and she and Ruth May spend their days in bed.

Book Three: The Judges

Back in the present, Orleanna insists to herself and to Ruth May that she was unable to do anything to prevent their suffering. She tells of Nathan's experience during World War II, in which he narrowly escaped the Death March from Bataan, which claimed the lives of all the men in his unit.

Orleanna and Ruth May are near death from malaria, which does not seem to concern Nathan. The three girls struggle to feed them all with no money to buy food. Anatole tells Leah about the current political situation in the Congo, noting the difficulties that Lumumba is having in his efforts to maintain independence. Whites are beginning to be attacked in the cities by black revolutionaries. Every night Orleanna begs Nathan to leave, but he persists in refusing.

While the sickness holds on to Ruth May, Orleanna slowly tries to pull herself together and take care of her family. She refuses to speak directly to Nathan. After her illness, she begins to speak her mind and insists she will get them out as soon as she can find a way. Leah begins to doubt her father's judgment as she recognizes that he is unable to take care of them.

Brother Fowles and his wife visit the Prices and present them with a much more benevolent view of the villagers that involves compromise and respect. When he and Nathan disagree about the interpretation of scripture and the best way to save the villagers, Nathan stomps off angrily. The Fowles give the family gifts of food and medicine.

Tata Ndu decides that he wants Rachel to be his wife. In order to escape that fate and a growing sense of danger, her father convinces her to pretend to be engaged to Axelroot. As they spend time together in a fake courting ritual, Rachel eventually grows to like him. Ruth May thinks about the diamonds she saw in the back of Axelroot's plane when she went with her father to see the doctor. She has told no one because Axelroot insisted that her family would get sick and die if she did. This discovery suggests that the pilot has been involved in smuggling operations.

Leah teaches at Anatole's school, and she and Anatole become good friends. Orleanna gives Rachel some of her jewelry for her seventeenth birthday. Adah notes that Ruth May has gotten better, but it seems as if the life has gone out of her. Leah begins to learn how to hunt in order to provide food for the family. She has difficulty though teaching the children who are becoming increasingly wary of whites during the political upheaval. She and Anatole have long talks about the black Africans' lives and culture in contrast to that of Americans. Axelroot tells Rachel that Lumumba is going to be murdered. Adah hears the same news while listening to his radio but with the added information that the Americans are behind the plot.

One night, the village is attacked by ants, which cover the ground, destroying everything in their path. All run to the river except Ruth May and Adah, who both need assistance. For the first time, Adah speaks out loud, asking for her mother's help. Orleanna is forced to make a choice, and she chooses Ruth May, abandoning Adah, who is later rescued by Anatole. He tells Leah that the villagers have taken the family to safety and that they have been looking out for them during these past months. Feeling that Anatole is the only person she can believe in now. Leah tells him that she loves him.

Book Four: Bel and The Serpent

In the present, Orleanna recalls the details of the political unrest in the Congo, noting that the U.S. government organized a coup that put Joseph Mobutu into power. Back in the Congo, the villagers hold an election and vote against accepting Christ as the savior of Kilanga.

Leah begins to openly defy Nathan after the vote. The villagers plan a hunt so that they will not die of starvation, and Leah participates. She kills an impala, but one of the villagers claims that he killed it. The chief cuts off a piece for her, but she throws it back, hitting the man who had argued with her. Rachel constructs a secret plan to have Axelroot take her away from the village.

In an effort to scare or punish anyone who supports the Prices, Tata Kuvundu, the village's spiritual leader, places a snake near Anatole's bed and another in the chicken house where Nelson sleeps. The latter one kills Ruth May. A devastated Orleanna prepares her for burial and then moves all of their possessions outside of the house, so that the villagers can take what they want.

Book Five: Exodus

After Ruth May's burial, Orleanna begins walking with her remaining daughters to Leopoldville, leaving Nathan behind. During the journey, they become sick with malaria. When they arrive at the village of Bulungu, they stop for a while as Orleanna decides what to do next. She eventually continues on with Adah, leaving Leah, who is delirious with fever, behind in Anatole's care until she is well enough to travel home. Rachel leaves with Axelroot. During her convalescence, Leah's love for Anatole deepens. When she gets better, she decides to stay in the Congo with him.

By 1962, Rachel and Axelroot are living together in Johannesburg, South Africa, where he works in the mining industry. Adah is back home in Georgia attending Emory University where she is studying medicine.

In 1964, Leah is staying in a convent in the jungle for protection as Anatole aids the revolutionaries and is eventually imprisoned by Mobutu's forces. She hears that Nathan is living in the jungle and is ill. Rachel has adapted well to segregated Johannesburg but decides to leave Axelroot who treats her badly. She seduces a French ambassador and soon marries him.

By Christmas of 1968, Adah has discovered that her condition had been misdiagnosed, and she is able to get rid of her limp. She is afraid, however, that she will lose her identity if she is cured of her disability. Leah comes to Georgia for a visit with Anatole, now her husband, and their son. Orleanna has become a civil rights worker. Adah fears that she will lose Orleanna to Leah and her family but soon realizes that her mother needs her and is comforted by the thought.

In 1974, Leah and Anatole now have three children. She constantly fears that Anatole will again be imprisoned. In 1978, Rachel runs the Equatorial, a resort near Brazzaville in the French Congo, left to her by her third husband. The resort, which was formerly a plantation, gets a good tourist trade, and Rachel is content there.

In 1981, Anatole has been sent back to prison after returning from a stay in the United States. Leah determines that her family needs to go back to the Congo because they have a responsibility to the country. Also, she insists "the air is just blank in America. . . . You can't ever smell what's around you." Leah is desperately lonely without Anatole. In the United States, Adah has become an expert in tropical diseases.

In 1984, the three sisters reunite in the Congo, a meeting that becomes, in Rachel's terms, "a sensational failure." She explains, "For the entire trip I think the three of us were all on speaking terms for only one complete afternoon." They argue mainly about their views of Africa and its people. Leah tells her sisters that their father has died. After an incident on the river when he tried to baptize some of the village children, their boat overturned, and the children drowned or were killed by a crocodile. As a result, the villagers set fire to a tower that Nathan had climbed up, and he burned to death.

In 1985, Orleanna moves to Sanderling Island off the coast of Georgia. By 1986, Leah has four sons and is living in the Congo, renamed Zaire, where she and Anatole work with farmers and try to establish a cooperative. They hope to be able to move to Angola, a truly independent nation beyond the reach of U.S. influence.

Book Six: Son of the Three Children

Rachel's resort has become quite profitable. Now living in Angola where she teaches health classes, Leah admits, "Quinine just barely keeps my malaria in check." Orleanna also suffers from the diseases she picked up in Africa.

Book Seven: The Eyes in the Trees

Ruth May controls the narrative in the final pages as she speaks to her mother and sisters, insisting that she will not judge them. She notes that Orleanna and her sisters tried to find her grave to say goodbye, but the village is no longer there. Ruth May forgives them and tells them, "Slide the weight from your shoulders and move forward. . . . You will forgive and remember."

Characters

Eeben Axelroot

Eeben Axelroot is the self-serving Afrikaner bush pilot, diamond smuggler, and CIA agent who helps Rachel escape Kilanga. They later live together in a common-law marriage until Rachel leaves him for a government official.

Brother Fowles

Brother Fowles, the missionary that had lived in Kilanga before the arrival of the Prices, "entered into unconventional alliances with the local people" and was consequently removed by the Mission League.38 He does not interpret the Bible as strictly as does Nathan and so can be much more flexible as he tries to help the villagers. His sympathetic and generous response to the villagers provides a model of what real missionary work can accomplish.

Tata Kuvundu

Tata Kuvundu, the village's spiritual leader, fears that Nathan will interfere with tradition and thus his power among his people. He tries to remove those whom he feels threaten his power by planting mamba snakes in their beds. One snake that was left in the chicken house for Nelson kills Ruth May.

Patrice Lumumba

Patrice Lumumba becomes the first elected president of the Republic of the Congo. His refusal to accept American influence in his country causes his ousting during a coup. He is later beaten to death by government forces. Anatole's support of Lumumba and the principles for which he stood makes him an enemy of Mobutu's government and as a result, he is frequently jailed.

Joseph Mobutu

Joseph Mobutu installs himself as president of the Republic of the Congo after leading a U.S. backed coup that ousted Lumumba from power. He ruled the country as a corrupt and tyrannical dictator for thirty years, enjoying a wealthy lifestyle while his people suffered in poverty.

Mama Mwanza

Mama Mwanza, one of the Prices' neighbors, had her legs burned so badly that they have become useless. She is able to move by scooting around on her hands. The Prices respect her resourcefulness, and Adah identifies with her.

Tata Ndu

Village chief Tata Ndu fears that Nathan and his teachings will usurp the chief's position among his people. Tata Ndu decides that he wants to take Rachel as one of his brides but does not pursue her when he is told that she is engaged to Axelroot.

Nelson

In exchange for a place to live, twelve-year-old Nelson, a village orphan who is one of Anatole's best students, helps the Price family after Mama Tataba leaves. He teaches the girls African customs and survival skills.

Anatole Ngemba

Anatole is the village schoolteacher who later becomes a revolutionary. He interprets Nathan's sermons and becomes sympathetic to the Prices' difficulty in adjusting to village life. Leah falls in love with him, and the two marry and have four children.

Pascal

Leah names her first child after nine-year-old Pascal who becomes her first friend in the Congo.

Adah Price

Adah suffers from a condition called hemiplegia, which makes the left side of her body useless. She blames her twin sister, Leah, for this infirmity, insisting that she grew weak in her mother's womb while Leah grew strong. Adah, who has decided not to speak, takes a cynical view of the world but notices everything. She claims, "When you do not speak, other people presume you to be deaf or feebleminded and promptly make a show of their own limitations." Since, according to her, she is "mostly . . . lost in the shuffle," she isolates herself from others. Diagnosed like her twin as gifted, she spends her time thinking of palindromes, poetry, and math.

Adah feels more accepted in the Congo where so many black Africans have disabilities that "bodily damage is more or less considered to be a byproduct of living, not a disgrace." As a result, she enjoys "a benign approval in Kilanga that [she has] never, ever known in Bethlehem, Georgia." She later admits that she has "long relied on the comforts of martyrdom." After she returns home, she is able to regain the use of her left side and becomes a researcher, studying deadly viruses that afflict Africans.

Leah Price

When she and her family arrive in the Congo, Leah is a firm believer in their mission and is devoted to her father, whom she idolizes. Initially, she is desperate for his approval and always wants to be with him. She never contradicts him or questions his autocratic rule of their family. Her compassionate nature, however, forces her to recognize her father's self-serving motives, and she rejects him as well as his religion. As she falls in love with Anatole, her new ideal, she becomes deeply involved with the plight of black Africans. Adah claims that "her religion *is* the suffering." Anatole warns her against trying "to make life a mathematics problem with [her] in the center and everything coming out equal." His nickname for her is "béene-beene," which means "as true as the truth can be."

Nathan Price

Nathan Price, the Baptist missionary who brings his family to the Congo, is an autocratic man whose religious zeal makes him rigid and unsympathetic. Orleanna recognizes that he could never love her because that "would have trespassed on his devotion to all mankind." He has antiquated views of women and their abilities, illustrated by his pronouncement: "Sending a girl to college is like pouring water in your shoes. . . . It's hard to say which is worse, seeing it run out and waste the water, or seeing it hold in and wreck the shoes."

His experiences during World War II made him "contemptuous of failure," and caused his "steadfast disdain for cowardice [to turn] to obsession." He had narrowly escaped the Death March from Bataan during the war, which claimed the lives of all the men in his unit except his because he had been evacuated due to an injury. Since then, he has carried the guilty suspicion and the fear that he was a coward, believing that God was always watching and judging him. As a result, he determined to prove his worthiness by saving more souls than were lost in his company. He "felt it had been a mistake to bend his will, in any way, to Africa," and so he became harder as time passed there. His monomaniacal pursuit of salvation for himself and the villagers blinds him to the dangers he and his family face, and so he refuses to let them leave.

Orleanna Price

Orleanna blames herself for her family's troubles. Adah's disability, she feels, was punishment for her own despair over getting pregnant with twins so soon after Rachel was born. She also blames herself for failing to protect her children from Africa and from their father, which results in Ruth May's death. When they first arrive, Orleanna tries to stand up to Nathan but is not strong enough to question the traditional role he forces upon her. Their difficult life in Africa begins to embolden her, however, as Ruth notes, "Mama has this certain voice sometimes. Not exactly sassing back, but just about nearly." When Ruth May dies, something in Orleanna snaps that gives her the courage to attempt to get her remaining daughters out of Africa. Ruth May's death, for which she continues to take responsibility, haunts her for the rest of her life.

Rachel Price

Rachael is a teenage prima donna when she arrives in the Congo, a status she struggles to maintain there. Her self-centered and materialistic nature does not change during the three decades that she lives in Africa. She does show certain resilience, however, as she weds three different men and eventually inherits a successful resort, all the while refusing to acknowledge the suffering that surrounds her.

Ruth May Price

Fierce, imperious Ruth May is "surprisingly stubborn for a child of five" and is always ready for a new adventure. Ironically, she is the one who is ultimately destroyed by Africa, which triggers feelings of guilt in her mother and her sisters.

Mama Bekwa Tataba

Mama Bekwa Tataba works as the Prices' servant after they arrive in the Congo. The girls initially are wary of her, but she teaches them how to survive. She also stands up to Nathan, who eventually frustrates her so much with his demands that the villagers submit to baptism that she leaves.

Mr. Underdown

Mr. Underdown and his wife are Belgian nationals who manage the finances for the missionary programs in the Congo. They represent the white ruling class in the Congo as they live in relative comfort in Leopoldville amidst of the overwhelming poverty of the black Africans. They flee immediately after the Congo gains independence.

Themes

White Supremacy

The novel chronicles the Belgian colonization of the Congo as well as U.S. efforts to control the country after it gains independence. The Price family unwittingly becomes involved in this process after they relocate to Kilanga. The doctor who sets Ruth May's broken arm tries to point this out to Nathan when he tells him, "We Belgians made slaves of [the black Africans] and cut off their hands in the rubber plantations. Now you Americans have them for a slave wage in the mines and let them cut off their own hands." He insists that Nathan and his family "are stuck with the job of trying to make amends." Nathan, however, refuses to accept this responsibility, insisting that "American aid will be the Congo's salvation."

Nathan and Rachel accept and insist upon the supremacy of their position in Africa, but the other members of the Price family feel a sense of guilt. Orleanna articulates this emotion when she notes, "I was just one more of those women who clamp their mouths shut and wave the flag as their nation rolls off to conquer another in war." Leah tries to alleviate some of the damage by devoting herself to improving the lives of black Africans.

Free Will

Free will is a term used to describe one's ability to make choices independently of internal compulsions or external, environmental influences. Those who believe that humans can exercise free will reject the Puritanical notion of predestination. The issue of free will relates to the interactions between Nathan and his family and the Africans. When he tries to impose his interpretation of Christian doctrine on the villagers, they are able to resist his control since they have already established their own spiritual and cultural views. Nathan's wife and daughters, however, who have not had the opportunity to establish a strong sense of themselves outside the family, have allowed Nathan to take control of their lives.

Their experiences in the Congo eventually prompt Orleanna and Leah to stand up to Nathan and determine their own destiny. After Leah observes her father's self-serving motives in his interaction with the Africans, she refuses to allow him to control her behavior and begins to adopt some of the villagers' customs.

While Orleanna also recognizes Nathan's cruel treatment of the Africans and his family members, her movement toward independence occurs much more slowly. During one of her monologues to Ruth May, she tries to explain why she chose to stay in the Congo as long as she did: "I wonder what you'll name my sin: complicity? Loyalty? Stupefaction? How can you tell the difference? Is my sin a failure of virtue, or of competence. I knew Rome was burning, but I had just enough water to scrub the floor, so I did what I could." Gradually, however, she becomes strong enough to exercise some measure of free will as she makes active choices in her attempts to protect her children.

Topics for Further Study

- Some critics have complained that the novel does not give Nathan a voice. Write one of the Price family's experiences in the Congo from his point of view.
- Read one of Kingsolver's novels that is set in the American Southwest, such as *Pigs in Heaven*. Compare and contrast in essay form the family dynamics in that novel and *The Poisonwood Bible*.
- Research and prepare a PowerPoint demonstration about missionary work in the Congo.
- How would you depict the novel's five narrative voices in a film? Write a screenplay of a portion of the novel that incorporates the Price family's different points of view.

After the wars of independence begin, Orleanna gains the courage to question Nathan's authority as she tries to convince him to leave the Congo even though she knows she will face his wrath. When the ants invade the village, she is able to make the difficult choice of which daughter to save, determining, "When push comes to shove, a mother takes care of her children from the bottom up." Ruth's death causes Orleanna to break away completely from Nathan's dominance and to take control of her family's destiny. Kingsolver suggests that the desire to determine one's own destiny can be strong enough to overcome impediments to free will.

Style

Narrative with Multiple Voices

Multiple voices narrate this book with the point of view shifting back and forth among Orleanna and her four daughters, providing different perspectives on the family's experiences in the Congo. Kingsolver employs these contrasting voices to suggest the subjective nature of observation and the impossibility of achieving a single objective point of view of other cultures and of personal experience. Each of the female voices in the narrative observes the Congo through her personal lens which has been shaped by experience. Orleanna, for example, relates her story of the Congo through a mother's eyes as she struggles to provide food and shelter for her family and keep her children safe. Thus, her focus is on what food is available and what dangers lurk outside the hut.

Each narrative angle also conveys contrasts between American attitudes toward the region. Rachel sees the Congo as an American materialist who is used to the comforts of home. Her response when they first arrive is an honest account of all of their feelings toward the naked villagers and the meal they offer them. She, however, maintains her initial assessment, while the others' views change over time as they learn more about their surroundings. Leah is the American idealist, first, following her father's missionary role, and then adopting Anatole's revolutionary stance. She ultimately rejects her American home for a difficult but satisfying African life that provides her with a sense of purpose and value.

Ruth May is the outgoing adventurer, making fast friends with the village children. Adah is the cynical observer, who is ultimately changed by her sympathetic response to the disease-ridden population. Orleanna becomes the voice of American guilt in consciousness of how Americans either allowed the corruption of colonization to occur or participated in the overthrow of governments for their own self interests. Nathan is not given a voice in the narrative, but his position is symbolized by the novel's title. Nathan's mispronounced declaration, "*TATA JESUS IS BANGALA*," which translates ironically to "Jesus is poisonwood," becomes a metaphor for the same self-serving arrogance that turns a noble ideal into poison. His misuse of the local language and the meaning he conveys accidentally in the process also suggest how the imposition of one set of cultural beliefs on a foreign culture is undermined by the outsider's inability to know the culture he is presuming to change.

Historical Context

The Colonization of the Congo

In the late 1870s, Leopold II, king of Belgium, gained control of the territories that made up the Congo in an effort to ensure his country's prosperity. He effectively set up a colonial empire there and established the International Association as a cover for his using the natural resources there as his own personal asset. Soon after, Leopold appointed himself head of the newly established, Independent State of the Congo, an ironic name since it was literally an enslaved state, which included the land known in the early 2000s as Zaire. Leopold took control of all land and business operations, including the lucrative trade in rubber and ivory as he ruled from a large estate in the region northeast of Kinshasa. Belgian-backed companies also took control of mining operations.

At the turn of the century, the public began to become aware of the harsh treatment of black Africans, especially those who worked for the rubber companies. As a result, the Belgian parliament wrested jurisdiction from Leopold in 1908 and established the Belgian Congo. Forced labor was eliminated under the new government, but European investments still controlled the country's wealth, and blacks were not allowed any part in the government or the economy. Black laborers worked the vast copper and diamond mining operations, while Europeans managed them.

The Struggle for Independence

In 1955, as calls for independence were mounting, Belgium constructed a thirty-year plan for independence, which the government hoped would ensure continued domination in the Congo and at the same time improve the lives of black Africans. However, nationalists such as Patrice Lumumba, who led the leftist movement called National Congolese, continued their protests against the Belgian-controlled government. In 1959, nationalists rioted in Kinshasa, initiating what became the steady decline in Belgian power.

In 1960, Belgium decided to give up the governance of the colony, and Lumumba became prime minister of the newly independent Republic of the Congo. Soon after, however, ethnic and personal rivalries threatened the stability of the new government. When the Congolese army mutinied, Lumumba sought aid from the Soviet Union as he tried to maintain control, but the country was soon seized by Joseph Mobutu who had Lumumba arrested and later murdered while allegedly trying to escape.

By the end of the 1960s, the Congo was divided into four parts, with Mobutu controlling the west, including Kinshasa. With U.S. weapons, Belgian soldiers, and white mercenaries, the central government stabilized, and in 1965, Mobutu proclaimed himself president. He ruled for thirty years with the backing of the U.S. government.

Bayei Village in Northern Botswana may provide a view of Africa similar to that experienced by the characters in The Poisonwood Bible

Critical Overview

Most reviews of *The Poisonwood Bible* were positive, though some stressed drawbacks while praising some parts. John Leonard wrote a glowing tribute in *The Nation* to Kingsolver's artistry. Leonard claims that in this novel, "Barbara Kingsolver has dreamed a magnificent fiction and a ferocious bill of indictment." Noting her shift from the domestic, southwestern American settings of her previous work, he concludes: "this new, mature, angry, heartbroken, expansive out-of-Africa Kingsolver—is at last our very own Lessing and our very own Gordimer, and she is, as one of her characters said of another in an earlier novel, 'beautiful beyond the speed of light.'"

Similarly impressed, Gayle Greene, in *The Women's Review of Books*, confesses, "not since *Beloved* have I been so engaged by a new work of fiction," and she praises "a story and characters that are gripping, a family saga that assumes epic and Biblical proportions." On the serious side, she applauds the novel's "strong political message, offering a scathing indictment of America's part in carving up Africa." But she also commends the novel's humor: "it has you laughing one moment and gasping with horror the next." In all, Greene finds it to be "a complex, textured work, its imagery patterns resonating across levels of meaning. . . . It is multivocal and multiphonic, its meaning not in a single voice but in the play of voices against one another."

Joining in, a reviewer for *Publishers Weekly* finds *The Poisonwood Bible* a "risky but resoundingly successful novel" that "delivers a compelling family saga, a sobering picture of the horrors of fanatic fundamentalism and an insightful view of an exploited country crushed by the heel of colonialism and then ruthlessly manipulated by a bastion of democracy." The reviewer praises its "marvelous mix of trenchant character portrayal, unflagging narrative thrust and authoritative background detail," and, like Greene, finds its humor "pervasive, too, artfully integrated into the children's misapprehensions of their world." The review concludes with the insistence that "Kingsolver moves into new moral terrain in this powerful, convincing and emotionally resonant novel."

Other reviewers were not as unconditional in their praise. Tim Stafford in *Christianity Today*, describing the novel as "grand and tragic," admits that "Kingsolver . . . writes beautifully and incisively of African village life." Stafford, however, finds fault with her characterization of Nathan Price, which, he claims, creates "a hole at the center of the book." He asserts that readers might "expect more insight" into this "incomprehensible" man. He also criticizes her "cartoonish story of idiot missionaries and shady CIA operatives destroying the delicate fabric of the Congo." Yet, her focus on the female members of the Price family "almost absolves the book of its shortcomings." He concludes: "Kingsolver writes luminously of these women who flex and cling to life, surviving, absorbing blows, still hoping. Their voices are unforgettable."

Stephen D. Fox in *Critique* criticizes Kingsolver's depiction of the villagers who, he claims, are "quite generalized, almost completely lacking in noteworthy or unique customs." Kimberly A. Koza in *Critique* concludes that the work "gains its power through [Kingsolver's] exploration of the Price women's struggles to judge their own complicity in both their family's fate and that of the Congo" but complains that her "shift to polemic in the second part of the novel often leads her to generalize and, at times, to oversimplify historical complexities."

Criticism

Wendy Perkins

Perkins is a professor of American and English literature and film. In this essay, she examines the theme of survival.

The threats to the Price family's physical survival in *The Poisonwood Bible* are obvious and immediate. They must find enough food to eat, stay away from poisonous snakes and tarantulas, and guard against dysentery and malaria. Less obvious but more complex are the personal obstacles that they face. One such problem is created by Nathan's religious fanaticism, fueled by his own insecurities, which prevents him from successfully adapting to his surroundings. His inability to overcome this obstacle ultimately destroys two lives—his and Ruth May's. The rest of the Price family are able to cope with many physical and personal trials during their time in the Congo. Yet, like the malaria that lingers in their systems long after their escape from Kilanga, emotional damage remains, which has a profound effect on the next three decades of their lives.

"For the next few decades, all of her daughters will be affected by these events, but none as much as Orleanna, who will experience a crippling sense of guilt."

As they are taught by the villagers to keep external dangers at bay, the Price women learn how to evade, to adapt, and to confront internal obstacles to their survival. Initially, they face a profound sense of culture shock compounded by their homesickness after their relocation to a foreign, often dangerous world. Their first response is to try to hold onto their American identity. They bring with them artifacts from American culture, like Underwood deviled ham, Band-Aids, Anacin, and number 2 pencils. As these goods run or wear out, however, they are forced to adapt to local customs regarding diet, farming methods, and social interaction—all except Rachel, who refuses to relinquish her American identity with its pronounced superiority and entitlement.

At first, Ruth May and Leah have the easiest time. Ruth May, who exhibits a child's natural adaptability, is the first to make friends with the village children. Leah soon makes friends of her own while she gains an appreciation of the beauty of the jungle, which she considers a heavenly paradise. Adah's gradual acceptance of her surroundings is made less complicated by her status as outsider. As she arrives in the Congo, she feels the same sense of disconnection she felt at home in a world that both pitied and ostracized her for her disability. When the villagers, who are used to physical deformities, do not treat her as more odd than they consider the rest of her family, she is able to settle into her new home. Orleanna's task is more difficult since her main focus is her family's health and security.

The family's process of adaptation is made more complex and challenging by Nathan's rigidity and righteousness. In his steadfast refusal to accept any point of view other than his own, he presses

What Do I Read Next?

- In her first novel *The Bean Trees* (1988), Barbara Kingsolver writes of the beginning of the relationship between Taylor Greer and her adopted Cherokee daughter, Turtle, a story that is picked up in the sequel, *Pigs in Heaven* (1993).
- Barbara Kingsolver's *Homeland and Other Stories* (1989) contains twelve short stories centering on various characters who struggle to form and maintain relationships.
- Ernest Hemingway's *Green Hills of Africa* (1935) is a stirring account of a two-month safari Hemingway and his wife Pauline joined in 1933. In the work, Hemingway reveals what the experience taught him about Africa and about himself.
- Beryl Markham's *West with the Night* (1942) chronicles her exciting life as an African bush pilot in the 1930s.

all to conform to his rules. His insistence that the villagers be baptized causes palpable tension between the family and the village that he refuses to try to alleviate. Adah complains that he speaks for everyone in his family since "he views himself as the captain of a sinking mess of female minds."

Adah and Rachel try to stay out of his way as much as possible to avoid his wrath. Orleanna, however, must deal with his tyranny on a daily basis as she struggles to protect and nurture her daughters. During their first few months in the Congo, she is "too dumbfounded to speak up for herself" or for her family when Nathan ignores their needs, since this is the role he has forced upon her from the beginning of their relationship. She admits, "Nathan was in full possession of the country once known as Orleanna Wharton. . . . Because in those days, you see, that's how a life like mine was known." In an attempt to justify her passive stance, she insists that she was "thoroughly bent to the shape of marriage," likening herself to the parrot Methuselah who, like she, had no wings.

Leah deals with her father's autocracy by fully accepting his dogma. She devotes herself to his mission wholeheartedly and spends her days trying desperately to please him. His garden becomes the focal point of her world as she tries to help him realize his vision of bringing new crops to the village. She begins, however, to question his beliefs and his character when she observes his refusal to address the real needs of the villagers and of his family. As Anatole presents her with a different view of the Congo and its people, Leah begins a move away from her dependence on her father. Anatole becomes her new ideal.

Orleanna tries to stand up to Nathan as her family faces new dangers during the country's revolutionary stirrings, but his will proves too strong for her, and defeated, she retreats to her bed, leaving her children to fend for themselves. Ruth May notes that when she looks in her eyes, "there isn't any Mama home inside there . . . Something in her is even worse hurt than what Adah's got." After a month in bed watching her daughters struggle to get food for them all, Orleanna summons the courage to resume her responsibilities; she declares that she will do anything that she can to help her daughters escape.

Orleanna is unable to get the family out, however, before two disastrous events occur: the ants' invasion that prompts her to choose one daughter over the other, and Ruth May's death. For the next few decades, all of her daughters will be affected by these events, but none as much as Orleanna, who will experience a crippling sense of guilt.

Rachel is the least affected by what she experiences in Kilanga. She admits that until the moment that Ruth May dies, she believes that she could go home and pretend the Congo never happened, which echoes the thoughts of the entire family. Yet she has learned how to survive comparatively unscathed. On the night the ants invade, she sticks out her elbows and is carried along by the crowd, which is what she continues to do for the rest of her time in Africa. What saves Rachel is her refusal "to feel the slightest responsibility" for what happens to the family in the Congo and her insistence that "there is no sense spending too much time alone in the dark."

Leah stays in Africa as well, but she does so because the continent has had a profound effect on her worldview. Her ideological focus has shifted from her father's distorted evangelicalism to Anatole's more inspiring vision of independence and activism. She has faced the devastating results of the colonialist enterprise in the Congo, which have shown her that "there is not justice in this world," but "there's the possibility of balance. Unbearable burdens that the world somehow does bear with a certain grace." Adah suggests that her sister feels guilt by association when she insists that Leah's mission in post-revolutionary Africa has become "like a hair shirt" to her.

Adah has also been intensely affected by her experiences in the Congo. After her mother chooses Ruth May to save during the invasion of the ants, Adah is crushed but is filled with a renewed desire to survive. When her mother takes her out of Africa and leaves Leah behind, she stops blaming her sister for her disability. Yet, she wonders, "How can I reasonably survive beyond the death of Ruth May and all those children? Will salvation be the death of me?" Eventually, she finds an unconditional salvation in her renewed relationship with her mother and in her own medical research.

The choice Orleanna is forced to make during the ant invasion, coupled with Ruth May's death, almost destroys Orleanna. Adah notes that since the ants, Orleanna "has been creeping her remorse in flat-footed circles around" her. After Ruth May's death, nothing matters to Orleanna except trying to ensure her family's escape. When her remaining daughters are safe, however, the burden of guilt becomes overwhelming. She continually talks to the deceased Ruth May, desperately trying to justify her own actions. After declaring, "I could have been a different mother . . . Could have straightened up and seen what was coming," she tries to insist that she could have done nothing to save her. Yet, Adah and Leah recognize that their mother has not forgiven herself for Ruth May's death. Adah explains, "Mother is still *ruthless*. She claims I am her youngest now but she still is clutching her baby. She will put down that burden, I believe, on the day she hears forgiveness from Ruth May herself."

Ruth May grants that forgiveness in the final pages of the novel, perhaps as a manifestation of her mother's need for absolution. She insists that she will forgive her as she tells her mother, "Slide the weight from your shoulders and move forward. You are afraid you might forget, but you never will. You will forgive and remember." Thus, the women in the Price family survive the physical and emotional impact of their time in the Congo as they recognize, in Adah's words, "The power is in the balance; we are our injuries, as much as we are our successes."

Source: Wendy Perkins, Critical Essay on *The Poisonwood Bible*, in *Novels for Students*, Thomson Gale, 2007.

Elaine R. Ognibene

In the following essay, Ognibene discusses the author's elucidation of how a dominating culture shrouds the truth about greed and power in the "scriptural rhetoric" of "righteous zeal and religious reckoning" while exploring the complexities of "clashing cultural views."

In his history of the Congo during the reign of Belgium's King Leopold (1876–1909), Adam Hochschild tells a riveting and terrifying story of greed and terror, as well as what he terms the "politics of forgetting" the hard truths that have emerged over the last hundred years or so. He shows how a dominant European and American technique for diverting attention from the truth involved a language of righteous zeal and religious reckoning, a scriptural rhetoric used to hide the real story of imperial greed. Several scholars from contemporary critical schools—deconstructionists, Marxists, and postcolonialists address the issue in a similar fashion. In the words of Phillipa Kafka, they work at "(un)doing the missionary position" in literature, advancing new notions of "exclusionary identity, dominating heterogeneity and universality or in more blunt language, White supremacy" (1997, xv), Relying on Henry A. Giroux's words, Kafka defines the missionary position as "monolithic views of culture, nationalism and difference" (xvi).

In *The Poisonwood Bible,* Barbara Kingsolver illustrates the hypocrisy of religious rhetoric and practice that sacrifices the many for the good of the few in power, drawing a clear parallel between a missionary's attitude and colonial imperialism. To the author, Nathan Price does not represent the missionary profession: he "is a symbolic figure . . . suggesting many things about the way U.S. and Europe have approached Africa with a history of cultural arrogance and misunderstanding at every turn" (http//www.kingsolver.Com/dialogue/12_questions.html). Nonetheless, Kingsolver does show how, contrary to popular opinion, religion and politics are not separate entities, but a powerful combined force used historically not only to "convert the savages" but to convert the masses to believe that what is done

"In *The Poisonwood Bible,* Barbara Kingsolver illustrates the hypocrisy of religious rhetoric and practice that sacrifices the many for the good of the few in power, drawing a clear parallel between a missionary's attitude and colonial imperialism."

in the name of democratic, Christian principles is done for the greater good.

Even King Leopold understood the power of public relations: he knew "that what matters, often, is less the substance of a political event than how the public perceives it" (1998, 251), or, as Hochschild says, "If you control perceptions, you control the event" (251). Leopold used democratic, religious rhetoric to control his rape and pillage of the Congo; he "recognized that a colonial push ... would require a strong humanitarian veneer," so he promised to abolish the slave trade and establish "peace among the chiefs ..." (Hochschild 1998, 45). Building the infrastructure necessary to "exploit his colony," Leopold raised money through the Vatican "urging the Catholic Church to buy Congo bonds to encourage the spread of Christ's word" (92). Using Catholic and Protestant missionaries to set up children's colonies, theoretically to offer religious instruction and vocational information, Leopold's true goal was to build his own kingdom. "He deployed priests, almost as if they were soldiers ... to areas where he wanted to strengthen his influence" (133–34). Describing 19th century colonizing behaviors, Hochschild observes, "In the Congo the Ten Commandments were practiced even less than in most colonies" (138). Ironic how almost a century after Leopold, deceptive and destructive "missionary" rhetoric persists and prevents human rights. In the United States, the rhetoric appears in a variety of groups from the Promise Keepers to the Kansas Board of Education, but the message is always one of righteous coercion. In post-colonial Africa, there is "still a form of neocolonialism" that denies human rights. As Raoul Peck, award winning filmmaker of *Lumumba*, states, "things haven't changed." Both at the time of Lumumbu's decolonization movement and now, the Congo is "too rich in resources to be left to the Congolese" (Riding 2001, 13, 26).

Numerous contemporary novels, such as *Crossing the River* by Caryl Philips, *Mean Spirit* by Linda Hogan, or *Comfort Woman* by Nora Okja-Keller provide examples of the missionary position gone awry. In these novels, authors often invert the journey motif. Men who see themselves as good Christians who lead good lives learn from their journeys that the concepts of Christianity upon which they have based their lives are inherently paradoxical. Some lose their way and sense of purpose, because neither scripture nor faith offers them an understanding of the disorder in their lives. Some ironically convert to "pagan" rituals and ways; others wander seeking answers to questions that have no answers and living isolated lives. Although locales shift and the specific religious affiliation, age and race of the missionary change, one recurring theme crosses culture and class lines: the men all see themselves as carriers of the "Word," superior to the populations they aim to convert. Over the course of the novels, most of the men alter their missionary position as their own words turn back upon them.

One man who does not change is Nathan Price. In *The Poisonwood Bible,* Nathan's evangelical, self-righteous, judgmental attitudes threaten the lives of his family, as well as the people in the remote Congolese village of Kilanga. A zealot, Nathan risks lives in pursuit of his obsessive vision. An abusive father, Nathan goes mad for the second time in his life, as he tries to convert the natives over a year and a half period of hunger, disease, drought, witchcraft, political wars, pestilential rains, Lumumba, Mobutu, Ike, and the CIA. The effects of Nathan's missionary position on his wife, Orleanna, his four daughters, and the Congolese become clear as Kingsolver parallels Nathan's behaviors to imperialist actions in the Congo.

Kingsolver uses multiple narrators to construct her political allegory. Orleanna, Leah, Adah, Rachel, and Ruth May tell their stories in contrapuntal turns, offering personal versions of the consequences of the Reverend's taking them to the Congo. Despite dramatically different voices, all, even Rachel, Ms. Malaprop of the novel, tell stories of change as well as discovery. Most reveal specifics about intellectual and spiritual awakenings; the loss of one kind of belief and birth of another. All, even five year old Ruth, draw some parallel between the tyranny of politics in the Congo and the war in their private lives. And all expose the missionary tactics of the man Adah calls "Our Father" as monolithic, abusive, and destructive. As the characters tell their stories in interrupted sequences that move back and forth among speakers, the narrative point of view creates a field of reciprocal subjects, all crucial to the story but none exclusive or central. The heart of the novel emerges only by stacking multiple renditions and discerning the similarities and differences that together shape the broader view. As tension builds up to crisis, their stories accomplish one of Kingsolver's stated aims: they "connect consequences with actions" in the Price family and the broader world as well (Sarnatoro 1998, 1).

In the beginning, "God said unto them . . . have dominion . . . over every living thing that moveth upon the earth" (Genesis 1:28). The Prices's journey into the heart of the Congo begins with Nathan, like King Leopold, taking the words of "Genesis" literally. The daughters' stories come from decades of journal-keeping but are recounted as circumstances unfolded; Orleanna's story comes from a kind of guilty hindsight. The voice that opens each of the first five chapters ("Genesis," "The Revelation," "The Judges," "Bel and the Serpent," and "Exodus") where scriptural titles set the themes is that of Orleanna Price, the wife of a man "who could never love her," a woman who tells her story to the ghost of her dead child, and a person who sees herself as "captive witness" to events that occurred during her year and one-half (1959–61) in the Congo. To Orleanna, "hell hath no fury like a Baptist preacher." Her narrative focuses upon the family stepping down "on a place [they] believed unformed," on their desire to have dominion, on their limited knowledge of almost everything, and on the unnameable guilt that she still carries with her. Orleanna's story illustrates the complicity that comes with silence and the "common hunger" shared by Nathan and others out to conquer the Congo.

In "The Revelation," Orleanna explains her initial ignorance about bringing Betty Crocker cake mixes into the jungle and her slow learning about Congolese cultural practices. She wanted to be a part of Kilanga and be Nathan's wife, but she acknowledges her true position: "I was his instrument, his animal. Nothing more . . . just one of those women who clamp their mouths shut and wave the flag as their nation rolls off to conquer another in war." Orleanna muses retrospectively on her political mistakes as well as her cultural ones, recognizing parallel behaviors between Nathan and national leaders. Thinking about Eisenhower's need for control and retired diplomat George F. Kennan's belief that the U.S. should not have " 'the faintest moral responsibility for Africa' ", she reconstructs Nathan's similar need for control, as well as his desire for distance from the consequences of his acts.

The longer she lives in Kilanga, the clearer Orleanna's vision becomes. Remembering a man who seduced her with promises of "green pastures," she now sees a "righteous" and unbending judge, an abusive husband and father for whom ownership is the norm. Trying to make sense of Nathan's transformation to a tyrant, Orleanna correctly identifies the turning point to be World War II and Nathan's escape from the Death March from Bataan that killed the rest of his company. Returning home a man who blamed others for his own sense of "sin," Nathan refuses her touch. When she jokes, Nathan hits her. When she listens to stories about the war on the radio, he tells her not to "gloat before Christ" about her "undeserved blessing." When they have sex, he blames her for her "wantonness." When she stands still, he condemns her "idleness." When she or one of the girls suffers, he accuses them of "a failure of virtue." Occupied by Nathan's mission "as if by a foreign power," she falls prey, allowing him "full possession of the country once known as Orleanna Wharton. . . ." Drawing parallel behaviors between Nathan and the colonizers, Orleanna sees how her own "lot was cast with the Congo . . . barefoot bride of men who took her jewels and promised the Kingdom."

Reconstructing the political espionage in the Congo, when America and Belgium "divided the map beneath [her] feet," the fifteen years after Independence, when Senator Church and his special committee looked into the secret operations in the Congo, Orleanna itemizes specifically the people and the politics involved. Appropriately she does so under the title heading of "Bel and the Serpent," a text from the Apocrypha; to most a book "of fear mongers who . . . want to scare people." Her history reveals the men who fit that description, including her husband. While the Congolese station chief, hired by CIA head Allen Dulles to arrange a coup, hired a scientist, Dr. Gottlieb, to make a poison that would kill or disfigure Patrice Lumumba, Orleanna was trying to protect her children and escape the "dreadful poison" raining down upon her from her husband's obsessive behavior. Sponging her five-year-old who was dying from malaria, Orleanna was oblivious to the "scent of unpleasant news" that she now knows: on that same August day, Mobutu Sese Seko was promoted to colonel in exchange for one million dollars in United States money to guarantee his loyalty; Lumumba is put under arrest in a house surrounded by "Mobutu's freshly purchased soldiers;" and, after Lumumbu's execution in January, the Congo is "left in the hands of soulless, empty men." Tracking the history of that period, author Bill Berkeley confirms that the Congo was left in the hands of tyrants, white and black, who, throughout Mobutu's thirty-four years of "brutality unmatched" in the colonial era and after, "took the jewels" and killed the people (2001, 117).

Plagued by unanswerable "if" questions, Orleanna closes her narrative in the "Exodus" chapter on a note that is sad, insightful, and redemptive. Free of Nathan's control, she chooses to speak and in voice comes redemption. She begins by defining the need to understand the deceptive nature of words, a recurring theme in the novel: "*Independence* is a complex word in a foreign tongue. To resist occupation, whether you're a nation or merely a woman, you must understand the language of your enemy. *Conquest* and *liberation* and *democracy* and *divorce* are words that mean squat . . . when you have hungry children . . ." Orleanna's wisdom about the space between words moves her to change. She accepts responsibility for her complicity and acquires the words for her story. For Orleanna, telling her story is a syncretic process, as she aims to reconcile what has gone before.

Like Orleanna, the highly intelligent fourteen year old twins, Leah and Adah, stand still and silent under their father's autocratic rule for much of their time in the Congo. They stand, however, at different ends of the Nathan continuum. Leah, an avid conversationalist, likes spending time with her father more than she likes "doing anything else," pays him due homage, and vows "to work hard for His favor, surpassing all others." She is, as her twin sister notes with disdain, "Our Father's star pupil." Adah, the twin who suffers from hemiplegia, loves palindromes, and does not speak until she is an adult, ridicules her father throughout her narrative with a brilliant ironic wit. Both, however, capture Nathan's destructive behaviors in their narratives. Leah via unconscious irony that grows into conscious knowledge and Adah via conscious understanding of her father's pride and ignorance. Both undergird their "Father" story with a narrative of domination and greed in the Congo, demonstrating similarities. By the end of the novel, their diverse views connect, and each woman names herself a pagan of sort, an "un-missionary." Like their mother they come to see that the Emperor, in this case "Our Father," is not wearing any clothes. Like their mother, they also believe that they are responsible in some way for the horrors that happen in Africa and they seek forgiveness.

Leah begins with stories about Nathan's arrogance and abuse. Watching Nathan correct Orleanna's mistaken notions about items to take to the Congo, she sees his disdain for the woman he associates with the "coin-jingling sinners" in the temple. Leah next observes Rachel fall victim to a strap thrashing when she paints her fingernails bubblegum pink, to Nathan a warning signal "of prostitution." A third example appears as the family lands in Leopoldville, and Nathan arrogantly dismisses Reverend Underdown's kind efforts as an attack on his self-reliance. Leah's comments upon landing in Kilanga are ironic: "He led us out . . . into the light. . . . Our journey was to be a great enterprise of balance. My father, of course, was bringing the Word of God—which fortunately weighs nothing at all." Leah is both wrong and right about "light" and "balance" in ways that she cannot yet imagine.

In Kalinga, Leah's sisters prefer to be mother's helpers, but she prefers to help father "work on his garden." Her garden story becomes a parable of the minister's inability to harvest either seeds or souls. Nathan plans his Garden of Eden to be his "first African miracle" and instructs his daughter while they work with a moral paradigm about the balance of God's "world of work and rewards." He states, "Great sacrifice, great rewards!" When Mama Tataba cautions Nathan about both his method and the poisonwood plant, he cites scripture and ignores her words. Next morning, with "a horrible rash" and swollen eye caused by the red dust from the tree, Nathan, one of "God's own," feels unjustly cursed. Denying responsibility for his own foolish acts, he screams out his rage at his family.

While Nathan heals, Mama Tataba reconstructs the garden shifting the design from flat to hills and valleys so that the seeds will grow, and later Leah watches as an angry Nathan levels it again. When Nathan does follow Mama Tataba's design, plants do grow but bear no fruit, because, they lack pollinators. To Leah, Nathan's failed efforts contradict his theory of balance and rewards, and his words about cause signify nothing: the Bible convention in Atlanta, Nathan tells Leah, "debated about the size of heaven . . ." and "there's room enough for everybody," especially the "righteous." Empty words, like empty vines, bear no fruit, Leah understands.

At fifteen, the more Leah learns about the ways of Kilanga, the more complicated her life becomes.

As the sisters spy on Eeben Axelroot, securing information about the CIA, guns, tools, army clothes, and "distant voices in French and English" that she will later comprehend, Leah also learns the language of Kikango and begins to recognize the wide gap between cultures, between American games like "Hide and Seek" and the Congolese children's game of "Find Food." Embarrassed by her father's ignorant and arrogant behavior, Leah shifts her ground. Catalysts are many, but the most important ones are her relationship with Anatole, an African teacher and co-worker whom she comes to love and marry; her increasing knowledge about war and politics, especially about Lumumba's revolutionary struggle; and her nursing Ruth May and Orleanna through a horrible bout of malaria. Each drives Leah to break the order of "Our Father" and join with "the inhabitants of this land" that she is coming to love.

The two episodes that solidify Leah's attitude about her father and her loss of his kind of faith are the election held by the villagers in Nathan's church and Ruth May's death. These two episodes also signify Kingsolver's testament to the power of language understood and her indictment of Nathan's rhetoric. During Sunday service, in the midst of Nathan's sermon about false idols from the "Apocrypha," the congregation is inattentive. Finally Tata Ndu, the tribal chief, stands and cuts Nathan off to hold "an election on whether or not to accept Jesus Christ as the personal Savior of Kilanga." Nathan shrieks that his behavior is "blasphemy," but Ndu hoists Nathan upon his own white imperialist petard. Ndu states that "white men have brought us many programs to improve our thinking . . . Jesus and elections" are two. "You say these things are good. You cannot say now they are not good." Leah feels a chill as her father begins speaking "slowly, as if to a half-wit" and then blows up, insulting the whole congregation. To Leah, Ndu "states truth" about Nathan's, and other white men's ignorance: "You believe we are *mwana*, your children, who knew nothing until you came here." Explaining the foolishness of such thought, Ndu clarifies the history of his learning handed down across generations, the philosophy of cultural sharing, the politics of a tribal government that teaches the need to listen to each man's voice before making a choice and then to select only if the entire community agrees, and the dangers of a majority vote capable of excluding up to forty-nine percent of the people. The congregation votes and Jesus loses, eleven to fifty-six. Leah sees how Nathan has no sense at all of the culture he wants to civilize; his message is as irrelevant as his Kentucky seeds to the Congo environment.

Kingsolver cleverly weds the personal and political in both Leah's reflections and Tata Ndu's connection of Nathan's actions to other white colonizers whose "Christian" rhetoric resounds with bigotry. Interestingly, writing about ongoing evil in Africa today, Bill Berkeley like Ndu, rebuts the views of two authors who, like Nathan, continue to perpetuate stereotypes of African inferiority. He dismisses as "nonsense" their notions that current violence results from a lack of "'Western enlightenment,'" a "'new-age primitivism'" or the "'superstitions'" that "supposedly flourish in tropical rain forests" (2001, 9).

Leah loses any faith that she had left in both her father and his God when Ruth May dies from a venomous snake bite, and her father has no words to explain the child's death, except that his youngest daughter "wasn't baptized yet." Seeing an "ugly man" who desired the personal glory of baptizing his child with all of Kilanga's children, the daughter who had idolized her father, now could not stand to look at him. Amidst torrential rains, Nathan appears like Lear, a mad father abandoned by his daughters, wandering in the wilderness and speaking in words that few can understand. Leah notes the bizarre and almost humorous irony, when Bwanga, one of Ruth May's friends, asks, "Mah-dah-mey-I?" The children remember Ruth May's game and echo her words, looking at her dead body and asking again and again in a rising plea: "Mother May I?" While the children chant to "Mother" seeking wisdom and permission, Father, Leah observes, continued his biblical oration without any clear idea of what was going on. Nathan lacks the wisdom that Lear gained from his suffering; Nathan is deaf to the truth just as he is deaf to the language nuances of the Congolese culture.

When Leah sings her part of the "Song of the Three Children," the song that closes the novel becomes a history and a promise. She knows that there is no justice in the world, but she sustains her belief in a certain kind of grace. Like Brother Fowles, she listens to the people, trusts in a dynamic Creation which will not "suffer in translation," and remains with Anatole and their family in Africa, the land she chooses as her own.

Adah begins her journey in a much different way than Leah. Although they are identical twins, Adah sees herself as a "lame gallimaufry" who is definitely not her father's "star pupil." Associating herself with both "Jekyll and Hyde" because of her dark desires and crooked body, Adah chooses silence, recognizing its advantages in certain circumstances, especially in Kilanga. Yet she aligns herself most often with Emily Dickinson, using her poetry as a kind of personal philosophy that guides her narrative: both liked to "dwell in the darkness" (i.e. a world of secrets and revelation), and both "Tell All the Truth *but tell it slant*." Her slanted truth carries a skeptical tone, especially about "Our Father," who punishes his children for being female or for straying from his puritanical path with the "dreaded Verse." Adah's words about her father are brilliant and caustic; there is little that she does not notice.

"Our Father speaks for all of us, as far as I can see," Adah says as she begins her analysis of Nathan's behavior in Kilanga. Not only does Nathan silence his family, but he insults them and has since the time of the twins' birth. Adah sarcastically surmises her father's attitude about her own condition: "Our Father probably interpreted Broca's aphasia as God's Christmas bonus to one of his worthier employees." She too comments upon her father's garden fiasco, his distance from and lack of concern about family members, and his passion for the Apocrypha. However, Adah's stories about "The Verse," her father's paradoxical sermons, and his persistent insult and abuse of family all connect, and each adds a specific dimension of Nathan's character that relates his behavior to broader public events.

"The dreaded Verse is our household punishment," states Adah, "we Price girls are castigated with the Holy Bible." Nathan writes some scriptural reference for the child-offender; the offense could be any act, from painting one's nails to saying damn, that "Our Father" considered a sin. Then the "poor sinner" must copy "Jeremiah 48:18 . . . and additionally, the ninety-nine verses that follow it." Her satiric commentary on her father's preference for "his particularly beloved Apocrypha" slides into a *reductio ad absurdum* set of questions that parallel Nathan's "impressive" outcomes with her own "grocery sums in the Piggly Wiggly" to the case of the "cursing parrot" Methuselah who was "exempt from the Reverend's rules . . . in the same way Our Father was finding the Congolese people beyond his power. Methuselah was a sly little representative of Africa itself, living openly in our household." Adah concludes with delicious wit: "One might argue, even, that he was here first."

From "Genesis" through "The Judges," Adah describes her father's ignorant errors as he attempts to convert the villagers to his point of view. Her palindrome for Nathan's sermonizing, his "high-horse show of force" is the "Amen enema." As the Reverend towers over the altar, Adah watches the congregation stiffen, and recalls the dead fish on the riverbank, one of her father's conversion mistakes. Nathan promised Kilanga's hungry people "the bounty of the Lord, more fish than they had ever seen in their lives," but he executes "a backward notion of the loaves and fishes," sending men out to pitch dynamite in the river. The villagers did feast all day, but there was no ice to save the thousands of fish that went bad along the bank. Nathan's destructive act won him no converts. To Adah, he appeared incapable of understanding why, just as he could not understand how saying "words wrong" led only outcasts to his flock.

Nathan's method is his meaning and that is his mistake, according to Adah: "Our Father has a bone to pick with this world, and oh, he picks . . . it with the Word. His punishment is the Word, and his deficiencies are failures of words. . . . It is a special kind of person who will draw together a congregation, stand up before them with a proud, clear voice, and say words wrong, week after week." Adah observes the Reverend shouting: "TATA JESUS IS BANGALA!" every Sunday, while people sit scratching themselves in wonder. "*Bangala* means something precious and dear. But the way he pronounces it, it means the poisonwood tree. Praise the Lord . . . for Jesus will make you itch." The irony seems clear to all but Nathan. He fails to see how the language of the region, rich in tonal ambiguities, describes far better than his English the complex antithesis that face people in his congregation. He expects only that they, like his family, will do as he teaches.

After the Congo achieves independence, after the family loses its stipend and all contacts with the larger world, after Orleanna and Ruth May fall "sick nigh unto death," the girls had to endure Nathan's "escalating rage" and physical abuse. Adah remembers the "bruises" and connects her father's abusive behavior with the secrets she learns about Ike and the planned assassination of Lumumba. Why the "King of America" wants a tall, thin man in the Congo to be dead is a shock to Adah. "How is it different," she wonders, "from Grandfather God sending the African children to hell for being born too far from a Baptist Church?" Adah wants to stand up in church and ask her father: "Might those pagan babies send us to hell for living too far from a jungle?" Adah never asks her father those questions, but she carries them with her when she leaves the Congo and decides to speak.

Free from Nathan's righteous rage, Adah finds her voice in a language of self-definition and science at Emory University, where she finds a future as a neonatal physician and researcher on AIDS and Ebola. Profaning her father's religious obsession, she states, "I recite the Periodic Table of Elements like a prayer: I take my examinations as Holy Communion; and the pass of the first semester was a sacrament." When she commutes back to her mother's house, searching for Nathan's military discharge to provide her tuition benefits, she discovers that his medal was not for "heroic service" but for "having survived." Though the conditions were "technically honorable . . . unofficially they were: Cowardice, Guilt and Disgrace." Adah finally understands why the Reverend could not flee the same jungle twice. Sixteen years later, Adah, like Orleanna and Leah, asks, "How many of his sins belong also to me? How much of his punishment?" She too tries to make sense of her complicity. Unwilling to engage in the "politics of forgetting," Adah tells the hard truth in her own poetic way.

The youngest and the oldest of the daughters, Ruth May and Rachel, lack the astute insight, sense of complicity for wrongs done in the past, and passionate commitment to make the world better for others than their twin sisters share. Both, however, each in her own humorous and sad way, show the evil results of their father's behavior, and both stories illustrate the consequences of white supremacy in ways the reader least expects.

Ruth May's time in the novel is short; she arrives in the Congo at age five and dies from the bite of a diabolical green mamba snake when she is six. Her words are few, but her naive voice reveals the prejudicial attitudes shaped by her father and a religious rhetoric of white superiority and biblical truth. Her statements about African people or blacks in general, her tales about parental conflict, and her "political" comments are never completely correct, but they illustrate well the outcomes of discrimination. Ruth May begins by repeating words of her father and expands into ordinary Georgia attitudes: "God says the Africans are the Tribes of Ham," the worst of Noah's three sons, and "Noah cursed all of Ham's children to be slaves forever. . . ." She thinks about "colored children" in Georgia, who are "not gifted" and, as Ruth May heard a man in church say, ". . . different from us and needs ought to keep to their own." Ruth May continues, telling readers about Jimmy Crow who "makes the laws" excluding blacks from stores, restaurants, and the zoo. She also tells about a classmate in Sunday school teaching her to talk like the "cannibal" natives: "Ugga bugga lugga." Ironically, these words parallel those of Khruschev in a newspaper cartoon that appears in an article on Soviet plans for the Congo. Holding "hands and dancing with a skinny cannibal native with big lips and a bone in his hair," Khruschev sings, "Bingo Bango Bongo, I don't want to leave the Congo!" words that sound amazingly like Ruth Ann's. A five year old's words, humorous as her mistakes may be, paralleled against the Khruschev cartoon, illustrate the breadth of white supremacist attitudes and the depth of Kingsolver's anti-imperialist ideology that undergirds the narrative. Her story about parental conflict adds to this understanding.

Ruth May hears her parents taking different positions on a range of issues related to the natives. For example, she watches malnourished children with distended stomachs and comments, "I reckon that's what they get for being the Tribes of Ham." Father "says to forgive them for they know not what they do." Mama says, "You can't hardly even call it a sin when they need every little thing as bad as they do." When Ruth May notices the lost legs, arms, eyes, and other physical disabilities of the natives, Father says, "They are living in darkness. Broken in body and soul. . . ." Mama says, "Well, maybe they take a different view of their bodies." Ruth May observes that "Mama has this certain voice sometimes . . ." and when Father states that "the body is the temple," Mama says, "Well, here in Africa that temple has to do a hateful lot of work in a day. . . ." Ruth May sees Father "looking at Mama hard . . . with his one eye turned mean," for talking back to him. Even Ruth May recognizes the undertow of her parents' relationship, but Kingsolver uses Ruth May's voice for more. Ruth May's story shows how her father places the people of Kilanga alongside his family, always beneath his feet, as she consistently challenges Nathan's and other exploiters' sense of superiority.

Nathan's physical abuse of both her sisters and herself, his assignment of "The Verse," his trying "to teach everybody to love Jesus" but breeding fear instead, all these acts are visible to Ruth May. So too are the broader politics that bring destruction to Kilanga. Ruth May's story is "off the mark" in words but on target in meaning. She observes the Belgian Army arrive, recognizes that the "white one knows who is boss" and sees the shoeless "Jimmy Crow boys" who hide out and say "Patrice Lumumba!" She listens to the doctor who sets her arm argue with her father about those "boys" and "missionary work" in the same debate. When the doctor says that missionary work "is a great bargain for Belgium but . . . a hell of a way to deliver the social services," listing the abuses of slavery, such as cutting off hands in the rubber plantations, Father becomes angry and shouts, "Belgian and American business brought civilization to the Congo!" Like other colonizers, Nathan associates "civilization" with his God, his language, and his culture.

These are the words Ruth May remembers; these are the words that make her "scared of Jesus." These are the words that tell her that her father isn't listening to anyone but himself. These are the words that when she has malaria make her believe she is sick "because of doing bad things." These are the words that make Ruth May believe that "being dead is not worse than being alive" but different, because the "view is larger."

Rachel, as clueless and morally neutral as she is, malaprops her way into the reader's critical vision, because she best represents America's material culture. Capable of entertaining her sisters with imitation radio commercials—"Medically tested Odo-ro-no stops underarm odor and moisture at the source!"—Rachel is "willing to be a philanderist for peace," but she can only go so "far where perspiration odor is concerned." For Rachel, fashion is more important than culture, politics or moral issues that she neither sees nor understands. Ironically, however, Rachel sees truth about things that concern her. For example, from the moment the Prices arrive in Kilanga, she sees the truth about Nathan's position, as well as the family's place in the Congo. "We are supposed to be calling the shots here," Rachel begins, "but it doesn't look to me like we're in charge of a thing, not even our own selves." Yet Rachel, like her father, takes for "granite" almost everything, although his assumptions are more serious than Rachel's expecting a "sweet-sixteen party" or a washing machines in their hut. Rachel's stories about the welcoming party planned by the natives and the Underdowns' visit, although only two of many often humorous tales, reinforce stories already told by her mother and the twins. But Rachel's narrative is different: her tone is one of contempt and her focus is on pragmatic issues, mainly her own gains and losses. Rachel finds herself a place among the exploiters. Even at the end of the novel, three marriages-of-sort later and not yet out of "the Dark Continent," Rachel still does not believe that "other people's worries" have "to drag you down."

When the Prices arrive in Kilanga, Rachel feels shoved "into heathen pandemony" as men drum and women sing, welcoming the family. Seeing women dancing and cooking "all bare chested and unashamed," she observes Father "already on his feet" with "one arm [raised] above his head like one of those gods they had in Roman times, fixing to send down the thunderbolts and the lightening." When Nathan begins to speak, "Rachel sees his speech as a rising storm." Initially the people cheer Nathan's passion, but Rachel's stomach knots because the Reverend "was getting that look he gets, oh boy, like Here comes Moses tromping down off of Mount Syanide with ten fresh ways to wreck your life." Rachel, despite her mistake, describes well the poison her father uses to destroy the people's spirit. As Nathan preaches about nakedness and the "sinners of Sodom," the natives' expressions "fall from joy to confusion to dismay." Nathan's words, unlike those of the Congolese, are not of welcome but of damnation, and throughout the novel, Nathan continues to use scripture as a weapon of attack.

When the Episcopalian Underdowns who oversee financial affairs for the Mission League bring news of uprisings and the need for the Prices to leave, Nathan's behavior shows how little he has changed. The Underdowns carry newspapers that cite Belgians as "unsung heroes" who come into a village and "usually interrupt the cannibal natives in the middle of human sacrifice." They also bring news about a Soviet plan for moving forward in the Congo, depriving "innocent savages of becoming a free society," and the election in May for June independence of the Congo. Rachel sees that for her father this news was a "fairy tale," and she states his response: "*An election* . . . [w]hy . . . [t]hese people can't even read a simple slogan. . . . Two *hundred* different languages . . . this is not a *nation,* it is the *Tower of Babel* and it *cannot* hold an election. . . . [T]hey don't have the . . . intellect for such things." Rachel misses the similarities between her father's words and the article's about "savages"; instead, she becomes angry at having her own wishes for leaving the Congo dashed. Rachel does, however, capture cause: "Father would sooner watch us all perish one by one than listen to anybody but himself." Refusing to heed any advice to leave, Nathan assumes his intractable position.

The remainder of Rachel's time in Kilanga is short. Under the pretense of engagement to Axelroot, the Afrikaner bush pilot, diamond smuggler, and CIA mercenary, Rachel learns about his espionage activities and eventually escapes with him to Johannesburg, South Africa, the beginning of her exodus experience. After three relationships, two real marriages, one divorce and one death, Rachel inherits her last husband's (Remy Fairley's) Equatorial Hotel for businessmen in Brassaville and never leaves the continent she so much wanted to escape. She does, however, create her "own domain." Although she credits herself with never looking back, her final words show that the memory of her father-as-antagonist remains; "Oh, if Father could see me now, wouldn't he give me The Verse!" Congratulating herself for not being like her father, for sounding "un-Christian," Rachel ironically misses the point that she is in a way most like him in her singlemindedness. Although in her own malapropism: "It's a woman's provocative to change her mind," Rachel never does.

Kingsolver ends her complex novel, leaving the reader with an uneasy sense of balance between loss and salvation. Nathan dies guilty, wandering in the jungle, speaking his rote messages about his foreign God, and sustaining his myth of purpose. Ruth Ann dies, and her spirit hovers over her mother offering forgiveness. Rachel, who cares little about others, does understand that she can reap the financial rewards of her white South African hotel. Orleanna and the twins, however, experience a redemptive sense of worth. Each in her own way learns, in Robert Coles's words, how "to hold secure one's own moral and spiritual self" amidst the "crushing institutional forces of the state . . . the marketplace, and . . . the church. . . ." Each is "driven by particular interests" and "passions" (1999, 167). All three women become advocates for justice: civil rights, medical research on AIDS, and revolutionary educational practices for the poor people in the Congo. The novel ends, but Kingsolver's story is not over. The net in which the Prices and the Congo are caught still exists, because the exploitation embodied in the "missionary" position remains to haunt not only the Congolese but a broader world as well.

At the beginning of the twenty-first century, one hundred years after Stanley preached the "gospel of enterprise," seeking men to work in Africa who would be "missionaries of commerce" (Hochschild 1998, 68), conflict in Africa continues in daily acts of violence and failed efforts at peace. As Tamba Nlandu, professor of philosophy and native of the Congo, explained, the country is divided into antagonistic sections that include multiple warring factions and wars continue even after "peace" treaties are established. Citing tribal and cultural conflicts, as well as power and greed as dominant motives for both Africans and outsiders alike, he sees peace as only a remote possibility (see also Fisher 1999; Fisher and Onishi 2000; Hranjskj 1999, 2000; Shaw 1999; and Traub 2000). Current information about wars appears in daily news stories about countless numbers of people succumbing to disease and hunger in burned, looted villages throughout the Congo. Citing the human toll of thirty-two months of war in "apocalyptic terms," Karl Vick estimates the dead at three million people, especially children (2001,A1,A5; see also Knickmeyer 2001, Nullis 2001). In late May 2001, Colin Powell, Secretary of State, traveled to Africa and promised to help combat disease and nurture democracy, a hopeful note. Yet Powell's promises are qualified by his own caution to avoid getting "too committed" and Defense Secretary Rumsfeld's desire for a sharp reduction in overseas commitments (Knickermeyer 2001, A1,A4). Richard Hollbrooke, former ambassador to the United Nations, worked hard but with little success to reduce Congressional antipathy for international peace keeping (Crossette 2001, 2–3). Despite promises of money to fight AIDS, the triumph of human rights is precarious at best, because as journalist David Rieff notes, an "entrenched moral absolutism" limits actions "to identifying atrocities, not doing good deeds" (1999, 40).

The "monolithic cultural views" that Kingsolver questions reappear in a recent interview with George Kennan. Questioned by Richard Ullman about the U.S. role in Russia, Kennan urges detachment: "I would like to see our government gradually withdraw from its public advocacy of democracy and human rights," establishing a clear distinction between Europe which "naturally, is another matter" because "we are still a large part of the roots of a European civilization" and anywhere else where struggle and violence occur (Ullman, 1999, 6). Half a century after Eisenhower, whether Russia or the Congo, Kennan feels "not the faintest moral responsibility."

The power of Kingsolver's novel lies in her ability to question that response. On the surface, *The Poisonwood Bible,* seems different from earlier works, such as *The Bean Trees* or *Animal Dreams,* fiction set mainly in South or Southwest America and occurring in a short span of time. In all her fiction, Kingsolver grapples with clashing cultural values, social justice issues, ecological awareness, and the intersection of private and public concerns. *The Poisonwood Bible,* however, is more complex; its images resonate across levels of meaning, allusions are multiple, and the stories of its narrators carry deep spiritual meaning. As retold narratives cross and refract, shedding different shades of light on the same truth, ethical questions multiply. Unlike authors such as Joseph Conrad, who, as Chinua Achebe states, "eliminate the African as a human factor" and reduce "Africa to the role of props for the break-up of one petty . . . mind," Kingsolver reverses expectations and roles; it is not the Congolese who are ignorant or "savage" or say the wrong words but the colonizers (North 2001, 40). Words, Kingsolver warns, have multiple meanings, especially in the Congo. To decode those meanings, readers must "look at what happens from every side and consider all the other ways it could have gone." Kingsolver dares us to do so and to discover the moments of truth in the telling. This essay offers one "particular" angled version of a multidimensional novel; it illustrates how in "(un)doing the missionary position," Kingsolver "connects consequences with actions" and challenges readers to do likewise.

Source: Elaine R. Ognibene, "The Missionary Position: Barbara Kingsolver's *The Poisonwood Bible*," in *College Literature*, Summer 2003, pp. 19–36.

Sources

Fox, Stephen D., "Barbara Kingsolver and Keri Hulme: Disability, Family, and Culture," in *Critique*, Vol. 45, No. 4, Summer 2004, pp. 405–18.

Greene, Gayle, "Independence Struggle," in *Women's Review of Books*, Vol. 16, No. 7, April 1999, pp. 8–9.

Kingsolver, Barbara, *The Poisonwood Bible*, HarperPerennial, 1998.

Koza, Kimberly A., "The Africa of Two Western Women Writers: Barbara Kingsolver and Margaret Laurence," in *Critique*, Vol. 44, No. 3, Spring 2003, pp. 284–94.

Leonard, John, "Kingsolver in the Jungle, Catullus and Wolfe at the Door," in *Nation*, January 11/18, 1999, pp. 28–30.

Review of *The Poisonwood Bible*, in *Publishers Weekly*, August 10, 1998, p. 366.

Stafford, Tim, "Poisonous Gospel," in *Christianity Today*, January 11, 1999, pp. 88–90.

Further Reading

Edgerton, Robert, *The Troubled Heart of Africa: A History of the Congo*, St. Martin's Press, 2002.

Edgerton chronicles the turbulent history of the Congo, from its pre-European colonization to the early 2000s.

Siegel, Lee, "Sweet and Low," in the *New Republic*, March 22, 1999, pp. 30–36.

Siegel critiques Kingsolver's characterizations of black Africans and what he considers her slanted view of Congolese politics.

Taylor, Jeffrey, *Facing the Congo: A Modern-Day Journey into the Heart of Darkness*, Three Rivers Press, 2001.

In this fascinating account of his journey on the Congo River in a canoe, Taylor brings his reporter's eye for detail to his descriptions of the landscape of this beautiful but sometimes treacherous country.

Walls, Andrew F., *The Missionary Movement in Christian History: Studies in Transmission of Faith*, Orbis Books, 1996.

Walls focuses on the theoretical background of the missionary movement in the Western and Eastern worlds as well as on specific missions.

Steppenwolf

Hermann Hesse

1927

Hermann Hesse's novel *Der Steppenwolf* (English translation, *Steppenwolf* [1929]), was first published in 1927. It is one of the major novels by the renowned German writer and was extremely popular amongst young people in the United States in the 1960s. The counterculture of that decade took inspiration from the fact that the protagonist of the novel, Harry Haller, makes use of sex and hallucinatory drugs as a means of fulfillment and self-discovery. Haller is a self-hating, fifty-year-old intellectual who despises the bourgeois culture in which he lives. Through encounters with various people, including two prostitutes and a drug-dispensing saxophone player, he embarks on a search for psychic wholeness and spiritual understanding. The novel combines realistic and surrealistic techniques and is strongly autobiographical, since between 1924 and 1926, when he was writing the novel, Hesse went through a crisis similar to that faced by Haller. Like Haller, whose initials the author shares, Hesse felt depressed and tried to shake it off by sensual indulgence. The protagonist of the novel resembles Hesse in other ways, too, including his temperament and his tastes in music and literature. In writing *Steppenwolf*, Hesse used the stuff of personal experience to create a dense novel that promotes uninhibited psychological exploration and spiritual aspiration.

Author Biography

German poet and novelist Hermann Hesse was born on July 2, 1877, in the small town of Calw, in the

Hermann Hesse The Library of Congress

German state of Württemberg. His father, Johannes, worked for a publishing house and had also, along with his wife Marie Gundert, been a missionary in India.

In 1891, Hesse entered the Protestant Theological Seminary at Maulbronn, but he ran away from the seminary after six months, and his father removed him from the school in May 1892. Even at this young age, Hesse had already decided he wanted to be a poet. He worked in a clock factory and then as an apprentice in a bookshop in Tübingen, during which time he read widely, especially the work of Goethe and the German Romantic poets.

Hesse's first volume of poetry was published in 1899, and his first novel, *Peter Camenzind* in 1904. The success of the novel ensured that Hesse was able to make a living as a freelance writer. He followed this with another novel, *Unterm Rad* in 1906 (*The Prodigy* [1957]; *Beneath the Wheel* [1969]), which was a fierce attack on the educational system.

Hesse married Maria Bernoulli in 1904, and they settled in Switzerland. They had three sons.

In 1911, Hesse traveled to India, which sparked his interest in Indian spirituality, an interest that culminated in the publication in 1922 of his novel *Siddhartha*, about the early life of the Buddha. From 1912 to 1919, Hesse lived in Bern, Switzerland. He volunteered for military service when World War I broke out in 1914 but was deemed unfit to serve. Instead, he was assigned to the German Embassy in Bern.

During the war, his wife developed a mental illness, and Hesse himself came close to a nervous breakdown. He underwent extensive psychoanalysis by a disciple of Carl Jung. His marriage finally broke up, and in 1919, he moved without his family to the village of Montagnola, near Lugano, in southern Switzerland, where he lived for the rest of his life. He became a Swiss citizen in 1923.

In 1919, Hesse published *Demian*, a novel that addresses the moral and spiritual crisis facing young people in Germany in the aftermath of the catastrophic World War I. The book was an immediate success, and it established Hesse's reputation as one of the foremost German writers of the period.

In 1924, Hesse married Ruth Wenger, but the marriage lasted only three years. He married for the third time, to Ninon Dolbin, in 1931.

Hesse's next major work was *Steppenwolf* (1927), followed by *Narziss und Goldmund* (1927) (*Death and the Lover* [1930]; *Narcissus and Goldmund* [1968]), and the work that many consider to be his masterpiece, *Magister Ludi* (1949) (*The Glass Bead Game* [1969]), which was published in 1943 in Zurich, Switzerland, after the Nazi authorities in Germany refused permission to publish. During World War II, Hesse's works were declared undesirable by Nazi Germany, and no reprints of his novels were allowed.

In 1946, Hesse was awarded the Nobel Prize for Literature and the Goethe Prize. After this, he wrote no more major works. Hesse died on August 9, 1962, at the age of eighty-five, in Montagnola, from a cerebral hemorrhage.

Plot Summary

Preface

The preface to *Steppenwolf* is told in the first person by a man who recalls his acquaintance with Harry Haller, the Steppenwolf ("wolf of the Steppes"). Haller was a man of about fifty who rented two rooms on the top floor of the house owned by the narrator's aunt. In the narrator's view, he was unsociable, shy, wild, and lonely, seemingly coming from another world than the comfortable bourgeois existence enjoyed by the narrator. However, Haller was a quiet, polite lodger, and the narrator's aunt took to him immediately. As the narrator gradually got to know Haller, he found him intellectually gifted and emotionally deep. The narrator had also suffered a lot and seemed full of self-hatred. Haller lived a disorderly life and followed no profession. He slept until late in the morning and spent his days with his books, which included many volumes of German poetry. He complained of poor digestion and insomnia. The narrator felt compassion for Haller's forlorn life, although one day he saw him happy in the company of an attractive young lady.

One day the Steppenwolf disappeared, and the narrator has no idea where he went. Haller left behind him a manuscript about himself, which the narrator sees as a document not only of the Steppenwolf's deeply troubled state of mind, but also of the sickness of the entire society.

Media Adaptations

- *Steppenwolf* was made into a film in 1974, written and directed by Fred Haines, starring Max von Sydow as Harry Haller and Dominique Sanda as Hermine. As of 2006, the film was in print and available for purchase in VHS format from Amazon.com and other Internet vendors.

Harry Haller's Records: "For Madmen Only"

Haller begins his manuscript by writing how he despises bourgeois comfort, the mediocre optimism of the middle classes. He hates the petty conventions of life, its comforts and domesticity, preferring extremes, either of pain or pleasure. He then goes on to describe how after a pleasantly mediocre day, he went for a walk in the evening. As he walks, he reviews his discontent with the age of spiritual blindness in which he believes he lives, and he recalls moments in which he awakened to a higher kind of life, although these moments never lasted for long. In a dark alley, he stumbles upon an old building on which he sees a sign: "Magic Theater: Entrance Not For Everybody." He also sees a sign: "For Madmen Only." But he cannot get into the building. He walks on and takes refuge in a tavern that he often visits. On his way home, he returns to the place where he saw the mysterious message, and a man he does not know hands him a little book.

Treatise on the Steppenwolf

When Haller returns home, he reads the title of the book: "*Treatise on the Steppenwolf. Not for Everybody.*" The treatise is an examination of the character and personality of Haller, written in the third person by an anonymous, objective observer. According to the treatise, Haller is divided between two natures, man and wolf. Each tries to sabotage the other. When he is a man, he is capable of beautiful thoughts and he behaves in a civilized way, but the wolf in him scorns this. When the wolf is the ascendant, he hates and despises humanity, valuing what is free and savage, strong and untamable. But then the man in Haller spoils the pleasure his wolf-like nature takes in being what it is. The Steppenwolf is, therefore, always in conflict with himself. Because of this intractable conflict, he has a tendency to suicide. When he was forty-seven years old, he vowed that he would take his own life on his fiftieth birthday, and this thought gives him some comfort.

The Steppenwolf stands as an outsider in bourgeois society which values comfort and a quiet life over principle and spiritual and intellectual integrity. In contrast to bourgeois mediocrity and compromise, the Steppenwolf knows the heights and the depths of life; he has an impulse to become either the saint or the sinner. It may be that he will be able to reconcile the conflicting elements in him, but he will have to look deeply into his own soul and know himself fully. Then he will realize that it is a simplification for him to see himself merely as a dual personality. He is, in fact a multitude of individualities, like everyone else, and to save himself he must know and embrace all aspects of his being, beyond his conscious personality.

Haller's Encounter with the Professor

When Haller has finished reading the treatise, he knows he must either take his own life or try to understand himself in a new way. Since he has been through many changes in his life and does not relish going through more upheavals, he resolves to take his own life in the near future.

One day he follows a funeral procession in town and listens to the service at the graveside. He is disgusted by the insincerity of the sentiments expressed. Walking on, he encounters an old acquaintance of his, a professor of oriental religion, who invites him for dinner that evening at his home. Haller accepts the invitation although he does not want to go. The evening turns out to be a disaster. The professor denounces as a traitor a man named Haller who is named in the newspaper as having stated that Germany was just as guilty as its enemies for the outbreak of World War I. The Steppenwolf does not tell the professor and his wife that he himself is the man named. After dinner, Haller makes an insulting remark about a small engraving of Goethe to which he has taken a dislike, without knowing that the engraving is one of the most treasured possessions of the professor's wife. Then Haller informs the professor that he is the man mentioned in the newspaper, and he rebukes the professor for his nationalistic and militaristic attitudes.

Meeting Hermine

After leaving the professor's house, Haller paces the streets. He cannot go home because he knows that if he does so, he will end up cutting his throat, and he fears death. Finding himself in an unfamiliar part of town, he enters a hotel called the Black Eagle, where he meets a charming young lady who takes an interest in him and asks him to dance. Haller is forced to decline since he has never learned to dance. He relates the story of his evening at the professor's home, and she tells him he is being childish. When she goes off to dance, he is so tired he falls asleep and dreams that he is meeting Goethe. When he wakes, the young woman returns. They agree to meet again for dinner the following Tuesday.

His spirits revived by the chance encounter with the woman and his dream of Goethe, Haller stays the night in a room at the hotel. When he meets the young woman at a restaurant, he learns that her name is Hermine. In spite of the fact that she is a prostitute, he is captivated by her. She seems to know everything about him, and she enables him to break through his isolation. She says that her purpose is to make him fall in love with her and that he must obey her every command. Her last command, she says, will be for him to kill her, but she does not explain what she means by this.

At the end of the evening, Hermine insists that he buy a gramophone so she can teach him the foxtrot in his rooms. He reluctantly agrees, and within a few days she gives him two dance lessons, both of which he hates, and then she announces that he must dance with her the next day at a restaurant. At the restaurant, he is persuaded by Hermine to ask a beautiful young woman to dance. Haller manages to pluck up his courage, and to his surprise, the young lady accepts his invitation. He later finds out that the woman is named Maria, and she is a friend of Hermine.

Haller's Awakening with Maria

Gradually, Haller gets used to dancing and to jazz, the kind of music he used to dislike. Before, he had despised people who went to dances and the like merely seeking pleasure, but now he becomes one of them, even though sometimes he feels he is a traitor to everything he regards as sacred.

One night he returns to find Maria in his bed, sent there by Hermine. He spends the night with her, and in subsequent days, she helps him discover the delights of the senses as well of dance halls, cinemas, bars, and other places where people gather for pleasure. He also indulges in drugs, such as cocaine and opium, supplied to him by Pablo, a saxophone player and friend of Hermine. This is a world in which Maria and Hermine are completely at home, although it is entirely new for Haller. For a few weeks, he is happy; it seems to him that Maria is the only woman he has ever really loved, although he knows that she has many other loves. But he also guesses that his happiness will be short-lived, and for some reason, he longs for the suffering that will make him ready to die.

One evening Haller attends a masked ball. He is nervous and does not arrive until late, having spent part of the evening at the cinema, watching a film about Moses and the Israelites in Egypt. When he arrives at the ball, he finds the atmosphere oppressive and is about to leave when his mood is suddenly transformed. He dances with a masked Spanish girl, who turns out to be Maria, and then he finds Hermine, who is dressed as a boy and reminds Haller of his boyhood friend, Herman. Haller dances for two hours with various women and is intoxicated by the atmosphere created by dancing, music, and wine. He feels the joy of merging his individual personality in the crowd.

The Magic Theater

When the ball is almost over, Haller encounters Pablo who invites him to a small room, gives him some opium and invites him to enter a "magic theater," a surreal world in which he experiences, as Pablo puts it, "the world of your own soul that you seek." Through the magic theater, Haller is to experience the unconscious elements of his personality, aspects of himself that he has ignored or pushed away. Looking at a large mirror on the wall, he sees a multitude of reflections of himself, at all ages and in all guises. Then he is alone again and opens a door that says, "GREAT HUNT IN AUTOMOBILES." He finds himself witnessing a war between men and machines. Taking the side of men, he and a former school friend named Gustav join the fight against a mechanized civilization based on narrow rationality that has impoverished life. They shoot at drivers and destroy several cars.

After this strange adventure ends, Haller stands again in the corridor and decides to goes through a door marked "GUIDANCE IN THE BUILDING UP OF THE PERSONALITY. SUCCESS GUARANTEED." In the room in which he finds himself, a man who resembles Pablo shows him through the use of a chessboard how the art of living is a game involving every element of the personality in constantly changing relationships. The next door Haller opens shows him the "MARVELOUS TAMING OF THE STEPPENWOLF," a bizarre scene from a booth in a fair in which first a man enslaves a wolf and then a wolf enslaves a man. Haller is horrified at this reminder of what he read in the treatise about the dual nature he believes he possesses. The next door he goes through, "ALL GIRLS ARE YOURS," is altogether more pleasant. He is once more a boy of fifteen with his first love, a girl named Rosa. But this time, instead of being too shy and polite to confess his love, he tells Rosa that he loves her. Starting with Rosa, Haller gets to relive all the loves of his life, but with happier outcomes in which his love is returned.

The final door Haller goes through in the magic theater is marked "HOW ONE KILLS FOR LOVE." After a surreal encounter with his idol, Mozart, Haller enters the last door of the magic theater. He sees Hermine and Pablo lying naked asleep on the floor, and it is obvious to him that they have just made love. He stabs Hermine under her breast, killing her. Although he is only killing her image in the magic theater, he does not at the time appear to know this, nor does he know whether his act was good or bad. Then Mozart enters, bringing with him a radio, which he arranges so that it plays some music by Handel. Haller recoils from the poor reproduction of the music he so much reveres, but Mozart rebukes him. What he hears is still the divine music of Handel. It may be distorted, but it can still be recognized, and there is a lesson in this for life, too. Life may distort the ideal, but it cannot wholly erase it.

Haller confesses to feeling guilty about having killed Hermine, and he imagines himself tried and convicted. But instead of being condemned to death as he desires, he is sentenced to "eternal life." In other words, there is to be no easy escape. Mozart consoles him, telling him he must keep listening to the wireless (radio) of life until he can learn to be like one of the immortals, to "reverence the spirit behind it" and also to laugh at its absurdities. Then Mozart suddenly turns into Pablo, who tells Haller that they are still in the magic theater, which will always be at his service. Haller feels that he understands everything now. He is ready to continue the game of life and traverse new roads of self-discovery.

Characters

Bourgeois Narrator

The bourgeois narrator is the nephew of Haller's landlady. He narrates the novel's preface, reporting on his acquaintance with Haller and his observations about Haller's character and personality. Unlike Haller, the middle-class narrator lives an orderly, respectable life, full of predictable routine; he goes to work at an office each day, and he values punctuality. Also unlike Haller, he neither smokes or drinks.

Erica

Erica is the estranged lover of Haller. He reports that he meets her occasionally, but for some reason she is angry with him and they quarrel.

Johann Wolfgang Goethe

Johann Wolfgang Goethe (1749–1832), a German poet, novelist, dramatist, and essayist, was one of the greatest writers Germany has produced. Haller is an admirer of Goethe, and he is greatly offended when, visiting the home of the professor, he sees a portrait of the great man that does not capture Goethe's true spirit. In one of the surreal episodes in the novel, Haller dreams that he meets Goethe. He reproaches him for being insincere in his work and presenting too optimistic a vision of human life. Goethe evades his question playfully, saying that Haller should not take things so seriously, and he laughs and dances.

Gustav

Gustav is Haller's boyhood friend. Haller meets him again through the "magic theater," when Gustav accompanies him in the war against the automobiles.

Harry Haller

Harry Haller, the protagonist and narrator of much of the novel, is known as the Steppenwolf. A divorced man nearing fifty years of age, Haller is an intellectual. He has published work on poetry and music and the metaphysics of art. He loves Goethe and Mozart and believes their work belongs on an immortal plane of life. But Haller is not a happy man. He is in poor health, suffering from gout and insomnia, and he does not fit well into bourgeois society. Living in two rented rooms in a city, he is an outsider, a solitary man, "a melancholy hermit in a cell encumbered by books," as he describes himself. He is lonely, since he sees his one friend, Erica, only occasionally, and even then they quarrel. But he will not seek out company because he despises comfortable, bourgeois respectability and mediocrity and prefers to experience the heights and depths of life, apparently through his appreciation of music and literature. When he finds himself drifting through tolerable days in which nothing much either good or bad happens to him, he says that he would sooner feel "the very devil burn in [him]" than accept this "slumbering god of contentment." He longs for strong emotions and sensations, not the kind of flat, sterile life that he believes is the bourgeois norm. He also finds himself at odds with the prevailing nationalism and militarism in Germany, convinced that it will lead to another war.

Haller has thought deeply about his own nature. He feels that he has a dual personality, divided between normal human emotions and feelings that lead to benevolent actions and what he describes as his wolf nature, which is strong, wild, ruthless, and solitary, and he despises humans for their vanity and stupidity. The man and the wolf in Haller are perpetually at war with each other. He can be sociable and friendly and pleasant, but then the wolf surfaces, and he behaves in socially unacceptable ways, as when he rudely criticizes the picture of Goethe in the professor's house. It is the wolf element within him that leads him to describe himself as "that beast astray who finds neither home nor joy nor nourishment in a world that is strange and incomprehensible to him." Haller feels so out of place in the world that he plans to commit suicide by cutting his throat with a razor. However, his life changes after he meets Hermine, who befriends him and introduces him to a world which formerly, because of his intellectual snobbery, he had despised. Instead of staying in his room reading his books of German poetry, he learns to dance and to enjoy worldly living, and doing so includes having a sexual relationship with the prostitute Maria. Through his new friends and his experiments with taking drugs given to him by Pablo that open him up to the unconscious elements of his mind, he learns to understand life in a more balanced way, accepting the many-sidedness of his being, instead of seeing himself divided into two fixed elements, man and wolf.

Herman

Herman was a childhood friend of Harry Haller. When Haller meets Hermine, her boyish appearance reminds him of Herman, a resemblance that becomes even more acute when Hermine dresses like a man at the fancy dress ball.

Hermine

Hermine is an friendly and charming prostitute, pale and pretty, whom Haller meets at a tavern called The Black Eagle. She has a rather boyish appearance, and Haller later realizes that she reminds him of his boyhood friend, Herman. When he first meets Hermine, Haller is in despair, but she listens to his tale of woe and seems to understand him. She takes charge of him and decides to teach him some of the simple things in life, such as dancing, that he, with all his intellectual accomplishments, has failed to learn. She refuses to accept any gifts from him, even though accepting such things from men is a part of her profession. Her role is to encourage Haller to experience all the sensual aspects of life that as a stiff intellectual he has scorned. She tells him not to take life so seriously, and she introduces him to Maria and sends her to his bed because she thinks it is high time he slept with a pretty young woman.

For his part, Haller is fascinated by Hermine. She is everything he is not, he observes. Unlike him, she is able to live in the moment, and she has a childlike ability to switch in an instant from seriousness to merriment. It is because of Hermine that Haller learns how to spend time enjoying himself at dances and listening to jazz in night clubs. She helps to end his sense of isolation.

Symbolically, perhaps, Hermine represents the feminine, sensual side of Haller himself (he says that when he looks at her it is like looking in a mirror). She may also represent his homoerotic desires, since she reminds him so much of his former male friend, Herman, and actually dresses as a man at the fancy dress ball. This symbolic dimension may help to explain why Haller kills the image of Hermine in the magic theater; because he has found in himself what she represents, she can no longer appear as a being outside of himself. He is, after all, only fulfilling her wish, amounting to a prediction, that he should eventually kill her.

Maria

Maria is a beautiful young woman who is a friend of Hermine. Like Hermine, Maria is a high-class prostitute, but there is also a kind of innocence about her. At Hermine's suggestion, she takes up with Haller, although she continues to see many other men as well. Haller falls in love with her. He believes that she is the kind of woman who lives only for love. Like Hermine, Maria makes Haller feel at home in the world of dance halls, cinemas, bars, and hotel lounges. She has no formal education, but, again like Hermine, she has the ability to live fully in the moment, in a sensual kind of way, and she knows exactly how to please her lovers. She also shows Haller that her love of the latest American popular songs can be as pure an artistic experience as his more exalted pleasure in classical music.

Wolfgang Amadeus Mozart

Wolfgang Amadeus Mozart (1756–1791) was one of the greatest composers in the Western musical tradition, famous for the almost heavenly beauty of his music. Haller venerates Mozart and regards his work as an expression of the eternal and the divine. In a surreal episode near the end of the novel, when Haller is in the "magic theater," he encounters Mozart and discusses music with him. Mozart reappears after Haller has murdered the image of Hermine and plays some music of Handel through a wireless. His purpose is to show Haller that even though the music is poorly reproduced, its divine quality can still be heard, and so Haller should also appreciate the presence of the divine in all the variegated expressions of human life. It is Mozart who refuses to pronounce the death sentence that Haller believes he deserves for killing Hermine. Instead, Mozart pronounces that Haller shall live, and by living, he will learn to revere life and also to laugh at it in the same way that the immortals laugh.

Pablo

Pablo is a saxophone player in a jazz band. Of South American or Spanish origin, he is a friend of Hermine and through her comes to know Haller. Pablo says little, but he is charming and seems to live on good terms with everyone. He is an excellent musician but, unlike Haller, sees little point in theoretical discussions about music. In Pablo's view, music should be played, not talked about, and he loves to play dance music that gets people moving and makes them happy. Pablo introduces Haller to mind-altering drugs, such as cocaine and opium, and he also suggests at one point that Haller join him and Hermine in a sexual encounter. Haller refuses, but the incident shows that Pablo does not conform to conventional notions of morality. The drugs Pablo gives to Haller enable Haller to enter the "magic theater" and so connect with his unconscious mind.

The Professor

The professor is a former acquaintance of Haller. They used to spend time together discussing oriental religion and mythology, which is the professor's specialty. When they meet again by chance in the street, the professor asks Haller to dinner. Haller's assessment of the professor is that his interests and knowledge are too narrow. He envelops himself in his scholarly work and believes in its value because he believes in evolution and progress. But he knows nothing of how the work of Einstein has changed the foundations of thought, because he thinks Einstein's work only concerns mathematicians. The professor is also a conventional, unthinking patriot who does not see that the militarism he supports will lead inevitably to the next war.

Themes

The Search for a Higher State of Consciousness

In a note to the novel written in 1961, Hesse declared that many readers had failed to understand the message of *Steppenwolf.* The book was not only about Haller's many miseries and failings. It pointed also to a "second, higher, indestructible world beyond the Steppenwolf . . . a positive, serene, superpersonal and timeless world of faith" (published as the "Author's Note" in the English translation of *Steppenwolf*). Hesse emphasized that the book was not about despair but belief.

This timeless world is glimpsed on a number of occasions by Haller. Since he is an extremely cultured, refined man, his knowledge and appreciation of the arts has given him moments of serene contemplation in which he is elevated into an eternal realm of the spirit, far above the messy push-and-pull of human life. He describes such moments early in the section of the novel entitled "Harry Haller's Records." One of them came when he attended a

Topics For Further Study

- Research the counterculture of the 1960s in the United States and make a class presentation that explains why *Steppenwolf* had such a strong appeal for young Americans during that decade.
- Read Hesse's novel, *Siddhartha*. Write an essay in which you discuss how Siddhartha's inner journey compares to that of Harry Haller. Are their spiritual quests similar? Do they reach the same kind of enlightenment? How do their methods differ? In what way is Vasudeva's instruction to Siddhartha to listen to the river similar to Mozart's instruction to Haller at the end of the novel that he must first learn to listen?
- Haller has a deep suspicion of technology and fears that it will debase the culture and adversely affect the human spirit. Why does he feel this? What reasons does he give? To what extent have his fears been realized? What are some of the dangers associated with technology that have become manifested in the years since *Steppenwolf* was first published? Make a class presentation with the results of your research.
- Harry Haller divides himself into two opposing qualities but later discovers how inadequate such a binary classification is. Write a short analysis like the "Treatise on the Steppenwolf" in which, taking yourself or someone you know well as your subject, you divide the whole personality into what you see as two main conflicting characteristics. Then show why these two characteristics are inadequate to describe a person's full nature. Is the treatise correct when it implies that every human being has a thousand different selves? What are the implications of that for the development of the personality?

concert. Listening to piano music, he was entranced, and a door opened to "another world," in which he "sped through heaven and saw God at work." It was a moment of complete acceptance, knowledge, and love in which he was able to contemplate all his human experiences in the light of eternity. The experience only lasted about fifteen minutes, but it gave him solace every time he thought about it in the many desolate days that followed. Sometimes he could for a moment see this other world clearly "threading my life like a divine and golden track." It came to him again in moments of spontaneous poetic inspiration or in reading poetry or contemplating a philosophical thought. At such moments, he felt complete and whole, and his heart was open to the truth of life, like a lover. Haller associates this world with the music of Mozart and Bach and the poetic world of Goethe. He refers to it as the realm of the immortals who live "in timeless space, enraptured, refashioned and immersed in a crystalline eternity like ether, and the cool starry brightness and radiant serenity of this world outside the earth." Hermine, in her capacity as another aspect of Haller's own mind, calls it the "kingdom of truth . . . the kingdom on the other side of time and appearances. It is there we belong. There is our home. It is that which our heart strives for." But Haller is bitterly aware of how hard it is to find this divine spark even for a moment in the humdrum human world. His abiding problem is how to achieve a higher state of consciousness, how to become one of the immortals, when he is confronted at every turn by the mediocrity of the bourgeois society in which he lives, its cultural decline, its obsession with the trivial and the degraded, with war and mechanization that debase the human spirit. Having once glimpsed this transcendental reality, he cannot forget it, and it is this that sets him apart from the rest of society: the man who sees the highest truth, however fleetingly, is doomed to be an outsider in a society that does not recognize its existence. At the end of the novel, it cannot be said that Haller has been successful in his quest to experience the divine level of life, but he is in a better position than he was at the beginning. He has been through the necessary processes of psychological healing (thanks to Pablo's "magic theater"), and with his new knowledge, he feels optimistic that the realm of the immortals is not beyond his grasp.

The Need for Psychological Wholeness

A precondition for attaining the highest spiritual perception, the novel seems to imply, is the need for Haller to repair his own psychological condition. He must first learn to experience the fullness of his own being. At the beginning of the novel, Haller, for all his intellectual power and refinement, is a psychologically maladjusted man. He is a misfit, at odds with the society in which he lives, rigid in his ways, tormented by what he sees as his dual personality, the "wolf" element in him—his desire to be independent, uncompromising, strong—always fighting with the human element that might otherwise be more sociable and agreeable, but is also cowardly and stupid. This psychologically crippled man, full of self-hatred, comes close to committing suicide since his life has become a "waste and empty hell of lovelessness and despair." He fails because he has been unable to live according to the truth of his own being. He has created a prison for himself by narrowing and limiting his concept of who he is. He thinks that the dual personality with which he so strongly identifies is fixed and immutable, not realizing that he is repressing a myriad of other selves, each of which in reality has a claim on him. "Harry consists of a hundred or a thousand selves," writes the author of the "Treatise on the Steppenwolf," according to whom the idea of a stable, unified personality is an illusion. In the treatise, Haller is compared to a gardener who cultivates a garden of a thousand flowers but then divides them into only two categories, edible and inedible. Since this is too crude a distinction, he misses nine-tenths of the beauty and value of the garden. According to the treatise, "This is what the Steppenwolf does with the thousand flowers of his soul. What does not stand classified as either man or wolf he does not see at all."

Since Haller represses so much of himself, and since the thrust of the psyche (according to the psychologist Carl Jung) is to wholeness and inclusion, he is fighting against the tide of life. At the most basic level, in his austere intellectual detachment, Haller has repressed his need for love and sex and his need to mix with others and enjoy himself socially. He must learn to be less stuffy, judgmental, and snobbish, to appreciate life in all its manifestations, both inner and outer. For this purpose, his new friends Hermine, Maria, and Pablo serve him well, opening him up to a new world of experience. The magic theater that Pablo encourages him to enter is "for madmen only"; that is to say, it is for those who are able to let go of the powerful grip of the rational mind and experience their unconscious desires and motivations. In particular, Haller is able to recover his erotic self through meeting once more the girls and women he has known in the past, but this time with more successful outcomes: "All the love that I had missed in my life bloomed magically in my garden during this hour of dreams." He learns that the personality is not fixed and rigid but contains a thousand different elements that can be moved around and recombined in different ways like so many pieces of a chessboard. This thinking frees him from the man/wolf dichotomy that has previously dominated and limited his awareness and makes him ready at least to attempt to experience the divine even within the hurly-burly of the human world.

Style

Realism and Surrealism

The novel is told on two levels, the realistic and the surreal. The bourgeois narrator's preface and the first part of "Harry Haller's Records" gives the reader a realistic picture of Haller's life. But when Haller is given the book, "*Treatise on the Steppenwolf*," a surreal element enters the novel, since from a realistic point of view, it is impossible for Haller suddenly to acquire a book written in this expository style which analyzes his own personality. Haller's dream of Goethe and his encounter with Mozart are other surreal events, as is the entire episode of the magic theater.

In Haller's encounter with Hermine, the realistic and the surreal levels are intertwined (although symbolic rather than surreal might be a better term in this context). At one level, Hermine is a shrewd courtesan who knows how to handle a new client; at another level, she is an incarnation of an aspect of Haller's own mind: she understands him perfectly, knows everything about him, and can read his thoughts, and he believes he can never have a secret from her.

Music Imagery

Music is a recurring motif, and different types of music illustrate the dichotomy between the ideal realm of the immortals and the bourgeois world; between spirit and flesh. In Haller's view, the music of composers such as Handel, Bach, and Mozart can express the divine and the eternal. By contrast, popular music, especially jazz, represents for Haller only cultural degeneration. In spite of this view, however, he acknowledges that jazz, even though he detests it, has "a secret charm" for him; its "raw and savage gaiety reached an underworld of instinct and breathed a simple honest sensuality." He also appreciates the happiness such music can convey. After he meets Maria, he comes to acknowledge that for those who enjoy the popular music of the day, it may provide them with an aesthetic experience that is just as valid and as profound as that provided by Mozart or other composers. This possibility suggests the bridging of the gap between spirit (represented by classical music) and flesh (jazz) that is part of the overall theme of the novel.

Mirror Imagery

The image of the mirror is used repeatedly to illustrate the point that the Steppenwolf must look at and examine himself unflinchingly in order to understand all aspects of his own nature. The mirror image occurs in the "*Treatise on the Steppenwolf*," for example, which states that Haller is well aware of the existence of such a mirror, as well as his need to look into it and his own terrible fear of doing so. The image of the mirror is used in connection with Hermine to convey the idea that she is an aspect of Haller's own self. When he looks into her face, it appears as "a magic mirror" to him. Near the end of the novel, Pablo shows Haller two mirrors, one in which Haller sees his accustomed wolf/man nature and which Pablo throws away before showing Haller another large mirror on the wall. In that mirror, Haller finally sees himself in a multitude of different guises. The mirror reveals to him the almost infinite facets and possibilities of his own self.

Historical Context

The Weimar Republic

In an attempt to create a parliamentary democracy in 1919 following World War I, German social democrats established the Weimar Republic in Germany. However, the Weimar Republic was beset by difficulties from the beginning. These included German resentment of the Versailles Treaty that followed World War I, which imposed punitive conditions on Germany in an attempt to ensure it would not threaten the victorious European powers again. Economic problems of Weimer included runaway inflation in the early 1920s and high unemployment during the worldwide depression in the early 1930s. Economic distress and social unrest combined to undermine the fledgling republic, which ended in 1933 with the establishment of the Third Reich by Adolf Hitler's National Socialist Party.

Significant issues in the literature of the Weimar Republic were the role of technology in society, nationalism, communism, and the cultural influence of the United States, among other countries. These were discussed by such figures as Thomas Mann (1875–1955), the greatest writer and intellectual of the Weimer Republic, who warned, along with others, against the dangers of fascism and authoritarianism. In *Steppenwolf*, Hesse made contributions to several of these issues. (Although during this period, Hesse lived in Switzerland, not Germany, he remained a German writer read by Germans.) Hesse's dislike of mechanization and technology can be seen in the surrealistic war on the automobiles and in Haller's negative comments about the radio and the gramophone. Equally prominent is Hesse's hatred of the kind of anti-democratic nationalism advocated by conservative forces in Weimar, as can be seen in the episode of Haller's dinner with the professor. Hesse's dislike of the cultural influence of the United States can be seen in Haller's contempt for jazz and American popular songs. In general, however, Hesse's novels during the period of the Weimar Republic were not political in tone. *Damien* (1919), *Siddhartha* (1922) and *Steppenwolf* (1927) are concerned mostly with the development of an enlightened personal vision; their interest is in psychology, spirituality, and the individual rather than society.

Psychological Theories of Freud and Jung

In the 1920s, the psychoanalytic theories of Sigmund Freud (1856–1939) were well known and widely accepted as groundbreaking contributions to human knowledge. In his studies of neurotic patients, Freud subjected the unconscious mind to rigorous investigation and showed how it influenced behavior. He believed that when people go through experiences that are too painful or threatening, they repress the memories of such experiences in the unconscious, where the memories become inaccessible to the conscious mind. Much of Freud's work dealt with repressed sexuality and aggression. He believed that dreams are the gateway to the unconscious mind and that by analyzing dreams the subconscious thoughts that affected behavior could be brought to the surface and the neurosis cured. One of Freud's most important works was *The Interpretation of Dreams* (1900).

Compare & Contrast

- **1920s:** Many in Europe are convinced that it is only a matter of time before another war breaks out on the continent. The prospect of war is connected to the fact that Germany resents the harsh conditions imposed on it in the Treaty of Versailles in 1919.

  Today: Having endured two major wars in the twentieth century, Europe is now involved in a network of economic and political relationships within the European Union that make a war between the principal powers of France, Britain, and Germany unlikely.

- **1920s:** In 1920, there are 7.5 million cars and trucks in the United States. The rise of the automobile industry in the United States and Europe leads to the development of infrastructure (new roads) and the decline of other modes of transportation such as horse-drawn vehicles, bicycles, streetcars, and interurban trains. Cars change everyday life for millions. Travel becomes easier and more convenient, increasing personal freedom and mobility. The growth of technology also leads some to fear the increasing mechanization of society and human subservience to machines, an attitude that Hesse dramatizes in the "war on the automobiles" section in *Steppenwolf.*

  Today: There are 220 million cars in the United States and 500 million cars worldwide. Cars are the main source of transportation in most developed countries. Rising gasoline prices and awareness of environmental pollution caused by the automobile lead to the development of hybrid vehicles that use electric power in addition to gasoline. Some of these cars yield as much as seventy miles to the gallon in freeway driving.

- **1920s:** Jazz, a form of music imported from the United States, becomes extremely popular in Germany. During the Weimar Republic, jazz becomes almost the national music, heard in cafés, dance halls, films and on gramophone records. American jazz musicians tour German cities.

  Today: Germany today remains strongly influenced by American culture, including jazz, television, and movies. Over 85 percent of movies playing in German cinemas are made in Hollywood. After Japan, Germany is the biggest foreign market for American films.

Hesse was a great admirer of Freud's work, and one of the key episodes in *Steppenwolf* is Haller's dream in which he meets Goethe. Before Goethe appears, Haller notices a scorpion climbing up his leg. He is aware that a scorpion can be "dangerously and beautifully emblematic of woman and sin." The image returns at the end of the dream, when Goethe presents Haller with a tiny effigy of a woman's leg. Haller falls in love with it, but when he reaches out to touch it, he fears it may be the scorpion, and he refers to his "hectic struggle between desire and dread." This incident suggests that sexual repression may play a part in fueling Haller's neurotic personality. The fact that Haller becomes much happier when he indulges in a sexual relationship with Maria seems to confirm this interpretation.

Swiss psychiatrist Carl Gustav Jung (1875–1961) was originally one of Freud's collaborators, but he broke with Freud in 1913 and developed his own system, which he called analytical psychology. Jung developed concepts such as archetypes, which he defined as recurring symbolic patterns in the mind, found in dreams as well as the mythologies of the world. Jung believed in the existence of a collective unconscious, not merely an individual one, in which these images were stored.

Hesse underwent Jungian psychoanalysis a decade before writing *Steppenwolf.* He later met and corresponded with Jung. Scholars usually identify Hesse's novel *Damien* as the one that shows the greatest influence of Jung, but there are elements of Jungian theory in *Steppenwolf,* too. One of the terms Jung used is the "shadow," the socially unacceptable aspects of the personality that are rejected by the conscious mind and pushed into the unconscious. This is close to what Hesse identifies in Haller as the wolf element within him. Jung also identified what he called the anima, the feminine element within a man, and this corresponds to the character Hermine in the novel.

Critical Overview

On first publication, *Steppenwolf* was praised highly by German writer Thomas Mann and was a bestseller in Germany in 1927, but in spite of that, the novel met some fierce criticism. Some readers saw in the prominence of sex and sensuality of this novel a betrayal of the asceticism and spirituality of Hesse's previous novel, *Siddhartha.* Hesse received many indignant letters from readers complaining about the novel's unusual form as well as the perceived immorality of its treatment of sex and its apparent endorsement of drug-taking. Hesse was also accused of being unpatriotic.

In England, the novel received a rather wary reaction from the reviewer for *The Guardian* newspaper, who objected to the "macabre" quality of the work and suggested "that post-war Germany is becoming rather too morbidly preoccupied with the intellectual insanity, which, according to Herr Hermann Hesse, overtakes human life when 'two ages, two cultures and religions, overlap.'" The reviewer's conclusion is:

> The author is at his best when his hero's thwarted idealism breaks into the foreground; for there is something malevolently Shavian about his forthrightness, and his bitter commentary on European civilisation is one of the few sane features of a maniacal book.

In the United States, *Steppenwolf* achieved far greater success than it did in Germany, although that success was over thirty years in coming. Beginning with the Beat Generation of the late-1950s, Hesse became something of a cult figure, and the Steppenwolf, as an outsider who opposed the materialist culture of his time, became a kind of hero. The popularity of the novel increased during the counterculture of the 1960s. The hippie culture of the young saw in *Steppenwolf* a guide and a philosophical justification for their experiments in hallucinogenic drugs and their opposition to the Vietnam War, which they viewed as an example of American greed and imperialism. The novel's status was such that a prominent rock band named itself after the title, and even in the early 2000s, there are several theater companies named Steppenwolf, in honor of the "magic theater" of the novel.

Mozart, one of the people whom Haller encounters in the magic theater The Library of Congress

Although Hesse's popularity in the United States waned during the 1970s, *Steppenwolf* remained highly esteemed by literary critics, some of whom regard the novel as Hesse's greatest achievement in the genre. Its form has been compared to that of James Joyce's *Ulysses*, and it has been interpreted in the light of the psychoanalytic theories of Carl Jung.

Criticism

Bryan Aubrey

Aubrey holds a Ph.D. in English and has published many articles on twentieth century literature. In this essay, he analyzes the role played by Pablo in Steppenwolf.

In the transformation of the Steppenwolf from an aloof, troubled intellectual to a person who engages wholeheartedly in all that life has to offer, a key figure is the saxophone player, Pablo. Haller meets him through Hermine at the Balance Hotel where Haller first dances in public with her. Pablo plays in the orchestra. He is young, dark, and good-looking, and his origins are either Spain or South America. He is clearly very different from the middle-aged, undistinguished-looking, northern European Haller. Hermine thinks very highly of Pablo and informs Haller that he is able to play every instrument there is and speak every language in the world. Haller, however, does not take to Pablo when he first meets him. He finds the musician agreeable and charming, but he is a little jealous of Pablo's friendship with Hermine. At this point, Haller does not feel at all comfortable in this dance hall environment, which he regards as a "world of idlers and pleasure seekers."

For some while, Haller continues to be unimpressed and indeed puzzled by Pablo. Haller is an intellectual whose currency is language. He deals in ideas, in intellectual theories, and scholarly knowledge, but Pablo is the opposite. He says almost nothing, no more than one word at a time, such as please or thank you. He gives Haller the impression that he does not think much, either. When Haller tries to talk to him about music, Pablo just smiles, and Haller takes this to mean that Pablo is unaware of any music other than jazz. Faced with this kind of vacuity, Haller assumes that Pablo lives only for playing the saxophone, in addition to being something of a dandy and a ladies' man. This is definitely not someone whom a man like Haller is going to take seriously. To the Steppenwolf, Pablo is like a child, "for whom there are no problems, whose joy it is to dribble into his toy trumpet and who is kept quiet with praises and chocolate," although he does learn from Hermine that Pablo is an expert in all kinds of drugs that will ease pain, aid sleep, and "[beget] beautiful dreams, lively spirits and the passion of love."

When Pablo finally does start responding verbally to Haller, he explains that he is a musician, not a professor. Whereas Haller's refined appreciation of music is gained by listening rather than playing, for Pablo, the purpose of music is to play it, not talk about it. He could, he says, make clever remarks about the music of Bach and Mozart, since he knows all their works—thus disproving Haller's notion that Pablo only knows jazz—but there would be no point in doing so. When Haller tries to convince him that Mozart's music is superior to the latest foxtrot, Pablo will not get drawn into an argument. He does not divide music into different layers, one eternal and the other ephemeral, the way Haller does. As a musician, he plays whatever is in demand, and he plays it as well as he possibly can since he loves to give people pleasure.

"Pablo represents that part of Haller's own mind that he has pushed out of his conscious awareness and into the unconscious. As Pablo calls that forgotten psychic energy awake, the impulses that Haller has repressed are unleashed."

This conversation is a telling one. Whereas Haller, despite the progress he is making, continues to be dominated by his intellect, which separates life into the dualities of spirituality/sensuality, man/Steppenwolf, classical music/jazz, high culture/low culture, Pablo makes no such distinctions. He has a more unified personality. As an enthusiastic participant in the sensual dance of life, he lives in the fullness of the moment. He does not make up theories about life or music; he is too busy living it.

When Haller takes up with Maria, he begins to see a lot more of Pablo, since Pablo and Maria are friends and also at some point have been lovers. During this time, Pablo sometimes gives Haller opium and cocaine, and they become friends. Haller's opinion of Pablo begins to change, although he still feels that he does not understand the younger man. He is shocked on one occasion when Pablo proposes that Haller and Maria join him in a "love orgy for three." Haller refuses abruptly. Some days later, Hermine remarks that Pablo may be a saint in hiding, since sometimes even sin and vice can be a way to saintliness. She is suggesting that Pablo is a spiritual seeker and that conventional notions of sin and vice may, in fact, be mere labels that bourgeois society places on behavior that contravenes its narrow moral standards.

What transpires as the novel progresses is that Pablo is indeed a kind of guru figure, a spiritual guide to Haller. Hesse drops a clue to this just after Pablo is introduced to the story. After meeting Haller, Pablo realizes immediately that he is a very unhappy man and tells Hermine that she must be nice to him. Pablo says, "Look at his eyes. Doesn't know how to laugh." The remark is meant literally, but it also has a deeper significance. Throughout *Steppenwolf* laughter is associated with the realm of

What Do I Read Next?

- Hesse's novel *Siddhartha* (first published in 1922) is the story of a young Indian man who seeks the path of spiritual knowledge and salvation. Modeled on the early life of the Buddha, the novel combines timeless Eastern wisdom about the ultimate reality of life with Hesse's distinctly original metaphysical and spiritual vision.
- Hesse's novella *Klingsor's Last Summer* (1920; first English translation, 1970) is about the last months in the life of an intense and passionate middle-aged painter called Klingsor. Like *Steppenwolf*, the novella has autobiographical elements and makes extensive use of the mirror motif. Also, just as Harry Haller gazes into the mirror before he enters the magic theater and sees all aspects of himself, so Klingsor expresses through his final self-portrait the entirety of his multi-faceted self.
- *Man and His Symbols* (1964) is a clear introduction, with many illustrations, to the theories of Carl Jung. It includes essays by Jung and other Jungian scholars, including Joseph L. Henderson, M.-L. von Franz, Aniela Jaffé, and Jolande Jacobi. The book explains Jungian concepts important for Hesse, such as the shadow, the anima and the animus, and the significance of dreams.
- Ralph Freedman's *Hermann Hesse, Pilgrim of Crisis: A Biography* (1978) is, as of 2006, the most thorough biography of Hesse available in English, especially strong on the autobiographical elements in *Steppenwolf*. In Freedman's view, Hesse resembles a character in one of his novels who eventually learns to reconcile his ideal of harmony with life on earth. He is able to live through crises while at the same time contemplating them in a detached manner.

---

the immortals. In Haller's dream of Goethe, for example, the revered old poet tells him that the immortals do not take things seriously. They like joking, and Haller hears him "[laughing] a still and soundless laughter." Later, in a moment of contemplation, Haller suddenly understands the full significance of this immortal laughter:

> It was a laughter without an object. It was simply light and lucidity. It was that which is left over when a true man has passed through all the sufferings, vices, mistakes, passions and misunderstandings of men and got through to eternity and the world of space. And eternity was nothing else than the redemption of time, its return to innocence, so to say, and its transformation again into space.

In this moment of understanding, Haller hears the laughter of the immortals, "a never-ending and superhuman serenity, an eternal, divine laughter." Laughter, it appears, is simply a metaphor for a mode of being in which there is no longer any attachment to the pleasures and pains of the world, only a timeless joy that is the essence of life, beyond any possibility of suffering.

When Pablo says Haller does not know how to laugh, he implies that Haller has no knowledge or understanding of this higher mode of being, a knowledge that Pablo himself possesses. Later, Haller will notice that there is always laughter in Pablo's eyes, and his actual laugh is "bright and peculiar"; it reminds Haller of the "strange and eerie laughter" that he associates with the immortals. It is Pablo who can show Haller the way.

Hesse has another surprise for the reader in connection with Pablo, although it will be no surprise to anyone who has been noting the layered nature of the narrative, which is at once realistic and symbolic. Pablo is in truth nothing more than an aspect—a long neglected aspect—of Haller's own mind. This becomes crystal clear towards the end of the novel when Pablo begins to prepare Haller and Hermine for the magic theater. "Why was Pablo talking so much?" Haller wonders. "Was it not I who made him talk, spoke, indeed, with his voice? Was it not, too, my own soul that contemplated me out of his black eyes . . . ?"

Pablo represents that part of Haller's own mind that he has pushed out of his conscious awareness and into the unconscious. As Pablo calls that forgotten psychic energy awake, the impulses that Haller has repressed are unleashed. The fact that Haller is beginning to realize this shows how far he has come from the time when he believed that he and Pablo were complete opposites with nothing at all in common. In a sense, of course, he was right, since Pablo represents everything within himself that Haller had tried so hard to deny. But he now realizes that, in the end, denying one's own nature is a lot harder than acknowledging it. The integrated self that emerges from such acknowledgement is just as Jung described it, a *coincidentia oppositorum*, a coexistence of opposites. One example of this concept occurs when Haller looks into the large mirror on the wall and sees a multitude of reflections of himself, all showing different characteristics, such as young and old, serious and comic, civilized and wild. One of these figures is an elegant young man who "leaped laughing into Pablo's arms and embraced him and they went off together." This is an allusion to the earlier incident in which Haller is repelled by Pablo's suggestion of a sexual encounter involving Pablo, Haller, and Maria. It suggests Haller's acceptance of his latent bisexuality, a motif that also occurs in his relationship with Hermine, who looks like a boy and who reminds Haller of his boyhood friend, Herman.

Pablo also functions as a teacher after Haller has "killed" Hermine. This incident of the killing has been variously interpreted. It may mean that Haller has recognized the feminine aspect of himself, and his destruction of the external Hermine means that he has reintegrated that self into his conscious awareness. But this interpretation is hard to reconcile with the negative terms, full of guilt and transgression, in which the incident is presented. An alternative explanation is what Pablo himself suggests, that Haller kills Hermine in a fit of jealousy. If this is so, it demonstrates that Haller has not yet fully learned what Pablo is trying to teach him, as Pablo himself points out. Haller has sunk back into a state in which he not only recoils from sensuality but also gets caught up in an ego-centered frame of mind, desperately needing to have exclusive control and ownership over the things to which he is attached in life. Then when he comes to his senses, he wallows in guilt, remorse, and the perceived need for retribution. Such is the human game as it is so commonly played, but Haller is being encouraged to play it differently. He gets some assistance from the sudden appearance of Mozart, who with the help

Johann Wolfgang Von Goethe, a famous German writer admired by the novel's protagonist, Harry Haller © Bettmann/Corbis

of the Handel-on-the-wireless analogy—the quality of the reproduction may be dreadful but the music it plays remains divine—grasps that life lived in the sphere of time is an expression, however distorted and disguised, of the qualities which he identifies as divine and which are summed up in that phrase, "divine laughter." It is not for Haller to criticize it or attempt to amend it; it is not for Haller to rail against the distortions of the ideal in the appearances of everyday life. Life is what it is. Mozart tells him that rather than tampering with it, "Better learn to listen first! Learn what is to be taken seriously and laugh at the rest."

When Mozart turns out to have been Pablo all along, Hesse springs his final surprise on the reader. Since Pablo and the wisdom he embodies is an aspect of Haller's own mind, then the same must be true of Mozart/Pablo. That ripple of divine laughter that appears to Haller as the eternal song emanating from some other, superior world inhabited by Mozart and the immortals is in fact no such thing. It is the voice of his own "higher" self, calling from within. All he has to do is listen.

Source: Bryan Aubrey, Critical Essay on *Steppenwolf*, in *Novels for Students*, Thomson Gale, 2007.

Kurt J. Fickert

In the following essay, Hesse's poetic use of the epiphany and "his expansion of its significance" is discussed.

In its literary dimension, the term "epiphany" refers to an occasion on which a character in a work of fiction is suddenly overtaken by a moment of insight into the tenor of his or her life. Originally the word had a religious connotation, since it refers to the experience of the biblical wise men who traveled to Bethlehem under the guidance of a bright star to bear witness to a miraculous birth. This element of a penumbra heightens the symbolic value of the epiphany in its figurative sense. A contemporary of Hermann Hesse, James Joyce made particular use of the epiphany as a poetic device in his early work. Striking examples appear in *A Portrait of the Artist as a Young Man* (1916) and in the prose poems he wrote to demonstrate the momentary illumination of the thoughts and commonplace objects that exalted him. There is no direct evidence that Hermann Hesse knew Joyce, although Joyce lived for a time and died (in 1941) in Zurich, a city quite familiar to Hesse and a primary location in the Steppenwolf's search for an identity. There is every reason to suppose, however, that Hesse would have been aware of, if not closely acquainted with, Joyce's linguistically challenging work. It is also likely that he was familiar with Joyce's concept of the role of the artist-writer in society, a subject of paramount interest to both writers. Within this frame of reference, this essay explores Hesse's use of the epiphany as a prototype in his most celebrated novel, *Der Steppenwolf* (1927), and will establish his expansion of its significance in a literary text.

Critics have paid markedly little attention to the subject of the moment of epiphany as Hesse puts it to use in his fiction; at the same time, they have repeatedly taken note of his practice of embellishing his realistic accounts with fantastic events and magical transformations. These occur with some frequency throughout Hesse's work, including the disappearance of Hermann Lauscher in the novel *Hinterlassene Schriften von Hermann Lauscher (Hermann Lauscher's Legacy of His Writings*, 1901) and of Hermann Hesse himself in the *Kurzgefasster Lebenslauf* (*Concise Autobiography*, 1924). Joseph Milek, in *Hermann Hesse: Life and Art*, explores the concept of the epiphany to a limited extent but holds it to be an aspect of the concept of grace. Milek postulates Hesse's propensity, acquired as a child raised in a Protestant household, to associate Christ's birth with God's gift of grace rather than with an occasion for the presentation of gifts. Through such an overlapping of general and private symbolism, Hesse uses the literary device of the epiphany to describe effectively the turmoil of his life and times and the transcendence beyond the resultant despair. It is this theme which underlies his fiction.

In his *Understanding Hermann Hesse*, Lewis W. Tusken has given the epiphany motif in *Der Steppenwolf* another designation, proposing that "Harry labels these magic moments Gottesspuren (traces of God)—Jung's 'flashes of insight.'" Oskar Seidlin leaves aside such religious and psychological connotations and summarizes Hesse's literary search for his selfhood in these terms: "[H]is entire work seems an endless recording of the process of awakening" (my emphasis). Ralph Freedman uses the philosophic concept of unio mystica to characterize the moment of sudden insight that overwhelms the protagonist in stories dealing with the experience of an epiphany. In accord with Freedman, David G. Richards describes the Steppenwolf's progress toward experiencing a corona-embellished rebirth in these words: "Haller's despair and thoughts of suicide may be seen as manifestations of this stage ('the dark night of the soul') which generally precedes the mystical experience of illumination (the unio mystica)."

Yet, critics of *Der Steppenwolf* have largely neglected to examine the exact nature of this moment of enlightenment in the novel. It occurs when the protagonist, a disillusioned writer and inveterate member of the bourgeoisie, experiences, like the reformer Martin Luther, a confrontation withthe equivalent of a symbolic lightning storm, namely, the moment of epiphany, which impels him to pursue his destiny. This event takes place only after Hesse has provided two descriptions, one magnifying the other, of Harry Haller's desperate state of mind. The book's first section is ostensibly the work of a first-person narrator, the landlady's observant, yet dispassionate, nephew. He gives an objective report about Haller's life of social isolation and personal wretchedness in a comfortable and orderly rooming house. The narrator has generously undertaken to prepare for publication the autobiographical papers Haller has left behind upon vanishing from his rooms. The second description is Harry's first-person narrative covering recent events in his life and their miseries.

The chief factor in Harry's recollections is his elucidation of the concept of "the Steppenwolf," as he has come to call himself. He recognizes a part of himself to be an antagonist, rebelling against the social constraints imposed on him by the bourgeois world into which he was born. He illustrates one of his exhibitions of self-destructive rage by portraying a visit he has made to the home of a professor, an old friend, whom he has just met again after a long period of separation. Harry finds himself incapable of communicating with his host and hostess and flees from their apartment after having wounded the feelings of the professor's wife. He has made scathing comments on her treasured portrait of Goethe, which, in Haller's view, depicts the German genius as a bourgeois idol. In recognition of his inability to conceal his hostility toward the superficiality of social norms, he condemns himself to living the life of an outcast and proclaims himself an "outsider" (Hesse uses the English word in his German text).

Under these circumstances, Harry is confined to roaming only ill-lighted and for the most part deserted city streets, while on occasion breaking up this routine with a visit to some dingy tavern where he orders a bottle of wine. On one of these nocturnal journeys, he experiences an epiphany that leads him to believe in the possibility of transforming his life into one in which he can achieve spiritual wholesomeness. The possibility of this transformation appears to him in the form of a fleeting vision. He glimpses a sealed-shut doorway with a pointed arch, now a part of a wall, at the opposite ends of which lie a church (symbolizing eternity) and a hospital (symbolizing life's fragility and brevity) concealed in darkness. The moving lighted letters of a sign above the portal illuminate the scene; the words become legible to Harry momentarily. They proclaim: "Magic Theater/Admittance not for everyone/—not for everyone." The message bewilders Haller; when his eyes look down at the mirroring surface of the street, darkened by rain, he sees the fading reflection of the advertisement's last words: "Only—for—the—Mad!" Harry cannot immediately fathom the meaning of this pseudo-slogan that seems to apply to him and his tormented life, but he suspects that his discovery of the hidden doorway will lead him to pursue a path into the inner depths of his being.

After Hesse's death (in 1962) an untitled manuscript was discovered among his papers and subsequently published in *Materialien zu Hermann Hesses "Der Steppenwolf,"* which can readily be looked upon as an earlier version of this episode. It tells the story of a writer, who, while on a journey, discovers in a way-station town a remarkable, forest-like garden, enclosed within a wall. Nearby

"The significance of the epiphany unfolds within Hesse's description of his search for release from an alienation from his self (the sense of being the lone wolf Harry Haller)."

there is a restaurant in which he has a conversation with a mysterious old man. The author gives him the name "Sparrow Hawk" (a prominent image in Hesse's *Demian*, 1919). The stranger provides the traveler with sage advice: "Make sure you act on your every wish [desire]." Later, the writer fulfills this prescription: wanting to see the garden, he climbs, with some effort, over the wall. He finds himself in a timeless world (Urwelt), a world of chaos, where wild delights and dismal fears contend with one another. Before the manuscript breaks off, the writer reveals that he believes the garden to be his own soul. As he listens to a piano being played, he concludes that for him every musical sound is a world in itself, is God himself. The supposition that the magic garden became, in *Steppenwolf*, the Magic Theater lies close at hand. This earlier draft is significant in that it provides a contrast to the final version, especially in regard to the omission of the scene of the epiphany and the entire section devoted to the Magic Theater. In comparing the neo-romantic writing in this fragment with the masterfully subtle writing in the finished novel, one cannot but agree with Thomas Mann's evaluation that "*Der Steppenwolf* [is] no less daring as an experimental novel than James Joyce's *Ulysses* [1922] and Andre Gide's *Les Faux-Monnayeurs* [1926]."

After Harry leaves the forest-like garden, where he has entered into the farther reaches of his mind or consciousness, the Steppenwolf's instinct is to seek out, in a reflex action, the thriving nightlife of the city. However, his thoughts remain focused on the promise of an incipient enlightenment that his epiphany has afforded him. He asks himself: "And who sought beyond the ruins of his life its disintegrating meaning, endured the seemingly senseless, experienced the seemingly irrational, hoped covertly to find nevertheless in an ultimate insane chaos revelation and the nearness of God?" Since the question has only one answer—the Steppenwolf—Haller is drawn back to the environs where the letters of the advertising sign had lit up the emptiness. Although only the darkness remains, Harry is light of heart. For his hopefulness he is rewarded by the appearance of a shadowy figure. It cannot be refuted that Harry's encounter with such denizens of the night represents reinforcing aspects of Harry's capability to go on with his soul searching. The man who is about to rush past him on the dark street appears to be a vendor, bearing a tray of brochures. In response to Haller's request, he is provided with one of these before the tout vanishes behind a door. It is, as he discovers back in his room, a treatise on the subject of the Steppenwolf written by members of a group joined together by their interest in the species.

Readers of the first edition of *Der Steppenwolf* were given the opportunity to consider the realistic aspects of the novel, since this part of the book was printed within inserted colored cover pages and was separately paginated. (It is now distinguished from the rest of the text merely by italicized type.) However, the symbolic overtones of this pamphlet are indeed of special significance. In an important critical appraisal of Hesse's work, Theodore Ziolkowski analyzes the form of *Der Steppenwolf* on the basis of a statement in one of the author's letters, dated 13 November 1930. Plainly, it consists of a third-person (in a figurative sense) introductory passage, a first-person narrative in two parts, and the interpolated tractate. Subsequently, Ziolkowski determines that the text takes the form of a sonata, with its repetitions and inversions. An equally valid conclusion about the book's format can be reached by considering its tripartite nature: an introduction to the Steppenwolf's personal revelations; the tractate; then prologue to, and elaboration of, the Magic Theater episode. This tripling of viewpoints can also be regarded as a part of a consecutive mirroring that indeed dominates the symbolism of the entire story. Each section serves to reflect and simultaneously magnify the other; none provides contrast. In the same way, the short-lived epiphany continues to illuminate Haller's journey. In a symbolic sense, it allows Haller to make the transition from hopelessness to an affirmation of life's meaningfulness. In a literal sense, he ceases, as a result of the epiphanic experience, to roam the city's midnight mazes, and instead explores the Magic Theater's splendiferous corridors with Mozart. Thus, before the advent of the epiphany he is lost in the realm of his darkest despair, whereas after it he ascends in the Magic Theater to his imagination's highest and most radiant peaks.

The significance of the epiphany unfolds within Hesse's description of his search for release from an alienation from his self (the sense of being the lone wolf Harry Haller). Although the "Tractate" restates to a considerable extent what the editorial prologue to Harry's confessions has already contended, it takes him a step further down the path that the epiphany on the city street has illuminated. The booklet convinces Harry (as the character Hermine will also do later) that he, like every human being, has not two but a multitude of selves. (For example, Hermine is the feminine in his nature.) It will be his task, as he forces himself to think beyond the concept of individuation, to imagine the many aspects of his personality and to examine the conflict between the author and the society with which he is inextricably involved, a core concept in Hesse's work. As the Steppenwolf tractate looks back on Harry Haller's dichotomous self, the analysis in the pamphlet also represents a bridge to the adventure of the Magic Theater (which the epiphany has created.)

While the three parts of the novel all deal with Harry's problematic character, it is the concluding section, the Magic Theater episode, which, although it again depicts his frustrations, affords him the knowledge of the "true self" promised him on the occasion of the epiphany. This kind of revelation will enable him to throw off the burden of living on the brink of madness and self-destruction. Thus, the slogan that appears at the end of the message provided by the epiphany is "Only for the Mad." These words become the motto for the tractate and subsequently the motto that prefaces Harry's experiences in the Magic Theater. According to Allemann, the main purpose of the booklet is to lead Haller in the direction of a resolution of his problems. The Steppenwolf then makes his first notable attempt to heal his dichotomous self by reading the pamphlet, which, in effect, generalizes his situation. In taking the tractate to heart, he confronts its authors, whom he will come to know as the Immortals of the Magic Theater, a construction of much greater sophistication than that of the previous version's sage in the restaurant at the edge of a magic forest. In her essay on *Der Steppenwolf* Mary E. Stewart states that Hesse's use of the motif of a suprahuman phenomenon "reflects the concern of many of [his] contemporaries to find some kind of timeless essence to set against the unanchored subjectivity of individual experience: Joyce's 'epiphanies' [and] Thomas Mann's interest in mythology." Hesse's interweaving of these psychological configurations follows the pattern of mirroring, which is the main feature of the symbolism in the novel's climactic episode.

Confronted with an eminently autobiographical text, the reader is led to assume that the story and the event of the epiphany are being told on a realistic level. The same kind of narration prevails in the account of the protagonist's desperate efforts to adjust to a life as a quasi-libertine in a cosmopolitan environment. However, in the ensuing Magic Theater episode, Harry's confessions unexpectedly and dramatically take on a bizarre aspect. In the occurrence that provides a resolution to Harry's problems in the novel, Haller (the name, in its relationship to "verhallen," suggests someone whose voice is fading away as though with his or her generation), as a half-bourgeois, half-beastly personality, becomes transformed. The first-person narrator is absorbed into the narrative when it becomes clear that the figure represents the author's search for wholeness. This ultimate state of existence is to be achieved, in consonance with the text's goal, by the integration of his many selves. It must be noted that this transformation does not constitute a final solution to the conflicts in Haller's life. Rather, it can only constitute a temporary one. The difficulties of the artist in his or her relationship to (bourgeois) society, according to Hesse, require ongoing attention.

The pre-Magic Theater stage of Harry's life in the city allows Hesse also to introduce the people of the demimonde and the bohemian world in the Zurich of the twenties. One of them, the prostitute Hermine, becomes prominent in her role as Harry's guide in the preternatural realm. Her name, which reminds Haller of his childhood friend Hermann (the author himself), suggests that she is Harry's anima, the creative (life-giving) self, an aspect of himself that he has suppressed in order to have a secure place in the bourgeois world. To prepare him for his experiences in the Magic Theater, Hermine has previously undertaken to educate him in worldliness, that is, to teach him how to enjoy the freedom of dance, jazz music, and the world of erotic, sensual pleasures. These activities bring to the fore a number of his many selves. The novel becomes the story of Harry's painful acquisition of the talents that allow him to function as a city-dweller in the post-World War One world. He finds he has the ability to drink to excess, to dance to "non-music," or jazz, and to consort with, and enjoy the favors of, prostitutes. At this point, the novel is a straightforward account of his life as he approaches the age of fifty. Along with the women of the night, Hermine and her friend Maria, Haller is also guided by the jazz musician Pablo, a name faintly reminiscent of two of Hesse's fellow artists: Pablo Picasso and Pablo Casals. They are her subtly presented as possible companions of Harry Haller in the hectic, pleasure-seeking activities of the bohemian inhabitants of a European metropolis. Their revelries reach a climax at a masked ball. It is at this point that the realism subsides, and the book becomes a surrealistic fantasy.

The symbolism in this concluding section of the novel is the outcome of a challenge that the author Hesse has put to himself. In his blatantly autobiographical essay "Krisis: ein Stuck Tagebuch," a second preliminary version of *Der Steppenwolf,* he acknowledges that a late-blooming but irrepressible urge to be strictly truthful and honest about himself led to his consciousness of the dark side of his nature. In a letter to Hugo Ball, who had been contracted to write Hesse's biography, Hesse stated this resolve. He also drew the conclusion that his, as he termed it, neurotic obsession with delving into the sicknesses of the times was indeed the result of those sicknesses (themselves the result of the excesses of individualism), which had overrun Europe like a plague. The treatment Hesse prescribed as a remedy for society's dissolute practices, namely, for example, the unending warfare among the nations, was to expose the wound that society had inflicted on itself. As a means to this end, Hesse chose to write an autobiographical account, detailing his bout with neurosis as an artist and intellectual.

In converting a hotel ballroom and its environs into a "magic theater," Hesse has created a cosmography of his own mind and soul. What are the features of this inner landscape? The figures Hesse conjures up to populate the scene are hyperbolic versions of the characters whom the Steppenwolf has met during his adventures in the nightlife of the metropolis. Hermine now serves to illuminate a psychological concept, that of the anima. According to the psychoanalytical theory of Carl Gustav Jung, the anima, in its capacity as a creative force in the mind, engenders healing in the fractured self. (Hesse was a patient of Jung and, more importantly, of Dr. Lang, one of Jung's disciples.) Against this background, the role that Hermine plays in the Magic Theater becomes clear: she brings Haller closer to understanding himself and his plight. Nevertheless, Harry's possibly feigned murder of Hermine, which occurs as his adventures in the deepest regions of the self come to a close, can but signify that he must abandon her as his guide and go the rest of his way alone. Further evidence that he has taken responsibility for his own life and way of living is the change in his thinking manifested by the transformation of Pablo, the saxophone player, into the image of Mozart. This puzzling interplay of symbols tends to place the reader back on the dark street where the glowing letters on the rain-darkened sidewalk spelled out the warning "Only for the Mad," that is, for those in an ultimate stage of distress. The turn of events in the Magic Theater cannot provide the ultimate solution either to the Steppenwolf's psychological problems or Harry Haller's confusions in a licentious society between the wars. As Beda Allemann has pointed out in his article "Der Traktat vom Steppenwolf," the author Hesse himself expressly presents his private insight into the means by which a society in turmoil can reacquire its equilibrium. The remedy requires, in Hesse's terms, a faith in "the higher, historical correlations of earthly existence."

In a letter written on 14 May 1931, following the publication of *Der Steppenwolf,* Hesse proclaimed: "One must be able to replace the idols of the age with a faith. This I have always done; in *Der Steppenwolf* this involves Mozart and the Immortals and the Magic Theater." Harry's adventures in the Magic Theater depict his attempt to resolve the conflicts that plague him (together with Hesse and all of bourgeois society) in the era of the twentieth century between two world wars.

In *Der Steppenwolf* Hesse does not champion escape from a world in upheaval by means of drugs that induce a false sense of security. Although licentious behavior occurs in the scenes that take place in the Magic Theater, these are a prelude to an episode of spiritual transcendence that occurs as a final consequence of Harry's epiphany. Neither does the Magic Theater have a resemblance to the Theater of the Absurd. When, in an episode in this section, Harry aims his pistol at the drivers of cars who race down the highways, they are for him symbolically destroyers of the natural world. He is protesting an act of vandalism perpetrated by a bourgeoisie too eager to solve problems by making use of machines. On a more personal level, Harry fulfills his youthful sexual desires by taking part in a charade in the theater's loges. In this latter adventure his Steppenwolf self whips his all-too-human self, and vice versa. These adventures serve mainly to lead him toward his ultimate adventure in the Magic Theater. Offering himself as a guide to Harry in reaching his goal, Mozart appears. Henry Hatfield, in an essay on Hesse's *Steppenwolf,* has pointed out that Mozart comes on stage at this point while reciting "a Joycean sort of 'pome.'"

Mozart is a many-faceted symbol. He stands, first of all, for the Immortals, namely, all creative artists. In a recent study of Hesse and his work, Karin Tebbin has associated artistic achievement with the process of becoming free of the bonds of the merely personal and reaching the lofty heights of the supra-personal; only from this vantage point can the writer share his views with the reader. In another capacity, Mozart symbolizes music and the power to express the ineffable. In a letter written on 10 January 1929, Hesse explains his decision to select Mozart from among other musical geniuses to reign in the Magic Theater. He posits that Mozart's operas were for him the very concept of theater. Significantly, Mozart also tries to teach Haller the art of laughter, the art of rising above the vicissitudes and dichotomies of life and above death itself.

At the conclusion of the climactic scene in which Mozart provides Haller with a key to the puzzles that he has confronted in the Magic Theater, this Immortal closest to Harry's heart vanishes. He leaves behind in Harry an intuitive sense of the meaningfulness of his experiences. As Ted R. Spivey explains, "[I]n a visionary moment [Harry] glimpses the archetype of the cosmic man." In regard to this archetype David G. Richards contends: "With mythopeic power Joyce and Hesse create figures originating in the archetype out of which the mythical heroes arose. They set out in search of the hero's image and power, which is awaiting discovery and activation in every individual." In this instance, Harry Haller, through Mozart and his compositions, begins to understand the cosmic aspect of the relationship between the artist and society, particularly bourgeois society, that has propelled the Steppenwolfs in its midst into madness. Harry Haller rids himself of his despair after his experience in the Magic Theater. The key function of the epiphany on the dark city street has been to bind together the three levels on which Haller's hegira tales place: the real world of Europe between the wars, the literary realm of the tractate, and the cosmic or eternal sphere of the Magic Theater. There the Steppenwolf momentarily puts aside his dual nature and transcends the ills of mortality.

As if to emphasize the tentative aspect of his achievement, Haller finds himself alone with the saxophone player Pablo (Mozart) at the end of his adventures and misadventures in the theater. Pablo berates him for having taken these too seriously and for having perhaps misinterpreted them. He reassures Harry that further experiments in reassembling

Max von Sydow as Harry Haller and Dominique Sanda as Hermine in the 1974 film version of Hermann Hesse's novel Steppenwolf © D/R Films/ The Kobal Collection

the many selves of the onetime dichotomous Steppenwolf can be made at his discretion. The open-ended nature of the conclusion of *Der Steppenwolf* establishes that the moment of epiphany initiated by the moving lighted text that Haller seeks to interpret is a signpost to the artist-writer. It directs artists and writers (and their public) in the direction of reorienting themselves in order to contend with a world gone mad. In the year in which *Der Steppenwolf* was first published, Hesse wrote to his biographer, Hugo Ball, and summarized what he had intended the novel to convey. Its message, so Hesse indicates, was that the writer's mission must be to become self-aware and thus bring, by establishing an inner equilibrium, harmony into a world beset with wars and moral decay. In his letter Hesse also proposes that the writer's objective must not be to affirm the goodness of life, but to explore its heights and depths so that readers and critics can become enlightened about the burden they bear in common with the writer.

Source: Kurt J. Fickert, "The Significance of the Epiphany in *Der Steppenwolf*," in *International Fiction Review*, January 2002, pp. 1–10.

Sources

"Beastly Nightmares," in *The Guardian*, June 21, 1929, n.p., http://books.guardian.co.uk/ (accessed April 26, 2006).

Field, G. W., *Hermann Hesse*, Twayne's World Author Series, No. 93, Twayne Publishers, 1970, pp. 86–108.

Hesse, Hermann, *Steppenwolf*, translated by Basil Creighton, Holt, Rinehart and Wilson, 1929.

Further Reading

Boulby, Mark, *Hermann Hesse: His Mind and Art*, Cornell University Press, 1967, pp. 159–205.

As of 2006, this was one of the most detailed readings available. Boulby discusses such topics as the significance of music for the novel's structure and theme; he views the novel as an optimistic one in which faith imposes order on chaos.

Mileck, Joseph, *Hermann Hesse: Life and Art*, University of California Press, 1978, pp. 174–97.

Mileck discusses such topics as the autobiographical elements in *Steppenwolf*. He doubts that Hesse himself took hallucinogenic drugs, even though Haller in the novel uses them to achieve self-knowledge.

Sorrell, Walter, *Hermann Hesse: The Man Who Sought and Found Himself*, Owald Wolff, 1974, pp. 83–93.

This is a concise overview of Hesse's life and work. Most interesting for an understanding of *Steppenwolf* is the chapter on Hesse's ironic brand of humor.

Tusken, Lewis W., *Understanding Hermann Hesse: The Man, His Myth, His Metaphor*, University of South Carolina, 1998, pp. 108–27.

Tusken gives a reading of *Steppenwolf* in mostly Jungian terms. The novel is an attempt to construct a literary metaphor for the Jungian concept of individuation, the development of all aspects of a person's individuality.

Toward the End of Time

John Updike

1997

John Updike's *Toward the End of Time*, published in 1997, is a mixture of science fiction, magic realism, and a journal account written by an older man who feels his world collapsing around him. The story is written as if it were the journal of Ben Turnbull, a retired financier who is living an economically comfortable life in New England despite the chaos and destruction around him. The majority of the story takes place in 2020, after a massive war between the United States and China. Despite the failure of the U.S. government, a depopulated Midwest, food shortages, and marauding teenagers who stone to death people whom they do not like, the self-indulgent protagonist enjoys sexual relations with young women and has time to golf and to play with his grandchildren. The narrator also drifts into fantasies which are presented so realistically they are hard to distinguish from what is real. Did Ben Turnbull really kill his second wife? Did he then have sex with a deer? Did he really witness Moses on the mountain? In the end, the protagonist, a man whom readers may not like, reveals a vulnerability with which they may identify.

Author Biography

John Updike was born on March 18, 1932, in Reading, Pennsylvania, located in what is known locally as Pennsylvania Dutch country. He spent the first thirteen years of his life, however, in the small community of Shillington, where his father, Wesley

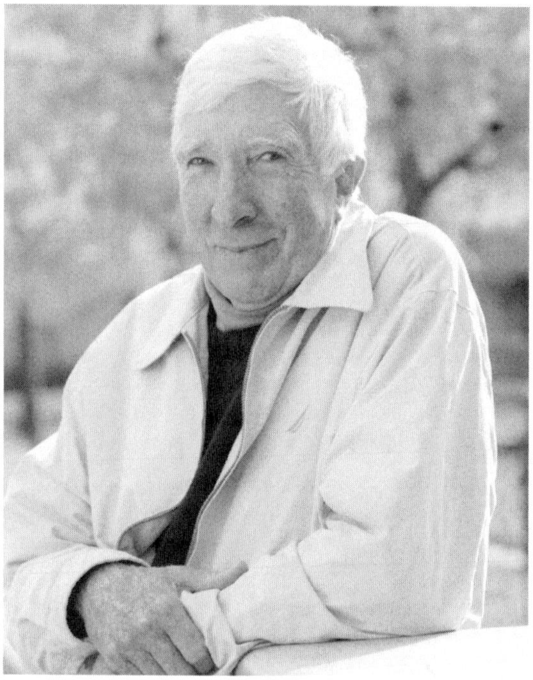

John Updike Photograph by Rick Friedman.

Updike, taught high school science. Updike's mother, Linda, encouraged her son's first attempts at writing in hopes that it might dispel Updike's tendency to stutter. She also supported his desire to attend Harvard when it came time for him to go to college. To their delight, Updike was awarded a scholarship to that university, an institution from which Updike and his parents realized many prominent authors had emerged.

In 1954, Updike graduated summa cum laude with a bachelor's degree and decided to pursue a second love, drawing. He attended the Ruskin School of Drawing and Fine Arts in Oxford, England. While in England, Updike's first short story, "Friends from Philadelphia" (1954), was published in the *New Yorker*, a huge accomplishment for any young writer. This first publication drew the attention of famed writer E. B. White, who helped Updike obtain a job at the *New Yorker* upon Updike's return to the States. While Updike was at the *New Yorker*, his writing is said to have come under the influence of J. D. Salinger (best known for his 1951 novel *Catcher in the Rye*) and John Cheever (most famous for his short stories, such as "The Swimmer" [1964]), whose works often appeared in the magazine at that time.

Four years after receiving his bachelor's degree, Updike published his first book, a collection of poems called *The Carpentered Hen and Other Tame Creatures* (1958). One year later, he published his first novel, *The Poorhouse Fair* (1959), a book about a home for the elderly. From this point on, Updike made his living solely by writing.

In 1960, Updike published the novel that introduced one of his most memorable characters, Harry Angstrom. This character appears in four successive novels, beginning with *Rabbit, Run*. *Rabbit Redux* appeared in 1971, followed by *Rabbit Is Rich* (1981) and *Rabbit at Rest* (1990). *Rabbit Is Rich* and *Rabbit at Rest* both won Pulitzer Prizes.

Updike has won many honors, including the National Book Award for his novel *The Centaur* (1963), a story about the relationship between a schoolmaster and his son; the National Book Award in 1982 for *Rabbit Is Rich*; and four medals: the National Medal of the Arts in 1989, the National Book Foundation Medal in 1998, the Caldecott Medal in 2000, and the National Humanities Medal in 2003, presented at the White House. Updike's *Terrorist* (2006) is his twenty-second novel to be published.

Updike has been twice married: Mary E. Pennington, whom he married in college in 1953, was his first bride. In 1977, Updike married Martha Ruggles Bernhard. Updike has four children and has lived most of his adult life in Massachusetts.

Plot Summary

Chapter I—The Deer

Toward the End of Time is written as if it were the journal of the protagonist, Ben Turnbull, and it begins with an entry written in late November of 2019, describing the first snow of the season. By the end of the first paragraph, the reader knows that the protagonist is somewhat depressed, unable to find even a trace of his "childhood exhilaration" and left only with "an unfocused dread of time." However, in the second paragraph, Ben is exhilarated, pleased with a new plastic snow shovel, an improvement over the metal ones of his childhood.

Along with many other subjects, the protagonist pays special attention to nature and all its transformations. He is also keenly aware of the people around him and the changes they go through. Ben analyzes his wife, Gloria, whom he says is always trying to tame nature by ordering people to trim one plant and uproot another. Deer have been eating the tender tips of his wife's shrubbery. Gloria wants Ben to shoot the animals. Ben believes that his wife secretly longs for his own death, too.

Ben and Gloria live in a sprawling old house on the shore of Massachusetts Bay. When Gloria spots a deer eating her bushes at night, she pushes Ben outside with a basket of old gold balls and tells Ben to throw them at the deer.

Gloria is Ben's second wife. Their relationship began as an affair, while Ben was married to another woman. On this particular night, Ben hopes that he and Gloria will have sex, but Gloria sees the deer again. She decides that she is going to borrow a gun from one of the neighbors so Ben can shoot it.

The next time that a deer appears, Gloria pushes Ben outside with the gun. She hollers for Ben to shoot, but Ben does not see the deer. When he returns to the house, Gloria calls him a "bastardly coward." Later, when Ben sees the deer again and fires a shot, Gloria promises to make love to him.

Next, in his journal, Ben ponders the word, "perhaps," thus introducing the quantum physics concept of probable lives, a theme that is developed later in the story. Ben also explores some details he has read about "Neandert(h)al man." He concludes that he, too, will one day be "as forgotten, as dissolved back into the compacted silt" as Neanderthal man. This comment introduces the subject of death that Ben ponders throughout the novel.

It is now January of 2020, and Ben, a retired partner of an investment broker firm, travels to Boston to take care of some clients whom he still serves. During his trip, the reader learns that there has been a war between the United States and China. Ben outlines some of the destruction that he sees, the result of heavy bombing.

The story takes a curious turn at this point, as Ben, at home again and in what can be described as a fantasy, watches a deer approach his house. Gloria is away. Ben sees the deer transform itself into "a young lean-bodied whore," whom he invites into the house. Ben and the deer have sex. "I tell myself she is a fantasy," he writes, "a branching not existent in the palpable universe." Not too much later, Ben writes about Deirdre Lee (whose first name bears a likeness to the word, deer), a prostitute who comes to service him. Deirdre is more human than the deer, but there are still allusions to her being deer-like. So it is not certain if she is real or imagined. Also confusing is Ben's statement: "It is not clear to me that Gloria is dead." Then he writes about having a faint memory of having shot Gloria. There is little explanation of these events. It is more likely that Ben has drifted into one of the probable worlds that he mentioned earlier in reference to quantum physics. Then, during one of their encounters, Deirdre and Ben decide to explore Ben's old house. This is a lead-in to Ben's discussion of Egyptian grave robbers, which ends the chapter.

Chapter II—The Dollhouse

It is early spring, and Ben notices flower buds that are all but ready to open. He recalls another spring, while he was still in college. Through this reverie, Ben introduces his first wife, Perdita. She was an art major and eventually bore Ben five children, and Ben relates that he now has ten grandchildren—nine boys and one girl.

Ben is reminded of Perdita when he sees his children and grandchildren. He then talks about the spouses of his children. One of his daughters has married an African man, whom Ben believes has taught his children and his first wife how to be a family, though they are now all separated.

Next, Ben provides a little more information concerning the aftereffects of the war. The population of the United States has been dramatically decreased, so much so that the current president has offered free farmland to any citizen who is willing to move to the now-depopulated Midwest.

Ben then refers to Deirdre as if she has moved into his house. They go shopping together for such domestic items as washcloths. When Ben looks into the faces of the people at the mall, he suspects that they think Deirdre is his daughter or an escort from a nursing home. When they are back at the house, Ben talks about how Deirdre is ridding the place of furnishings, especially those belonging to Gloria. Deirdre makes Ben carry rugs and other furniture to the barn. Memories are stirred when Ben goes into the barn and sees old children's toys, including some that were his. He remembers the doll house that he once tried to build for his oldest child, Mildred. While still married to Perdita, Ben would go to the cellar to work on the doll house. But the atmosphere in the cellar was anything but inspiring. He felt the weight of the house, the mortgage, his children, and his pregnant-again wife pressing down on his head. Instead of being inspired, Ben would think about his death, that of his daughter Mildred, and even the death of the dolls for which the house was being made. "There was no God," Ben had thought at that time, "just Nature, which would consume my life as carelessly and relentlessly as it would a dung-beetle corpse in a compost pile." He could not stand it in the cellar. But when he would go back upstairs, even though

Perdita would try to help relieve his stress, he would blame her for trying. Finally, Ben buys a doll house for Mildred from a store.

Spin and Phil come for Ben's monthly payment for protection. When Ben looks like he might balk, Phil insinuates that Ben might find his barn or house burned down if he does not produce the money. Deirdre comes out and tells Spin and Phil to leave. Deirdre tells Ben that she and Phil went to school together. Deirdre refers to Ben as her husband and butts her head into Phil's and Spin's bellies (like a deer might do). Later, Ben notices a smashed window in his barn. He discovers that things are missing. He also hears people in the woods around his house.

In a new episode, Ben goes skiing with Ken and Red. There are not many people at the ski resort, and the equipment is in need of repair. When he returns home, Ben is stiff from the experience but not too tired to notice that something has changed. "An infinitesimal measurement had been made, and Deirdre and I were in another universe." Ben suspects Deirdre has been with another man, but Deirdre denies it.

At Easter, Deirdre takes Ben to church. The preacher talks about Mary Magdalene and how she wept when she found that Jesus was not in the sepulcher where his body had been buried. A man appears, according to scripture, and Mary recognizes him as the Master. This figure tells Mary Magdalene not to touch him. Ben then says that it was at this point that Christ was in what in quantum theory is called "superposition—neither here nor there . . . He was Schrödinger's cat."

Spin and Phil show up again and warn Ben of some teenagers from Lynn, presumably the town in Massachusetts. The kids have been threatening local people. Deirdre suggests that the teens from Lynn might just get Spin and Phil if they do not watch out. Later, Deirdre tells Ben she is getting bored living with him. When Deirdre watches television, Ben searches the Bible, looking for the story of St. Paul. Ben recites part of the history. It was Paul, Ben concludes, who marketed Christianity to the world. Quite abruptly, Ben becomes part of the Biblical story and is with Paul, and the narrator and the timeframe of the story changes. The narrator is now John Mark. He is traveling with Paul. This narrator claims he is the one who wrote about the encounter on the mountain between Moses and God.

Ben goes to visit his oldest son, Matthew. When Ben returns, he finds a note from Deirdre, stating that she can no longer take it. She is now with Phil. They have taken more things from Ben's house because Phil suggested that it is a woman's right to do so.

Chapter III—The Deal

Gloria returns in the third chapter. Ben is surprised and asks where she has been. Gloria responds: "You *never* listen when I tell you where I'm going." Ben hopes Gloria will not notice the missing furniture. Their lives just pick up where they left off. Gloria complains about the deer.

Ben goes to Grandparents' Day at the school of his grandson, Kevin. Perdita, Ben's first wife, is there. Ben is still struck by Perdita's beauty; he and she still communicate well and understand one another with just a few words, often completing one another's sentences. When he gets home, Gloria is obviously jealous, assuming that Ben enjoyed seeing Perdita.

Ben follows a scientific line of thinking. It begins with his noticing an object in the sky that is "at least twenty times wider than the moon" and three times larger than an object that was made on Earth and projected into the heavens before the war with China. No one knows for sure what it is. There is speculation that it may have existed "in prehistory." All anyone really knows for sure is that it is some kind of spaceship. No communications, however, have been received from it. Scientists have speculated that whoever owns it has "found a way to travel from point to point by the power of the mind." On Earth, Ben continues, the human mind has learned to coexist with matter, whereas those who travel in the mysterious object in the sky have learned to control matter with the mind. This realization makes Ben feel as insignificant as an ant. The object hangs in the sky, he states, "like a dead man's open eye." Ben feels as if the intelligence inside the object is studying life on Earth, like a zoologist might study a group of chimpanzees.

Ben discovers three young teens in the woods below his house. The teens have gathered pieces of wood and are putting together a make-shift shelter. Ben tells them to get off his property. One of the boys mentions Phil and Deirdre. The boys suggest that Ben allow them to stay there for Ben's protection. All kinds of troublemakers are moving this way, the teens tell Ben, who threatens to go to the police. After that, the boys mock him. They know that there are no police. Ben leaves them alone, rationalizing that he does not really use that part of his property. He does not tell Gloria about the incident. He does not want her to investigate the teens because they might tell her about Deirdre. The teens keep a close eye on Ben's house and know personal details about his life.

Ben continues to talk about nature. It is the only ordered aspect of his circumstances. Nature follows the cycle of the seasons each year, no matter what kind of confusion and chaos is occurring in human affairs. It is now summer. Ben goes back down toward the beach to check on the teenagers. This time he carries the rifle that Gloria borrowed for Ben to scare away the deer. Ben is shaking with fear, but he hopes the gun will convince the teens that he has authority on his land. Ben has no intention of using the gun. When Ben gets down to the beach, he finds a young girl among the teenagers. The girl's presence subdues the boys slightly. Ben takes this opportunity to be slightly more aggressive. He mentions Spin and Phil, believing that this will scare the teens away. Maybe Spin and Phil are known as dangerous thugs or gangsters. But the teens are not impressed. They tell Ben that Spin and Phil will not be coming around any more. The boys tell Ben that he should change his routine and make his protection payments directly to them. If he does not, the boys threaten to burn down Ben's barn, or worse. A few days later, Ben finds Spin's rotting corpse in his barn. Ben rushes to his house to call the police. No one answers. By the time he returns to the barn, the body is gone. It was meant as a message, Ben concludes. He is shaken but goes down to the teens and asks them how much they are charging for their protection.

Later, Ben visits the teens more often. He even offers them advice on how to get his neighbors to give the teenagers protection money. Ben suggests that the kids burn down a neighbor's beach cottage and kill another neighbor's cat.

Chapter IV—The Deaths

The girl on the beach, now identified as Doreen, attracts Ben. One day when Ben goes down to the beach, he finds Doreen alone. She tells Ben that the teen boys have left the message that Ben can touch her, but he cannot penetrate her.

Ben is diagnosed with prostrate cancer and has an operation. Still in pain from the operation after a few weeks, Ben wanders down to the beach. Everything that the teens had built is pulverized. Ben finds small fragments of bone and flesh. He is not sure whose bodies are in the ruins. He believes "metallobioforms," some cross between a biological life form and metal, are to blame for the deaths. These creatures rise from the ground and devour their victims from the feet up.

The FedEx driver, who turns out to be Phil, now collects protection money, and the U.S. government may move from Washington, D.C., to Memphis, the center for FedEx. Mexico has repossessed Texas, New Mexico, Arizona, and lower California.

Ben's world is changing rapidly. He wears diapers now and cannot perform sexually. His friends, Red and Ken, finally come to visit him. They have little to say, and Ben cannot understand how he once enjoyed their company. Gloria hires a man to kill the deer that eat her plants. Winter is rushing in, marking the end of the cycle noted in Ben's journal. Although the seasons repeat one after another, seemingly unchanged, the same is not true for Ben's life. Even Gloria is drifting away from Ben. She even insists on sleeping in her own bed because Ben is now incontinent. Ben begins to feel like some plant in Gloria's garden, which she is constantly trying to train through pruning, tying back, and various forms of poisons.

> Slurping my soup, picking my nose even in the dark of the movie theatre, putting on a striped tie with a checked jacket—all these harmless self-indulgences excite her to flurries of admonition, and perhaps I am wrong to take offense. She merely wants to train me, like a rose up a trellis. As I age and weaken, I more and more succumb to her tireless instruction.

Ben is fading, much like the large object in the sky that suddenly, one day, disappears.

Chapter V—The Dahlia

The last chapter opens with Ben discussing the two life forms on earth: humans and a fungus. The fungus grows all over the land in various forms. The narrator (it is not clear if this is Ben) wanders around, picking and eating it.

John, the man who is to kill the deer, arrives at Ben's house, dressed in camouflage. He will kill the deer with a bow and arrow. In order to lure the doe, John brings a fawn blat that mimics the cry of a young deer. When John finally gets the deer, he guts it and shows off the carcass to Gloria. John explains in detail how he killed the doe. Gloria is ecstatic. John offers Gloria and Ben a deer steak. They tactfully refuse.

Near the end of the novel, Ben wants to find the dahlia tuber that Gloria has safely stashed away. She had won a prize for the flower in the summer and has packed it away for the winter. Ben does not want to ask Gloria where it is because he realizes that she does not trust him with it. He also realizes that the greatest moment of that year for Gloria probably was the winning of the dahlia prize.

Characters

Adrien

Adrien, who is from the African country of Togo, is married to Ben's daughter Irene. He and Irene have two children, Olympe and Etienne. Adrien teaches computer science at a local prep school. Ben gives Adrien credit for helping to teach Ben's fractured family how to stay together. Adrien's cultural definition of family influences Ben's children.

Beatrice

Beatrice, one of Ben's daughters-in-law, is married to Allan. She is overweight, has a drinking problem, and has trouble controlling her two sons. She visits Ben and announces that she is pregnant. Ben is slightly jealous of his son's license to seduce Beatrice.

Ken Dixon

Ben's golf buddy, Ken, is a retired airline pilot. Though Ben often plays golf with Ken, he really does not know much about Ken until after Ben has surgery. Ken comes by to see Ben, but the two men do not have much in common.

Doreen

The teenager Doreen hangs out with the three boys who camp out at the edge of Ben's property, the ones who offer Ben so-called protection from other troublesome youths. Ben lusts for Doreen, and Doreen notices. She tells him one day that the boys have told her that Ben can play with her sexually, but he is not to have intercourse with her. At the end, Doreen is killed or just disappears.

Geoff

Geoff shows up with Perdita during Grandparents' Day at the school of one of Perdita's grandsons. Geoff lives with Perdita. He is an artist and noticeably younger than she. Ben thinks Geoff might be gay.

Irene

Irene, Ben's middle daughter, is married to Adrien. She and Adrien have two children.

John

Gloria hires John to kill the deer that eats her flowers and bushes. John chooses to use a bow and arrow to do so. He arrives near the end of the novel to perform this act. John claims he can feel the deer and patiently waits for weeks before he finally takes the opportunity to kill the deer. Glory believes that John is much more sensitive than Ben, despite the fact that Ben did not have the heart to kill the deer.

José

José is one of the teens who force Ben to pay protection money. He is the biggest of the boys and appears to be potentially the most violent.

Deirdre Lee

Twenty-three-year-old Deirdre is a prostitute whom Ben often likens to a deer. For instance, he refers to her as brown-skinned and heavily furred. She comes to Ben's house during Ben's fantasy of having killed Gloria, his second wife. When Deirdre is finished having sex with Ben, she steals items from his house. She never reappears in the story, but she is discussed. She ends up with Phil, who continually refers to her as a whore. In the end, Ben asks Phil about her. Phil insinuates that she has returned to prostitution.

With Deirdre, Ben has his most fulfilling sexual experiences. Of the two women with whom Ben lives, Deirdre seems to be the more caring. Gloria, by contrast, seems only to tolerate Ben, maybe for his money.

Manolette

Manolette is the youngest of the three teenage boys who build a hut on Ben's property. Ben guesses that Manolette is about twelve. He is the quietest and least demanding of the trio.

Mildred

Mildred is Ben's oldest child and daughter. Ben tries to build a doll house for her.

Phil

Phil is one of the thugs who come to Ben's house and threaten to hurt him or his property unless Ben pays them for protection. Phil is heavy set and wears crumpled suits. Phil went to school with Deirdre and is not afraid to tell her to keep out of his dealings with Ben. When Deirdre leaves Ben, she goes to Phil. At the end of the story, Phil is a FedEx driver. FedEx has taken over the protection business.

Ray

Ray is one of the older teens who have camped out on Ben's land. Ben refers to Ray as the little lawyer. Ray appears to be the most rational person in the group.

Red Ruggles

Red Ruggles is Ben's golf buddy. Red owns a fish business and is often on his cell phone when the men are together, talking to managers of his business and to international suppliers. When Red comes to visit Ben after Ben's operation, Ben gets a different impression of the man. He used to tolerate Red when they played golf together, but Ben does not understand why.

Spin

Spin and his buddy Phil are referred to as the ambassadors. Spin comes to Ben's house to collect protection money. Spin has a red and gray mustache. He often has a toothpick in his mouth. Spin is more aggressive than Phil. In the end, his aggression may contribute to his being brutally murdered. The teenage boys stone Spin to death, sending a message to Ben that Ben better pay them the protection money he used to give Spin.

Allan Turnbull

Allan, Ben's son, has, according to Ben, most closely followed in his father's footsteps. Allan has made his profession in finance. He has two sons, Quentin and Duncan.

Ben Turnbull

Ben, the protagonist, grew up poor but made a lot of money working for an investment company. He is now retired and living comfortably but not too happily. Ben has five children, all of them fairly well off financially. He has been married twice. Neither marriage was successful. He was not faithful to either Perdita, his first wife, or to Gloria, his second wife. However, he seems have been more in love with Perdita than with Gloria.

Ben has unsatisfied sexual appetite. He lusts after women, no matter what their ages. He even feels sexually drawn to one of his daughters-in-law. He has a low opinion of women, yet he needs them. His sexual drive seems to be his main focus; ironically, he becomes impotent due to prostrate cancer. By the end of the novel, he appears to grasp a hint of an awakening. He has always been observant of nature, but at the end, its beauty is more important to him.

Gloria Turnbull

Gloria, Ben Turnbull's second wife, likes to rearrange nature. She pushes Ben and seems rather negative toward him. Ben suspects that she wants him dead. She disappears completely for a large section of the book. Ben fantasizes that she is dead. In her absence, Ben invites Deirdre into the house.

Gloria appears to see little worth in Ben. She does not trust him and believes he is not sensitive to her needs. When Ben has his operation, Gloria is distracted by her business and completely withdraws from him. In the end, Gloria shows more feminine warmth toward John, who kills the deer for her, and Phil, who collects protection money from her. She belittles Ben and takes full charge of their lives.

Perdita Turnbull

Perdita was Ben's first wife. Ben and she met in college. Perdita was an art student. She bore him five children in the course of their marriage. When Ben sees her during Grandparents' Day celebration at the school of one of their grandsons, he refers to her as the "gaunt old witch" who "contains a beauty that I am one of the last on earth to still descry." Ben was not faithful to Perdita while married to her. One of his affairs was with Gloria, who eventually pulls him away from Perdita. However, Ben does not seem to be completely over Perdita. He senses his love for her when he sees her. Gloria senses it too and is jealous of Perdita, who may be the only person in the novel for whom Ben has deep feelings.

Themes

Lust

Lust is a driving force in Updike's protagonist, Ben Turnbull, in *Toward the End of Time*. Lust seems to keep Ben alive. Ben's lust broke up his first marriage, driving him toward his second wife. Even though Ben is retired and elderly, his desire for women is constant. Whenever Ben watches his second wife, Gloria, he sees her in a lustful way and wants to have sexual intercourse with her. But whenever Gloria is away, Ben either fantasizes about bringing another woman into the house or actually sneaks another woman in. If neither of these options works, Ben resorts to his pornographic magazines. He pays to have a prostitute come to his house. The prostitute is in her twenties, at least forty years younger than Ben. After the prostitute leaves him because she is bored, Ben engages sexually relations with a teenage girl who has camped out on his property. When he goes shopping or travels to Boston, he lusts after any attractive woman who crosses his path. Sex seems always to be on his mind. So long as he can dominate a woman, he knows he is superior, that he is himself.

Ben is diagnosed with prostate cancer and becomes impotent and incontinent afterward his operation. Gloria will have nothing to do with him

Topics For Further Study

- Read a book written for the general public on some of the theories of quantum physics as applied to everyday life. Suggested authors are Amit Goswami's *The Quantum Doctor: A Physicist's Guide to Health and Healing* (2004) or Fred Wolf's *Matter into Feeling* (2002) or watch the movie *What the Bleep Do We Know*? (2005). List some of the concepts that most appealed to you or made you think about life in a different way. Discuss these ideas with your class.
- Read some literary criticism on Updike's *Toward the End of Time*, looking at the ways in which the criticism evaluates the work. Then write an essay in which you argue either that the novel succeeds or that it fails, using quotations from the criticism you read to support your argument. Present your paper to your class.
- Updike presented his view of what the year 2020 will be like. What is your view? Write an essay in which you describe what your neighborhood, your city, your country, or the world will be like in 2020. Will it be better or worse than it is now? You may want to consider global warming, globalization of industry, and the political scene as well as situations closer to home such as what your daily life might be like.
- Research the political relationship between the United States and China. What did your research indicate were the possibilities of China and the United States engaging in a war? Does China have the potential of becoming a military threat? What about an economic threat? Is there any chance that China might one day dominate the world such as the United States does today? You may want to include information about the balance of trade and U.S. national debt. Present your findings to your class.

---

and even refuses to sleep in the same bed with him. The young teenage girl tells Ben that he can sexually play with her, but he is not allowed to have intercourse with her. Of course, this restriction is not necessary, since Ben cannot perform sexually anyway. When Ben's body begins to deteriorate, he cannot do much about his sexual appetite. His condition connects with the pervasive decay conveyed through his old age and Ben's thoughts of dying. His sexual impulse also is related to the destruction all around Ben, in his country, his government, and his society. Everything is deteriorating, even the one factor—sexual drive—that has motivated Ben most of his life. The loss of male sexual prerogative is the chief sign of deterioration and death. Living is reduced to this one dynamic: male sexual gratification through dominating females. But death ultimately levels that hierarchy.

Death

Death recurs in the novel. The protagonist is dying. Death is present in many elements in this story. Ben's journal begins with the first snow then progresses through the seasons, ending with winter once again. Winter suggests death, as leaves fall off the trees and plants die back.

Gloria wants a deer killed. Ben refuses to kill it, but by the end of the story, Gloria has found a hunter to do the job. This hunter shoots the deer with a bow and arrow, guts the doe, and offers Ben and Gloria a piece of the meat. The deer, which caused only minor damage to some of Gloria's plants, is sacrificed. Ben believes that Gloria secretly wants him shot, too. In the end, it is not the hunter but Ben who is sensitive to the cruel fate of the young doe.

Then, too, Spin is killed. Spin is kicked and stoned to death by a group of teens who want to prove a point. Spin's death is a message to Ben that he had better meet the teens' demands. Spin's life is meaningless to these young kids, just as meaningless as Ben feels his own life is when he looks up at the huge spaceship in the sky. These teenagers, then, are eaten by the metallobioforms.

These half-mechanical, half-biological widgets are indiscriminate about what they consume. The teens, like the deer, are in the wrong place at the wrong time, and so they are devoured.

The title of this story, of course, says it all. The end of time suggests the death of everything: the country, the Earth, the atmosphere, and all forms of life. As Ben ponders his own death, as he experiences the deterioration of his body, he also thinks about the end of everything that he has known. He realizes that everything eventually dies, just as the Neanderthal population became extinct. This thought presses down on him especially hard as he attempts to make a dollhouse for his daughter. He cannot manage to focus on the project after he realizes that even his daughter will die one day. Everything will disappear, will be wiped out, just as certainly as the war has wiped out vast numbers of people both in the United States and in China. Ben realizes that death may be the only certainty.

Illusions

With the failure of the government and the erosion of law and order, chaos rules Ben Turnbull's world. At least, Ben calls it chaos. However, in large part, Ben's world is barely affected by the breakdown. There are no police; there is little food left in the stores; thugs demand protection money but offer no services. Yet Ben continues to play golf, to go on ski trips, to satisfy most of his desires. Is the chaos, then, just an illusion, like some of Ben's fantasies? He imagines having sex with a deer-like creature The deer walks into his house as a deer, but it seems to change once it gets into Ben's bed. Perhaps, Ben only thinks that the deer comes into his house, and he really has sex with a prostitute. Later, however, the prostitute refers to Ben as her husband. But this is not as strange as Ben believing that he has killed his wife, Gloria.

Updike may be exploring the concept of multiple, coexisting realities. Gloria is absent from the scene, and Ben cannot remember where she is or if she is alive. According to him, she may be both dead and alive. Likewise, Deirdre may be both a deer and a young woman, both a prostitute and Ben's wife. Ben could be both John Mark, a character that he pulls out of history, and himself. He could also be an old, incontinent, and impotent man and someone who is still virile enough to act sexually with a teenage girl.

Ben speaks directly about illusion when he describes the large object that hangs in the sky as a second moon. No one knows for sure what it is, and when it fades into the atmosphere, Ben suggests that the object may, in fact, be the result of mass illusion. Ben also speculates that the beings in the spacecraft may have advanced intelligence. In order for them to appear in the skies in such a large ship, Ben believes, they must have mastered mind over matter. If they have done so, then perhaps all reality is an illusion.

Style

Journal Writing

Toward the End of Time presents itself as the journal of the protagonist, Ben Turnbull. The daily details contained in the journal provide the plot. For example, the journal reports on the arrival of Phil and Spin, who demand protection money. These two characters are eventually replaced with the teenaged boys. Their deaths are recounted, too. The journal also records Ben's sexual encounters, although it is unclear if Ben actually has these experiences or just fantasizes about them. The journal describes Ben's married life with his second wife, Gloria. Readers are privy to the slow disintegration of Ben and Gloria's relationship as Ben gives in to his wife's commands. Ben also records some details concerning his bout with cancer, his operation, and recuperation.

But the journal contains more than outward daily occurrences (including the seasons as described in terms of the cyclical budding, blossoming, and fading away of plants, which Ben carefully chronicles). The journal also reflects Ben's emotions as he explores why he reacts to the situations in which he finds himself. These thoughts are often written in a loosely associative way, similar to stream-of-consciousness writing. One thought leads to another, and pretty soon, Ben is off on a tangent that might explore a story from the Bible or a speculation in a scientific magazine.

Ben's journal writing is significant to him. Its importance is evident in the frequency of his writing in it and in the periods when he cannot write. As Ben becomes ill and does not want to write anything in his journal, he leaves lines blank, as if he is honoring the spirit of the journal. This construction in the novel helps the reader to understand Ben better. The protagonist shows his vulnerability in his journal, which causes readers to feel more empathy for him. Readers may suspect that Ben can only be honest in his journal.

Magical Realism

Related to surrealism, magical realism enriches reality by incorporating dimensions of the imagination. Realistic and fantastic parts are presented as equally real, though these disparate parts may fit together quite illogically. For example, Ben imagines making love to a deer and the action is presented as though it literally occurs or as if the animal morphs into a woman. Gloria wants Ben to shoot the deer, and his feelings extend beyond the ordinary; the deer enters his house, turns into a human being who maintains some deer-like characteristics; and Ben makes love to her. "She becomes," Ben relates, "a young lean-bodied whore, whom I invite into the house." Later, Deirdre is described as "heavily furred." When Deirdre leaves, Ben describes how she "bound[ed] down through the woods with her lifted tail showing more white than anyone could expect." Magical realism allows Updike to probe the boundaries of reality and to suggest that fantasy and thought are as real as matter, and they shape the nature of what people take as the external world.

Science Fiction

Science fiction is a type of fantasy writing in which scientific information and theories are used as the basis of the story or to explain it. Several elements in the novel suggest science fiction. For example, Updike creates a huge object in the sky that the narrator sometimes refers to as the second moon. The journal reports that scientists have been unable to detect what the object is. At times, Ben wonders if it is a projection of mass illusion. However, at other times, Ben believes (or at least ponders the possibility) that the unknown object is a spaceship, created by beings that are much more advanced than humans. He supports this idea by considering the destruction and chaos caused by a war between the United States and China. Matter and mind on Earth, Ben concludes, are equally vital, whereas those beings in the spaceship surely must have minds that have learned to control matter.

Updike also inserts what he calls metallobioforms. These science fiction creatures combine inert matter and biological life. The metallobioforms kill humans just as often as humans destroy material objects. Metallobioforms are a strange hybrid of metal and a biological life form. These creatures live underground and can be heard ticking. They rise out of the ground slowly and devour human beings (as well as other matter) from the ground up. The metallobioforms eventually destroy the teenagers who camp on Ben's land. Science fiction imagines a futuristic world by stretching the limits of the known and taking scientific information and creating something new with it. In this way, Updike creates a world quite unlike the one inhabited by his readers, an act of imagination which allows the characters to move across realities and extend them.

Historical Context

Quantum Physics

Concepts connected to quantum physics and quantum mechanics are suggested in Updike's novel *Toward the End of Time*. On the quantum (or submicroscopic) level of existence, scientists have discovered that tiny bits of matter, such as electrons and protons, have indeterminate being. This means they may or may not exist. They exist as probabilities. In Newtonian physics, larger objects are said to either exist or not exist, but they do not exist as probabilities.

When extremely small bits of matter can be measured, they are said to exist. Scientists have shown that when quantum particles are not seen or cannot be measured, they exist only in what is referred to as potential reality. An electron, for example, can exist in multiple possibilities of realities, like a cloud of possibilities, and is, therefore, said to exist in a superposition. This is true, however, only as long as it is not observed or measured. Quantum particles can potentially be, therefore, in two different places at once.

In 1935, Erwin Schrödinger proposed an illustration for the quantum theory of superposition. In his illustration, he suggested that a cat be placed into a steel container. In the container with the cat was a contraption that could possibly open a vial of hydrocyanic acid, which would in turn kill the cat. Those observing the steel container (all they could see was the outside walls of the container and not what was inside it) could not determine if the contraption had or had not been triggered to release the vial of acid, nor could they determine if the cat was dead or alive. Since the observers could not tell if the cat was dead or alive, Schrödinger said the cat existed in a superposition and was both dead and alive at the same time. Superposition is known to exist on the quantum level. Whether it also exists in the larger reality is not known.

Throughout his novel, Updike uses concepts associated with quantum physics to create mystery and to suggest multiple levels of reality. Like Schrödinger's cat, which, according to one theory, is both dead and alive, Updike's characters (and storyline) incorporate multiple possibilities. The idea that there can be multiple and simultaneous realities suggests that interpretation of the text should remain open-ended. Within this framework, readers are encouraged not to seek a single truth in the details but to focus instead on how multiple levels of reality invite various interpretations of the novel.

Relationship between the United States and China

In the early 2000s, China was not considered an enemy of the United States; neither was it trusted fully as an ally. One point of disagreement between the two countries concerned Taiwan: China claimed it as its own territory; the U.S. government and certain business interests supported Taiwan's efforts to remain independent.

Despite this potential area of conflict, the United States and China had reasons to work together. One reason was economical. Between 1970 and 2000, U.S. manufacturers outsourced production to other countries. One country that benefited from this practice was China. While U.S. businesses and the U.S. economy benefited from cheaply produced goods, China's economy was strengthened so that urban areas could be modernized; China also increased its military strength.

In an annual report to Congress presented by the secretary of defense in 2005, China's rapid military expansion was noted. Training as well as military weaponry improved sharply between 1995 and 2005, possibly as a result of China's hope to reclaim Taiwan. Were China to try to force Taiwan to give up its independence, the U.S. position in support of Taiwan independence might draw the United States into a conflict with China on the side of Taiwan. In the early 2000s, the United States supported an independent Taiwan, which broke away from China, both philosophically and politically after the 1940s. China, however, did not recognize the separation and continued to claim Taiwan as one of its provinces. The military buildup in China was seen by the secretary of defense as possibly signaling that China was considering a showdown with the Taiwanese.

Critical Overview

Updike's *Toward the End of Time* received mixed reviews. Some critics really liked it; others did not. For instance, a critic for *Publishers Weekly* commends "this magnificent new novel" for "its futuristic setting." The same critic concludes that the "book . . . has all the hallmarks of a classic."

From another point of view, Jeff Giles, writing for *Newsweek*, states that Updike's *Toward the End of Time* "is one of the author's rare misfires, a dull, disjointed roadside accident of a novel." In a similar tone, Marvin J. LaHood, writing for *World Literature Today*, states that *Toward the End of Time* is one of Updike's "worst." LaHood continued: "There is nothing noble about Turnbull [the protagonist]. His mind is filled with tawdry images and erotic desires; his attitude toward women is demeaning and contemptible." LaHood concludes that Updike "seems one of the most uneven of American writers." Updike can write great books, LaHood concedes, but *Toward the End of Time* is definitely not one of them.

Writing for the *New Statesman*, Jan Dalley points out that "to complain about Updike's attitude to women is like complaining that a cat has claws." Since the sexism is inescapable, Dalley cautions readers: "If you don't think that the vibrant beauty of his prose and the taut rhythm of his ideas are worth the price, then you just have to read another writer." At the end of her review, Dalley states that Updike's "quirks are infuriating as always, but his imaginative brilliance and ferocious commitment to his truth are undimmed." Then Dalley adds: "His gaze is as unflinching as ever; as ever, its contempt for others is richly matched by its self-disgust. That is Updike. If you don't like the cat's claws, get a dog."

Will Manley, writing for *Booklist* begins his review of *Toward the End of Time* with strong praise for Updike's style:

> His work is uplifted by a prose style of beauty and precision and a narrative skill of perceptiveness and sensitivity. Updike is a captivating storyteller with an insightful eye and a wonderful mastery of the English language. His characters are memorable, his dialogue is real, and his plots speak to us with directness and meaning.

This is Manley's view before reading *Toward the End of Time*. After reading this "wretched" book, however, Manley concludes: "Updike is indeed human, maybe not like you and me, but human all the same." Flawed as all humans are, the great author is fully able to write a terrible book.

The author Margaret Atwood, writing a review for the *New York Times* paradoxically states that *Toward the End of Time* "is deplorably good." Atwood continues: "Surely no American writer has written so much, for so long, so consistently well."

Atwood praises the book and its "brilliant metaphors." She asserts that "As a writer, Updike can do anything he wants." Atwood concludes that this novel could "scarcely be bettered."

Coming down between the admirers and detractors, Edward B. St. John, a critic for the *Library Journal*, describes the novel as "uneven" but nonetheless evincing "the bittersweet, elegiac quality of *Rabbit at Rest.* "

Criticism

Joyce Hart

Hart is a published author and former writing teacher. In this essay, she examines Updike's descriptions of and references to women in order to explain why some readers think the author is a misogynist.

Some literary critics, even those who do not refer to themselves as feminists, have stated that John Updike, as represented through some of his writing (including *Toward the End of Time*) is a misogynist. As a matter of fact, there is a lot of reading material on the subject, including interviews in which Updike confronts this charge and does not quite conclude that his critics are in error.

Misogyny is the hatred of women. The Greek roots of this word are "misein," which means "to hate," and "gyne," which means "woman." Misogyny is hatred based on sex, and it can take many different forms, some more overt than others. In all, the prejudice assumes that women are inferior to men or are to be used by men. Possibly even the misogynist does not always recognize his prejudice. Misogyny may be subconscious, acted out without the person who has the prejudice recognizing his own bias. However, there are telltale signs of misogyny and a whole vocabulary of reasons for it. The intent of this essay is not to analyze misogyny but rather to examine how Updike refers to women in *Toward the End of Time* in order to explain how he may have earned this label.

There are four types of women in Updike's novel: the wife, the daughter, the lover, and the prostitute. These types are not always mutually exclusive and discrete. For example, the prostitute type and the wife may overlap at one point and the daughter (step-daughter, daughter-in-law) sometimes overlaps with the lover. Noting how Updike describes these different types, portrays them, and then has his protagonist, Ben Turnbull, react to them, should indicate some of the beliefs that the author has about women, or if not the author's concept then the concept of the narrator who may serve as the author's mouthpiece.

First is Ben's current wife, Gloria. Ben states quite noisily throughout his journal that Gloria wants to control everything in her presence. She wants to control Ben, her business, and all of nature that surrounds her. She wants deer killed, trees uprooted, and flowers encouraged, all according to her definition of aesthetics. Gloria, as Ben depicts her, is a bully. She calls Ben "a bastardly coward," when he refuses to shoot the deer that eats her shrubs. She also promises to have sex with him if he will scare the deer away by shooting over the deer's head or killing it.

Ben is passive-aggressive in response to Gloria. He pretends to recognize her strengths, but at the same time, he puts Gloria down and, therefore, diminishes her. She may think she is the dictator of the household, but Ben portrays her as frivolous, such as when she has one plant dug up only to replace it with a similar one, all for no logical reason. When Gloria barks a command (or even when she pleads and cajoles), Ben only pretends to go along with her ideas. He listens to her instructions to do this or that, but if he moves to the sound of her voice, he does so only according to his own fancies. Gloria hands him a gun, which Ben takes outside, but he does not (and never intends to) shoot the deer.

Overall, Gloria is depicted as the hen-picking stereotype of a wife. This image blurs, however, when Ben remembers what she was like before he married her. Then Gloria's character more closely resembled a prostitute. Ben remembers Gloria for the sexual gratification that she once provided him and for the costly gifts that he bought for her afterward. The narrator, at one point, offers: "Just as she, I thought, was helpless to do anything but attempt to direct and motivate me: ferocious female nagging is the price men pay for our much-lamented prerogatives, the power and the mobility and the penis." He puts up with her, in other words, as long as she puts out.

Gloria disappears for a while in the story, and Deirdre appears next. Deirdre is seen first as an animal that arouses Ben as he imagines a deer loping into his house and then into his bed. The deer morphs into Deirdre, whom Ben defines as a prostitute. Deirdre is another example of Ben's passive-aggressive reaction to Gloria. While Gloria is away, Ben cheats on her by inviting a prostitute into their house. He justifies this betrayal by convincing himself that Gloria is dead, that he has, in fact, killed her. Gloria no longer satisfies Ben sexually. "In our old age," Ben relates about his and Gloria's relationship, "we had to carefully schedule copulations that once had occurred spontaneously, without forethought or foreboding." Ben and Gloria have grown complacent and programmatic; now they schedule their sexual interactions. Ben even states that facing the deer, eye to eye, was "more exciting than anything I had done lately, including making love to Gloria." Deirdre is more exciting; she is also younger.

Before Gloria leaves the scene, at least temporarily, Ben daydreams about what he would do if Gloria were to die. He had once thought that he would look up old girlfriends to see if they might still be interested in him. But he has changed his mind. Now, he would "seek out only young whores, with tight lower bodies and long, exercise-hardened limbs." He would seek these women because they would have what it takes to handle his "erratic erections" and assure him of a gratifying sexual experience. Old girlfriends mean emotional baggage. Young prostitutes, on the other hand, are adept at servicing him without further expectation. Their sole purpose would be to figure out how to re-stimulate his sexual passion, "like a tricky tax matter laid before a well-paid accountant on a clean, bed-sized desk." It is all numbers to Ben, all rational interactions. He pays; the women provide the service. This is Ben's fantasy female relationship, which he partially makes come true through Deirdre. Ben's arrangement with Deirdre works for a while, at least until Deirdre begins to refer to herself as Ben's wife. "Deirdre is becoming a little too familiar," Ben states. "Instead of submitting to my sexual whims, she prefers to give me the benefit of her feminist rage." Then their relationship deteriorates. Ben loses interest; Deirdre eventually leaves.

However, while Deirdre is still with him, Ben ponders prostitutes. He estimates that, since the so-called collapse of civilization, the "quality of young women who are becoming whores has gone way up." Instead of "raddled psychotics," Ben states, now women who might have otherwise become "beauticians or editorial assistants, nurses or paralegals, have brought efficiency and comeliness to the trade." Ben is not glorifying prostitution for the sake of the women who are involved in it. Rather, he is glorifying himself. He has not stooped so low, in other words, that he has invited a person who is half-crazed into his house. Instead, he has asked for the services of a woman from an acceptable, albeit secondary, profession. That is the picture Ben paints for his own sake.

"In Ben's pursuits of health and sexual fulfillment, no woman is safe. There are no women outside his sexual radar. He knows no boundaries."

Then Ben treats Deirdre badly. At one point, Ben states: "It had not occurred to me until this moment to hurt her. Now it seemed an inviting idea." He enjoys hurting Deirdre and thinks the pain arouses her, too. Ben slaps her so hard that "she tumbled onto her back, her eyes stung into life by the blow." In slapping Deirdre, Ben thinks he proves his power over her. This is emphasized shortly after he slaps her, when he sees Deirdre as a child. He looks at her and sees "her face like the face of a girl being mussed in the backseat of a family Chevrolet." Then as he attempts to hurt her by plunging himself inside her, he notices her body "stiffening like a scared child." Here, the man plays the master who subjugates his slave, or even worse than that, the adult male forcing himself on a female child. Ben degenerates from misogynist to pedophile.

Ben assumes that his right to be sexually gratified justifies his abuse of others. Women are objects, vehicles by which he satisfies himself, and he feels most alive when he has made a new conquest. When he reminisces about his first wife, he remembers how he cheated on her. He realizes that eventually he will be caught, and it will cost him his marriage. Ben, however, turns this in some strange, twisted way to his advantage. He states: "My marriage, I knew, was doomed by this transgression or by those that followed, but I was again alive, in that moment of constant present emergency in which animals healthily live." The word, "healthily" sums up Ben's contradictory attitude. Deluding himself, he excuses his behavior by equating it with health and vigor. His activities are positive. They make him feel healthy, and he does not care at whose expense.

In Ben's pursuits of sexual fulfillment, no woman is safe. There are no women outside his

What Do I Read Next?

- Updike is probably best known for his so-called Rabbit series—novels having the same main character, Harry "Rabbit" Angstrom. The first of these novels made Updike famous. The series was collected in a book called *Rabbit Angstrom: The Four Novels: Rabbit, Run; Rabbit Redux; Rabbit Is Rich; Rabbit at Rest* (collected in 1995). Most reviewers believe that the Rabbit novels are Updike's best.
- Phillip Roth is a contemporary of Updike and often compared to him. Roth's most famous novel is *Goodbye, Columbus* (1959), a story of romance and a clash of class and culture. Readers who would like to read a more recent novel with an older protagonist by Roth may want to try his *Human Stain* (2001).
- Saul Bellow's work is often compared to the work of Updike. Bellow's *Herzog* (1964) is often referred to as the author's best work. It tells the story of a man who has suffered many setbacks. The book consists of a series of letters through which the protagonist tries to gain a perspective on his life.
- Updike was trained as an artist before he became a writer. In 2005, he published a series of essays on American art, *Still Looking: Essays on American Art*. Updike uses his gift with language to help broaden readers' appreciation of certain American masterpieces.
- In 1990, Updike published *Self-Consciousness: A Memoir* about his life and philosophy. Critics have proclaimed that this book goes much further than just autobiography because readers are able to glimpse the way the author thinks.

sexual radar. He knows no boundaries. At Christmastime, for instance, Ben's daughters-in-law stay at his house. While describing them, Ben admits that two of his daughters-in-law stir him sexually. "They seem," Ben adds, "for all their impenetrable grooming and manners, not quite content." In Ben's fantasies, he assumes he can satisfy them. Later, when his daughter-in-law, Beatrice, comes to visit, Ben states that her being in the house with him when Gloria is not at home "had a lyrical illicit side, an incestuous shadow." Ben sees yet another female only in relation to sex. He adds: "The languor of the child's [Ben's grandson's] frail, unambitious white limbs disturbingly suggested to me how my daughter-in law would dispose herself in bed." And when Beatrice bends over to pick something up, Ben cannot take his eyes off her. "How nice it would be, I thought, to be beneath her and feel her breasts sway, heavy and liquid, across my face." When Beatrice gets ready to leave, Ben admits: "My exchange with Beatrice had been all irritable foreplay, ending in biological jealousy of my son." He is lusting after his son's wife, which he admits without guilt or shame. According to him, Beatrice is the object designed for male gratification; she is not a person, and she certainly does not have equal status to the male who wants to use her.

Updike wrote the novel; that he has Ben writing his journal removes the text just slightly from Updike's own hand. The author who creates the world of the novel is responsible for the images of women the protagonist envisions. In this novel, women are dissected into parts, and those parts are all sexual in nature and presented to satisfy the male and at the female's expense. Women's thoughts are insignificant. Their emotions go unnoticed or are ridiculed or demeaned. Female intelligence is not acknowledged. In the world of this novel, if women have any power, it is the reflexive power that men allow them so that women can satisfy men.

There is only one female in the novel toward whom no sexual impulse is implied. She is Ben's only granddaughter. Ben cuddles her, feeds her, and enjoys her as the human being she is. If this story continued and that granddaughter matured, who knows what Ben's attitude would be toward her?

Source: Joyce Hart, Critical Essay on *Toward the End of Time*, in *Novels for Students*, Thomson Gale, 2007.

Robert Boyers

In the following review, Boyers comments on the author's promotion of "cranky local obsessions to a level of universality" and the demoralization of Updike's character in the wake of a catastrophe and while facing physical extinction.

John Updike's new novel is set in the year 2020, not long after a brief but devastating war in which millions of American and Chinese citizens were killed. We see none of this killing, and we are told nothing of the causes that led to the war or that brought it to a close. Occasional references are made to the resultant aftermath, to a collapsed national economy and deteriorating office buildings, to a "depopulated" Midwest and abandoned neighborhoods; but we do not tour those neighborhoods or feel in any way the effects of the reported disaster. A passing reference to Chinese missiles, or to Mexico as a golden land of opportunity, will remind us that something consequential has happened, that the world out there is a place different in many ways from the world of 1997. But in virtually every respect the local world in which Updike immerses us is our—or rather, his—familiar world. It is not at all surprising to the reader of this novel that for Updike's eloquent alter ego, Ben Turnbull, "the collapse of civilization" amounts to little more than an inspiring rise in "the quality of young women who are becoming whores."

A retired investment counsellor with a large extended family living nearby in the Boston area, Turnbull is neither an idiot nor a monster. He is 66, and his depravities are practiced on a modest scale. He is as susceptible as the next man to twinges of remorse and pity; or so we are to believe. If the collapse of civilization seems to him remote, it is in part because his routine preoccupations and his immediate prospects have been little affected by the conflagration. When he speaks, casually, of "rapacity, competition, desperation, death to other living things" as "the forces that make the world go around," he is repeating a settled conviction that took root in him long before the recent disastrous events. He did not need reports of "the plains [as] a radioactive dust bowl" to instruct him on "the forces that make the world go around."

It matters to Ben very little, so far as we can tell, that the dollar is worthless, for in its place he spends a "scrip" issued by "corporations, states and hotel chains," and he can apparently buy whatever he wants, from private security guards to gardening supplies, from gasoline to Federal Express service. When he is ill, he drives to Boston from his suburban home to see a doctor, and he receives first-rate treatment at a hospital. He visits his grandchildren, attends parties, and carves turkeys precisely as he would have done if no apocalypse had occurred. For such a person, war and change are things that happen to other people. None of his children are said to have been lost or threatened by the nuclear exchange, and his eleven grandchildren would seem to face only the garden varieties of rapacity and desperation that fall to each of us.

"Updike is content to give us creatureliness without ethical dimension. His character refers now and again to transgression or trespass, but he is fundamentally a complacent man, forgiving himself everything, pitying his frailty and his fate, extracting a sensual enjoyment even from his occasional self-lacerations."

Updike betrays no anxiety about the glaring inadequacy of his novel as an account of drastic political and social upheaval. He places his narrative in the hands, in the voice, of a man who sees what Updike usually sees. Turnbull is a bright man who can be counted on to say bright things in a language so precise and so fluent that he often reminds us of his creator. And he, too, has the habit of lingering for a time in the ample forests of his own prose. He reads books, entertains theories, and argues with himself about the status of virtue and the Nietzschean notion of ressentiment. He has little patience for actual politics, and he likes to retreat efficiently from troubling questions to manageable problems. These are tendencies of his temperament that Updike has no wish to condemn.

Ben Turnbull is a guide to nothing but the vagaries of his own frequently compelling intelligence.

He acknowledges the facts of political reality much in the way that he examines more proximate facts, with a cool empathy, an almost aesthetic detachment. He is more than a little dreamy, eager to lose himself in "cosmic feeling" and to ride the surfaces of life for their "transcendent sparkle." He is more comfortable speaking about entropy than about hope or action. When he recites the facts—this happened, then that, then that—he is already pulling back from the thicknesses of history, drawing around himself a circle of certainty within which existence proceeds as it must, without the possibility that events in the great world will drastically disrupt his security and his routine.

He knows, of course, that events do sometimes disrupt, and that lives have been destroyed, or ended, as a result of particular conflicts. He registers changes in society; but for all his acute powers of observation, he has little sense of society as a contention of forces in which individual will and intelligence may often play a significant role. He knows how to hurt and to flatter, how to give and to resist, how to get on in the world; but he feels that he can no more control the local, small-scale forces impinging on his life than he can control the forces governing the nuclear exchange between China and the United States. He is a very observant quietist, whose passivity is the condition of his acuity. Amused that anyone would presume to learn or to grow by studying the world; he swells with a cruel satisfaction when he tells his young hooker-mistress "that I don't much care what happens in the world. . . . What Spin and Phil and the kids from Lynn do with the world is up to them. I just want to buy a little peace, day by day."

In the course of his retirement on a small but comfortable property not far from Boston, Turnbull is visited by a bunch of sleazy racketeers offering to sell him protection. Collectors for "local crime overlords," they are likened to "old-style" movie actors; and Updike is so in thrall to their banal cinematic features—one "rolls around in his mouth" a trademark toothpick, another issues sick threats "with a quick hitch in his shoulders"—that he is unable to invest them with even a trace of genuine malice or menace. The federal government can no longer protect its citizens, and the local police are without the resources to do much. How this can have happened we are not permitted to ask. It just happened. And in the same way we must accept that the predators can be kept more or less out of one's way, so long as they are paid. They may fight among themselves, but they represent no direct threat to Turnbull's well-being. Suspicious and a little put out at first, he learns quickly to accept what is a necessary evil, and becomes increasingly curious about his protectors. Ben accepts that people do what they must do to get along, extortionists no less than homeowners. What we call social order is an arrangement we do well not to look at too closely. Curiosity about this element or that is perfectly acceptable, so long as it is not underwritten by a nagging interest in social justice.

Ben's relations with these thugs resemble his relations with most other persons. He never gets too close to anyone, though he is curious about selected aspects of wives, children, lovers, clients. His present wife Gloria seems to him now and then a killer, eager for his death or his disappearance, though she sometimes ministers to him with a puzzling ardor. A former wife, Perdita, "loyal if unenraptured," with her "thick and rounded" soles and "little toes," sometimes seems less a person than a pretext for recalling odd potencies and transgressions. His prostitute mistress Deirdre, a thief and a preternaturally avid sex toy with "silken rivers of dark body hair," betrays, now and again, "as in every woman," "the hormones of nest-building." In all, Ben doubts most things, including his own unstable view of them. He wants from life nothing more than the same old paltry satisfactions that he derides. Now and then he wonders at "the mysteries of overplenteous life," or (somewhat less sublimely) at "the miraculous knit of the jockey underpants stretched across [his] knees" as he sits on the toilet; but these epiphanies rarely prevent him from feeling "dull" and unresponsive.

The action of the novel is very limited. Ben stays close to home, only occasionally venturing out to the office to do a bit of work, finding few colleagues who miss him. He golfs, reads, visits his grandchildren. When his wife is away, he shares his bed with Deirdre, who stirs him up and eventually leaves him for a more exciting criminal companion. He reaches out, at first reluctantly, then more eagerly, to the band of adolescent racketeers living in a makeshift shed on the outskirts of his modest property, offering them advice on extortion and, in the end, mildly mourning their demise. His thoughts range from "the vibrant magenta of crabapple" to marriage as "a mental game of thrust and parry played on the edge of the grave." He remembers his many failures and his frequent derelictions, but consigns almost everything in his experience to "Sisyphean repetitiveness" and "triviality." By far the most important event in his account of himself is his bout with prostate cancer, his struggle "in a narrow wedge of space-time beneath the obliterating imminence of winter." He issues resonant utterances about meaning and meaninglessness, about change and entropy, but he barely moves from the place he has settled in, and his special gift is to avoid "any thought that will tip [him] into depression."

What action there is in the novel is provided by Ben's rarely sluggish imagination. His journal entries move from one sensation to another, from the smell of a crotch to the dread of humiliation, from the springy hair on the head of a half-black grandchild to the "muffled thrumming" sounding through an open storm window. Often the impressions of the visible world are mild, picturesque, reassuring: "sunlight reflected from the granite outcropping warms the earth." A robin startled into flight, "a stuffy bird, faintly pompous in its portly movements, spoiled by the too many songs and poems unaccountably devoted to him," is a quaint emblem, familiar, comforting, literary. Calmly attentive to every little thing, Updike's narrator is especially alert to "repositories"—"in garages and basements and closets and attics"—that "pledge our faith in eternal return," though he is all too aware of an encroaching entropy, "when there is not a whisper, a subatomic stir, of surge."

Still, Ben is subject to powerful surges, to panics and to nostalgias and to seizures of fervor. He lurches uncontrollably from one time plane to another, trying on identities with a promiscuous, relaxed abandon. His journal entries allow for several varieties of free association: a narrative of Egyptian grave robbers, a fragment from the life of Saint Mark, the reverie of an early Christian monk, the brutal churnings of a uniformed Nazi, a so-called "good German recruited to guard an extermination camp." What the primary narrative lacks in tension and variety, these fragmentary narratives, with their air of peremptoriness and incompletion, of bluff yet authoritative improvisation, would seem to provide.

Yet it is Updike's sureness of touch that is generally sacrificed in these interpolations. The music of the prose remains intact, the full voice of a confident and exacting speaker recognizable even where, as in the musings of the early Christian monk, the language becomes slightly arch, the sentence structures noticeably more symmetrical, the perspective strained to accommodate "our Lord's birth of a meek virgin" and a "Providence in its miraculous patience [lending] scope so as to accumulate ungainsayable proofs toward the eternal damnation of their souls." It is exhilarating to move, without transition, from "one busy summer day" on which "it fell to [Ben] to f—— three women" to the reflections of a monk in sackcloth about to be put to the sword; but though we are disposed to applaud the sackcloth theater, we must wonder what purpose is served by these showy fragments.

We do not require conventional transitions, which in any case Updike occasionally provides, as when the sight of a Jewish doctor, naked in a locker room, suddenly stirs Ben to contrive the sequence in the Third Reich. But the fragments do not exfoliate. They tell us nothing about Ben except that, like any literate person, he can identify briefly with people about whom he has read in books. The sequences have no urgency in the design of the novel. Updike sticks with each of them just long enough to satisfy a modest aesthetic imperative. These fragments are shapely, clever, deftly edged, and intermittently poignant, but they amount, in the end, to discrete triumphs of superfluity.

Of course, the fragments belong to Ben Turnbull, and their telling us so little about him leads us to ask what instead they may reveal about the novelist. Is "antiquity" a key to Updike's vision in a way we had not previously suspected? Probably not. No more do the words "early Christian church" or "Holocaust" provide a critical lead. If the interpolations tell us little about Ben, they tell us little about the novelist; or little that we did not know before. It is hard not to see in Ben many of the standard views and obsessions that the novelist has expressed in many other writings. Ben is by turns wise and foolish, refined and coarse, playful and tendentious. He has an eye for color, line, and form, and also a predilection for philosophical or scientific speculation. Occasionally guilty or dissatisfied, he mostly gets on with his instincts and his appetites; and he is rarely restrained by the higher moralities. He displays a sometimes disarming affection for small things, for mannerisms and foibles. Like other Updike narrators, he is good at taxonomy and elegy, and though he finds little cause for optimism, he is frequently consoled by the comely surfaces of simple things. Saddened by the theft of a fine living room rug, he brightens when "its absence exposed a maple parquet whose beauty had been long obscured."

But Ben is most recognizably a standard Updike male in his sexual obsessions. He rightly describes himself as "like some horn-brained buck." Ben's erotic fantasies include a decidedly sadistic component; he is turned on by thoughts of desecration and enslavement. He is regularly aroused by the exposed shoulders of a step-daughter or a glimpse of a daughter-in-law's thigh. He cannot comprehend his married son's "patently monogamous affection" for his wife; fidelity seems to him peculiar, an atavism associated with a time before the disappearance of the gods. He is perpetually in search of erotic intoxication, of inflammation and submission. The "flesh-knot" of the anus is to him a recurrent temptation, and he likes the thought that the woman who "serves [him] with a cold, slick expertise" is also a teasing, "money-grubbing c——" who can be screwed "until she squealed for mercy."

All of this, as Ben knows, is cast in the language of standard sexual fare, "constructed mainly of images from popular culture." Now, for a certain kind of writer—Don DeLillo, or Robert Coover—these susceptibilities and influences would be an irresistible opportunity to probe the inner consequences of mass culture, to consider its pernicious invasion of our dreams and our desires. But Updike, who no doubt sees as clearly as anyone else what has become of us, has no wish whatever to explore this aspect of American fate. The brief observation about "popular culture" has no significant relation to anything else in the novel, and in effect serves merely to indicate that Updike himself is too clever to be entirely taken in by the language that he has given to his character. To allow Ben to follow up on his observation would be to violate as essential complacency.

To note, in passing, the origin of erotically charged language is to be smart; but to ask further questions about it might suggest that something ought to be done to liberate us from, or to make us critical of, an unfortunate susceptibility. But that would be the sort of wishful thinking in which no self-respecting realist can indulge. This satisfied sense of the dominant reality is nicely revealed in the following passage:

> There is a warmth in the proximity of a man who has f—— the same woman you have. It is as if she took off her clothes as a piece of electric news she wished him to bring to you. He has heard the same soft cries, smelled the same stirred-up scent, felt the same compliant slickness, seen the same moonlit swellings and crevices and tufts—it was all in Phil's circuitry, if I could but unload it. . . . My sexual memories had become epics of a lost heroic age, when I was not impotent and could shoot semen into a woman's wincing face like bullets of milk. Deirdre's flanks in memory had acquired the golden immensity of temple walls rising to a cloudless sky and warmed by an Egyptian sun. Whore though he thought her, a nimbus of her holy heat clung to Phil—his oily black pubic curls had tangled with hers. . . .

We learn from this passage much of what is real to Updike's character. Potency is real, and the loss of potency. Scent and touch and soft cries are real, and an intimacy based upon shared physical sensation. The young man whose "pubic curls had tangled with [Deirdre's]" feels "indignant" when he realizes that "he mattered to [Ben] only as an emanation of our shared c——," but Ben has no recourse to indignation. For all his thinking, for all his reading, he is only appetite and tropism. Words such as "sacred" and "holy" and "nimbus" are to him an oil to lubricate the passage of sexual energy. His post-operative impotence is affecting because we feel that he is lost without the faculties that are most real and important to him, but Updike does not permit us to forget who and what this man is. A dark, voluptuous, obscene electric charge is carried by the erotically loaded sentences that Ben constructs. We are stirred, but also repelled, by his efforts "to drag with [his] tongue the sweet secret of [a woman's] name out of the granular dark of [his] memory cells." And we wonder at Updike's reluctance to build into the novel any figure who might offer some resistance to Ben, who might be repelled by him as we are repelled.

But the character is most fully revealed in the way he confuses realms, swings wildly between celestial and obscene, worships "the little flesh-knot between the glassy-smooth buttocks visible in moonlight . . . at just the right celestial angle." All the intermittent talk of celestial angles and tempting white church collars and "the risen Jesus" serves mainly to reveal the speaker's baffled desire for something other than what he knows and has. His is a rhetoric of disappointed love, of an obscuring, unsubstantiated ambivalence. Ben desires epiphany but he subsists on shame. He cultivates a barren, hopelessly repetitive eroticism. ("She was a choice cut of meat and I hoped she held out for a fair price.") Absorbed by the glamours and the corrosions of the flesh, he has not the strength to think through his confusion. Like everything else, it is a given fact of his condition. And Updike has no wish to think it through, either.

What excites Ben Turnbull is not, apparently, a subject fit for moral or psychological criticism. Updike is content to give us creatureliness without ethical dimension. His character refers now and again to transgression or trespass, but he is fundamentally a complacent man, forgiving himself everything, pitying his frailty and his fate, extracting a sensual enjoyment even from his occasional self-lacerations. He counsels the thugs on his property on the ways of the world, advising them to "mention casually" to prospective clients "that [they] would hate to see any of their children kidnapped," and that "if they don't pay up [protection money]" the boys "might think about killing one of their cats." Nor does he beat himself up about his relations with the 14-year-old girl of the gang, whom he visits when the others are away. There are traces of tenderness in their carefully delimited transactions. "She was cool to the touch, surprisingly, and clean-smelling." Ben notes. "Her breasts smelled powdery, like a baby's skull, and her nipples were spherical, like paler, smokier versions of honeysuckle berries." There is nothing in this of Nabokovian decadence or play. The man is merely not a bad guy, and he has no reason not to be tender to a young girl who allows him to place his tongue where he likes.

"She graciously offered to touch me, where I jutted," he goes on, but he had earlier promised the boys "no penetration," and the "hand-job" offered by the sweet young thing "would penetrate my soul." This is as close as we come, in this novel, to "renunciation." But the lapse into soul-fear is without conviction. Ben fears only exposure by his wife, the possible loss of "the island of repetitive safety [he] had carved from the world." His little intoxications are pathetic things, as he well knows. Not for him a full-fledged Dionysian rebellion, any more than a crisis of conscience. In the suburbs this *homme moyen sensuel* can savor the acid taste of teenage honeysuckle on his tongue while daydreaming through the sumptuously appointed living room, "a breezy, translucent person, a debonair proprietor."

Toward the End of Time will call to mind earlier novels by Updike, especially *Rabbit at Rest,* with its self-destructive, relentlessly unappetizing protagonist Harry Angstrom. Like Ben Trunbull, Rabbit regards few things as "his problem" and accepts that he "never was that great" as father or husband. Both characters are unapologetic womanizers. In part an emblem of his society. Rabbit sees that in his America—as in the America of 2020—"everything [is] falling apart," and though—like Ben Turnbull—he is at least mildly interested in many things, from science to history, he is resolutely unamenable to improvement or edification. Rabbit—like Ben—wins a modest claim on our sympathy principally by confronting premonitions of death, by acknowledging "something more ominous and intimately his: . . ." Ben is a more articulate person than Rabbit, less of a slob, but Updike grants him no greater portion of grace and discovers in his failings fewer occasions for satire or merriment.

Toward the End of Time is a simpler and less attractive book than *Rabbit at Rest.* For it is defiantly not a book about anything remediable, or about the way we live now. For all of its technical beauties, its proficiencies of diction and syntax, Updike's new novel is especially disheartening in its specious and half-hearted attempt to situate its private malaise in the aftermath of a terrible historical catastrophe. The book is not only indifferent to history, it exploits history. It uses the moral and historical grandeur of a world war to promote its cranky local obsessions to a level of universality and interest that they do not deserve. The near-destruction of the world notwithstanding. *Toward the End of Time* is just the familiar Updikean dystopia. The war in this book is an empty device, and spiritual exhaustion is written all over its pages.

There is in Ben Turnbull, as also in Updike's other characters here, no possibility of growth, and what passes for redemption is at most an activity of consciousness for which genuine advance is reducible to mechanical invention. The novel's easy acceptance of a long cosmic view—the "silently clamorous, imperiously silver and pure" rotation of the stars—merely flattens every prospect of judgment, penance, reconciliation, and change, and reduces it to triviality and illusion. In Updike, the words "transcendent" and "trust" and "virtue" have never before seemed so frivolous. The book seems a reflex of frustration and bitterness. To mistake one's own spiritual condition for the final measure of reality, to confuse one's own aggrieved, attenuated shadow on the wall with being itself in all its variety, is to offer a terribly impoverished version of experience. The wonder of it is that Updike, brilliant as ever in evoking the profusion of surface life, in making palpable what he once called "the skin of a living present," seeks here only to distract us from the essential demoralization, the sense of nullity that holds even the novel's most vivid particulars firmly in its grip.

Source: Robert Boyers, "Bullets of Milk," in the *New Republic*, Vol. 217, No. 20, November 17, 1997, pp. 38–42.

James Yerkes

In the following review, Yerkes praises Updike on the insights he brings to the psychology of his character, who reflects on and ruminates about his life while advancing toward death.

It's about time. Since 1958 John Updike has published at least one book a year—except for 1961, 1967, 1973 and 1980. With this new novel, he is again on time, and the book itself is about

> **"A consistent theme in his work, abundantly evident here, is the tortured ambiguity of human existence. Life is a maddening collision of vague hints of transcendent meaning and merciless blows of absurdity."**

time. It's the story of a man moving toward death from prostate cancer at age 66 and about the ruminations, recollections, regrets and awkwardness which attend that trajectory.

Ben Turnbull is a retired investment counselor living in a large house overlooking the sea just north of Boston in the year 2020. Nuclear war between China and the U.S. has thinned the continental population and a kind of regional segmentation of the country has occurred, making the federal government an irrelevant entity and producing a confederation of local interests that ensure social survival. Massachusetts issues its own currency, but security is managed by gang-style arrangements and protection payoffs to young toughs. In the sky orbits the shining speck of a U.S. space station, left as a result of the war, its astronauts long dead.

Within this fragmented cultural setting Ben maintains his cool married relationship with compulsive Gloria; his fantasy with a desirable young whore (his term), Deirdre; his lecherous dalliance with a 13-year-old "moll," Doreen; his regretful memories about his first wife, Perdita; and his endearing relationships with his ten grandchildren.

Far more convincing than the futurist scenario is Ben's experience of "an unfocused dread of time itself" as his physical powers deteriorate and existential questions loom ever larger. "What doesn't fade into the void? . . . Some day I will be as forgotten, as dissolved back into the compacted silt, as your typical grunting, lusting, hungry, broken-boned Neanderthal man. I simply cannot believe it! And that is simply stupid of me."

Updike's reflections on ultimate meaning in the face of sure physical extinction move in the ambiance of ancient and yet ever new metaphysical and religious questions, questions that revolve around the nature of time—personal, cosmic, seasonal. The exploration of personal time includes the narration of Ben's inner reflection, which moves searchingly back into his past with regret and guilt. It is also the time of physical deterioration—with more frequent trips for urination and the attendant pinch of pain. It is the time of confronting the truth of a cancer diagnosis and the time of self-pity, when the look in a spouse's and one's friends' eyes records their expectation of one's imminent death. It is the time of anticipating the odd and bracing finality of one's personal death.

Updike also explores time in cosmic context, drawing on the "many universes" theory derived from the indeterminacy principle of quantum physics. At one point it is unclear whether in fact he has killed Gloria with his shotgun, because at that moment "the universe branched and crackled." This makes possible the entrance of Deirdre, and a myth-like emergence of a connection between Deirdre and a deer eating Gloria's flowers and shrubs.

We are also given a full treatment of big-bang or big-crunch cosmology and the eventual reversed implosion of our universe's time and space. One cannot help being arrested by the physics and metaphysics of this tale and by its clear, readable exposition, deftly maneuvered into the plot of Ben's own impending demise.

Nature's seasonal time is also explored with Whitmanesque attention and Vivaldi-like progression through the seasons, winter through fall. That seasonal order is not incidental to the psychological and spiritual movement of the plot. It also suggests the eternal return to fecund sources and the sacred source, to use the terms of Mircea Eliade, the historian of religion. This is a connection we are meant to notice, for one of Ben's daughters is married to a Carol Eliade, son of Romanian immigrants, and their child, Ben's grandson, afflicted with dyslexia, is said to have inherited a personal form of "post-linearity."

Updike's meditations also include subterranean burrowings inside an Egyptian pyramid, theological disputations by the feisty apostle Paul as he trudges along the high sea slopes of Asia Minor; chilling conversations with an SS guard in a Jewish death camp; and bizarre encounters with newly emergent evolutionary "metallobiological" creatures the size of the tree shrews, with chainsaw-like heads. This is not an altogether convincing mix of fiction and fantasy, but it illustrates Updike's career-long interest in constantly reinventing himself as a writer.

A consistent theme in his work, abundantly evident here, is the tortured ambiguity of human existence. Life is a maddening collision of vague hints of transcedent meaning and merciless blows of absurdity. Standing inside the realms of nature and culture, one cannot gain any fixed elevation, no Archimedean point of soul-certainty about some ultimate meaning.

Still, Updike seldom fails to name fairly clearly the Christian possibility, the scandalous possibility, of an unexpected word of hope spoken to humanity from beyond these realms. To be sure, this often happens, as in the current novel, in a frame of sarcastic contrasts: Christmas lights are "our part of the annual pretense that God descended to earth in a baby's body." "Christianity said, God is a man. Humanism said, Man is a god. Today we say . . . everything is nothing." Acceding to Deirdre's desire to go to Easter service, after she comments it would be "bad luck not to go," Ben observes:

> Thus Christianity, once an encompassing cathedral built on swords and crowns, holding philosophy in one transept and music in the other and all the humanity of Europe and the Americans in its nave, has died back to its roots of mindless superstition. We went to the nine o'clock service in the church of her childhood, a shabby United Something (Presbyterian and Methodist? Congregational and Reformed?) . . .

Elsewhere, Ben describes his memory of going down to the basement to work on a dollhouse for his daughter:

> There was no God, each detail of the rusting, moldering cellar made clear, just Nature, which would consume my life as carelessly and relentlessly as it would a dung-beetle corpse in a compost pile. Dust to dust: each hammer's stroke seemed dulled by cosmic desolation, each measurement for my rust-dulled crosscut saw seemed part of the grid of merciless laws that would soon extinguish me. I couldn't breathe . . .

Anyone who has not felt the power of this genuinely annihilationist possibility will find little of power or comfort in a faith that runs, as Updike has said, at right angles to this stern materialism. I believe theologian Stephen Webb is on target when he suggests that "Updike models a new way of doing religion in fiction, a kind of negative theology of fiction, that honors the secularity of his readers, but also maintains the integrity of religious forms of life, as antiquated but still livable."

Updike's sexual characterizations and descriptions are sure to be noted. Ben's bedroom scenes with Deirdre, his exploitative multiple-orifices lust, and his molesting, pedophilic dalliance with Doreen are explicitly described. Updike has been unrepentant in defending the novelist's role of recording the hard facts. The fatally ill Ben confesses, "I still peer out of the windows of my eyes with the unforgiving spirit of a young man on the make. . . . In the same shameful nook of me that craves immortality, I am as carnal as ever." One is reminded of Ann-Janine Morey's comment about male-oriented fiction in general and Updike in particular "Women, functioning as embodied inspirations for longing, are experienced as both vast and absent holes for some unseen world." There is no question that Updike regards this blind drive to fill all the holes as a compulsive surrogate expression of a religious quest for an absconded God.

It is also important to note, however, that in no work does Updike ever describe or condone abusive physical coercion or violence in sexual encounter. Sex in Updike may be seamy and steamy, but it is never abusively violent. It is always ultimately consensual, moral or not.

Finally, Updike focuses on the profound dilemmas of our experience of the natural world. Nature copiously gives birth in beauty and kills without mercy; it simultaneously sustains us in health and pleasure and destroys us in disease and suffering; it both inscrutably generates life and propels everything toward extinction.

So what are we to make of the metaphysics of time, religiously speaking? How are we to interpret its unilinear irreversibility, the dominating intractability of natural causes, the unavoidability of death for each living thing—which only humans, apparently, so painfully reflect upon? What could be the ultimate reason or purpose for a cosmos that generates this whole process, yet seems ineluctably headed for its own self-destruction? The philosopher Pythagoras asked 2,500 years ago, "Why is there something and not nothing?" Given our modern cosmological understanding, as Updike suggests, we might well ask the reverse, "Why will there be nothing after something?" After his diagnosis of cancer, Ben exults:

> Alive. I'm alive, I sometimes think now, listening to the rain in the gutters, feeling the extensions of my limbs in space, beneath the soft sheets. What bliss life is, imagined from the standpoint of a stone or of a cubic yard of black water in the icy ocean depths. Even there, apparently, conglomerated molecules managed to light a tiny candle of consciousness. The universe hates death, can it be? If God be for us, who can be against us. Nor height, nor depth, nor any other creature, shall be able to separate us. . . . Alive. A pitiable but delicious reprieve from timelessness.

In his remarks accepting the Jesuit Campion Award in New York recently, Updike commented,

"The modern Christian inherits an intellectual tradition of faulty cosmology and shrewd psychology." The new physics requires a new metaphysics of time that squares better with big-bang, big-crunch theory. Not that this particular theory should be considered final. The role of theology is neither to dictate nor to bless the cosmological theory of the present, and it certainly is not to spend its time trying to repristinate outmoded Christian cosmologies of the past. Its forte is the life of the soul, the anxious psychology of finitude which Isaac Watts articulated so clearly:

> Time, like an ever-rolling stream, Bears all its sons away; they fly, forgotten, as a dream Dies at the opening day.

There is no question that Updike understands this psychology very well and brilliantly describes the life that hovers always between the hints of hope and the blows of despair. When Updike has felt free to speak his own personal stance, as in his memoir *Self-Consciousness,* there seems no question that he would align himself with the conclusion of Watts creed:

> Before the hills in order stood, Or earth received her frame, From everlasting thou art God; To endless years the same. O God, our help in ages past, Our hope for years to come, Be thou our guard while troubles last, And our eternal home.

Christian faith is indeed about time—both its creation and its redemption, from beyond time. This novel suggests what we need to be clear about that, as both we and the cosmos drift, wonderingly, toward the end of time.

Source: James Yerkes, Review of *Toward the End of Time*, in the *Christian Century*, Vol. 114, No. 33, November 19, 1997, pp. 1079–82.

Sources

Atwood, Margaret, "Memento More—but First, Carpe Diem," in *New York Times Book Review*, October 12, 1997, pp. 9–10.

Dalley, Jan, Review of *Toward the End of Time*, in *New Statesman*, Vol. 127, No. 4372, February 13, 1998, p. 46.

Giles, Jeff, Review of *Toward the End of Time*, in *Newsweek*, Vol. 130, No. 15, October 13, 1997, p. 78.

LaHood, Marvin J., Review of *Toward the End of Time*, in *World Literature Today*, Vol. 72, No. 2, Spring 1998, pp. 374–75.

Manley, Will, Review of *Toward the End of Time*, in *Booklist*, Vol. 94, No. 7, December 1, 1997, p. 589.

Review of *Toward the End of Time*, in *Publishers Weekly*, Vol. 244, No. 32, August 4, 1997, p. 62.

St. John, Edward B., Review of *Toward the End of Time*, in *Library Journal*, Vol. 122, No. 15, September 15, 1997, pp. 103–04.

Updike, John, *Toward the End of Time*, Fawcett Columbine, 1997.

Further Reading

De Bellis, John, *John Updike: Critical Responses to the "Rabbit" Saga*, Praeger Publishers, 2005.

The collected twenty-seven essays, including some by Updike, explore Updike's writing and explain the Rabbit series.

Goswami, Amit, *The Self-Aware Universe*, Tarcher, 1995.

The physicist Amit Goswami of the University of Oregon has brought together spirituality and quantum physics in a language that lay people can easily understand. Like Ben Turnbull in Updike's novel, Goswami searches for a way to understand the universe and the meaning of life through science and religion.

Pritchard, William H., *Updike: America's Man of Letters*, University of Massachusetts Press, 2005.

Pritchard examines all of Updike's novels as well as his memoirs in an attempt to provide a clear picture of the author's work.

Updike, John, and James Plath, *Conversations with John Updike*, University Press of Mississippi, 1994.

These thirty interviews on Updike's work give the reader an intimate view of Updike's thought and the progression of his ideas.

We Were the Mulvaneys

Joyce Carol Oates

1996

Although Joyce Carol Oates has been a fixture of American literature since her debut novel in 1964, her twenty-sixth novel *We Were the Mulvaneys*, published in 1996, was the first one to reach the top of the *New York Times* bestsellers list. The book tells the story of the Mulvaney family, a close-knit clan of social achievers who live in a rural community in upstate New York from the 1950s through the 1980s and how their peaceful existence is fractured when the daughter is molested after a high school dance. The aftermath of the event drives different family members into isolation, alcoholism, and a revenge scheme that includes kidnapping and murder. As with many of Oates's works, the sudden realization that violence can break out at any moment forces the characters to reconsider what they thought they knew about the world. Unlike many of her books, though, *We Were the Mulvaneys* has a life-affirming conclusion in which the characters finally make peace with the demons that have haunted them. Oates's eye for detail and understanding of the emotions of damaged and fragile human beings allow readers to follow six individuals on their separate paths while never losing sight of what makes each one of them a Mulvaney.

Author Biography

Joyce Carol Oates was born on June 16, 1938, in Lockport, a small town in rural western New York State, similar to the setting of many of her works,

Joyce Carol Oates © Nancy Kaszerman/Corbis

including *We Were the Mulvaneys*. Her father worked as a tool and die designer, and her mother was a homemaker. As a child, Oates spent much time on her grandparents' farm and attended a one-room schoolhouse. She completed her first novel at the age of fifteen, but it was not published.

Oates attended Syracuse University on a scholarship, graduating as valedictorian in 1960; as an undergraduate, she won the *Mademoiselle* magazine College Fiction Award for one of her short stories. She received her M.A. from the University of Wisconsin in 1961. After graduation, she and her husband, Raymond Joseph Smith (with whom Oates co-founded the *Ontario Review* in 1974) moved to Detroit. While she was teaching at the University of Detroit, one of her short stories was published in the annual *Best American Short Stories* anthology, reinforcing her commitment to writing. Her writing in her years in Detroit is characterized by a gritty urban vision best displayed in her novel *them*. From 1967 to 1978 she taught at the University of Windsor, in Windsor, Ontario, Canada.

Oates's first few novels, starting in the early 1960s, did not gain much public attention, although they did earn her critical praise. From the beginning of her career, she garnered accolades from her peers, winning National Endowment for the Arts grants in 1966 and 1968; a Guggenheim fellowship in 1967; nominations for the National Book Award in 1968 and 1969; and an actual National Book Award in 1970. From there, her list of publications becomes massive, with a list of awards to match, including nominations by the Pulitzer Prize committee, the American Theater Critics Association, and the Horror Writers of America. As of 2006, she was one of the most prolific writers living, having published over a hundred titles, including novels, short story collections, poetry collections, plays, collections of essays, children's books, and nonfiction studies. In addition to the massive body of works published under her own name, she has also published eight novels under the pseudonym Rosalind Smith.

Since 1978, Oates has taught at Princeton University, first as a visiting writer, then as a professor, and as of 2006 as the Roger S. Berlind Distinguished Professor in the Humanities.

Plot Summary

I. Family Pictures

We Were the Mulvaneys begins in the voice of the youngest member of the family, Judd Mulvaney, who serves as narrator intermittently throughout the novel. He introduces readers to the Mulvaney family, which was socially prominent in their rural upstate New York community, where they lived from 1955 to 1980. The father, Michael Sr., ran a successful roofing company. The mother, Corinne, watched over the household, High Point Farm, which was busy with four children, pets, and farm animals, all while running a small antiques business out of one of the barns on the property. The Mulvaney children—Mike Jr., Patrick, Marianne, and Judd—were popular and successful in school. Mike Jr. was a football star, Marianne was a cheerleader, Patrick had top academic honors, and Judd, born considerably later, was the treasured youngest of the family.

The first few chapters of the novel establish the situation, with Judd explaining that he felt left out of the family's brightest moments, the events such as huge parties and visits from interesting friends, that helped define the Mulvaneys as one of the most popular families in the Chautauqua Valley.

The story begins in the chapter titled "Valentine's Day, 1976." Marianne, after attending the Valentine's Day dance in town at Mt. Ephraim High School, spends the night at a friend's house

Media Adaptations

- *We Were the Mulvaneys* was available as of 2006 in an abridged form on audio cassette and CD, read by J. Todd Adam. It was released by HighBridge Audio in 2001.
- The book was adapted to a movie by the Hallmark Network in 2002. Starring Blythe Danner and Beau Bridges, it was nominated for three Emmys (lead actress, lead actor, and music). As of 2006, the film was available on DVD from Hallmark Entertainment.
- An excellent essay on this book written by Oates herself is available at the Oprah Book Club website http://www.oprah.com/obc/pastbooks/joyce_caroloates/obc_20010124_essay.jhtml (accessed April 26, 2006).

in town and phones the next day for a ride home. After Patrick drives into town for her and brings her back in a snowstorm, she goes to her room then takes a bath, not telling her family what happened after the dance: a senior boy, Zack Lundt, got her drunk and raped her.

Because her family revolves around the cheery demeanor generated by Corinne, Marianne keeps the news of the rape to herself. She blames herself, not the boy, for what has happened. In the middle of a weekday morning, another mother tells Corinne that she has seen Marianne going into the Catholic Church, although school is in session and the family is Protestant. Corinne goes to the church and gets Marianne. En route home, the car runs over something in the road that seems to be a small animal, and Marianne becomes hysterical. Corinne takes her to the family doctor, who examines her and explains that Marianne has been raped.

When Michael comes home and Corinne tells him the news, he races over to the Lundt's house, bursts in, and tries to strangle Zachary Lundt, but he is stopped by the police whom Corinne called as he raced out into the night. The news of his assault against the boy and his father, a friend of Michael's, spreads around town. When Marianne goes back to school in a few weeks, there are rumors and jokes whispered that imply she is promiscuous. Marianne, in a fragile mental state, refuses to testify against Zachary Lundt, and a lawyer advises the Mulvaneys that there is not much legal recourse.

Michael Mulvaney begins drinking heavily, which makes him miss work. He starts spending more time in the working-class bars that he used to frequent before his roofing business prospered and the Mulvaneys became socially prominent. Old friends avoid him and his family, which feeds his resentment. One night, an old acquaintance who runs a seedy inn and tavern where the Mulvaneys used to go when they were a young married couple calls: he tells Corinne that she has to come and get her husband, who has been hurt in a fight. Spending the night with him in one of the inn's rooms, Corinne realizes that her main commitment is to her husband.

Soon after, without any discussion with the rest of the family, the parents arrange to send Marianne away to live with a distant relative. They do this because Michael cannot bear the constant reminder of his powerlessness in the face of what happened to her.

II. "The Huntsman"

After Marianne leaves, the family slowly dissolves. Mike Jr. moves out of the house, living in town and working for Mulvaney Roofing. He drinks and hangs around with a wild crowd, arguing constantly with his father. After a car accident which he survives, but which does serious injury to his fiancée, who is riding with him, Mike Jr. joins the Marines and is seldom heard from throughout the rest of the novel.

Patrick leaves home to attend Cornell University a few months after Marianne is sent away. Before leaving, he gives the valedictorian speech at graduation at Mt. Ephraim High School. Embittered because the boy who raped his sister is part of the school's popular group, Patrick arranges for noxious fumes to spray through the audience during the commencement ceremony, a plot so cleverly planned and orchestrated that no one even suspects him. At college, Patrick has no friends. He seldom comes home during breaks, and when he does, he leaves soon.

Even with Marianne gone, Michael continues to drink and act belligerent in public, driving his business into the ground. He hires lawyers to determine who he can sue for redress over his grievances, forcing him to take out thousands of dollars in loans to pay them.

Two years later, Marianne travels by bus to visit Patrick. It is 1978, and she has left the home of the distant cousin to attend Kilburn State College, where she attends class infrequently. She is a member of the Green Isle Co-Op, a community of coworkers who grow food and bake breads and sell their goods in local stores when they can. Patrick is astounded at how little she looks like the cheerleader she once was: her hair is chopped, and she is undernourished, and he mistakes her at first for a twelve-year-old boy.

Michael Sr. goes to the Mt. Ephraim Country Club one afternoon and notices a group of his former friends sitting together, laughing. Drunk, he pours a glass of beer on the head of a district judge, which leads to his arrest for assault and a newspaper article about the incident. The results are further erosion in Mulvaney Roofing and more attorney bills.

Feeling himself to be something of an outcast, Patrick goes to see a rock band on campus. He does not feel comfortable with the crowd, but while there he notes a boy that he mistakes at a distance for Zachary Lundt. Patrick gets the idea to kidnap Lundt and kill him. He contacts Judd, telling him to take one of the rifles from the house and meet him at a secret location in the woods near the family home, and he calls the Lundt house, pretending to be one of Zachary's old high school friends and finds out when he will be home for Easter break. One night, Patrick goes out to a bar where Zachary is with his friends and abducts him at gunpoint. He takes him deep into a nearby swamp, where Lundt falls under water and is about to drown before Patrick realizes that he does not want to kill his worst enemy. He reaches into the mud and saves Lundt's life and then leaves Lundt in the wilderness.

III. "The Pilgrim"

Marianne works hard at the Green Isle Co-Op, waiting for the day when her mother will call her up and say that her father wants her to return home to High Point Farm. She is loved and respected by her co-workers, but she avoids closeness. She cries when she is by herself. When the director's assistant leaves, the director discovers that Marianne has the drive and intelligence to be second in charge; he increases her responsibilities. Like most of the young women at the co-op, Marianne has a crush on Abelove, the director, and is honored to work closely with him.

When news of her grandmother's death reaches her, Marianne resolves to go to the funeral and to renew her connection to her family. A shy boy from the co-op named Hewie Miner offers to drive her across the state to the town where Corinne was raised. After traveling several hours, though, Marianne finds that she does not have it in herself to enter the chapel: she watches from outside and sees her mother and Judd, but neither of her other brothers or her father. On the way home, she has Hewie drive through Mt. Ephraim, past the Mulvaney Roofing building, through the streets she knew as a child, and past High Point Farm, realizing how removed she is now from it all.

After her day-long journey, Abelove approaches Marianne and asks if she and Hewie are in love. She assures him that they are not, and he then offers her an even higher position in the Green Isle Co-op: associate director. As he is explaining how much everyone at the co-op loves her, Abelove confesses that he is in love with her, too. Marianne leaves, telling him that she wants to think about what he has said: that night, she packs her things and leaves the Green Isle Co-op, her home and life's obsession for several years, without saying goodbye to anyone.

IV. Hard Reckoning

In the spring of 1980, Judd finishes junior year of high school in a new town: the dwindling Mulvaney Roofing business and mounting legal bills have forced the family to sell High Point Farm and move to nearby Marsina. Michael Sr. has been consistently drunk and angry, spending time away from home, so that selling the house and finding a new house have fallen to Corinne. Michael's vague attempts to restart the roofing business in the new town fail. The family hears from Mike Jr., Patrick, and Marianne intermittently.

Marianne ends up in Spartansburg, as the companion of an older, wheelchair-bound writer, Penelope Hagström. Miss Hagström respects Penelope's intelligence and trusts her with her household business.

One night, when he arrives home late and drunk, Michael is rough with Corinne, and Judd intervenes against his father. The next day, Judd moves out and finds his own apartment.

The roofing business goes bankrupt, and all of the family's remaining assets, including the new house, are sold. With the dissolution of the house, Michael and Corinne go in different directions. He lives in a series of smaller apartments and then rented rooms, taking jobs that he cannot keep because he drinks, is unable to work on roofs or do heavy labor, and is too belligerent to take orders from men who once would have been his employees.

In 1988, Corinne finally contacts Marianne, who is twenty-nine years old, to tell her that her father is dying and has called for her. Marianne had left Miss Hagström several years earlier when the older woman offered to increase her responsibilities. She had moved to a small town, rented a room, and taken a job in a grocery store. But one day, when her cat Muffin, the one reminder of life at High Point Farm, fell ill, she had rushed him to a local animal hospital, run by Dr. Whittaker West, a veterinarian whose dedication had earned his hospital and animal shelter an excellent nationwide reputation. Soon Marianne had moved into the huge mansion that houses the shelter and had become West's assistant. When the time came to euthanize Muffin, Dr. West, while consoling Marianne, admitted that he was in love with her.

In Rochester, where Michael Mulvaney has been taken, Judd and Corinne insist that he has called Marianne's name, but he does not seem to recognize her or anyone around him. To her ear, he seems to have spoken his older sister's name, Marian. He dies, and Mike Jr. returns to join the family in scattering his father's ashes on a hill above High Point Farm.

Epilogue. Reunion: Fourth of July 1993

The Mulvaneys are all invited to a Fourth of July reunion at a farm that Corinne and her friend Sable Mills have bought and turned into an antique shop. The business is prospering, and the farm, though not as grand as the one at High Point Farm, is expansive enough for the two women, and it is adjoined by a creek that ran past the old family property, about eighteen miles away. Judd is the editor of a small newspaper, the *Chautauqua Falls Journal*. Marianne is married to Whit West, and they have a young son. Mike Jr., who is now a civil engineer in Wilmington, Delaware, has a wife and two children, and they are expecting another. Patrick, who has not been back to the area since the night he abducted Zachary Lundt, has traveled from California by motorcycle with his girlfriend, showing an entirely different personality than the bookish introvert that he was when he left. In all, twenty-seven people have gathered at the home of Corinne Mulvaney, giving her children time to reacquaint themselves with each other and get to know their extended family and their mother's friends.

Characters

Abelove

Abelove is the charismatic leader of the Green Isle Co-op. His background is a mystery: no one even knows his true first name, which is described as "something odd and awkward like 'Charlesworth.'" He is a peaceful man who talks about helping the poor, extolling Christian principles while at the same time worrying about expanding the financial range of the co-op. All of the women at the co-op, including Marianne, are secretly in love with Abelove.

Patrick is suspicious of Abelove. Corinne banters with him throughout a meal, but she turns abruptly against Abelove when he comments on Marianne's personality.

After Marianne has risen in rank to become his valuable assistant, and rumors have spread through the co-op that she might be involved with Hewie Miner, Abelove confesses to Marianne that he is in love with her and wants to marry her. Though it is her desire, she sneaks away that night, unable to cope with such potential happiness.

Birk

Birk, once one of Abelove's students at Kilburn College, serves as assistant director at the Green Isle Co-Op when Marianne is there. He disappears without a trace one day, leaving behind all of his belongings.

Button

See Marianne Mulvaney

Della Rae Duncan

A mentally challenged girl from the poor area of Mt. Ephraim, Della Rae is molested by a group of boys from the football team.

Miss Penelope Hagström

On the road by herself, Marianne is taken into the home of Miss Hagström, an elderly, crippled poet. Famous nationally for her writing, Miss Hagström is known in her own town of Spartansburg as an unfortunate woman who was abandoned by her fiancée years ago and has been weakened over the decades by multiple sclerosis. She is a sharp wit and is usually kind to Marianne, seeing in her the intelligence and capability which Marianne does not see in herself. At times, though, Miss Hagström can be bitter and sarcastic.

When Miss Hagström offers to elevate Marianne's position, to make her the associate director of the Hagström Foundation for the Arts in addition to being her personal assistant, Marianne finds the increased involvement uncomfortable and leaves her one night without saying goodbye to Miss Hagström.

Miss Ethel Hausmann

When it is decided that Marianne cannot stay at High Point Farm with her family, she is sent to live in Salamanca with Ethel Hausmann, a relative on Corinne's side. Miss Hausmann is not familiar to the family. She is in her early fifties and has never had children of her own; she has worked for a podiatrist for thirty years, silently in love with him.

Haw Hawley

When they were first married, Corinne and Michael Mulvaney spent their time with a rowdy crowd at the Wolf's Head Inn, owned by "Haw" Hawley. Corinne looks down on him as a drunk, but he is polite and helpful the night that he calls her to the inn to help Michael, who has been injured in a fight.

Zachary Lundt

Zachary Lundt is the boy who rapes Marianne Mulvaney. He is a senior, the same age as Patrick and a year older than Marianne, when she catches his eye at the Valentine's dance, and he offers to drive her home when her date has to leave early. In his car, he gives Marianne liquor and tells her he has a confused life and he feels comfortable talking with her about serious philosophical matters. He tells her that she brings out the best in him. After a while, though, he becomes angry and rapes her.

Because Zach is a popular member of the football team, what he has done does not reflect badly on him. The other students at Mt. Ephraim High support him, turning against the Mulvaneys, spreading rumors that Marianne was his willing sexual partner.

Years later, when Zach is away at the state university at Binghamton studying business administration, he comes home for spring break and is abducted outside a bar by Patrick Mulvaney. Taken at gunpoint to a nearby bog, Zach denies knowing what Patrick is talking about regarding the girl he raped, and he begs shamelessly to have his life spared.

Sable Mills

Sable shares a house with Corinne in 1993, the time at which the book ends. It is an arrangement that provides both women with financial security and companionship. The two met after running into each other repeatedly at antique auctions and with their shared interest have opened an antique store, Alder Antiques, on the farm they share.

Sable is ten years younger than Corinne and attended the same high school. She has been married and divorced three times and has children and grandchildren. While Corinne is a natural homemaker, Sable is a natural businessperson, making their partnership well-rounded and fulfilling.

Hewie Miner

Hewie Miner is the worker at the Green Isle Co-op who agrees to drive Marianne across the state to her grandmother's funeral. He is shy but kind and on suspension from college for having loaned his lab notes to another student. Hewie hardly talks over the course of the thirteen-hour trip. When they return to the co-op, Hewie tells her that he would be glad to do anything for her because he is in love with her. Rumors circulate that Marianne and Hewie are romantically linked, spurring Abelove to confess his own love for Marianne.

Mule

See Mike Mulvaney

Corinne Mulvaney

Corinne is the mother of the Mulvaney family and its spiritual center. She is highly spirited with a zest for life. At first, her enthusiasm infects her children, driving them to be successful in school. After Marianne has been raped, though, Corinne alienates her children by making the decision to stand by her husband, so that when he finds it too painful to live with Marianne, she agrees to send her daughter away to live with a distant relative. She tries to remain positive during the turmoil that tears her family apart, but her cheerfulness is just seen as self-delusion.

Corinne is a devout churchgoer. A formative episode from her childhood occurred when she and her mother were in a car accident in a blizzard when she was seven: they walked through the snow and became lost, and probably would have frozen if their way were not lit by a swarm of fireflies. Improbable as everyone else finds the story, Corinne looks back on the incident as a sign from God.

After Marianne is raped on Valentine's Day in 1976, Corinne finds herself able to talk to a therapist and a few friends about what happened, though she is not able to use the word, "rape." She tries to be supportive but is defensive about her husband and agrees to send Marianne away for his sake. Corinne talks with Marianne infrequently. As Michael sinks deeper and deeper into alcoholism, she takes control of family matters, including the most painful to her, the sale of High Point Farm. Still, she loses her husband.

In the end, Corinne is happy, living with her friend Sable Mills on a farm not far from the one where she raised her family and running an antique store like the one she ran at High Point Farm. She hosts the family reunion at the end of her book and is surrounded by children, grandchildren, friends, and church members.

Judd Mulvaney

Judd, the narrator of the book, is the youngest Mulvaney, born several years after his next older sibling, which leaves him with a feeling that the peak years of the Mulvaney family life, the ones that were most legendary, came before he arrived and that subjects are being discussed that he is does not know about. In 1976, when Judd is thirteen, his siblings leave home in quick order: Marianne is sent to live with relatives, Mike goes into the Marines, and Patrick goes to college.

When Patrick decides to kill the boy who raped Marianne, he phones Judd from college and enlists him in the plan, instructing Judd to secretly remove one of the rifles from the house. Judd is frightened, but he also admires his brother and vows not to let him down. He delivers the gun to Patrick and later picks it up without ever finding out what happened with it.

Judd is left with his parents and watches his father's downward spiral as he loses his business and the house. Then one night in 1980 he and his father come to open physical confrontation, and Judd, still in high school, moves out and takes his own rented room in a ramshackle building.

At the end of the book, Judd is thirty, the editor of a twice-a-week local newspaper.

Marianne Mulvaney

The story of the destruction of the Mulvaney family centers on the rape of seventeen-year-old Marianne. She is a happy, popular teenager, a member of the 4-H club and the cheerleading squad, until Zachary Lundt gets her drunk after the Valentine's dance and rapes her. After that, Marianne finds herself ostracized: first at school, where she is treated as though she is promiscuous, and at home, where her father is unable to come to grips with his own failure to protect her.

Marianne internalizes the blame for the rape, feeling that she is just as responsible as Zach Lundt was for what happened because she was drinking in his car. Having been sent away, she waits patiently for years, expecting to be called back home. In later life, she finds herself unable to deal with emotional attachments or responsibilities: when Abelove, whom she has had a crush on, declares his love and asks her to marry him, she runs away from the co-op without telling him, and when Penelope Hagström offers to promote her to an executive position in her charitable organization, Marianne again runs off without a word. She eagerly races to her father's death bed when she hears he has called for her, only to find that he is too far gone to recognize her.

Marianne ends up happily married to Whit West, a veterinarian who runs a shelter for animals. Her childhood on the farm, and her love for her horse Molly-O and her cat, Muffin, who is her traveling companion throughout the book, are reflected in her eventual sense of security at Dr. West's clinic.

Michael Mulvaney Sr.

Michael Mulvaney is the father of the Mulvaney family, their protector and the source of their dissolution, dying estranged from his wife and children, addled by alcohol, and bitter.

Michael Mulvaney came from a large Irish Catholic family, leaving home at age eighteen to get away from his drunk, abusive father: because he left, his father insisted that no one in the family would ever contact him for the rest of his life. After marrying Corinne, his family grew, and his business, Mulvaney Roofing, prospered, growing into one of the largest in the county. As he succeeded, Michael left behind his working-class friends and began associating with others who were prosperous.

After attacking the boy who raped Marianne and finding out that the law will not prosecute him, Michael begins drinking heavily. His business suffers, and he loses money on lawyer fees. He becomes increasingly bitter toward the people he thought were his friends and even toward his family. He cannot bear to see Marianne anymore, so she is sent away, which angers his sons.

Michael loses his business; he loses the farm; he argues with Corinne and leaves her. Late in his life, after he has taken jobs from men he would not have even hired at Mulvaney Roofing, he spends an evening with his son, Mike, who finds that his father barely has a grasp on reality anymore. Eventually, Michael is found lying in the street, and his family is called to his deathbed. He is thought to have called for Marianne, to whom he has not talked in the years since she was banished, but it could also be that he actually spoke the name of his favorite sister, Marian.

Mike Mulvaney Jr.

Michael Mulvaney Jr. is the most obscure family member, in part, because he is the most distant from the book's narrator, Judd, and in part because he moves away early. When Marianne is molested, Mike is already out of high school and working for his father's roofing company. He is a former high school football hero, and his younger brother and sister are reminded of his social position by the trophies in school that bear his name. Although he has a sense of honor, like all the Mulvaneys, he also bears the shame of not interfering with his friends when he knew they were raping a girl.

After Marianne is raped, Mike, like his father, soothes his anger with drinking. He becomes known to local police because of his reckless driving, but his football hero reputation saves him from serious charges. After he injures a girl badly in a car accident, he joins the Marines. For most of the novel, he is away. He ends up with a wife and two children, working as a civil engineer in Wilmington, Delaware.

Patrick Mulvaney

Patrick is a boy genius, with a keen scientific mind but none of the social skills that the other members of his family enjoy. He attends high school with Marianne, one grade above her: after she is raped, Patrick has to live with the school gossip that she has been promiscuous and got what she deserved. He becomes so bitter that he sabotages his graduation, at which he is speaking as valedictorian, with a stink bomb in the air ducts.

In college, Patrick finds himself even more an outcast. He goes to a concert, attempting to behave in the way that normal college students behave, and he sees someone who resembles Zachary Lundt: this association leads to the revelation that Lundt's assault on his sister has caused all of the troubles that have torn apart the Mulvaney family and the idea that he can correct the family's problems by killing Lundt. He kidnaps at gunpoint the man he considers his enemy and takes him to a deserted bog, but at the last minute he realizes that killing him will not make life better for the Mulvaneys.

After realizing the futility of revenge, Patrick quits school and travels. He is not in contact with the family often and cannot be reached when his father dies. It is a surprise when he shows up at the family reunion at the end of the book well-adjusted: he is physically fit, has a beautiful girlfriend, and has a peaceful outlook on life.

Pinch

See Patrick Mulvaney

Ranger

See Judd Mulvaney

Dr. Whittaker West

West is a veterinarian who has a clinic for stray animals, Stump Creek Hill, that has gained national attention. He divides his time between treating animals and lobbying politicians for grants to support his work. On her own, living in a rented room with her cat Muffin, Marianne goes to West's clinic one day when the cat is sick. She becomes involved with the animal refuge and moves in, taking on more and more duties. When Muffin dies, West tells her that he is in love with her. They show up at the family reunion, years later, married, with children.

Themes

Estrangement

In this novel, Oates dramatizes how trauma and loss can disrupt a group's self-concept and cohesiveness. The Mulvaneys are not able to maintain their group identification as prosperous and successful once an attack intrudes and injures one of the family members. Once that loss occurs, the self-concept of the group and its collective sense of its place in the world alter. When this shift occurs, the group no longer coheres, and individuals disperse literally or insulate themselves in other ways. This loss of coherence is most conspicuous in Marianne who is sent away from the family because her father cannot live with the realization that his family is vulnerable to violent acts and that he is powerless to protect his children from them. After being molested by Zachary Lundt, Marianne is sent away from her previously close-knit family. Psychologically, she replicates that removal by withdrawing from potential relationships and from

Topics For Further Study

- The animals that the Mulvaneys raise on their non-producing farm are central to this story. Make a list of all of the animals mentioned in the novel, and then write a chart that shows what it would cost to feed them all in today's dollars.
- Michael Mulvaney's slide into alcoholism follows a fairly standard pattern. Interview a member of Alcoholics Anonymous and find out what that person thinks of Michael's behavior, as you present it. Then report to the class the steps that your interviewee said Michael or Corinne could have taken.
- Examine the statistics linking rape and alcohol abuse in your state, and write a letter to Marianne Mulvaney explaining what happened to her and whether she has a case against Zachary Lundt that would stand up in court.
- Author Jonathan Franzen's novel *The Corrections* was chosen for Oprah's Book Club, just as this novel was, but Franzen declined the offer, even though it would have meant thousands of more copies would sell. Research the controversy over Franzen's refusal, and conduct a debate representing both sides of the argument.
- Much is made in the novel of the fact that the Mulvaney parents disagree about joining the Mt. Ephraim Country Club and about Michael's eventual expulsion from it. Contact at least three country clubs to find out what a person would have to do to join and what a person would have to do to be thrown out, and then write the rules that you would use if you were to start your own private club. Present your rules to your class with explanations.

opportunities to progress professionally. Though the victim in the initial instance, she is punished; having learned that she is to blame, she is driven by shame to continue that punishment by denying herself good. Oates symbolizes her guilt and shame with the torn, bloodied dress that Marianne hides in the back of her closet. Significantly, Marianne's mother knows where to find the dress, and she disposes of it without a word to Marianne, allowing her daughter to fixate in a self-punishing mental state. The aftereffects of the assault harden into a pattern of withdrawal and self-sabotage which assures Marianne's future unhappiness. If her parents could have accepted Marianne as changed by her experience and loved her despite that change, her trauma would have likely had less effect and those effects would have neutralized sooner. Banning her from the family underscored the guilt Marianne was quick to feel for the assault perpetrated on her. The novel seems to suggest that if victims and their families do not have sufficient support to work through trauma and loss, these disrupting, violent acts can change both the victim and the family dynamics permanently.

Revenge

In Patrick Mulvaney's response to the assault on his sister, Oates is able to explore both the attraction of revenge and its uselessness. Patrick's prank during commencement and his later, much more dangerous kidnapping of Zachary Lundt are impotent responses to a violent assault. Fortunately, Patrick gains some insight into the futility of revenge when he witnesses Lundt's near drowning. Patrick realizes that acting hurtfully now cannot revise the past. He realizes that hurting Lundt solves nothing. Though the novel does not follow his life for many years, Oates makes clear in the end that Patrick has been able to find peace chiefly because he realizes that revenge cannot give him peace.

Alcoholism

In the head of the family, Michael Mulvaney Sr., Oates explores the ever widening destruction caused by progressive alcohol addiction. Mulvaney's downfall follows the typical downward spiral of alcoholism. Moreover, his abuse of alcohol is not just a reaction to the assault on his daughter. Oates shows that Michael is a likely candidate for alcoholism even if the rape had not occurred and triggered his behavior. For one thing, his father was an abusive alcoholic, and studies show that alcoholism is usually repeated in subsequent generations, either because of genetic or learned factors. Also, Michael's younger days, before the responsibilities of a growing business and family reined him in, were characterized by drunken weekends when he caroused at the tavern at Wolf's Head Lake, following the path of Haw Hawley, who ends up broken and divorced himself. As Corinne realizes later, when Michael takes up with his old drinking buddies again, the life that they built at High Point Farm (which constituted the "high point" in their marriage) may have "only postponed Wolf's Head Lake in their lives." Alcohol, which is first understood as a means of enjoying a weekend, later becomes a deadly weapon of self-torture, self-sabotage, and the destruction of relationships with others. Oates's novel dramatizes this widening sphere alcohol affects. As a response to trauma and loss, alcohol is a self-medicating insulation in the present moment serving as a barrier to unbearable pain. Over the long haul, however, alcohol is the thief that steals everything away from Michael Mulvaney Sr., his business, his social circle, his family. Ironically, Michael Sr. chooses to drink, and that choice is much more pervasively destructive than Marianne's choicelessness in being assaulted by Zack Lundt.

Optimism

In spite of the travails of the Mulvaney family, Corinne, the mother, continues to hold on to the hope that things will eventually be set aright again. The family's life at High Point Farm, where they are happy together, is built around Corinne's view of the world: she is the one who grew up on a farm and values socializing and religion. Her family values rub off on her husband and children, but their hold on them is not as strong as Corinne's. After the rape of Marianne, the others stray from the family's optimistic outlook; they feel vulnerable, subject to the same hardships that befall others. But Corinne holds on to her positive attitude.

The novel uses the cowbell to symbolize diminished and ascendant hope. It is the focus of an early chapter, in which Corinne uses it to call Patrick in from his wanderings to tell him to pick Marianne up in town. Neither realizes then that this moment marks the end of innocent life at High Point Farm, which is, after the rape, clouded with secrets, suspicion, guilt, and anger. For contrast, Oates brings back the cowbell at the end of the novel, when the extended family is gathered at Corinne's new farm: this time, when Corinne rings the bell, it suggests the advent of a bright future for the family members. Judd describes her "Laughing like one of her own grandchildren, the color up in her cheeks, tugging the cord of the old gourd-shaped cowbell to summon us all to eat, at last." In Corinne's optimism lies the energy for the recreation of her life. Perhaps Oates is suggesting that a positive outlook provides the energy necessary to transform one's life.

Style

Denouement

The French word, denouement, literally means "the unraveling" and is commonly used to describe the part of a story that comes after the action is completed, when the plot complications that have been put in motion throughout the story have reached their climax and the issues explored are settled. The main part of *We Were the Mulvaneys* ends with the scattering of Michael Mulvaney's ashes. It is a poignant moment, one that gives some closure to some family members, but it still leaves unanswered questions: Patrick is still missing after having abducted a man at gunpoint years earlier, and Marianne's relationship with Dr. West has just been mentioned, leaving open the possibility that she may repeat with him the self-sabotaging choices she made in previous relationships. Corinne is left alone and penniless.

The book's epilogue, set some years later, might be seen as the author's way of pasting a happy ending onto an unhappy story, but it actually is necessary for telling readers the results of the family's struggles. The fact that the Mulvaneys end up as functional adults in their separate lives is not a reversal of the events of the book, but a reasonable result of the growth process. Although Oates skips years in the lives of her characters, she lets readers know, when the story has unraveled, exactly where the events of the story have led each of them.

First-Person Narrator

We Were the Mulvaneys is told from a first person point of view, narrated by Judd Mulvaney. However, Oates modifies or adapts the point of view as needed. In some places Judd speaks in first person about his experiences, referring to himself as "I" or "me." He experiences Green Isle Co-op for himself on a trip there with his mother, and he knows more than anyone else about Patrick's plan to abduct Zachary Lundt because Patrick has involved Judd in the plan. But some events lie beyond Judd's firsthand knowledge, such as the rape or the gunpoint abduction or his parents' night at the Wolf's Head Inn; in these cases, perhaps readers can assume that he is reporting on what he has heard or learned, perhaps even filling in gaps with his imagination.

In addition, some events are reported in third person point of view. The third person narrative reports on Marianne's life apart from her birth family, her stay at the Green Isle Co-op, her time with Miss Hagström, her move to Sykesville where she meets Whit West; similarly, long sections focus on Patrick's life at Cornell and his thoughts about his mentor and fellow students. For these parts, Oates uses third person.

Historical Context

Rural New York

Though New York City is a huge and densely populated urban center, much of New York State is rural farmland. The area that stretches north toward the state capital, Albany, and west toward Buffalo is referred to as upstate New York. The western part of the state is mostly rural, with more in common culturally with the farmlands of Pennsylvania and Indiana than with life in New York City. In this western area, Oates set several of her works, including *We Were the Mulvaneys*.

The fictional town of Mt. Ephraim in upstate New York is described as being "in the Chautauqua Valley approximately seventy miles south of Lake Ontario." New York does have a Chautauqua County, but it is unlikely that it is the location Oates has in mind, since this area, along New York's westernmost border with Pennsylvania, is the adjacent to Lake Erie, not Lake Ontario. The area she describes is further east, toward the Finger Lakes Region, named after a series of narrow lakes that look a little like fingers flared out and stretching southward.

Agriculture plays an important role in the economy of New York State, providing about a $3 billion business annually. About a quarter of the state's land is used for farm production, including apples and grapes (western New York is considered one of the country's best climates for producing quality wines); corn, oats, and soybeans; and livestock and dairy products, which account for more than 60 percent of the state's agriculture. New York is the country's third largest dairy production state.

The fact that High Point Farm in the novel is not used for agricultural production is an accurate reflection of the transformation that began about 1960 and continued into the early 2000s in New York State and across much of the country. Advances in transportation and communication have made once isolated areas reasonably accessible, which enables people to commute to work in cities and yet live in rural area. Since the 1970s, population movement has been away from cities: while suburbia once constituted those towns adjacent to a large city, suburban sprawl has driven housing into what was once farmland. Although the remote area discussed in the novel is not directly affected by the flight of city dwellers from urban centers, it is part of the same desire, which began in the 1960s, a longing to escape man-made environments and enjoy a spacious, natural setting. Although Oates's Chautauqua Valley is located in the middle of farmland and the people live on farms, no one among the Mulvaneys' social circle (except the poor family that leases land from them) actually practices farming. Like the members of the Green Isle Co-op, the people living in and around Mt. Ephraim live like farmers, although they are not farmers themselves.

Critical Overview

With few exceptions, *We Were the Mulvaneys* accomplishes the rare yet often hoped-for balance of being embraced by both critics and the book-buying public. With an initial 1996 print run of 75,000 copies, the novel was clearly expected to be popular. Attention to the book soared, however, when it was announced as the first selection of 2001 for Oprah's Book Club. After that, hundreds of thousands of copies were bought. Though the 2002 movie adaptation was made for a cable television network, its three Emmy award nominations helped draw attention to an even wider audience.

When the book debuted, most critics were enthusiastic about it. For example, Joanne V. Creighton, writing in the *Chicago Tribune*, announces at the start of her review, "*We Were the Mulvaneys* is a major achievement that stands with Oates' finest studies of American life," going on to call it, "capacious, riveting and moving." This assessment is echoed by a reviewer for *Publishers*

Weekly, who describes the book as "Elegiac and urgent on tone," and who concludes, "the prose is sometimes prolix, but the very rush of narrative, in which flashbacks capture the same urgency of tone as the present, gives this moving tale its emotional power." A *Booklist* reviewer notes that "Oates' latest novel is a tragic, compelling tale," and adds the prediction: "Her legion of fans will be pleased."

Reviewing the book for the *Washington Post*, Dwight Garner points out how easy it would be to "undervalue" the work of a writer who is as productive as Oates. "By now it's become trite to exclaim at the length of Oates' books, or at the sheer abundance of them." He later insists: "It would be a mistake, however, to underestimate *We Were the Mulvaneys*." Garner finds that the book's subject justifies Oates's style: "The busy spill of her sentences is a perfect match for the tumble of big-family life."

A 1996 review in *Glamour*, however, uses a less serious tone: "Injustices pile up," its reviewer writes after a short summary, "and so, unfortunately, do Oates' essentially familiar themes: Life is Random! People are cruel! One wrong turn and you're finished! Still, Oates makes her twenty-sixth novel fresh and psychologically affecting as she probes the destruction and resurrection of an American nuclear family." While that review hints at sarcasm, the review by Gayle Hanson in the *Washington Times* a few months later is openly disdainful, noting that "Joyce Carol Oates' *We Were the Mulvaneys* is long on cliché-driven verbiage and short on insight, with a plot that could have been lifted from a community college course called the Dysfunctional Family in American Literature."

Criticism

David Kelly

Kelly is an instructor of literature and creative writing. In this essay, he proposes that the turn of events in the epilogue of the novel is actually the logical result of the events that come before it.

Some critics have viewed Joyce Carol Oates's *We Were the Mulvaneys* as the tragic tale of a happy family brought low by an act of violence, to which the author has chosen to add an optimistic but unlikely happy ending. This view seems to derive from a few fairly obvious facts about the book. For one thing, the lives of all five surviving members of the Mulvaney clan shift from emptiness to fulfillment after the narrative stops studying them, so that they suddenly show up in the book's epilogue financially secure and emotionally sound. In real life, the chances of such a spontaneous outbreak of contentment would be unlikely, and Oates's way of handling their changes in fortune outside the book's narrative only serves to make readers suspicious. Another aspect that calls out to skeptics is that this particular book, with an ending that is unusually upbeat for Oates, has become the bestselling novel, prompting the suspicion that she may have deliberately damaged the story's natural flow to provide a crowd-pleasing conclusion.

If the epilogue reverses the course of the novel for no reason other than commercial ones, the choice would assure an artistic failure, regardless of the novel's sales numbers. That fact is far from clear, though. That Oates does not give the details of family life between 1990, when Michael Mulvaney Sr. dies, and Independence Day of 1993, which is given as the date of the cheerful family reunion, does not mean that the story picks up after the break in an unrelated place. It just means that the story has developed from the elements Oates earlier set in place.

We were the Mulvaneys is a story about identity. From the first line—"We were the Mulvaneys, remember us?"—to the last, which ends with "back when we were the Mulvaneys," the novel is presented as a story about what it means to be a Mulvaney and the ways that two parents and their four children regrettably lose touch with that identity. The violent rape of Marianne, the one daughter, is an obvious catalyst for changes in Mulvaney family persona, and the epilogue suggests the family's unrecorded struggle to reclaim its original identity. If this reading makes sense, then, yes, the time that is unexplained, between the scattering of Michael Mulvaney's ashes and the epilogue, is indeed unfinished business.

However, the novel actually gives every indication that the opposite is more likely the case, namely that Corinne, Mike Jr., Patrick, Marianne, and Judd are happy in the end precisely because the years have allowed them to shed their Mulvaney identity and develop on their own. In the end, they have not returned to the happiness they once had; rather, they have survived the burden of being Mulvaneys that should have had a much more limited influence over their lives. Being Mulvaneys, in the grand sense which Judd pines for at the book's start, turns out to have not been a solution to their problems, but the cause.

The book offers many definitions of what it once meant to be a Mulvaney. The family members have nicknames; they have a coded way of talking that hints at things left unsaid; and for their values, the Mulvaneys look to each other, leaving them slightly puzzled by the world at large. Any family or other social group creates its own rules and forms its own identity. In this case, though, readers do not get a clear picture of the Mulvaney group persona because all of the facts are filtered through the consciousness of Judd, who tends to idealize the family, projecting onto it a fading greatness that may not have existed after all.

Judd is the one who calls the home, High Point Farm, a "Storybook House." When Judd says, "For a long time you envied us, then you pitied us," and "For a long time you admired us, then you thought, *Good!—that's what they deserve*," he conveys an outsider's perspective on the family that applies to some degree to himself. When he says, in the book's second sentence, "You may have thought that our family was larger," he shows that *he* is the one who thinks of the era that he did not experience firsthand as a sort of golden age of Mulvaneys. Though Judd says that he is telling this story to get to the truth, Oates makes it clear that his memories are clouded by nostalgia. The reality of the family's structure comes out through the telling of the story, and it is different than what the youngest Mulvaney's enthusiasm might lead readers to believe.

The Mulvaney family at its best is a fabricated construct, drawn together by the sheer will of the parents, Michael and Corinne, who have the desire to create an ideal household but not the experience or temperaments to make it happen. Each parent contributes to the family's life in the affluent upstate New York countryside in the late twentieth century. From Michael come a gift of friendliness and an interest in social attention, visible in his strong desire, over Corinne's objection, to join the local country club. Corinne contributes domestic gifts: she sets the pace for life at High Point Farm and provides the family with its moral values. Their differences ensure that their children will be well-rounded, but their differences also practically guarantee that the family will fail.

The problems with the family extend back as far as the history given in the book. For one thing, Michael and Corinne, well-meaning as they are, are just not family-oriented people at heart. Michael was banished by his own father, sent out into the world in his teens. His eventual banishment of his daughter, which may seem surprisingly cruel, reflects the treatment he received as a youngster. Corinne's family is local but conspicuously absent from the Mulvaneys' lives: the cousin to whom Marianne is sent to live is not familiar to the children, and Corinne's mother, though she lives only about a hundred miles away, is never talked about except for one striking childhood memory about fireflies in winter. The idea that the Mulvaneys are perfect is undermined by what readers learn about the parents' backgrounds.

"As their social status dwindles due to social prejudice, fear, shame, and given Michael's quick descent into alcoholism, the members of the family find that they have to face the world as individuals, not as representatives of a group."

When they are growing up, the Mulvaney children are not so much happy as, like their father in his roofing business, successful. They have the drive to be successful in sports and academics. This kind of success is driven by outward perceptions, a mark of the way they handle themselves among non-Mulvaneys. Even at High Point Farm, their social interactions are mitigated by the dogs, cats, birds, and horses. It makes sense that the Mulvaney family identity would be attractive to Judd, since he looks at it as an outsider; the family identity is constructed to respond to outsiders best. But the assault on Marianne separates the family from the socially acceptable world (and, not coincidentally, the animals, which stop being the media for Mulvaney communication immediately after the assault). As their social status dwindles due to social prejudice, fear, shame, and given Michael's quick descent into alcoholism, the members of the family find that they have to face the world as individuals, not as representatives of a group. At this point, they find that they are lost.

The change affects Marianne most profoundly, of course. In the short term, she turns to Catholicism to cope with her guilt and shame. In the long term, she internalizes the shame to such a degree as to sabotage her own successes in coming years, running away from Abelove once it becomes

What Do I Read Next?

- Brenda Daly's *Lavish Self-Divisions: The Novels of Joyce Carol Oates*, published by University Press of Mississippi in 1996, the year that *We Were the Mulvaneys* appeared, gives readers a critical survey of Oates's previous work.
- Oates's twenty-ninth novel, *Broke Heart Blues*, is considered her next great novel after *We Were the Mulvaneys*. Published in 2000, it is about John Reddy Heart, a popular boy in an affluent Buffalo suburb during the 1960s, who becomes an iconic figure when one of his mother's boyfriends is murdered.
- *Songs in Ordinary Time*, a novel by Mary McGarry Morris, concerns a young woman raising three children and struggling with an alcoholic husband. Set in Vermont in 1960, the book is similar in some ways to *We Were the Mulvaneys*. It was published by Penguin in 1996.
- Greg Johnson's biography of Joyce Carol Oates, *Invisible Writer* (1998), covers her life approximately up to the time of the publication of this novel. In preparing his book, Johnson had access to private family papers and was allowed to interview family members. His biography traces connections between the novels and the life of Oates and also debunks certain myths that have surrounded the author.
- Oates's collection *The Faith of a Writer: Life, Craft, Art* (2003) gathers together essays that explain her view of writing, drawing from her life story.

apparent that her love for him might be returned and, as if to demonstrate that her psychosis is not just a fear of men, running from an offered promotion at the home of her patron, Miss Hagström. Marianne's psychological damage is expectable, perhaps even unavoidable. The effect on her siblings, though, shows how shaky the family structure is to begin with: Mike Jr. is the first to leave: realizing that his life after high school is degenerating into drunkenness and bitterness, he gets himself into the structured environment of the Marines and is seldom seen at High Point Farm again. Patrick, who spends a few years wondering why he is unable to reach his intellectual potential, decides that his failures are the fault of the boy who raped Marianne, but eventually he finds that it is better to save a life than to take one. Judd tries to support his mother, who accepts her husband's increasingly abusive behavior, until he decides that he cannot help her, and he makes the healthy choice of going out into the world to find his own way.

The break-up of the family is, of course, exacerbated by the actions of Michael Sr., who sends Marianne away and then alienates the whole town with his anger, public drunkenness, and business negligence. Oates makes it clear, through the information she gives about his childhood and early courtship of Corinne, that Michael's behavior, though triggered by his realization that he cannot protect his daughter, is in his nature all along. The rift with his father suggests the sort of world view that he knew first; as a young man, he was a heavy drinker, as resentful of the social superiority of college students as Marianne's rapist proves to be of her; as a young husband, he hunts and drinks with a rowdy crowd at Wolf's Head Lake. The only thing that has made it possible for the Mulvaneys to become a socially acceptable family at all is that Corinne has been able to suppress Michael's nature, even though she could not change it. After the rape, she makes the decision to dedicate herself to this flawed man at the expense of her children.

It is no coincidence that the Mulvaneys are able to find contentment only after the death of Michael Sr. One reading of the book might have it that the violent act against Marianne twists Michael Sr. in such a way that the family, as dysfunctional families do, wraps itself around his demons, leaving Corinne and the children time to find themselves only when he is gone. An even broader view, though, would be that the family members are a bad fit from the start, that Michael Mulvaney tries too hard to seem socially acceptable, in the way that his son Patrick ends up trying to feign being "normal." The happy people that are reintroduced to the readers in the book's epilogue are happy because they are individuals and are in control of their own lives. It is significant that Corinne's new friend and roommate, Sable Mills, has never heard of the Mulvaneys, the legendary family introduced in the book's first pages: they all end up happy once they are freed of the job of living up to the responsibility of happiness.

Source: David Kelly, Critical Essay on *We Were the Mulvaneys*, in *Novels for Students*, Thomson Gale, 2007.

Ellen G. Friedman

In the following excerpt, Friedman demonstrates how Oates "redraws" the family unit through a departure from the Oedipal pattern and aligning the father with cultural changes.

Particular narrative practices that depart from tradition draw our attention not only for their literary values but also for what can be read in such departure concerning cultural meaning. The arguments proposed here presume agreement on this issue: social practices and meanings are figured in fiction, and fictional narratives stay within a geography of cultural possibility. Despite the instability of signs, instabilities circulate within borders that are made visible in the interactions between literature and social institutions and practices. Such legitimating and disciplinary attributes of narrative have been connected to the unconscious of narrative, to oedipal sources. "Every narrative" Roland Barthes wrote in *Pleasure of the Text,* leads "back to Oedipus." In his view, the Father, as a figure for origin and law, is the rationale for all storytelling: "If there is no longer a Father, why tell stories [. . .]? Isn't storytelling always a way of searching for one's origins, speaking one's conflicts with the Law?"

Oedipus's centrality in current explanatory cultural narratives is emphasized even in philosophical texts written to oppose it. Gilles Deleuze and Felix Guattari resist oedipal determinism in *Anti-Oedipus: Capitalism and Schizophrenia* against the prevailing ideas of cultural and orthodox psychoanalysts: "They all agree that, in our patriarchal and capitalist society at least, Oedipus is a sure thing [. . .]. They all agree that our society is the stronghold of Oedipus." Deleuze and Guattari assess the fascination with oedipus as profound, and with exasperation declare that he "is demanded, and

"The family has not only survived without the patriarchal head, but they have thrived. Although they still carry the patronymic, they have moved quietly and unobtrusively beyond the Name of the Father."

demanded again and again." In his introductory remarks to the book, Mark Seem, one of its translators, summarizes the revolutionary effort it would take to disengage from the oedipal thrall: "The first task of the revolutionary [. . .] is to learn [. . .] how to shake off the Oedipal yoke and the effects of power, in order to initiate a radical politics of desire freed from all beliefs. Such a politics dissolves the mystifications of power through the kindling, on all levels, of anti-oedipal forces [. . .] forces that escape coding, scramble the codes [. . .]."

Because the trope of the father, particularly the oedipal father, is repeatedly invoked in explanations of culture and narrative, this essay theorizes the new role of the father before turning its attention to the texts that exemplify this pattern and its narratological and cultural implications. [. . .]

Joyce Carol Oates's *We Were the Mulvaneys*, published a year after *Synonym for Love*, repeats this pattern in a complex family narrative that is even more insistent than Moore's text in its refusal of the inevitability and finality of the oedipal family pattern. The process of the plot transforms the father from a "punishing imago" to an inhabitant of the world of flesh and releases his family into the present and the promise of a future. The text centers on an ideal nuclear family consisting of mother, father, three sons, and a daughter. They live in a paradisiacal farm called "High Point" in upstate New York from 1955 to 1980. The father, a self-made man, a benign Sutpen when we first meet him, has made the family rich and is a pillar of the community. Oates is blunt about his representational status as an originating patriarch. He describes himself as having created a new Garden of Eden whose inhabitants bear his name, Mulvaney: "Like God said gazing upon his creation in the Garden of Eden, it *was* good [. . .]. The Mulvaneys who bore his name, not just the kids but the woman, too."

This Eden's destruction is managed through a Freudian plot: the daughter, Marrianne, is raped at a dance and thus made useless as exchange value to insure the paternal legacy. The text baldly tells us the significance of this rape: "Did you know Marianne: how by breaking the code that day, you broke it forever? For us all?" The oedipal family then unravels. The father embarks on a frenzy of destructive revenge, mostly through lawyers, which costs him all his wealth and land. He cannot look at his daughter, and his wife obliges him by sending her away. One by one, the children leave; the father turns into a drunkard; and the mother tries to survive. The narrative follows each of the children as they slowly build lives away from the patriarchal center. As the father becomes indigent and finally dies and is cremated, turned to ashes, the mother gains a life. She makes a business out of antiques, sets up a household with another woman, and prospers.

Oates is quite deliberate in making her readers aware of the difference between the possible ending and the new one she is writing. The novel "proper" ends with the father's cremation, his ashes tossed out on the wind by two of the brothers: "shaking out the last of the grit and ashes. As the wind took them, so roughly. And gone." However, the death of the patriarch does not initiate yearning. Rather, it is followed by an epilogue that takes place on Independence Day. Called "Reunion: Fourth of July 1993," it emphasizes the family members' independence from the oedipal. Moreover, since the holiday celebrates freedom from the parent nation, England, and the initiation of the US, it intimates the possibility of new cultural configurations once loosened from the víse of the paternal narrative. At a Fourth of July family reunion, uncles, cousins, mother, children, and grandchildren gather, and the missing father is hardly registered. Each has succeeded despite what had seemed for many years like a horrific decentering of family. The family has not only survived without the patriarchal head, but they have thrived. Although they still carry the patronymic, they have moved quietly and unobtrusively beyond the Name of the Father. The last sentence of the epilogue, in which the narrator speaks of his brother, suggests such a beyond: "I laughed, poking Patrick in the arm, had to laugh at that expression his face he'd had when we were boys, when we were the Mulvaneys." Although individual Mulvaneys continue, *the Mulvaneys*—the individual members organized in an oedipal family led by the father—are past. This ending redraws the family epic, reimagining and expanding its representational possibilities. The father has moved out of the center and is a family figure among others, unexceptionally mortal and fallible.

In another register, this ending on Independence Day also suggests a rethinking of a sense of nation partially anchored in a sacred notion of the Founding Fathers. Coincidentally, the television documentary film *Thomas Jefferson: A View from the Mountain*, which brought to general public attention Jefferson's affair with Sally Hemings and the living descendents of that affair, aired in 1995, a year before Oates's novel was published. It was given a great deal of play in the popular media and awakened national doubt about the mythical, idealized figures that Americans have been schooled to revere as the nation's father, such as Jefferson. The resulting complications in the nation's sense of Jefferson—his hypocrisy above all—was the national equivalent to the trajectory of the father in postpatriarchal fiction, in which in his fallibility he becomes more ordinary and relieved of mythic power.

Such an affiliation between world and text allows discourse between the two registers; the changed treatment of the father in *We Were the Mulvaneys* resonates with the changed treatment of cultural fathers, such as Jefferson. Thus another attribute of this relation is that fictional narratives serve a fundamental function of cultural legitimation; in Jerome Bruner's vocabulary they are "normative." Or in Foucauldian terms, in its relation to social institutions and practices, the novel has surveillance and disciplinary functions. Although the function of narrative in relation to social practices may be variously described, that relation is rarely in contention; whether that relation be normative or disciplinary, narrative has a privileged ethical relation to culture and to readers. In the move beyond the Name of the Father in *We Were the Mulvaneys*, as well as other narratives, we read social change. [. . .]

Like the fathers in postpatriarchal fiction, Jefferson has gone from mythic proportions to embodied, fallible man. He is the Jefferson for our age; his fall into the somatic is in many ways enabling. It enables the nation, perhaps one instance at a time, to let go of its oedipal romance to allow for a more pluralistic understanding of what it is. Acknowledging black descendents of Jefferson sheds a necessary critical light on the construction of national ideals as well as extending who is entitled by their legacy. Just as the Mulvaneys are past, so in the sense of patriarchal iconic entity is Jefferson. Making him past has made others, such as his black descendents, so much more publicly present. The 1990s was also the decade that saw the "year of the woman" prompted by the Thomas-Hill hearings, in which Anita Hill did not get use of the "master's voice" as Thomas did. Toni Morrison's *Paradise* registers this national drama in another, larger more resonant and historical key. In her postpatriarchal beyond, the most tentative of those discussed here, women contest, challenge, destabilize oedipal assumptions and power, thus providing opportunities for alternatives. [. . .]

These authors write perhaps against the past but also for the present toward the future. If contemporary US writers can imagine beyond the patriarchal narratives, refuse and refute the oedipal imperative, and if they are registering or in some sense policing a cultural shift, perhaps it is not too much to say that the promises implied in the pluralistic democracy that is the US seem that much less improbable.

Source: Ellen G. Friedman, "Postpatriarchal Endings In Recent US Fiction," in *Modern Fiction Studies*, Vol. 48, No. 3, Fall 2002, pp. 693–713.

Valerie Miner

In the following review, the reviewer explores Oates's questioning of family instincts and survival as symbolic of humanity's evolution.

To be without a family in America is to be deprived not just of that family, but of an entire arsenal of allusive material as cohesive as algae covering a pond.

We Were the Mulvaneys: If they *were* the Mulvaneys, who are they now? What happened? How did it happen? Examining systems and shifts within an upwardly/downwardly mobile white American family between 1955 and 1993, Joyce Carol Oates has written an uncharacteristically cathartic book with a provocatively happy ending.

Oates's twenty-sixth novel questions instinct and survival. She employs social theory, theology and science to ask whether changes within the family are emblematic of evolution within the species. Is the Mulvaney story a tale of predetermination, adaptation or self-creation?

Audacious speculation is nothing new for Oates, one of our best contemporary novelists, who combines a nineteenth-century political and moral range with a twentieth-century psychoanalytic sensibility. Perhaps this talent for thinking is one reason Oates writes better novels than short fiction. While her stories often seem raw, the extended enterprise of a novel affords her adequate space to filter emotional dilemmas through action and consequence.

"Is this really Joyce Carol Oates, intrepid archeologist in the dark, sticky folds of the contemporary psyche? Witnessing redemption on the Independence Day baseball diamond? Perhaps she's right. Perhaps sentimentality—forget divine will or scientific logic—is the perversely simple secret survival code of the American family."

Oates is under-appreciated in a culture suspicious of artist as intellectual and artist as productive worker. Her fiction consistently raises philosophical issues within an examination of American violence. Some critics have an almost prudish response to her prolific (promiscuous) output. Even those who appreciate her seem to read each new book for evidence that her speedy literary metabolism stems from psychological compensation or glandular defect. But Oates's unblinking curiosity about human nature is one of the great artistic forces of our time.

The Mulvaney family has an American Dream–like cache of midcentury luck. Dad, Michael Mulvaney, graduates from working-class bitterness to middle-class success. His pretty, quirky wife, Corinne, proves her talent for family choreography by raising four charmed kids: Mike Jr., a handsome athlete; Patrick, a science prodigy; Marianne, a sweet apprentice homemaker; and Judd, the earnest little Mulvaney caboose whom everyone, distractedly, loves.

In any text of evolutionary theory, authorship determines credibility. The first-person omniscient narrator here is young Judd, who has grown up into a truth-seeking journalist. Judd is the most peripheral Mulvaney, the repository of secrets and heir to family progress. His voice ranges from sardonic to awestruck to mournful. Judd becomes an agile, broadly empathetic storyteller, entering the minds of his parents and siblings, sometimes even referring to himself in the third person.

The crucible of Mulvaney identity is High Point Farm, outside Mt. Ephraim, New York, an expansive, picturesque registered landmark built in 1849. Classy yet unpretentious, it gets photographed for local calendars.

> The gravel drive is lined with tall aging spruces. Around the house are five enormous oaks and I mean enormous—the tallest is easily three times the height of the house and the house is three storeys. In summer everything is overgrown, you have to stare up the drive to see the house—what a house! In winter, the lavender house seems to float in midair, buoyant and magical as a house in a child's storybook.

Look closer, and something is always awry, like "the sprawling, overgrown and somewhat jungly farm itself, blurred at the edges as in a dream where our ever-collapsing barbed wire fences trailed off into scrubby, hilly, uncultivated land. (On a farm, you have to repair fences continually, or should.)" Broken fences and broken clocks—Corinne's antique clocks, each telling a different time.

The midseventies are a blessed period for the Mulvaneys. Dad, a flourishing businessman, finally gets accepted into the Mt. Ephraim Country Club. Mike Jr. is courted with numerous college football scholarships. Patrick excels in school. Corinne's antique collection swells. Marianne, a popular cheerleader, is elected Valentine princess. Then crisis strikes: Zachary Lundt, a high school student, rapes the beautiful, innocent Marianne.

The novel becomes a saga of shame and redemption. Gossip travels fast in Mt. Ephraim, and disgrace falls not on the rapist but on the Mulvaneys. Each family member internalizes the rape as a personal attack for being what Lundt calls a "hot s—— Mulvaney." Each follows a different avenue to revenge, penance and/or refuge. Mike Jr. leaves home, joins the Marines and eventually marries back into the domestic dream. Patrick retreats inside his head as the nerdy Cornell genius. Michael Sr. drinks his way through a tangle of real and imagined betrayals. Corinne and Marianne take different doses of Christianity: Corinne charitably suspends judgment of her family, while Marianne humbly retreats into forgiveness, self-effacement and self-erasure. Judd's way of dealing with his shame is to tell secrets, as a small-town newspaperman and as the narrator of this book.

Oates eloquently employs daily details, cataloguing Corinne's antiques, mapping Patrick's Ithaca jogging route, calculating the number of paint gallons required to spruce up High Point Farm. She is a vivid storyteller, and the occupations, names and places are rich in allusive imagery. Michael Sr., a roofer, climbs his way into the middle class. Marianne's neo-Marxist-Christian guru is called "Abelove." Corinne's romantic antiques serve as icons for pious Marianne, who identifies with a picture called *The Pilgrim,* and also for fierce Patrick, who admires a woodcut called *The Huntsman*: "The young hunter was blond, beardless, hatless, in plain clothing of a bygone era; the mountain ram was a magnificent beast with curly black wool, remarkable curling horns, a high-held head. . . . Both were heroic figures, very male."

As modern huntsman, Patrick torments his sister's rapist, this man-boy he blames for destroying the family. He meticulously plans Zachary's murder and then, at the moment of execution, he realizes Zachary is no longer the cocky teenager and Marianne no longer the violated cheerleader. They have all changed, all adapted.

Oates is fascinated by the markings of kinship. Particularly impressive is her shaping of siblings' passions, allegiances and resentments. She reveals the special affinities between Mike and Judd—eldest and youngest—as well as between middle children Patrick and Marianne. She observes the erotic and competitive tensions among brothers and sister as they negotiate for notice and immunity from their parents, coping with the essential contradiction of being an individual within a family.

As in other novels (*Son of the Morning, American Appetites, Because It Is Bitter, and Because It Is My Heart*), Oates here combines the analytic intellect of Iris Murdoch with the cinematic enterprise of Stephen King. One of her most nuanced and painful scenes is this détente in a cheap cafe between down-and-out father and successful eldest son:

> He'd taken out his wallet, was offering the ravaged old dad some bills, and the dad was protesting, "No! No thanks, son," almost convincingly, "—you're an old married man now, soon there'll be babies and you'll need all the money you can get." Breaking off then to cough, as if coughing were a signal of sincerity, but there was a cigarette in his fingers and he'd inhaled wrong and the coughing veered out of control. *This is how you'll die the bulletin came puking up your lung-tissue.* But Mike was insisting that his dad accept the money, the kid's big-boned handsome face dark with blood and eyes glistening with misery. . . . Giving in then and the son in the tall muscled Marine-body slipped cash into his shyly opened hand.

I *wish* I could believe the last chapter: a July 4 picnic and baseball game—almost all the Mulvaneys reunited after years of recrimination, punishment, individuation, evolution. "Mom must have seen it in my face, that happiness that's almost too much to bear, she stood beside me lifting her glass, voice rapturous, 'I'm just so, so happy every one of you is here! It just seems so amazing and wonderful and, well, a miracle, but I guess it's just ordinary life, how we all keep going, isn't it?'"

Is this really Joyce Carol Oates, intrepid archeologist in the dark, sticky folds of the contemporary psyche? Witnessing redemption on the Independence Day baseball diamond? Perhaps she's right. Perhaps sentimentality—forget divine will or scientific logic—is the perversely simple secret survival code of the American family.

Source: Valerie Miner, "Independence Day," in the *Nation*, October 28, 1996, pp. 62–64.

Thomson Gale

In the following essay, the critic gives an overview of Oates's life and work.

For over four decades, Joyce Carol Oates has produced a large body of work consisting of novels, short stories, criticism, plays, and poetry. Few living writers are as prolific as Oates, whose productivity is the cause of much commentary in the world of letters. Not a year has gone by since the mid-1960s in which she has not published at least one book; occasionally as many as three have been released in a single year. Her contributions to the field of poetry alone would be considered a significant output. "Any assessment of Oates's accomplishments should admit that the sheer quantity and range of her writing is impressive," observed a *Contemporary Novelists* essayist. The essayist added: "Oates is a writer who embarks on ambitious projects; her imagination is protean; her energies and curiosity seemingly boundless; and throughout all her writing, the reader detects her sharp intelligence, spirit of inquiry, and her zeal to tell a story."

A prodigious output means nothing if readers do not buy the books. Oates has established a reputation for consistently interesting work, ranging in genre from stories of upper-class domesticity to horror and psychological crime, but everywhere she reveals "an uncanny knack for understanding middle America, suburbia, and the temper of the times," to quote the *Contemporary Novelists* critic. Violence and victimization often feature in Oates's stories and novels, but existential questions of self-discovery abound as well. In an era of postmodernism and deconstruction, she writes in a classic mode of real people in extreme situations. As one *Publishers Weekly* reviewer put it, "Reading an Oates novel is like becoming a peeping tom, staring without guilt into the bright living rooms and dark hearts of America."

"Although, as with much of her fiction, Oates has denied any autobiographical basis for *We Were the Mulvaneys* other than a familiarity with the northern New York setting and once owning a cat answering to the description of the title family's household pet, the creative process involved in creating the novel is almost as evocative as personal experience."

In *Book* Oates said, "I am a chronicler of the American experience. We have been historically a nation prone to violence, and it would be unreal to ignore this fact. What intrigues me is the response to violence: its aftermath in the private lives of women and children in particular." Susan Tekulve in *Book* felt that, like nineteenth-century writer Edgar Allan Poe, "Oates merges Gothic conventions with modern social and political concerns, creating stories that feel at once antique and new. But she also shares Poe's love of dark humor and a good hoax." *New York Times Book Review* correspondent Claire Dederer found the author's novels "hypnotically propulsive, written in the key of *What the Hell Is Going to Happen Next?* Oates pairs big ideas with small details in an ideal fictional balancing act, but the nice thing is that you don't really notice. You're too busy rushing on to the next page."

Oates has not limited herself to any particular genre or even to one literary style. She is equally at ease creating realistic short stories—for which she won an O. Henry Special Award for Continuing Achievement—or parodistic epics, such as the popular Gothic novels *Bellefleur*, *A Bloodsmoor Romance*, and *Mysteries of Winterthurn*, all published in the 1980s. She attracts readers because of her ability to spin suspenseful tales and to infuse the ordinary with terror. As Oates stated in a *Chicago Tribune Book World* discussion of her themes, "I am concerned with only one thing: the moral and social conditions of my generation." Henry Louis Gates, Jr. wrote in the *Nation* that "a future archeologist equipped with only her *oeuvre* could easily piece together the whole of post-war America."

Born into a working-class family, Oates grew up in rural Erie County, New York, spending a great deal of time at her grandparents' farm. She attended a one-room school as a child and developed a love for reading and writing at an early age. By fifteen, she had completed her first novel and submitted it for publication, only to discover that those who read it found it too depressing for younger readers. Oates graduated from Syracuse University in 1960 and earned her master's degree the following year from the University of Wisconsin. It was at Wisconsin that she met and married her husband, Raymond Joseph Smith, with whom she has edited the *Ontario Review*. The newlyweds moved to Detroit, where Oates taught at the University of Detroit between 1961 and 1967. After one of her stories was anthologized in the *Best American Short Stories*, she decided to devote herself to creative writing.

Urban issues are a major theme in Oates's writing, such as her 1969 novel *them*, which earned a National Book Award in 1970. However, her early work also reveals her preoccupation with fictitious Eden County, New York, a setting based on her childhood recollections. Betty De Ramus is quoted in the *Encyclopedia of World Biography* as saying: "Her days in Detroit did more for Joyce Carol Oates than bring her together with new people—it gave her a tradition to write from, the so-called American Gothic tradition of exaggerated horror and gloom and mysterious and violent incidents."

The novel *them* chronicles three decades, beginning in 1937, in the life of the Wendall family. The novel "is partly made up of 'composite' characters and events, clearly influenced by the disturbances of the long hot summer of 1967," Oates acknowledged. Although regarded as a self-contained work, *them* can also be considered the concluding volume in a trilogy that explores different subgroups of U.S. society. The trilogy includes *A Garden of Earthly Delights*, about the migrant poor, and *Expensive People*, about the suburban rich. The goal of all three novels, as Oates explained in the *Saturday Review*, is to present a cross-section of "unusually sensitive—but hopefully representative—young men and women, who confront the puzzle of American life in different ways and come to different ends."

A story of inescapable life cycles, *them* begins with sixteen-year-old Loretta Botsford Wendall preparing for a Saturday night date. "Anything might happen," she muses innocently, unaware of the impending tragedy. After inviting her date to bed with her, Loretta is awakened by the sound of an explosion. Still half asleep, she realizes that her boyfriend has been shot in the head by her brother. Screaming, she flees the house and runs into the street where she encounters an old acquaintance who is a policeman. Forced to become his wife in return for his help, Loretta embarks on a future of degradation and poverty. The early chapters trace Loretta's flight from her past, her move to Detroit, and her erratic relationships with her husband and other men. The rest of the book focuses on two of Loretta's children, Jules and Maureen, and their struggle to escape a second generation of violence and poverty.

New York Times reviewer John Leonard wrote, "*them*, as literature, is a reimagining, a reinventing of the urban American experience of the last thirty years, a complex and powerful novel that begins with James T. Farrell and ends in a gothic dream; of the 'fire that burns and does its duty.'" Leonard added: " *them* is really about all the private selves, accidents and casualties that add up to a public violence." *Christian Science Monitor* contributor Joanne Leedom also noted the symbolic importance that violence assumes and links it to the characters' search for freedom: "The characters live, love, and almost die in an effort to find freedom and to break out of their patterns. They balance on a precipice and peer over its edge. Though they fear they may fall, they either cannot or will not back away, for it is in the imminence of danger that they find life force. The quest in *them* is for rebirth; the means is violence; the end is merely a realignment of patterns."

Throughout the 1970s, Oates continued her exploration of American people and institutions, combining social analysis with vivid psychological portrayals: *Wonderland* probes the pitfalls of the modern medical community; *Do with Me What You Will* focuses upon the legal profession; *The Assassins: A Book of Hours* attacks the political corruption of Washington, DC; *Son of the Morning* traces the rise and fall of a religious zealot who thinks he's Christ; and *Unholy Loves* examines shallowness and hypocrisy within the academic community. In these and all her fiction, the frustrations and imbalance of individuals become emblematic of U.S. society as a whole.

Oates's short stories of this period exhibit similar themes, and many critics judged her stories to be her finest work. "Her style, technique, and subject matter achieve their strongest effects in this concentrated form, for the extended dialogue, minute detail, and violent action which irritate the reader after hundreds of pages are wonderfully appropriate in short fiction," *Dictionary of Literary Biography* contributor Michael Joslin observed. "Her short stories present the same violence, perversion, and mental derangement as her novels, and are set in similar locations: the rural community of Eden County, the chaotic city of Detroit, and the sprawling malls and developments of modern suburbia."

One of Oates's most popular and representative short stories is "Where Are You Going, Where Have You Been?" Frequently anthologized, the story first appeared in 1966 and is considered by many to be a masterpiece of the short form. It relates the sexual awakening of a teenage girl by a mysterious older man through circumstances that assume strange and menacing proportions; it is a study in the peril that lurks beneath the surface of everyday life.

The protagonist, fifteen-year-old Connie, is a typical teenager who argues with her mother over curfews and hair spray, dreams about romantic love with handsome boys, and regards her older, unmarried sister as a casualty. One Sunday afternoon Connie is left home alone. The afternoon begins ordinarily enough with Connie lying in the sun. "At this point," noted Greg Johnson in *Understanding Joyce Carol Oates*, "the story moves from realism into an allegorical dream-vision. Recalling a recent sexual experience as 'sweet, gentle, the way it was in movies and promised in songs,' Connie opens her eyes and 'hardly knew where she was.' Shaking her head 'as if to get awake,' she feels troubled by the sudden unreality of her surroundings, unaware—though the reader is aware—that she has entered a new and fearsome world."

Shortly afterward, a strange man about thirty years old appears in a battered gold convertible. His name is Arnold Friend. Excited by the prospect but also cautious, Connie dawdles about accepting his invitation to take a ride. Friend becomes more insistent until, suddenly, it becomes clear that Friend has no ordinary ride in mind. He makes no attempt to follow Connie as she flees into the house, but he also makes it clear that the flimsy screen door between them is no obstacle. As Mary Allen explains in *The Necessary Blankness: Women in Major American Fiction of the Sixties*, "his promise not to come in the house after her is more disturbing than a blunt demand might be, for we know he will enter when he is ready."

Oates explores another genre with her Gothic novels *Bellefleur*, *A Bloodsmoor Romance*, and *Mysteries of Winterthurn*. These novels are an homage to old-fashioned Gothics and were written with "great intelligence and wit," according to Jay Parini. Oates told Parini that she considers the novels "parodistic" because "they're not exactly parodies, because they take the forms they imitate quite seriously." The novels feature many of the stock elements of conventional Gothics, including ghosts, haunted mansions, and mysterious deaths. But the plots are also tied to actual events. "I set out originally to create an elaborate, baroque, barbarous metaphor for the unfathomable mysteries of the human imagination, but soon became involved in very literal events," Oates explained in the *New York Times Book Review*. Her incorporation of real history into imaginary lives lends these tales a depth that is absent from many Gothic novels. Though fanciful in form, they are serious in purpose and examine such sensitive issues as crimes against women, children, and the poor, as well as the role of family history in shaping destiny. For these reasons, Johnson believed that "the gothic elements throughout her fiction, like her use of mystical frameworks, serve the larger function of expanding the thematic scope and suggestiveness of her narratives."

Bellefleur is a five-part novel that encompasses thousands of years and explores what it means to be an American. It is the saga of the Bellefleurs, a rich and rapacious family with a "curse," who settle in the Adirondack Mountains. Interwoven with the family's tale are real people from the nineteenth century, including abolitionist John Brown and Abraham Lincoln, the latter who in the novel fakes his own assassination in order to escape the pressures of public life. In his *New York Times Book Review* assessment of the book, John Gardner wrote that its plot defies easy summarization: "It's too complex—an awesome construction, in itself a work of genius," and summarized it as "a story of the world's changeableness, of time and eternity, space and soul, pride and physicality versus love." *Los Angeles Times Book Review* contributor Stuart Schoffman called the Bellefleurs' story "an allegory for America: America the vain, the venal, the violent." Wrote *New York Times* critic Leonard: "On one level, *Bellefleur* is Gothic pulp fiction, cleverly consuming itself. . . . On another level,

Bellefleur is fairy tale and myth, distraught literature. . . . America is serious enough for pulp and myth, Miss Oates seems to be saying, because in our greed we never understood that the Civil War really was a struggle for the possession of our soul." Oates herself has acknowledged that the book was partially conceived as a critique of "the American dream," and critics generally agreed that this dimension enhances the story, transforming the Gothic parody into serious art. Among the most generous assessments was Gardner's; he called *Bellefleur* "a symbolic summation of all this novelist has been doing for twenty-some years, a magnificent piece of daring, a tour de force of imagination and intellect."

In 1990 Oates returned to familiar themes of race and violence in *Because It Is Bitter, and Because It Is My Heart.* The story tells of a bond shared between Jinx Fairchild, a black sixteen-year-old living in the small industrial town of Hammond, New York, and Iris Courtney, a fourteen-year-old white girl who seeks help from Jinx when a town bully begins harassing her. During a scuffle, Jinx inadvertently kills the boy, and the story follows Jinx and Iris as their lives are guided by the consequences of this event. Encompassing the years 1956 to 1963, the book explores the issues of racial segregation and downward mobility as the two characters struggle to overcome their past by escaping from the confines of their hometown. "Iris and Jinx are linked by a powerful bond of secrecy, guilt and, ultimately, a kind of fateful love, which makes for a . . . compelling . . . story about the tragedy of American racism," wrote Howard Frank Mosher in the *Washington Post Book World.*

In *American Appetites*, Oates also explores life among the upper-middle class and finds it just as turbulent and destructive beneath the surface as the overtly violent lives of her poorer, urban characters. Ian and Glynnis McCullough live the illusion of a satisfying life in a sprawling suburban house made of glass, surrounded by a full social life and Glynnis's gourmet cooking. When Glynnis discovers her husband's cancelled check to a young woman they once befriended, however, the cracks in their carefully constructed lifestyle are revealed, leading to a fatal incident. *American Appetites* is a departure for Oates in that it is told in large part as a courtroom drama, but critics seem not as impressed by Oates's attempt at conveying the pretentiousness of this group of people as with her grittier tales of poverty and racism. Hermione Lee, writing in the London *Observer*, felt that the theme of Greek tragedy and its "enquiry into the human soul's control over its destiny . . . ought to be interesting, but it feels too ponderous, too insistent." Likewise, Robert Towers in the *New York Times Book Review* praised Oates's "cast of varied characters whom she makes interesting, . . . places them in scrupulously observed settings, and involves them in a complex action that is expertly sustained," but somehow they produce an effect opposite of the one intended. "We're lulled into a dreamy observation of the often dire events and passions that it records," Towers concluded. Bruce Bawer in a *Washington Post Book World* review found the device of conveying ideas "through intrusive remarks by the narrator and *dramatis personae*" ineffective and "contrived." However, Bawer suggested that although *American Appetites* conveys "no sense of tragedy . . . or of the importance of individual moral responsibility," it does "capture something of the small quiet terror of daily existence, the ever-present sense of the possibility of chaos."

Oates reconstructs a familiar scenario in her award-winning *Black Water*, a 1992 account of a tragic encounter between a powerful U.S. senator and a young woman he meets at a party. While driving to a motel, the drunken senator steers the car off a bridge into the dark water of an East Coast river, and although he is able to escape, he leaves the young woman to drown. The events parallel those of Senator Edward Kennedy's fatal plunge at Chappaquiddick in 1969 that left a young campaign worker dead, but Oates updates the story and sets it twenty years later. Told from the point of view of the drowning woman, the story "portrays an individual fate, born out of the protagonist's character and driven forward by the force of events," according to Richard Bausch in the *New York Times Book Review.* Bausch called Oates's effort "taut, powerfully imagined and beautifully written . . . it continues to haunt us." A tale that explores the sexual power inherent in politics, *Black Water* is not only concerned with the historical event it recalls but also with the sexual-political power dynamics that erupted over Clarence Thomas's nomination for Supreme Court Justice in the early 1990s. It is a fusion of "the instincts of political and erotic conquest," wrote Richard Eder in the *Los Angeles Times Book Review.*

Oates's 1993 novel *Foxfire: Confessions of a Girl Gang* recounts in retrospect the destructive sisterhood of a group of teenage girls in the 1950s. The story is pieced together from former Foxfire gang member Maddy Wirtz's memories and journal and once again takes place in the industrial

New York town of Hammond. The gang, led by the very charismatic and very angry Legs Sadovsky, chooses their enemy—men—the force that Legs perceives as responsible for the degradation and ruin of their mothers and friends. The girls celebrate their bond to one another by branding each others' shoulders with tattoos. But as they lash out with sex and violence against teachers and father figures, they "become demons themselves—violent and conniving and exuberant in their victories over the opposite sex," wrote *Los Angeles Times Book Review* contributor Cynthia Kadohata. Although Oates acknowledged to *New York Times Book Review* critic Lynn Karpen that *Foxfire* is her most overtly feminist book, she wanted to show that though "the bond of sisterhood can be very deep and emotionally gratifying," it is a fleeting, fragile bond.

In portraying the destructive escapades of these 1950s teenagers, Oates is "articulating the fantasies of a whole generation," remarked *Times Literary Supplement* contributor Lorna Sage, "putting words to what they didn't quite do." Likening the book to a myth, Oates told Karpen that *Foxfire* "is supposed to be a kind of dialectic between romance and realism." Provoking fights, car chases, and acts of vandalism, the Foxfire gang leaves their mark on the gray town—antics that get Legs sent to reform school, "where she learns that women are sometimes the enemy, too," noted Kadohata. *New York Times Book Review* critic John Crowley likened the novel to a Romantic myth whose hero is more compelling than most of the teen-angst figures of the 1950s. Legs, Crowley noted, is "wholly convincing, racing for her tragic consummation impelled by a finer sensibility and a more thoughtful daring than is usually granted to the tragic male outlaws we love and need."

Sexual violence invades another upstate New York family in Oates's *We Were the Mulvaneys*, published in 1996. In sharp contrast to the isolated, emotionally impoverished family introduced in *First Love*, the Mulvaneys are well-known, high-profile members of their community: Michael Mulvaney is a successful roofing contractor and his wife, Corinne, dabbles at an antiques business. As told by Judd, the youngest of the three promising Mulvaney sons, the family comes unraveled after seventeen-year-old Marianne is raped by a fellow high school student. Ashamed of his daughter's "fall from grace," proud and patriarchal Michael banishes her to the home of a relative, an action that drives him to the drunken state that results in the loss of home and job. Meanwhile, other family members succumb to their individual demons. The saga of a family's downfall is uplifted by more positive changes a decade later, which come as a relief to readers who identify with the Mulvaneys as compelling representatives of the contemporary American middle class.

Although, as with much of her fiction, Oates has denied any autobiographical basis for *We Were the Mulvaneys* other than a familiarity with the northern New York setting and once owning a cat answering to the description of the title family's household pet, the creative process involved in creating the novel is almost as evocative as personal experience. "Writing a long novel is very emotionally involving," Oates told Thomas J. Brady in the *Philadelphia Inquirer*. "I'm just emotionally stunned for a long time after writing one." *We Were the Mulvaneys*, which at 454 pages in length qualifies as "long," took many months of note-taking, followed by ten months of writing, according to its author. After being chosen by Oprah Winfrey as one of her book club editions, the novel became the first of Oates's works to top the *New York Times* bestseller list.

Throughout her prolific writing career Oates has distributed her vast creative and emotional energies between several projects at once, simultaneously producing novels, stories, verse, and essays, among other writings. In her 1995 horror novel, *Zombie*, she seductively draws readers into the mind of a serial killer on the order of Jeffrey Dahmer. While straying from fact far enough to avoid the more heinous aspects of Dahmer-like acts, Oates plugs readers directly into the reality of her fictitious protagonist, Quentin P., who "exists in a haze of fantasies blurred by drugs and alcohol and by his inherent mental condition of violent and frenzied desires, thoughts and obsessions," according to *New York Times Book Review* critic Steven Marcus. Through the twisted experimentation on young men (involving, among other things, an ice pick) that Quentin hopes will enable him to create a zombie-like companion who will remain loyal to him forever, Oates "is certain to shock and surely to offend many readers," warned *Tribune Books* critic James Idema, "but there could be no gentler way to tell the story she obviously was compelled to tell."

Within her nonfiction writing, Oates's foray into sports philosophy resulted in the book-length essay *On Boxing*, which led to at least one television appearance as a commentator for the sport. She also submitted a mystery novel to a publisher under a pseudonym and had the thrill of having it accepted before word leaked out that it was Oates's creation. Inspired by her husband's name, in 1988 Oates published the novel *Lives of the Twins* under the name Rosamond Smith. "I wanted a fresh reading; I wanted to escape from my own identity," Linda Wolfe quoted Oates as saying in the *New York Times Book Review*. She would use the Smith pseudonym again for several more mystery novels, including *Soul/Mate*, a story about a lovesick psycho-killer, *Nemesis*, another mystery concerning aberrational academics, and *Snake Eyes*, a tale of a tattooed psychopathic artist.

Oates's 1997 novel *Man Crazy* is a reverse image of *Zombie;* it tells the first-person story of a "pathological serial victim," Ingrid Boone, who through a rag-tag childhood, a promiscuous and drugged-out adolescence, and a stint with a satanic motorcycle cult, has her personal identity nearly destroyed. *New York Review of Books* critic A. O. Scott commented that Oates "continually seeks out those places in our social, familial and personal lives where love and cruelty intersect. . . . Oates is clearly interested in exploring the boundary between a world where cruelty lurks below the surface of daily life and one in which daily life consists of overt and constant brutality."

Published in 2000, one of Oates's most successful novels to date is *Blonde*, a fictional reworking of the life of Marilyn Monroe. Oates told a writer at *Publishers Weekly* that, while she was not intent upon producing another historical document on the tragic star, she did want to show "what she was like from the inside." According to some critics, Oates was successful in her endeavor. *Booklist* contributor Donna Seaman commented that the author "liberates the real woman behind the mythological creature called Marilyn Monroe." A *Publishers Weekly* reviewer found the novel "dramatic, provocative and unsettlingly suggestive," adding that Oates "creates a striking and poignant portrait of the mythic star and the society that made and failed her." In *World Literature Today*, Rita D. Jacobs concluded that *Blonde* "makes the reader feel extraordinarily empathetic toward the character Marilyn Monroe and her longing for acceptance and a home of her own."

Oates's first published works were short stories, and she has continued to pen them throughout her career. Her collections of short fiction alone amount to more work than many writers finish in a lifetime. A *Publishers Weekly* reviewer remarked that with her short works Oates has "established herself as the nation's literary Weegee, prowling the mean streets of the American mind and returning with gloriously lurid takes on our midnight obsessions." Whether in macabre horror stories such as those in *The Collector of Hearts: New Tales of the Grotesque* or in realistic works such as those found in *Faithless: Tales of Transgression*, Oates offers "a map of the mind's dark places," wrote *New York Times Book Review* contributor Margot Livesey. *Orlando Sentinel* correspondent Mary Ann Horne stated that in *Faithless*, Oates "does what she does best . . . delving into the dark areas of ordinary consciousness, bringing back startling images from the undercurrent of modern fears and secrets."

Oates uses secrets as a diving board for her exploration of a small town's psyche in *Middle Age: A Romance*, published in 2001. The book opens with the drowning death of sculptor Adam Brandt as he tries to rescue a child. His death becomes a catalyst for the residents of Salthill-on-Hudson, New York. Adam's former lovers begin to investigate his life, dissatisfied husbands become inspired to finally leave, and singles find their soul mates. In *Booklist*, Carol Haggas approved of the title: "Few caught in the throes of middle age would categorize it as 'romantic,' yet what makes Oates's characters romantic is how well they fare on their journeys of personal reinvention and whether they, and the reader, enjoy the trip." While the book received some criticism for lack of a linear plot, *New York Times* critic Claire Dederer viewed that as a strength of Oates's writing. "Naked of a compelling plot, in a strange sense Oates's remarkable ability is clearer than ever. We have time to notice the careful construction of theme, the attention to a cohesive philosophy, the resonant repetition of detail." More than one reviewer noted that the ending of *Middle Age* proves more redemptive than most of Oates's previous fictions. As Beth Kephart summarized in *Book*, "There is light, a lot of it, at the end of this long book." A *Publishers Weekly* contributor concluded it is "reminiscent of her powerful *Black Water*, but equipped with a happy ending, Oates's latest once more confirms her mastery of the form." *St. Louis Post-Dispatch* reviewer Lee Ann Sandweiss likewise noted that *Middle Age* is "Oates's most compassionate and life-affirming work to date. . . . This novel establishes, beyond any doubt, that Joyce Carol Oates is not only [one of] America's most prolific writers but also one of our most gifted."

From the introspection of middle age, Oates moved to the self-discovery of early adulthood in *I'll Take You There*. Called her most autobiographical novel to date, the book deals with an unnamed protagonist as she comes of age at Syracuse University in the early 1960s. Like Oates, "Anellia" (as she calls herself) is raised on a farm in western New York state and is the first in her family to go to college. Anellia cloaks herself in guilt and low self-esteem, bequeathed to her by her brothers and father. They blame her for her mother's death from cancer developed shortly after Anellia was born. Desperate for a mother figure and female companionship, the poor Anellia joins a snobby, bigoted sorority where she seems to be singled out for torment because of her finances and lack of grooming. She feels special pain from the antagonistic relationship she has with the sorority's British housemother, Mrs. Thayer. She uncovers Mrs. Thayer's excessive drinking and both of them are forced to leave the house, humiliated.

Still desperate for love and affection, she starts an affair with African-American philosophy graduate student Vernon Matheius. Vernon is intent on ignoring the civil rights struggles of the times, believing that philosophy is his personal salvation. Their relationship is categorized by discord and Anellia also snoops through his life and uncovers the fact that he has a wife and children he is denying. As Anellia deals with the fallout from her discovery and her separation from Vernon, she receives word that her father, who she thought dead, is dying in Utah. She travels west to be with him at his bedside, hoping to gain a sense of familial kinship. In a twist of irony, she is not allowed to look directly at her father, but steals a glimpse of him through a mirror, which kills him from distress when he sees her.

Critics and fans described *I'll Take You There* as a hallmark of Oates's consistent excellence in style, form, and theme. *Los Angeles Times Book Review* critic Stanley Crouch praised Oates's "masterful strength of the form, the improvisational attitude toward sentence structure and the foreshadowing, as well as the deft use of motifs." Even perceived weaknesses by some critics are regarded by others as quintessential Oatesian mechanics. In Rachel Collins's review for *Library Journal*, she questioned the heavy use of characterization and psychological backgrounding that takes place in about the first 100 pages. A *Publisher's Weekly* reviewer reflected that "Oates's fans will be pleased by the usual care with which she goes about constructing the psychology of Anellia and Vernon." Collins went on to call the book "a bit formulaic," noting that the romance between Anellia and Vernon lacks "the intense sexual energy present in Oates's other works." *Booklist* contributor Donna Seaman wrote that the scenes with Anellia and Vernon are "intense and increasingly psychotic" and Oates's "eroticism verges on the macabre and the masochistic." Vicky Hutchings in the *New Statesman* concluded the book is neither "depressing nor dull, but full of edgy writing as well as mordant wit."

Published in 2003, *The Tattooed Girl* is the story of thirty-nine-year-old writer Joshua Seigl, who has been diagnosed with a debilitating nerve condition. In need of an assistant, he interviews and rejects a number of graduate students, and impulsively hires the vacuous Alma Busch. While it seems like an act of charity, Seigl is increasingly patronizing to Alma, thinking that he has "rescued" her. Alma is described as dim-witted and slow, suffering from a lack of self-esteem and scarred by past sexual trauma, which resulted in the crude tattoo on her face. Seigl, of course, is unaware of Alma's anti-Semitism, which is born of her disfigurement and fueled by her sadistic waiter boyfriend, Dmitri Meatte. As Seigl's health deteriorates, Alma gains psychological strength to sabotage Seigl's health, finances, and mental well-being and eventually hatches a plan to take his life.

While a *Kirkus Reviews* contributor called *The Tattooed Girl* "better-than-average Oates," some reviewers found the characterization of Seigl, Alma, and Dmitri inconsistent. *New York Times* writer Michiko Kakutani said, "The novel gets off to a subtle and interesting start. . . . Oates's keen eye for psychological detail seems to be fully engaged in these pages." Yet she argued that "the attention to emotional detail evinced in the novel's opening pages—in which she limned Seigl's fears of mortality and his anxieties about his family and work—evaporates by the middle of the book, replaced by horror-movie plots and cartoony characters." In the *New York Times Book Review* Sophie Harrison noted that Alma, Seigl, and Dmitri's actions "contradict their given characters, and the irony doesn't always feel intentional." The *Kirkus Reviews* contributor observed that "Oates is onto something with the bruised, malleable figure of Alma," but the secondary figures of Dmitri and Seigl's hypomaniac sister Jet "have nothing like its principal's realness." Even so, Oates continued to receive praise for her style, including a review in *Booklist* which described *The Tattooed Girl* as a "mesmerizing, disturbing tale" told with "her usual cadenced grace."

Also published in 2003 was Oates's second book for young adult readers, *Small Avalanches and Other Stories*, in which she reprises some of her previously published short stories for adults as well as new material. The twelve stories all deal with young people taking risks and dealing with their consequences. As with her adult fiction, Oates maintains her dark tone. *School Library Journal* reviewer Allison Follos observed, "The stories have a slow, deliberate, and unsettling current." James Neal Webb on the *BookPage* Web site echoed that "Oates's trademark is her ability to tap, uncontrived, into the danger that's implicit in everyday life."

In 2004 Oates began publishing suspense novels under a new pseudonym. Writing as Lauren Kelly, Oates has been true to her prolific nature. Indeed, the first three novels published under the moniker were released in less than two years. In the first novel, *Take Me, Take Me with You*, research assistant Lara Quade is mysteriously sent a ticket to a concert. When she redeems the ticket, she finds that her seatmate, Zedrick Dewe is there under identical circumstances. As the story progresses, Lara and Zed's relationship begins to grow, and they eventually discover that their pasts are linked. Reviewing the novel for *Library Journal*, Stacy Alesi called the story "haunting and beautifully written." Interestingly, a *Kirkus Reviews* critic used similar terms to describe the second Kelly novel, *The Stolen Heart*. The critic stated that the novel is "a haunting portrait of grief and psychological fragilityy." *The Stolen Heart* begins when Merilee Graf is twenty-six years old. When Merilee was ten years old, one of her classmates vanished and was never found. Sixteen years later, Merilee's chance encounter with the missing girl's brother coincides with the death of her own father. Merilee's recollections of the disappearance are then triggered by these events. Although a *Publishers Weekly* contributor thought the story is "overwrought," they also noted that it is "oddly compelling."

In addition to her fiction and poetry, Oates lays claim to a large body of critical essays, ranging in subject matter from literature and politics to sports and quality of life. Although she has said that she does not write quickly, she also has admitted to a driving discipline that keeps her at her desk for long hours. In an era of computers, she continues to write her first drafts in longhand and then to type them on conventional typewriters. She told *Writer:* "Writing to me is very instinctive and natural. It has something to do with my desire to memorialize what I know of the world. The act of writing is a kind of description of an inward or spiritual reality that is otherwise inaccessible. I love transcribing this; there's a kind of passion to it."

Source: Thomson Gale, "Joyce Carol Oates," in *Contemporary Authors Online*, Thomson Gale, 2006.

Joanne V. Creighton

In the following essay, Creighton discusses factors infuencing Oates's intellectual and emotional development, which may subsequently have influenced her writing, and the place of the self and the mind in Oates's writing.

Personal and Cultural Contexts

In a 1988 essay, "Does the Writer Exist?," Joyce Carol Oates is bemused by the often disorienting "contrast between what we *know* of a writer from his or her work—the private self—and what we are forced to *confront* in the irrefutable flesh—the 'public' self." Certainly, the contrast between Joyce Smith, the seemingly quiet, serene, cultivated, and sensitive woman, and Joyce Carol Oates, who writes of violence, brutality, sordidness, sexual compulsion, and emotional duress, has often struck observers.

Earlier, she carefully guarded the life and self that exist outside of her written work. Only the baldest facts were revealed. In recent years Oates has been somewhat less self-protective, letting out more information about her family background, acknowledging the autobiographical underpinnings of her works, commenting about personal experiences.

We can now fill in more about the "powerful appeal of certain personalities" and places in her life. Among the most potent influences are her parents and the "vanished world" of their lives and her childhood: "To say *my father, my mother* is for me to name but in no way to approach one of the central mysteries of my life." Oates is more explicit about how much her writing is an attempt, in part, "to memorialize my parents' vanished world; my parents' lives. Sometimes directly, sometimes in metaphor." She goes back actually and psychically into her family's past in her recent writing. There is a coming-home quality—a reappraisal of the past from the mellow perspective of midlife—about Oates's latest work, which is more openly autobiographical and personal. She went back to the realm of her childhood, for example, to prepare to write the novel *Marya: A Life* (1986), which is, she acknowledges, a deliberate conflation of her mother's experiences and her own. Similarly, in *You Must Remember This* (1987), she claims to have "tried consciously to synthesize my father's and my own 'visions' of an era now vanished" ("Father," 84).

Oates is bemused by the "genteel" literary community that misunderstands and criticizes the harsh and violent world of much of her fiction. This world, Oates insists, is part of her literal and psychic inheritance. She tells of the tremendous tension she experienced writing *Marya*, "the most 'personal' of my novels." She had the feeling that she was "trespassing—transgressing?—in some undefined way venturing onto forbidden ground." She discovers belatedly that she had fictionally recapitulated an incident from her family's past that had not been disclosed to her: the murder of her maternal grandfather in a barroom brawl, after which her mother was "given away" to be reared by her aunt's family. In an uncanny way, she was drawn to invent (or to remember) this subject from her family's past.

There are other violent events and family secrets only recently revealed. Oates's paternal grandfather, Joseph Carlton Oates, abandoned her grandmother and father when her father was only two. Twenty-eight years later he reappeared, bearing a grudge against his son, wanting to fight him, but the son, Frederick Oates, would not participate. Joyce Carol Oates comments sardonically that perhaps the most unintentionally generous gesture of her grandfather was his abandonment of his family, for "it is likely, given his penchant for drinking and aggressive behavior, he might very well have been abusive to his wife and to my father, would surely have 'beaten him up' many times—so infecting him, if we are to believe current theories of the etiology of domestic violence, with a similar predisposition toward violence." Oates learned recently that when her father was 15 her great-grandfather tried unsuccessfully to kill his wife in a fit of rage and then killed himself ("Father," 45, 84).

While her father did not duplicate the violent patterns of behavior of his father and grandfather, he was fascinated with the "romance of violence" and its transmutation into masculine sport, "which excludes women," and he retained a "conviction that there is a mysterious and terrible brotherhood of men by way of violence." He took his daughter to boxing matches, inculcating in her the same lifelong fascination with the sport (and with violence). For her, however, as we shall see, boxing is a study of "the other": "Boxing is for men, and is about men, and *is* men." Frederick Oates also enjoyed another quintessentially "male" sport, flying—the "romance of the air," as Oates calls it, "transcending space and time and the contours of the familiar world in which you work a minimum of 40 hours a week, own property in constant need of repair, have a family for whom you are the sole breadwinner[.] What is

"In her faith in the aspiring human spirit, Oates is prototypically American and finds her place within the traditions of American romanticism. But it is romanticism with a difference, with an ironic postmodernist recognition that 'the "I," which doesn't exist, is everything.'"

flying but the control of an alien, mysterious element that can at any moment turn killer—the air?" He and his flying buddies performed loops and turns and rolls, and sometimes buzzed friends' and neighbors' houses. It was her father, Oates claims, who inspired the flying scenes in her novel *Bellefleur* (1980). He also sometimes took his young daughter Joyce for rides ("Father," 84–85), which appears, curiously, to have precipitated the fear of flying that compelled the adult Oates to eschew air travel whenever possible.

What most impresses Oates about her father and mother is their representative and exemplary survival and "transcendence" of "a world so harsh and so repetitive in its harshness as to defy evocation, except perhaps in art" ("Father," 84). They survived and prevailed despite family turmoil and the wrenching hardships and dislocations of the Great Depression. Her mother, creative with flowers and in decorating the house, still makes her daughter's clothes. Her father, who had to quit high school, who was laid off work several times, and who worked most of his life as a tool-and-die designer, has innate musical ability and, at over 70 years of age, enrolled in classes in English literature and music at the State University of New York at Buffalo.

They are neither self-pitying nor nostalgic about the hard times of the past. Of her father Oates writes, "If there was anger it's long since buried, plowed under, to be resurrected in his daughter's writing, as fuel and ballast." That Oates is, for example, the first member of her family to graduate from high school, let alone college, evokes in her a "class" anger, but she makes clear that it is "a personal anger, not one I have inherited from my family." From her parents Oates claims to have learned the genius of happiness, an "instinct for rejoicing in the life in which they have found themselves," and a predilection for useful employment: "we love to work because work gives us genuine happiness, the positing and solving of problems, the joyful exercise of the imagination" ("Father," 108).

What is critical in understanding Oates's relationship to American traditions and culture, I believe, is that she sees her parents' lives, and her own, as emblematically American. Her parents' survival and triumph over hardship—and, similarly, her own "transmogrification" of their vanished world into art—are examples of the aspiring and triumphant human spirit.

Oates's family is prototypically American in its multicultural immigrant origins: Irish, German, and Hungarian. Her maternal grandparents were Hungarians who emigrated to the United States in ship steerage at the turn of the century and settled in the Buffalo area. Her grandfather's name was Bs, Americanized to Bush; her grandmother's name was Torony. She says, "I never read Upton Sinclair's *The Jungle* without a powerful reaction; surely Sinclair was describing my grandparents' lives as well as those of his hapless Lithuanian immigrants." She was raised "American" with most of what was ethnic "ignored, or denied, or repressed, very likely for reasons of necessity." The temperament of her Hungarian grandfather, for example, might seem to "sound flamboyant and colorful" only "if seen through the retrospective of years and the prudent filter of language." Similarly, her grandmother's refusal to learn to read English, reasoning that it was "too late" when she had come to the States at age 16, although she lived into her eighties, "is associated in my mind with a peculiar sort of Old World obstinacy and self-defeat." There was no contact for over 60 years with relatives in Hungary, and she and her brother learned no Hungarian as children. Yet when she visited Budapest in May of 1980, she experienced a kind of unsettling recognition. For one thing, she is "struck by the disquietingly familiar look of strangers glimpsed on the streets: the eyes, the cheekbones, skin coloring, the general bearing." Some resemble her, she thinks, more than her brother or parents: "Uncanny sensation!—as if I had stepped into a dream." She is disoriented by the realization that Joyce Carol Oates is widely read in Hungary—another indication, no doubt, of uncanny correspondence. Most dominant is the visceral "tug of recognition, pleasurable yet disturbing" with the people: "I have been told that beneath their gaiety Hungarians are melancholy people and of course it's true: I know the temperament from within" ("Budapest," 331–35).

Budapest is one of the memorable cities that engraves itself on the author's psyche. "Lovely Budapest": I don't know where I am, but I think I am at home" ("Budapest," 343). Oates's experiences while on tour in Eastern-bloc countries inspired some fine stories, such as "Old Budapest" and "My Warszawa: 1980" in her volume of short stories *Last Days* (1984).

Indeed, the shaping effect of place is critical to an understanding of Joyce Carol Oates. The quintessential world of her fiction remains the geography of her childhood—both the countryside around Millersport in upper New York State, where she lived on her grandparents' farm, and the small city, Lockport, where she attended school. The latter locale becomes her fictitious and symbolic Eden County, akin to Faulkner's "little postage stamp world," Yoknapatawpha County. This Eden County world is skillfully evoked in a number of works, from her first, such as *By the North Gate* (1963), *Upon the Sweeping Flood* (1966), and *With Shuddering Fall* (1964), through her most recent, including: *Son of the Morning* (1978), *Bellefleur, Marya: A Life, You Must Remember This*, and *Because It Is Bitter, and Because It Is My Heart* (1990). Oates's childhood world remains the generating core of her fiction, infusing her work with resonance and authenticity.

Lockport, with its distinctive Erie Canal, Oates explains, is "the city of my birth, my paternal grandmother's home, suffused forever for me with the extravagant dreams of early adolescence—I attended sixth grade in Lockport, and all of junior high school there; the city is probably more real to me, imaginatively, than any I have known since." Lockport is sometimes, as in *Marya*, imagined as "Innisfail," evoking Yeats's lost romantic world. Sometimes, as in *You Must Remember This*, Lockport becomes fused with another city of Oates's experience, Buffalo, to become the fictitious city "Port Oriskany." Oates claims to have had a map of Port Oriskany taped to her wall during the writing of *You Must Remember This* so that she could stare at it and "traverse its streets, ponder its buildings and houses and vacant lots, most of all that canal that runs through it" (Preface to *Y*, 380).

Not only is the Eden County world described with authenticity, so also is the quintessential Oatesian experience associated with that place: female adolescence. Repeatedly in her stories and novels, Oates portrays with convincing resonance the inchoate identity of the adolescent girl who plays alternatively at being good and being wild. Oates captures so well the dreamy narcissism of the adolescent, her infatuation with sleazy charms, her experimental flirtation with danger, temptation, and even death.

Second only to the world of her childhood is the impact of Detroit on the writer. Detroit is, Oates acknowledges, the place "which made me the person I am, consequently the writer I am—for better or worse." She acknowledges that much of the writing of her early period, between 1963 and 1976, "has been emotionally inspired by Detroit and its suburbs (Birmingham, Bloomfield Hills, to a lesser degree Grosse Pointe) that it is impossible for me now to extract the historical from the fictional."

In an essay entitled "Visions of Detroit" she asks: "Why do some events, some people, some landscapes urban or rural fall upon us with an almost inhuman authority, dictating the terms of our most private fantasies, forcing upon us what amounts very nearly to a second birth—while others, most others, make virtually no impression at all and quickly fade." There's "never an answer," she concludes; but she does think, in retrospect, that "the extraordinary emotional impact Detroit had" on her must have been partly due to the awakening of "submerged memories of childhood and adolescence in and around the equally 'great' city of Buffalo, New York" ("Detroit," 348).

Detroit has, for Joyce Carol Oates, a representational and visceral effect: she characterizes it as "ceaseless motion, the pulse of the city. The beat. The beat. A place of romance, the quintessential American city." Its "brooding presence, a force, larger and more significant than the sum of its parts" offered "a sentimental education never to be repeated for me" ("Detroit," 347, 349). For those of us who, like Oates, have lived in Detroit, she does indeed convincingly evoke the city—its streets and neighborhoods, its institutions, its geographical and social stratifications, its raw and seamy violence, its vaguely threatening but hauntingly vital "pulse."

Detroit offered Oates a vivid canvas on which to explore the "larger social/political/moral implications of my characters' experiences." While detailing the lives of specific characters, Oates's novels encapsulate important phenomena of American culture: the migration of poor to the city, like the Wendalls in *them* (1969); the sterility of the suburban rich, as in *Expensive People* (1968); the effects of social upheavals such as the Detroit riot in *them;* and the malaise of the sixties, as in *Wonderland* (1971). A number of Detroit novels look critically at major societal institutions—medicine, law, education—and the struggles of radically dislocated characters who look to these structures for stable concepts of identity. Most often a male character dominates the early Oates novel, and the central movement of the novel is his attempt to free himself from intolerable constraints, often through violence—a mode of action particularly suited to Detroit, the reigning "murder capitol."

Joyce Carol Oates observes the gaudy drama of this prototypical city from her comparatively serene and protected residence in the university. The university, in fact, is another important place in Oates's fictional world. All of her adulthood—from age 17 on—Oates has lived within the culture of a university. Yet for a significant period of Oates's career, the university is dwarfed by the city. The conflict between the city and the university, between the demands of the raw external environment and the lures of the seemingly protected world of academia, is an important tension in Oates's work: it is a conflict played out in her Detroit fiction as well as in her later works.

Sister Irene in "In the Region of Ice" (*The Wheel of Love*, 1970) cannot minister to the raging emotional needs of her student, Allen Weinstein. Maureen in *them* accuses her teacher "Joyce Carol Oates" of being off in a world of books, unaware of the demands of the world in which her students live. Maureen has throughout her harsh young life looked to the library and books quite literally as a sanctuary from reality, and she sets out on a quest to beg, borrow, and steal her way into the protected environment of academia: she becomes, through determined husband-stealing, the wife of a college instructor. The university is vaguely implicated in the social unrest of the sixties: Jules Wendall becomes part of the foolish-sounding, incendiary counterculture around Wayne State University at the time of the Detroit riot.

Others of Oates's characters are not peripheral hangers-on but legitimate students who attempt to make themselves anew within a university culture, such as Jesse (*Wonderland*) in his medical studies at the University of Michigan. He, like Marya in a much later book, discovers that it is not easy to slough off the past and construct a new self.

Sometimes the academic world itself becomes the central setting of Oates's work: it is not portrayed sympathetically. In *The Hungry Ghosts* (1974), set at "Hilberry University" in southwestern Ontario (and probably inspired by Oates's experiences at the University of Windsor), Oates takes a satiric perspective, stressing the insecurities, pedantry, fears, and phobias within a claustrophobic academic culture. That satiric perspective continues with another academic fiction, *Unholy Loves* (1979), set at "Woodslee University" in upper New York State, although the novel is also a serious study of the "holy love" of art, and the validity and sanctity of the artist's vocation.

Increasingly, Joyce Carol Oates's fiction is about the attractions and the dangers of the life of the mind, and gradually women take central stage. Whereas a number of Oates's early novels focus on male protagonists and their quests for liberation from intolerable constraints, often through violence, the novels of Oates's middle period portray a number of intelligent, gifted, sensitive young women, who are more identifiably like the author herself: Laney in *Childwold* (1976), Brigit in *Unholy Loves*, Monica and Sheila of *Solstice* (1985), Marya in *Marya: A Life*, Enid in *You Must Remember This*, Iris in *Because It Is Bitter, and Because It Is My Heart*—not to mention the more fanciful characterizations of Deidre in *A Bloodsmoor Romance* (1982), and Perdita in *Mysteries of Winterthurn* (1984).

Oates circles back to her childhood world as she depicts more frequently young women with a developing interest in books and ideas—an interest sharply at odds with the tough, mindless, backcountry environment in which many of them are situated. Some of the bright young girls of Oates's fictional world find genuine, if fitful, joy in their awakening to the inner life. They go far beyond the vacuous and frightened women of Oates's earlier fiction—the Maureen Wendalls who try to steal their way into the academic world, to cocoon themselves from the harshness of the external world.

For example, Kasch in *Childwold* describes Laney's awakening: "You stir, you wake, you come to consciousness, heaved upon the sands of consciousness; but where are you, why have you gone so far? The books you read are not my books, the language you use is not my language." *Marya* describes the formative awakening of a young girl's intellectual life at a university. Marya—like Enid, Brigit, and Sheila—is also drawn to the artistic life and to the attractions and the dangers of the unconscious, the generating source of creativity. Oates depicts in these young women the developing sensibilities of the female artist. Portrayed, as well, is the uneasy residence of the artistic sensibility within the academy, the conflicting pulls of the conscious and the unconscious, the intellectual and the instinctual—conflicts that are dramatized, for example, in the symbiotic relationship of the artist and teacher, Sheila and Monica, in *Solstice*.

Since Oates both literally and figuratively lives within a university culture—now that of Princeton University, where she is the Roger S. Berlind Distinguished Professor in the Humanities—it is not surprising that her work, both creative and critical, is very much informed by and set within the context of intellectual traditions. While Oates is at times critical of the academy, its failed teachers, its fears and phobias and petty politics, she is also very aware of its value: its sanctification of the inner life, its rich heritage of ideas and art. A distinguished teacher; a learned critic; a provocative and insightful reviewer and commentator; a coeditor, along with her husband, Raymond Smith, of the *Ontario Review* and the Ontario Review Press; a major writer of novels, stories, plays, and poems: Oates is indeed, as John Updike has suggested, aptly described as a "woman of letters."

Conceptual and Aesthetic Contexts

It is the mature woman of letters, the Joyce Carol Oates within her published work, about whom I am most concerned in this study of the novels of the middle years. Where does this voice fit within intellectual and literary traditions? Oates's provocative and astute critical essays continue to offer both valuable insights into her views of the artistic process and useful perspectives from which to view her fiction.

Subscribing to romantic and modernist logocentricism, Oates argues in her critical essays that the author's voice and vision are encapsulated in a work of art. Not for her is the postmodern view that "texts" (which she calls "that most sinister of terms") unravel, deconstruct on the page. Rather, "the greatest works of art sometimes strike us as austere and timeless, self-contained and self-referential, with their own private music, as befits sacred things." Reading is "the sole means by which we slip, involuntarily, often helplessly, into another's skin; another's voice; another's soul." As writing is a search for the "sacred text," criticism is "the profane art," the "art of reflection upon reflection . . . [a] discursive commentary upon another's vision." In direct challenge to poststructuralist theories that would "decenter" the author, Joyce Carol Oates insists on the essentially rhetorical and pleasurable nature of writing and of reading: art provides an opportunity for communication between the consciousness of the writer and the reader.

Oates is unconcerned about the "anxiety of influence" described by Harold Bloom. An erudite person, she readily acknowledges, "I've been influenced in many ways by nearly everyone I've read, and I've read nearly everyone." But Oates does not take the structuralist view that devalues the individual and asserts the primacy of external shaping forces (language, culture, history). Rather, she retains (to be sure, with some skepticism and questioning) the romantic notion of the uniqueness and the primacy of the individual.

The private, fluid, ultimately mysterious core of the self is a subject of bemused speculation in a number of Oates's essays and fictional works. In a 1984 essay she looks back to a time in 1972 and comments that "I seemed to have been another person, related to the person I am now as one is related, tangentially, sometimes embarrassingly, to cousins not seen for decades." Yet she claims to have had then, while very sick, a "mystical vision." Although now the very term seems "such pretension," the experience impressed her enormously. She envisioned

> the "body" [as] a tall column of light and blood heat, a temporary agreement among atoms, like a high-rise building with numberless rooms, corridors, corners, elevators shafts, windows.... In this fantastical structure the "I" is deluded as to its sovereignty, let alone its autonomy in the (outside) world; the most astonishing secret is that the "I" doesn't exist!—but it behaves as if it does, as if it were one and not many. In any case, without the "I" the tall column of light and heat would die, and the microscopic life particles would die with it . . . will die with it. The "I," which doesn't exist, is everything.

So, the deluded sovereignty of the nonexistent "I" is a matter of some irony to Oates, and she equates this irony with a postmodern perspective: "as a novelist of the 1980s, my vision is postmodernist, and therefore predisposed to irony" ("Pleasure," 197). Yet her postmodern irony does not discredit the intellectual and literary heritage of humanism and modernism. The elusive self, "individual, stubborn, self-reliant, and ultimately mysterious," is at the center of Oates's work. *Marya* (1986), for example, is prefaced by a quotation from William James—"My first act of freedom is to believe in freedom"—and the spirit of James, Oates says, pervades the novel. What she says about James's views is equally applicable to her own: "It is the fluidity of experience and not its Platonic 'essence' that is significant, for truth is relative, ever-changing, indeterminate; and life is a process rather like a stream. Human beings forge their own souls by way of the choices they make, large and small, conscious and half-conscious.... identity (social, historical, familial) is not permanent" (Preface to *M*, 377–78).

Oates's perspective, then, is very human-centered. Only with human consciousness, human perception, human creativity is the world given significance. For her it is not an overstatement to say, along with Emily Dickinson, "The Brain—is wider than the Sky—." She argues that "most human beings, writers or not, are in disguise as their outward selves . . . their truest and most valuable selves are interior" ("Exist," 52). But the interior self is dualistic, made up of both conscious and unconscious contents, and ideally what needs to be achieved is some happy balance between the two: "that mysterious integration of the personality that has its theological analogue in the concept of grace."

Joyce Carol Oates sounds very Jungian when she argues that the psyche "seems to be at its fullest when contradictory forces are held in suspension" ("Soul," 185). Like Jung, Oates has a tremendous respect for the dark other within the self. It is out of the human psyche that all that is mysterious has arisen—all the wonderlands perpetuated across time, all the Jekyll/Hyde dualities, all the collective fantasies we call culture. There are intimations of a Jungian collective unconsciousness in some of Oates's remarks, or at the very least a recognition of universal commonalities in human experience, and especially in American cultural experience. The artist is exceptionally receptive to them as they well up, with their own undeniable authority, out of the unconscious: "Something *not us* inhabits us; something insists upon speaking through us" ("Beginnings," 14).

Just as the self is ideally balanced between conscious and unconscious contents, so too does the writer attempt to achieve a balance between unconscious motives and conscious technique. Technique—"the dams, dikes, ditches, and conduits that both restrain emotionally charged content and give it formal, and therefore communal, expression"—act as the writer's defense against the "white heat" of the unconscious: "Clearly the powerful unconscious motives for a work of art are but the generating and organizing forces that stimulate consciousness to feats of deliberation, strategy, craft, cunning." Oates describes her own practice as a writer as "an active pursuit of 'hauntedness': I can't write unless I am preoccupied with something sometimes to the point of distraction or obsession." Being in the grip of a literary obsession "has the force of something inhuman: primitive, almost impersonal, at time almost frightening" ("Beginnings," 7, 19, 14).

Oates, raised a Catholic, appears to have no belief in a transcendent God, but she does subscribe to a sense of immanent (albeit metaphoric) godliness within the inner life, the human psyche: "To say that the kingdom of God is within is, in one sense, to speak simply in metaphor, and very simply. To say that most people are very rarely interested in the kingdom of God (at least as it lies within, and not without) is to speak the most obvious truth." Oates places the highest possible value on the godlike creativity of the artist: it is not outrageous to think that "we live the lives we live in order to produce the art of which we believe ourselves capable" ("Soul," 172, 177).

In her repeated borrowing of theological metaphors to describe the nature of art, Oates echoes the high modernist tradition of Joyce and Yeats: "The secret at the heart of all creative activity has something to do with our desire to complete a work, to impose perfection upon it, so that, hammered out of profane materials, it becomes sacred: which is to say, no longer merely personal" ("Dream," 43).

To achieve such a sacred text is a kind of triumph, a transcendence of the profane. Throughout her work, Oates is concerned with transcendence of various kinds, with human attempts to overcome limitations and obstacles. "Can it be true, or is it a useful fiction," she asks, "that the cosmos is created anew in the individual?—that one can, by way of a defiant act of self-begetting, transcend the fate of the nation, the community, the family, and—for a woman—the socially determined parameters of gender?" Her characters are groping toward wholeness, struggling to grow. She says, "in my fiction, the troubled people are precisely those who yearn for a higher life—those in whom the life-form itself is stirring. . . . only out of restlessness can higher personalities emerge, just as, in a social context, it is only out of occasional surprises and upheavals that new ways of life can emerge" (Boesky, 482).

To be sure, the difficulty of such transcendence is dramatized again and again in Oates's fiction: she is aware of the hubris, the Faustian overreaching, that is often a part of such a struggle. Moreover, her characters are deeply embedded within entangling familial and social groups, and within recognizably American geographical, historical, cultural, political, and ethical contexts. Oates claims that she "could not take the time to write about a group of people who did not represent, in their various struggles, fantasies, unusual experiences, hopes, etc., our society in miniature" (Boesky, 482).

In her faith in the aspiring human spirit, Oates is prototypically American and finds her place within the traditions of American romanticism. But it is romanticism with a difference, with an ironic postmodernist recognition that "the 'I,' which doesn't exist, is everything." She says, "Our past may weight heavily upon us but it cannot contain us, let alone shape our future. America is a tale still being told—in many voices—and nowhere near its conclusion." She herself—the Joyce Carol Oates who doesn't exist in the flesh but who is a voice incarnated in an impressive body of work—is one of the preeminent tellers of that tale.

Source: Joanne V. Creighton, "The 'I,' Which Doesn't Exist, Is Everything," in *Joyce Carol Oates*, Twayne's United States Authors on CD-ROM, G.K. Hall & Co., 1997; previously published in 1992.

Sources

"American Dreams and Nightmares," in *Glamour*, Vol. 94, No. 9, September 1996, p. 132.

Creighton, Joanne V., "Dealing with Devastation," in Chicago Tribune, September 22, 1996, p. 3.

Garner, Dwight, "When Bad Things Happen," in *Washington Post*, September 22, 1996, p. X04.

Hanson, Gayle, "Tale of Family Breakdown Falls Apart," in *Washington Times*, December 22, 1996, p. B7.

Oates, Joyce Carol, *We Were the Mulvaneys*, Penguin, 1997.

Review of *We Were the Mulvaneys*, in *Booklist*, Vol. 93, No. 22, August 1996, p. 1855.

Review of *We Were the Mulvaneys*, in *Publishers Weekly*, August 5, 1996, p. 430.

Further Reading

Cologne-Brookes, Gavin, *Dark Eyes on America: The Novels of Joyce Carol Oates*, Louisiana State University Press, 2005.

This academic survey of Oates's works contains a lengthy analysis of *We Were the Mulvaneys*.

Nussbaum, Carol, *Sex and Social Justice*, Oxford University Press, 1999.

In addition to discussing the ways in which society treats sexual transgressions, this book refers to Oates's description of the gang rape of Della Rae

Duncan in the novel as an example of ritualistic group assault behaviors.

Oates, Joyce Carol, "Art and 'Victim Art,'" in Where I've Been, and Where I'm Going: Essays, Reviews, and Prose, Plume, 1999, pp. 69–75.

Because she often includes acts of violence, particularly sexual violence, in her works, Oates is frequently accused of using victimization as a literary tool; here, she responds to this observation.

Watanabe, Nancy Ann, *Love Eclipsed: Joyce Carol Oates's Faustian Moral Vision*, University Press of America, 1998.

One of the most scholarly overviews of Oates's work published as of 2006, this book draws from a wide selection of literature throughout history—Shakespeare, Pope, Goethe, and Rousseau, to name just a few—to explain her oeuvre as one that greatly deserves its world-wide following.

Glossary of Literary Terms

A

Abstract: As an adjective applied to writing or literary works, abstract refers to words or phrases that name things not knowable through the five senses.

Aestheticism: A literary and artistic movement of the nineteenth century. Followers of the movement believed that art should not be mixed with social, political, or moral teaching. The statement "art for art's sake" is a good summary of aestheticism. The movement had its roots in France, but it gained widespread importance in England in the last half of the nineteenth century, where it helped change the Victorian practice of including moral lessons in literature.

Allegory: A narrative technique in which characters representing things or abstract ideas are used to convey a message or teach a lesson. Allegory is typically used to teach moral, ethical, or religious lessons but is sometimes used for satiric or political purposes.

Allusion: A reference to a familiar literary or historical person or event, used to make an idea more easily understood.

Analogy: A comparison of two things made to explain something unfamiliar through its similarities to something familiar, or to prove one point based on the acceptedness of another. Similes and metaphors are types of analogies.

Antagonist: The major character in a narrative or drama who works against the hero or protagonist.

Anthropomorphism: The presentation of animals or objects in human shape or with human characteristics. The term is derived from the Greek word for "human form."

Antihero: A central character in a work of literature who lacks traditional heroic qualities such as courage, physical prowess, and fortitude. Antiheroes typically distrust conventional values and are unable to commit themselves to any ideals. They generally feel helpless in a world over which they have no control. Antiheroes usually accept, and often celebrate, their positions as social outcasts.

Apprenticeship Novel: See *Bildungsroman*

Archetype: The word archetype is commonly used to describe an original pattern or model from which all other things of the same kind are made. This term was introduced to literary criticism from the psychology of Carl Jung. It expresses Jung's theory that behind every person's "unconscious," or repressed memories of the past, lies the "collective unconscious" of the human race: memories of the countless typical experiences of our ancestors. These memories are said to prompt illogical associations that trigger powerful emotions in the reader. Often, the emotional process is primitive, even primordial. Archetypes are the literary images that grow out of the "collective unconscious." They appear in literature as incidents and plots that repeat basic patterns of life. They may also appear as stereotyped characters.

***Avant-garde*:** French term meaning "vanguard." It is used in literary criticism to describe new writing that rejects traditional approaches to literature in favor of innovations in style or content.

B

Beat Movement: A period featuring a group of American poets and novelists of the 1950s and 1960s—including Jack Kerouac, Allen Ginsberg, Gregory Corso, William S. Burroughs, and Lawrence Ferlinghetti—who rejected established social and literary values. Using such techniques as stream of consciousness writing and jazz-influenced free verse and focusing on unusual or abnormal states of mind—generated by religious ecstasy or the use of drugs—the Beat writers aimed to create works that were unconventional in both form and subject matter.

***Bildungsroman*:** A German word meaning "novel of development." The *bildungsroman* is a study of the maturation of a youthful character, typically brought about through a series of social or sexual encounters that lead to self-awareness. *Bildungsroman* is used interchangeably with *erziehungsroman,* a novel of initiation and education. When a *bildungsroman* is concerned with the development of an artist (as in James Joyce's *A Portrait of the Artist as a Young Man*), it is often termed a *kunstlerroman.* Also known as Apprenticeship Novel, Coming of Age Novel, *Erziehungsroman,* or *Kunstlerroman.*

Black Aesthetic Movement: A period of artistic and literary development among African Americans in the 1960s and early 1970s. This was the first major African-American artistic movement since the Harlem Renaissance and was closely paralleled by the civil rights and black power movements. The black aesthetic writers attempted to produce works of art that would be meaningful to the black masses. Key figures in black aesthetics included one of its founders, poet and playwright Amiri Baraka, formerly known as LeRoi Jones; poet and essayist Haki R. Madhubuti, formerly Don L. Lee; poet and playwright Sonia Sanchez; and dramatist Ed Bullins. Also known as Black Arts Movement.

Black Humor: Writing that places grotesque elements side by side with humorous ones in an attempt to shock the reader, forcing him or her to laugh at the horrifying reality of a disordered world. Also known as Black Comedy.

Burlesque: Any literary work that uses exaggeration to make its subject appear ridiculous, either by treating a trivial subject with profound seriousness or by treating a dignified subject frivolously. The word "burlesque" may also be used as an adjective, as in "burlesque show," to mean "striptease act."

C

Character: Broadly speaking, a person in a literary work. The actions of characters are what constitute the plot of a story, novel, or poem. There are numerous types of characters, ranging from simple, stereotypical figures to intricate, multifaceted ones. In the techniques of anthropomorphism and personification, animals—and even places or things—can assume aspects of character. "Characterization" is the process by which an author creates vivid, believable characters in a work of art. This may be done in a variety of ways, including (1) direct description of the character by the narrator; (2) the direct presentation of the speech, thoughts, or actions of the character; and (3) the responses of other characters to the character. The term "character" also refers to a form originated by the ancient Greek writer Theophrastus that later became popular in the seventeenth and eighteenth centuries. It is a short essay or sketch of a person who prominently displays a specific attribute or quality, such as miserliness or ambition.

Climax: The turning point in a narrative, the moment when the conflict is at its most intense. Typically, the structure of stories, novels, and plays is one of rising action, in which tension builds to the climax, followed by falling action, in which tension lessens as the story moves to its conclusion.

Colloquialism: A word, phrase, or form of pronunciation that is acceptable in casual conversation but not in formal, written communication. It is considered more acceptable than slang.

Coming of Age Novel: See *Bildungsroman*

Concrete: Concrete is the opposite of abstract, and refers to a thing that actually exists or a description that allows the reader to experience an object or concept with the senses.

Connotation: The impression that a word gives beyond its defined meaning. Connotations may be universally understood or may be significant only to a certain group.

Convention: Any widely accepted literary device, style, or form.

D

Denotation: The definition of a word, apart from the impressions or feelings it creates (connotations) in the reader.

***Denouement*:** A French word meaning "the unknotting." In literary criticism, it denotes the resolution of conflict in fiction or drama. The *denouement* follows the climax and provides an outcome to the primary plot situation as well as an explanation of secondary plot complications. The *denouement* often involves a character's recognition of his or her state of mind or moral condition. Also known as Falling Action.

Description: Descriptive writing is intended to allow a reader to picture the scene or setting in which the action of a story takes place. The form this description takes often evokes an intended emotional response—a dark, spooky graveyard will evoke fear, and a peaceful, sunny meadow will evoke calmness.

Dialogue: In its widest sense, dialogue is simply conversation between people in a literary work; in its most restricted sense, it refers specifically to the speech of characters in a drama. As a specific literary genre, a "dialogue" is a composition in which characters debate an issue or idea.

Diction: The selection and arrangement of words in a literary work. Either or both may vary depending on the desired effect. There are four general types of diction: "formal," used in scholarly or lofty writing; "informal," used in relaxed but educated conversation; "colloquial," used in everyday speech; and "slang," containing newly coined words and other terms not accepted in formal usage.

Didactic: A term used to describe works of literature that aim to teach some moral, religious, political, or practical lesson. Although didactic elements are often found in artistically pleasing works, the term "didactic" usually refers to literature in which the message is more important than the form. The term may also be used to criticize a work that the critic finds "overly didactic," that is, heavy-handed in its delivery of a lesson.

***Doppelganger*:** A literary technique by which a character is duplicated (usually in the form of an alter ego, though sometimes as a ghostly counterpart) or divided into two distinct, usually opposite personalities. The use of this character device is widespread in nineteenth- and twentieth-century literature, and indicates a growing awareness among authors that the "self" is really a composite of many "selves." Also known as The Double.

***Double Entendre*:** A corruption of a French phrase meaning "double meaning." The term is used to indicate a word or phrase that is deliberately ambiguous, especially when one of the meanings is risqué or improper.

Dramatic Irony: Occurs when the audience of a play or the reader of a work of literature knows something that a character in the work itself does not know. The irony is in the contrast between the intended meaning of the statements or actions of a character and the additional information understood by the audience.

Dystopia: An imaginary place in a work of fiction where the characters lead dehumanized, fearful lives.

E

Edwardian: Describes cultural conventions identified with the period of the reign of Edward VII of England (1901–1910). Writers of the Edwardian Age typically displayed a strong reaction against the propriety and conservatism of the Victorian Age. Their work often exhibits distrust of authority in religion, politics, and art and expresses strong doubts about the soundness of conventional values.

Empathy: A sense of shared experience, including emotional and physical feelings, with someone or something other than oneself. Empathy is often used to describe the response of a reader to a literary character.

Enlightenment, The: An eighteenth-century philosophical movement. It began in France but had a wide impact throughout Europe and America. Thinkers of the Enlightenment valued reason and believed that both the individual and society could achieve a state of perfection. Corresponding to this essentially humanist vision was a resistance to religious authority.

Epigram: A saying that makes the speaker's point quickly and concisely. Often used to preface a novel.

Epilogue: A concluding statement or section of a literary work. In dramas, particularly those of the seventeenth and eighteenth centuries, the epilogue is a closing speech, often in verse, delivered by an actor at the end of a play and spoken directly to the audience.

Epiphany: A sudden revelation of truth inspired by a seemingly trivial incident.

Episode: An incident that forms part of a story and is significantly related to it. Episodes may be either self-contained narratives or events that depend on a larger context for their sense and importance.

Epistolary Novel: A novel in the form of letters. The form was particularly popular in the eighteenth century.

Epithet: A word or phrase, often disparaging or abusive, that expresses a character trait of someone or something.

Existentialism: A predominantly twentieth-century philosophy concerned with the nature and perception of human existence. There are two major strains of existentialist thought: atheistic and Christian. Followers of atheistic existentialism believe that the individual is alone in a godless universe and that the basic human condition is one of suffering and loneliness. Nevertheless, because there are no fixed values, individuals can create their own characters—indeed, they can shape themselves—through the exercise of free will. The atheistic strain culminates in and is popularly associated with the works of Jean-Paul Sartre. The Christian existentialists, on the other hand, believe that only in God may people find freedom from life's anguish. The two strains hold certain beliefs in common: that existence cannot be fully understood or described through empirical effort; that anguish is a universal element of life; that individuals must bear responsibility for their actions; and that there is no common standard of behavior or perception for religious and ethical matters.

Expatriates: See *Expatriatism*

Expatriatism: The practice of leaving one's country to live for an extended period in another country.

Exposition: Writing intended to explain the nature of an idea, thing, or theme. Expository writing is often combined with description, narration, or argument. In dramatic writing, the exposition is the introductory material which presents the characters, setting, and tone of the play.

Expressionism: An indistinct literary term, originally used to describe an early twentieth-century school of German painting. The term applies to almost any mode of unconventional, highly subjective writing that distorts reality in some way.

F

Fable: A prose or verse narrative intended to convey a moral. Animals or inanimate objects with human characteristics often serve as characters in fables.

Falling Action: See *Denouement*

Fantasy: A literary form related to mythology and folklore. Fantasy literature is typically set in nonexistent realms and features supernatural beings.

Farce: A type of comedy characterized by broad humor, outlandish incidents, and often vulgar subject matter.

***Femme fatale*:** A French phrase with the literal translation "fatal woman." A *femme fatale* is a sensuous, alluring woman who often leads men into danger or trouble.

Fiction: Any story that is the product of imagination rather than a documentation of fact. Characters and events in such narratives may be based in real life but their ultimate form and configuration is a creation of the author.

Figurative Language: A technique in writing in which the author temporarily interrupts the order, construction, or meaning of the writing for a particular effect. This interruption takes the form of one or more figures of speech such as hyperbole, irony, or simile. Figurative language is the opposite of literal language, in which every word is truthful, accurate, and free of exaggeration or embellishment.

Figures of Speech: Writing that differs from customary conventions for construction, meaning, order, or significance for the purpose of a special meaning or effect. There are two major types of figures of speech: rhetorical figures, which do not make changes in the meaning of the words, and tropes, which do.

***Fin de siecle*:** A French term meaning "end of the century." The term is used to denote the last decade of the nineteenth century, a transition period when writers and other artists abandoned old conventions and looked for new techniques and objectives.

First Person: See *Point of View*

Flashback: A device used in literature to present action that occurred before the beginning of the story. Flashbacks are often introduced as the dreams or recollections of one or more characters.

Foil: A character in a work of literature whose physical or psychological qualities contrast strongly with, and therefore highlight, the corresponding qualities of another character.

Folklore: Traditions and myths preserved in a culture or group of people. Typically, these are passed on by word of mouth in various forms—such as legends, songs, and proverbs—or preserved in customs and ceremonies. This term was first used by W. J. Thoms in 1846.

Folktale: A story originating in oral tradition. Folktales fall into a variety of categories, including legends, ghost stories, fairy tales, fables, and anecdotes based on historical figures and events.

Foreshadowing: A device used in literature to create expectation or to set up an explanation of later developments.

Form: The pattern or construction of a work which identifies its genre and distinguishes it from other genres.

G

Genre: A category of literary work. In critical theory, genre may refer to both the content of a given work—tragedy, comedy, pastoral—and to its form, such as poetry, novel, or drama.

Gilded Age: A period in American history during the 1870s characterized by political corruption and materialism. A number of important novels of social and political criticism were written during this time.

Gothicism: In literary criticism, works characterized by a taste for the medieval or morbidly attractive. A gothic novel prominently features elements of horror, the supernatural, gloom, and violence: clanking chains, terror, charnel houses, ghosts, medieval castles, and mysteriously slamming doors. The term "gothic novel" is also applied to novels that lack elements of the traditional Gothic setting but that create a similar atmosphere of terror or dread.

Grotesque: In literary criticism, the subject matter of a work or a style of expression characterized by exaggeration, deformity, freakishness, and disorder. The grotesque often includes an element of comic absurdity.

H

Harlem Renaissance: The Harlem Renaissance of the 1920s is generally considered the first significant movement of black writers and artists in the United States. During this period, new and established black writers published more fiction and poetry than ever before, the first influential black literary journals were established, and black authors and artists received their first widespread recognition and serious critical appraisal. Among the major writers associated with this period are Claude McKay, Jean Toomer, Countee Cullen, Langston Hughes, Arna Bontemps, Nella Larsen, and Zora Neale Hurston. Also known as Negro Renaissance and New Negro Movement.

Hero/Heroine: The principal sympathetic character (male or female) in a literary work. Heroes and heroines typically exhibit admirable traits: idealism, courage, and integrity, for example.

Holocaust Literature: Literature influenced by or written about the Holocaust of World War II. Such literature includes true stories of survival in concentration camps, escape, and life after the war, as well as fictional works and poetry.

Humanism: A philosophy that places faith in the dignity of humankind and rejects the medieval perception of the individual as a weak, fallen creature. "Humanists" typically believe in the perfectibility of human nature and view reason and education as the means to that end.

Hyperbole: In literary criticism, deliberate exaggeration used to achieve an effect.

I

Idiom: A word construction or verbal expression closely associated with a given language.

Image: A concrete representation of an object or sensory experience. Typically, such a representation helps evoke the feelings associated with the object or experience itself. Images are either "literal" or "figurative." Literal images are especially concrete and involve little or no extension of the obvious meaning of the words used to express them. Figurative images do not follow the literal meaning of the words exactly. Images in literature are usually visual, but the term "image" can also refer to the representation of any sensory experience.

Imagery: The array of images in a literary work. Also, figurative language.

***In medias res*:** A Latin term meaning "in the middle of things." It refers to the technique of beginning a story at its midpoint and then using various flashback devices to reveal previous action.

Interior Monologue: A narrative technique in which characters' thoughts are revealed in a way that appears to be uncontrolled by the author. The interior monologue typically aims to reveal the inner self of a character. It portrays emotional experiences as they occur at both a conscious and unconscious level. Images are often used to represent sensations or emotions.

Irony: In literary criticism, the effect of language in which the intended meaning is the opposite of what is stated.

J

Jargon: Language that is used or understood only by a select group of people. Jargon may refer to terminology used in a certain profession, such as computer jargon, or it may refer to any nonsensical language that is not understood by most people.

L

***Leitmotiv*:** See *Motif*

Literal Language: An author uses literal language when he or she writes without exaggerating or embellishing the subject matter and without any tools of figurative language.

Lost Generation: A term first used by Gertrude Stein to describe the post-World War I generation of American writers: men and women haunted by a sense of betrayal and emptiness brought about by the destructiveness of the war.

M

Mannerism: Exaggerated, artificial adherence to a literary manner or style. Also, a popular style of the visual arts of late sixteenth-century Europe that was marked by elongation of the human form and by intentional spatial distortion. Literary works that are self-consciously high-toned and artistic are often said to be "mannered."

Metaphor: A figure of speech that expresses an idea through the image of another object. Metaphors suggest the essence of the first object by identifying it with certain qualities of the second object.

Modernism: Modern literary practices. Also, the principles of a literary school that lasted from roughly the beginning of the twentieth century until the end of World War II. Modernism is defined by its rejection of the literary conventions of the nineteenth century and by its opposition to conventional morality, taste, traditions, and economic values.

Mood: The prevailing emotions of a work or of the author in his or her creation of the work. The mood of a work is not always what might be expected based on its subject matter.

***Motif*:** A theme, character type, image, metaphor, or other verbal element that recurs throughout a single work of literature or occurs in a number of different works over a period of time. Also known as *Motiv* or *Leitmotiv*.

Myth: An anonymous tale emerging from the traditional beliefs of a culture or social unit. Myths use supernatural explanations for natural phenomena. They may also explain cosmic issues like creation and death. Collections of myths, known as mythologies, are common to all cultures and nations, but the best-known myths belong to the Norse, Roman, and Greek mythologies.

N

Narration: The telling of a series of events, real or invented. A narration may be either a simple narrative, in which the events are recounted chronologically, or a narrative with a plot, in which the account is given in a style reflecting the author's artistic concept of the story. Narration is sometimes used as a synonym for "storyline."

Narrative: A verse or prose accounting of an event or sequence of events, real or invented. The term is also used as an adjective in the sense "method of narration." For example, in literary criticism, the expression "narrative technique" usually refers to the way the author structures and presents his or her story.

Narrator: The teller of a story. The narrator may be the author or a character in the story through whom the author speaks.

Naturalism: A literary movement of the late nineteenth and early twentieth centuries. The movement's major theorist, French novelist Emile Zola, envisioned a type of fiction that would examine human life with the objectivity of scientific inquiry. The Naturalists typically viewed human beings as either the products of "biological determinism," ruled by hereditary instincts and engaged in an endless struggle for survival, or as the products of "socioeconomic determinism," ruled by social and economic forces beyond their control. In their works, the Naturalists generally ignored the highest levels of society and focused on degradation: poverty, alcoholism, prostitution, insanity, and disease.

Noble Savage: The idea that primitive man is noble and good but becomes evil and corrupted as he becomes civilized. The concept of the noble savage originated in the Renaissance period but is more closely identified with such later writers as

Jean-Jacques Rousseau and Aphra Behn. See also Primitivism.

Novel of Ideas: A novel in which the examination of intellectual issues and concepts takes precedence over characterization or a traditional storyline.

Novel of Manners: A novel that examines the customs and mores of a cultural group.

Novel: A long fictional narrative written in prose, which developed from the novella and other early forms of narrative. A novel is usually organized under a plot or theme with a focus on character development and action.

Novella: An Italian term meaning "story." This term has been especially used to describe fourteenth-century Italian tales, but it also refers to modern short novels.

O

Objective Correlative: An outward set of objects, a situation, or a chain of events corresponding to an inward experience and evoking this experience in the reader. The term frequently appears in modern criticism in discussions of authors' intended effects on the emotional responses of readers.

Objectivity: A quality in writing characterized by the absence of the author's opinion or feeling about the subject matter. Objectivity is an important factor in criticism.

Oedipus Complex: A son's amorous obsession with his mother. The phrase is derived from the story of the ancient Theban hero Oedipus, who unknowingly killed his father and married his mother.

Omniscience: See *Point of View*

Onomatopoeia: The use of words whose sounds express or suggest their meaning. In its simplest sense, onomatopoeia may be represented by words that mimic the sounds they denote such as "hiss" or "meow." At a more subtle level, the pattern and rhythm of sounds and rhymes of a line or poem may be onomatopoeic.

Oxymoron: A phrase combining two contradictory terms. Oxymorons may be intentional or unintentional.

P

Parable: A story intended to teach a moral lesson or answer an ethical question.

Paradox: A statement that appears illogical or contradictory at first, but may actually point to an underlying truth.

Parallelism: A method of comparison of two ideas in which each is developed in the same grammatical structure.

Parody: In literary criticism, this term refers to an imitation of a serious literary work or the signature style of a particular author in a ridiculous manner. A typical parody adopts the style of the original and applies it to an inappropriate subject for humorous effect. Parody is a form of satire and could be considered the literary equivalent of a caricature or cartoon.

Pastoral: A term derived from the Latin word "pastor," meaning shepherd. A pastoral is a literary composition on a rural theme. The conventions of the pastoral were originated by the third-century Greek poet Theocritus, who wrote about the experiences, love affairs, and pastimes of Sicilian shepherds. In a pastoral, characters and language of a courtly nature are often placed in a simple setting. The term pastoral is also used to classify dramas, elegies, and lyrics that exhibit the use of country settings and shepherd characters.

Pen Name: See *Pseudonym*

***Persona*:** A Latin term meaning "mask." *Personae* are the characters in a fictional work of literature. The *persona* generally functions as a mask through which the author tells a story in a voice other than his or her own. A *persona* is usually either a character in a story who acts as a narrator or an "implied author," a voice created by the author to act as the narrator for himself or herself.

Personification: A figure of speech that gives human qualities to abstract ideas, animals, and inanimate objects. Also known as *Prosopopoeia.*

Picaresque Novel: Episodic fiction depicting the adventures of a roguish central character ("picaro" is Spanish for "rogue"). The picaresque hero is commonly a low-born but clever individual who wanders into and out of various affairs of love, danger, and farcical intrigue. These involvements may take place at all social levels and typically present a humorous and wide-ranging satire of a given society.

Plagiarism: Claiming another person's written material as one's own. Plagiarism can take the form of direct, word-for-word copying or the theft of the substance or idea of the work.

Plot: In literary criticism, this term refers to the pattern of events in a narrative or drama. In its simplest sense, the plot guides the author in composing the work and helps the reader follow the work. Typically, plots exhibit causality and unity and have a beginning, a middle, and an end. Sometimes, however, a plot may consist of a series of disconnected events, in which case it is known as an "episodic plot."

Poetic Justice: An outcome in a literary work, not necessarily a poem, in which the good are rewarded and the evil are punished, especially in ways that particularly fit their virtues or crimes.

Poetic License: Distortions of fact and literary convention made by a writer—not always a poet—for the sake of the effect gained. Poetic license is closely related to the concept of "artistic freedom."

Poetics: This term has two closely related meanings. It denotes (1) an aesthetic theory in literary criticism about the essence of poetry or (2) rules prescribing the proper methods, content, style, or diction of poetry. The term poetics may also refer to theories about literature in general, not just poetry.

Point of View: The narrative perspective from which a literary work is presented to the reader. There are four traditional points of view. The "third person omniscient" gives the reader a "godlike" perspective, unrestricted by time or place, from which to see actions and look into the minds of characters. This allows the author to comment openly on characters and events in the work. The "third person" point of view presents the events of the story from outside of any single character's perception, much like the omniscient point of view, but the reader must understand the action as it takes place and without any special insight into characters' minds or motivations. The "first person" or "personal" point of view relates events as they are perceived by a single character. The main character "tells" the story and may offer opinions about the action and characters which differ from those of the author. Much less common than omniscient, third person, and first person is the "second person" point of view, wherein the author tells the story as if it is happening to the reader.

Polemic: A work in which the author takes a stand on a controversial subject, such as abortion or religion. Such works are often extremely argumentative or provocative.

Pornography: Writing intended to provoke feelings of lust in the reader. Such works are often condemned by critics and teachers, but those which can be shown to have literary value are viewed less harshly.

Post-Aesthetic Movement: An artistic response made by African Americans to the black aesthetic movement of the 1960s and early '70s. Writers since that time have adopted a somewhat different tone in their work, with less emphasis placed on the disparity between black and white in the United States. In the words of post-aesthetic authors such as Toni Morrison, John Edgar Wideman, and Kristin Hunter, African Americans are portrayed as looking inward for answers to their own questions, rather than always looking to the outside world.

Postmodernism: Writing from the 1960s forward characterized by experimentation and continuing to apply some of the fundamentals of modernism, which included existentialism and alienation. Postmodernists have gone a step further in the rejection of tradition begun with the modernists by also rejecting traditional forms, preferring the anti-novel over the novel and the antihero over the hero.

Primitivism: The belief that primitive peoples were nobler and less flawed than civilized peoples because they had not been subjected to the tainting influence of society. See also Noble Savage.

Prologue: An introductory section of a literary work. It often contains information establishing the situation of the characters or presents information about the setting, time period, or action. In drama, the prologue is spoken by a chorus or by one of the principal characters.

Prose: A literary medium that attempts to mirror the language of everyday speech. It is distinguished from poetry by its use of unmetered, unrhymed language consisting of logically related sentences. Prose is usually grouped into paragraphs that form a cohesive whole such as an essay or a novel.

***Prosopopoeia*:** See *Personification*

Protagonist: The central character of a story who serves as a focus for its themes and incidents and as the principal rationale for its development. The protagonist is sometimes referred to in discussions of modern literature as the hero or antihero.

Protest Fiction: Protest fiction has as its primary purpose the protesting of some social injustice, such as racism or discrimination.

Proverb: A brief, sage saying that expresses a truth about life in a striking manner.

Pseudonym: A name assumed by a writer, most often intended to prevent his or her identification as the author of a work. Two or more authors may work together under one pseudonym, or an author may use a different name for each genre he or she publishes in. Some publishing companies maintain "house pseudonyms," under which any number of authors may write installations in a series. Some authors also choose a pseudonym over their real names the way an actor may use a stage name.

Pun: A play on words that have similar sounds but different meanings.

R

Realism: A nineteenth-century European literary movement that sought to portray familiar characters, situations, and settings in a realistic manner. This was done primarily by using an objective narrative point of view and through the buildup of accurate detail. The standard for success of any realistic work depends on how faithfully it transfers common experience into fictional forms. The realistic method may be altered or extended, as in stream of consciousness writing, to record highly subjective experience.

***Repartee*:** Conversation featuring snappy retorts and witticisms.

Resolution: The portion of a story following the climax, in which the conflict is resolved. See also *Denouement.*

Rhetoric: In literary criticism, this term denotes the art of ethical persuasion. In its strictest sense, rhetoric adheres to various principles developed since classical times for arranging facts and ideas in a clear, persuasive, appealing manner. The term is also used to refer to effective prose in general and theories of or methods for composing effective prose.

Rhetorical Question: A question intended to provoke thought, but not an expressed answer, in the reader. It is most commonly used in oratory and other persuasive genres.

Rising Action: The part of a drama where the plot becomes increasingly complicated. Rising action leads up to the climax, or turning point, of a drama.

***Roman a clef*:** A French phrase meaning "novel with a key." It refers to a narrative in which real persons are portrayed under fictitious names.

Romance: A broad term, usually denoting a narrative with exotic, exaggerated, often idealized characters, scenes, and themes.

Romanticism: This term has two widely accepted meanings. In historical criticism, it refers to a European intellectual and artistic movement of the late eighteenth and early nineteenth centuries that sought greater freedom of personal expression than that allowed by the strict rules of literary form and logic of the eighteenth-century neoclassicists. The Romantics preferred emotional and imaginative expression to rational analysis. They considered the individual to be at the center of all experience and so placed him or her at the center of their art. The Romantics believed that the creative imagination reveals nobler truths—unique feelings and attitudes—than those that could be discovered by logic or by scientific examination. Both the natural world and the state of childhood were important sources for revelations of "eternal truths." "Romanticism" is also used as a general term to refer to a type of sensibility found in all periods of literary history and usually considered to be in opposition to the principles of classicism. In this sense, Romanticism signifies any work or philosophy in which the exotic or dreamlike figure strongly, or that is devoted to individualistic expression, self-analysis, or a pursuit of a higher realm of knowledge than can be discovered by human reason.

Romantics: See *Romanticism*

S

Satire: A work that uses ridicule, humor, and wit to criticize and provoke change in human nature and institutions. There are two major types of satire: "formal" or "direct" satire speaks directly to the reader or to a character in the work; "indirect" satire relies upon the ridiculous behavior of its characters to make its point. Formal satire is further divided into two manners: the "Horatian," which ridicules gently, and the "Juvenalian," which derides its subjects harshly and bitterly.

Science Fiction: A type of narrative about or based upon real or imagined scientific theories and technology. Science fiction is often peopled with alien creatures and set on other planets or in different dimensions.

Second Person: See *Point of View*

Setting: The time, place, and culture in which the action of a narrative takes place. The elements of setting may include geographic location, characters' physical and mental environments, prevailing cultural attitudes, or the historical time in which the action takes place.

Simile: A comparison, usually using "like" or "as," of two essentially dissimilar things, as in "coffee as cold as ice" or "He sounded like a broken record."

Slang: A type of informal verbal communication that is generally unacceptable for formal writing. Slang words and phrases are often colorful exaggerations used to emphasize the speaker's point; they may also be shortened versions of an often-used word or phrase.

Slave Narrative: Autobiographical accounts of American slave life as told by escaped slaves. These works first appeared during the abolition movement of the 1830s through the 1850s.

Socialist Realism: The Socialist Realism school of literary theory was proposed by Maxim Gorky and established as a dogma by the first Soviet Congress of Writers. It demanded adherence to a communist worldview in works of literature. Its doctrines required an objective viewpoint comprehensible to the working classes and themes of social struggle featuring strong proletarian heroes. Also known as Social Realism.

Stereotype: A stereotype was originally the name for a duplication made during the printing process; this led to its modern definition as a person or thing that is (or is assumed to be) the same as all others of its type.

Stream of Consciousness: A narrative technique for rendering the inward experience of a character. This technique is designed to give the impression of an ever-changing series of thoughts, emotions, images, and memories in the spontaneous and seemingly illogical order that they occur in life.

Structure: The form taken by a piece of literature. The structure may be made obvious for ease of understanding, as in nonfiction works, or may obscured for artistic purposes, as in some poetry or seemingly "unstructured" prose.

***Sturm und Drang*:** A German term meaning "storm and stress." It refers to a German literary movement of the 1770s and 1780s that reacted against the order and rationalism of the enlightenment, focusing instead on the intense experience of extraordinary individuals.

Style: A writer's distinctive manner of arranging words to suit his or her ideas and purpose in writing. The unique imprint of the author's personality upon his or her writing, style is the product of an author's way of arranging ideas and his or her use of diction, different sentence structures, rhythm, figures of speech, rhetorical principles, and other elements of composition.

Subjectivity: Writing that expresses the author's personal feelings about his subject, and which may or may not include factual information about the subject.

Subplot: A secondary story in a narrative. A subplot may serve as a motivating or complicating force for the main plot of the work, or it may provide emphasis for, or relief from, the main plot.

Surrealism: A term introduced to criticism by Guillaume Apollinaire and later adopted by Andre Breton. It refers to a French literary and artistic movement founded in the 1920s. The Surrealists sought to express unconscious thoughts and feelings in their works. The best-known technique used for achieving this aim was automatic writing—transcriptions of spontaneous outpourings from the unconscious. The Surrealists proposed to unify the contrary levels of conscious and unconscious, dream and reality, objectivity and subjectivity into a new level of "super-realism."

Suspense: A literary device in which the author maintains the audience's attention through the buildup of events, the outcome of which will soon be revealed.

Symbol: Something that suggests or stands for something else without losing its original identity. In literature, symbols combine their literal meaning with the suggestion of an abstract concept. Literary symbols are of two types: those that carry complex associations of meaning no matter what their contexts, and those that derive their suggestive meaning from their functions in specific literary works.

Symbolism: This term has two widely accepted meanings. In historical criticism, it denotes an early modernist literary movement initiated in France during the nineteenth century that reacted against the prevailing standards of realism. Writers in this movement aimed to evoke, indirectly and symbolically, an order of being beyond the material world of the five senses. Poetic expression of personal emotion figured strongly in the movement, typically by means of a private set of symbols uniquely identifiable with the individual poet. The principal aim of the Symbolists was to express in words the highly complex feelings that grew out of everyday contact with the world. In a broader sense, the term "symbolism" refers to the use of one object to represent another.

T

Tall Tale: A humorous tale told in a straightforward, credible tone but relating absolutely impossible events or feats of the characters. Such tales were commonly told of frontier adventures during the settlement of the west in the United States.

Theme: The main point of a work of literature. The term is used interchangeably with thesis.

Thesis: A thesis is both an essay and the point argued in the essay. Thesis novels and thesis plays share the quality of containing a thesis which is supported through the action of the story.

Third Person: See *Point of View*

Tone: The author's attitude toward his or her audience may be deduced from the tone of the work. A formal tone may create distance or convey politeness, while an informal tone may encourage a friendly, intimate, or intrusive feeling in the reader. The author's attitude toward his or her subject matter may also be deduced from the tone of the words he or she uses in discussing it.

Transcendentalism: An American philosophical and religious movement, based in New England from around 1835 until the Civil War. Transcendentalism was a form of American romanticism that had its roots abroad in the works of Thomas Carlyle, Samuel Coleridge, and Johann Wolfgang von Goethe. The Transcendentalists stressed the importance of intuition and subjective experience in communication with God. They rejected religious dogma and texts in favor of mysticism and scientific naturalism. They pursued truths that lie beyond the "colorless" realms perceived by reason and the senses and were active social reformers in public education, women's rights, and the abolition of slavery.

U

Urban Realism: A branch of realist writing that attempts to accurately reflect the often harsh facts of modern urban existence.

Utopia: A fictional perfect place, such as "paradise" or "heaven."

V

Verisimilitude: Literally, the appearance of truth. In literary criticism, the term refers to aspects of a work of literature that seem true to the reader.

Victorian: Refers broadly to the reign of Queen Victoria of England (1837–1901) and to anything with qualities typical of that era. For example, the qualities of smug narrowmindedness, bourgeois materialism, faith in social progress, and priggish morality are often considered Victorian. This stereotype is contradicted by such dramatic intellectual developments as the theories of Charles Darwin, Karl Marx, and Sigmund Freud (which stirred strong debates in England) and the critical attitudes of serious Victorian writers like Charles Dickens and George Eliot. In literature, the Victorian Period was the great age of the English novel, and the latter part of the era saw the rise of movements such as decadence and symbolism. Also known as Victorian Age and Victorian Period.

W

***Weltanschauung*:** A German term referring to a person's worldview or philosophy.

***Weltschmerz*:** A German term meaning "world pain." It describes a sense of anguish about the nature of existence, usually associated with a melancholy, pessimistic attitude.

Z

***Zeitgeist*:** A German term meaning "spirit of the time." It refers to the moral and intellectual trends of a given era.

Cumulative Author/Title Index

Numerical

A

B

C

D

I

J

K

L

W

Y

Z

Cumulative Nationality/Ethnicity Index

Asian American

Asian Canadian

Australian

Barbadian

Canadian

Chilean

Chinese

Colombian

Czechoslovakian

Danish

Dominican

English

European American

French

German

Hispanic American

Subject/Theme Index

*Boldface denotes discussion in *Themes* section.

Subject/Theme Index